HISTORY
& MYSTERY

VOL 2

BERNIE L. CALAWAY

Copyright © 2021 by Bernie L. Calaway

All rights reserved. No part of this publication may be reproduced, distributed, or transmitted in any form or by any means, including photocopying, recording, or other electronic or mechanical methods, without the prior written permission of the author, except in the case of brief quotations embodied in critical reviews and certain other noncommercial uses permitted by copyright law.

ISBN: 978-1-64314-459-7 (Paperback)
        978-1-64314-485-6 (Ebook)

AuthorsPress
California, USA
www.authorspress.com

FOREWORD TO THE ESSAYS AND ENCYCLOPEDIA

ARE YOU AWARE THAT the major task of a prophet is *not* to predict stuff? Has your neighbor used the term "eschaton" and left you puzzled? Having trouble with the details of those multi-horned monsters in the book of Revelation? Don't know how to properly use an athame?

Fear not. The *History and Mystery: The Complete Eschatological Encyclopedia of Prophecy, Apocalypticism, Mythos, and Worldwide Dynamic Theology* has arrived to help you out. Few of us have the leisure of thumbing through thick Bible dictionaries or clicking on twenty websites, only to find there are no definitions that differentiate the apocalyptic from the eschatological material. (Uh, what *is* apocalyptic and eschatological substance anyway?) Nor is it convenient to stop a study here and there along the way wondering what exactly one is reading. To push the idea a bit more, an attempt has been made to introduce Bible names and terms that not only pertain directly or exclusively to prophecy and eschatology, but also to history, science, the mystery religions, ecclesiology, philosophy, ethics, religious aberrations and cults, anthropology, pagan or foreign religions and many other disciplines. The word reviews are as thorough as possible but back away from tedious. Or, as one reviewer put it, "These aren't definitions; they're explanations." A person can actually *understand* them.

The encyclopedia you are clutching is unique. The first segment of the five-volume set is a series of some sixty essays relating to prophetic or theological topics that may be a bit "difficult" or begging for fuller explanation. The information provides a good base from which to start the search for information and understanding and is therefore placed in front. Next door to the explanations come the definitions themselves. Prophetic or esoteric words and phrases are identified and defined. Here is everything from Aaron to Zwingli. But still, more is needed since the interpretation of such a complex subject must delve into myth, religious history, and worldwide concepts of beliefs that are required for a comprehensive perspective. You will find terms not readily available in most standard Bible dictionaries or encyclopedias, either conveniently online or in print.

Surely, there are risks when a solitary person (*i.e.,* without resources from specialized researchers, editors, brains, etc.) attempts to compile a glossary. The words must be carefully chosen and neither too detailed nor too generalized. Edgar Allen Poe once effused: "A definition is that which so describes its object as to distinguish it from all others." By contrast, the philosopher F.C.S. Schiller said, "All words cannot be defined." Somewhere within this annoying juxtaposition somebody has to try for the practical. Within the hubris of theology versus mysticism, that task is even more daunting. All words and every nuance of definition are not included—that's an impossible task. If the subject is too vast to be reasonably explored, only the most common references are listed. But the important terms are present, at least all those I could think up or look up. Biblical and historical figures have been selectively chosen with more expansion in the essays. Both the expositions and the dictionary carry a Christian, perhaps even an evangelical, bias that seems logical and consistent to the purpose of the research.

Still, the questions keep piling up. What does a kiss have to do with apocalyptic judgment? How did the Moabites help form Hebrew and Christian eschatology? How does Roman Catholic end time doctrine line up with the Baptists? or a Hindu? Why do Branch Davidian types and Islamic terrorists seek suicide in apocalyptic fervor but the general public lends it scant attention? How can a lamb be ferocious and a wolf be a pacifist? Why did the Vikings see the world ending in violence but the ancient pharaohs only heard a gentle whimper? How is magic different from foreordination? And who cares? To hear the Almighty, do we need a God helmet or a prophet's mantle? My Social Security number has three sixes in it. Should I upgrade? Am I a universalist or a premillennialist? Who started the odd Quaker apocalyptic movement? Was the wizard Merlin a better prophet than Robin Goodfellow? How come the Mayans got it wrong? Is the UN about ready to tax your unleaded gasoline and your diet sodas? How are prophecies

History and Mystery

related to miracles? Puzzles like that can slow your metabolism and keep you up all nights.

Nobody knows all the answers, and even fewer of the questions, but we can learn something. Certainly, it's a great help to have a dictionary at hand. As a tip to the user, bear in mind that different translations of the Scripture and other sources may employ alternate words for the same subject. In most cases, the New International Version is the preferred Bible translation used here with scholarly essay for the remaining supply. If that doesn't work, I am confident you're smart enough to find another approach to the solution. Be a valiant, intrepid reader.

This lexicon edition hits church history (heavily American) and the human condition (both ancient and modern) with more than a gentle tap. Those features are intentional because our living faith today (and certainly beyond today) is the lasting bequeathal of the prophetic thrust. All is not done. Everything relates. Even the pagan and the modernist feed off each other sometimes. Those high-octane technical words are also important because they're the language of the theologians. The extended *"See also"* sections following most of the definitions are sure to aid in further study if desired, as will the consulting bibliography at the end. Also, don't forget to use the "history and mystery of…" section of the lexicon for a sort of mini-index to related or linked subject matter. And you will need assistance to facilitate your research, being aware that aside from the Scripture, world culture and local usage also show multiple terms that may be identical or may differ from our own common understanding. Or there may be several meanings. Despite what may be a violation of accepted dictionary alphabetizing, any "s" within parentheses to indicate the plural is ignored when arranging alphabetically. As to all those words that think they should be capitalized—who knows? Most major characters of the Old and New Testaments are identified to enhance clarity and give the "human" touch. Only the most prophetically, historically, and theologically pertinent titles and terms are cited in the encyclopedia, lest the texts become unwieldy. Even so, there are around 10,000 entries throughout the five volumes in an effort to be comprehensive.

A word of caution may be in order next. Some may feel offended that certain individuals, groups, or institutions are classed within the textbook as "cults," false prophets, or some other seemingly maligned description. If such there be, I see no remedy for it. The work is, after all, written in the Christian perspective and that which is considered clearly outside the bounds of that faith can only be; it is what it is. Certainly there is no subtle pleasure or ulterior motive associated with the treatment of any term defined or explained. Remember, Christianity itself is (and always has been) hardly immune to negative labeling, worthy of it or not and true or not. Striving for artificial political correctness would inevitably drive both dictionary essays into the ditch of mediocrity.

One more caveat needs careful explanation. The reader will hardly fail to notice the prominence of dispensational and premillennial theology in both the expositions and the dictionary. The predominance of those themes is almost inevitable. Furthermore, knowledge dealing with dispensationalism and premillennialism are the most complex and detailed structures of modern eschatology and apocalyptic writing whereas other viewpoints are relatively straightforward. According to non-dispensational theories, all apocalyptic description in the Bible is either: (1) symbolic or metaphorical—almost never literal, (2) such language and the apocalyptic style of writing were common in the first century and in post-Babylonian Judaism but is practically unfathomable today, (3) various Bible renditions have mistranslated some of the text, which can therefore, be manipulated according to a favorite interpretation, (4) apocalyptic language, and its sister non-literal genre (poetry), must always be taken in as romantic or esoteric writing—never historically, (5) all apocalyptic scenes and descriptions are whole within themselves and bear little or no relation to similar paradigms, (6) details of dispensational eschatology are being foisted upon the uniformed and youthful generation who are incapable of full comprehension and should thereby be subject to vilification or, at least, refutation, (7) the Bible does not discuss the end of the age anywhere at any time. Any one of the assumptions mentioned can easily "explain" eschatology in such a context for it refers only to a theology of symbolic hope and steadfast perseverance in times of trouble. That essentially makes eschatology practically irrelevant to our times, except in its last remaining function as encourager to the believer. Premillennial and dispensational thinking, however, require far more investigation and explanation to expound the doctrine fairly. So then, the emphasis in the word list exceeds the simple "comfort and hope" purposes for the future and develops, not necessarily from the author's personal hermeneutics, but from sheer necessity.

Finally, (sigh mournfully) something you need may have been omitted, or maybe an error is made somewhere. I regret that (really) but am not to be surprised by it. So then, accept my humble apologies beforehand. Kindly try to remember the writing is from the perspective of biblical scholarship, not stupefying theology.

Here's hoping that what is presented will be interesting and helpful. If that happens, I'm one happy old writer dude.

Bernie L. Calaway
Myrtle Beach, SC

CONTENTS

Foreword to the Essays and Encyclopedia iii

Encyclopedia of Eschatological and Mystical Terminology

Aaron—azymes 1-253
Ba.—Byzantine Church...254-408
Cabala—Cyrus the Great (Cyrus II) 410-675
da Casale, Umbertino—Dystopia 676-821

Bibliography 823

Encyclopedia of Eschatological and Mystical Terminology

A

Aaron: first high priest of Israel and brother to Moses and Miriam. The name means "enlightened." He was the center of the Aaronic Covenant, which provided a perpetual priesthood for the nation. Aaron was chief spokesman for Moses in the presence of Pharaoh, as well as his valuable assistant on the Exodus journey. God even named him (Ex. 7:1) as "Moses' prophet." From time to time, he has been called "the savior of Israel" because he was brave enough to venture forth into the midst of the Exodus Israelites in his priestly robes and jeweled accouterments, carrying holy incense to check the avenging angel of the plague recorded in Numbers 16:45. Aaron's career was somewhat marred when he cast the calf idol while Moses was delayed on Mount Sinai receiving the tablets of the Law (Ex. 32). He died on Mount Hor before entering the Promised Land and was succeeded by his son Eleazar. Tradition says that his burial was near Petra, close to his sister Miriam. *See also* Aaronic Covenant; Aaron's rod that budded; Miriam; Moses; Mount Hor; priest(s).

Aaronic Covenant: a contract of God with Israel, through Aaron the high priest, which pledged that the nation would always have a sacerdotal system from his descendants and a worship ritual acceptable to God (Ex. 40:15). *See also* Aaron, Aaron's rod that budded; Abiathar; Abimelech; clean clothes for Joshua; Eleazar; Judaism; Levitical Covenant; Phinehas; priest(s); Zadok.

Aaron's rod that budded: a miraculous act that verified the Lord's determination that Aaron, and he alone, was indeed the chosen of God to be high priest of Israel. When challenged in his leadership, twelve staffs (one from each of the Hebrew tribes) were presented before the Lord but only that of Aaron bloomed and even produced almonds (Num. 17). The miraculous artifact was kept as one of the sacred objects in the Holy Place of the tabernacle. No doubt, the wonder of the budding rod could be considered a reaffirmation of the Aaronic Covenant. It is interesting that Aaron's rod that budded was also the one that consumed the rods-that-became-snakes belonging to the magicians of Pharaoh's court (Ex. 7:8–13). *See also* Aaron; Aaronic Covenant; almond; almond tree branch; flora, fruit, and grain, symbology of; Jannes and Jambres; tabernacle, the.

Abaddon: 1. the Hebrew name for the demonic leader or "king" of the horde of the Abyss issued from the fifth trumpet (Rev. 9:11); the Greek term for the same evil entity is Apollyon. Both terms mean "Destruction" (as found in paradigms like Proverbs 27:20 and Job 26:6). 2. some Bible translations use the name (as in Psalm 88:11) to identify the place of the dead, or *Sheol*. *See also* Abezi-Thibod; Adramelech; Anammelech; Apollyon; Asmodaeus; Azazel; Azrael; Baal-zebub; death; Death and Destruction; demon(s), demonism; destroyer; devils; Dibbuk; Dubbi'el; Gadreel; idol(s); Legion; Lilith; Mastema; names, symbology of; Pazuzu; Sammael; Sceva; scorpion; *Sheol*; slave girl of Philippi; Syrophoenician woman; underworld; Valley of Decision; woman of Canaan.

Abba: the Aramaic word for "Father," used relatively infrequently in the Bible (Mk. 14:36; Rom. 8:15). Most linguists agree that the term is a rather personal one, coming close to our appellation "Dad" (*pater*). It is possible that the word was part of the response formula to early Christian baptism as well. If so, the proper response to the baptizer's question from the candidate would be "Abba, Father" and would articulate the first expression of testimony after the baptismal act by the new Christian. *See also* abba; abbess; abbey; abbot; Father, father; names (titles) for God.

abba: 1. the official ecclesiastical title for a Syrian or Coptic bishop. 2. a camel's hair cloak, striped with colors or black and white, used as an outer garment worn by Bedouin men and cinched with a leather belt or sash, in which a dagger or pistol can be stowed. *See also Abba;* abbess; abbot; Bedouins; bishop(s); Coptic Church; Syrian Orthodox Church.

Abbahu, Rabbi: a Talmudist of Israel (ca. A.D. 279-320) known as a collector of Hekalots and an authority on weights and measures. He is considered one of the more respected and learned of the early Jewish teachers. *See also* Jew(s).

Abbasid Caliphate: Islamic Empire rule dating from A.D. 750, making it the second caliphate headquartered in Baghdad. *See also* Ayyubid dynasty; caliph; caliphate; Fatimid Caliphate; Islam; Quarmatians; Rashidun Caliphate; Umayyad Caliphate.

abbess: the female head of a nunnery, abbey, or similar retreat center. *See also* abba; abbey; abbot; agapetae; ancress; cenobium; Eastern Orthodox Church; hegumene; monasticism; mother superior; orders; Roman Catholic Church.

abbey: a community of monks or nuns led by an experienced abbot or abbess. Sometimes the term names the monastery of residence as well. Many in a monastic setting are of Roman Catholic, Eastern Orthodox, or Eastern religions, but the practice is common enough in ecclesiastical circles. *See also* abba; abbess; abbot; agapetae; cenobium; cloister; convent; Eastern Orthodox Church; hegumene; monastery; monasticism; monk(s); mother superior; nun(s); orders; priory; Roman Catholic Church.

abbot: a title meaning "father" given to the head of a monastery. *See also Abba;* abba; abbess; abbey; cenobium; clergy; Eastern Orthodox Church; ecclesiastic(s); Father, father; monastery; monasticism; monk(s); orders; Roman Catholic Church.

Abbott, Lyman: former lawyer turned Congregationalist minister (1835–1922). Abbott worked in the American Union Commission, a group of clergy and laypersons designed to advise the government on matters of Reconstruction in the South after the Civil War. He was an early advocate of the Social Gospel movement and succeeded Henry Ward Beecher as pastor of Plymouth Congregationalist Church in Brooklyn. *See also* Beecher, Henry Ward; Congregationalists; Social Gospel; Social Darwinism; social issues.

Abdiel: a prominent figure in Jewish folklore (but not Scripture) as the angel who fought against Satan's rebel warriors. In Milton's *Paradise Lost* he is pictured in that role because his name means "servant of God." *See also* angel(s).

Abdon: the eleventh named judge in Israel (Jud. 12:13–15), an Ephraimite. He served eight years and seems to have held exceptional status since he had seventy sons and grandsons who rode about on seventy ass colts. Josephus reported he had a peaceful administration with little occasion for heroic deeds. *See also* judge(s); Judges as Old Testament book.

Abednego: the Babylonian name for one of the three wise companions of Daniel who were rescued from the fiery furnace. Abednego's Hebrew name was Azariah ("God has helped") but was altered to honor one of the gods of the Babylonian pantheon, most likely Nebo. *See also* Azariah as exile; Belteshazzar; Daniel; Hananiah the exile; Meshach; Mishael; Nebo; Nebuchadnezzar; Shadrach; Sumerian and Babylonian pantheon.

Abel: second son of Adam and Eve (Gen. 4:2). He was murdered by his brother Cain but became a pivotal prophetic theme as history progressed. Many consider him a prophet since Jesus seemed to refer to him as the first (Lk. 11:51) with that designation. Abel is important to the prophecy theme since he is considered a type for the first Christian martyr, Stephen. *See also* Abel to Zechariah; Cain; martyr(s); prophet(s); Stephen of Jerusalem.

Abelard, Peter: a Roman Catholic theologian (1079 – 1142) of the old school. Abelard was a charismatic academic, philosopher, accomplished poet, and monk, but his life ended in disgrace at the monastery in Cluny. He had been accused of seducing, impregnating, and secretly marrying Heloise, his young student and a niece of the canon at Notre Dame. Heloise's uncle took revenge by arranging Abelard's castration and confinement. Heloise was sent to a convent. Letters exchanged between the two lovers gave rise to a celebrity status for both until Abelard was declared a forerunner of Satan and officially defamed. He did issue texts that interact with church tradition and Scripture. The Protestants later used him as the poster boy for all they perceived as wrong with Catholic theology and morality. *See also* monasticism; monk(s); Roman Catholic Church; scholasticism.

Abel-Mehola: the region of the prophet Elisha's home in the Jordan Valley.

Abel to Zechariah: a rather generically specified generation of evildoers and murderers of the prophets when taken in its broadest meaning. Jesus condemned a certain age group that he held guilty for the blood of all the prophets shed from Abel to Zechariah [A–Z] (Gen. 4:8; 2 Chr. 24:20–22). Genesis records the death of Abel (the first martyr) at the hand of his brother Cain. Second Chronicles recites the death of the last Old Testament martyr, a prophet named Zechariah. The accusation of Jesus was pointed at the population of his day who continued their vindictive persecution of God's messengers sent to them, including himself as the greatest of the prophets and the very Son of God. As a race, we all share to some extent the guilt of such mistreatment and rejection. The totality of meaning for the phrase may be in Revelation 18:24 which laments the blood of the prophets, the saints, and all who have been killed on the earth. *See also* Abel; alpha; Alpha and Omega; author and perfecter (finisher) of our faith; Beginning and the End, the; First and the Last, the; martyr(s); martyrdom; prophet(s); Zechariah as true prophets; omega.

Abernathy, Ralph David: Baptist and close associate of Martin Luther King, Jr. (b. 1926), active in the Civil Rights Movement. He assumed leadership of the Southern Christian Leadership Conference after King was assassinated. *See also* Afro-American theology; Baptists; King, Martin Luther, Jr.; social issues.

Abezi-Thibod: a demon of Jewish folklore who was said to be the spirit who aided Pharaoh's magicians in opposition to Moses and Aaron. The Jews saw him as a kind of patron demon over Egypt. The name means "father lacking counsel." *See also* Abaddon; Adramelech; Anammelech; Apollyon; Asmodaeus; Azazel; Azrael; Baal-zebub; Dibbuk; demon(s), demonic; devils; Dubbi'el; Gadreel; idol(s); Jannes and Jambres; Legion; Lilith; Mastema; Pazuzu; Sammael; Sceva; slave girl of Philippi; Syrophoenician woman; woman of Canaan.

Abgar: the customary name given to various kings of Edessa, but also known as a particular person in some writings where he is called Abgarus Uchama or Abgar V the Black. Edessa is now Urfa, Turkey. As one of the Edessaian rulers, King Abgar V has possible eschatological connections and was already renowned for his valor among the nations east of the Euphrates. However, his body was wasting away with a strange disease. He heard about Jesus and his curative powers and sent a letter to request him [Jesus] to come and heal him. There was no curative at the time he asked but Jesus was said to have replied in a return epistle. Later, it is reported, the apostle Thomas sent Addai to heal the king. Other accounts say the messenger was Thaddeus. The legend continues with the story that Jesus also sent the king a healing towel called the *Mandylion*. This object was later carried to Constantinople as a sacred relic. The healing miracle and correspondence mentioned in the legend almost certainly did not happen because, as far as we know, Jesus wrote nothing (possibly excepting the doodling in the dirt before the woman accused of adultery in John 8:1–11). *See also* Addai; Edessa; Judas; king(s); Mandylion, the Holy.

Abiathar: son of Ahimelech, the leading priest of Nob. Abiathar alone escaped the massacre by Saul as revenge for aiding David's flight from the king's jealous persecution. He immediately joined David in exile and became his priest (1 Sam. 22:20–23). Abiathar remained loyal to David (even when co-priest with Zadok) during the rebellion of

Absalom but sided with Adonijah in a later attempt to seize the throne. Abiathar was deposed, thus ending the line of Eli and replacing it with that of Eleazar under Zadok in accordance with earlier prophecy. Abiathar had a son named Jonathan, who acted as a spy for David's cause during the rebellion of Absalom. Solomon expelled Abiathar to the village of Anathoth at the outset of his reign but kept Zadok since the latter was descended in the Aaronic line through Aaron's son Eleazar and his grandson Phineas (a more legitimate lineage). Abiathar was a member of the house of Eli at Shiloh through Aaron's son Ithamar, which was condemned for abusing the priestly office in 1 Samuel 2. *See also* Aaronic Covenant, the; Ahimelech; Doeg; Eleazar; Ithamar; Jonathan; Nob; Phinehas; priest(s); Zadok.

Abihu: a son of Aaron. He and his brother Nadab were slain for unauthorized sacrifice before the altar of God (Lev. 10:1–3) and both men died childless. *See also* Eleazar; Jaazaniah; Nadab; priest(s); strange fire; Zadok.

Abijah as Old Testament personalities: 1. an unworthy son of the prophet Samuel appointed by his father as judge of Israel after him (1 Sam. 8:1–3). The people rejected Abijah's leadership (along with his brother Joel) and demanded a king instead. 2. also called Abijam, the second king of Judah who reigned after his father Rehoboam (913–911 B.C.) for a brief three years. He attempted to reunite the kingdom under David's line but was resisted by Jeroboam, the first king of Israel. God showed favor to the house of David, however, and preserved Abijah's army even though the odds were stacked in Jeroboam's favor. 3. a young son of Jeroboam I who became ill. Despite his mother's frantic pleas to the prophet Ahijah, the boy died as a sign of God's displeasure because his father had set up the idolatrous golden calves in Israel. 4. the name of King Hezekiah's mother (2 Chr. 29:1). *See also* Ahijah; Jeroboam I; judge(s); king(s); kings of Israel and Judah; kings of Israel and Judah in foreign relations; Joel.

Abijah as priestly division: a priestly designation of which Zechariah, the father of John the Baptist, was a member. The various courses or rosters of all the priests at that time allowed each to function in some capacity and for some appropriate duration in the Temple. Without such a duty list, some would be denied opportunity to serve their reasonable time. *See also* priest(s); Temple.

Abijam. See Abijah as Old Testament personalities.

Abimelech: 1. a usurper to leadership of a section of the tribal divisions after the death of the judge Gideon (Jud. 9). He was cursed in a prophetic fable by the only surviving son of Gideon, Jotham, a prophecy that eventually proved itself in Abimelech's death because he had murdered all of Gideon's seventy sons with the aid of the people of Shechem. For this atrocity, both the town and Abimelech himself were destroyed. 2. a king of Gerar deceived by Abraham, who withheld the fact that Sarah was his wife, pretending she was his sister (Gen. 20:1–18). Because Sarah was exceptionally beautiful, Abraham feared he would be killed and his wife taken from him. There seems to have been another king of Gerar also named Abimelech (or perhaps the same who associated with Abraham), who had contact with Isaac in much the same situation as Abraham's encounter (Gen. 26:1–33). 3. Others were named Abimelech (less often spelled as Ahimelech) so the name may have been a generic term for a foreign king. *See also* Abraham; fable(s); Jotham; judge(s); Judges as Old Testament book; king(s); millstone; Sarah; Segub; trees and the thornbush, fable of the.

Abington School District vs. Schempp: a 1963 Supreme Court trial involving a Seventh Day Adventist who was seeking unemployment compensation because she could not find a job that would excuse her Saturday day of worship. The justices ruled that government must have a compelling state interest (otherwise known as the "strict scrutiny" process) to pursue any action impinging on the personal rights of individuals. *See also* Allegheny County vs. ACLU;

antidisestablishmentarianism; Backus, Isaac; Baptists; *Booke of the General Lawes and Libertyes;* Caesar cult; caesaropapacy; civil religion; collegialism; disestablishmentarianism; Edict of Milan; Edict of Nantes; Edict of Toleration; Emerson vs. Board of Education; emperor worship; Establishment Clause and Free Exercise Clause; Geghan Bill; Government Regulations Index (GRI); Johnson Amendment; Leland, John; Lemon vs. Kurtzman; Massachusetts Body of Liberties; National Day of Prayer; *Pontifex Maximus; princeps; principis;* public square; Shubert vs. Verner; state church; Toleration Act of 1649; ultramontanism; Virginia's Religious Disestablishment law.

Abiram: 1. a Reubenite, the brother of Dathan and a co-conspirator with Korah's rebellion (Num. 16). 2. the firstborn son of Hiel, the man who rebuilt Jericho (1 Ki. 16:34) from the ashes of Joshua's siege. Abiram and his brother were sacrificed by their father as children when Jericho was reconstructed. The youngster's death during the laying of the foundations of the city was said to be a fulfillment of Joshua's curse on that place many years before (Josh. 6:26). *See also* Dathan; Hiel; Jericho; Korah; Segub.

Abishag: a young woman renowned for her beauty cited in 1 Kings. She was assigned to be a concubine to the elderly and enfeebled King David; her duties were to serve him as a companion and lie alongside to keep him warm. *See also* concubine.

Abishai: a cousin of David and brother of Joab, one of the king's most loyal generals. He commanded one of the three regiments that managed to subdue the rebellion of Absalom and later aided in the pursuit of the rebel Amasa. Speculation indicates he was also one of those who risked his life to bring the fugitive David a drink of water from the well at the king's hometown, Bethlehem. He also rescued David from a Philistine giant and slew 300 troops with his spear. Abishai participated in many battles and his devotion to David was irrepressible. *See also* Abner; Amasa; Asahel; Benaiah; David; David's generals; giant(s); Joab.

abjuration: a renunciation under oath of heresy committed by a Christian of the Roman Catholic Church who wants to be reconciled to the faith. *See also* ascesis; *metanoia;* penance; recant; repent, repentance; rogation; Roman Catholic Church.

ablegate: a papal envoy or legate. *See also* apocrisiarius; auxiliary ministries; ecclesiastic(s); nuncio; Roman Catholic Church.

ablution: pertaining to the ceremonial washing before prayer or other religious function, purification distinct from washing for cleanliness. Sometimes the name *lustration* is substituted. Jewish priests, in particular, were required to wash their feet in the vessel provided (or molten sea in the Temple) before attending before the Lord (Ex. 40:30–32; Heb. 9:10). Muslims also practice the ritual. The Pharisees were criticized by Jesus for their pretentious washings which meant nothing except hypocrisy (Mt. 15:1–15; Mk. 5:1–13). The baptism practices of John the Baptist could be seen as an ablution for sins in preparation for the coming kingdom of God (Mk. 1:1–8). *See also* Essenes; foot washing(s); Great Sea, the; Islam; *lavabo;* liturgical year; liturgy, Christian; liturgy, Jewish; nipper; washings, ceremonial.

Abner: a cousin of Saul and commander of the king's army (1 Sam. 14:50–51). After the death of Saul and Jonathan, Abner made the only surviving son, Ish-Bosheth, king in the place of his father. Abner was subsequently offended by Ish-Bosheth, however, who then attempted to realign himself with David. Josephus described him as erudite, well-spoken, and good natured. He was killed shortly thereafter by his rival Joab in a blood feud (2 Sam. 3:27). *See also* Abishai; Amasa; Benaiah; David; David's generals; Joab.

abolitionist: one opposed to the practice of slavery and is active to abolish it. *See also* slave, slavery.

abomination: a concept of revulsion, especially in a religious context. The term can refer to an object, an action, a word, or even a thought that is disreputable or contemptuous toward God (Pro. 15:26; Ezk. 14:6). Idols were considered an atrocity before the Lord and an unrelenting target for almost all the prophets. *See also* abomination of desolation, the; blasphemy; idol(s); idolatry.

abomination of desolation, the: also known as the abomination that causes desolation, the abomination causing horror, and the overspreading of abomination. The phrase originated with the prophet Daniel, who used it to describe the defiant act of Temple desecration performed by Antiochus Epiphanes. That tyrant sloshed swine broth on the altar in the Jerusalem sanctuary and/or erected a statue to Zeus there. The act has taken on apocalyptic meaning and was used by Jesus to designate the ultimate desecration of the future Temple of the Jews during the time of Tribulation. Most scholars assert that this final act of evil intent, the Antichrist's raising up a statue of himself in the Holy Place of the Tribulation Temple (or his physical presence there), will constitute the ultimate act of blasphemy against God. The pagan and Greek Syrian equivalent of the abomination would be *Baal Shamayin,* or "Lord of Heaven." This the Jews punned in Hebrew to *Shiqquts* ("abomination") and *shomen* (*Shamyim*), which we read as "abomination of desolation." *See also* abomination; beast, image of the; Daniel's vision of the destroying monster; idol(s); idol(s); idol of jealousy; Lord of Heaven; statue erected by Nebuchadnezzar; statue of the beast; wing of the Temple.

abortion: the intentional termination of an unborn fetus, legal or not. The United States has seen some 55 million abortions since 1973, the year of the Supreme Court ruling on the matter called *Roe vs. Wade*. In all, there are likely about 50 million abortions annually worldwide, sometimes using the body parts for scientific experimentation. Controversy has swirled concerning the practice of abortion since many consider it an international ethical issue which they equate to murder. Some opponents make exceptions for conception resulting from rape or incest but others do not. The earliest known abortion records may extend back to ca. 1550 B.C. in the Egyptian Ebers Papyrus but the practice has never ceased throughout history. Sometimes mass exterminations of the unborn were in evidence like the burial monuments to the chief Phoenician female deity Tanit and her spouse Baal Hammon. Roman Catholic authority may well be the leading opponents of open abortion but others, called the "abortion grays" (who may well be the majority of the population), object to the practice but do not want to see it criminalized. *See also* contraception; eugenics; infanticide; murder; *pharmakeia*; Sanger, Margaret Higgins; social issues.

abracadabra: an invented word with association to both esoteric and entertainment magic formed sometime in the first or second century and spoken in Aramaic. The term coincides with the first few letters of the Phoenician alphabet, and when strung together, comprises the name of an ancient demon of disease. Conjurers employed the name as a spell to be spoken as "may the thing be destroyed." Today, it is more recognized as a sort of *Voila*! expression to show off something supposedly appearing from nowhere, as in stage magic. Other sources define the word as "curses" or "damnation." Some Jewish Cabbalists assert the four Hebrew letters in the word can be set in the form of an inverted triangle to make up a magic formula signifying "May your lightening be banished until death." *See also* Eudo de Stella; Fox sisters; grimoire; Harry Potter; hocus-pocus; Houdini, Harry; Magical Papyri; magic, magick; mumbo jumbo; names, symbology of; Saint Germain, Comte de; thaumaturgy.

Abraham: "the friend of God," the first patriarch and source of blessing to Israel and the nations (active around 2000 B.C.). He was originally called Abram (meaning "exalted father"), but God changed his name to Abraham, meaning "the father of a multitude" or "father of many nations." The Jews affectionately call him *Avraham Aveinu* (Abraham our Father). In the New Testament, he is called "father of the faithful" or "man of faith" (Gal. 3:9). He was the center of one of the most important covenants, the very one that guaranteed God's chosen would have a homeland and a populous existence as a nation. Further, he is considered the base of blessing for all nations. Genesis 17:6 specifically states: "I will make you very fruitful; I will make nations of you, and kings will come from you." This promise has assuredly been active since even unlikely peoples like the Parthians, some citizens of Pergamum, and the Lacedemonians (Spartans), according to some historians, are to share the ancestry of Abraham in some degree. Extra-biblical sources, including the *Genesis Rabbah*, tell us that Abraham grew up as the son of an infamous idol maker named Terah, and Abraham himself was a Chaldean astronomer. With his gained faith in the one God, Abraham destroyed his father's idols, causing his persecution by the wicked king Nimrod. Abraham is often classed as a prophet, as well as a patriarch. *See also* Abrahamic Covenant; Aram, Arameans; Esau; Hagar; Hagar and Sarah; Haran; Hebron; Ibri; Jacob; Judaism; Keturah; names, symbology of; Nimrod-bar-Cush; patriarch(s); prophet(s); Sarah; seed of Israel; Sumer, Sumerian(s); Terah.

Abrahamic Covenant: the agreement God made with Abraham granting a perpetual existence for His chosen people (Gen. 12:1–3). Initially, however, the promises to Abraham pertain to himself and his family personally. He was to have provision and protection. But the covenant was broadly extended and consisted of at least eight stipulations from God who would: 1. make Abraham a great nation, 2. bless Abraham, 3. make Abraham's name great, 4. make Abraham a blessing to the nations, 5. bless those who will bless Abraham, 6. curse any who curse Abraham, 7. bless all peoples of the earth through Abraham and, 8. give the land of Canaan possession to the Jews. The covenant was later reaffirmed to Isaac (Gen. 17:21) and to Jacob

(Gen. 35:10–12). The treaty ratification was marked by an elaborate ceremony (Gen. 15) as a ritual of certification. The Abrahamic Covenant is unique and of interest because it grants a general blessing through Abraham, whose obedience to God was renown. It is correct to state that, through Abraham, "all families of the earth" are to be blessed. Those who hold this promise to be "spiritual" and not literal defy what Abraham himself believed and what God's actual intentions are for the human race. *See also* Abraham; Abraham's seed; covenant(s), biblical; circumcision; covenant ceremony; Jew(s); Judaism; remnant; seed of Israel.

Abraham's bosom. See bosom of Abraham.

Abraham's sacrifice: an incident in the life of the patriarch Abraham in which he was commanded by God to sacrifice his only son, Isaac. Following directions, father and son journeyed to the very site where the future Temple would be constructed on Mount Moriah. There Abraham prepared the sacrifice. At the last moment, God directed that the boy's life be spared, and He substituted a ram for the holocaust offering instead. Abraham then called the place *Jehovah-jireh*, "the Lord will provide." Abraham's test has mighty prophetic significance in that it operates as a type of God's then pending sacrifice of his only Son, Jesus Christ. The occasion is detailed in Genesis 22. *See also* Isaac; mountain of the Lord; Mount Moriah.

Abraham's seed: an identifying phrase which, in certain contexts, embraces the groups of people called natural Israel, spiritual Israel, or the Church. *See also* Abrahamic Covenant; Jew(s); remnant; seed of Israel; Seed, the.

Abraxas: the supreme deity of the Gnostic Basilides, who was contemporary with Jesus. The term also represented the multi-layered heavens with their non-corporeal guardians, which must be overcome to reach enlightenment. The god of Basilides is to be studied with connection to the Great

Archon and always with mystical properties. The seven letters of the name may represent the major planets—sun, moon, Mercury, Venus, Mars, Jupiter, and Saturn. Some gemstones had the name engraved and were surely charms. *See also* Aeons; Archons; aerial toll houses; Basilideans; Basilides; Gnosticism, Gnostic(s); idol(s); planets as gods, the.

abrogation: the cancellation of a revealed teaching brought on by a later revelation. The practice seems to be exclusive to Islam and some fringe cultic groups. The *Qur'an*, for example, is oddly formatted—the longer suras (chapters) are placed first and the shortest last. This lack of any logical or chronological order, combined with abrogation, makes an accurate reading difficult if not impossible. Simply put, abrogation occurs when one revelation contradicts a later one, at which point the earlier doctrine is cancelled or explained in another manner. Treaties and agreements can also be "broken" or abrogated. *See also* biblical criticism; lower criticism; source criticism.

Absalom: a son of David who rebelled against his father in hopes of becoming king of united Israel. He was killed during the ensuing civil war when his long hair became entangled in the branches of a tree. David's grief over his son's death almost demoralized the nation until he was upbraided by Joab.

absolute: in the realm of religious philosophy, a concept of a Being that transcends the ordinary, mundane, or physical. The term has been suggested as similar in meaning to Logos and remarked upon as representing "the God of the Universe." *See also* Logos.

absolution: the formal act of a bishop or presbyter in pronouncing forgiveness of sin to a repentant Christian. The more important absolution, however, is that granted by the blood of Jesus for the remission of sin and the pledge of eternal life. On occasion, the prophets were permitted to absolve others, especially kings, for their transgressions before God if instructed to do so and if the situation merited. *See also* atonement; *ego te absolvo;* forgiveness; liturgy, Christian; liturgy, Jewish; redemption; Roman Catholic Church; shrive.

absolutism: the conviction that absolute truth exists, the antonym of relativism.

abstinence: to refrain from consuming certain foods (often meat) or drink (especially alcoholic) for religious reasons or duty. Rejection of certain items in the diet, even of short duration, is a form of self-denial said to be beneficial to spiritual growth and renewal. *See also* Black Fast, the; fast, fasting; Lent; temperance.

Abu-Bakr: the first caliph to succeed Mohammed, as recognized by the Sunni sect of Islam. He was one of the few whom Mohammed promised paradise without martyrdom. *See also* Islam; Sunni Islam.

Abuk: the first woman, according to the Dinkas of the Nile River basin—a mother deity. She was worshiped in Sudan and Ethiopia as the goddess of rain, fertility, and gardens. Her familiar is a small snake. *See also* Egyptian pantheon; Eve; idol(s); woman (women).

Abulfaragius: an obscure Arab Christian historian of the 13th century. The eminent Orientalist Thomas Hyde (1636–1703) quotes him as saying that Zoroaster was a pupil of the Hebrew prophet Daniel, and that it was he who predicted to the Magians of Persia that a new star would appear to notify them of the birth of a royal child in Judea. It was that announcement that launched the Magi toward Bethlehem. *See also* Daniel as prophet; Magi; Zoroaster, Zoroastrianism.

Abyss, the: the dark "pit," "bottomless pit," or "holding pen" that seems to have been specifically designed to imprison particularly wicked fallen angels. Revelation 9:1–11 speaks of opening the pit to release the demonic hordes contained there with the sounding of the fifth trumpet. The Abyss is to be the place of banishment for Satan, who will be incarcerated there for a time after his capture before he is cast into the lake of fire. Also it names the very place to which the Gadarene demons cast out by Jesus begged not to be sent (Lk. 8:26–39). *See also* binding of Satan; Bolos; bound angels; deep, the; hell; Jahannam; lake of fire; loosing of Satan; Perdition; pit; *Sheol;* Tartarus; underworld; Xibala.

acacia. See shittim.

Acan: the Mayan god of wine. *See also* idol(s); Itzamna; Mesoamerica.

Accadian. See Akkadian.

accept Christ, to: Christian jargon for the personal experience of one who accedes to the spiritual drawing power of the Holy Spirit and voluntarily but sincerely repents of sin and acquests to a life of faith. *See also* altar call; "asking Jesus into my heart"; born again; birth from above; Christianese; confession(s) of faith; conversion; "plead the blood"; profession of faith; regeneration; "saved"; "turn your life [heart] over to Jesus"; "walking the aisle"; "washed in the blood."

acceptable year of the Lord, the. See Jubilee Year.

accideme: the science of words and word formation. The practice, along with lexicography (word definitions) and syntax (relationship of words), is considered essential to textual research and language. *See also* alliteration; apostrophe; apothegm; assonance; autograph; Bible; Bible manuscripts; Bible translations; biblical criticism; chiasmus; conflict story; *constructio ad sensum;* context; contextualization; dittography; double sense fulfillment; doublets; doubling; edification; eisegesis; epanadiplosis; epigrammatic statements; etymology; exegesis; figure of speech; folio; form criticism; gattung; gloss; gnomic sayings; grammatical-historical interpretation; *hapax legomena;* haplography;

hermeneutic(s); higher criticism; homographs; homonyms; homophones; *homoteleuton;* hyperbole; idiom; *inclusio;* interpolation; interpretation; inverted nun; irony; isagogics; *itture sopherim;* jot and tittle; kere; *kethib;* "L"; liberalist interpretation; literal interpretation; litotes; loan words; lower criticism; "M"; Masoretic Text; minuscule(s); mystery of God; omission; onomastica; onomatopoeia; palimpsest; papyrus; paradigm; parallelism; parchment; *paroimia;;* pericope; personification; Peshita; pointing; point of view; polyglot; principles of interpretation; proof texting; pun(s); "Q"; redaction; revelation, theological; rhetorical criticism; rhetorical devices; riddle; satire; *scripto continua;* scriptorium; *sebirin;* simile; similitude; source criticism; sources, primary and secondary; special points; strophe; superscription; symbol(s); synecdoche; syntax; synthetic parallelism; text; textual criticism; *tiggune sopherim;* Time Texts; Torah; translation; transposition; trope; type(s); typology; uncial(s); vellum; verbicide.

accidie: an expression in literary works used to illustrate spiritual sloth, boredom, discouragement, and the like with one's faith.

accommodation: 1. the doctrine or idea that God "accommodated" (some say the term should be "condescension") Himself to the earth and the people on it as the only way in which He could interact with us who are tainted by the curse of the Fall. There is truth in the belief, certainly. But we must, at the same moment, remember that Christ not only accommodated himself to become Jesus the man—he *was* Jesus the man. Since we are created in the image of our Maker, we are closer to Him than is at first apparent. By the "accommodation" of the incarnation and the cross, Christ made eternal fellowship with God possible. Still, it was a real cross with real nails and real blood, real pain, and real separation from the Father. And the resurrection was the coming to life in a real body even if was a kind of accommodation of his appearance to ours or, more accurately, our accommodation to his body. 2. an adaptation of a word or expression in the Bible contrary to the original meaning, usually an error in translation. *See also* biblical criticism; curtain of the Temple; gloss; hermeneutic(s); interpretation; principles of interpretation.

accuser of our brothers: Revelation's name for the dragon **of** (Rev. 12:10). The literal meaning of the word *satan* is "accuser." *See also* angel of light; Anointed Cherub; Baal-zebub; Baphomet; Beelzebub; Belial; Cupay; Day Star; dragon; Evil One, the; father of lies; Ghede; goat; god of this age, the; guardian Cherub; Hahgwehdaetgah; Iblis; idol(s); *Kategor;* kingdom of the air; kingdom of this world; king of Babylon; king of Tyre; Light-Bringer; lion; Lucifer; Mastema; Morning Star, the; prince of demons; prince of the power of the air; prince of this world; red dragon; ruler of the kingdom of the air; Sanat Kumar; Satan; seed of the serpent; serpent; Shaytan; son of the morning, son of the dawn.

Aceldama (Akeldama). See Field of Blood; potter's field.

acephali: literally, "no head." The term refers to those churches, sects, or movements without recognized leadership. Such a name may have been inspired by the ancient stories of legendary races with no heads; their eyes and mouth were in the breast. *See also* autocephalous; church, administration of the early; church models; conciliarism; congregational polity; connectional polity; ecclesiology; episcopate; faith and order; Free Church(es); hierarchical polity; magisterium; plebania; polity; prelacy; presbytery; representative polity; rite; ritual; shepherding (cultic); shepherding (discipleship); shepherding (pastoral); sobornost.

Achamoth. See *Sophia.*

Achan: one of the tribe of Judah participating in the attack on Jericho (Josh. 7). After the victory there, Achan appropriated some looted valuables in violation of the holocaust restriction imposed by the Lord that Jericho was to be wholly destroyed. His sin caused the subsequent defeat of the Israelite army at Ai. Lots were employed to discover the guilty after which he and his family were stoned to death in the Valley of Achor. Josephus and some other manuscripts said that his name was Acher, probably a variant of Achan. *See also* Ai; ban; corporate punishment; Valley of Achor.

Acher: meaning "the other," a reference to Rabbi Elisha ben Abuyah, who supposedly entered Paradise (heaven) via a vision. There he reported seeing Metatron (as the translated Enoch) sitting before God. Since only deity can do that, Acher exclaimed there were *two* Gods present. Because of the Jewish prerequisite of monotheism, Elisha was condemned as a heretic, cursed, and tagged as "Acher." The Talmud explains that Metatron's presumption was permissible because he was the heavenly scribe and must assume a sitting posture to do his duties. *Third Enoch* speaks of all Israel being saved, except poor Acher. Some early Christians who read *3 Enoch* thought the sitting figure might be Jesus. *See also* Jew(s).

Acheron: the "river of pain" or "river of woe," one of the five Greek mythological rivers of Hades. Some legends assert Acheron was the son of Helios and Gaea or Demeter but was changed into the water flow as punishment for aiding the Titans against Zeus by giving them refreshing drink. *See also* Charon; Demeter; Gaia (Gaea); Helios; hell; idol(s); Olympian pantheon; Styx; underworld.

Acherusia. See Lake Acherusia.

Achiacus: a convert welcomed by Paul because his visit supplied needed goods and refreshment for his spirit (1 Cor. 16:17).

Achish: son of the king of Gath, David's Philistine sponsor during his exile as an outlaw from Saul. Achish showed favor to David even though the two peoples, the Hebrews and the Philistines, were adamant enemies. *See also* Gath.

Achtariel: an angel of Jewish lore identified as the Old Testament "angel of the Lord." The claim is also made that Achtariel is the "real" name of the Lord in heaven. *See also* angel(s); angel of the Lord, angel of Yahweh.

acolyte: an accensor, from the Greek meaning "follower" or "attendant." In Roman Catholicism and other High Church liturgy, an acolyte performs minor duties during religious services; often these servers are adolescents. Some Protestant denominations also make use of acolytes. In Eastern Orthodoxy, the closest job description to acolyte would be an altar server. A thurifer is an altar boy (or sometimes a girl) with a censer. *See also* Eastern Orthodox Church; orders; Roman Catholic Church.

acosmism: the theological or philosophical idea that the material world is an illusion. There may be a "God" or god-type in the universe, but if so, he is neither personal nor intimate with creation or humanity. The doctrine is common in many Eastern religions. *See also* Cathars; deism; maya.

Acre: Akko in Hebrew, a site twelve miles from Haifa in Palestine. The place was the maritime gateway and chief port during the Crusader period. It was the temporary headquarters of the kingdom of Jerusalem (Outremer), the Knights Templar, and the Hospitallers when threatened by Mameluke forces. Acre was captured in 1291 and all survivors were beheaded, thus essentially ending all productive Crusader ventures in the Holy Land. The city was leveled as a fortress and forever lost as the grandest construction of the era. *See also* Castle Blanc; Crusades; knighted orders; Outremer; Palestine; Tortosa.

acrostic poem: a psalm, hymn, recitation, or similar composition of which specified lines begin with the successive letters of the alphabet. Psalm 119 and the book of Lamentations are a pair of ready examples of a Hebrew acrostic poem. Often, the arrangement was employed as a memorization technique. *See also* antithetic parallelism; chiasmus; climatic parallelism; doubling; music; poetry (biblical); psalm; synthetic parallelism.

Act Concerning Religion. See Toleration Act of 1649.

Act of Conformity: official statement under Queen Elizabeth I that assured uniformity and practice in the newly formed Church of England. *See also* Act(s) of Supremacy; Church of England.

Act of Contrition: a recitation for confession of sin formulated by the Roman Catholic Church. It may be prayed formally via auricular confession or privately. There are several versions of the text, but the popular English wording as taught in catechism reads: "My God, I am sorry for my sins with all my heart. In choosing to do wrong and failing to do good I have sinned against you whom I should love above all things. I firmly intend, with your help, to do penance, to sin no more, and to avoid whatever leads me to sin. Our Lord Jesus Christ suffered and died for us. In His name, my God, have mercy." *See also* confession; Roman Catholic Church.

act of God: some unexplained action attributable to the divine. It is a common phrase for natural disasters and the like used often by insurance companies (much to the chagrin of most theologians).

Act(s) of Supremacy: official decrees of the king and parliament of England that defined the power of the monarchy versus the legislature. The first, a statute (enacted 1534), reserved all ecclesiastical authority in the Church of England to the Crown under Henry VIII. The edict named the king as the only supreme head on earth of the Church of England but, aside from officially breaking with Rome and the pope, the new church remained largely Catholic in practice and polity. The separation arose due to Rome's refusal to grant Henry VIII a marriage annulment from this then-wife Catherine of Aragon. All Catholic monasteries and abbeys were confiscated for their wealth and property but Roman Catholicism in the country changed little of its beliefs and practices. The second decree, issued during the reign of Elizabeth I, and the parliament (in 1558), required the place of the Crown in matters of the church and the state would remain indisputably supreme with the Crown. However, the second diktat did reverse some of the more restrictive elements of freedom of religion from the earlier decree. The state was seen to be superior over the Church of England and free from all foreign pressure nevertheless. *See also* Act of Conformity; Church of England; Henry VIII, King.

Act of the Six Articles: an edict approved by King Henry VIII and parliament in 1539 which allowed canon (church) law to modify or consolidate civil legislation with severe penalties for disobedience. Even though the decree pertained to religious matters, it was viewed as law for English citizens no matter their faith preferences. Six articles, lifted directly from Roman Catholic and Anglican practice, were affirmed: transubstantiation, withholding the cup for laity at Communion, clerical celibacy, mandatory obedience to chastity vows, permission for private masses, and the importance of auricular confession. Protestants called the legislation "the bloody whip with six strings." *See also* Church of England; Henry VIII, King.

Acts as New Testament history: a basic history of the Church, written by the physician and historian Luke and following the Gospels in the New Testament. The record begins with the ascension of Christ and records the arrival of the Holy Spirit at Pentecost; it ends with a glimpse of Paul at Rome in his final days of missionary activity. Important eschatological treatises include judgment, the Millennium, the Davidic Covenant, and other end time themes. *See also* Acts 29; Christianity in the Roman Empire; church, administration of the early; church, divisions of the early; history of the Church; Luke as missionary.

Acts 29: church-talk for the progress and actions of the Church since the close of the book of Acts (which ends with Chapter 28, not 29). World outreach, missions, and worship did not cease with the record by Luke but continues to this day and is worthy of commentary. *See also* Acts as New Testament history; Christianese.

actualization: a New Age religion teaching or methodology based on pantheism. The premise is that all humans possess a Christ-centered element that makes them united to the universal Father-Mother Creator God, whether they know or acknowledge it or not. *See also* Christ-consciousness; New Age religion.

acupuncture and acupressure: methodologies of ancient Chinese medicine by which needles or pressure are applied to certain parts of the body in order to balance the *yin* and *yang* within. The process is said to open blocked meridians (pathways) and open the chakras so Chi (the life energy) can freely flow. The application has health benefits but is often involved in certain esoteric belief systems as well. *See also* chakra; Chi; contemplative prayer movement; kundalini; meridians; Shakti.

A.D. See *Anno Domini*.

Adad: 1. the ancient Mesopotamian god of tempest and rain. 2. the name or title (though proof positive evidence is missing) of one or more kings of Aram during the era of Israel's divided kingdom. *See also* Hadad; idol(s); king(s); Mesopotamia; Sumerian and Babylonian pantheon.

Adam: the first man, carrying a meaning delivered as "of the soil" or "taken from the red earth," an appropriate derivation since God made Adam from the dust of the ground. He is said to be a type for Jesus according to Paul. In this model position, Adam was the recipient of a covenant of works whereby he and his helpmate were to tend the Garden of Eden in exchange for long life and blessing. He and Eve lost their place in Paradise because of disobedience after yielding to the temptation of the serpent. As federal head of the human race, Adam is responsible for the world's alienation from God, our difficulty with sin, and the source of our need for the redemption in Christ. *See also* Adamic Covenant; Edenic Covenant; covenant of works; Eve; Fall, the; federal theory of guilt; image of God; Lilith; man; names, symbology of; Original Sin; Pre-Adamites; second Adam; son(s) of man (men); works, salvation by.

Adamic Covenant: the first covenant initiated by God. Adam was to care for Eden in exchange for continued blessing, protection, and long life. The treaty failed because of the first couple's sin of pride and disobedience. *See also* Adam; covenant(s), biblical; Edenic Covenant; Eve; Fall, the; federal theory of guilt; Original Sin; works, salvation by.

Adamites: a rather licentious Christian religious group active in North Africa from the second through the fourth centuries. They routinely practiced their worship in the nude supposedly to copy the innocence of pre-fallen Adam and Eve. A later group with similar practices and doctrines sprang up in Europe. *See also* cult(s); sect(s).

Adar as calendar month: the sixth month of the Jewish civil year of the Hebrew calendar and the twelfth in the ecclesiastical menology. The nomenclature Adar I, Adar II, or Ve-adar (*Ve* means "and thus") are also relative to various aspects of the dating. Adar occurs in the February reckoning but in leap years it is preceded by a thirty-day intercalary month called Adar Aleph. The first letter of the Hebrew alphabet, *aleph*, relates to the March time period and is critical in determining when the Jewish Feast of Purim is to be celebrated. *See also* calendar (Hebrew); feasts and special days of Judaism; Purim, Feast of.

Addai: (sometimes Addeus or Thaddeus) traditional founder of the Syriac-speaking church at Edessa in Northern Mesopotamia. He holds eschatological interest because he was, according to the *Testament of James*, entrusted with the revelations of James the Just that Addai alone was to receive secretly, and then open after ten years had elapsed. That tradition is Gnostic in origin but Addai is venerated in Eastern Orthodoxy because it is believed he was sent by the apostle Thomas to cure King Abgar V of Edessa, who had fallen ill. It is said then that Abgar and Jesus corresponded often following the miraculous healing. *See also* Abgar; Edessa; Judas; Mandylion, the Holy.

Additions to Daniel: apocryphal shorter writings that supplement the book of Daniel. They include *Song of the Three Young Men, Daniel and Susanna,* and *Bel and the Dragon [Snake]. See also* Apocrypha, the; *Bel and the Dragon;* Daniel as Old Testament prophecy; Susanna.

Adelphi Organization: a small communal cult established by Richard Kieninger (d. 2002). One community is located near Dallas, Texas, and the other in Stelle, Illinois. Both are established on the esoteric philosophy of Kieninger and the preparation for doomsday soon to visit the earth. *See also* communal communities; cult(s); Kieninger, Richard.

adelphopoiesis: literally, "brother-making," an ecclesiastical process or ceremony in Roman and Orthodox churches that united same-sex (usually male) partners in a special relationship. There is controversy as to whether the action was to create a "blood-brother" relationship or to sanction same sex union in some form. The practice ended for Roman Catholicism in the 14th century and for Eastern Orthodoxy in the 18th century. *See also* brother(s); civil unions; Eastern Orthodox Church; Roman Catholic Church; Sergius and Bacchus.

adept: an individual recognized as having attained a specified expertise or knowledge, especially in magical practice or the occult. *See also* idolatry; magic, magick; New Age religion; occult, occultic; witchcraft.

***ad hominen* argument:** any attempted polemic against a person or position based on character assassination and guilt by association. The process appeals to emotion and prejudice rather than intellect or reason. It is a common accusation of the church and religious practice today from those who oppose them, an attack sometimes justified to some extent.

The prophets, too, like us, were not immune to this type of unfair censure. The Church itself is not immune to *ad hominen* action when not behaving properly in its attitude and practice.

adiaphora: literally, "matters of indifference." The 16th century Reformers coined the term for the purpose of avoiding divisive debate on non-essentials of faith. What a woman wears to church gatherings, for example, is of no theological consequence and therefore should not be an item of dispute. "Warn them before God against quarreling about words; it is of no value" (2 Tim. 2:14).

adjacent possible: Stuart Kauffman's concept of the increasing acceleration of human knowledge and technology, which is predicted to be so rapid in the future that it will fundamentally change who we are as a race of peoples. *See also* Five Ways, the; Jumping Jesus Phenomenon, the; Law of Accelerating Returns, the; point of infinity; teleology; timewave, the; zero state.

Admah: one of the cities of the plain near the Dead Sea (Gen. 10:19; 14:2, 8). It was destroyed along with Sodom and Gomorrah but lived on in infamy as a symbol of wickedness and a warning to subsequent generations in Israel (Hos. 11:8). *See also* cities of the plain; Pentapolis; Sodom; Sodom and Gomorrah; Zeboiim; Zoar.

Adonai: also *Adonay*, a common appellation for God in the Hebrew language. The term was used in place of the holy name *Yahweh*, which was considered too sacred to speak or write. The Greek translation in the LXX is *Kyrios*, which defines both Adonai and Yahweh. *Kyrios* also names Christ. *See also* Christ; El; Elohim; 'Emeth; I AM WHO I AM; Jah; Jehovah; Jesus Christ; Messiah; name known only to Christ; Name, my; Name of the Lord, the; names (titles) for God; names (titles) for Jesus; name that is above every name, the; name that no one knows, the; Name, your; omnific word; Sabaoth Adoai; Shemhamforesh; Yahweh.

Adonijah: a son of David who sought to be king of Israel as his father's death approached. He was aided by Joab and Abiathar but opposed by Nathan the prophet, Bathsheba, and other military officials and priests who favored Solomon. The rebellion failed and Adonijah was later slain on Solomon's order.

Adonis: the Greek god of beauty and desire worshiped mostly by women. His cult was central among the many mystery groups in operation at that time and shows a basic structure from the sect of Tammuz. Adonis was beloved of Aphrodite, who tendered his care as a child to Persephone. The latter was also enamored and refused to return him when he became of age. Adonis was killed by a wild boar in the ensuing conflict of jealousy among the gods. By order of Zeus, Calliope settled the dispute by decreeing that Adonis would be required to spend one-third of his time with Aphrodite, a third with Persephone, and the remaining third reserved to his own discretion. His multiple deaths and rebirths mark him as a central vegetation renewal deity. *See also* Aphrodite; fertility gods; idol(s); Olympian pantheon; Persephone.

Adonizedek. See Melchizedek.

adoption: the theological concept whereby believers are received into God's family, making them joint-heirs with Christ, by the will of God and not by human demand. *See also* glorification; grace; justification; regeneration; salvation; sanctification; theology.

Adoptionism: the theological idea that God "adopted" Jesus to be the Son at some point in his ministry, usually noted to be the moment of his baptism. At the point of selection, it is claimed that Jesus was empowered by the Spirit to be a healer and teacher until his death on the cross, a process known as "dynamism." *See also* Adoptionism; Anomoeans; appropriation; Arianism; Arius; complementarian view of the Trinity; Donatism; dualism; Dynamic Monarchianism; dynamism;

dyophysitism; eternal subordination of the Son; "four fences of Chalcedon"; *homoiousios; homoousios;* hypostatic union; incarnation; *kenosis;* kenotic view of Christ; miaphysitism; modalism; monarchianism; monoenergism; monophysitism; Nestorianism; Nestorius; *ousia;* patripassianism; Pelagianism; *perichoresis;* psilanthropism; Sabellianism; Socianism, Socinian; subordinationism; theanthroposophy; *Theophorus;* Trinity; two natures, doctrine of the; unipersonality.

Adramelech: the "king of fire," a false god whom the ancients may have recognized as a first-rank devil of hell (called Satan's chancellor) and as the source behind the womanizing spirit. The spirit was a form of sun-god related to Moloch, which Judeo-Christian sources named as a demon requiring child sacrifice. It even appears in Milton's *Paradise Lost* and in Friedrich Klopstock's epic poem *The Messiah*. The name also applies to the spirit force causing females to mate with animals and was worshiped in synch with the female demon Anammelech. *See also* Abaddon; Abezi-Thibod; Anammelech; Apollyon; Asmodaeus; Azazel; Azrael; Baal-zebub; demon(s); demonic; devils; Dibbuk; Dubbi'el; Gadreel; idol(s); Legion; Lilith; Mastema; Pazuzu; Sammael; Sumerian and Babylonian pantheon.

Adso: a monk who wrote to Gerberga, sister of Otto I of Germany (ca. A.D. 950) in which he warned of the near approach of the Antichrist. The letter was widely copied and circulated around Europe. Adso's prediction centered the Antichrist on earth after the last of the Frankish kings was gone. His research, in obedience to the Queen's command, was recorded as *Little Work on Antichrist* in A.D. 954. He believed an antichrist spirit was manifested in dictators like Antiochus, Nero, and Domitian, but a personal one would arrive later from the Jewish tribe of Dan. *See also* monasticism; monk(s).

Adullam: an ancient city in the Shephelah region of Judah. Here was the headquarters of David when he was an outlaw on the run from Saul and not far from the place where he killed Goliath. The prophet Micah envisions the area as a place of blessing from the one who is the glory of Israel (Mic. 1:15).

adulteress: a female unfaithful in the marriage relationship. The description rests on Religious Babylon (Rev. 17), named because of her unrighteous and abusive liaison with the earth's inhabitants, which describes her as being "drunk with the wine of her adulteries." Some translations speak of "the passion of her immorality" and similar terms. The description derives from *porneia* from which we get the word pornography. *See also* adultery, adulteries; dog(s); fornication; Great Prostitute, the; idolatry; prostitute, prostitution; Religious Babylon.

adultery, adulteries: illicit sexual activity, technically between couples, one or both of whom are married. The term is a frequent apocalyptic description of moral and religious infidelity used frequently in Scripture. Faithless and immoral religion is often classed as harlotry and infidelity. *See also* adulteress; dog(s); fornication; idolatry; prostitute, prostitution; Religious Babylon.

Advent: the period of time on the calendar that anticipates the celebration of Christmas. The word is appropriate in that its meaning responds to "arriving." Most churches recognizes the four Sundays prior to December 25 as the days of Advent, each of which usually entails some form of special emphasis in the worship occasions. Some see the days as the "little Lent" when sorrow and shame for sin change to the joy and hope of Christmas. *See also* advent(s) of Christ; Advent wreath; carol(s); Christingle; Christmas; Christmas tree; *epiphaneia;* feasts and special days of high liturgy faiths; feasts and special days of Protestantism; First Advent; Gaudete Sunday; Lent; Lessons and Carols; liturgical year; liturgy, Christian; Noel; Yule.

Adventism, Adventist(s). See Seventh-Day Adventism.

advent(s) of Christ: an arrival or an "appearing" of the Savior. Advents are spoken of as plural when the First (the birth and ministry of Jesus) is discussed along with the Second (the *Parousia* or Second Coming). *See also* Advent; Advent wreath; appearing, the; appointed time, the; Christmas; consummation, the final; day he visits us, the; Day, that; End, the; *epiphaneia;* eschatology, eschatological; First Advent; fullness of time; Glorious Appearing; "here, there, or in the air"; rapture; Second Coming; Second Coming procession; secret rapture.

Advent wreath: a common enough Christmas artifact in many homes and churches evident in the Advent season. The wreath, its arrangement, and its symbolism represent the four weeks of year prior to Christmas Day by advertising the light of Christ coming into a sin-darkened world. Various traditions and ritual are assigned to the representation but there are some common themes. The wreath itself is evergreen—perhaps a holdover from pagan festivals of the warding of evil and evil spirits—now representing the life of vitality for the believer. If cones are added, they can signify the resurrection of Christ and of the believer. Its circular arrangement adds the sign of eternal life and the defeat of death. Traditionally, the round stand holds five candles—three purple, a rose, and one other (usually centered and larger) of white. Purple suggests the liturgical color of Lent, for repentance and fasting; pink is for joy; white is for purity. One candle is lit each Sunday of Advent with the last (white) lighted on Christmas Eve or Christmas Day. The first candle (purple) is the Prophecy candle or candle of hope. God is faithful and will keep His promises. The second (purple) is the Bethlehem candle or candle of peace. We are to "get ready" to welcome the Lord born in Bethlehem. The third (pink) is the Shepherd's candle or candle of joy. Advent is good news as announced to the humble shepherds on the Judean hillsides. The fourth light is the Angels' candle or candle of love. God sent His

Son because He loves us as testified by the angel chorus above Bethlehem. The fifth is the Christ candle (white). The spotless lamb of God has been sent to banish our sin and provide the fellowship of Jesus to all who will receive him. Alternative symbolism is just as valid. Some prefer blue candles (the color of life) to the three of purple to distinguish the wreath somewhat from Lent and Advent. In some instances, the four encircling candles represent the patriarch, the prophets, John the Baptist, and Mary. Or, the third may honor Mary in feminine pink. The surrounding four tapers can number the 4,000 years since the birth of Christ. *See also* Advent; Christingle; Christmas; Christmas tree; colors, liturgical; flora, fruit, and grain, symbology of; Gaudete Sunday; liturgy, Christian; symbol(s); white; wreath.

Adversus Judaeos: certain anti-Semitic writings of the early church fathers (Cyril, Chrysostom, Augustine, Eusebius, Justin, Origen, Jerome, and others). The Jews were labeled as "Christ killers," demons, plague carriers, bloodthirsty pagans who sought to drink the blood of children at Easter, lechers, etc. *See also* anti-Semitic; Concordant of Collaboration; conspiracy theorists; Day of Pardon; *Entdectes Judenthum;* "Protocols of the Elders of Zion"; *Simonini Letter.*

advocate: 1. to testify for or support a given proposition or person. 2. a lay protector and legal representative for a monastery. 3. The Holy Spirit is sometimes described as an advocate to the Father for the believer (Jn. 14:16). *See also* Eastern Orthodox Church; monastery; monasticism; names (titles) for the Holy Spirit; Roman Catholic Church.

advowson: the right under English law to nominate or present a clergyman to a vacant posting. *See also* Church of England.

adytum: the most sacred or secret place in a temple. The Zion Temple Holy of Holies could be called an adytum. *See also* furniture and furnishings of the modern church; Holy of Holies; temple(s).

Aelia Capitolina: the Roman name for Jerusalem around A.D. 135 A.D., an event brought about by order of Emperor Hadrian. The city was designated as a pagan municipality after it was somewhat restored from its destruction in A.D. 70. *See also* Hadrian; Jerusalem as city; Jerusalem, invasions of; Roman Empire.

Aeneas: a bedridden paralytic in Lydda who had held his malady for eight years (Acts 9:32–35). Peter healed him in the name of Jesus.

Aeons: residents or divisions of the heavenly spheres, according to Gnosticism, which must be penetrated by the possessors of secret knowledge in order to reach perfection. The name infers "emanations from God and takes on a number of names and functions depending on the type of Gnosticism being investigated. *See also* Archons; Basilideans; Demiurge; emanations, doctrine of; Gnosticism, Gnostic(s); idol(s); Pleroma; *Sophia*.

aerial toll houses: an Easter Orthodox belief (not sanctioned by all) that the human soul is escorted to heaven by God and angels. Along the way, however, there are encounters with wicked spirits located at "toll houses" that fling accusations and accuse the soul of sin. If possible, they will drag the accused to hell. *See also* Abraxas; Aeons; Archons; Eastern Orthodox Church; Gnosticism, Gnostics; idol(s).

Aesculapius. See Asclepius.

Aesir: a collective name for the grouping of gods and goddesses of ancient Norse mythology. Asynjur (the goddesses of the group) and Vanir (the gods of the collection) were associated anthropological classifications useful to scholars for sorting ancient Norse theology. Often the Vanir are seen as one group of Norse gods associated with fertility, wisdom, nature, magic, and the ability to foresee the future; the other arm of gods is the Aesir. *See also* Alfheimr; Armanenschafft; Asa; Asatru; blyt; frost giants; giant(s); idolatry; Norse and Old Germanic pantheon; seior; Valupsa; volva; Wotanism.

aetiology. See etymology.

affusion: baptism by pouring water over the head. *See also* aspersion; baptism; immersion.

African Independent Churches: or African Indigenous Churches, faith groups based in African culture to some extent. Some congregations may hold variations of Western denominations but others carry more tribal or existing local traditions from the native countries. *See also* Afro-American theology; church bodies in America (typed); denomination(s); denominationalism.

African Methodist Episcopal Church: largest black denomination in the United States. In 1787, a group of black churchgoers (led by ex-slave Richard Allen) withdrew from the segregated Saint George's Methodist Episcopal Church in Philadelphia. They built a new congregation on land owned by Allen and Francis Asbury and dedicated the building, which was named Bethel. From that beginning, several schools and overseas missionary outreach efforts were promoted, including Wilberforce College in Ohio. That school is named after the English abolitionist William Wilberforce. *See also* Afro-American theology; Allen, Richard; church bodies in America (typed); denomination(s), denominationalism; "invisible institution, the"; Revels, Hiram Rhoades; Seabury, Samuel; Vesey, Denmark; Wilberforce, William.

African Methodist Episcopal Zion Church: Methodists of the black tradition began in New York in 1796. *See also* Afro-American theology; church bodies in America (typed); denomination(s), denominationalism.

Africanus, Scipio: the Roman general and statesman who defeated the Phoenician general Hannibal (235-183 B.C.). He was a worshiper of Jupiter and a priest of Mars but exhibited some interest in eschatology. In fact, he claimed to be prescient, and predicting the future was one of his major occupations. *See also* Roman Empire.

Africanus, Sextus Julius: a Roman (possibly Libyan) biblical commentator (ca. A.D. 160–240) who claimed the world would end 6,000 years after the creation, which he calculated to be no later than A.D. 500. Julius Africanus was one of the earliest great scholars of the ancient world who was an able Christian and apologist for the faith. He was an itinerate philosopher type, a historian, and heavily influenced Eusebius. *See also* Roman Empire.

Afro-American theology: or black theology, a movement popular in the 1960s and still recognized, which was intended to identify the Afro-American method of study and preaching when experienced in that culture. Their view of prophecy and theology in general is often dynamic and expressive, although there are definitely "High Church" (liturgical) expressions of worship as well. The Afro-American style of worship can trace its roots to slavery days when blacks benefitted from the Great Awakenings then sweeping the country. Specifically, a number of black denominations emerged at the time, including the African Methodist Episcopal Union with other black Baptists congregations and associations. Black Protestants make up about eight percent of the United States population. Much of the music also springs from the era which created the folk/worship harmonies, the so-called "Negro Spirituals," those expressions fused from the revivalism of the times and those repetitions and rhythms of what they remembered from Africa. In some cases, black theology tends to slide easily into political activities, including the civil rights movement. *See also* Abernathy, Ralph David; African Independent Churches; African Methodist Episcopal Church; African Methodist Episcopal Zion Church; Allen, Richard; Church of God in Christ; Elijah Mohammed; Fard, Wallace (Wali) Dodd; Farrakhan, Louis; Great Awakenings, the; Graham, William; Harris, William Wade; "invisible institution, the"; Jackson, Jesse Louis; Jubilee Singers; King, Martin Luther, Jr.; Kwanzaa; Malcolm X; Million Man March; music;

National Baptist Convention; Nation of Islam; Powell, Adam Clayton; Restoration Movement in America; Revels, Hiram Rhoades; Sharpton, Charles "Al" Jr.; Spirituals; Wheatley, Phillis.

afterlife: the common term for life after death. The Old Testament speaks little of it (though it is not silent on some aspects of the subject), and most ancient Jews had scant interest in it. Plato talked of people as having a "soul," which might reflect a divine force beyond itself. The Sadducees, Essenes, Pharisees, and Zealots took on varying degrees of differences from each other concerning the world beyond. The Essenes were the most keen to learn of it, and the Sadducees were the most skeptical. Intertestamental writings, especially the earliest (called *Wisdom of Solomon*), saw a proliferation of records of the subject. *See also* Abraham's bosom; Annwn; Aralu; Arcadia; Asgard; Avalon; Dis; Duat; Elysium; eschatology, eschatological; eternal life; future life, doctrine of the; Gehenna; Hades; happy hunting ground; heaven; hell; Hy-Breasail; Hyperborea; intermediate state; Jade Empire, the; Jahannam; Janna; lake of fire; life after death; limbo; *Limbus Puerorum;* metempsychosis; Mictlan; new heaven and new earth; Nirvana; Otherworld; Paradise; paradise of God; paraeschatology; Pardes; Perdition; Promised Land, the; Pure Land, the; purgatory; rebirthing; reincarnation; Shambhala legends; *Sheol;* soul sleep; space doctrine; Summerland; Thule, land of; Tir na nOg; underworld; Upper Gehenna; Utopia; Valhalla; world to come, the; Xibala.

after one's own lusts: or "ungodly desires," a negative phrase indicating humanity's bent to selfishness and immorality (*e.g.,* 2 Peter 3:3, Jude 18). The words inevitably convey a sense of disgust inherent in the mortal infatuation with indulgent sin and are an apocalyptic sign of the increasing apostasy of the age. *See also* debauchery; demimondaines; depravity; harmartiology; hedonism; moral relativism; sin(s); social issues.

History and Mystery

Agabus: a prophet from Jerusalem (Acts 11:27–30) who predicted a widespread famine in the Roman Empire. At one point, he symbolically bound himself with Paul's belt to warn the apostle of impending imprisonment if he persisted on his journey to Jerusalem. Josephus related that this famine prophesied by Agabus actually occurred during the procuratorships of Fadus and Tiberius Alexander. *See also* prophet(s); Izatus, King; Helena.

agape. See love.

Agapemone: an English communal experiment that began around 1850 by Henry James (1811 – 1899), Samuel Starkey, and some others. They were known at that time as "The A." The sect was a breakaway from the Church of England that formed itself into a commune. With the advent of J. H. Smyth-Pigott (ca. 1890), however, the institution changed since their new leader claimed to be Jesus reincarnated. *See also* communal communities; sect(s).

agapetae: churchmen and churchwomen living together in celibacy. *See also* abbey; communal communities; ecclesiastic(s); monasticism; Roman Catholic Church.

agathodaimon: Greek for "good demon" or "good spirit." The ancient Greeks believed that every person possessed one—a guardian spirit who watched over him or her throughout life. When Christianity appeared, it was an easy transition to a similar belief. *See also* bugbears; daemons; demon(s), demonic; demonology; guardian angel(s); *psychopomps*; tutelary.

age: 1. a period of more or less indeterminate but lengthy time in which a single historical theme may be traced. In religious history, one may speak of the church age, the age of lawlessness, ages past, the ages to come, etc. (1 Cor. 10:11, *et al.*). 2. the length of a person's life, usually reckoned around 70—80 years by our standards, but less for the ancients (Ps. 90:10). 3. the world or the historical course of the world as it is counted off in history and time (Heb. 1:2; Eph. 2:2). Apocalyptically speaking, the term is often expanded as "the present age and the new age" or "this world and the world to come." *See also aion; eon;* eschatology, eschatological; *olam.*

age of accountability: the chronological or psychological stage of maturity of a boy or girl wherein the child is recognized as old enough and mature in faith enough to determine the true concept of religious conviction as an individual. For Jewish boys, the time is age thirteen but most other faith groups are not so precise. The term is therefore relative. As such, those denominations in quest of childhood dedication do not baptize infants and may defer church membership until satisfied that the candidate understands the commitment fully. *See also* Bar and Bat Mitzvah; Confirmation; credo-baptism; pedobaptism.

Age of Aquarius: the approaching zodiac age (symbolized as the water-bearer) that will replace the present dispensation of Pisces (the fish). The latter segment began around the time of Jesus, and the Age of Aquarius will commence sometime around the year 2025. Such an advent held some importance to the Founding Fathers as they believed that the new nation would have significant impact in that future. It was also central to the so-called "hippie era" of the 1960s and 70s and to most New Agers today, because it portends more to a chance to break away from traditional Christian-dominated values of this era and promote more of the ancient wisdom and mantic philosophy. At the core of the belief, there appears to be a not-so-subtle affirmation that the human race will finally achieve the ability to think for itself and shed its need for religious instruction and protection. Meanwhile, the changeover period (now) is a time of unparalleled confusion, apprehension, and extremism. This is so because the new waves of occultic or spiritual energy being generated is in flux as the two ages merge and convulse. *See also* astrology, astrologists; constellations; Damanhur; Fourth Density; harmonic conversion; New Age religion; zodiac.

History and Mystery

age of grace: the time of the present when the Church is extant and responsible for proclaiming the gospel of grace (the favor of God offered to all persons even though it is unmerited) to the entire world. The reference is posited as superseding the age of law, or the daunting Old Testament dependence on Judaic regulation and ritual. *See also* age of the Gentiles; fullness of the Gentiles; Gentiles; grace; "great parenthesis, the"; prophetic postponement; times of the Gentiles.

age of lawlessness: a future time when the world's evils will multiply, termed by Paul as "terrible times in the last days" (2 Tim. 3:1–9). *See also* day of evil; day of God, the; day of (our Lord Jesus) Christ; day of Revenge; day of the Lamb's wrath, the; day of [their] visitation; day of the Lord; day of trumpet and battle, a; day of vengeance of our God; "days of Elijah"; "days of Noah"; great and dreadful day, that; wrath, the coming.

Age of Reason: history's unofficial designator for the 1700s. The era identified a time when many educated people became skeptical of the Bible and Christian belief and began to be convinced that human reason might be the answer to the human dilemma. Not all, scientist or otherwise, held to the new beliefs however. *See also* clergy scientists; Renaissance.

age of redemption: a phrase the rabbis declared would be operative when the regathering of Israel transpires, or when the exiles are reconvened from their *Diaspora*. Some recognize that the creation of the state of Israel in 1948 began such an era. Many Christian theologians and laypersons would understand the time to note an era of later Jewish repentance and reoccupation of millennial Jerusalem by the Jews. *See also* restoration of all things; restoration of Israel (the Jews); second Exodus.

age of the Gentiles: the present age of the world in which non-Jews, sometimes called "the nations," take center stage in history. Revelation 11 speaks of a time when part of the Temple will be trampled under by the Gentiles. The period indicated is usually intended in a negative sense toward religious history unless the "*church* of the Gentiles" is its object. *See also* age of grace; fullness of the Gentiles; Gentiles; "great parenthesis, the"; prophetic postponement; times of the Gentiles.

Age of Violence: an artificial dispensational era suited for the church at Sardis (Rev. 3:1-6). The approximate historical date is noted as A.D. 1328–1648 when the church seemed to indulge in persecution of its own constituency, as well as those outside the faith.

age to come: a shorthand reference to the Millennium. *See also* eschatology, eschatological.

Aggadah: a rabbinic commentary covering all of the Old Testament. It tries to motivate the reader to pious living by use of legends, quotations of the elders, proverbs, mysticism, practical advice, etc. The title means "telling" or "something told" and is essentially a compilation of rabbinic homilies. The collection is essentially literary productions of various descriptions heavily laced with Jewish folklore. They are a sort of body of figures and incidents based somehow on biblical characters and events. *See also* Aqiba, Rabbi Joseph ben; Bible Code; Cheiro; Gemara; *gematria;* Halakha; *isopseplia;* Judaism; Masseket Hekalot; Midrash; Mishna; *notarikon;* Qabbala; *Sefiort;* Talmud; *Tanakh;* Targum(s); *temoorah;* Torah; torah; Zevi, Shabbatai; *Zohar.*

aggiomamento: "modern" ideas of the established Roman Catholic Church that have come slowly over the centuries, often with little discernible difference in doctrine. The councils of Vatican I and II are usually cited as the most progressive. *See also* Council of Trent; Roman Catholic Church; Vatican I and Vatican II.

agnosticism, agnostic(s): a term attributed to Professor Thomas Henry Huxley in 1869 that defines a person who claims he or she cannot know God with certainty. *See also* apatheist;

atheism, atheist(s); Brights, the; Huxley, Thomas Henry; possibilianism.

Agnus Dei: an anthem common in the Roman mass but with origins in the East. The words "Lamb of God" give its title followed by "who takes away the sins of the world." The prayer is highly repetitive and is addressed specifically to Christ as present in the Eucharist. *See also* Eastern Orthodox Church; liturgical year; liturgy, Christian; music; Roman Catholic Church.

Agobard: bishop of Lyons (ca. A.D. 779–840). He believed that the arrival of the Antichrist was near and advised Emperor Louis the Pious to hoard and protect the church's teachings concerning the matter. *See also* Roman Catholic Church.

agora: public open space of a town, countryside, or city where people of the ancient world could congregate. It was ideal for marketing, bazaars, street entertainment, and social, business, or legal interaction. Political debate and even executions were often enacted there. Thus it was near-essential community real estate which naturally led to religious exchange and actions of all descriptions as well. *See also* Areopagus.

Agpeya: the Coptic book of hours. At its core are seven prayers from the Psalms and readings suitable for prime, tierce, sext, nones, vespers, and compline. *See also* canonical hours; Coptic Church; liturgical year.

Agrapha: unwritten units of tradition regarding the life of Christ. The collective knowledge inherent in the cache of information is small in volume and mostly apocryphal, but some parts survive in Acts, Paul's epistles, and once in the book of James. None, to our present knowledge, are referenced in the Gospels. *See also* Apocryphal Gospels; Gospel(s); "L"; *logia;* "M"; oral tradition; "Q"; source criticism; unwritten prophecies.

Agrippa. See Herod Agrippa I; Herod Agrippa II.

Agrippa Books: enormously-sized books used by devotees of the occult. The references were said to be thick, five-foot-tall volumes with pages made of human skin. The works were supposedly collected by Heinrich Cornelius Agrippa, a philosopher and dabbler in the demonic during the 1500s. The books were said to contain the names of the demons and the spells that would bring them forth, along with other useful information. The set was reputed to be so evil that they were kept wrapped in chains in empty rooms so the devil would not escape. *See also* alchemy; *arcanum arcandrum; Arcanum,* the; *Book of Abramelin, The;* cantrip; *Corpus Hermecticum;* demon(s), demonic; demonology; Emerald Tablet of Hermes, the; *Golden Bough, The;* grimoire; Hermeticism; Hermetic wisdom; Hermetic writings; idolatry; magic arts; magic, magick; mana; mantic wisdom; occult, occultic; parapsychology; *Picatrix;* secret wisdom; spell names; *Spiritas Mundi.*

Agur. See Lemuel.

Aha!: an exclamation of malicious joy, often showing contempt for the good or for the discomfiting fortunes of another (Ps. 35:21; 70:3; Ezk. 25:3). The Hebrew drama of striking one's hands together while exclaiming "*ah*" illustrates the cry of sorrow or surprise with a base meaning of "ach!" Today's use of the expression is more uplifting. *See also* clapping hands and stomping feet; striking hands and striking the thigh.

Ahab: the seventh king of Israel (874–853 B.C.) and one of the most wicked. He fostered Baal worship as influenced by his queen, Jezebel (a Tyrian princess). Ahab's reign was long and prosperous in its political components but was continually criticized in a religious and humanitarian sense by the prophet Elijah. The king's jealous murder of Naboth to gain his ancestral vineyard (a scheme hatched by Jezebel) earned him the prediction that canines would lick up his blood and Jezebel would be devoured by feral dogs. The savage purge by Jehu resulted in both prophecies' literal fulfillment. Ahab was killed in battle against the Syrians who had broken the treaty secured earlier by him, and then joined with his enemies. *See also* Jezebel; king(s); kings of Israel and Judah; kings of Israel and Judah in foreign relations; Naboth.

Ahab and Zedekiah: a pair of false prophets among the exiles to Babylon (Jer. 29:21–23). According to legend, the two habitually seduced other men's wives, even trying their perfidy on a concubine or daughter of King Nebuchadnezzar. It is possible that they were the source material for the apocryphal book of "Daniel and Susanna." *See also* False Prophet, the.

Ahasuerus. See Xerxes.

Ahaz: the twelfth ruler of Judah (735–715 B.C.) who shared rule with Jotham, his father, for part of his time on the throne. Ahaz was numbered among the evil kings of the Southern Kingdom and became a prey for Syria and Israel when these two nations joined against him. Ahaz appealed to Tiglath-pileser of Assyria for help when Jerusalem was besieged by a coalition of Israel and Damascus. On the advice of Isaiah the prophet, Ahaz refused to submit and Jerusalem was subsequently saved by a supernatural act of God. Assyria's aid proved more of a hindrance than a help, however, as Judah was now subservient to that kingdom. Ahaz worshiped the idols of Assyria, even sacrificing his own son, earning him Isaiah's severest criticism. In 320 B.C., Ahaz confiscated the Temple treasure, broke up the furnishings, and stripped its gold to pay the necessary protection money to Tiglath-pileser (2 Ki. 16:8–18; 2 Chr. 28:21, 24). He then installed a Syrian altar on Mount Zion. *See also* king(s); kings of Israel and Judah; kings of Israel and Judah in foreign relations.

Ahaziah of Israel: the eighth king of Israel, the eldest son of Ahab (853–852 B.C.). Ahaziah continued the wicked religious policies of his father, though not as severely. He did earn the rebuke of Elijah, however, who announced that Ahaziah would not recover from the injury he sustained in a fall. Ahaziah had even sent messengers to inquire of the Philistine god Baal-zebub about his health rather than consult Yahweh. *See also* king(s); kings of Israel and Judah; kings of Israel and Judah in foreign relations.

Ahaziah of Judah: the sixth king of the Southern Kingdom (841 B.C.) sometimes called Jehoahaz or Azariah in some translations (the latter is probably a gloss). His reign was short because he found himself in the wrong place at the wrong time. He was visiting Joram of Israel at Jezreel when Jehu's furious *coup-d'état* began. Ahaziah was swept up in the action and killed along with many of his family. Meanwhile, Baal worship continued unabated in Judah because of the influence of his mother, Queen Athaliah, the daughter of Ahab and Jezebel. *See also* Jehoahaz of Judah; king(s); kings of Israel and Judah; kings of Israel and Judah in foreign relations.

Ahijah: 1. a prophet who met the future king of the Northern Kingdom, Jeroboam, on the contender's return from exile in Egypt, where he had been in seclusion for fear of Solomon. The seer tore his garment into twelve pieces at that meeting, giving ten of the remnants to the prospective ruler. The demonstration announced that Jeroboam would control the ten northern tribes as the state of Israel, while Judah and Benjamin would constitute the Southern Kingdom under Rehoboam (1 Ki. 11:29–39). Later, when Jeroboam's son Abijah became ill, the king sent his wife in disguise to inquire of the prophet whether the child would survive. Ahijah, now blind, nevertheless recognized the queen and announced that the child would die (1 Ki. 14:1–8). 2. a priest of Israel under King Saul, a great-grandson of Eli (1 Sam. 14:3). *See also* priest(s); prophet(s).

Ahikam: Jeremiah's invaluable political protector against the godless court of King Jehoiakim (Jer. 26:24). He was eventually put to death for supporting the prophet. Ahikam was the son of Gedaliah, the Babylon appointee over Judah.

Ahikar: also Archiacharus, the hero of a seed story in *Tobit* and other folk tales. Ahikar was supposedly an official in Assyria under both kings Sennacherib and Esarhaddon. Being falsely accused of treason, Ahikar was eventually rescued and reinstated at court. *See also Story of Ahikar.*

Ahimaaz: one of the two sons of Zadok who was serving as high priest when Absalom arose in rebellion against David (2 Sam. 15:27). With Jonathan, the son of Zadok, he acted as David's spy, receiving information from Zadok and Abiathar in Jerusalem and passing it to David. He also insisted that he be allowed to be a runner that conveyed the news of David's victory over Absalom's army. Upon reporting, however, he wisely withheld the information that Absalom, the king's son, had been killed in the battle. *See also* Jonathan; priest(s).

Ahimelech: 1. the priest of Nob who aided David and his men when David was a fugitive from Saul. Ahimelech provided the sacred bread of the tabernacle for David and his famished loyalists, a humanitarian act that caused his vengeful death along with all the priests of Nob, except Abiathar, at the hand of Saul. 2. Others in the Old Testament were named Ahimelech (or Abimelech), including the son of Abiathar and co-priest with Zadok under David. The reference to Abimelech in the AV and RV translations of 1 Chronicles 18:16 is probably a scribal error intended to be written as Ahimelech. There was also a Hittite loyal to David by that name (1 Sam. 26:6). *See also* Aaronic Covenant, the; Abiathar; Doeg; Eleazar; Ithamar; Nob; Phinehas; priest(s); Zadok.

ahimsa: a term prominent in Hinduism, Buddhism, and especially Jainism that conveys a message of nonviolence – doing no harm nor wishing it. The principle shows in India as veneration for cows and vegetarianism; the Jainists are known to sweep the ground before him or her so as not to harm even an insect. Gandhi (1869–1948), Martin Luther King, Jr., and the Dalai Lamas were all influenced by the *ahimsa* concept. *See also* Buddhism; cow; Hinduism; Jainism; *satyagaha*.

Ahithophel: David's most accomplished advisor in matters of state (2 Sam. 16:23). He betrayed his king and joined Absalom's rebellion. Absalom, however, was deceived by David's spies and foolishly rejected Ahithophel's advice regarding the conduct of the war. Ahithophel then committed suicide. The implied lesson is that one should be slow to reject prophecy or the judicious counsel of a wise person.

Ahmad, bin Abd Allah Muhammad: Islamic false *Mahdi* (1844–1885) in Sudan. He led an effective campaign against the Turkiyah oppression of the Sudanese at the time. Ahmad was tagged as "the mad *Mahdi* of the Sudan" because of his extremism and Wahhabis beliefs. His party was called the Samaniyya. *See also* Islam; terrorist(s).

Ahmadinejad, Mahmoud: former militant president of Iran, a Shiite Muslim. Ahmadinejad embraces a definite and personal apocalyptic agenda and has proclaimed that he has a role to play in the end time by welcoming the *Mahdi*, or the Twelfth Imam. His destiny, as self-proclaimed, is to ferment disaster to the world with plans of precipitating Armageddon. Ahmadinejad almost always began every political speech (including those at the United Nations) with reference to the *Mahdi* and claimed to have had regular help from his Messiah. Iran's persistent development of nuclear power may presage such an agenda for that country and consternation for the world of today. *See also* anti-Semitic; Iranian military; Islam; jihad; *Mahdi;* Shiite Islam; terrorist(s); Twelfth Imam, the.

Ahmad, Mirza Ghulam: Islamic writer and false *Mahdi* (1839–1908) born in India. Ahmad founded the Ahmadiyya Muslim Community, which promoted the peaceful spread of Islam as opposed to *jihad*. He claimed that Jesus survived the cross and migrated to Kashmir. Ahmad and the communal cult leader John Alexander Dowie, once entered into a prayer battle. Ahmad challenged Dowie, stipulating that the one who died first would be proven false since both men claimed to be incarnations of the Coming One. Dowie died in 1907 and Ahmad in 1908. *See also* Christian Catholic Apostolic Church; communal communities; Dowie, John Alexander; Islam.

Aholah and Aholibah. See Ezekiel's Oholah and Oholibah allegory.

Aholiab: the Danite artist craftsman who constructed worship vessels for the tabernacle under Moses (Ex. 31:6). *See also* art, religious; Bazaleel.

Ahriman: the evil spirit recognized in Zoroastrianism as the dualistic representative of chaos, also known as Angra Mainyu, or the Druj. *See also* Ahura Mazda; idol(s); Zoroaster, Zoroastrianism.

Ahura Mazda: or Ohrmazd, the god of goodness as encountered in the dualism of Zoroastrianism. *See also* Ahriman; idol(s); Zoroaster, Zoroastrianism.

Ai: 1. the small city centering the second military skirmish by the army of Joshua in Canaan. The Israelite light infantry had some difficulty subduing the city because of sin in the camp (precipitated by Achan) but were eventually successful. Archeologists have had some difficulty locating the site so it may have been confused with Bethel. 2. a city east of the Jordan in Ammonite territory mentioned by Jeremiah in his curse of that nation (Jer. 49:3). *See also* Achan.

aikido: an Eastern term roughly translated as "way of the harmonious spirit," a modern Japanese martial arts sect. The techniques were developed by Marihei Weshiba between the 1930s and 1960s. *See also* sect(s).

Aina religion: the Aina indigenous people of Japan and their religious practices. As a culture, they were persecuted and driven north into the country, then eventually assimilated into Japanese culture. *See also* idolatry; sect(s).

Aion: a god of both destruction and creation and associated with the zodiac. He is pictured as cast in human form with a lion's head and a serpent entwined around his body and is often depicted as ithyphallic and standing on a globe surrounded by the stars of the zodiac. His statue in the Vatican shows him with wings and nude, except for a Masonic-type apron. In Hellenistic culture, Aion is the god of "time unbounded" whereas Chronos can be fractured into past, present, and future. *See also* idol(s); Mithraism; Olympian pantheon; reptilian theory.

aion: and *aionios,* the Greek word for "age" or "time" but which seems to imply eternity or unending time. An equivalent Hebrew word might be *olam. Aion* may also mean "world" which has fostered some confusion as to the meaning when Jesus used it, along with *kosmos* (the world) to help him lecture about the end of days. Phrases such as "the end of the world" and "the end of the age" are sometimes used synonymously though that usage is not technically correct. *See also* age; eon; *olam.*

Aisha: daughter of Abu-Bakr and third wife to Muhammed (614–678), his favorite after his first spouse, Khadija. Aisha was married at the age of six, and the consummation supposedly took place at age nine. She persevered despite political intrigue and eventually became a dynamic force in her own astuteness. *See also* Fatima; Islam; Khadijah.

Aitken Bible: the first English-language Bible printed in America (1781). Before the American Revolution, the only Bibles available were imported from England but the supply was embargoed by the British when the war began. Despite attempts by the Continental Congress to import them from other countries, the shortage was never filled until the post-war Congress approved local production through

History and Mystery

the efforts of the Philadelphia printer Robert Aitken. *See also* Bible.

Akae: the name of the great and mysterious heavenly oath after its revelation to the holy angels, according to noncanonical writings. The oath was officially in the charge of the archangel Michael and reputedly holds great power in the universe. *See also* Beqa; Kesbul; oath(s); secret name, the; "sign, the"; symbalon.

akathist: a musical rendition dedicated to a saint, a holy event, or the Trinity used in Eastern Orthodox worship. A selection is called an "unseated hymn" since the congregation remains standing during the singing. *See also* Eastern Orthodox Church; liturgical year; music.

Akiba ben Yosef: learned rabbi (c. 50 – 132 A.D.) and a leading contributor to the Mishna and many other theological writings. He was executed by the Romans following the Bar Kokhba revolt. His topical arrangement of the Mishna is of particular interest to Judaism. *See also* Akiba's classification of the Mishna; Jew(s).

Akiba's classification of the Mishna: Rabbi Akiba's arrangement of the subject matter in the Mishna. The compilation is not theological but topical but is, nevertheless, an aid to interpretation. The several categories include: 1) Seeds (*Zeraim*)—laws about agriculture, the seventh year, and the kinds of tithes. This section is prefaced by a series of prayers called *Berakhoth* which holds the Shema (Deut. 6:4-5), the eighteen benedictions, grace at meals, and other prayers; 2) Festivals (*Moed*)—feasts, fasts, festivals, and Sabbath laws; 3) Women (*Nashim*)—laws pertaining to marriage, the place of widows, vows, etc.; 4) Injuries (*Nezikim*)—civil and criminal laws, oaths. The *Pirke Aboth* is appended to this section; 5) Holy Things *(Kodashim)*—sacrifices, meal offerings, the first-born, excommunication, measurements of the Temple, etc.; 6) Clean Things (*Toharot)*—vessels, defilement from a corpse, leprosy, the red heifer, ritual and purification baths for women, childbirth, sexual intercourse, etc. *See also* Akiba ben Yosef; Judaism; Mishna; *Pirke Aboth.*

Akitu: the new year festival of ancient Babylon in honor of the chief god Marduk. The observance featured a mock battle between the king of Babylon and the dragon of the deep symbolizing Marduk's defeat of chaos. *See also* Babylon, Babylonians; Marduk; Sumerian and Babylonian pantheon; Tiamat.

Akkad: the first world power to break the power of Sumer, perhaps the world's most ancient civilization. Around 2400 B.C., King Sargon began to rule unified Mesopotamia. His monarchy was short, however, and the area soon split into Babylonia (south) and Assyria (north). Nevertheless, the language (Akkadian) and some of the cultural aspects of Akkad survived. *See also* Akkadian; Sargon of Akkad.

Akkadian: or Accadian, the ancient tongue of Akkad and the court language of Babylon during the time of Daniel. The speech seems to have been difficult to learn and use but the prophet appears to have had a fine grasp of it. *See also* Akkad.

Akra: sometimes seen as Acra, a fortified citadel for troops used by the Seleucid Syrians in Jerusalem. The defense proved formidable until Judas Maccabee was able to subdue it and thereby assure Judea's brief period of independence. *See also* Antonia Fortress; Jerusalem, landmarks of; tower.

alabaster: hard marble-like material that can be shaped into figurines, vases, sculptures, and the like. The ancients used them to contain expensive perfumes and oils. *See also* Mary; woman with a jar of ointment.

Aladura: a religion of Western Nigeria founded ca. 1918; it means "Church of the Lord." The sect is a mix of Anglicanism and traditional African ritual. Ministers carry an iron pole about 2′ × 5″ with a loop on the top as a symbol of office.

Vestments and gowns are a common feature for worship and rosaries are used to purify water and when praying the Psalms. *See also* idolatry; sect(s).

alamoth: most likely a musical term even though we do not know exactly how it was employed, except that it was part of the Temple musical service (1 Chr. 15:20). The sound was possibly in a higher octave than the *sheminith* and intended to be sung with the female voice or a soprano. Some researchers claim it was a musical instrument of some description. *See also* music; musical instrument(s); *Selah; sheminith; shigionoth*.

***al-Aqsa* Mosque:** a Muslim worship center situated today squarely on the Temple Mount in Jerusalem. The name refers to "a distant place" (as distant from Mecca) and is a true mosque as opposed to the Dome of the Rock, which is considered more of a shrine. The site has eschatological consequence since it is a possible hindrance to the Temple rebuilding by the Jews. The site served as a headquarters for the Knights Templar when they controlled the area. Its damage or removal would surely precipitate a worldwide crisis. *Al-Aqsa* was originally attributed to the entire Temple Mount, as though it marked the high-water mark of Muslim ambition. It was here that Mohammed allegedly received a vision of ascending into Paradise and is considered Islam's third holiest site. *See also* Dome of the Rock; Dome of the Spirits; Islam; Jerusalem, landmarks of; knighted orders; mosque; shrine(s); Suleiman the Magnificent.

alas. See woe(s).

al-Assad, Bashar: embattled dictator of Syria (a Shi'ite) during the country's recent civil rebellion. Al-Assad was determined to keep the republic under his personal vision of Islamic control. The rebellion began in 2011 as part of the surging "Arab Spring" of dissent in the Middle East and quickly evolved into a multi-faction and prolonged conflict. *See also* al-Baghadi, Abu Bakr; "Arab Awakening"; Arab Spring; Islam; Syria; terrorist(s).

Alawis: a sect of Islam in the Shi'ite tradition, mostly settled in Syria where they once held their own state. They were subject to persecution by the Sunni sect of Islam because of their rebellion and nonconformity. Although the Alawis are considered Muslim, they have taken over the celebration of Christmas from the Christians and practice certain ceremonies of pagan origin. *See also* Druze; idolatry; Islam; Ismailis; Quarmatians; Syria.

al-Baghadi, Abu Bakr: terrorist leader of ISIS who moved his radicalized army to Syria against Bashar al-Assad in an extension of his power in the region. Hardly a more extreme criminal could be named in all of history. *See also* al-Assad, Bashar; Islam; Islamic State in Iraq and Syria (ISIS or ISIL); terrorism; terrorist(s); Syria.

Albertus Magnus: a teacher to Thomas Aquinas and contemporary of Roger Bacon. He was born in A.D. 1200 in Lauingen, Germany, then became a Dominican and bishop. The early church called him Dr. Universalis or Dr. Expertus. Albertus was a specialist in many subjects of his day including logic, psychology, philosophy, natural science, theology, and many others. *See also* Aquinas, Thomas; clergy scientists; Dominicans; Roman Catholic Church.

Albigenses: a religious group centered in the southern French town of Albin during the 12th and 13th centuries, that was considered heretical by the established church. They believed there are two Gods in the world—one being evil (the Old Testament God) and the other good (the New Testament God), something akin to Gnosticism and the Manicheans. To them, all matter was evil, including the human body. They were also called Cathars, the "purified ones." The Roman popes considered these peaceable people a blight in the land and launched a vindictive Crusade that destroyed them all. *See also* Cathars; Inquisition, the; Manicheanism; martyr(s); sect(s).

alchemy: sometimes called "the Royal Art," a philosophy and esoteric chemical experimental skill primarily focused on the attempt to change base metals (*i.e.*, lead, into precious ones, mainly gold). The alternate name *chymistry* was sometimes used. Alchemists trace their genesis to Hermes Trismegistus who is sometimes identified with the Egyptian god Thoth and a smaller number of other progenitors, even including the Hebrew leader Moses. No doubt Hermes Trismegistus was never a single person but became a sort of idiom meaning "thrice-greatest" representing a form of the *logos*. Devotees of Trismegistus' work set his mark on their products which evolved to the "hermetic" seal for airtight containers. Early alchemists began with the assumption that all metals were composed of only three elements—sulfur (fire), mercury (liquid), and salt (solid) in varying amounts which could be manipulated. Only later did the Persian physician Rhazes (A.D. 865? – 925?) put forward that the elements were actually animal, vegetable, and mineral. The number of *elements* (a late term for basic natural material) at one point became four—earth, fire, water, and air. Now we know there are over 100 in the periodic table. Before modern scientific nomenclature, the alchemist might employ exotic substances like powder of algaroth, Pampholix, oil of tarter, or butter of arsenic. Interestingly, nuclear physicists have managed to turn base metal into gold on a limited scale and succeeded somewhat where the alchemists failed. The practice of alchemy also employed the search for "the elixir of life" which would cure all diseases, along with the futile hunt for the mysterious philosophers' stone. What is less commonly recognized is that alchemy was also a spiritual discipline and may even be considered the precursors of both organic chemistry and metaphysics and may have energized the search for the Holy Grail. It would be remiss not to mention a number of prominent alchemists who contributed their art through the ages. Albertus Magnus (1193 – 1280) was a Dominican and bishop. Ramon Lull (1232 – 1315) was a Spanish philosopher, Francisco Giorgi (1466 – 1540) a Venetian Franciscan monk, and Paracelsus (1493 – 1541) a Swiss physician and surgeon. Roger Bacon (1214 – 1292), perhaps the most famous of all the experimenters along with the legendary Christian Rosenkreuz, was a Franciscan. Giordano Bruno (1548 – 1600) was also a Dominican monk turned Calvinist and Lutheran and Jabir ibn Hayyan (Gerber) was a mathematician (c. 721 – c. 815) whose work was so esoteric it coined the term "gibberish." *See also* Agrippa Books; *arcanum arcandrum; Arcanum,* the; Bacon, Roger; *Book of Abramelin, The;* cantrip; clergy scientists; *Corpus Hermecticum;* "Dionysius Artificers, The"; dot within a circle; electrum; element(s); Emerald Tablet of Hermes, the; *Golden Bough, The;* grimoire; Hermes Trismegistus; Hermeticism; Hermetic wisdom; Hermetic writings; Holy Grail; idolatry; *khemeia; Kybalion;* magic arts; magic, magick; *mana;* mantic wisdom; Moses; natural elements, the four; occult, occultic; od; Order of the Rosy Cross; *ormus;* parapsychology; philosophers' stone; *Picatrix;* powder of projection; Rosenkreuz, Christian; secret wisdom; spell names; *Spiritas Mundi;* Therapeutae; transmutation.

Alcibiades: (Elchasai) producer of a heretic Gnostic group promoting female angels, and a new method of sin remission according to his writings. He also promoted incantations, circumcision, reincarnation, and astrology He also taught that Christ was a mere man. *See also* Gnosticism, Gnostic(s).

Aldebert: an eighth century false Messiah and ex-bishop of the Roman Catholic Church. In his apostasy, Aldebert claimed to be in possession of certain artifacts, which he claimed were given to him by an angel in the guise of a man. With these, he could conjure any wish. He also claimed to know the sins of any without hearing their confessions. He was defrocked by a synod of the church in A.D. 744 and imprisoned. To the embarrassment of the ecclesiastical authorities, he escaped but evidently made no more public claims of messiahship. *See also* Roman Catholic Church.

History and Mystery

Aleph: (or Aum Supreme Truth) the modern name of the cult more familiarly called *Aum Shinri Kyo,* a bioterrorist doomsday sect based in Japan. *Aum Shinri Kyo* applies to a Japanese expression for "Supreme Truth," a nationalistic cult with some apocalyptic leanings founded by convicted criminal Shoho Ashara (Chizno Matsumoto). They were charged with the Tokyo subway gassing in 1995 that resulted in the deaths of eleven commuters. Numerous other instances of murder, torture, and assassination are attributed to the cult as well. The group had promulgated November 29, 2003, as the end of days. Supposedly, their doctrine of violence has modified, but the Japanese government watches them very closely. Ashara was hanged for his crimes by the Japanese government in 2018. *See also* Ashara, Shoko; cult(s); idolatry; terrorism; terrorist(s).

Aleppo Codex: regarded as perhaps the oldest complete Hebrew Bible in the world. The writing was completed around 30 A.D. near the Sea of Galilee and is now included in the international Memory of the World Register by UNESCO in order to protect its heritage. It resides in the Shrine of the Book in Israel after it was smuggled out of Syria. *See also* Bible; Bible manuscripts; Bible translations.

Alexander Jannaeus: a member of the Maccabee dynasty who ruled Judea 103–76 B.C., the successor to John Hyrcanus. His wife was Alexandra who occupied the throne after Jannaeus' troubled reign of twenty-seven years. Alexander was a son of John Hyrcanus but one despised by his countrymen, of whom he slaughtered many as punishment for their disrespect and ingratitude to him. Despite his self-sacrificial efforts and wars against the Jewish oppressors, Alexander found no peace in his accomplishments, and the Jews were in great distress during his rule. In frustration, he was not above crucifying political adversaries who opposed him (which he did by the thousands) and slitting the throats of their wives and children before those condemned. To add to the country's woes, the Pharisees and Sadducees were locked in a vicious power struggle at that time; many of those executed by Alexander were Pharisees. *See also* Alexandra; Hasmonean dynasty; Hyrcanus, Jew(s); John; king(s).

Alexander of Alexandria: bishop of the church at Alexandria (d. 328). His tenure saw the outbreak of the Arian controversy, which he strongly opposed as heresy. *See also* Roman Catholic Church.

Alexander of Ephesus: a companion of Paul who was seized in the riot at Ephesus instigated by Demetrius the silversmith. Alexander and his friends, Gaius and Aristarchus, were endangered but eventually released unharmed (Acts 19: 23–41). *See also* Artemis.

Alexander the blasphemer: one whom Paul denounced as having "made a shipwreck of his faith" (1 Tim. 1:19–20). He and his partner, Hymenaeus, were condemned because of their blasphemy. Alexander's error, or at least one of them, may have involved false teachings concerning the resurrection (2 Tim. 2:17–18). Both were excommunicated by Paul and condemned to Satan. *See also* Hymenaeus.

Alexander the Great: (356–323 B.C.) one of the greatest conquerors of all time and an unsurpassed military genius of the Macedonian kingdom. In a brief eleven years, he managed to conquer most of the known world at that time. Alexander was a student of Aristotle and already a leader at age twenty. He was successful in overpowering the massive Persian Empire among many others and was keen to establish Hellenism wherever his conquests led him. Josephus reported that Alexander spared Jerusalem amid his conquests because he had dreamed of the city and its priests before his planned attack, only to be met outside the city limits by the citizens and leaders exactly as his vision had portrayed. Legend says he favored Jerusalem when shown the accurate prophecies of Daniel about him (probably Dan. 7:6; 8:5–8, 20–22; 11:3, and related passages). Alexander died of fever and dissipation in Babylon, reputedly despondent that there were no more worlds to conquer. Most conservative scholars identify him, or the Ptolemaic and Seleucid kingdoms he fostered, as the bronze belly and thighs of Nebuchadnezzar's stratified statue of Daniel 2, the winged leopard of Daniel's dream in Daniel 7, and the unihorned flying goat (a rhinoceros or unicorn?) of Daniel 8. Likely, he is also "the mighty king" mentioned in Daniel 11:3. *See also Diadochi;* flying goat, the; Greece; Greek as nationality; Hellenism, Hellenization; king(s); philosophy of the Greeks; ram and the goat, the; winged leopard, the.

Alexander the metalworker: one strongly opposed to the gospel who gave Paul considerable trouble (2 Tim. 4:14–15). Paul warned Timothy to beware of him.

Alexander the priest: a member of the high priestly family at Jerusalem when Peter and John were on trial there before the Sanhedrin (Acts 4:6). It is possible that this Alexander is the same as mentioned by Josephus as the alabarch (governor) of the Jews in Alexandria, and brother to Philo. *See also* Jew(s); priest(s).

Alexander the son of Simon: the son of Simon of Cyrene and brother to Rufus. The father, Simon, was forced to carry the cross of Christ (Mk. 15:21) part of the way to Golgotha. *See also* Rufus; Simon.

Alexandra: the wife of Aristobulus I, then Alexander Jannaeus of the Hasmonean lineage. She ruled Judea on her own (quite ably) after her second husband from 76–67 B.C. Her first husband was noted for his cruelty and as the instigator who changed the Hasmonean theocracy of Judah into a secularized political kingdom. Practically speaking, the Pharisees actually ruled the nation through her. She then married the brother of Aristobulus, Alexander Jannaeus. Alexandra left two sons, Hyrcanus II (63-40 B.C.) and Aristobulus II (67–63 B.C.). The brothers quarreled about the succession.

Hyrcanus eventually took the high priesthood while Aristobulus seized the civil authority. Civil war resulted but was settled by the Romans who set Antipas (Antipater) the Idumean in charge under the pretended authority of Hyrcanus. Shortly after, the rule of the Jews fell to Herod the Great. *See also* Alexander Jannaeus; Aristobulus I; Hasmonean dynasty; Jew(s); queen(s).

Alexandria as city: metropolis of North Africa founded by Alexander the Great that he intended to be a masterpiece of Greek culture. It became the recognized center for those ancient scholars who attempted to blend Christian and Jewish theology with Greek philosophy. The city boasted the largest library in the ancient world until most of it was destroyed by fire. The library inventory was increased substantially when Mark Antony gave all 200,000 volumes at the library of Pergamum (the second largest in the world) to Cleopatra and moved them to Alexandria. *See also* library of Alexandria; patriarchate(s); School of Alexandria; seven wonders of the ancient world.

Alexandria as patriarchate. See patriarchate(s).

Alexandrian school. See School of Alexandria.

Alfheimr: a mystical land north of inhabited Scandinavia according to Norse legend. The name meant "land of the elves" as these creatures were believed to be nature spirits helping and guiding humans to the gods. Directly north of Alfheimr lay Asgard, the land of the god where Odin lived and where Valhalla was situated. *See also* Aesir; Asa; Asatru; Asgard; blyt; idolatry; Norse and Old Germanic pantheon; seior; tree of life, the; Valhalla; volva; Wotanism.

Alhambra Decree: the order of King Ferdinand and Queen Isabella which expelled all Jews from Spain. *See also* Conversos; Inquisition, the; *Tisha b'Av*.

alien: 1. a person from another country or another world. 2. one disassociated from the current religious or political culture where he or she is presently abiding. Moses, when exiled to Midian from Egypt, experienced this sensation. He even named his first son "Gershom" because the Hebrew term sounds like "an alien there." 3. a visitor from outer space. *See also* alien abduction; Alien Disclosure Event; alien immersion; alien Jesus; egregores; Fermi paradox; UFO.

alien abduction: an experience claimed by some in which they were abducted by alien beings. Often the victims maintain they were transported to alien spacecraft where invasive physical and mental experiments were performed on them against their will. *See also* alien; Alien Disclosure Event; Ancient Astronaut Theory; Anunnaki; *Chariots of the Gods?*; Human Enhancement Revolution (HER); panspermia theory; UFO.

Alien Disclosure Event: a phrase inspired by the Disclosure Project, an anti-conspiracy group dedicated to unveiling possible secrets associated with extraterrestrial contact. Their research hints that alien life forms have visited our planet and that certain other facts about their threat potential are being officially withheld from the public. The Alien Disclosure Event anticipates the day and action when authorities finally admit the truths concerning otherworldly contacts. *See also* alien; alien abduction; Ancient Astronaut Theory; Area 51; Black Vault; conspiracy theorists; panspermia theory; UAP; UFO.

alien immersion: or alien baptism, a baptism performed by a minister or representative of a denomination of which the candidate is not a member. Some church bodies and officials allow and accept the baptismal experience of another affiliation while others do not. *See also* alien; baptism; close Communion, open Communion; credo-baptism; pedobaptism.

alien Jesus: the far-fetched pronouncement that Jesus was an alien who, along with certain other space travelers, visited the earth intent on manipulating the DNA and historical destiny of earth's population. The idea may have been first floated by a London cab driver named George King who, in 1954, claimed to have received a message from extraterrestrials on Venus revealing the alien guest story (along with other "Cosmic Masters" like Confucius, Buddha, and Sri Krishna). He eventually formed the Aetherius Society to promote the theory. *See also* alien; Ancient Astronaut Theory; Alien Disclosure Event; Fermi paradox; UFO.

Alighieri, Dante: or more accurately Durante degli Alighieri, master Italian poet and philosopher (1265–1321 A.D.). Dante (as he is universally known) was called "the Supreme Poet" of the Middle Ages. His masterpiece, *The Divine Comedy* (in three parts) won instant acclaim. The author was almost constantly caught up in the vicissitudes and cutthroat politics of the day and suffered in his person and fortune most of his life. Caught up in the politics of his native Florence, Dante favored the so-called "Whites"—those who yearned for more freedom from the Roman Church, led at the time by Pope Boniface VII, over the "Blacks"—those who favored firm loyalty to the pontiff and his influence. He was an advocate of the separation of church and state, an attitude far ahead of his time. Some adversarial contemporaries, as well as general enemies both in and outside the Roman Catholic Church at the time, unabashedly appear in Dante's allegorical hell, purgatory, or paradise. *See also Divine Comedy*, the; Roman Catholic Church.

Ali ibn Abi Talib: the cousin and son-in-law of Mohammed (? A.D. 598-600) whom the Shi'ite branch of Islam declares to be the legitimate successor to Mohammed and the first imam. He is considered the "Fourth Rightly Guided Caliph." Thus, they are in dispute with the rival Sunni party which named Abu-Bakr as the true leader. *See also* Fatima; Husain; Islam; Shi'ite Islam.

Alinski, Saul: a Jewish-American political community organizer among the poor (1909 – 1972). His organizational skills were superb even though based on "manufactured crises" to stimulate his actions. From the practice we can easily interpret the motto "Order out of Chaos" and he even dedicated his book, *Rules for Radicals*, to the greatest of all the organizers—Lucifer. He expressed a wish before his death that he would go to hell and not heaven. Alinski's ideals influenced Barak Obama, Hillary Clinton, and many others of more liberal political persuasions in and out of power positions. *See also* Jew(s).

Alkalai, Rabbi Yehuda: Jewish leader (1798–1878) who predicted that the Balkans and most of Eastern Europe will return to Israel because we are in the Messianic age. He is considered to be a pioneer for the budding Zionist movement and a hero of Israel. *See also* Jew(s); Zionism.

Alka-Seltzer Christians: certain believers, usually new to the faith, who enter their life-changing experience with God with energy and exhilaration but quickly fade in purpose. The phrase brings to mind the advertising jingle "plop plop, fizz fizz" denoting enthusiasm until the excitement vanishes into obscurity and disappears without a trace. *See also* Christianese; slurs, religious.

Allah: the Islamic name for God. Mohammed claimed the term and called it *al-Ilah*, "the God," which was later shortened to "Allah." Even so, the name predates Islam and Mohammed's time since it was in use much earlier to refer to an Arabian deity, a fact which probably made the new religion more acceptable to the indigenous population. The word is Arabic for *the* God or *any* God. In pre-Mohammedan days there were 360 of them represented in the Ka'bah. The one for the tribe of Quraysh, to which Mohammed belonged, was named Hubal. When the prophet conquered Mecca, and in response to his visions, he turned out all 359 of the other Allahs but kept his own Hubal and declared him to be supreme and singular in the Arab world. Henceforth, Hubal was only to be referred to as Allah and monotheism became the primary law of Islam. It is possible Hubal was imported from Baal to the north which would make him an import of the Levant. There is absolutely no hint of Trinitarian doctrine associated with the title, a belief that according to Islam, makes Christianity polytheistic. The second article of the Muslim statement of faith is spoken and read as: "I bear witness that there is no God but Allah, and Mohammed is his prophet." The character of Islam's view of God is different in many fundamental respects from that of Judaism and Christianity. There is sharp debate as to whether the Islamic God Allah is the same as the Christian designation. Given the history of the Arabic name for Allah and its current understanding, they most definitely are not. Modern Islam has now conceived "the 99 Beautiful Names of Allah," some of which are lifted from the *Qu'ran* and others not. *See also Alluha Akbar;* idol(s); Islam; names (titles) for God.

Allegheny County vs. ACLU: the 1989 Supreme Court ruling declaring that religious holiday symbols on public property do not violate the First Amendment if there are other differing symbols present. A Jewish Menorah and a Christmas tree together, for instance, is legal but a single depiction of an exclusive religious symbol may not pass the test. *See also* Abington School District vs. Schempp; antidisestablishmentarianism; Backus, Isaac; Baptists; *Booke of the General Lawes and Libertyes;* Caesar cult; caesaropapacy; civil religion; collegialism; disestablishmentarianism; Edict of Milan; Edict of Nantes; Edict of Toleration; Emerson vs. Board of Education; emperor worship; Establishment Clause and Free Exercise Clause; Geghan Bill; Government Regulations Index (GRI); Johnson Amendment; Leland, John; Lemon vs. Kurtzman; Massachusetts Body of Liberties; National Day of Prayer; *Pontifex Maximus; princeps; principis;* public square; Shubert vs. Verner; state church; Toleration Act of 1649; ultramontanism; Virginia's Religious Disestablishment law.

allegorical interpretation: a.k.a. *tropology,* a system of biblical interpretation, springing chiefly from Origen and promoted by Augustine, which the latter scholar applied to prophecy. The methodology downplays, or even discards, the general or usual meaning of the text in favor of a more spiritualized or esoteric sense. The process relies heavily on finding "hidden" meanings behind the actual words that will uncover what the author really intended. Almost every paradigm of Scripture, especially apocalyptic language, should be given a figurative or metaphorical interpretation, which only the erudite scholar can adequately discover and explain. The essence of allegorism is that it centers on the reader's experience and ideas while neglecting the more obvious message of the text. The whole concept of allegorization seems to have sprung from a single dubious proof text of John 6:63: "The Spirit gives life; but flesh counts for nothing." Allegory was spiritual; the literal was fleshly. Early on, most church authorities, particularly Augustine and Origen, insisted Revelation and other apocalyptic works should be interpreted allegorically. In fact, the terms chosen for the methods in use reveal a certain bias in that the allegorical was called the "spiritual" method but the literal was called "carnal." *See also* allegorical vision(s); allegorism; allegory, allegories; analogical interpretation; Augustine, Aurelius; biblical criticism; Christoplatonism; dynamic equivalence; empyreanism; fourfold interpretation; grammatical-historical interpretation; hermeneutic(s); higher criticism; idealism; illumination; inspiration; interpretation; liberalist interpretation; literal interpretation; multiple sense prophecy; Origen; Pardes; plenary inspiration; principles of interpretation; revelation, theological; rhetorical criticism; source criticism; text; textual criticism; threefold sense of interpretation; translation; transmission history.

allegorical vision(s): a sometime description of certain eschatological revelations explained in revelatory form (*e.g.*, those in Daniel 7 and 8 and in 2 Esdras 11–12). *See also* allegorical interpretation; allegorism; allegory, allegories; dreams and visions; vision(s).

allegorism: a spiritualized or metaphorical interpretation of a given passage of Scripture. The process was widely used by the Alexandrian school among the ancient theologians for explaining difficult passages and is a favored method today despite its obvious deficiencies. The practice often ends with manifold interpretations, depending on the experience and mind-set of the reader. *See also* allegorical interpretation, allegorical vision(s); allegory, allegories; empyreanism, Fourfold Interpretation; idealism; multiple sense prophecy; Pardes; prophecy types; Victor of Hugo (Victor Hugo).

allegory, allegories: an extended metaphor or tropology. Allegories are similar to fables or parables but are often longer and contain more extensive figurative language. The subject of the story is treated under the guise of another topic to present a more abstract or spiritual narrative yet still using concrete or sensible forms. The most obvious allegories in the Scripture are: the so-called "shepherd Psalm" (Ps. 23), the grape vine (Ps. 80:8–14), God's vineyard (Isa. 5:1–7), the great eagles (Ezk. 17:1–10), the lioness (Ezk. 19:1–9), the vine (Ezk. 19:10–14), the bread of life (Jn. 6:26–59), the sheepfold and the shepherd (Jn. 10:1–21), the vine and branches (Jn. 15:1–7), the expert builder (1 Cor. 3:10–17), the armor of God (Eph. 6:10–17), and the comparison of Hagar and Sarah (Gal. 4:21–31). *See also* allegorical interpretation; allegorical vision(s); allegorism; Augustine, Aurelius; metaphor; Origen; parable(s); Pardes.

Alleluia. See Hallelujah.

all-encompassing theory: the idea that presumably proves that everything we believe, feel, or do can be explained by some theory or thought process. Those who assert, for example, that evolution (the process of natural selection in nature) is an all-encompassing theory place heavy assumptions in the validity of their conjectures to the point where it is no longer science but philosophy. Almost certainly no human thinking can formulate a one-size-fits-all theorem for the complete understanding of any subject and thus the belief is an impossible worldview. *See also* theory of everything, the.

Allen, Richard: organizer of America's earliest African Methodist Episcopal Church and its first bishop (1760–1831). Allen was a former slave born in Delaware but gained his freedom and became active as a Methodist minister. In 1787 he was manhandled by an usher at Saint George's Methodist Episcopal Church in Philadelphia when he tried to pray in the whites only section, a congregation in which he was technically a member. Outraged, Allen stormed out of the assembly and began his own institution, an assembly called Bethel. *See also* African Methodist Episcopal Church; Afro-American theology; "invisible institution, the."

All Hallows' Eve. See Hallowmas; Halloween.

alliteration: a stylistic device of writing in which a series of words (or close together) have the same consonants or sounds. The approach can be appealing to the mind and there are examples in the Bible—mostly in the poetry. The use does not, however, guarantee accuracy of preciseness of meaning. *See also* accideme; apostrophe; apothegm; assonance; autograph; Bible; Bible manuscripts; Bible translations; biblical criticism; chiasmus; conflict story; *constructio ad sensum;* context; contextualization; dittography; double sense fulfillment; doublets; doubling; edification; eisegesis; epanadiplosis; epigrammatic statements; etymology; exegesis; figure of speech; folio; form criticism; gattung; gloss; gnomic sayings; grammatical-historical interpretation; *hapax legomena;* haplography; hermeneutic(s); higher criticism; homographs; homonyms; homophones; *homoteleuton;* hyperbole; idiom; *inclusio;* interpolation; interpretation; inverted nun; irony; isagogics; *itture sopherim;* jot and tittle; kere; *kethib;* "L"; liberalist interpretation; literal interpretation; litotes; loan words; lower criticism; "M"; Masoretic Text; minuscule(s); mystery of God; omission; onomastica; onomatopoeia; palimpsest;

papyrus; paradigm; parallelism; parchment; *paroimia; paronomasia;* pericope; personification; Peshita; pointing; point of view; polyglot; principles of interpretation; proof texting; pun(s); "Q"; redaction; revelation, theological; rhetorical criticism; rhetorical devices; riddle; satire; *scripto continua;* scriptorium; *sebirin;* simile; similitude; source criticism; sources, primary and secondary; special points; strophe; superscription; symbol(s); synecdoche; syntax; synthetic parallelism; text; textual criticism; *tiggune sopherim;* Time Texts; Torah; translation; transposition; trope; type(s); typology; uncial(s); vellum; verbicide.

Allogenes: a Gnostic identity the same as Seth and possibly representing Jesus, or a Jesus figure. The name means "he who comes from another race" or "the stranger." *See also* Gnosticism, Gnostics; idol(s); Seth; Sethianism.

Allouez, Claude Jean: a Jesuit missionary to the Great Lakes region of North America (1622–1689). While in liaison with the French fur traders, Allouez mapped the coastal areas of the lakes for the first time. He was made vicar general in 1663 and opened a mission at De Pere, Wisconsin, where he ministered to the Illinois and Miami Indians. *See also* missions, missionaries; Roman Catholic Church; Society of Jesus.

All Saints' Day. See Hallowmas.

All Souls' Day. See Hallowmas.

"all these things": a cautionary phrase used by Jesus in his Olivet instruction concerning the end time. The context occurs with the indicator that "this generation" would not pass away until "all these things happen." The meaning seems to be that the generation to see the "things" of the end will also see the end itself. All that transpires beforehand then are preludes or signs of the last days, and they must become apparent and should be heeded before the setting for the end is made ready. *See also* advent(s) of Christ; age of lawlessness; apocalyptic, apocalypticism; apocalyptic time; appearing, the; appointed time, the; coming ages, the;

consummation, the final; day he visits us; day of the Lamb's wrath, the; "days of Elijah"; "days of Noah"; day of the Lord; day of evil; day of God, the; day of (our Lord Jesus) Christ; day of Revenge; day of the Lamb's wrath, the; day of the Lord; day of trumpet and battle, a; day of vengeance of our God; day of [their] visitation; Day that (the); due time, in; *elthnen;* end of all things; end of the age, the; End, the; end, the; end time; eschatology, eschatological; eschaton; fullness of time; Glorious Appearing; great and dreadful day, that; "here, there, or in the air"; rapture; Second Coming; Second Coming procession; secret rapture; TEOTWAWKI; termination dates; time; time is near, the; times and the seasons, the; times of fulfillment; until he comes; wrath, the coming.

Alluha Akbar: "God is greater," or "God is great," the common prelude battle cry to all acts of violence by Muslim extremists promoted by *jihad* or terrorism. *See also* Allah; al-Qaeda; al-Shabab; anti-Semitic; Boko Haram; Daesh; *Deus Volt!;* Fatah; Hamas; *harem;* Hezbollah; House of War; Islam; Islamic State in Iraq and Syria (ISIS or ISIL); *jihad;* Muslim Brotherhood; Nusra Front; Palestinian Islamic Jihad (PIJ); Palestinian Liberation Organization (PLO); radicalized; Salafi; Taliban; terrorism; terrorist(s); Velayat Sinai; Wahhabism; wild animals (beasts) of the earth.

all who have been slain on the earth: a phrase or its equivalent language throughout Revelation (*e.g.*, Revelation 5:9, which describes the fate of those killed in the Tribulation). Most deaths occur at the hands of the Antichrist or his wicked political arm, Babylon the Great. In fact, Babylon herself may be a participant of beginning atrocities in the Tribulation even though she is not mentioned until Revelation 14:8. *See also* eschatology, eschatological; martyr(s); martyrdom.

almah: in Hebrew, a girl who has reached puberty but still under the protection and guidance of her family. The word may refer to "a virgin" (as in Isaiah 7:14) and has raised controversy as to the translation of the Isaiah passage. Is the word "young woman" or "virgin"? The answer has significant impact on the prophecy of Christ's virgin birth prediction. *See also* virgin birth; virgin(s), virginity; woman (women).

Almighty, the: the name for God (*Pantokrator* in Greek) highly favored in much of the Old Testament and in Revelation past chapter 3. It seems to be the preferred title for those calling on God other than members of the Church, who usually prefer the more intimate name, "Father." The term is not limited to the New Testament certainly. The name has been long in use; even Naomi, the mother-in-law of Ruth, and many others in Hebrew history voiced it (Ruth 1:20). The title is Hebrew is *Shaddai*. *See also* Most High (God), the; names (titles) for God; Pantocrator.

almond: an important nut crop for the peoples past and present, including Judah. To the ancients, the almond represented semen and thus aligned itself with reproduction and immortality. It was associated with hope and abundance. Aaron's rod that budded was of this product (Num. 17:8), an act that showed God's power over political uprising. Almond symbology pertained to the auto-generative power of the bud and represented rejuvenation, vigilance, and delicacy. *See also* Aaron's rod that budded; almond tree branch; flora, fruit, and grain, symbology of.

almond tree branch: a vision of Jeremiah (Jer. 1:11–12) in which the prophet sees the branch of an almond tree. Since the Hebrew word for "watching" sounds like "almond tree," the Lord is saying He is watching His people to see if they will be faithful and fruitful and if His word will be fulfilled in them. *See also* Aaron's rod that budded; almond; flora, fruit, and grain, symbology of.

almsgiving: charity or philanthropy. Jews, Christians, and Muslim are steady in admonishing that the poor should not suffer, and our time, talents, and money should be on the line to assist wherever possible. *See also* charity.

Aloros I: the first king of the earth, according to Babylonian myth, some 432,000 years before the Great Flood. Details are given in Berossus' history called the *Babyloniaca*. *See also Babyloniaca;* Berossus; king(s); Oannes and the Seven Sages.

alpha: the first letter of the Greek alphabet. The character has explicit apocalyptic significance when describing Christ as "the first." *See also* Alpha and Omega; alphabet; author and perfecter (finisher) of our faith; Beginning and the End, the; First and the Last, the; omega.

Alpha and Omega: The Lamb's (Christ's) description of himself in Revelation 1:8 and elsewhere. The intent is to describe the Lord as having no beginning or end, the Lord of history, since the Alpha and the Omega are the first and last letters of the Greek alphabet (A–Ω). Modern usage might produce "from A to Z." *See also* Abel to Zechariah; alpha; alphabet; author and perfecter (finisher) of our faith; Beginning and the End, the; First and the Last, the; names, symbology of; omega.

alphabet: a series of pictographs or letters that make up a written language. The term itself is derived from the first two letters of the Greek language—alpha and beta. Any alphabet is the essential tool for creating and forwarding writings, including sacred literature, from generation to generation. Our earliest inscriptions in the North Semitic script date to the ninth century B.C. but some form of lettering had been in use much earlier, usually written in cuneiform. Where and when writing with syllables and vowels actually began is disputed or unknown in its detailed history. Most scholars agree, however, that early alphabets sprang directly from Egyptian hieroglyphics (technically not a true alphabet) and an early Sinai peninsula script called proto-Sinaitic, as well as possibly a Sumerian-derived style from ancient Ugarit, as early as the 14th century B.C. Finally, the Phoenicians perfected a good commercial text. Certainly, we know that the Old Testament was written principally in Hebrew, an old language in its own right (especially when palaeo-Hebrew is included) and the New Testament was composed in Greek. To the Phoenicians goes the credit for exporting their alphabet (from about 900 B.C. or earlier) to the existing world. *See also* alpha; Alpha and Omega; alphanumeric code; angelic language; cuneiform; *Babyloniaca;* Dee, John; element(s); Enochian; Estrangela; *gematria; isopseplia;* jot and tittle; literomancy; Oannes and the Seven Sages; Ogham; omega; onomastica; Phoenicia, Phoenicians; rune(s); Shaw, George Bernard; Stephen of Perm; Sumer, Sumerian(s); Syriac; theomatic numbers; Ugarit; Ulfilas; Yiddish.

Alphaeus: the name for two men mentioned in the New Testament as fathers of two of the disciples—Matthew and James. Some scholars claim they are the same man but the theory is unlikely since Matthew and James are never identified as brothers and their backgrounds are radically different. There is further dispute as one or both are sometimes confused with Clopas (Cleophas) who, himself, is not clearly identified. *See also* Clopas; James; Matthew as apostle.

alphanumeric code: a method of using letters of an as equivalent to numbers in order to cipher or decipher certain terms (*gematria*). The process only "works" with languages like Hebrew, Latin, and Greek which have letters with corresponding numerals to match. Not surprisingly, the most famous of all attempts to use the system involve Revelation's mysterious number 666. Most who employ the technique end up identifying one or more Roman emperors whose names can be evolved from the letters and numbers of the name and/or title. The pattern is notoriously unreliable since manipulation easily slips into the process and uncertainty abounds as to which language Revelation is using in its code. *See also* alphabet; Antichrist; apocalyptic calculation; 888; *gematria;* numbers, symbology of; 616; 666; theomatic number(s).

Alpha Ovule: a spirit, the "divine spark" within every human which had to be released from the bonds of ignorance or conditioning to shine free in the world, according to the cult of the Arcane and Magickal Order of the Knights of Shambhala (AMOOKOS). The exercises necessary to its discharge allowing humanity's work toward self-awareness, knowledge, and wisdom are known almost solely to AMOOKOS, a cult established by Shri Gurudeva Mahendranath in 1978, an occult organization. *See also* bugbears; Gnosticism, Gnostic(s); idolatry; sect(s); occult, occultic.

al-Qaeda: sometimes al-Qaida or al-Quida, a global militant Islamist terror organization founded by Osama bin Laden sometime before 1989. The name means "the base." Today, it is probably the central target of anti-terrorist nations. It and its many sister fanatic units target all democracies but mainly the United States (which Muslim extremists call the "Great Satan") and Israel (the "little Satan"). *See also Alluha Akbar;* al-Shabab; anti-Semitic; beast(s); bin Laden, Osama; Boko Haram; Daesh; Fatah; Hamas; *harem;* Hezbollah; House of War; Islam; Islamic State in Iraq and Syria (ISIS or ISIL); *jihad;* Muslim Brotherhood; Nusra Front; Palestinian Islamic Jihad (PIJ); Palestinian Liberation Organization (PLO); radicalized; Salafi; Taliban; terrorism; terrorist(s); Turkistan Islamic Party; Velayat Sinai; Wahhabism; wild beasts (animals) of the earth.

already not yet: a phrase sounding like a near-contradiction which attempts to explain the temporal nature of God's kingdom. It is with us now but not fully here in its complete expression. The meaning tells us God is active and among us but will not totally manifest until the eternal phase of the Kingdom of God to come, a truism that Christianity cannot deny. *See also* Christianese; kingdom of God.

al-Shabab: an extremist faction of militant Islam native to Somalia. The group has ties to al-Qaida and is notorious for beheadings in the region. *See also Alluha Akbar;* al-Qaeda;

anti-Semitic; beast(s); Boko Haram; Daesh; Fatah; Hamas; *harem;* Hezbollah; House of War; Islam; Islamic State in Iraq and Syria (ISIS or ISIL); *jihad;* Muslim Brotherhood; Nusra Front; Palestinian Islamic Jihad (PIJ); Palestinian Liberation Organization (PLO); radicalized; Salafi; Taliban; terrorism; Turkistan Islamic Party; Velayat Sinai; Wahhabism; wild beasts (animals) of the earth.

Alsted, Johann Heinrich: Reformed Protestant scholar (1588–1638) who calculated the date of the world's end to be 1694. He ferreted out his concept not with the Bible, but through hermetic wisdom. *See also* Reformed Churches.

altar: furniture used in ritual worship, usually the focus of adoration or attention for those in observance. The root term suggested "bringing" or "sacrifice" which described its purpose. The word is a frequent metaphor in apocalyptic language because it is closely linked to the practice of sacrifice. Examination seems to suggest there is a heavenly prototype altar (Rev. 16:7) from which earthly ones can be copied. Today the altar in most churches is the center of attention and the base for offering the Eucharist, receiving monetary gifts, and sharing Communion. *See also* altar call; altar, consecration of the; altar guild; altar of incense; altar of sacrifice; altar, washing of the; "approach the holy altar"; Ariel; furniture and furnishings of the modern church; harg; *masseboths;* sacred stones; stone(s); tabernacle, the.

altarage: a stipend or extra gratuity paid to a priest (a prebend). *See also* benefice; benefit of clergy; carrodian; *cathedraticum;* love offering; mensa; papal revenue; pounding; prebend; stipend.

altar board: a rectangular piece of wood embossed with a cross or other emblems used by Eastern Orthodox clergy. The board is sacramentally anointed so, if necessary, the Eucharist can transpire as long as the altar board is in use. *See also* altar, consecration of the; Eastern Orthodox Church; furniture and furnishings of the modern church; osculatorium.

altar call: a procedure employed by any number of evangelical churches, also called "the invitation" or "walking the aisle." The old tent revivalists called the act "walking the sawdust trail." The action is an appeal in which the uncommitted, the unchurched, the unaware, and others with spiritual issues are urged to make public confession of personal religious needs by approaching the altar to be met by the pastor or designated counselors. The petition is usually accompanied by congregational singing of hymns with an appropriate repentance theme and prayers either private or oral. The solicitor may request the personal salvation of God or present an appeal to the Holy Spirit to request or recite a special prayer, affirm public testimony or rededication of one's life, apply for church membership, or for any reason as prompted by the Holy Spirit. The invitation is normally offered near the end of the worship and may be extended in time as long as the leadership deems advisable. The process can be an excruciating emotional trauma for some and may evolve into a harangue of sorts from the preacher. When used responsibly, however, the effect can be positive and cathartic. *See also* accept Christ, to; "asking Jesus into my heart"; birth from above; blood of Christ; blood of the Lamb; born again; Christianese; confession(s) of faith; conversion; evangelist(s), evangelism; fishers of men; gospel; liturgy, Christian; lost; "nail-scarred hands, the"; profession faith; "plead the blood"; regeneration; "saved"; "sawdust trail, the"; soul-winning; "turn your life [heart] over to Jesus"; "walking the aisle"; "washed in the blood."

altar, consecration of the: the liturgical act of consecrating (dedicating) an altar in preparation for its sacred use. Most such procedures are High Church orientated and involve anointing the altar with oil from a chrism that has been blessed by a bishop. The articles or accouterments, such as patens and chalices, can be dedicated at the same moment. *See also* altar; altar board; altar guild; altar, washing of the.

altar guild: a more or less informal association of laypersons responsible for the care of the altar and its furnishings within a church or chapel setting, including the availability and good order of all needed articles for the worship ritual. *See also* altar; altar, consecration of the; altar, washing of the.

altar of incense: a small hestia in the Hebrew tabernacle and temples on which incense was burned. The smoke signified prayers rising to God. Revelation 8:3–5 pictures a holy angel approaching the altar of incense in heaven with intent to burn a fragrance there. This action produced smoke ascending to represent the prayers of the Tribulation saints. The angel then filled a censer of fire from the altar and flung it to the earth. Results of that act produced thunder, lightning, and an earthquake. *See also* altar; altar of sacrifice; incense; tabernacle, the.

altar of sacrifice: the large altar of the Hebrew tabernacle and temples on which animal and cereal sacrifices were offered to God. Hebrew sacrificial altars were made of stone; smaller ones for differing purposes were of precious metals. Christians claim that the bloody offering is a type for the shed blood of Jesus on the cross. *See also* altar; altar of incense; tabernacle, the.

altar, washing of the: the practical yet ceremonial cleaning of the altar and its immediate area. First, it is stripped of its linen and utensils, then washed and perhaps anointed. Maundy Thursday is most often chosen as the opportunity for this task. Of course, the sacred objects used in service at the altar are also maintained. *See also* altar; altar, consecration of the; altar guild; Maundy Thursday; washings, ceremonial.

Alternative Service Book: the ASA, perhaps the most popular printed worship guide in the Church of England. The book contains the order of service and is noted for the many prayers contained inside. *See also Book of Common Prayer*; Church of England; liturgical year; liturgy, Christian; Protestant Episcopal Church; Zebra Book.

Alt-right: an extreme, and sometimes radical, supremacist movement that advocates rejection of democracy and dismantling the Constitution. The replacement desired is a fundamentalist dictatorship. *See also* Christian Identity Movement (CIS); militant domestic organizations; Patriot Movement, the.

alukah: a leech, a vampire, a werewolf, or a demon. The name is often associated with the female demon Lilith and it appears on lists naming Solomon's subjected demons. *See also* Asmodaeus; demon(s), demonic; Dibbuk; Dubbi'el; Legion; Lilith; mythological beasties, elementals, monsters, and spirit animals; Sammael.

al-Zarqawi, Abu Musab: terrorist mastermind in Iraq during most of the Gulf Wars fighting there; he was killed by coalition forces in 2006. *See also* beast(s); Islam; terrorism; terrorist(s); wild animals (beasts) of the earth.

A.M. See *Anno Mundi*.

Amalek, Amalekites: a semi-nomadic people of the Negev Desert. They were descendants of Esau (Amalek was a grandson of Esau) and consistent enemies of Israel from the time of Moses until David nearly exterminated them. Sometimes they would join forces with other opponents of Israel, including the Midianites. Balaam called them "the first among the nations" (Num. 24:20a), either because they were the first to attack Israel or because of their antiquity in the region. Perhaps it can be said that of all the national enemies of Israel, the Amalekites were the most hated, and their extinction was prophesied by both Moses (Ex. 17:14–15) and Balaam (Num. 24:20b). It is possible that the prophecies obtained a boost in the purge by the Jews as recorded in the book of Esther. According to Josephus, 75,800 of them were killed in one day. David was forced to lead reprisals against them because Saul had refused to execute their king, Agag (2 Sam. 15:9–33), in clear disobedience to God and the prophet Samuel. The last remnant was wiped out by 500 Simonites at Mount Seir during the reign of Hezekiah (1 Chr. 4:43). Jewish legend tells us that the monstrous offspring of the Watchers resided with the Amalekites. So then, when Saul did not exterminate them at God's direction he infected Israel with evil spirits. *See also* Esther as Hebrew heroine; Esther as Old Testament book; Haman; Mordecai; Purim, Feast of; Watchers, the.

Amana Community: or Amana Society, one of the more successful and enduring of the several 19th century religious communal movements in America (1842 – present). The community was established by Christian Metz (1794–1867) as a product of Protestant cooperative experiments in Germany, a movement at the time called "the Community of True Inspiration." The American group was organized on a farm near Buffalo, New York, where work and worship were intertwined and all was equally shared. Later, in 1855, Metz moved the followers to cheaper land in Iowa that he commissioned as "Amana," the name he insisted was divinely inspired. All labor, supplies, and profits were shared equally among the seven villages of farms, factories, and facilities eventually established at the height of the enterprise. The Amana Community still exists, in altered form, specializing in household appliances and operated by its member stockholders. *See also* church bodies in America (typed); communal communities; Inner Light Churches.

Amanitere. See Candace.

Amasa: the general chosen by Absalom during his rebellion against his father, David, to replace Joab, who had remained loyal to David. David had intended to replace Joab with Amasa as his commander because the former had slain his son Absalom in the rebellion. However, Joab treacherously murdered Amasa, as he had done to Abner, but vengeance for the crime only came in the reign of Solomon. *See also* Abishai; Abner; Asahel; Benaiah; David; David's generals; Joab.

Amasis: the Egyptian pharaoh defeated by Nebuchadnezzar of Babylon. *See also* Amenhotep II; Egypt, Egyptians; Hophra; king(s); Menes; Merneptah; Necho II; pharaoh; Pharaoh of the Exodus; Ramses II; Sesostris; Shabaka; Shishak; So; Tirhakah.

Amaury, Arnauld: reputed to be the heartless knight monk of Rome's Catholic army which subdued the Cathars during the Albigensian Crusade (1209–1229). At the village of Baziers in southern France, the entire population of 20,000 was massacred and the town burned. When asked what to do about separating the surviving Catholics from Cathars, he replied, "*Caedite eos. Novit enim Dominus qui sunt eius.*"—("Slay them. God knows his own.") The more modern rendition of the injunction is: "Kill them all and let God sort them out." *See also* Caesarius of Heisterbach; Cathars; monk(s); Roman Catholic Church.

Amaziah: the ninth king of Judah (796–767 B.C.). His father Joash had been the victim of an assassination, but Amaziah moved quickly to punish the perpetrators and rebuild the military after an invasion by Syria. He intended to hire 100,000 Israelite mercenaries but finally conceded that this course was unwise since Israel was considered a traitorous breakaway nation. That attitude cost him more trouble with the Northern Kingdom. Amaziah was able to return Edom to his power by defeating them in a vicious encounter. He slaughtered 10,000 Edomites in battle and threw another 10,000 off a cliff. He even brought back the idols of Edom and fostered their worship in Jerusalem. Despite the warning of the unnamed man of God (2 Chr. 25:15–16), Amaziah continued his headlong rush to ruin. Meanwhile, the dismissed mercenaries had returned to Israel in an angry mood. Subsequently, Amaziah was determined to punish Israel as he had done to Edom. King Jehoash of Israel warned Amaziah in a parable not to accost him, but to no avail. Judah was subsequently routed in disgrace for Yahweh had determined to punish them for their idolatry.

Amaziah was taken prisoner but was eventually released after the walls of Jerusalem were breached and the Temple looted. Soon after, however, he was killed in a palace *coup*. *See also* cedar of Lebanon and a thistle, parable of the; king(s); kings of Israel and Judah; kings of Israel and Judah in foreign relations.

amber: a color or substance recognized by its pale yellow or gold-shaded appearance. It is mentioned prophetically in Revelation 1:15 and parts of Ezekiel where it is described as "glowing metal" or "glowing bronze" and used as an aid to describe the deity. In Revelation 21:18, it depicts the color or material of the New Jerusalem – perhaps an opaque hue of a soft-glowing yellow intended to represent pure beauty. In that sense, the color amber could be a symbol of the presence of God. The ancients might understand amber as a mix of gold and silver or a mysterious but precious metal of the time called electrum. In any case, amber in these references does not normally name the tree resin or marine fossil of the same name ordinarily fetched from the seas. *See also* bronze; bronze feet; electrum; gold, golden; New Jerusalem; street(s) of gold.

Ambrose: bishop of Milan in Lycia of Asia Minor (ca. 337–397). Ambrose was a generous, intelligent, and forceful church leader, especially in his opposition to Arianism. His theology, however, was perhaps more liberal than many of his time. His most notable prophetic act was no doubt his confrontation with Emperor Theodosius I. The emperor had massacred 7,000 people in Thessalonica in revenge for the murder of the Roman governor by rioters in 390. Ambrose refused the Eucharist or any worship opportunity for Theodosius until the emperor repented, thus demonstrating the strength of the Eastern Church at that time. *See also* Ambrose Rite; Doctors of the Church; liturgical year; Roman Catholic Church; *Te Lucis*; Theodosius I.

History and Mystery

ambrosia: a fruit salad or dessert from pineapple, mandarin oranges, shredded coconut, miniature marshmallows, and sometimes nuts. It is traditionally popular as a Christmas delight but ancient myth names it as the food, drink, or ointment of the Greek and Roman gods. *See also* flora, fruit, and grain, symbology of; fruit; Olympian pantheon.

Ambrosian Rite: the Roman Catholic rubric named for Ambrose, Bishop of Milan in the fourth century. It is practiced in either the ancient or traditional form but differs from the more recognized Roman ritual of our day. *See also* Ambrose; feasts and special days of high liturgy faiths; liturgical year; liturgy; liturgy, Christian; Roman Catholic Church.

Amen: 1. a word meaning "so be it" or "thus it is or will be." The Hebrew expression springs from the root '*mn*, which carries a meaning of truthfulness, stability, or affirmation of something another has spoken. The term is used to testify to one's agreement with another, accept a mission, assume an oath, or express a deeply moving liturgical response or prayer. As such, the word is far more than a convenient way to end a benediction, prayer, or sermon. The term can convey affirmation ("so be it"), supplication ("so let it be"), expectation ("let it be" – a thought closely associated with Jesus), confidence ("it shall be"), necessity ("it must be"), certainty ("it is"), or acquiescence ("let it be even so.") The word, with "alleluia," is the only one recognized in all the world's languages. Sometimes Jesus reversed the formula and stated the Amen first as to say "truly" or "verily," which indicated he was about to speak great truths and that he should be heeded. Amen then is an affirmation, a praise, a commitment, and a worship expression in a single flavorful word that has proven to be more complex and comprehensive than commonly considered. 2. the Egyptian mythical god of the underworld, a dwelling called the Amente. *See also* Amente; Amen, the; Egyptian pantheon; Hallelujah; idol(s); underworld.

Amenemope: an Egyptian wise man quoted in Proverbs 22:17–24. His life dates from the 13th century B.C. and helps give selected Hebrew wisdom writing an interesting touch. *See also* Egypt, Egyptians.

Amenhotep II: Egyptian pharaoh (1450–1420 B.C.). Many scholars believe he was the Pharaoh of the Exodus and thereby in direct conflict with Moses. Others claim the Pharaoh of the Exodus was Merneptah (1235 B.C.) or Ramses II (1300 B.C.). *See also* Amasis; Egypt, Egyptians; Hophra; king(s); Menes; Merneptah; Necho II; pharaoh; Pharaoh of the Exodus; Ramses II; Sesostris; Shabaka; Shishak; So; Tirhakah.

Amente: 1. the accuser in the underworld according to *The Apocalypse of Paul*. The apostle is assured his righteousness would prevail against the power of Amente during Paul's alleged visit there so that he could pass unmolested. 2. a somewhat obscure Egyptian underworld or hell. *See also* Amen; angel(s); Aralu; Dis; Duat; Gnosticism, Gnostic(s); hell; idol(s); Jahannam; Perdition; *Sheol;* underworld.

Amen, the: a name for Christ. In Revelation 3:14, Jesus identified himself as the physical "Amen," the embodiment of the truth of God that heaven itself declares to be the final and most complete affirmation of the deity. Jesus described himself to the church at Laodicea as "the Amen, the faithful and true witness, the ruler of God's creation." *See also* Amen; names (titles) for Jesus.

American Baptist Churches USA: an ethnically diverse Protestant denomination with an estimated 1.3 million adherents in about 5000 local congregations, mostly in the United States and Puerto Rico. Beginnings date to the early 17th century and the denomination has remained loyal to their guiding doctrinal principles of biblical authority, independence of the local congregation, missions, service, and evangelism. *See also* Baptists; church bodies in America (typed); denomination(s), denominationalism.

History and Mystery

American Bible Society: an active, and probably the largest Bible translation and distribution organization in the world. The institute has stated that its mission is to provide a Bible for every person in a language and format each can comprehend and afford. As of the year 2016, some one billion people worldwide have no access to the Scriptures, eighty-nine million in the United States do not read the Word, and there are yet 2000 languages into which a full Bible has not been translated. *See also* Bible; Bible societies; Founding Fathers; Gideons International; religious education; religious organizations; Society of the Propagation of the Faith in Foreign Parts; Society for the Propagation of the Faith in New England.

American folklore: those legends, tall tales, music, customs, art, popular beliefs, proverbs, jokes, oral history, and myths that make up the unique culture and character of the United States. Each ethnographic episode contributes its own humor and entertainment that make the country what it is at the simple heart of its people. Whether the talent demonstrated is from history, religion, geographical section, or ethnic lore, the product paints the character of the nation that only native talent and natural skill can invent. Colorful characters are at the center of almost every myth and song the populace has produced. Who can resist the likes of Paul Bunyan and his blue ox Babe? Or Casey Jones and Mike Fink? Others would nominate Pecos Bill and his wife Sluefoot Sue and his horse Widowmaker. None should neglect Johnny Appleseed (John Chapman), John Henry, Old Stormalong, Febold Feboldson, Tisayac, Joe Magarac, Sally Ann Thunder Ann Whirlwind Crockett, Bowleg Bill, Rip Van Winkle, Tony Beaver, Deadwood Dick (Nat Love), Calamity Jane (Martha Jane Canary), Kemp Morgan, and a host of others. *See also* bugbears; Celtic folklore and religion; Chapman, John; charivari; fable(s); folklore; folk religion; mythological beasties, elementals, monsters, and spirit animals.

American Party: the "Know-Nothings," an anti-Catholic and anti-immigration secretive political movement in the United States begun in 1854. The tide of Irish and German immigrants at the time alarmed many Americans who thought that their jobs were being jeopardized by the aliens. The Know-Nothings actually sabotaged an early attempt to erect the Washington Monument because it contained so many Masonic and foreign symbols in the design. The unusual tag name for the group grew from their habit of meeting in secret lodges and answering all questions with, "I know nothing." The sect attempted to limit immigration, establish a twenty-one-year residency requirement for citizenship, and politically targeted the Roman Catholic Church in America, sometimes resorting to riots and violence. In 1856, the Know-Nothings nominated former president Millard Fillmore for the high office, but their candidate was defeated by James Buchanan. After that, the party faded away. The American Party discussed above is not to be confused with that of the same name, or the American Independent Party and its clones from the late 1960s. Certain racists organizations are also sometimes referred to as "American parties." *See also* anti-Semitic; Aryan Nation; Covenant, The Sword, and the Arm of the Lord, The (CSA); Christian Identity Movement (CIM); Fenians; Knights of the Golden Circle; Knights of the White Camellia; Ku Klux Klan; militant domestic organizations; Molly Maguires; Neo-Nazi(s); Patriot Movement, the; Red Shirts; terrorism; terrorist(s).

"American Pie": a pop music song by singer Don McKean in 1971 which some believe refers to the America's end in some of its lyrics. It became the music craze of the decade. The mystery words have baffled listeners for years but most agree there are references to Karl Marx, Vladimir Lenin (or more likely John Lennon), the Fab Four, the Byrds, James Dean, Charles Manson, and Jackie Kennedy. Still others suspect the words were inspired by Deuteronomy 32 known as the Song of Moses. McLean has since sold the manuscript for over a million dollars and we still don't know the identity of "Miss American Pie" for certain. The name also appears as the title of a teen comedy movie released in 1999 by Adam Herz. *See also* Lenin, Vladimir; Manson, Charles; Marx, Karl; music; Song of Moses.

American Society for the Promotion of Temperance: the first national temperance organization in America. The faction was formed by clergy and laymen in Boston in 1826; it eventually managed the passage of the Maine Law (1851), the earliest legislation prohibiting the manufacture and sale of liquor. The Temperance Movement then was started by men but expanded and mostly energized thereafter by dynamic women like Susan B. Anthony, Elizabeth Cady Stanton, Carry Nation, and Frances E. Willard. Their efforts birthed the likes of the Anti-Saloon League, the Women's Temperance Society, and the Prohibition Party in politics. The issue of women's suffrage became embroiled with the effort and resulted in the passage of the eighteenth and nineteenth Amendments to the United States Constitution. The eighteenth Amendment was eventually repealed when it became obvious that national temperance was not enforceable and bred more crime than it eliminated. Temperance before that time, however, was spurred by countless clergy, including the fiery Billy Sunday, Theobald Mathew, and Thomas Wentworth Higginson. A number of denominations were also active, including the Church of the Brethren, Dunkards, Quakers, and Southern Baptists. *See also* Anti-Saloon League; Baptists; Dunkards; Higginson, Thomas Wentworth; intoxication; Mathew, Theobald; religious organizations; social issues; Sunday, Billy; temperance; Woman's Christian Temperance Union.

Amicale: an anti-colonial rebellion in French Equatorial Africa launched by Andre Matsoua (1899–1942). Followers of the sect were called *Matswanistes* and named Matsoua as the Messiah after his death. They then formed themselves into a secluded religious sect. *See also* cult(s); idolatry; Matsoua, Andre.

***Amidah*:** a Jewish prayer extant for over 2,000 years and a common recitation for the faithful. The word means "standing" since that is the assumed stance for the worshiper to address God. The prayer is to be recited three times daily. Within are some nineteen blessings and eighteen benedictions, making it (with the *Shema*) one of the most beloved and obligatory in all of Judaism. So basic is the prayer it is simply called *Tefillah*, "the prayer." *See also* gestures; prayer(s); *Shema*.

amillennial, amillennialism: the doctrinal position which states that there will be no literal 1,000 years of peace in which Christ rules the world (the Millennium). Technically, however, amillennialists *do* grant a Millennium of sorts in that it constitutes the present age in which we live, what might be termed "realized amillennialism" or "realized eschatology." We are in the Millennium now inasmuch as the Church is making and moving the kingdom of God forward as best as we can on earth. The current church age is the Millennium in that Christ is reigning spiritually over the Church but not the world. The saints in the intermediate heaven are governing there even as the Church is doing the same on earth. They further assert that, indeed, the Second Coming of Christ will be a real and dramatic event, along with the resurrection of the dead, but those actions will not produce a millennial era. So then, amillennialists view the First Advent of Christ as more significant than the Second. Because of the ministry and sacrifice of Christ, the kingdom of God has already come, Satan is bound, and sin is overcome. They would not go so far as to assert that Satan is totally inactive, that sin is abolished, or that this kingdom experience is the best we're going to get. Obviously, that does not describe our world today. They would insist, however, that evangelism is unstoppable, although not everyone will accept the gospel. The "Millennium" is "here" now but it is not "fully here." Amillennialists see Daniel and Revelation as highly symbolic books whose images must not be taken at face value. Old Testament prophecies are much the same in that they are already fulfilled, or soon will be. They view Judaism as irrelevant to God's present and future plans. Perhaps it is correct to say it is the most popular theory among Christian theologians today and has been for some time. It appears to have much less adherence among the general public. *See also* biblical criticism; eschatology, eschatological; postmillennial, postmillennialism; premillennial, premillennialism; preterism; Schism of Nepos; Tyconius.

Amish: also Amish Mennonites, a sister organ of the Mennonite Church but probably in a somewhat stricter practice of doctrine, life, and worship. The fellowships are active in a number of sects (Pennsylvania Dutch, German, various Amish subgroups, Old Order Amish, etc.). They are known universally for their simple living, plain dress, and disinclination to modernism or technology of almost any description. The groups exist in tightly centered and closed societies in a modified but Spartan communal setting even though they live amid a noisy and busy world. The church began in Switzerland in 1693 led by Jakob Amman, following a dispute with certain Alsatian Anabaptists. The first group settled in Pennsylvania in 1727. Little has changed in the fellowship's history because the rule of the population, the *Ordnung*, is incumbent upon everyone. At age eighteen, however, Amish boys and girls are free to decide whether to accept baptism and remain in the Amish life or go out into the world. Trespassers within the community norm are "disciplined," better understood sometimes as "punished." Amish are universally pacifistic and prefer to be un-communicative to outsiders, those whom the Pennsylvania Dutch call "the English." Current to this writing, they are the fastest growing denomination in the United States, due primarily to a high birth rate. *See also* church bodies in America (typed); communal communities; Hutterites; Mennonites; Pennsylvania Dutch; rumspringa; shunning.

Ammia: a respected female prophet active in ancient Philadelphia of the first century. *See also* prophetess(es).

Ammon, Ammonites: the son of Lot by his younger daughter. His descendants, then called the Ammonites, thrived as semi-nomadic peoples northeast of Moab from 1200 to about 600 B.C. The principal settlement in the land was probably Rabbah. The Ammonites were perpetual enemies of Israel. The two nations warred frequently and Ammonite idolatry was a threat to the worship of Yahweh; both countries were consistently cursed by the prophets on those occasions. Ammon has some apocalyptic interest in that Daniel 11:41 states that it, along with Moab and Edom, will be spared the rampages of the "northern king." No nation exists today by that name, nor did it in Daniel's time. Most likely, some modern equivalents will be allied with the Antichrist in the end days and escape his punishments. *See also* Edom, Edomites; Edom, Moab, and Ammon; Moab, Moabites; Molech.

Amnon: a son of David killed by Absalom on account of his violation of their sister Tamar (2 Sam. 19:38).

Amon: 1. the fifteenth king of Judah (642-640 B.C.). Like his father Manasseh, Amon was a wicked and godless king. He was eventually assassinated by an anti-Assyrian party within two years of gaining the throne. 2. an idol of Egypt also known as Amon-Re in subsequent developments of his position as chief god in the land (Jer. 46:25). The name also appears as Ra-Atum—the Egyptian sun-god, perhaps the principal deity of the land whose great temple was at Karnak in the city of Thebes. Unlike most of the Egyptian pantheon which featured animal figures for identification, Re was represented by the plain solar disc. At one point in Egyptian history, Pharaoh Akhenaton even decreed a short-lived monotheism of heliolatry. The Egyptian word *amon* means "hidden." Egypt held an expansive pantheon of gods and goddesses but the Bible mentions only a limited number of them, either by name or inference 3.

the biblical No-Amon was an Ammonite god. *See also ba;* Draco; Egyptian pantheon; Heliopolis; idol(s); *ka;* king(s); kings of Israel and Judah; kings of Israel and Judah in foreign relations; Levant pantheon; *maat;* sun worshipers.

amora: (plural amoraim) a title for wise elders or rabbis who are talented preachers or teachers. The word means "those who say," or "those who speak over the people." *See also* Assemblies of the Wise; atrahasis; elder(s); ensi; *Hasidim; maskilim;* prophet(s); prophetess(es); wisdom; wise, the; zaddik.

amoretti. See *putti.*

Amorites: an ancient race of nomads, but at other times in their history settlers in Canaan and Mesopotamia, a civilization active around the 21st century B.C. They may have had a peaceful association with Abraham but were encountered as enemies by Moses and the migrating Israelites. In the conflict at that point, the Amorites and their king, Sihon, were defeated. Sometimes the Old Testament seems to treat the Amorites as a kind of generalized name for all the Canaanites. They were an idolatrous people that eventually disappeared as a distinct population in Palestine. At least once (in Ezekiel 16:3,45) they, along with the Hittites, are classed as the parents of sinful Judah. Such similes are commonly applied to ancient enemies of Israel because of blatant idolatry so prominent in the lands.

Amos as Old Testament prophecy: an early prophetic book that contains the preaching of the prophet Amos. Within its contents are a number of significant eschatological features including a vivid description of "the day of the Lord," perceived as a time of trouble and hardship for the Jews and a designation for the Tribulation. There are a number of prophetic visions and a promise that the two kingdoms of Israel and Judah (then divided) will someday be reunited. Amos is credited with several miraculous interventions for Israel and a number of visions from God: 1. a plague of grasshoppers turned back (Amos 7:1–3), 2. a judgment of fire averted (Amos 7:4–6), 3. vision of the plumb line (Amos 7:7–9), 4. vision of the basket of ripe fruit (Amos 8), 5. vision of the Lord beside the altar (Amos 9:1–10). One essential eschatological statement occurs in Amos 3:7: "Surely the Sovereign Lord does nothing without revealing his plan to his servants and the prophets." The sentence validates that the purpose of foretelling prophecy and assures us adequate warning will always be issued before the great deeds of God are enacted. *See also* Amos as prophet; curses of Amos.

Amos as prophet: a shepherd and "pincher of sycamore buds" (a farmer) from Tekoa. Though he was from the southern kingdom, he preached mainly in Israel. At the time of his ministry, society and religion were bankrupt throughout the land. The rich were oppressive, even "selling a slave for a pair of shoes." He dared to describe the pampered women of the cities as "fat cows of Bashan." Amos attacked these injustices vigorously, along with the prevalent corrupted religion in Israel. He was a rather simple, plain man but uncompromising in his zeal. *See also* Amos as Old Testament prophecy; prophet(s); prophets as martyrs.

Amphictyonic League: the confederation of the Israelite tribes after they had more or less secured all the Promised Land under Joshua and other leaders. The League, as loose or as cohesive as it may have been, did serve to keep order and provide some cooperation among the tribes. However, the Israelite unity among its own was not as consistent or effective as may be generally believed. Such affinity, as it rose and fell, was based on a few central themes distinctive to them alone: 1. the promises of the fathers (covenant pledges of a homeland and a people to Abraham, Isaac, and Jacob), 2. deliverance (they were rescued from slavery under Moses), 3. covenant (God Himself had guaranteed a land for settlement to be held in perpetuity), 4. wilderness wandering (remembering the land was not taken early as it should have been because of the nation's rebellion in the wilderness), 5. conquest or inheritance (the land was taken by force, for the most part, and only those participating were deemed suitable to rule). *See also* amphictyony.

amphictyony: government via tribal confederation. The ancient Hebrews were essentially an amphictyony or at least a loose confederation of tribes. Despite the prophets' characteristic universalism, the tribal association remained important to their society. The book of Judges is our best example of how the system operated, a poor experiment at best, when tested religiously and militarily. *See also* Amphictyonic League.

Ampliatus: a disciple in Rome greatly beloved by Paul (Rom. 16:8).

Amram and Jochebed: the parents of Moses, Aaron, and Miriam (Ex. 6:20) from the tribe of Levi. Josephus named Amram as a prophet because, according to the historian, but not Scripture, Amram had a vision of God directing him as to how he was to save the life of Moses since Pharaoh had decreed the death of all boy babies at the time. *See also* prophet(s).

Amraphel: an ancient ruler of Shinar who joined forces with other kings in the area to battle in the valley of Siddim during the days of Abraham (Gen. 14). Some experts have attempted to identify him as being the same as Hammurabi or Nimrod-bar-Cush but the comparisons do not glue well together. Others claim the name locates an Amorite tribe between Elam and Babylonia about 1800 B.C. *See also* king(s).

Am Shinri Kyo. See Aleph.

amulet(s): a small item of jewelry or token often associated with magical practices or charms. *See also* ankh; Celtic wheel; charm(s); crucifix; gris-gris; Hand of Fatima; idol(s); juju; magic, magick; Medusa; talisman(s); teraphim; wanga.

Amum: widely considered to the chief of the ancient Egyptian pantheon. His name, if uttered intentionally or accidently, would produce havoc so he was considered the most mysterious and powerful god of the Egyptian pantheon.

To the Hebrews, the awe of Amum may be something of a parallel affinity in the unspeakable Tetragrammaton of God—*Yahweh*. *See also* Egyptian pantheon; idol(s); Yahweh.

Amyraldism: the doctrine advocated by Moses Amyraut (1596–1664), a French Protestant who confirmed the four major points of Calvinism. There is a vital addition, however, in that Amyraut also insisted that Christ died for all people, thus making salvation theoretically possible for everyone. The belief is then sometimes called "hypothetical salvation." *See also* Arminian churches; Arminianism; Arminius, Jacobus; Calvinism; Calvin, John; Canons of Dort; conditional election; election; fall from grace; Five-Point Calvinism; free will; Grotius, Hugo; monergism; "once saved, always saved"; Pelagianism; perseverance of the saints; predestination; Remonstrants; *Remonstrance, the;* sect(s); solifidianism; Synod of Dort; total depravity; TULIP.

Amytis: the Median-born wife of Nebuchadnezzar II, perhaps still active in the days of Belshazzar. It was for her that the famous Hanging Gardens of Babylon were constructed since she was lonely for the lush flora and fauna of her homeland. *See also* Hanging Gardens of Babylon; Nebuchadnezzar II; queen(s).

Anabaptists: radical dissenters who originated in Switzerland but quickly spread to Austria, Moravia, and elsewhere after A.D. 1523. The term means "baptized again" since they abjured the rite for infants. At that time, however, the name merely defined those of radical views in that era. Anabaptists stood in direct opposition to most Roman Catholic doctrine, then authoritative in the day, since they advocated personal belief before baptism (thus pedobaptism was not sanctioned), biblical authority, separation of church and state, elimination of sacramental and sacerdotal grace, the centrality of the gathered church, the restoration of New Testament love as the pattern of Christian conduct, and holy living produced by the experience of regeneration

History and Mystery

in the individual by the Holy Spirit. They were violently opposed to the point of sentenced to drowning at first, followed by outright persecution of every description. They grew rapidly to great numbers but the maltreatments they suffered destroyed almost all adherents. *See also* Bockelson, Jan; Evana; Hoffman, Melchior; martyr(s); martyrdom; Matthys, Jan; Mennonites; Reformed churches; sect(s); Simon, Menno.

anachronism: an historical misalignment or error (*e.g.*, to report the presidency of Thomas Jefferson at the time of the Civil War in America) would be an anachronism. It is quite reasonably considered a mark of poor research and authorship. *See also ex eventu* prophecy.

Anada: a cousin and disciple of Buddha in the sixth century B.C. He is said to have memorized all the sermons of his master and proclaimed them far and wide. *See also* Buddhism.

Anagignoskomena: deuterocanonical scriptures accepted by the Easter Orthodox Church that also include *3 Maccabees*, Psalm 151, *Prayer of Manasseh,* and *3 Esdras.* The Gregorian Orthodox also accepts *4 Maccabees. See also* Eastern Orthodox Church.

Anak: tribal progenitor of the Anakim (plural), or giants, in Palestine during the time of Joshua and after (Num. 13:22). The term means "long-necked" (or some depiction of the neck or a necklace) or simply "a tall one." Those of the breed may have been demon/human hybrids and the most direct cause of God's command to eradicate the entire race in Canaan because of their evil pollution of the land. *See also* Anunnaki; Cyclopes; Fir Bolg; Fomorians; frost giants; giant(s); Laestrygonians; Nephilim; Semyaza; Titans; transhumanism; Watchers, the.

Anakim. See giant(s).

Analects: the implied sayings and conversations of Confucius. *See also* Confucius, Confucianism; *li.*

analogical day theory: the stratagem that posits the six days of creation described in Genesis are to be taken analogically. The Bible's use of the word "day" could mean an unspecified length of time. The theory is an undisguised attempt to fit the literal creation story into the evolutionary concept. *See also* analogical interpretation; big bang theory; big crunch theory; chaos theory; cosmogony; cosmology; *creatio ex nihilo*; creation; creationism; creation science; Creator; day-age theory; evolution; evolution, theistic; framework hypothesis; gap theory of creation; intelligent design; involution; Omphalos Hypothesis; progressive creationism; "six-day theory, the"; uniformitarianism; Young Earth Creationist Movement.

analogical imagination: a religious perspective that stresses the expression of God in all aspects of His sovereignty. Dialectical imagination, on the other hand, emphasizes the individual and the perceived withdrawal of God away from the sinful world of our habitation. Both hypotheses were advanced by Andrew Greely who believed, probably erroneously, that Catholics were more dialectical and Protestants analogical. *See also* dialectical imagination.

anagogical interpretation: a method of scriptural interpretation taught by some theologians in the Middle Ages. These scholars presumed Origen's threefold sense of understanding—the literal, the moral, and the spiritual—were correct but subdivided the last (spiritual) into two parts:—the allegorical and the anagogical. Succinctly, the anagogical approach adds a layer to the allegorical sense, somehow making it even more "spiritual." For example, if the allegorical interpretation suggested the phrase "let Christ be love," we can arbitrarily add a fuller explanation by stating "may we be led by Christ's love to glory." *See also* allegorical interpretation; analogical day theory; biblical criticism; dynamic equivalence; Fourfold Interpretation; grammatical-historical interpretation; hermeneutic(s); higher criticism; idealism; illumination;

inspiration; interpretation; liberalist interpretation; literal interpretation; Origen; plenary inspiration; principles of interpretation; revelation, theological; rhetorical criticism; source criticism; text; textual criticism; threefold sense of interpretation; translation; transmission history.

analogy of being: (*analogia entis*) the idea from Thomas Aquinas espousing that an analogy exits between the created order and God the Creator. Theologians can then safely draw conclusions about God from objects around us and from the composition of the natural order. *See also* analogy of faith.

analogy of faith: (*analogia fidei*) the principle that any interpretation of the Scripture must conform and harmonize with the totality of the teachings of the Bible as a whole on that given subject. The foundation of the thinking is that God cannot contradict Himself. The approach assumes that an historical or biblical parallel used for determining the meaning or fulfillment of a given passage must be in accord with the overall theological meaning and based upon solid faith principles. The hermeneutical expression was first formed by the Reformation theologians and smoothed by Karl Barth who insisted that any connection between the created order and God is only established on the basis of God's self-revelation to us. The Bible is the best interpreter of itself. As Paul admonished: "Compare spiritual things with spiritual things" (Rom. 12:6; 1 Cor. 2:13). *See also* analogy of being.

Anammelech: an Assyrian goddess worshiped as an associate of the sun-god Adramelech. She is named a demon who takes the form of a quail. *See also* Abaddon; Abezi-Thibod; Adramelech; Apollyon; Asmodaeus; Azazel; Azrael; Baal-zebub; demon(s), demonic; devils; Dibbuk; Dubbi'el; Gadreel; idol(s); Legion; Lilith; Mastema; mythological beasties, elementals, monsters, and spirit animals; Pazuzu; Sammael; Sumerian and Babylonian pantheon.

Anamnesis: the remembrance of God's sacred deeds on behalf of His people through His Church. Such contemplation is intended to ignite praise and thanksgiving within the worshiper. At a minimum, the recollection includes meditation on the passion, resurrection, and the Second Coming of Christ. As a formal act of worship, the anamnesis is usually limited to High Church liturgy. As a prayer, the act calls up the death and resurrection of Christ. *See also* liturgical year; liturgy, Christian; prayer(s).

Ananias and Sapphira: disciples in Jerusalem who sold some of their property with the pretext of sharing in the common distribution of goods practiced by the early church. They cheated, however, and held back some of the gain for themselves. The duplicity and lies to cover their theft were disclosed and both were slain by the Holy Spirit (Acts 5:1–11).

Ananias of Damascus: a devout Christian disciple in Damascus when Paul (then called Saul) was led to that city in blindness (Acts 9:10–19). Ananias may also be a prophet, although this identification is not noted in the passage. Ananias was instructed by God to receive Paul, restore the apostle's sight, baptize him, and vouch for his authority as an emissary to the Gentiles. He obeyed despite his fear of Saul the Pharisee and subsequently received the apostle's commendation. *See also* prophet(s).

Ananias the priest: a high priest appointed by Herod, king of Chalcis, around A.D. 48. In A.D. 58, Paul was arraigned before him, and he appeared as chief prosecutor before the procurator Felix (Acts 23:2; 24:1). Ananias was assassinated in 67 A.D., according to Josephus. *See also* Jew(s); priest(s).

Ananke: the Greek goddess of necessity, fate, or destiny. Her three daughters became the Three Fates of Greek mythology. *See also* idol(s); Olympian pantheon.

Ananus of Jerusalem: the high priest emeritus at the time of the Jewish revolt against the Romans. He was of noble character, a just and persuasive man who was nearly successful in preventing the Jewish War, the wholesale slaughter of his people, and the devastation of the Temple because of his astute leadership. He was slain, however, by the Zealots in alliance with the cruel Idumeans. His able assistants were also killed, Jesus the priest and Zecharias the high priest among them. With them perished 12,000 innocent civilians, and this was before the Romans even attacked Jerusalem. Josephus counted the murder of Ananus as the true end of political Jerusalem, a perfidious act that caused God to determine punishment for His people and the purge of His sanctuary by fire and blood. *See also* Jewish War; priest(s).

Anaphora: the Eucharistic prayer and consecration of the Communion, the high point of any Roman Catholic or Orthodox Mass. The Greek original carried the meaning of "I carry up" or "I offer up (in sacrifice)" and ends with the *Sanctus*. *See also* consubstantiation; elevation; epiclesis; Eucharist; liturgical year; liturgy, Christian; prayer(s); Roman Catholic Church; sacrament(s); *Sanctus*, the; transubstantiation; wafer; wine.

Anastasis: the great domed rotunda over the supposed tomb of Jesus in Jerusalem completed in A.D. 340. *See also anastasis;* church; Church of the Nativity; Church of the Holy Sepulcher; Edicule; Jerusalem, landmarks of; Martyrium.

anastasis: Greek for "raising up" or "resurrection." *See also* Anastasis; ascension; resurrection(s).

Anath: or Anat, a savage Canaanite goddess of fertility, sexuality, and violence, a sister and companion of Baal. She has been depicted as wearing a belt of heads and hands of human beings, many of whom were sacrificed children. The Israelites were not immune to her worship or those of her ilk. The Bible makes no direct reference to her but does mention her sister idols since frequently all the fertility goddesses are somewhat fused in ancient thinking. Most, including Ashtoreth, were worshiped as the spouse or consort of Baal (Jud. 10:6; 1 Sam. 7:4). *See also* Ashtoreth(s), Ashtaroth; Baal; idol(s); Levant pantheon; queen of heaven; Venus.

anathema: someone or something devoted or cursed to destruction (Mal. 2:2; 1 Cor. 16:22). Often enough, refusal to heed the words of the prophets or apostles (which are, in essence, the Word of God) invited divine anathema. An anathema then is that which is forbidden. The word may also mean something horrid or accursed. *Anathema Maranatha* (lifted from 1 Corinthians 16:22) warns that anyone who does not love the Lord Jesus at his coming is condemned or "accursed when the Lord comes." From time to time the Roman Catholic Church has seen fit to "pronounce the anathema" upon a person or nation which the popes perceive as having fallen outside official stance and considered bound for hell. *See also* ban; *harem;* Roman Catholic Church.

Anathoth: the hometown of Jeremiah the prophet in the territory of Benjamin. The prophet's neighbors were angered at his pessimistic preaching and plotted his death. God warned Jeremiah, however, and decreed the death of the conspirators even as retribution into the next generation (Jer. 11:21-23).

Anatolia: the land mass today composing most of Turkey but known to the ancient Greeks as Asia Minor. The region is bordered by the waters of the Black Sea, the Mediterranean, the Aegean, and the Sea of Marmara. Numerous tribes and kingdoms are found in the history of the region, among the oldest to be named being the Hattiam, Hurrianian (Assuwa), Phrygia, Ionia, Lydia, Cilicia, Caria, Lysia, and Mysia. *See also* Cappadocia.

Anaxagoras: philosopher of ancient Greece (ca. 500–428 B.C.) who founded an early teleological interpretation of the cosmos. His idea was centered on the mind which controlled the soul. A specified belief in a deity, however, had no distinct place in the scheme. *See also* philosophy of the Greeks.

History and Mystery

ancestor reverence: the ancient practice (still in vogue in some cultures today) by which deceased ancestors, or their spirits, are honored with attendance, votive offerings, food, etc. The process of the rituals involved, at least in rural parts of China, seldom varies and are enacted with veneration. First, the name of the deceased in written on a wooden tablet and placed in the home or at the graveside. Devotion may be pronounced at home, the burial site, or a temple. The body is wrapped in a pall, white being the color of grief. Male mourners dress in red; the women in blue. The eldest son always leads the devotion, even if the young man is adopted. Fireworks are set off at the gravesite and sometimes performances are rendered. The deceased is thought to have three souls, each of which must be placated. The grieving period normally lasts three years. The reverence ritual has been commonly labeled "ancestor worship," but the designation is not precisely correct. *See also* Badimo; bugbears; cult of the dead; Day of the Dead; idolatry; Kirant; Loa Loas; necrolatry; necromancy; sect(s).

anchor: a maritime device of some weight used to fasten a ship to the seabed. It was, then, a navigational device symbolic of safety. The early Christians adopted the symbol, giving it a higher meaning aspiring to the hope of eternal life. Though mentioned only four times in Scripture (three in Acts and once in Hebrews 6:19), the ship's anchor became a favorite logo of Christian hope. Its natural design with a transverse bar suggests a cross and the figure appears often in the catacombs. According to tradition, it was the symbol of Clement of Rome who was supposedly bound to an anchor by Emperor Trajan and cast into the sea. Some early churches and cathedrals also showed the ceiling as an inverted ship with its keel above the viewer for similar reasons. The anchor was also a pagan device, sometimes seen with a rope or serpent clamoring up the vertical shaft, representing the tortured soul making its way from the depths of earthly life. *See also* Clement of Rome; cross; hope.

anchorites. See desert mystics; monasticism.

Ancient Astronaut Theory: the idea that the earth has been visited by extraterrestrials, a theory popularized by Erich von Daniken and Zechariah Sitchin. These alien beings, perhaps gods or avatars, are said to have fostered the great cultures of the ancient Egyptians, Mayans, Druids, and many others. The theory points to certain ancient artifacts, writings (including the Bible), myths, structures, and artworks as proof of Earth's visitation. Even Alexander the Great is reputed to have seen alien spacecraft. Such structures as the megaliths of Stonehenge and Easter Island, the pyramids of Egypt and Mesoamerica, Baalbek in Lebanon, and the Nazca lines of Peru are said to exist only because the celestial beings taught the ancients how to construct them. Certain depictions in art look like flying saucers and other airborne machines. Some strange inventions like the mysterious Antikythera Mechanism (a clock-like device) seem to have a special purpose; the Baghdad batteries of Babylon might be capable of storing electricity, for example. Ancient avionic devices and gliders of Egypt and South America appear capable of flight, provided they are not simply replicas of ordinary birds. Some Paleolithic cave drawings appear to resemble suited astronauts of today. *See also* alien; alien abduction; Alien Disclosure Event; alien Jesus; Anunnaki; *Chariots of the Gods?;* Chintamani Stone; Fermi paradox; Guardians; Igigi; lulu; panspermia theory; Sitchin, Zecharia; transhumanism; UFO; von Daniken, Erich.

Ancient of Days: a particularly awesome description of God the Father as related in Daniel 7:11–14. In the vision, a heavenly throne room is pictured dominated by the Ancient of Days. The display is apocalyptic in which we are shown a celestial court with thrones, twirling wheels, fire, countless attendants, books of law, and other grand accouterments, all set in place to pronounce eternal judgment of wickedness on a universal scale. All civil governments, including that of Antiochus Epiphanes (whom the vision mocks) and that of the Antichrist (which it typifies), will perish before the judgment of God. Such earthly kingdoms will endure "for a time and a season" but will be banished with finality on the day of judgment. *See also* names (titles) for God.

ancress: a female religious recluse. *See also* abbess; desert mystics; monasticism; nun(s); Roman Catholic Church.

Anderson, Sir Robert: biblical scholar (1841–1918) who perhaps deserves most credit for theological contributions in several prophetic areas. It is his perception of Daniel's seventy weeks vision, however, that gained unparalleled acclaim. One of his more incisive works of that theme is entitled *The Coming Prince. See also* seventy weeks, prophecy of the.

Andreae, Johann Valentinus: a German theologian (1586–1654) and principal leader of the sect known as the Order of the Rosy Cross, a part of Rosicrucianism. *See also* Order of the Rosy Cross; Rosicrucianism; sect(s).

Andrew as apostle: one of the original twelve apostles and one of the four prominent spokesmen asking specific prophetic questions of Jesus on the occasion of the Olivet Discourse. He was the brother of Peter and is sometimes called the patron of evangelism. *See also* apostle(s); disciple(s); liturgical year; martyr(s); prophets as martyrs.

Andrew van der Bijl: (b. 1928), a Dutch missionary known worldwide as Brother Andrew. In 1955, he began smuggling Bibles behind the Iron Curtain, then expanded his operation. Around the word he has become known as "God's smuggler." *See also* colportage, colporteur; missions, missionaries.

Andromeda: daughter of King Cephas and Cassiopeia of Greek legend. When her mother bragged that Andromeda was fairer than the Nereids, or that she herself was prettier than the sea nymphs, the ocean god Poseidon chained Andromeda to a rock and called the beast Cetus to destroy her. She was rescued by Perseus, her future husband. *See also* Arethusa; Cassiopeia; Daphne; elemental(s); household deities; idol(s); Medusa; nymph; Olympian pantheon.

Andronicus: 1. a possible heir to the Seleucid kingdom during the time of Antiochus IV Epiphanes. Andronicus murdered his brother Antiochus who had been a hostage in Rome. He, in turn, was killed by Antiochus IV, an act that helped Antiochus Epiphanes secure the throne of Syria even though he was not a legitimate candidate. 2. a relative and fellow prisoner with Paul at Rome (Rom. 16:7). He was a Jewish convert to Christianity and was in the faith before Paul.

anele. See unction.

angel(s): often described as celestial beings created immortal by God. In point of fact, however, angels cannot be technically tagged as eternal because they were created and therefore had a beginning; furthermore, they can be killed or otherwise have an ending which gives some of their number no infinite future. The beings, in some form or another, are represented in all cultures and all eras of civilization, including our own. The name angel (*angelos*) means "messenger" (*mal'ak*), a frequent activity among the many and varied duties of angels in service to their Maker. "Are not all angels ministering spirits sent to serve those who will inherit salvation?" (Heb. 1:14). Their principal role is to worship and serve the Trinity, but they frequently are called to speak to humans, to assist them, to protect them, or to discipline them. The heavenly beings may bring a message of judgment, encouragement, hope, or mission, but they are always trying to clearly communicate their revelations when tasked. Aside from the generic name for angels the word also describes one of the so-called "lowest" classification of power and authority; these include the principalities, archangels, and angels in that ranking. The "middle" section holds the dominions, Virtues, and powers. The "highest" order contains the Thrones in third place, the Cherubim next, and Seraphim as the penultimate. As a categorization system, each grouping names three ranks in three courses. There are other methods of classification but the above represents the most instructive in simplicity and clarity as catalogued by Jewish specialists. Angels, then, are personal beings (sometimes called spirits or "ministering spirits") but higher in position than humankind. Even so, angel and archangel are not normally capitalized when writing though, in some contexts, they can represent a ruling class in heaven. Human eyes cannot commonly perceive the angelic hosts now (though creditable witnesses have said they have witnessed and interacted with them on many special occasions) because we are mortals of a different realm. Certain Bible actors certainly did. However, Scripture testifies that we will see them someday in the blessed kingdom as promised to Nathaniel of the Gospels (Jn. 1:31). Furthermore, we are appointed to be positioned as judges over them (1 Cor. 6:2-3). Clearly the angelic orders have organization and structure; we know of at least four divisions—archangels, Cherubim, Seraphim, and servant angels—with a further New Testament subdivision as rulers, principalities, authorities, powers, dominions, thrones, and world rulers according to Colossians 1:16. Popular identification of rankings is headed by the traditional nine divisions: 1. Seraphim (the highest order and closest attendants to the throne of God), 2. Cherubim (guardians of God's glory and second in rank over all angelic dimensions), 3. Thrones (over peace and submission), 4. Dominions or Lords (for ordering of the world), 5. Virtues or Strongholds (over the elements), 6. Powers or authorities (warriors), 7. principalities or rulers (commanders of the lower angels and tasked to ensure obedience to God's directives concerning the universe), 8. Archangels (over the gospel), 9. Angels (messengers and most familiar to us humans). Fallen angels, on the other hand, are described as having the same essence as the holy ones, but are evil in nature. Satan is their prince. The generally accepted theory is that demons were once good angels who rebelled against their Originator because of jealousy over the creation of mankind. Gabriel and Michael are named in Scripture on the good side, and Satan and Apollyon on the evil side. Almost forty percent of all angelic references in the Bible are found in the book of Revelation. Their depiction in art often sport wings, but that accouterment probably does not suit their actual composition. Specified angelic visions of the hierarchy describe wings of some description (certainly not feathers) associated to a quantity of them but ordinary ones have none. A summary of angelic powers would include the facts that they: 1. act as messengers for the divine (Gen. 19:15), 2. have spirits (Ps. 104:4) but can assume substantial shapes (Gen. 18), 3. kill and defend (2 Ki. 19:35; Rev. 9:15), 4. praise God (Lk. 2:13; Heb. 1:6; Rev. 7:11), 5. touch either with force or gentleness (Gen. 32:24; 1 Ki. 19:5; Acts 12:7), 6. walk through fire (Dan. 3:28) or penetrate solid objects, 7. appear and disappear at will (Num. 22:31; Jud. 6:11; Lk. 22:43), 8. control animals and animals can perceive them (Dan. 6:22; Num. 22), 9. operate in a military-like structure or as members of the council of God (Mt. 26:53; Rev. 9:11); 10. enter human dreams (Gen. 31:11, 1 Sam. 3; Mt. 1:20), 11. prevent speech (Lk. 1:20) or permit it, 12. change form at will (Gen. 3; Ex. 3:2; Jud. 13:6; 2 Cor. 11:14; Heb. 13:2), 13. escort the dead (Lk. 16:22), 14. control or govern the elements (Jud. 6:21; Rev. 7:1; 14:18), 15. cure illness (Jn. 5:4), 16. use telekinesis (Acts 12:7), 17. move between heaven and earth (Gen. 28:12; Lk. 2:15; Jude 6), 18. influence time (Lk. 4:5), 19. operate various vehicles or other unknown modes of travel (Ps. 68:17), 20. induce unconsciousness or sleep (Acts 12:10), 21. consume food (Gen. 18; Ps. 78:25) (though not of dietary necessity), 22. tell lies if they are impious or have an agenda to do so (Gen. 3; 1 Ki. 22:22; Gal. 1:8), 23. are good or iniquitous (Ps. 78:49), 24. learn and dispense knowledge (1 Pe. 1:12), 25. sin if it their will (2 Pe. 2:4), 26. fight each other in the roles of good vs. evil (Rev. 12:7), 27. are innumerable in population (Ps. 68:17), 28. do not marry (Mk. 12:25) and presumably do not procreated as they, themselves, are created beings, 29. have their own speech (1 Cor. 13:1), 30. desire (the holy) or refuse (the fallen) worship of God (Col. 2:18; Rev. 19:10), 31. honor God, escort the Son, and act for the Holy Spirit (Mt. 25:31; Rev. 21:12), 32. protect children (Mt. 18:10), individuals, nations, and churches (Rev. 1:20), and 33. will be agents of divine judgment and be subject to judgment themselves (Job 4:18; 1 Cor. 6:3; Mt. 13:37-41; 2 Pe. 2:4). Perhaps angels are best studied in our sparse knowledge of them according to their 1) nature (who they are), 2) status (their hierarchical rank), and 3) function (what they do). We may see them identified or implied by various names in either Greek or Hebrew: archangels, armies (*sebaot*), bodies, hosts (*saba*), assembly (*mo 'ed; elah*), authorities (*exousia*), sons of God (*bene ha elohim*), brigades (*degalim*), wheels, electrum (Ez. 1:4) (perhaps symbolizing mystery and uniqueness), chrysolite (Dan. 10:5-6), archers (*sin 'an*), heroes, divisions, stars (Rev. 1:20) (*kokebim; stratia*), children of God, congregation (*qahal; edah*), court (*din*), the divine council (*sod; adat el*), spirit or spiritual beings, doves (Mt. 3:16) (descriptive of movement only), elders (Rev. 4:4), the elect, escorts, demons (*shedim*), fire or flames of fire, the divine family, gods (*elohim*), warriors, watchers (*irin*), witnesses, heavenly angels (*samayim*) or heavenly ones (*epouranioi*), holy ones (*qedosim; hagiais*) or holy angels (*malakim qodes*), lights (*photon*), messengers (*mal' ak*), mighty ones (*quibborim; abbirim*), ministers (*seret*) or ministering spirits (*ruhot; pneumata*), powers (*dynamis*), dominions (lords) (kyrios), princes or commanders (*sar*), rulers (*archai*), principalities (*arche*), servants (*leitourgos*), shepherds, thrones (*thronos*), winds, mediators (*melis*), troops (*gedudim*), cherubim (*kervuim*), seraphim (*serapim*), guardians, glorious ones (*doksai; hagiais*), world rulers (*kosmokrator*), or simply "men." See *also* Abdiel; Achtariel; *agathodaimon;* Akae, the;

altar of incense; Amente; angelic language; angelic miracles; angel of Babylon's fall; Angel of Darkness; angel of death; angel of his presence; Angel of Light; angel of light; angel of the Abyss; angel of the covenant; angel of the east; angel of the fire; angel of the incense; angel of the little scroll; angel of the Lord, angel of Yahweh; angel of the millstone boulder; angel of the sun; angel of the Temple; angel of the waters; angel of the wedding supper of the Lamb; angelology; angelophany; angelotry; Angels' Chorale; angels of measurement; angels of nature; angels of the churches; angels of the Euphrates; angels of the harvest; angels of the heavens; angels of the Lord's presence; angels of the nations; angels of the Revelation; angles of the winds; angels of touring; angels of transport; angels of vengeance; Annunciation, the; Anpiel; Antiphonal Amen; archangel(s); Ariel; Arioch; armies of heaven; attending spirits; authorities; Azazel; beast(s); Bene Elohim; Beqa; *Book of Abramelin, The;* bound angels; burnished man, the; Cainites; celestial court, the; chariot(s); chasmal; Chashmallim; Chayoth; Cherub, Cherubim; council of God; council of heaven; council, the heavenly; court of heaven; daemons; Daniel's vision from the revealing angel; death angel; deceiving spirits; demon(s), demonic; devils; Dionysius the Areopagite; divine council; dominions; dove; *dulia;* eagle(s); eagle (angel) of woe, the; El; elder(s); electrum; elect, the; *elohim;* Erelim; ethnarch; Eularia; evil (unclean) spirit(s); Ezekiel's report of the scribe clothed in linen; Ezekiel's vision of the Cherubim and the departed glory; fallen angel(s); fallen star; familiar spirits; fellow servants; fire; flying angels, three; four angels of the Euphrates; four living creatures of Ezekiel; four living creatures of Revelation; frog(s); Gabriel; Galgallim; gates of the New Jerusalem; glory; goetia; Gregori; guardian angel(s); Guardian Angels, Feast of the; guardian Cherub(s); Habib; Hashmallim; Hayyot; Heavenly Council; heavenly court; Herod Agrippa I; high priest cleansed and robed; holy one of heaven; holy ones; hosts of heaven; Husk(s);

History and Mystery

idol(s); Ishim; Israel; Jacob; Jael and Zarall; judgment of the angels; Kesbul; liturgical year; Lot's wife; loud command; Lucifer; *mal'ak;* man (men); man among the myrtle trees; man from Macedonia; man (men); manna; Manoah; man of God, a (the); man with a linen cord and a measuring rod; man with a measuring line; Maroni; Melchizedek; messenger of Yahweh; Metatron; Michael; Michaelmas, Feast of; monastic vows; Morning Star, the; Ophanim; Phanuel; powers; Pravuil; prince of Greece; prince of Persia; prince who protects your people, the; prince, your; principalities; *psychopmps; putti;* Radueri'el; Rahati'el; Raphael; Raquel; Remuel; saints of the Most High; Sandalforn; Saraquel; Sarathiel; scribe clothed in linen; Semyaza; Seraph, Seraphim; servant; Sethites; seven spirits before the throne; seventy shepherds; Shabbat angels; shepherd/shepherdess; Sim Kiel; sin (rebellion) of the angels; six destroying warriors; Song of Moses and the Lamb; son of the morning, son of the dawn; sons of God; spirit; spirits in prison; spiritual warfare; star(s); Tartarus; taxiarch; territorial spirits; thrones; transporting angel of Ezekiel, the; trumpet call of the elect; twenty-four elders, the; 200,000,000 invaders; Uriel; Virtues; voice of the archangel, the; war in heaven; Watchers, the; wind(s); Yoel; your prince; Zechariah's vision of the man with a measuring line.

angel coin: a coin, first minted in the 1400s, with one side showing the archangel Michael slaying the dragon (Satan). Until the 1700s, people of England who contracted the "King's Evil" (the skin disease scrofula) could present themselves to the current regent who was obligated to touch them, then present the token called an "angel." *See also* angel slices.

angelica: a vegetable from Iceland (although in the rest of the world an angelica is an herb, not a veggie). It is used as a flavoring and a mixture for perfumes because of its "heavenly" aroma. Thus, its association with the angels (as well as a popular name for girls). Further, angelica names a musical instrument called the lute in the 1600s. *See also* flora; fruit, and grain, symbology of; musical instruments; perfumes, ointments, and spices.

angelic language: the legendary concept that humans can speak with angels via the Enochian alphabet. Such a syllabus was thought to be lost before the Noah flood but was "rediscovered" by John Dee around 1581 with the aid of an occultic seer. The concept was a common one in Dee's time. If one could talk to the angels, they could be summoned and people could interact with them. The script, which he called "Angelical," was supposedly the language God used to address Adam and the angels and His method of speaking the world into existence. The alphabet itself is a phonic representation of twenty-one letters in both print and script. In photographs, the characters resemble a simplistic mix of Chinese and Hebrew. *See also* alphabet; angel(s); Dee, John; Enochian.

angelic miracles: supernatural actions by the angelic beings that testify to God's prophetic witness. Examples include: 1. blinding the Sodomites and destroying Sodom and Gomorrah following their stay as guests of the Patriarch Abraham at Mamre (Gen. 19), 2. burning Gideon's sacrifice (Jud. 6:19–24), 3. feeding Elijah by ravens (1 Ki. 19:5–7), 4. destroying the Assyrian army (2 Ki. 19:35), 5. rescuing the Hebrew servants from the fiery furnace (Dan. 3:25–27), 6. rescuing Daniel from the lions' den (Dan. 6:–24), 7. a future action prophesied as the regathering of Israel (Mt. 24:31), 8. rolling the stone from Jesus' tomb (Mt. 28:2), 9. opening prison doors for the incarcerated disciples (Acts 5:19–23), 10. giving of the law (Acts 7:53; Gal. 3:19; Heb. 2:2–3), 11. freeing Peter from prison (Acts 12:1–17), 12. enacting the death of Herod Agrippa I (Acts 12:23), 13. rescuing Moses' body from Satan (Jude 9), 14. pouring out the wrath of God in Revelation 6–16 and other places throughout that apocalyptic letter. *See also* angel(s); angels of the Euphrates; angels of the harvest; angels of the Revelation; Anne, Queen de la Palude; Annunciation, the; Bethsaida; Bethlehem; body of Moses, dispute over the; Bokim; Daniel's experience in the lions' den; furnace; harvest of the earth; Herod Agrippa I; hip; holding back the four winds; Jacob's ladder; miracles; Passover; remnant; resurrection of Jesus; Sodom and Gomorrah; war in heaven; wrath, the coming.

angel of Babylon's fall: the powerful and authoritative angel of Revelation 18:1 who announces the fall of Babylon the Great at the hand of God. *See also* angel(s); angels of the Revelation; Babylon, Babylonians; Babylon the Great; city of power; desolate and naked; filth of her adulteries; "glorified herself"; great city, this; Great Prostitute, the; haunt (prison) for every unclean and detestable bird; merchant(s); Mystery Babylon the Great the Mother of Prostitutes and Abominations of the Earth; Religious Babylon; Secular Babylon; smoke of her burning; whore of Babylon; wine of her adulteries.

Angel of Darkness: the supernatural entity, according to the beliefs of the Essenes, expected to oppose the righteous at the end of the age as he combats the Angel of Light. *See also* Angel of Light; Dead Sea Scrolls; Sons of Darkness; Teacher of Righteousness; *War of the Sons of Light Against the Sons of Darkness;* War Scroll; Wicked Priest.

angel of death: sometimes called "the destroyer." An angelic representative (or perhaps more than one) of the Lord assigned to enact the penalty of execution or threat of death on portions of the population. The death angel was God's heavenly agent who was charged to dispense the ultimate penalty at the Lord's command, often in great numbers (*i.e.,* Exodus 11; 12:23; 2 Kings 19:35; 1 Chronicles 21:16). It could be said that the death angel was in essence God Himself acting in vengeance for committed sin or disobedience. An alternate translation to identify the being is found in 1 Corinthians 10:1–3 as "the destroying angel." Other scriptural renditions of the life forms and their actions include: 1. before Eden with flaming sword (Gen. 3:24), 2.

over Egypt to accomplish the death of the firstborn (Ex. 12:21–30), 3. before Balaam and his donkey (Num. 22:21–35), 4. at the destruction of Sodom and Gomorrah (Gen. 19), 5. before Joshua at Jericho (Josh. 5:13–15), 6. against Meroz at the battle of the Kishon River (Judg. 5:23), 7. before David at Jerusalem (2 Sam. 24:15–17; 1 Chr. 21:13–21), 8. against the Assyrians (2 Ki. 19:35–36; Isa. 37:36), 9. against Herod Agrippa I (Acts 12:23), 10. any number of accounts of angelic vengeance enacted in the book of Revelation. Early Jewish legend claimed that the death angel could be defeated because he tracked with the person's name. The remedy, then, was to change one's name on the deathbed with the aid and ministry of a rabbi and thus confuse the hunting angel. *See also* angel(s); angel of the Lord.

angel of Ezekiel's transposition. See transporting angel of Ezekiel, the.

angel of his presence: a reference from the Exodus experience that describes God's sharing in the affliction of His people who were then enslaved in Egypt (Ex. 3:7–10). In the Lord's compassion, He sent the angel of His presence to save the people under duress, a heavenly messenger who acted as a vanguard for the liberated Hebrews (Ex. 14:19; Num. 20:14–16). The angel of the presence also appears prominently in Isaiah (Isa. 63:9) as Israel's protector and provider. *See also* angel(s); angel of the Lord, angel of Yahweh; angels of the Lord's presence.

Angel of Light: (or Prince of Light) the supernatural leader for the Qumran community expected to lead the righteous against the Angel of Darkness in the eschaton. *See also* angel of light; Dead Sea Scrolls; Sons of Darkness; Teacher of Righteousness; *War of the Sons of Light Against the Sons of Darkness;* War Scroll; Wicked Priest.

angel of light: a holy messenger—an angel of heaven bathed in righteousness. At least one reference to such beings in Scripture, however, carries a negative connotation in that the devil is capable of masquerading as an angel of light (2 Cor. 11:14). *See also* accuser of our brothers; angel(s); angel of the Lord, angel of Yahweh; Anointed Cherub; Baal-zebub; Baphomet; Beelzebub; Belial; Cupay; Day Star; dragon; Evil One, the; father of lies; Ghede; goat; god of this age, the; guardian Cherub; Hahgwehdaetgah; Iblis; idol(s); *Kategor;* kingdom of the air; kingdom of this world; king of Babylon; king of Tyre; Light-Bringer; lion; Lucifer; Mastema; Morning Star, the; prince of demons; prince of the power of the air; prince of this world; red dragon; ruler of the kingdom of the air; Sanat Kumar; Satan; seed of the serpent; serpent; Shaytan; son of the morning, son of the dawn.

angel of the Abyss: the mighty angel of Revelation 20:1 who captures the dragon (Satan) and forces him into the pit of the Abyss for 1,000 years of imprisonment. *See also* Abyss; angel(s); angels of the Revelation.

angel of the covenant: a special messenger of Yahweh (*Eliyahu ha-Navi* in Hebrew) showing the importance of the presence and promises of God with His chosen. Perhaps it is not far off the mark to view such an agent as the most unique in descriptions of covenantal theology with the Jews and with the Church, most clearly predicted in Malachi 3:1. From these and other appearances, the messenger of the covenant has taken on mystical, and even prophetic, associations with Abraham, Elijah, John the Baptist, and Jesus. It is the covenant angel who gives the "little book"—a *covenant*—to John in Revelation 7:13–17. *See also* angel(s); angel of the little scroll; angel of the Lord, angel of Yahweh; covenant(s), biblical; little scroll, the; messenger of the covenant; Sandalforn.

angel of the east: the heavenly being of Revelation 7:3, the keeper of the heavenly seal. It is he who will label the 144,000 faithful witnesses in preparation for their work on Tribulation earth. *See also* angel(s); angels of nature; angels of the Revelation; seal(s).

angel of the fire: the angel of Revelation 14:18 who directs the harvest of the grapes. *See also* angel(s); angel of the Temple; angles of nature; angels of the harvest; angels of the Revelation; harvest of the earth.

angel of the incense: a special angelic being (some claim he is Christ himself) who appears before the Tribulation altar in Revelation 8:3. His arrival follows the seven seals of judgment previously opened and precedes the seven angels (or archangels) who will sound the trumpets. His purpose seems to set the stage in prayer for the remaining catastrophes, then to ignite them by casting fire on the earth from the heavenly altar of incense. Revelation calls this eighth heavenly being "another" angel, no doubt because he succeeds the previous actions of the typical set of seven with a related mission but not part and parcel with the preceding group. *See also* angel(s); angels of the Revelation; incense.

angel of the land and sea. See angel of the little scroll.

angel of the little scroll: the heavenly messenger of Revelation 10 whose job is to tender the scroll of ministry to John so it can be consumed by the writer. This librarian angel of splendid appearance is robed in a cloud, wears a rainbow as a headdress, shows skin of fired bronze, and forms a giant of such proportions that he can straddle land and sea. Yet his only equipment is the small scroll he is charged to deliver to John. *See also* angel(s); angel of the covenant; angels of nature; angels of the Revelation; little scroll, the.

angel of the Lord, angel of Yahweh: a theophany expression representing a kind of Christ-like or godly figure who speaks and acts for God. Often, the tasks of the angel of the Lord were deadly and enacted in war or fierce destruction performed in God's name (*e.g.,* Zechariah 12:8–9). The angel of the Lord could also be a figure (or the similitude of many of them) who are seen as protectors. Psalm 34:7 reads: "The angel of the Lord encamps around those who fear him, and he delivers them." Many Christian theologians see the angel of the Lord as Christ himself in his pre-incarnate form busily at work in the Old Testament era. Jewish folklore, however, even gives the angel of Yahweh a name—Achtariel. *See also* Achtariel; angel(s); angel of death; angel of his presence; angel of the covenant; Christophany; theophany.

angel of the millstone boulder: the heavenly being who dramatically illustrates the joyous fall of Babylon the Great by splashing a great rock into the sea. Its disappearance into the depths symbolizes the definite and eternal loss of the evil city, never to be seen again. *See also* angel(s); angel of Babylon's fall; Babylon the Great; angels of the Revelation; city of power; filth of her adulteries; great city, this; merchant(s); millstone; Secular Babylon; smoke of her burning; whore of Babylon; wine of her adulteries.

angel of the sun: the angel of Revelation 19:17 standing in the sun to call forth the birds of carrion to feast on the carcass of fallen Babylon. *See also* angel(s); angels of nature; angels of the Revelation.

angel of the Temple: the angel of Revelation 14:15 who directs the wheat harvest episode. *See also* angel(s); angel of fire; angels of the harvest; angels of the Revelation; harvest of the earth.

angel of the waters: an angelic being commissioned in Revelation 16:5 to empty the third bowl of God's wrath on the waters of earth. As he did so, he proclaimed that this judgment and that of all the bowls were just. Each pouring serves as contributing to the victory of the Lamb because all were ordained by the Holy One. Furthermore, the perpetrators deserve the punishments because of their unspeakable crimes against the innocent. *See also* angel(s); angels of nature; angels of the Revelation; waters.

angel of the wedding supper of the Lamb: the angel of Revelation 19:9 who pronounces blessing on the soon-coming marriage of the Lamb and his Church. See also angel(s); angels of the Revelation; marriage supper of the Lamb.

angel of woe, the. See eagle (angel) of woe, the.

angelology: the study of the constitution and action of angels. See also angel(s); angel coin; angel(s) of the churches; angelotry; angel slices; Opus Sanctorum Angelorum; sons of God; "where angels fear to tread."

angelophany: a miraculous angelic appearance, a phenomenon occurring frequently enough in scriptural accounts. It is practicable, if not totally accurate, to esteem an angelophany and a theophany as the same incident. Or the two may appear together as in the vision of Jacob's ladder at Bethel (Gen.28: 10–22). Other appearances include: guarding Eden after the Fall (Gen. 3:24), guardian of Ishmael and Hagar (Gen. 16), saviors of Lot and his family from Sodom (Gen. 19), preventer of the sacrifice of Isaac (Gen. 22), at the burning bush (Ex. 3), wrestling with Jacob (Gen. 32), at the Red Sea (Ex. 14), death dealer to the Egyptians at Passover (Ex. 12), before Balaam and his donkey (Num. 22-24), at the battle of Jericho (Josh. 5:13 – 6:7), at Bochim (Jud. 2), with Gideon (Jud. 6), prior to Samson's birth (Jud. 13 – 16), at the census plague of David (2 Sam. 24:10 – 17), before armies (1 Ki. 22:19), to refresh Elijah (1 Ki. 18), to aid Elijah (2 Ki. 1), with Israel and Hezekiah before Sennacherib (2 Ki. 18 – 20), at the court trial of Job (Job 1:6), touching Isaiah's tongue with a live coal (Isa. 6), with Daniel's friends in the fiery furnace (Dan. 3), with Daniel in the lions' den (Dan. 6), as Daniel's interpreter (Dan. 8), the "man" clothed in linen (Ezk. 9 – 10), encounters with Zechariah (Zech. 1, 5), in Joseph's dreams (Mt. 1:20 – 21; 2:13 – 23), to announce the births of John the Baptist and Jesus Lk. 1 – 3), at the pool of Bethesda (Jn. 5:4), comforting Jesus in the wilderness and on the Mount of Olives (Lk. 4, 22: 42 – 43), after the resurrection (Mt. 28:2 –4, 20:12), with the apostles in prison (Acts 5), with Philip the evangelist (Acts 8:26 – 39), conversing with Cornelius and Peter (Acts 10), releasing Peter from prison (Acts 12), causing the death of Herod (Acts 12:23), in shipwreck with Paul (Acts 27), various encounters in Revelation with John, and elsewhere. Angels may appear as humans, Cherubim, Seraphim, or another disguise. After several centuries of rare angel appearances we seem to be experiencing an increase of sightings; some may see this occurrence as a sign of the end times. *See also* angels(s); angels of the Revelation; eschatology, eschatological; theophany.

angelotry: the forbidden practice of worshiping angels. The heavenly beings do not desire it, nor does God condone it. John of Revelation made the error twice (Rev. 19:10, 22:8–9) and was chastised on both occasions. Angelotry should not be confused with angelology which is the study of angels. *See also* angel(s); *dulia*; hyten.

Angels' Chorale: a contrived but descriptive title for the praise offered by myriads of angels in Revelation 5:12. *See also* music; praise paradigms of Revelation, the.

angel slices: cookies made with pecans and coconut. Legend has it that Saint Peter gives one to every child entering heaven to help them recover from homesickness for earth. *See also* angle coin.

angels of measurement: those heavenly beings of Revelation 11:1 and 21:15 who supervise the careful measuring of the Temple and New Jerusalem. *See also* angel(s); angels of the Revelation; canon of the Scriptures; Ezekiel as Old Testament book; Ezekiel's vision of the man with a measuring line and rod; measuring line; measuring rod; Zechariah as Old Testament book; Zechariah's vision of the man with a measuring line.

angels of nature: those angelic beings supposedly assigned governance over various aspects of the natural world. Some of their numbers appear to be routinely allocated positions in the world over birds, fish, wind, water, agriculture, or any number of duties relating to the earth. Certain verses in Revelation may come closest to affirming such designations when they speak of angel agents manipulating the natural realm under God's authority, such as the winds or rivers and the like. All others specifically designated and named, rightly or not, are arbitrarily applied from human sources. *See also* angle(s); angel of the east; of fire; angel of the little scroll; angel of the sun; angel of the waters; angels of the Euphrates; angels of the harvest; angels of the winds; Anpiel.

angels of the churches: the mysterious ones named as titular heads of each of the seven Revelation churches in Revelation 2 and 3. Each church angel is addressed separately but their true identities are obscure, although several possibilities have been put forth to explain them. Some see the angels as the various pastors (or elders) of the several churches, or the human messengers who carried the Revelation letter to them. Others suggest they are symbolic of a particularly bright attitude or worthy program within each congregation. Still others claim they are literal angels who protect and spiritually govern the congregations. Suggestions have been forwarded that the angels are in place as fellow prophets with John, the writer of Revelation, to assist him in reading and interpreting his letter. What is obvious is that they are "held aloft" by the right hand of Christ for it is He who gives both angel and church their stability and direction. *See also* angel(s), angelology; angelotry; angels of the Revelation; eagle(s); Essenes; guardian angel(s); seven churches of Asia Minor, the; sons of God; star(s).

angels of the Euphrates: those heavenly beings, four in number, described in Revelation 9:13–16. Their task was to remain "bound" to the river until given divine permission to open the waterway to invasion by 200,000,000 conquerors. There is debate as to whether this quartet is malevolent or holy. These four are confined at the Euphrates River (Rev. 9:14) in strict accord with the will of God for a specified purpose and a specified time. The release of these beings precipitates the sounding of the sixth trumpet (the second woe). The loosing of these formerly restricted beings launches an invasion of 200,000,000 troops (or demons) which will kill a third of mankind during the Tribulation. Some researchers confuse the identity of the armies of the sixth and seventh trumpets, considering them to be either both human or both demonic militia. The description of each, however, makes it clear that the sixth horde are evil spirits and the seventh are flesh and blood soldiers. *See also* angel(s); angels of nature; angels of the Revelation; bound angels; eschatology, eschatological; Euphrates River; Great River, the.

angels of the harvest: a pair of angelic beings who enact the drama of the harvest scene of Revelation 14:14–20. One is described as "like a son of man," crowned with gold, and astride a cloud carrying a sharp sickle; the other also wields a sickle and both act together to gather the wheat and grapes as supervised by other angels on scene. *See also* angel(s); angel of the fire; angels of nature; angel of the Temple; angels of the Revelation; cyclorama; eschatology, eschatological; harvest of the earth; one "like the son of man."

angels of the heavens: those angelic beings said to govern the stars, constellations, and other celestial objects of the universe. *See also* angel(s); constellations; Rahati'el; star(s).

angels of the Lord's presence: a collection of angels, according to *The Testament of Levi*, who attend the throne of God to make expiation for sinners who acted unwittingly. They also offer sweet bloodless sacrifice. Angels below them are another corps who bear prayers upward to the angels of the Lord's presence. *See also* angel(s); angel of his presence.

angels of the nations: ancient Jewish and Christian belief that God has ordained an angel to safeguard and guide the nations of the world. Individuals can experience them as well in some traditions. Daniel 10 relates that the messenger to the prophet was delayed because there was conflict in heaven between him and Michael against the prince of Persia and Greece. The Jews claimed that Satan was the angel of Rome. No guardian angel operates on the behalf of Israel for God Himself has made them His chosen. The archangel Michael is given another title or task in that respect and is named as the guardian of Israel. *See also* angel(s); ethnarch; Eularia; guardian angel(s); Michael; prince of Greece; prince of (in) Jerusalem; prince of Persia; seventy shepherds.

angels of the Revelation: a series of angelic beings, or their prototypes or voices, abound in the Apocalypse. We can discern the announcing angel (Rev. 1:1), the seven angels of the churches (Rev. 1:20) [if they are truly angels over the congregations], the angels of heaven who witness the names of the book of life (Rev. 3:5), the twenty-four elders (Rev. 4:4) [if these two dozen are truly angels], the four living creatures (Rev. 4:6b) [if this quartet are really Cherubim as suspected], the mighty angel seeking a seal-breaker (Rev. 5:2), multitudes of angels surrounding the throne of the Lamb (Rev. 5:11), the four angels of the winds (Rev. 7:1), the angel of the sunrise (Rev. 7:2), more multitudes of angels surrounding the throne of the Lamb (Rev. 7:11), the seven angels of the trumpets (Rev. 8:2), the angel of the golden censer (Rev. 8:3), the "eagle" angel announcing woes (Rev. 8:13), the falling "star" angel of the Abyss (Rev. 9:1), the four angels of the Euphrates (Rev. 9:15), the mighty angel in the cloud and rainbow with the little scroll (Rev. 10:1), the archangel Michael and his angelic army (Rev. 12:7), the three "preaching" angels (Rev. 14:6 –11), an angel "like the son of man" (Rev. 14:14), the angel commanding the harvest angels (Rev. 14:15), the angel with a sickle (Rev. 14:17), the angel of fire (Rev. 14:18), the seven angels with the bowl plagues (Rev. 15:1), the angel of the waters (Rev. 16:5), the mighty angel of splendor and Babylonian interpreter (Rev.

18:1), the angel with the giant millstone boulder (Rev. 18:21), the angel of invitation to the wedding supper of the Lamb (Rev. 19:9) [if he is different from the boulder angel], the angel standing in the sun (Rev. 19:17), the angel with the key to the Abyss (Rev. 20:1), the angels at the pearly gates (Rev. 21:12), and the angel with the measuring rod (Rev. 21:15) [if he differs from the angel of Rev. 21:9], the angel of the river of life (Rev. 22:1), [if he is different from previous speakers], the angel of Christ's testimony (Rev. 22:16). Those heavenly beings named in the Apocalypse, then, are either commissioning angels, judgment angels, warring angels, or worshiping angels. Specific tasks seem to be emphasized. Evil angels and servants of Satan are also present here and there. Some have named the angel of the pit as evil since he is reported to have "fallen" and because he opened the Abyss to free vicious minions on the earth; he most certainly is not a malevolent being for he operates under the Lord's direction. *See also* angel(s); angelic miracles; angel of Babylon's fall; angel of the Abyss; angel of the east; angel of fire; angel of incense; angel of the little scroll; angel of the millstone boulder; angel of the sun; angel of the Temple; angel of the waters; angel of the wedding supper of the Lamb; angels of measurement; angels of the Euphrates; angels of the harvest; angels of the winds; angels of touring; angels of vengeance; angelophany; eagle (angel) of woe, the; eschatology, eschatological; Michael; New Jerusalem.

angels of the winds: a quartet of heavenly beings introduced in Revelation 7. Their assigned task is to hold back any winds of disturbance until the 144,000 faithful witnesses can be sealed with divine protection. Sometimes, in artistic renditions, we see them as small figures with puffed cheeks at the four corners of an illustration. *See also* angel(s); angels of nature; angels of the Revelation; eschatology, eschatological; four winds of earth; four winds of heaven; holding back the four winds; wind(s).

angels of touring: a number of angelic messengers described in Revelation assigned as docents in order to acquaint John (and us) with the various images and symbology of the book (*e.g.,* Revelation 17:1; 22:1.) It is their task to explain, describe, and otherwise educate us as much as possible to Revelation's apocalyptic message much like a docent. *See also* angel(s); angels of the Revelation; eschatology, eschatological.

angels of transport: angels tasked with moving persons or objects from one place to another. Whether the movement of persons is a physical dislocation or a disembodied one is frequently a question of uncertainty. Examples of angels engaged in such activity include Zechariah 5:5-11, Revelation 17:3, and Ezekiel 8:1-3. Such transpositions usually involve obtaining a better or more comprehensive view of some object or action that serves to educate the viewer or to remove one from danger. Oftentimes, the angel or Spirit may simply direct an individual via the mind to change his location for some purpose (*cf.* Acts 8:26). *See also psychopomps*; transporting angel of Ezekiel, the; Zechariah's vision of the woman in a basket.

angels of vengeance: a series of servant angels who facilitate the eradication of evil from the earth at the command of the Lamb. Their responsibilities include actions involving the seals, the trumpets, and the bowls. *See also* angel(s); eschatology, eschatological; vengeance.

Angelus: a morning devotional prayer commemorating the incarnation. The name is taken from the *angel's* announcement to Mary of the coming birth of Jesus. *See also* Anamnesis; Confiteor; liturgical year; prayer(s).

Anglicanism: the form and practices of the Church of England. The name is taken from the Latin *ecclesia angelica,* "the English Church." (The more anti-liturgical Protestants of the time called it "prelacy".) The American version of Anglicanism is the Protestant Episcopal Church of the United States of America, a name chosen after the Revolutionary War to better fit the spirit and mind-set of the new nation. That experiment, and following the time, consisted mostly of the wealthy gentry of the land and, as a denomination, did not experience exceptional growth. The Anglican Church and its American cousin are both considered Protestant churches even though they closely resemble Roman Catholicism in belief and practice. The Anglican communion is active in the British Isles and elsewhere. *See also* Act of Conformity; Act of Supremacy; advowson; Alternative Service Book; Articles of Religion; Bangorian Controversy; banns; Becket, Thomas; Black Fast, the; Black Letter Days; Black Rubric; *Book of Common Prayer;* Bray, Thomas; Church of England; Canterbury; cardinal(s); Caroline Divines, the; Charles I, King; Chicago-Lambeth Quadrilateral; Clapham sect; coadjutor; compass rose depiction; Cranmer, Thomas; Cromwell, Thomas; curate; diocese; *episcopi vaganti;* flying bishop(s); Hales, Stephen; Hampton Court Conference; Henry VIII, King; High Church, Low Church; Jones, Hugh; Ken, Thomas; Latitudinarians; Laud, William; Low Sunday; Malthus, Thomas Robert; Manteo; Mass; metropolitan; monstrance; More, Thomas; Newman, John Henry; normative principle; parish; Philadelphians; pram service; prelacy; primate; Pole, Cardinal Reginald; pram service; Protestant Episcopal Church; Protestant Reformation, the; Raikes, Robert; rector; Reformed Churches; Seabury, Samuel; Society for the Promulgation of the Gospel in Foreign Parts; sodality; *Te Deum Laudamus;* Thirty-Nine Articles, the; three cornerstones of Anglicanism, the; tippet; Tractarianism; verger; vestry; vicar; vicar general; warden; Weems, Mason Locke; William and Mary.

Anglo-Israelism: sometimes British Israelism, a once prominent cult in the United Kingdom and the United States also known as the Worldwide Church of God. Promoted by Herbert W. Armstrong and his son, Garner Ted,

Anglo-Israelism asserts that Britain and the United States are heirs to the ten lost tribes of Israel. At the risk of misrepresenting some minor point of doctrine, it may be noted that Britain represents the tribe of Ephraim, America is Manasseh, Ireland and Denmark are Dan, Germany notes the Assyrians, Italy names the Babylonians, and other Western nations account for the remaining tribes of Israel (some twenty-two countries in all). The movement believed the Celts to be one of the lost tribes of Israel. At one point, the group had a wide following, a strong publishing effort, and a worldwide radio ministry called *The World Tomorrow*. *See also* Armstrong, Herbert W.; Brothers, Richard; Celtic folklore and religion; cult(s); idolatry; lioness and her cubs and the vine, the; lions, the young; lost tribes, the ten; Millennial churches; Pack. David C.; sect(s); tribes of Israel, the; twelve tribes; Worldwide Church of God.

Angra Mainyu. See Ahriman.

anhypostasis: a doctrinal stance assumed by some later prominent Protestant writers which denies the independent existence of Christ's humanity. The incarnation was a deliberate choice of Christ to take on flesh and be complicit with human nature. Anhypostasis is the opposite position of enhypostasis. *See also* enhypostasis.

aniconism: refusal to use or adore icons. *See also* Iconoclasts, War of the; icons, iconography.

Animal Apocalypse, The: a Jewish apocalyptic writing, one of a few which survived the eschatological purge of such products by the early rabbis, mostly because they were protected and studied by Christian theologians. The work is a kind of Pseudepigraphal history of the world (part of the dreams of Enoch) but one in which the author chose to display all the main characters as animals. *The Book of Watchers* is another production in the same vein, also rescued by Christian scholars. *See also* bestiary; book(s); *Book(s) of Enoch*; fable(s); Pseudepigrapha, the; Watchers, the.

animal magnetism: a term coined by F. A. Mesmer referring to a force or fluid that he believed was capable of being transferred from one person to another. The experience developed into what is now called "mesmerism" or hypnosis, two more appealing terms that have lost the attachment to animals. *See also* hypnosis; magnetism; mesmerism; occult, occultic; psi; physic vampires.

animals, birds, and insects, symbology of: animals or insects that are symbolically descriptive of an idea related to their species. In Revelation, for example, a dragon represents Satan, beasts describe evil persons, and, in Revelation 13:2, the seven-headed beast is further described as being part leopard, bear, and lion. Daniel contains many more animal representatives, usually to denote some nation or empire in his day or in times to come. Oxen were a symbol of strength (Num. 23:22) and other cattle often portrayed idol worship. Common symbols of desolation or wilderness include owls, ostriches, wild goats, wild donkeys (onagers), hyenas, and jackals. Jesus is often spoken of as the "lion of the tribe of Judah." As to actual animals (symbology completely aside), it may be theologically sound to believe that they, as part of God's living creation, may share the next life with us even as they do now, though their spiritual essence is certainly different from our own. Without certain of the animals that provided pre-Christian and pre-Judean sacrifices, there would have been no blood redemption, nor would we enjoy the companionship of pets, food, clothing, shelter, or the wonders of the animal kingdom. For convenience, insects, birds, and mythological beasts are classified with animals in symbology. The Bible appears to specify around twenty-four shore and sea creatures, about seventy for the land, near sixty of the air, and close to twenty-two arachnids and insects. Mythology could utilized almost any animal in its complex symbolism but favorites seem to be cats, dogs, wolves, owls, snakes, dragons, bears, bulls, crows or ravens, lions, and goats. *See also* animal(s); animism; ant; Anpiel; ashes of the red heifer; ass; Azazel; badger; Baphomet; Baraminology; bear; beast(s); beast from the land; beast from the sea; bees; bees of Assyria, the; Behemoth; bells of the horses; bestiary; bird; black horse; black lamb; blood of the Lamb; blood overflowing; bridle of the horse; bull; Bull of Heaven; Buraq; calf; camel; cattle and oxen; chimera; cow; crawling creatures on the wall; crocodile; crow; deer; dog; donkey; dove; dragon; Ezekiel's lioness and vine allegory; fable(s); familiar; flies of Egypt; flocks and herds; flora, fruit, and grain, symbology of; fly; flying goat, the; four chariots into the world; four creatures of Revelation; four horsemen of the Apocalypse; fox; frog(s); Fu Xi and Nuwa; gnat; goat; golden calf; goose; grasshoppers; hen; horn(s); hornet; horse; hound(s) of hell; hunched bear, the; jackal; jaguar; lamb; Lamb and the Lion, the; leopard; Leviathan; lion; lion and the yearling (calf), the; Lion of the tribe of Judah; lions, the young; locusts; moth; mule; mushrishu; mythological beasties, elementals, monsters, and spirit animals; names, symbology of; owl; owl of Minerva; pale horse; Pegasus; pig; pigeon; Python, python; Rahab; ram; ram and the goat, the; red dragon; red horse; raven; rider on the white horse; rooster; sacrifice; salt; scorpion; serpent; seven-headed cobra; sheep; sheep and the goats, judgment of the; Sky-Bellower; Sleipnir; sparrow; stork; tiger; two-horned ram, the; unclean animals, Peter's vision of; white horse; wild beasts (animals) of the earth; winged leopard, the; winged lion, the; wolf; wolf will live with the lion, the; worm; zoophilia.

anima sola: "the lonely soul," one who finds himself in purgatory and helpless to extricate the soul or change its condition. Contemporary prayer in the real world on behalf of such spirits is considered advantageous by some religious persuasions. The belief is especially popular in Roman Catholicism, Mormonism, and certain folk religions like Santeria. *See also* Church of Jesus Christ of Latter-Day Saints, the; prayer(s) for the dead; purgatory; Roman Catholic Church; Santeria.

History and Mystery

animism: the belief that all natural objects, especially animals, and the universe itself possess a soul or describe credence in spiritual beings. It is perhaps the most primitive of religions. Hebrew and Christian theology regale against such ideas and the prophets considered animism and its various expressions as idolatry. The cult is also known in some contexts as animal worship or zoolatry or *zoolatria*. *See also* animals, birds, and insects, symbology of; Druidism; henotheism; idolatry; kathenotheism; mana; monism; New Age religion; pagan practice; panentheism; pantheism; polytheism; sect(s); totemism; Wicca.

ankh: an ancient Egyptian religious symbol represented as a cross topped by a circle. It has been called the *crux ansata*, the "cross with a handle." The ankh symbolized heaven and earth joined and was the key of Osiris, who used it to progress souls to the afterlife. The design is ubiquitous in ancient Egypt art and literature and can be construed to represent the totality of living, both in the present and in the afterlife. Further, it represented spirit, fertility, prosperity, and health—just as the systematic ebb flow of the Nile demonstrated the ideal naturally. Specifically, the Egyptians believed the soul was composed of five elements: *Jb* (the heart), *Ren* (one's personal name), *Sheut* (the person's shadow or silhouette), *Ba* (personality), and *Ka* (the vital spark of life). Together, they formed the *Ha*, or the total person that exists forever. Later, the Coptic Christian Church adopted it as their official logo and any number of organizations or movements has done similar borrowing. *See also* amulet(s); charm(s); Coptic Church; crucifix; Egypt, Egyptians; Egyptian pantheon; gris-gris; Hand of Fatima; idol(s); juju; *Ka; maat;* magic, magick; penates; talisman(s); wanga; zoe.

Anna: the aged prophetess and widow who was continually to be found in Herod's Temple because of her piety and prophetic abilities. She is said to be one of the godly remnant (Lk. 2:36–38) and was present when Joseph and Mary brought the infant Jesus to be dedicated. Her blessing on the child was in the form of thanksgiving for his birth and testimonies to his future blessings on Israel in the presence of any who would listen. *See also* liturgical year; prophet(s); prophetess(es).

Annas: high priest, with his son-in-law Caiaphas as unofficial co-priest, in the year John the Baptist began his ministry (Lk. 3:2). Each of his five sons eventually became high priests also, as well as Caiaphas who followed him. Annas was instrumental in the condemnation of Jesus and participated in the trial of John and Peter (Acts 4:6) before he was deposed around A.D. 15. Despite his dismissal, Annas remained virtually in control of the Temple. His influence perhaps sprang from his appointment by Quirinius of Syria and because of his seniority and reputation; that may explain why Jesus was tried first before him. *See also* priest(s).

Anne, Queen de la Palude: in Brittany, France, the saint of all who live from the sea or lie beneath it. Saint Anne (1477–1514) was a Breton duchess who was forced to marry Charles VIII, king of France, who promptly exiled her when she became pregnant. At the French seaside, legend says a "ship of glory" was provided for her, piloted by an angel, and was taken to the Holy Land where she gave birth to Mary, the mother of Jesus. As she aged, Anne begged to return to Brittany and was again ferried there by the ship of glory and its angelic helmsman. She died in her homeland as an impoverished but beloved queen of the Britons. *See also* queen(s); Roman Catholic Church.

annihilationism: also known as "conditionalism" or "conditional immortality," the belief that the soul perishes after death. The idea is present in some cults and sects but is not a biblical truism. *See also* nihilism; Nirvana; Pralaya.

Anno Domini: Latin for "after divinity" or "the year of the Lord," more commonly expressed simply as "A.D." A.D. is the common method of dating history centered on the presumed date of Christ's birth. The exact date of Christ's nativity is uncertain, however, and calendar makers have made mistakes in dating. Any calendar developed from the selected arbitrary date will serve well enough for our purposes. The dating system was first set out by the Roman monk Dionysius Exiguus, also called Dennis the Short (A.D. 525), who made a number of errors in his calculations. *See also* B.C.; B.C.E.; C.E.; calendar (Gregorian); calendar (Julian); Roman Empire.

Anno Mundi: a calendar designation that when abbreviated is noted as A.M., or "the Year of the World." The notation is used by some historians and redactors in the context of the Jewish accounting of time. The Hebrew calendar dates from the perceived creation of the world and A.M. is used exclusively to that perspective. *See also Anno Domini;* B.C.; B.C.E.; C.E.; calendar; calendar (Gregorian); calendar (Julian); calendar (Hebrew).

annulment: an official declaration by Roman Catholic authority that a marriage has become null and void. According to most additional dogma of the question, remarriage cannot take place without the pronouncement which states, in essence, the first union never transpired. *See also* divorce; matrimony; Roman Catholic Church.

Annunciation, Feast of the: Catholic liturgical devotion commemorating the announcement of Gabriel to Mary that she was to be the mother of Jesus. *See also* Annunciation, the; feasts and special days of high liturgy faiths; liturgical year; *Magnificat;* Mary; Roman Catholic Church.

Annunciation, the: the term recognizing the announcement of the angel Gabriel to the Virgin Mary that she was to be the mother of Jesus. A liturgical church festival celebrates the event on March 25. *See also* Annunciation, Feast of the; Gabriel; liturgical year; *Magnificat;* Mary.

Annwn: the Welsh Hades. It possessed kings, chiefs, and commoners, who are somewhat like us but far superior

– known as "the comeliest and best equipped people ever seen." *See also* Abaddon; Abraham's bosom; afterlife; Aralu; Arcadia; Asgard; Avalon; death; Dis; Duat; Elysium; eternal life; future life, doctrine of the; four horsemen of the Apocalypse; Gehenna; grave; Hades; happy hunting ground; Harrowing of Hell, the; heaven; hell; Hy-Breasail; Hyperborea; idol(s); intermediate state; Jade Empire, the; Jahannam; Janna; lake of fire; life after death; limbo; *Limbus Puerorum;* Mictlan; netherworld; Nirvana; Olympian pantheon; Otherworld; Paradise; paradise of God; paraeschatology; Pardes; Perdition; Promised Land, the; Pure Land, the; Pluto; purgatory; Shambhala legends; *Sheol;* soul sleep; space doctrine; Summerland; Tartarus; Thule, land of; Tir na nOg; Tophet; Tyropoeon Valley; underworld; Utopia; Valhalla; Valley of Decision; Valley of Hinnom; Valley of Jehoshaphat; Valley of Slaughter; world to come, the; Xibala.

Anointed Cherub: a title used only once in Scripture to identify Satan in his pre-fallen state. The interpretation is that he as Lucifer was appointed with higher beauty and power than other angels before he turned adversary and accuser. *See also* accuser of our brothers; angel of light; Baal-zebub; Baphomet; Beelzebub; Belial; Cupay; Day Star; dragon; Evil One, the; father of lies; Ghede; goat; god of this age, the; guardian Cherub; Hahgwehdaetgah; Iblis; idol(s); *Kategor;* kingdom of the air; kingdom of this world; king of Babylon; king of Tyre; Light-Bringer; lion; Lucifer; Mastema; Morning Star, the; prince of demons; prince of the power of the air; prince of this world; red dragon; ruler of the kingdom of the air; Sanat Kumar; Satan; seed of the serpent; serpent; Shaytan; son of the morning, son of the dawn.

Anointed One, the: Jesus Christ as ordained by the Father God to be King of kings and Lord of lords. The Hebrew term is "Messiah" and the Christian designation is "Christ." Cyrus the Great was also, in a sense, "anointed" as God's chosen vessel (Isaiah and the historian Xenophon both call him "my [God's] shepherd)," but not with the power and authority of Jesus. The angel Gabriel also uses the title to refer to the Messiah (Dan. 9:25). This anointed one in Daniel has been variously identified in trying to interpret the associated "seventy sevens" prophecy. Is he to be known as Cyrus the king, Onias III of Syrian Palestine priest, Zerubbabel the prince, Joshua the postexilic priest, Ezra the priest and scribe, Nehemiah the governor, or Jesus? Hebrew priests, kings, and prophets were often anointed with oil to ritually sanctify their ordination. Christians were admonished to anoint the sick. Such action imitates the anointing of Jesus but no person, other than Christ, is ever called "the Anointed *One*." *See also* anointing; Christ; coming prince (ruler), the; Cyrus the Great (Cyrus II); Mary's anointing; names (titles) for Jesus; seventy weeks, prophecy of the.

anointing: the act of applying a sanctified fluid on the head and shoulders of any chosen servant dedicated to be a priest or king. A prophetic anointing might be akin to assuming the "mantle" of a prophet—the burden of such a ministry. Usually, a horn of sweet olive oil was dribbled or poured over the head to mark the ordination. Psalm 23:5 contains the praise for such an honor in the statement, "You anoint my head with oil." Jesus Christ is frequently called "the Anointed One," a title with superior designation in his role as Messiah. The Lord was anointed on one occasion with expensive ointment by an unnamed woman of Mark 14:1–11 (the same service was done by Mary in John 12:1–8), but he interpreted those actions as a burial ritual of devotion presaging his death. The body could also be anointed for medicinal, funeral, or cosmetic reasons. James (Jas. 5:14) instructs the elders to anoint the sick (traditionally performed by touching or smearing the forehead with accompanying prayer). The disciples often performed this custom as part of their ministry of healing, which is considered one of the gifts of the Holy Spirit. Christ's baptism may more accurately depict his anointing for ministry. The sacrificial altar was appropriately anointed with blood as the Law of God demanded. One of four materials or concepts may be used to anoint, depending on the purpose and occasion (*viz.*, oil, water, blood, or a "spiritual" anointing without use of any physical liquid matter). As an example of the last implication, Hebrews 1:9 speaks of the ritual as "anointing you with the oil of joy." In another sense, the apostle John says that God Himself has "anointed" all believers, an act which most accept as the Father promoting the Holy Spirit within us (1 Jn. 2;27–28). Thus, one who is touched by a spiritual revelation or challenged to a ministry, as examples, may be said to have been anointed by the Spirit of God. Such a mighty gift, which is the true mark of a Christian, will make us confident and unashamed at his coming. That loving act makes God's special anointing an awesome apocalyptic experience. *See also* Anointed One, the; burial; call(ing); charism; Church of the Holy Sepulcher; Cyrus the Great (Cyrus II); gestures; *ghaliloun;* hair; healing; holy water; laying on of hands; liturgy, Christian; mantle; Mary's anointing; oil of anointing; olive oil; ordination; perfumes, ointments, and spices; unction; wine; woman with the jar of ointment.

anoint the most holy (or holy one), to: one of the six important goals named in Daniel 9:20–24 that God desires to accomplish before final victory over evil can be announced. The goal is to sanctify the earth as holy, especially as the millennial Temple is cleansed and/or the Holy One (Christ) is honored. *See also* atone for wickedness; Big Six Clauses, the; end sin; finish transgression; inaugurate eternal righteousness; names (titles) for Jesus; seal up vision and prophecy.

Anomoeans: a.k.a. "Dissimilarians" in Latin, a more radicalized group of Arians of the early church who asserted that, not only was Jesus not *like* God (as the Arians believed), but he was also decidedly *unlike* Him. *See also* Adoptionism; Adoptionism; appropriation; Arianism; Arius; complementarian view of the Trinity; Donatism; dualism; Dynamic Monarchianism; dynamism; dyophysitism; eternal subordination of the Son; "four fences of Chalcedon"; *homoiousios; homoousios;* hypostatic union; incarnation; *kenosis;* kenotic view of Christ; monoenergism; miaphysitism; modalism; monarchianism; monophysitism; monoenergism; Nestorianism; Nestorius; *ousia;* patripassianism; Pelagianism; *perichoresis;* psilanthropism; Roman Catholic Church; Sabellianism; Socianism, Socinian; subordinationism; theanthroposophy; *Theophorus*; Trinity; two natures, doctrine of the; unipersonality.

Anpiel: according to Jewish folklore, the angel who protects birds. He is said to be a resident of the sixth heaven and is sometimes named as the angel who escorted Enoch to the afterlife. Anpiel can be arbitrarily referenced as a kind of generic of his angelic type who are apparently assigned duties covering some particulars of nature. There are said to be, for example, angels over fish, the earth, water, sky, and other aspects of the natural world. Most subject designations are not scripturally based but play a role in veneration and appeals for aid from some believers who do not directly access Christ alone in their prayers and attentions. *See also* angel(s); angels of nature; animals, birds, and insects, symbology of.

Anselm: archbishop of Canterbury, scholastic, theologian, and philosopher (1033–1109). He is credited with creating the ontological argument in an attempt to prove the existence of God. He also advocated that some penalty is a requirement of God for personal sin. *See also* Church of England; Investiture Controversy; liturgical year; ontology.

ant: an insect profuse in Palestine and most other parts of the world. When used as analogy, the crawler symbolizes foresight because it lays up stores for winter and demonstrates diligence, teamwork, and unceasing activity (Pro. 6:6; 30:25). *See also* animals, birds, and insects, symbology of.

antediluvian: "before the flood," referring to Noah's deluge recorded in Genesis 6–8.

ante-Nicene fathers: those influential theologians and bishops, with their writings, who constitute the finest of early church scholarship of which we have knowledge. The time period is usually reckoned as ending around A.D. 325. A solid, if not exclusive, list of ante-Nicene scholars would feature Clement of Rome, Clement of Alexandria, Ignatius, Justin Martyr, Irenaeus, Barnabas, Polycarp, Hermas, Papias, Hippolytus, Lactantius; Novatian, Cyprian, Caius, Victorinus, Tertullian, Theophilus of Antioch, Origen, Mark Minucius Felix, Lactantius, Commodianus, Gregory Thaumaturgus, and Dionysius. Certainly there were others. *See also* biblical criticism; bishop(s); Eastern Orthodox Church; patristic period; patrology; Roman Catholic Church.

anthem: a special musical presentation by solo or choir. Traditionally, the anthem evolved from a musical setting drawn from the Psalms or some other Scriptures. It has undergone extensive style changes but remains one of the largest productions and often technically challenging to musicians. An anthem is also commonly named as the official tune or composition of a nation. *See also* Anthem to the Triune God; liturgical year; liturgy, Christian; music.

Anthem of the Triune God: a contrived but descriptive title for the praise section in Revelation 4:8 voiced by the four living creatures. *See also* anthem; music; praise paradigms of Revelation, the.

Anthony, Susan Brownell: prominent American female social activist (1820–1906) who helped pave the way for passage of the long-overdue nineteenth Amendment to the Constitution granting the right to vote to women. Anthony was also active in the abolitionist and temperance movements and worked closely with such notables as Fredrick Douglass, Parker Pillsbury, Wendell Phillips, William Henry Channing, William Lloyd Garrison, Amelia Bloomer, and Elizabeth C. Stanton. She was a Quaker in religious background. The U. S. Mint has long been eager to strike a Susan B. Anthony dollar coin to save production costs but Americans have resisted in favor of a folding bill. *See also* Mott, Lucretia Coffin; slave, slavery; Society of Friends; Stanton, Elizabeth Cady; suffragan; temperance.

Anthony the recluse. See Antony.

Anthropocentric and Anti-Trinitarian churches: a classification of religious bodies that generally deny the doctrine of the Trinity and tend to be human-centered in theology. Such bodies may include Unitarian Universalists, Church of the New Jerusalem (Swedenborgianism), Christadelphians, American Ethical Union, and Judaism. The eschatology beliefs of the group (excluding Judaism) is practically nil because of their anthropocentric emphasis. *See also* anthroposophy; church bodies in America (typed); Judaism; sect(s); Socinianism; Swedenborg, Emmanuel; Swedenborgianism; Trinity; Unitarian Universalists.

anthropomancy: a form of divination determined by psychic readings of the entrails of a human sacrifice. *See also* anthroposopcy; apotropaic magic; aretology; astral plane; astral projection; astrolabe; astrology, astrologers; athame; audition; augury; automatic writing; bagua; belomancy; bibliomancy; black arts; black mirror; blood moon(s); cartomancy; chaos magic; chiromancy; clairaudience; clairsentience; clairvoyance; cleromancy; cone of power; conjure; crop circles; cryptesthesia; crystallomancy; crystal skulls; curious acts; divination; dream(s); dreams and visions; ecstasy; enchantment; enneagram; esoteric texts; evil eye; extrasensory perception (ESP); foreknowledge; foretelling; geomancy; grimoire; gris-gris; hepatoscopy; Hermetic wisdom; Hermetic writings; hex; hierscopy;

horoscope(s); hydromancy; idol(s); idolatry; ifa; incantation; juju; labyrinth walk; lecanomancy; literomancy; locution; magic arts; magic, magick; magic square; magnetism; mana; mantic wisdom; mantra; miracle(s); monition; necromancy; New Age religion; numbers, symbology of; mystery religion(s); occult, occultic; omen; oneiromancy; oracle(s); otherworldy journeys; ouija board; out-of-body experiences OBEs); paranormal; parapsychology; past life regression; peace pole(s); pentagram; philosophers' stone; planchette; planets as gods; portent; precognition; prediction; prefiguration; premonition; prodigy; prognostication; prophecy, general; psi; psychic(s); psychic healing; psychic reading; psychomancy; psychometry; psychonautics; pyramidology; rebirthing; remote viewing; retrocognition; revelation; rhabdomancy; scrying; séance; secret societies; secret wisdom; sorcery, sorceries; spell; spell names; spiritism; stigmata; supernatural; superstition; tarot; telegnosis; telepathy; telesthesia; theugry; third eye, the; thoughtform; totemism; vision(s); vision quest; visualization; voodoo; voudou; wanga; warlock(s); Web-Bot; witchcraft; wizard(s); *ya sang*; yoga; Zen; zodiac; *zos kia* caucus.

anthropomorphism: a description of God using human or mortal terminology. Such an idiom is common in theology, especially apocalyptic language, as an aid to comprehension of God's identity and action. As one example, "the hand of God" is an anthropomorphism since Yahweh has no bodily extremities. *See also* theophany.

Anthroposophical Society: an intellectual and quasi-philosophical movement founded by Rudolf Steiner (1861–1825) in 1913. The association aims for what the members describe as soul-nurturing. Worldwide affiliation of those interested in their brand of the arts, science, spirituality, and culture is generally practiced as "spiritual science." *See also* anthroposophy; religious organizations; sect(s).

History and Mystery

anthroposophy: an occult movement begun in the late 19th century by Rudolf Steiner (1861 – 1825), a German reformer who hoped his invention would change the education, health, and agriculture of his time. The doctrine drew heavily from Theosophy, Hinduism, and reincarnation. Steiner believed that the body had three physicals—for willing, feeling, and thinking and that the self continues to develop in a spirit world. *See also* Anthroposophical Society; aretology; Ariosophy; curious acts; esoteric sects; Hinduism; locution; mantic wisdom; monition; occult, occultic; paranormal; reincarnation; secret societies; secret wisdom; sect(s); sorcery, sorceries; supernatural; telegnosis; Theosophy; Zen.

Antichrist: the one identified in apocalyptic literature as a future superman of evil, the most familiar name or title among twenty-six mentioned in Scripture. More than 100 passages of Scripture discuss his person, work, and character and there are about twenty-five titles for him. The name may mean "one who opposes Christ" or "one who counterfeits Christ." He is to be active in the Tribulation years and in possession of the shared power of his sponsor, Satan. The Antichrist is pictured in Revelation 13:1–10 as a multi-headed beast arising from the sea (the world populations), but he was typed much earlier as the Greek/Syrian dictator Antiochus Epiphanes. He is to be charismatic in personality at the start of his career (springing from the first broken seal of Revelation 6:1) but will quickly show his scurrilous spirit of evil and mayhem. Before that, somewhere early in the end time process, Antichrist will actually becomes Israel's protector—at least until his betrayal at the half-way point of the Tribulation. Only the restrainer keeps him in check during our times. The apostle Paul identified him as the "man of lawlessness," "the wicked one," "the man doomed to destruction," or "son of perdition." Daniel called him "the little horn." In fact, the Antichrist has many other aliases: the beast (Rev. 13:1), the little horn (Dan. 7:8), a king, insolent and skilled in intrigue (Dan. 8:23), the prince who is to come (Dan. 9:26), the one who makes desolate (Dan. 9:27), a contemptible person (Dan. 11:21), the king who does as he pleases (Dan. 11:36 – 45), a foolish shepherd (Zech. 11:15 –17), the rider on the white horse (Rev. 6:2). Some commentators see the three great tasks of Antichrist to be: 1. to invite or coerce the world to come under the power of Satan, 2. to cause the worship of Satan, and 3. to muster a huge army to defy Christ at his Second Coming and thereby win the world for Satan. In other words, his objective is one world government dominance, one religion, and one global social society. The Antichrist is also a prominent figure in the pseudepigraphal writings. In *The Apocalypse of Daniel*, he is pictured as the leader of the final assault on Christians. Jews, demons, and nature herself are to participate in this persecution, but all will ultimately be defeated. The writing also provides a bizarre physical description of Antichrist and relates the tale of his futile attempt to perform a miracle and to defeat the "three holy men" in a vain effort to stave off his downfall. Some scholars see another portrait of the Antichrist in Zechariah 11:17 where the evil shepherd is described as wounded in his arm and blinded in the right eye. The passage reminds one of the eerie renditions of Antichrist of Revelation with his healed wound. Debate rages as to whether this "resurrection" of Antichrist is a legitimate coming to life or some form of genetic or medical manipulation. Those who do not subscribe to a literal expectation for Antichrist's advent as an actual person may claim that the idea is a myth, a mere principle of evil, or an institution of evil on some level. *See also* abomination of desolation, the; alphanumeric code; Antichrist as a Muslim; antichrist, spirit of; anti-Semitic; Antiochus Epimanes; Antiochus IV Epiphanes; *Armilus;* Baphomet; beast from the sea, the; beast, image of the; Black One, the; contemptible person, a; covenant of death; *Dajjal;* Daniel's vision of the destroying monster; Daniel's vision of the four beasts;

Daniel's vision of the kingdom beasts; eighth king, the; eschatology, eschatological; False Church; False Prophet, the; Gigith; Haman; Illuminati Tyrant; little horn, the; man of lawlessness; names, symbology of; Nimrod-bar-Cush; restrainer, the; seven years covenant with Israel; 616; 666; Solomon; son of perdition; third eye, the; three antichrists theory; world ruler; worthless (wicked) shepherd, the.

Antichrist as a Muslim: a recent and somewhat startling (but perhaps purely logical) assumption that the eschatological Antichrist is to be a Muslim and not a European as has been traditionally assumed. For centuries, from Hippolytus to modern scholarship, the culmination of the four empires of Daniel's metal statue and his rendition of the weird beasts was assumed to be Rome. The reference is important because most conservative scholars agree these visions prophesy the source of the coming strongman of evil, the Antichrist. Now, the new assertion is that the Antichrist cannot be European but must be an Arab, and that the Antichrist's future dominion (usually considered to be the so-called Revived Roman Empire) cannot be connected to ancient Rome but has to do with Islam. The error of the old thinking, if there is one, has to be blamed on the fact that parts of the prophecy of Daniel have been sealed, *i.e.*, hidden, until the time of their unveiling in the end of days. The term "end times," almost by common agreement in the new way of thinking, is now. Some are even insisting that the first rider on the white horse of Revelation 6 has already broken out of his seal and is, in fact, a contemporary Muslim. Further, the new theory states the seven-headed kingdom beasts of Revelation are to be identified as 1) Egypt, 2) Assyria, 3) Babylon, 4) Persia, 5) Greece (Macedonia), 6) Rome, and 7) the Islamic realm. In modern times, the new collection would be identified as Egypt, Syria, Iraq, Iran, Albania, Turkey, and the Islamic republics of the new regime. Four end time "signposts" have been designated to show us where we are along the time scale: seal # 1 = Saddam Hussein's rise and fall (the winged lion of Daniel), seal # 2 = the Sunni-Shia war (Daniel's bear and ram), seal # 3 = the four nation confederacy which will rebuff the actors of seal # 2 (the leopard of Daniel), and seal # 4 = the emergent Antichrist (the little horn of Daniel). The interpretation of the Gog and Magog scenario (never clearly or fully enunciated) has also changed. Now the ten nation alliance that make up the God and Magog invaders have been tentatively identified as 1) New Turkey (Magog, Tubal, Meshech, and Gomer), 2) New Egypt (Egypt), 3) New Albania (Sinai), 4) New Iran (Persia), 5) Sudan (Cush), 6) Libya? (Put), 7) Algeria? (Put), 8) Turkmenistan? (Togarmah), 9) Uzbekistan? (Togarmah), and 10) Kazakhstan? (Togarmah). Perhaps the most innovative thinkers to launch and advocate for the new Islamic Antichrist theory are an author writing under the name of Mark Davidson and the blogger Joel Richardson. If their efforts have merit, the ideas are surely to change eschatological thinking to a large degree in the immediate future. *See also* Antichrist; eschatology, eschatological; *Dajjal;* Daniel's vision of the destroying monster; Daniel's vision of the four beasts; Daniel's vision of the kingdom beasts; Gog and (of) Magog; Islam; little horn, the; Revived Roman Empire; seven years covenant with Israel; stratified man, dream of the; three antichrists theory; world ruler.

antichrist, spirit of: a pervasive attitude of evil, godlessness, and selfishness extant in our own age but predicted to intensify and spread as end time events approach. John warns the world (1 Jn. 2:18–19) that the anti-Christian mind-set that exists today will solidify into the Tribulation dictator called Antichrist during the Tribulation era. Some theologians support what is termed the "dynamic" view of the antichrist spirit wherein opponents argue that 1John 2:18 carries no definite article in the phrase "the last hour." The passage should be translated *an* hour of crisis and not *the* future end time moment of crisis. According to their thinking, the term "antichrist" refers to more than a person for his influence has been present throughout church history. *See also* Antichrist; eschatology, eschatological.

antichrists, three theories of. See three antichrists theory.

antidisestablishmentarianism: said to be the longest word in the English language; it, however, has a rather simple meaning. The term establishes the opposition to the idea that there should no longer be an official church within any given country. *See also* Abington School District vs. Schempp; Allegheny County vs. ACLU; caesaropapacy; *Booke of the General Lawes and Libertyes;* civil religion; collegialism; disestablishmentarianism; Edict of Milan; Edict of Nantes; Edict of Toleration; Emerson vs. Board of Education; Establishment Clause and Free Exercise Clause; Geghan Bill; Government Regulation Index (GRI); Johnson Amendment; Lemon vs. Kurtzman; Massachusetts Body of Liberties; *Pontifex Maximus; princeps; principis;* public square; Shubert vs. Verner; state church; ultramontanism; Toleration Act of 1649; ultramontanism; Virginia's Religious Disestablishment law.

Antigonus II: the last king in Palestine (40–37 B.C.) during Judah's brief period of independence. Antigonus is held by some to be the fulfillment of Zechariah's prophecy (Zech. 11:8–9) contained in the parable of the two shepherds because he prevented his uncle, Hyrcanus II (63–40 B.C.), from becoming high priest by cutting off his ears. Any physical deformity disqualified a candidate for the priesthood in Israel (Lev. 21:17–24). Antigonus is considered the official end of the Hasmonean line. In the final days of the kingdom, Herod besieged Jerusalem in order to secure the crown, which had been given to him by the Romans. He was aided in this effort by the Roman general Sosius and some mercenary troops. The Jews resisted strongly, but the city was finally stormed after a long siege. Rapine and pillage ensued until Herod managed to stop the purge by buying off the soldiers with his own money. Herod then bribed Mark Antony to kill Antigonus, which, according to Josephus, was accomplished by his beheading in Antioch. The period of Jewish autonomy had lasted 126 years. *See also* Aristobulus II; Hasmonean dynasty; Jew(s); Judas the Essene; king(s).

Antilegoma, Antilegomena: an early church compilation of writings that at one time were potentially New Testament books but not finally found in the accepted canon. Those more acceptable to more scholars were called *Homologoumena*. *See also* canon of the Scriptures.

antinomianism: a term meaning "without law" or "against law," that asserts Christians are free to transgress the moral code of God because divine grace covers any sin. While technically correct (provided true repentance is involved), believers are not at liberty to indulge in indiscriminate or continual sin for authentic and sensible reasons, as Paul explained in Galatians 5:13–6:10. Antinomianism often equates to "libertinism" or even amoral behavior. Certain radicals of the 16th century in England, called "Ranters," were the extremists of the belief. They considered themselves specially called of God with knowledge superior to that of the Bible and were free of any human or divine restrictions. It was acceptable to scandalize respectable people or practice any form of social taboo. On the positive side, however, Antinominianism is friendly to the bedrock Protestant belief that faith is gained by grace alone, not by obedience to moral law. *See also* covenant of grace; covenant of works; demimondaines; grace; hedonism; law and gospel; monergism; Nicolaitans; salvation; social issues; *sola Christo, sola fide, sola gratia, sola Scriptura, soli Dei gloria*; solifidianism; works, salvation by.

antinomy: two truths presented that seem to contradict each other. The Bible contains such revelations that require research, faith, and intuitive knowledge to either refute or coalesce.

Antioch as patriarchate. See patriarchate(s).

Antiochene Rite: an early catalog of renditions of the Eastern Orthodox liturgy. *See also* Eastern Orthodox Church; liturgical year; liturgy, Christian.

Antiochian school. See School of Antioch.

Antioch of Pisidia: a large metropolis about 300 miles west of Antioch of Syria which was a fortified Roman city at Pamphylia north of Perga in present-day Turkey. Paul and Barnabas enjoyed considerable preaching success there, especially in recruiting Gentiles to the faith (Acts 13:13–52). Since the mission was successful, Paul was able to appoint elders for the church and continue to shepherd their growth. It is advisable to wrestle with geography when noting the cities of Antioch for there were sixteen of them in that day.

Antioch of Syria: a population center of Syria, the third largest city in the Roman Empire. Several ancient historians, including Josephus, also named it as the third greatest for culture and commerce in the Roman Empire after Rome and Alexandria. It was located about 200 miles north of Damascus. Many believers fled there following the stoning of Stephen where they preached to fellow Jews and to Gentiles as well. It achieved early importance as a satellite of the Jerusalem mother church and later a center for conservative or orthodox theology and a patriarchate. The church was large, influential, and active and boasted a substantial number of Gentile believers. It was here that the followers of Christ were first called "Christians" (Acts 11:26) when that name was intended to be an insult. *See also* patriarchate(s); School of Antioch; Syria; Tyche.

Antiochus Epimanes: Jewish tag name for Antiochus Epiphanes. Antiochus' rage and cruelty prompted the nickname, which means "the madman." *See also* Antiochus IV Epiphanes; king(s); little horn, the; Seleucia, Seleucids; Syria.

Antiochus II Theos: one of the Syrian "allies" of Daniel 11:6 (261–246 B.C.) who strived for an alliance with his Ptolemaic rival, Ptolemy II Philadelphus. The plan was to arrange a marriage between Ptolemy's daughter Berenice and Antiochus, who had hoped to subvert the South via the common practice of royal matrimony political intrigue. The scheme failed, however, because Ptolemy died shortly after. The action is likely depicted in Daniel 11:17. *See also* king(s); Seleucia, Seleucids; Syria.

Antiochus III the Great: one of the more successful Greek conquerors of the Seleucid North (223–187 B.C.). He is likely the king mentioned in Daniel 11:10–19. Antiochus managed to raise his kingdom to prominence for a time, but through failed expeditions in European and by giving asylum to the Carthaginian general Hannibal, he alienated Rome against his realm. Rome's legions quickly drove him across the Hellespont and he was sorely defeated at the battle of Magnesia (190 B.C.). The Syrian kingdom was eventually overrun by Pompey and made a part of the Roman Republic (63 B.C.). *See also* Cleopatra of Syria; king(s); Pompey; Seleucia, Seleucids; Syria.

Antiochus IV Epiphanes: Greek-Syrian despot of the intertestamental era. He was the eighth ruler in the Seleucid dynasty (175–163 B.C.). Keen to promote Hellenism and the worship of Olympian Zeus, Antiochus was noted for his cruelty and disregard of any culture not resonating to the Greek ideal. The Jews were especially hated by him and were the object of some of his most savage treatment. After his stand-down on the orders of Rome, Antiochus returned to Jerusalem in vengeance and slaughtered 40,000 Jewish men, women, and children in a mere three days. *First Maccabees* calls him the "wicked root." Antiochus is undoubtedly the role model for the abomination of desolation cited in Daniel 9:27. To gain that approbation, Antiochus erected a statue of Zeus in the Temple and sloshed the broth of a sacrificed pig on the altar. He was opposed, and eventually overcome, by the Maccabee patriots, thus gaining Judea a short interval of independence. *See also* Antichrist; anti-Semitic; abomination of desolation, the; Antiochus Epimanes; king(s); little horn, the; Popilius Leanas; Seleucia, Seleucids; Syria.

Antipas the martyr: a name singled out within the church at Pergamum (Rev. 2:13) as representative of the martyr's suffering in that city. It is uncertain if his mention identifies a righteous individual by that name living at the time or if it is a generic title typifying all who suffer for the sake of righteousness. The name is Greek meaning "against all." *See also* martyr(s); martyrdom; names, symbology of; witness(es).

Antipas the tetrarch. See Herod Antipas.

Antipater. See Herod Antipater.

antiphon: a responsorial Psalm or a short chant sung in association with a Psalm. The Israelites once worshiped God in their newly conquered territory with antiphonal responses. Half of the people stood atop Mount Gerizim and half on Mount Ebal to shout the blessings and curses provided in the Law of Moses (Josh. 8:30–35). *See also* Antiphonal Amen; *Intermerata;* liturgical year; liturgy, Christian; liturgy, Jewish; music; responsive reading; versicle.

Antiphonal Amen: a contrived but informative title for the praise section in Revelation 7:12 and 15–17 voiced by angels, the four living creatures, and the twenty-four elders. *See also* music; praise paradigms of Revelation, the.

antiphoner: a choir-book with printed liturgical chants for singing the canonical hours. *See also* canon(s) of the church; liturgy, Christian; Defnar; music.

antiphony: a collection of liturgical chants to be sung antiphonally by a choir in public adulation as the worship occasion suggests. *See also* chant; chantry; liturgy, Christian; music.

antipope(s): a series of personalities (numbering about forty) who throughout Roman Catholic history have claimed title to the papacy but were outside the See at Rome or whose reigns were not wholly or officially supported. From the third to the 15th centuries, various dissident cardinals and secular kings have supported outsiders with varying degrees of accomplishment. Victor IV, a rival leader in Sicily in the third century, is considered the first. Some are mentioned in Malachy's "Prophecy of the Popes" which makes it difficult to accurately identify the final one from his vision. *See also* Babylonian Captivity of the Church; Council of Constance; John XXIII, Pope; Malachy; Pope Joan; "Prophecy of the Popes"; Roman Catholic Church.

Anti-Saloon League: one of the more powerful and influential temperance organizations of the early 20th century. It was most active perhaps in its local affiliates which were based mainly in mainline church denominations like the Methodists, Baptists, Congregationalists, and Disciples. Its influence even overshadowed the earlier Woman's Christian Temperance Union. Prominent leaders included mostly men (with fewer women who generally preferred other organized alcohol protests) including founders Wayne Wheeler, Howard Hyde Russell, Purley Baker, Edward Young Clark, and Ernest Cherrington. The League was politically and publicity involved (including support to the Prohibition Party) to great effect. Today the remnants are known as the American Council on Alcohol Problems. *See also* American Society for the Promotion of Temperance; blue laws; religious organizations; social issues; temperance; Woman's Christian Temperance Union.

anti-Semitic: or anti-Semitism, a term in use for only about 150 years. The word stands for prejudice or hostility against Jews, a designation which somehow eventually filtered to that race alone from among the many Semitic peoples of the ancient world. The attitude is the longest-held and deepest hatred in human history. The mind-set is

History and Mystery

long-standing and intense at certain times and in certain cultures but is pervasive almost everywhere and in all times as had been a particular target of Satan since Adam and Eve. A large number of religious slurs have arisen to designate a Jew including Hymie (with particular reference to Brooklyn, New York, popularized by Jesse Jackson), JAP (Jewish American Princess, especially women and girls of social class), Shiksa (the Yiddish of Poland and Germany; also, a non-Jewish girl or woman within the Jewish community), Yid (Yiddish), Abbie, Heeb or Hebe, Ikey or Ikey-mo, (Jewish males in America), Kike (illiterate Jews who immigrated through Ellis Island and signed their names with a circle—a *kikel*—instead of a cross), Mokey (monkey?), and Shylock (from Shakespeare's "Merchant of Venice"). Anti-Semitism is to be a prominent feature of a large volume of millennial or apocalyptic speculation and doctrine to be experienced in the future. In point of fact, the Jews have been targets for genocide from any number of cultures and nationalities, including Egypt, Assyria, Babylonia, Persia, Grecian Syria, Rome, the Crusaders, and the Nazis of Germany and persecutions will likely continue to the end. The most violent pogroms were the depredations of the Roman Empire, the Crusades, the Inquisition, the Holocaust, and the current Islamic terrorist campaigns directed against Jews. Anti-Semitism is particularly odd in Christianity since the faith started as a sect of Judaism. Jesus, the twelve apostles, and all the first Christians were Jews by birth. It is true the Gospels portray the Jews as the arch-enemy of Jesus but they also share the guilt with the Romans. The Christian Church has been a major investor in Jewish disparagement. The church Fathers were among the notorious Jew-haters on record including notables like Justin Martyr, Irenaeus, Tertullian, Eusebius, Constantine, Jerome, John Chrysostom, Augustine, Martin Luther, Thomas Aquinas, and the entire Council of Nicea in A.D. 325. *See also Adversus Judaeos;* Ahmadinejad, Mahmoud; *Alluha Akbar;* al-Qaeda; al-Shabab; American Party;

Antichrist; Antiochus IV Epiphanes; Anusim; Apion; Arafat, Yasser; Aryan Nation; Atta, Mohammed; ban; bin Laden, Osama; blood libel; *B'nai B'rith;* Boko Haram; Christianese; Concordant of Collaboration; Conversos; Coughlin, Charles E.; Christian Identity Movement (CIM); Covenant, The Sword, and the Arm of the Lord, The (CSA); Crusades; crypto-Jew; Cyril of Alexandria; Daesh; Defamation of Religious Resolution, the; *Entdectes Judenthum;* Establishment Clause and Free Exercise Clause; Esther, book of; Fatah; Felix; Festus, Porcius; Flagellants; Florus; genocide; Gog and (of) Magog; Haman; Hamas; *harem*; Hellenism, Hellenization; Herod Agrippa I; Hezbollah; Hitler, Adolf; Holocaust, holocaust; Holocaust Remembrance Day; Icke, David Vaughan; Illuminati; Intifada; Inquisition, the; Islam; Islamic State in Iraq and Syria (ISIS or ISIL); Jewish persecutions; *jihad;* Khomeini, Grand Ayatollah Ruhollah Musavi; king who exalts himself, the; Knights of the Golden Circle; Knights of the White Camellia; Ku Klux Klan; little horn, the; "Little Satan"; Marrano; Mordecai; Mujahidin; Muslim Brotherhood; *nakba;* Nation of Islam; Neo-Babylon; Neo-Nazi(s); "never again"; Newton, Thomas; Niebuhr, Reinhold; Nusra Front; Ottoman Turks; Palestinian Islamic Jihad (PIJ); Palestinian Liberation Organization (PLO); Palestinians; persecutions; Patriot Movement, the; Patronius; Penn, William; philo-Semitism; Pilate, Pontius; pogrom; preacher's kid(s); procurator(s); "Protocols of the Elders of Zion"; Ptolemy, Ptolemaics; radicalized; rice Christians; Roman Empire; Salafi; Samaritan(s); Seleucia, Seleucids; Semitic(s); serpent seed doctrine, the; seventy shepherds; Shi'ite Islam; *shoah; Simonini Letter;* slurs, religious; Smith, Gerald Lyman; Society of Friends; stern-faced king, the; Sunni Islam; Taliban; terrorism; terrorist(s); Tertullian; Thule Society; time of Jacob's trouble; *Tisha b'Av;* Toleration Act of 1649; Varus; Velayat Sinai; Wahhabism; Wandering Jew; Waqf; WASP; willful king, the; Williams, Roger; Zeresh; Zionism.

antitheism: the conviction that God, nor any gods, does not exist. *See also* agnosticism, agnostic(s); areligious; apatheist; atheism, atheist(s); atheism, the new; meta-atheist; O'Hair, Madelyn Murray; Nietzsche, Frederich; Russell, Bertram; scoffers; theism.

antithesis: a contrast or opposition in literary and philosophical terminology, such as the juxtaposition of the concepts we call *right* and *wrong*. In rhetoric, the process is achieved by placing a sentence or part of a sentence against another to which it is opposed and from which a balanced contrast can be discerned. In theology, the term is a technical one and refers to six of the sayings of Jesus contained in the rhetorical structure of the Sermon on the Mount wherein Jesus cites the Mosaic Law "You have heard..." (thesis) "but what I tell you is this..." (antithesis). *See also* Hegel, Georg Wilhelm Friedrich.

antithetic parallelism: a writing of two lines of Hebrew poetry in which the second echoes the first in a contrasting way (*e.g.,* Psalm 1:6). *See also* acrostic poem; chiasmus; climatic parallelism; colon; doubling; poetry (biblical); synthetic parallelism.

antitype: an historical event that ensues as a result of a previously occurring "type," or representation of that event which predicted it. An antitype can be seen as the fulfillment of a prophecy in the correct context. *See also* fulfillment; type(s).

Antonia Fortress: a fortified structure Josephus called the Tower of Antonia, a citadel rebuilt by Herod the Great—who named it after Mark Antony—on the northwest side of the Jerusalem Temple. It was used as barracks for the Roman military of occupation and to store the garments of the high priest (only to be issued for necessary use in the festivals). Paul was imprisoned there prior to his journey to Rome under arrest. For a time, early Christians understood the Antonia to be the Praetorium, the judgment seat of Pilate before whom Jesus was tried. Most archeologists now believe that the true Praetorium is part of Herod's palace. Even before the time of David there were citadels (fortifications or towers) in Jerusalem. *See also* Akra; Gabbatha; Jerusalem, landmarks of; Lithostrotos; Praetorium; Roman Empire; tower; Tower of David.

Antony: sometimes Anthony, Antony the recluse, or Anthony of the desert, the first truly influential hermit who withdrew into the monastic life in the third century. At age thirty-five, he secluded himself in an old fort on the Nile River and lived there twenty years until his death around A.D. 350. He was said to be 105 at his end. Named a saint, he is noted for his instructions to followers who centered around him and for his physical warfare with demons. Antony was famous for his fidelity, intellect, compassion, and asceticism, the latter of which he frequently abandoned to answer pleas for teaching, healing, and leadership among the people. He was known regularly fighting devils and evil spirits in defense of the gospel. The villagers near his retreat called him "God's Friend." Athanasius wrote his biography which has been proven to be faked. *See also* Athanasius; Basil; desert mystics; Evagrius; liturgical year; monasticism; monk(s); mysticism, mystics; near death experiences (NDEs); Paul of Thebes; Roman Catholic Church.

Anu: ancient Mesopotamian sky god, also the name for their highest heaven. *See also* idol(s); Sumerian and Babylonian pantheon.

Anubis: ancient Egyptian god of the underworld and embalming known as the "dog god." He was the son of the goddess Nephthys, who abandoned him in the Nile for fear of her husband, Seth. The infant was rescued and fostered by Isis even though there was suspicion that the real father was her own husband/brother Osiris. Anubis is symbolized as a jackal head on a human body and was revered as a guide to the afterlife. He was a watchdog for the gods, a healer, and an embalmer. *See also* Egyptian pantheon; idol(s); Isis; mythological beasties, elementals, monsters, and spirit animals; Nephthys; Osiris; Seth; underworld.

Anunnaki: (Annunaki) "those who from heaven have come," viewed as extraterrestrials who colonized Earth according to the legend and interpretations of the Sumerian texts. The original landing party was said to consist of fifty beings called "gods." Some of them, and their offspring, were said to reign over the lower Mesopotamian city states for thousands of years in a single lifetime. Some researchers equate them with the Old Testament Nephilim. *See also* alien abduction; Anak; Ancient Astronaut Theory; *Chariots of the Gods?*; cities of the gods; cuneiform; Cyclopes; demi-god(s); Enki and Enlil; *Enuma Elish; Epic of Gilgamesh, The; Fir Blog;* Formorians; frost giants; giant(s); Guardians; idol(s); Igigi; Laestrygonians; lulu; Mesopotamia; Nephilim; Nibiru; panspermia theory; reptilian theory; Sumerian and Babylonian pantheon; Sumerian Tablets; Sumer, Sumerian(s); Table of Destinies; Tiamat; Titans; transhumanism; UFO; von Daniken, Erich; Watchers, the.

Anusim: the process by which Jews were compelled to abandon their traditional faith and forced to convert to another religion. The term means "forced one" or "coerced one." *See also* anti-Semitic; Conversos; Judaism; Marrano.

"any moment rapture": a premillennial doctrine advocating immanency—that the rapture could occur at any time of God's choosing. There are no prophesied events scheduled to transpire between now and the rapture, so far as we know. *See also* eschatology, eschatological; rapture.

apatheist: a person who thinks God's existence is irrelevant and unimportant. Apatheism is essentially the lack of concern whether a supreme being exists or not. *See also* agnosticism, agnostic(s); antitheism; areligious; atheism, atheist(s); meta-atheist; scoffers; theism.

apathela: the state of being in control of one's emotions or to be unmoved by passion, according to Coptic Christian belief. *See also* Coptic Church; nepsis.

Apelles: 1. a tested disciple in Rome who found Paul's favor (Rom. 16:10). 2. a Gnostic who agreed that Jesus came in the flesh but after the resurrection he disintegrated his body. *See also* Gnosticism, Gnostic(s).

aphorism. See apothegm; proverb(s).

Aphrodite: Greek goddess and patron of love and beauty. She was named the "foam born" because she supposedly sprang from the sea. She was married to the blacksmith Hephaestus but lover of Ares, the god of war. Her Roman counterpart was Venus and was heavily worshiped in the church at Smyrna (Rev. 2:8–11). *See also* Ares; idol(s); Olympian pantheon; Venus.

Aphthartodocetism: the belief, originated around the sixth century, that the body of Christ was incorruptible and his sufferings were purely voluntary.

Apion: a.k.a. Plistonices, a sophist living in Alexandria (ca. 30–20 B.C.–A.D. 45–85) known for his blatant anti-Semitic propaganda. Among other outrageous accusations, he accused the Jews of worshiping a golden ass' head. In an even more incredulous accusation, he states that the Jews annually captured a Greek traveler, imprisoned him in the Temple, fattened him up, and then cannibalized his entrails to show contempt to the Greek nation. Apion was, at one point, the Alexandrian ambassador to the Roman court. Some insight into his character may be seen in Emperor Tiberius' name for him, *Cymbalum Mundi*—"the human drum." Apion's concerted but ridiculous attacks on the Jews prompted Flavius Josephus to write an effective and erudite rebuttal. Josephus's debate, contained in his *Against Apion*, is actually two books. The second of the pair is a direct attack on Apion himself but the first is more generally directed against influential Greeks who refused to believe the antiquity of the Jewish race as ascribed by Josephus (some 5,000 years of history). The collection was written somewhere between A.D. 95-100. On the positive side, Apion is famous for writing the tale "Androclus and the Lion." *See also* anti-Semitic; Epaphroditus; Josephus, Flavius.

'apiru. See Habiru.

Apis: the sacred bull of Memphis sometimes depicted with a solar disk between his horns. The black bull-calf was arguably the most important animal deity in Egypt and of interest to the Greek writers as well. Apis is said to have been conceived by a ray from heaven. *See also* Egyptian pantheon; idol(s); mythological beasties, elementals, monsters, and spirit animals; Olympian pantheon.

apocalupsis: the first word of the Greek text of Revelation meaning "apocalypse"—to reveal. *See also* Apocalypse, the; apocalyptic, apocalypticism; Revelation as New Testament book.

Apocalypse of Baruch: an apocryphal selection in two sections, the first being a collection of prayers and revelations to Baruch, the aide to Jeremiah; the second consists of a letter to the nine and one-half tribes of Israel. Baruch was interested in knowing the fate of his people in the trying circumstances of the Babylonian Exile—something God supplies in visions and omens. *See also* apocalyptics; Apocryphal Apocalypses; Apocrypha, the; *Baruch, Book(s) of.*

Apocalypse of Esdras: an apocryphal writing claiming to be expanded revelations of Ezra the scribe. The writing has been in existence since the second century and was included in the first edition of the King James Bible in 1611. The work appears to be a hybrid of fiction and fact, typical of many of the pseudepigraphal collection. Its interest in prophecy is centered in chapters 11–12 which detail a complex allegory about a three-headed eagle with its wings and body. Many prophecy students claim that this section is a pointed expose of the rise of Papal Rome and Eastern Orthodoxy and predicts their doom. That may explain why the book never shows in Catholic theology. *See also* apocalyptics; Apocryphal Apocalypses; Apocrypha the.

Apocalypse of Paul: one of the more curious of the pseudepigraphal writings of interest to Christians. The book supposedly relates the details of Paul's revelations in the third heaven (2 Cor. 12:2–4). According to its history, the *Apocalypse of Paul* was deposited at the apostle's house in Tarsus, following the directives of an angel who ordered it buried under the floor. When the container was subsequently recovered, again at the direction of an angel, the diggers found a white marble box. Being fearful of its contents, the retrievers took the find to a judge, and, since it was sealed with lead, he sent it on to Emperor Theodosius. Inside were the manuscript and a pair of Paul's footwear that he had worn on his missionary journeys. It is said that the work helped inspire Dante in his descriptions in *The Divine Comedy*. *See also* apocalyptics; Apocryphal Apocalypses.

Apocalypse, the: an alternate name for the last book of the New Testament. The first word of the Revelation letter is *apocalupsis,* which translates to "apocalypse" (revealing) and produces the source of the title. *See also apocalupsis;* little Apocalypse; Revelation as New Testament prophecy.

Apocalypsis Nova: a simulated dialogue about Christian doctrine with the archangel Gabriel. The work was written by Friar Amadeus of Portugal (1420 – 1482), of which parts are a commentary on Revelation. Later, the transcript was spoofed at least once which may have been an indication of its value to the early church. *See also Piagnoni;* Utopia.

apocalyptic, apocalypticism: a style of writing featuring fast-paced narrative, esoteric descriptions, fantastic imagery, and colorful symbolism. The method was popular shortly before, during, and for some time after the intertestamental period. It is the principal literary vehicle for expressing eschatological thought and doctrine. Daniel and Revelation are the Bible's two best representatives of the method, but many other scriptural texts and large numbers of noncanonical apocalyptic transcripts in that style are available for reading and study. Apocalypticism is nearly always crisis orientated and shapes itself as a form of protest against some troublesome element of society or conflict in the spirit realm. It may, and frequently does, offer comfort to the righteous under duress while also promoting a strong resistance to evil. These twin aspects of the genre, hope and conflict, should never be bifurcated. Apocalypticism emerged from the postexilic thought within Judaism but was influenced by Hellenism, along with ideas from Persia, Babylonia, Egypt, Greece, Rome, and even some Canaanite cultures. The apocalyptic literary tradition has certain features in common—an ordeal of human suffering is encountered at the hands of evil or an evil figure, the arrival of a divine savior, a final conflict between the forces of good and evil, a time of cosmic judgment, and, finally, an era of perfection that may provide for the punishment of the wicked but certainly reward for the righteous. Apocalyptic writers generally clutched a pattern of belief centered on at least four core values: 1. They were pessimistic about history, at least human history. No culture or person could significantly change the nature of our existence. True righteousness could only come from God. 2. They had a deep interest in the justice of God. 3. The doctrine of the resurrection of the dead was central to their philosophy. 4. They were virtually preoccupied with the end of the world. Later, Christian apocalypticism reworked some of the Jewish versions to make them more closely resemble the Christian world view. The style has suffered through the ages by either viewing it as irrelevant to modern society or as the playground of extremists. *See also* advent(s) of Christ; age of lawlessness; "all these things"; apocalyptic calculation; apocalyptic fervor; apocalyptic folk; apocalyptics; apocalyptic themed books and movies; apocalyptic time; apocryphal; Apocryphal Acts; Apocryphal Apocalypses; Apocryphal Gospels; Apocrypha, the; appearing, the; appointed time, the; Bozrah; catabolic collapse; celestial disturbances; coming ages, the; consummation, the final; Daniel's dream of the kingdom beasts; Daniel's interpretation of Nebuchadnezzar's statue dream; Daniel's interpretation of Nebuchadnezzar's tree dream; Daniel's vision from the revealing angel; Daniel's vision of end time; Daniel's vision of the destroying monster; Daniel's vision of the four beasts; Daniel's vision of the seventy "sevens"; Daniel's visions of the mighty kingdom; day he visits us, the; day of evil; day of God, the; day of the Lamb's wrath; day of the Lord; day of (our Lord Jesus) Christ; day of Revenge; day of [their] visitation; day of trumpet and battle, a; day of vengeance of our God; "days of Elijah"; "days of Noah"; Day, that (the); *Dies Irae;* doomsday; Doomsday Clock, the; doomsday cult(s); due time, in; Edom, Moab, and Ammon; *elthnen;* end of all things, the; End, the; end, the; end time; *en takhei;* eschatology, eschatological; eschaton; Ezekiel's vision of the new Temple and new land; Ezekiel's vision of the restored theocracy; Ezekiel's vision of the valley of dry bones; fullness of time; future life, doctrine of the; futurist(s); futuristic interpretation; Glorious Appearing; great and dreadful day, that; great sign, the; great signs, the; Great Wall, the; "here, there, or in the air"; judgment on the great Day, the; judgment seat of Christ; judgments, general and particular; *kairos;* last day(s), the; last hour, the; last trumpet, the; *Mirror of History;* Nemesis; omega point; Pella; Petra; point of infinity; polar shift; rapture; remnant; Second Coming; Second Coming procession; secret rapture; sign of the Jew; sign of the Son of Man, the; signposts of the end time; signs and wonders; signs in heaven; "signs of the times"; singularity; TEOTWAWKI; termination dates; time; time is near, the; time line, eschatological; time of fulfillment; times and the seasons, the; times of the Gentiles; time, the present; time, understanding (knowing) the; "until he comes"; "waiting for the Lord"; wrath, the coming.

apocalyptic calculation: or apocalyptic numbers, an attempt to measure time or duration as perceived in apocalyptic language, whether by ancient writers or modern. The process is imprecise at best because the wisdom writers used nonstandard measures and because the very nature of apocalypticism tends to obscure such reckonings. Jesus warned us never to attempt to discern the exact date of his appearing, although there are hints, or "signs," of that event. Computation of apocalyptic data is any attempt, by calendar or mathematics, to determine the times and dates of eschatological events. Some such investigations are fenced with divine restrictions (*e.g.*, to discern the date of the Second Coming). Other attempts are difficult or even futile because we do not know a precise starting or ending date, nor do we know all the methods the ancients used to reckon dates, and often enough, these were not uniform among cultures. That is not to say, however, that no accounting can be attempted; in fact, it should be when history, knowledge, and biblical authority allow its feasibility. *See also* alphanumeric code; apocalyptic, apocalypticism; apocalyptic fervor; apocalyptic journey; apocalyptics; apocalyptic time; appointed time, the; Bible code; coming ages, the consummation, the final; date-setting; day of God, the; day of (our Lord Jesus) Christ; day of the Lord; day of the Lord's wrath, the; "days of Elijah"; "days of Noah"; Day, that (the); Divine Proportion, the; doomsday; Doomsday Clock, the; doomsday cult(s); due time, in; 888; eleven; *elthnen;* end of all things, the; end of the age, the; End, the; end, the; end time; *en takhei;* eschatology, eschatological; eschaton; "fingerprint of God, the"; "forcing the time"; forty; fullness of time; *gematria;* heptad(s); *kairos;* last day(s), the; last hour, the; law of the sevens, the; Millerites; Miller, William; nine; numbers, symbology of; Pythagorean Theorem; seven; Seventh-Day Adventism; seventy-two; seventy weeks, prophecy of the; 616; 666; ten; TEOTWAWKI; termination dates; theomatic number(s); thirty-seven; three; time; time is near, the; time of fulfillment; time is near, the; twelve; twelve eagles prediction; "until he comes"; wrath, the coming.

apocalyptic fervor: a popular term for describing the more radical and fantastic aspects of end time expression. The phenomenon seems to rise and fall with imprecise but regular seasons, especially increasing during times of crisis. Certainly, the emotion can evolve into an embarrassing and unhelpful preoccupation with those terrible aspects of the end time. When taken reasonably and appropriately, however, the sentiment can be commendable and an aid to the eschatological inquirer. *See also* apocalyptics, apocalypticism; apocalyptic calculation; apocalyptic themed books and movies; apocalyptic time; camp meetings; cosmophobia; Doomsday Clock, the; doomsday cult(s); eschatology, eschatological; "eschatomania"; eschatophobia; "forcing the time"; Great Awakenings, the; great sign, the; great signs, the; last day(s), the; last hour, the; millennial madness; noise; Restoration Movement in America; revivalism; "sawdust trail, the"; "waiting for the Lord."

apocalyptic folk: a.k.a. neo-folk, uber-folk, folk-noir, a modern genre of music (most often heard band-style) with despondent themes such as social decline, cultural decay, and hopelessness. The style is said to be a replacement for the protest songs of the 1960s and 70s but still has appeal to the extreme political left and right, the occult, and some environmentalists. The underlying philosophy appears to be that nothing in the present world can last. *See also* apocalyptic, apocalypticism; music.

apocalyptic journey: known as a visionary journey and some other terms, an apocalyptic style of writing in which the storyteller goes back and forth in time or up and down in space through the inspiration or imagery of the mind. Along the way, the dreamer usually encounters mythical and fantastic beasts or sights that have eschatological meaning. Daniel and Revelation are certainly apocalyptic journeys, as is *2 Esdras* and Ezekiel. Charles Dickens's *A Christmas Carol* allows Scrooge to meet the ghosts of Christmas past, present, and future whom he uses to reform his parsimonious and ill-humored attitude. Dorothy and her friends make their way to the Emerald City in *The Wizard of Oz* through adventure and discovery. Dante's *Inferno* is another example among many. See also astral projection; apocalyptic, apocalyptical; apocalyptics; multivalent language; night journey, the; otherworldy journey(s).

apocalyptics: prophecies or literary descriptions that deal with end time events. Perhaps the most intense apocalyptic passages in the New Testament are Mark 13 (with its parallels in Luke 21 and Matthew 24–25), 1 Thessalonians 4:13–5:1), 1 Corinthians 15, 2 Thessalonians 2:1–12, 2 Peter 3:1–13, and Jude. The most dynamic apocalyptical material in the Old Testament is probably Ezekiel, Daniel, Zechariah, and Joel. It has been noted by some alert prophecy scholars that the book of Daniel is best suited for Gentiles, Ezekiel for the Jews, and Revelation for Christians. A sampling of the strongest noncanonical apocalyptics would include the *War Scroll* of Qumran, the *Testament of Moses, Testament of the Twelve Patriarchs, Testament of Job*, some of the *Sibylline Oracles, 1 and 2 Esdras, 1 Enoch, Assumption of Moses, 2 Baruch, Apocalypse of Abraham*, and large parts of lesser known intertestamental offerings. See also apocalyptic, apocalypticism; apocalyptic journey; Apocryphal Apocalypses; Daniel's decipher of the hand writing on the wall; Daniel's dream of the kingdom beasts; Daniel's interpretation of Nebuchadnezzar's statue dream; Daniel's interpretation of Nebuchadnezzar's tree dream; Daniel's vision from the revealing angel; Daniel's vision of the destroying monster; Daniel's vision of end time; Daniel's vision of the destroying monster; Daniel's vision of the four beasts; Daniel's vision of the seventy "sevens"; Daniel's visions of the mighty kingdom; eschatological parable(s); eschatological text(s); eschatology, eschatological; Ezekiel's vision of the new Temple and new land; Ezekiel's vision of the restored theocracy; Ezekiel's vision of the valley of dry bones; little Apocalypse, the; miracles of Jesus with eschatological emphasis; *Mirror of History;* Olivet Discourse, the; parables of Matthew 13.

apocalyptic themed books and movies: thousands of art and literature productions have been created through the ages on the apocalyptic topic but a few in the 21st century seem to have set the tone for our age. The Bible, of course, still leads the way in apocalyptic literature followed by other more modern books like *Oryx and Crake* (Margaret Atwood), *The Road* (Cormac McCarthy novel and 2009 film), the short story "There Will Come Soft Rains" (Ray Bradbury), *The Exorcist* (William Peter Blatty novel in 1971 and movie in 1973), *When the Wind Blows* (comic book by Raymond Briggs and animated film in 1986), *The Decameron* (Giovanni Boccaccio from c. 1351), *Riddley Walker* (Russell Hoban), *The Book of Dave* (Will Self), *World War Z* (Max Brooks), *Station Eleven* (Emily St. John Mandel), *The Passage* (Justin Cronin), *The 5th Wave* (Rick Yancy), *Life as We Knew It* (Beth Pfeffer), *Angelfall* (Susan Ee), *Alas, Babylon* (Pat Frank), *The Girl with All the Gifts* (M. R. Carey), *The Stone Sky* (N. K. Jeminsin), *Happy Doomsday* (David Sesnowski), *The Stand* (Stephen King novel in 1978 and TV series in 1994), and *The Cabin at the End of the World* (Paul Tremblay). Films are next including the *Planet of the Apes* series, *Mad Max* series, *Buffy the Vampire Slayer* series, *The Hunger Games* series(books by Suzanne Collins), *28 Days Later,* and *Hitchhikers Guide to the Galaxy.* Film critics and fans all have favorites, certainly, but few would omit the following: *When Worlds Collide* (1951), *The War of the Worlds* (1953 and 2005), *Invasion of the Body Snatchers* (1956 and 1978), *On the Beach* (1959), *The Day the Earth Caught Fire* (1961), *Dr. Strangelove or: How I Learned to Stop Worrying and Love the Bomb,* (1964), *Rosemary's Baby* (1968), *The Omen* (1976) and *The Omen: 666* (2006), *The Day After* (1983), *Threads* (1984), *The Quiet Earth* (1985), *The Sacrifice* (1986), *The Seventh Sign*

(1988), *The Rapture* (1991), *12 Monkeys* (1995), *Last Night* (1998), *The Omega Code* (1999), *Donnie Darko* (2001), *Time of the Wolf* (2003), *The Day After Tomorrow* (2004), *Doomsday* (2008), *The Book of Eli* (2009), *4.44 Last Day on Earth* (2011), *Melancholia* (2011), *Take Shelter* (2011), *The Turin House* (2011), *The Cabin in the Woods* (2012), *Seeking a Friend for the End of the World* (2012), and *This is the End* (2013). Three more TV series should be mentioned: *The Walking Dead* (2010), *American Horror Story* (2011), and *Legion* (2017). *See also* art, religious; arts, the; apocalyptic, apocalypticism; apocalyptic fervor; book(s); *Decameron, The; Fifteen Signs of Doomsday, The;* Dystopia.

apocalyptic time: an accounting of apocalypticism in the mind or heart. For people immersed in the eschatological theme, apocalyptic time is an aroused sense of excitement, foreboding, or expectation for what the eschaton means and how life changing it can be. Many people today sense that we are living in apocalyptic time. *See also* advent(s) of Christ; age of lawlessness; "all these things"; apocalyptic, apocalypticism; apocalyptic calculation; apocalyptic fervor; apocalyptics; appearing, the; appointed time, the; coming ages, the; consummation, the final; day he visits us, the; day of evil; day of God, the; day of (our Lord Jesus) Christ; day of Revenge; day of [their] visitation; day of the Lamb's wrath; day of the Lord; day of trumpet and battle, a; day of vengeance of our God; "days of Elijah"; "days of Noah"; Day, that (the); due time, in; *elthnen;* end of all things, the; end of the age, the; End, the; end, the; end time; *en takhei;* eschatology, eschatological; eschaton; "forcing the time"; fullness of time; Glorious Appearing; great and dreadful day, that; great sign, the; great signs, the; Great Wall, the; "here, there, or in the air"; *kairos;* last day(s), the; last hour, the; rapture; Second Coming; Second Coming procession; secret rapture; TEOTWAWKI; termination dates; time; time is near, the; time line, eschatological; time of fulfillment; times and the seasons, the; times of the

Gentiles; time, the present; time, understanding (knowing) the; "until he comes"; "waiting for the Lord"; wrath, the coming.

apocatastasis: or *apokatastasis*, the restoration or restitution to the original or primordial condition of the human race. The doctrine, or philosophy if preferred, is an old one but occupies few mainstream advocates today when the theological term "apocatastasis" is used. Part of the doctrine of *apocatastasis* claims all will find heaven; even Satan and his demons and hell will be emptied. It is a cardinal principle of Unitarian Universalism. The word can also be narrowed to explain the final restitution of all things at Messiah's appearance. *See also* Ballou, Hosea; universalism; Unitarian Universalists; Winchester Platform of 1803.

apocrisiarius: or aposcrisiary, an ambassador or diplomat, the equivalent of a papal nuncio. The office was active from about A.D. 452 – 743 when the Roman pope was prone to send a legate to the Patriarchy of Constantinople. *See also* ablegate; nuncio; Roman Catholic Church.

apocryphal: a term originally meaning "hidden" or "things concealed." The definition persists for noncanonical apocalyptic writing, but modern usage carries a more pejorative tag as something of questionable authority. *See also* Apocrypha, the.

Apocryphal Acts: the general designation for a group of stories of legends concerning the apostles. Most were written in the second or third century and include such titles as *The Acts of: Andrew, John, Paul, Peter, and Thomas*. The latter, written in Syriac, is the most complete and possibly the most famous. *See also* Apocryphal Apocalypses; Apocryphal Gospels; Apocrypha, the.

Apocryphal Apocalypses: any number of apocryphal writings with a decidedly eschatological theme. Among the titles encountered include the following most acclaimed or most prominent for apocalyptic study: *Apocalypse of Baruch, Ascension of Isaiah,*

Assumption of Moses, Book(s) of Enoch; 4 Ezra, Jubilees, Book of; Sibylline Oracles, and *Testament of the Twelve Patriarchs. See also Apocalypse of Baruch; Apocalypse of Esdras; Apocalypse of Paul;* Apocryphal Acts; Apocryphal Gospels; Apocrypha, the; apocalyptics; *Ascension of Isaiah; Assumption of Moses; Book(s) of Enoch; 4 Ezra; Jubilees, Book of;* multivalent language; *Sibylline Oracles; Testament of the Twelve Patriarchs.*

Apocryphal Gospels: those noncanonical writings that purportedly describe the life, words, and deeds of Jesus but from unverifiable authenticity. Most are in fragments and many are Gnostic in origin and theme. The most acknowledged Apocryphal Gospels include such titles as: *Apocryphon of John, Book of Thomas the Contender, Dialogue of the Savior, Epistle of the Apostles, Gospel of Bartholomew, Gospel of Peter, Gospel of Mary, Gospel of the Ebionites, Gospel of the Egyptians, Infancy Gospel of Thomas, Letter of Peter to Phillip, Pistis Sophia, Protoevangelium of James, Second Treatise of the Great Seth, Secret Book of Mark; Sophia of Jesus Christ. See also* Agrapha; Apocrypha, the; Apocryphal Acts; Apocryphal Apocalypses; Apocrypha, the; apocalyptics; "Book of Thunder"; Carpocratians; Nag Hammadi library; Gnosticism, Gnostic(s); Gospel of Nicodemus; Sethians; *Thomas the Contender, Book of.*

Apocrypha, the: a collection of extrabiblical writings in the apocalyptic style. The name suggests material that is mysterious or secretive and is extant in something less than twenty titles; scholars may differ a bit on which are to be counted. Some reflect Hellenistic influences and many are found among the Essene scrolls of the Dead Sea. The major titles among the Apocrypha include *Judith, Additions to the Book of Esther, 1* and *2 Esdras, Prayer of Manasseh, Ecclesiasticus (Sirach), Baruch, Epistle of Jeremiah, Prayer of Azariah and the Three Young Men (*additions to Daniel*), Susanna, Bel and the Dragon, Tobit, Lives of the Prophets; 1,2,3,* and *4 Maccabees, and Wisdom of Solomon.* Virtually all of the apocryphal books are rather careless with details such as dates and times of events as well as many geographical locations, historical facts, and personalities being referenced; more errors are obvious than those of the canonical Scriptures. Most of the above titles are represented in the Roman Catholic, Greek, and Slavonic Bibles. A number of the most apocalyptic themes of the Apocrypha and Pseudepigrapha might include *Acts of Peter, Acts of Thomas, Apocalypse of Abraham, Apocalypse of Peter; Assumption of Moses, Epistle of Barnabas, Epistle of Clement, Epistle to the Laodiceans, 1 Enoch, 1 Esdras, 4 Ezra, Gospel of Judas, Gospel of Mary, Gospel of Thomas, Prayer of Manasseh, Protoevangelium of James, 2 Baruch, 2 Ezra, 2 Esdras* (chapters 3-14 only), and *Testimony of Truth.* Some Roman Catholic Bibles include a few titles of the Apocrypha as suitable for study. *See also* Additions to Daniel; *Apocalypse of Baruch; Apocalypse of Esdras; Apocalypse of Paul;* apocryphal; Apocryphal Acts; Apocryphal Apocalypses; Apocryphal Gospels; apocalyptics; *Assumption of Isaiah; Assumption of Moses; Barnabas, Epistle of; Baruch, Book(s) of; Bel and the Dragon;* Books of Adam; deuterocanonical books; *Esdras;* 1 and *2 Maccabees; 4 Ezra; Infancy Gospel of James;* Infancy Gospels; *Jubilees, Book of; Lives of the Prophets;* Nag Hammadi library; Pseudepigrapha, the; *Sibylline Oracles;* Susanna; Tobias; *Tobit.*

apodictic formula: to reason or expound by way of argument. The prophets used the method extensively. An example of the process is expounded in Isaiah 1:18: "Come now, let us reason together, says the Lord." Sometimes, the prophets were not averse to applying the apodictic formula to debate with God Himself. *See also* apology, apologetics.

apodictic law: statutes or rules intended to be applied universally. The Ten Commandments are a prime example of apodictic law. *See also* canons of the church; Capitulary; caustic law; Mosaic Law; rede; statute(s); Ten Commandments, the.

Apollinarius, Apollinarianism: bishop of Laodicea (A.D. 310–390) who showed some interest in eschatology. Since the emperor Julian the Apostate refused the Scriptures to be recognized or circulated, Apollinarius produced the Old Testament in Homeric and Pindaric poetry so they could remain in some form. As an influential bishop of the early church, he set about to combat Arianism. His answer to the question of the substance of Christ was to promote that Jesus had a body and soul but not a changeable mind; the Logos has simply assumed flesh. Christ was "divine mind" (the *logos*) present in a human body. Since the idea tended to lessen Jesus' humanity, it was rejected by the standards of the day and Apollinarius seceded from the church in 375. *See also* Logos; *logos*; Roman Catholic Church.

Apollo: a Greek and Roman deity, the handsome god of healing, music, poetry, prophecy, and masculinity. He was the brother and lover of his twin sister Artemis. Apollo's son was Aesculapius, the god of surgery and medicine. The emergence of the Apollo legend really begins when he arrived with a group of men at Delphi in search of the Python. He had come from his birthplace on the island of Delos where he and his sister were placed by their mother, the Titaness Leta. Their father was Zeus but a jealous Hera demanded an escape. Artemis was born first, nine days before her brother. Both matured quickly (Artemis was even able to assist in her twin's birth). In search of fame and adventure, Apollo managed to slay the Python snake with a single arrow to the heart and the Mount Parnassus area became the locus of his worship. The Sibyl priestesses were dedicated to him as worshipers and messengers. *See also* Artemis; Asclepius; Daphne; Delphi, Oracle of; Hippocratic Oath; idol(s); Mount Parnassus; Olympian pantheon; *Pytho*; Python, python; perdition; Sibyl(s).

Apollonarius of Hierapolis: bishop of Hierapolis and Christian apologist (d. second century). He wrote a brief tract against the Montanists. *See also* Montanus, Montanism; Roman Catholic Church.

Apollonia: a deaconess of Alexandria who suffered persecutions under the reign of Decius and before. In A.D. 249, there was an anti-Christian riot in the city n which several believers were killed. Apollonia was captured and struck in the face, knocking out her teeth. A large fire was started in the street and threatened her with death in flames if she did not renounce Christ. Apollonia's answer was to walk into the blaze to her death. *See also* liturgical year; martyrs; Roman Catholic Church.

Apollonius of Tyana: an austere, ascetic philosopher who was born about the time of Jesus' crucifixion. Julia Domna, the wife of the Roman emperor Septimius Severus, wrote a biography of Apollonius where he is presented as a miracle worker, healer, and visionary like Jesus. Apollonius came into disagreement with the emperor Diocletian and barely escaped with his life to Ephesus. There, it is reported, he could view the murder of Diocletian with satisfaction. Much of the lore of Apollonius, who was set up to be a rival to Jesus, is fiction from before but he did have an impact on the early church. Eusebius of Caesarea even wrote an attack on him a century later. *See also* Roman Empire.

Apollos: eloquent preacher from Alexandria who was quite learned in the Scriptures and an aggressive pastor and missionary. There is evidence that he and his companions knew only the baptism of John and not the baptism of faith in Christ then in use by the Church. He was further instructed in the faith by Aquila and Priscilla (Acts 18:24–28). Apollos and Paul were mutually supportive even though some of their loyalists tended to favor one man or the other (1 Cor. 1:12). *See also* missions, missionaries.

Apollyon: the Greek name for the demonic leader of the hosts erupting from the Abyss in the fifth trumpet (Rev. 9:11); the name means "Destruction." *See also* Abaddon; Abezi-Thibod; Adramelech; Anammelech; Asmodaeus; Azazel; Azrael; Baal-zebub; demon(s), demonic; devils; destroyer; Dibbuk; Dubbi'el; Gadreel; idol(s); Legion; Lilith; Mastema; names, symbology of; Pazuzu; perdition; Sammael; Sceva; scorpion; slave girl of Philippi; Syrophoenician woman; woman of Canaan.

apology, apologetics: the art or practice of theological debate and defense of certain faith principles, also called polemics in a more negative sense. Apologetics does not imply regret for behavior or speech, as the normal definition suggests today, but is a polished and aggressive defense of established faith. Since the term is usually applied to Orthodox doctrine, it is seldom extended to arguing for or against obscure doctrine nor is it normally noticed as part of the heretical arsenal of debate. Applicable terms infer an attitude and action of "answering back" or "defending" as suggested in Paul's appeal "in defense of the gospel" (Phil. 1:7, 17). *See also* apodictic formula; polemics.

apophatic: the theological perception that God cannot be understood or known in terms of categories. The term is derived from the Greek *apophasis* meaning "negation" or "denial." Apophatic language refers to God negatively or in refutation of His functions (*i.e.*, in terms of how God differs from humans).

Apophis: a devil figure of ancient Egypt, also known as Typhon. He is classed as the spirit of evil, darkness, and destruction usually cast as a serpent. *See also* Baal-zebub; Baphomet; Beelzebub; Behemoth; Belial; Cupay; Egyptian pantheon; giant(s); Hahgwehdaetgah; Iblis; idol(s); *Kategor;* Leviathan; lion; Mastema; mythological beasties, elementals, monsters, and spirit animals; Olympian pantheon; Rahab; reptilian theory; Sammael; Sanat Kumar; Satan; Seth; Shaytan; Typhon.

Apophis asteroid: a space rock originally designated Asteroid 2004MN4 which, when originally detected, was predicted to strike the earth on April 13, 2029. Since then, calculations are that it will miss but will coincide with the appearance of the crescent of the New Moon on that date. Some apocalypticists attribute importance to this event and sometimes associate it with dangerous comets hurtling at us near the same time. *See also* apocalyptic, apocalypticism; astronomy, astronomists; celestial disturbances; cosmology; impact event; Nemesis, Nibiru.

apophthegm. See apothegm.

Apopi: the Egyptian symbol of the Demon of Desire. *See also* Egyptian pantheon; idolatry; mythological beasties, elementals, monsters, and spirit animals.

aposcrisiary. See apocrisiarius.

apostasy: the term (*apostasia*) that denotes a grievous turning away from the true faith; the rebel may then be labeled by church authority as an *apostate*. It is always marked in Scripture as a great sin leading to religious disunity and ecclesiastical chaos. Christian eschatology, along with any number of other religions, predicts a cascading increase of disbelief and violence before the end of the age. Our future troubled age will be marked by the breakdown of family life, cheating and bullying in school, workplace, organizations, and the home, loss of ethics in business, religious and political insensitivity, careless research in medicine, health, and treatment, increasing crime rate and intensified violence, censure of our military, scandal in the church, unchecked misbehavior in sports and entertainment, declining racial tolerance, rampant materialization and out-of-control debt, squishy judgments in the courts, epidemic substance abuse, lack of civility in public behavior, and many more examples of lapses of integrity and faith. *See also* apostasy, the great; apostate church, the; backslide; church abuse; fable(s); "falling into sin"; godless myths; heresy; heretic; old wives' tales; Satan's so-called deep secrets; turned to fables (myths); unsound doctrine.

apostasy, the great: a severe "falling away" from the faith as predicted by Paul and others near to, and conditioned by, the rise and rule of the Antichrist. Such a pronounced retreat from pure belief is the result of "the restrainer" (the Holy Spirit and/or the human agencies which help him) being made less active by the will of God (2 Th. 2:7) at that time. *See also* apostasy; eschatology, eschatological.

apostate church, the: an occasional name for the future religious coalition to be led by the False Prophet in the Tribulation.

It bears no resemblance to the Church today as the bride of Christ, or to any association of saints that may come to exist in the Tribulation. *See also* apostasy; False Church; False Prophet, the.

apostle(s): one sent forth as a messenger. The term easily fits the original twelve disciples (eventually minus Judas the betrayer) who were active during and for a generation after the ministry of Jesus. They were promised special rewards in heaven, and all except John were almost certainly martyred. All (with Matthias or Paul likely added later to make the required twelve), are to sit on thrones in judgment of Israel (Lk. 22:29–30). This eschatological prophecy is again pictured in Revelation 21:14 where the names of the apostles are on the foundations of New Jerusalem. Before that time, however, Jesus told them that their earthly ministry would be in the form of a servant, not that of ruler (Mk. 10:42–44). Those original apostles, properly called disciples, listed in the Gospels are named as: Simon Peter, Andrew, John, James, Philip, Nathaniel (also called Bartholomew), Matthew (also called Levi), Thaddaeus (also called Judas or Jude), James the Less, Simon the Zealot, Thomas, and Judas Iscariot (the traitor). Matthias was selected to replace Judas. Paul, Barnabas, Silas, and James the brother of Jesus are also numbered among the premier apostles plus many more as time progressed. Such other worthies are designated apostles in the New Testament and legitimately called by that title if they met the qualifications of having seen the Lord personally and were divinely called to that position. Frequently the apostles were called "disciples," a correct description, although that idiom is a more generalized grouping; all followers of Christ in any capacity and in any age are appropriately called disciples but there are no more apostles after the last, John, was deceased. *See also* Andrew as apostle; call(ing); charisms; disciple(s); James; John as apostle; Judas; liturgical year; Matthew as apostle; Matthias; Nathaniel; Paul as apostle; Peter as apostle; Philip; *presbuteros;* prophets as martyrs; Simon; Thomas as apostle; spoons, apostle.

Apostle's Creed: the statement of faith used for both liturgical and catechetical purposes by many church bodies today and in the Christian past. An alternate title less in vogue is "Symbol of the Apostles." Most likely, the entire creed was intended to be a refutation of Gnosticism and is respected in our time for its great antiquity and simple content. Today, it is used in forms peculiar to each persuasion by Roman Catholicism, Lutheranism, the Anglican community, and Western Orthodoxy. It is also popular with Presbyterians, Methodists, and Congregationalists. The text affirms: "I believe in God, the Father Almighty, maker of heaven and earth. And in Jesus Christ, his only son, our Lord, who was conceived by the Holy Spirit, and was born of the virgin Mary, suffered under Pontius Pilate, was crucified, died and buried. He descended into hell. On the third day he rose again from the dead. He ascended into heaven and sits at the right hand of God the Father Almighty. From there he will come to judge the living and the dead. I believe in the Holy Spirit, the forgiveness of sins, the resurrection of the body, and the life everlasting. Amen." *See also* Athanasian Creed; confession(s) of faith; Gnosticism; Harrowing of Hell, the; liturgical year; liturgy, Christian; Nicene Creed.

Apostolic Age: in church history, the period generally noted as A.D 40-100 when many of the early church apostles were yet active. Dispensationalists use the same dates but claim it represents the early church (recorded in Revelation as the church of Ephesus) in its purity but already lacking is its love for Christ. *See also* Apostolic Church; dispensation(s); dispensational theology; Ephesus.

Apostolic Brethren: a group of believers founded in A.D. 1260 by Gerard Sagarello in northern Italy. They were opponents of the Roman Church in power at the time, causing their leader to be burned at the stake in 1300. A second leader named Brother Dolcino assumed command and quickly achieved success within the movement. He died in 1307, but by then the main tenets of the fellowship were established.

There are indications that the group was pre-Tribulational in doctrine, believed that Enoch and Elijah were to be the two super witnesses in the Tribulation, and were confident that Brother Dolcino and his followers would descend with Christ at the Second Coming. If we have interpreted the standards of the church correctly, the Apostolic Brethren were one of the earliest premillennial advocates in the church age. *See also* dispensational theology.

Apostolic Church: a contrived name for the period of history noted in dispensational theology representing the church at Ephesus (Rev. 2:1–7). The fitting date is A.D. 40-100, a time of growth and consolidation through evangelism and early church organization, although it was already losing some of its first love in Christ. *See also* Apostolic Age; dispensation(s); dispensational theology.

apostolic succession: the Roman Catholic tenet that the see of Rome holds manifest destiny to be the leading bishopric of Christendom because Peter was connected to it, even as its first pope for twenty-five years. The authority for such a conclusion comes from Jesus' pronouncement in Peter's presence that he would build his Church on his type of stalwart faith (Mt. 16:17–19). Peter's name means "rock." However, it should be noted that this Roman tradition is not strong. It appeared late, and other patriarchate territories also had excellent apostolic support. "The rock" statement also occurs in additional references to the other apostles, whereas Peter was even called Satan by Jesus at one point (Mt. 16:23) only a short time after his great confession. Peter was likely martyred long before he could establish any solid leadership tradition in Rome. Further, Jesus addressed Peter in the masculine second person plural but spoke of "this rock" in the feminine first person singular. Those terms could not have been more different despite the same use of the noun *rock*. In the first instance, Jesus addressed Peter personally, but in the second, he referenced himself or that faith in him that Peter had just voiced. Pope

Boniface III was the first to assume the title "Universal Bishop" in A.D. 606 which set up the primacy of the Roman branch of the church. Most would consider the assumption an arrogant act. What then is "the rock" referenced by Jesus? Chrysostom said it was the faith of the confession from Peter. Ambrose claimed it was the profession of universal faith. Jerome and Augustine understood the rock to be Christ himself. The other apostles, and the New Testament itself, hardly acknowledged Peter as an absolute authority, although he was recognized as prominent among the twelve; in fact, James was president of the Jerusalem church and both he and Paul overruled Peter on more than one occasion. All of Scripture is hesitant to name any person as holding a supreme office or function. The prophets, for example, are never ranked on such an idea. *See also* binding and loosing; *Donation of Constantine;* keys of the kingdom; Leo I, Pope; Peter as apostle; "Pseudo-Isidorian Credentials"; rock(s); Rock (my, the); Roman Catholic Church; Schism, the Great.

apostrophe: 1. in literary criticism, a technique for addressing an absent person or object (*e.g.,* calling out the name of someone who has already died). 2. a grammatical mark for showing possession. *See also* accideme; alliteration; apothegm; assonance; autograph; Bible; Bible manuscripts; Bible translations; biblical criticism; chiasmus; conflict story; *constructio ad sensum;* context; contextualization; dittography; double sense fulfillment; doublets; doubling; edification; eisegesis; epanadiplosis; epigrammatic statements; etymology; exegesis; figure of speech; folio; form criticism; gattung; gloss; gnomic sayings; grammatical-historical interpretation; *hapax legomena;* haplography; hermeneutic(s); higher criticism; homographs; homonyms; homophones; *homoteleuton;* hyperbole; idiom; *inclusio;* interpolation; interpretation; inverted nun; irony; isagogics; *itture sopherim;* jot and tittle; kere; *kethib;* "L"; liberalist interpretation; literal interpretation; litotes; loan words;

lower criticism; "M"; Masoretic Text; minuscule(s); mystery of God; omission; onomastica; onomatopoeia; palimpsest; papyrus; paradigm; parallelism; parchment; *paroimia; paronomasia;* pericope; personification; Peshita; pointing; point of view; polyglot; principles of interpretation; proof texting; pun(s); "Q"; redaction; revelation, theological; rhetorical criticism; rhetorical devices; riddle; satire; *scripto continua;* scriptorium; *sebirin;* simile; similitude; source criticism; sources, primary and secondary; special points; strophe; superscription; symbol(s); synecdoche; syntax; synthetic parallelism; text; textual criticism; *tiggune sopherim;* Time Texts; Torah; translation; transposition; trope; type(s); typology; uncial(s); vellum; verbicide.

apothegm: 1. a brief saying or proverb from the Gospels or a tersely pointed saying (like an aphorism) usually found in an equally brief context. Examples usually refer to those types of sayings from Jesus when referencing the New Testament. Other terms, including "paradigm," "pronouncement story," or "proverb" are sometimes used with similar meaning. 2. in the Coptic Christian tradition, often spelled as apophthegm, the term represents memorable sayings of an "old man," symbolic of wisdom. In the practice of the desert mystics, the phrase "give me a word" was an invitation to impart uplifting acumen and salvation that could be integrated into one's life to profit. *See also* accideme; alliteration; apostrophe; assonance; autograph; Bible; Bible manuscripts; Bible translations; biblical criticism; chiasmus; conflict story; *constructio ad sensum;* context; contextualization; Coptic Church; dittography; double sense fulfillment; doublets; doubling; edification; eisegesis; epanadiplosis; epigrammatic statements; etymology; exegesis; figure of speech; folio; form criticism; gattung; gloss; gnomic sayings; grammatical-historical interpretation; *hapax legomena;* haplography; hermeneutic(s); higher criticism; homographs; homonyms; homophones; *homoteleuton;* hyperbole; idiom; *inclusio;* interpolation; interpretation;

inverted nun; irony; isagogics; *itture sopherim;* jot and tittle; kere; *kethib;* "L"; liberalist interpretation; literal interpretation; litotes; liturgy, Christian; loan words; lower criticism; "M"; Masoretic Text; minuscule(s); mystery of God; "old man"; omission; paradigm; pericope; proverb; wisdom; onomastica; onomatopoeia; palimpsest; papyrus; paradigm; parallelism; parchment; *paroimia;* pericope; personification; Peshita; pointing; point of view; polyglot; principles of interpretation; proof texting; pun(s); "Q"; redaction; revelation, theological; rhetorical criticism; rhetorical devices; riddle; satire; *scripto continua;* scriptorium; *sebirin;* simile; similitude; source criticism; sources, primary and secondary; special points; strophe; superscription; symbol(s); synecdoche; syntax; synthetic parallelism; text; textual criticism; *tiggune sopherim;* Time Texts; Torah; translation; transposition; trope; type(s); typology; uncial(s); vellum; verbicide.

apotheosis: the act of raising a mortal hero type to the status of divinity, something Greco-Roman politics were prone to do. To state the philosophy bluntly, apotheosis is "man becoming [as] God." Roman emperors, especially, were notorious to elevate themselves to godhead or were agreeable for others to do it for them. The process is also common in a number of Eastern religions. The understanding is that reincarnation of a human leader into a deity is accomplished, or an ascension to that position has been successful. The painting on the Capitol dome in Washington, D.C. depicts George Washington in such a glorification, though that depiction is likely artistic expression or metaphorical. *See also* avatar; Caesar cult; caesaropapacy; idolatry; Palamism; *Pontifex Maximus;* theogony; theophany; theosis.

apotropaic magic: "to ward off," a method of sympathetic magic employed to avoid bad luck, the evil eye, and the like by use of a charm (an amulet) or a gesture ("knock on wood"). *See also* anthropomancy; aretology; Ariosophy; astral plane; astral projection; astrolabe; astrology, astrologers; athame;

audition; augury automatic writing; bagua; belomancy; belomancy; *besom;* bibliomancy; black arts; black mirror; blood moon(s); cantrip; cartomancy; charm(s); chiromancy; chaos magic; chiromancy; clairaudience; clairsentience; clairvoyance; cleromancy; cone of power; conjure; crop circles; cryptesthesia; crystallomancy; crystal skulls; curious acts; curse(s); divination; dream(s); dreams and visions; ecstasy; enchantment; enneagram; esoteric sects; evil eye; execration; extrasensory perception (ESP); foreknowledge; foretelling; *geis;* geomancy; grimoire; gris-gris; hellbroth; hepatoscopy; Hermetic wisdom; Hermetic writings; hex; hierscopy; horoscope(s); hydromancy; idol(s); idolatry; ifa; imprecation; incantation; intoxication; juju; labyrinth walk; lecanomancy; literomancy; locution; lotus-eaters; magic arts; magic, magick; magic square; magnetism; mana; mantic wisdom; mantra; miracle(s); monition; mystery religion(s); necromancy; New Age religion; numbers, symbology of; occult, occultic; omen; oneiromancy; oracle(s); otherworldy journeys; ouija board; out-of-body experiences (OBEs); paranormal; parapsychology; past life regression; peace pole(s); pentagram; *pharmakeia;* philosophers' stone; planchette; planets as gods; portent; pow-wow; precognition; premonition; prodigy; prognostication; prophecy, general; psi; psychic(s); psychic healing; psychic reading; psychomancy; psychometry; psychonautics; pyramidology; rebirthing; reincarnation; remote viewing; retrocognition; revelation; rhabdomancy; scrying; séance; secret societies; secret wisdom; sorcery, sorceries; spell; spell names; spiritism; stigmata; supernatural; superstition; taboo; tarot; telegnosis; telepathy; telesthesia; theugry; third eye, the; thoughtform; totemism; vision(s); vision quest; visualization; voodoo; voudou; wanga; ward; warlock(s); Web-Bot; Wicca; witch(es); witchcraft; wizard(s); *ya sang*; yoga; Zen; zodiac; *zos kia* cultus.

apparition: a ghostly appearance—any extraordinary but immaterial phenomena that hints of the presence of some specter or phantom. Extrabiblical history relates at least three such events that are of apocalyptic interest. One report from *2 Maccabees* tells us that Heliodorus, the greedy tax collector for the Seleucids, was prevented from looting the Temple in Jerusalem when a threatening apparition opposed him. Another tale came from Josephus. When King Herod entered the sepulcher of David and Solomon, he proceeded to loot all the costly goods inside. Desiring more, he proceeded further into the tomb, close to the place where the bodies lay. It was then that a blast of fire erupted and killed two of the king's guards. Herod was so frightened that he attempted amends by erecting a costly pillar near the site as an encomium. Josephus further relates certain fantastic events just before the destruction of Jerusalem by the Romans. He reports a star resembling a dangling sword stood over the city. Then a comet passed overhead visible for an entire year. At Passover, during the Feast of Unleavened Bread, on the eighth of Nisan at the ninth hour of night, a great light shown around the altar and Holy Place making the vicinity like daylight and lasting half an hour. At the same festival, a heifer being led by the high priest to be sacrificed, calved a lamb in the midst of the Temple precincts. A few days later, on the twenty-first day of Jyar, chariots and soldiers in full battle dress were seen running to and fro across the heavens just before sunset. At Pentecost, as the priests were entering the Inner Court on duty, they felt an earthquake and heard a great noise. This was followed by the voices of multitudes saying, "Let us remove hence." Moreover, the Eastern Gate of the Temple (which was made of brass, quite heavy, and bolted firmly into its foundations) mysteriously opened of its own accord during the nighttime. The strength of twenty men was required to close it again. Perhaps the most astounding of the signs concerns one Jesus, son of Ananus, a farmer on pilgrimage to Jerusalem. We may rightly call him a prophet as he began to shout aloud, "A voice from the east, a voice from the west, a voice from the four winds, a voice against Jerusalem and the holy house, a voice against the bridegroom and the brides, and a voice against the whole people! Woe, woe to Jerusalem!" This he cried for seven years and five months despite being lashed to the bone many times. His throat never became hoarse, nor did his litany change, day or night. His final utterance came from the wall itself during the siege when a stone from a Roman trebuchet struck him dead. The Talmud relates similar events: forty years before the Temple's destruction and around the time of Jesus' death, the lot for the Lord's offering during the sacrifice of the scapegoat kept appearing in the priest's left hand whereas it should have come up in the right. The scarlet thread on the Temple door refused to turn white to assure the people their sins were forgiven. The westernmost light on the Temple Menorah would not stay lit. The wise of Jerusalem perceived these apparitions and signs rightly to be filled with dread but most took them as presages of God's deliverance. If we trust the journalist of *2 Maccabees* and Josephus the historian (and there is no pronounced reason to discredit them) the assumption is to attribute this phenomenon to divine action. So-called appearances of the virgin Mary reported here and there around the world may be termed apparitions in some circles. Belief in wandering spirits was surely acceptable to the ancients; even the apostles were convinced they were seeing a ghost when Jesus walked toward them on the waters of Lake Galilee (Mk. 6:49). *See also* astral body; bugbears; familiar spirit; Fatima, Our Lady of; Garabandal visions; ghost(s); Guadalupe, Our Lady of; Heliodorus; Herod the Great; La Salette, vision of; Lourdes, Our Lady of; Mariolatry; paranormal; Sergius and Bacchus; spirit; theophany; vision(s); witch of Endor.

appearing, in view of his. See his appearing, in view of.

appearing, the: a sort of shorthand expression to describe the Second Coming of Christ. *See also* apocalyptic, apocalypticism; apocalyptic time; appointed time, the; consummation, the final; day he visits us, the; day of the Lord; day of God, the; day of (our Lord Jesus) Christ; Day, that; *en takhei;* eschatology, eschatological; Glorious Appearing; great and dreadful day, that; rapture; Second Coming; Second Coming procession; secret rapture; time; time is near, the.

Apphia: a disciple, possibly married to Archippus, who hosted a church congregation in her home (Phm. 2) at Colossae. She was called "our beloved." *See also* Archippus.

Applewhite, Marshall: founder of the cult called "Heaven's Gate." Applewhite was born in Texas on May 17, 1931 and died with his cult as a suicide on March 26, 1997. The religion he founded (with Bonnie Nettles) was a UFO style sect that planned to rendezvous with alien space ships said to be arriving behind the Hale-Bopp Comet. He and Nettles, known as Ti and Do, grew their sect mostly via the Internet. Applewhite and his followers died by poison (laid in ritual position and backed up by plastic bags over the heads) in groups of fifteen on the twenty-fourth of March, fifteen on the twenty-fifth, and nine on the twenty-sixth. *See also* cult(s); Heaven's Gate; Nettles, Bonnie.

applied kinesiology. See kinesiology, applied.

appointed time, the: an important apocalyptic expression referring to the day determined by God to end His season of wrath and assume His authority over heaven and earth and allowing for no other time. The phrase is used most often in Daniel but it appears elsewhere in Scripture as well. Theologically speaking, the "appointed time" is that instance when God acts as He has determined to act (Ps. 102: 13,16). *See also* apocalyptic calculation; apocalyptic time; appearing, the; consummation, the final; day he visits us, the; day of the Lord; day of God, the; day of (our Lord Jesus) Christ; Day, that; due time, in; *en takhei;* eschatology, eschatological; "forcing the time"; Glorious Appearing; great and dreadful day, that; rapture; Second Coming; Second Coming procession; secret rapture; time; time is near, the.

"approach the holy altar": the right or received permission to partake of Holy Communion in most High Church protocol. In 567 A.D. the twenty-third canon of the Council of Tours proclaims: "Let all those who appear to persist in their folly of performing around any stones, trees, or fountains, manifest sites of paganism, acts that are incompatible with the rules of the church, be driven from the Holy Church and let none permit them to approach the holy altar." *See also* altar; Entrance Rite; Eucharist.

appropriation: the theory that each personhood of the Trinity has specific functions even though all are involved in every task. The most common illustration of the idea is that God can be seen primarily as Creator, the Son as savior, and the Holy Spirit as sanctifier. Each, however, never acts in isolation from the others. *See also* Adoptionism; Anomoeans; Arianism; Arius; complementarianism view of the Trinity; Donatism; dualism; Dynamic Monarchianism; dynamism; eternal subordination of the Son; "four fences of Chalcedon"; *homoiousios; homoousios;* hypostatic union; incarnation; *kenosis;* kenotic view of Christ; modalism; Monarchianism; monophysitism; monoenergism; Nestorianism; Nestorius; *ousia;* patripassianism; Pelagianism; Pelagius; *perichoresis;* psilanthropism; Sabellianism; Socianism; Socinians; subordinationism; theanthroposophy; *Theophorus;* Trinity; two natures, doctrine of the; unipersonality.

a priori: an assumption or presupposition. Some discussions of doctrine, for instance, begin with an assumption of the truth of certain positions to be debated. *See also* theologoumenon.

Apse: the Babylonian god of lakes and fresh water. *See also* idol(s); Sumerian and Babylonian pantheon.

Aqiba, Rabbi Joseph ben: also known as Akiba or "Tana," the Torah master who taught that a hidden meaning lies under every written form of the Law of Moses (ca. A.D. 50–135). Naturally, he favored the allegorical method of interpretation. *See also* Bible Code; Cheiro; *gematria;*

Haggada; Halakha; *isopseplia;* Jew(s); Masseket Hekalot; Midrash; *notarikon;* Qabbala; *Sefiort; temoorah;* Zevi, Shabbatai; *Zohar.*

***Aqsa* Mosque.** See *al-Aqsa* Mosque.

Aquila: 1. husband of Priscilla introduced in the New Testament. Together they made up an effective husband-wife team who were faithful co-workers with Paul. They were able and tireless workers to whom Paul and Apollos were deeply indebted and even risked their lives for Paul's comfort and safety (Acts 18:1–3, 18, 26; Rom. 16:3; 2 Tim. 4:19). 2. a Jewish proselyte called Pontus from Sinope, Turkey, (A.D. 130) who translated the Old Testament into Greek. He may be the same individual known as Onkelos. *See also* Aquila, translation of; Priscilla.

Aquila, translation of: a Greek translation of the Old Testament made by a Jewish proselyte of Pontus named Aquila in the second century. The Jews thereafter preferred this work to the Septuagint, which had become the Old Testament of the Christians. *See also* Aquila; Bible translations; Hexapla; Septuagint.

Aquinas, Thomas: learned Dominican theologian and prolific writer (ca. A.D. 1225–1274), an Italian. Despite his all-consuming commentaries on almost every theological subject imaginable, Aquinas never addressed the rapture theme or related subjects. This omission may partly explain the minimal expression of openly expressed eschatology in Roman Catholic theology. The writings of Aquinas, called "Thomism," have become the virtual academic guide for almost all branches of Roman Catholic theology. The religious studies of Aquinas are both abstract and practical in its parts, heavily laced with the philosophy of Plato. He once said in his work, "It seems that we can use no words at all to refer to God." The thought is a bit ironic since his writings run to some sixty-one volumes in the English edition and remained unfinished at his death. As a student,

Thomas was called "a dumb ox" because of his obesity and ponderous methods. Yet, he is said to have been able to dictate three books at once and never lost logical thinking. Now he is known to Roman Catholic authorities as the "Angelic Doctor." Aquinas's most profound work is his *Summa Theologica*, which applies Aristotelian methods to Christian theology. Despite his mistrust and ridicule of the supernatural, it is reported that he refused to complete his great treatise because of a dramatic dream from God that caused him to cease writing and assert what he had composed was "straw." He died three months later. *See also* desert mystics; Five Ways, the; infused righteousness; liturgical year; *Quinque Viae;* Roman Catholic Church; scholasticism; *Summa Theologica;* teleology.

Arabah, Sea of. See Dead Sea.

"Arab Awakening": a newspeak description of recent upheavals in many Muslim nations in the previous decade or so of the 21st century. A number of Islamic nations have been, or are presently involved, in political and religious disturbances that have caught the attention of the world. Certainly Iran, Egypt, Syria, Tunisia, Yemen, Bahrain, Libya, Iraq, and, to some extent, all Islamic nations of the Middle East have seen democratic uprisings, terrorist activity, and ideological turmoil never before experienced in modern memory. Afghanistan, Pakistan, and a number of Muslim southern African countries have also undergone similar upheaval. No matter what one's political or eschatological stance, such activities surely carry apocalyptic import. *See also* Arab Spring; Islam; *nakba*.

Arabia: a peninsula holding the borders between the Suez Canal and ancient Persia. The land mass is 1500 miles long and 800 wide. It is mostly desert with scattered oases and, in Bible times, sparsely settled. There were numerous nomadic peoples in the area loosely called Arabs, many of whom were, and are, dire enemies of Israel. Islam spread rapidly from there, started even before the death of Mohammed and accomplished by war and intense missionary zeal. Today most of the area is called Saudi Arabia and retains its fierce anti-Semitic sentiment. *See also* anti-Semitic; Bedouins; Cush, Cushites; Dedan; Islam; *Ka'aba;* Kedar; madrassas(s); Mecca; Medina; Meunites; Midian, Midianites; Pillars of Mina, the Sacred; Moors; Queen of Sheba; Rashidun Caliphate; Seba, Sabeans; Sheba; Sinai; Uz; Wahhabism; Well of Zam-Zam; Zimri.

Arab Spring: a Muslim uprising in a number of Arabic countries in the early decades of the 21st century attempting to throw off the fanatical and dictatorial elements of Islam. Few participants, however, held a true understanding of the complexities of democracy and the results have hardly proven especially productive to freedom. Hostilities began on December 17, 2010, in Tunisia but quickly spread to Egypt, Libya, Bahrain, and Yemen. Violent demonstrations also erupted in Iraq, Iranian Khuzestan, Jordan, Sudan, Oman, Morocco, Algeria, Kuwait, and Lebanon. *See also* "Arab Awakening"; Islam.

Arafat, Yasser: long-time leader of the Palestine Liberation Organization (PLO) and ardent hater of Israel. Despite most assumptions, Arafat was born in Egypt, not Palestine (August 24, 1929–November 11, 2004), bearing the legal name Mohammed Yasser Abdel Rohman Raouf Arafat al-Qudwa al-Husseini. His recalcitrance in negotiating and terrorist sponsorship finally caused the Israelis to seclude him by force for two years until his death under somewhat uncertain circumstances. Arafat was the nephew of the mufti of Jerusalem in the 1920s, Haj Amin al-Husseini, the Muslim official who is said to have invented the story that it was from the site of the Dome of the Rock that Mohammed ascended to Allah. Some view Arafat and his actions as a model antichrist. *See also* anti-Semitic; Fatah; Islam; Middle East Peace Initiatives; Oslo Accords; Palestinian Liberation Organization (PLO); terrorism; terrorist(s).

Aralu: the Babylonian Hades, similar to the Greek concept of the underworld and the Hebrew view of *Sheol. See also* Abraham's bosom; afterlife; Amente; Annwn; Arcadia; Avalon; Dis; Duat; Elysium; eschatology, eschatological; eternal life; future life, doctrine of the; Gehenna; Hades; happy hunting ground; heaven; hell; Hy-Breasail; Hyperborea; intermediate state; Jade Empire, the; Jahannam; Janna; lake of fire; life after death; limbo; *Limbus Puerorum;* Mictlan; new heaven and new earth; Nirvana; Otherworld; Paradise; paradise of God; Pardes; Perdition; Promised Land, the; purgatory; Pure Land, the; Shambhala legends; *Sheol;* soul sleep; space doctrine; Sumerian and Babylonian pantheon; Summerland; Thule, land of; Tir na nOg; underworld; Upper Gehenna; Utopia; world to come, the; Xibala.

Aramaic: the *lingua franca* of the ancient world during, before, and after the time of Jesus. The language is an old one and appeared in many regional dialects. Some Aramaic words are found in Ezra, Daniel, Jeremiah (a gloss), and even a couple of words in Genesis. The New Testament also contains words of Jesus from the cross spoken in Aramaic: *"Eloi, Eloi, lama sabachthani?"* (Mt. 27:46). The translation of his plea appears as: "My God, My God, why have you forsaken me?" The Hebrew language faded during the Babylonian Exile (as verified in Nehemiah 13:24) and was replaced by Aramaic for ordinary speech and for facility of bartering in the marketplace and for formal legalistic transactions. Aramaic became the vernacular of the Jewish population, while Hebrew remained for use in the synagogue and academia. *See also "Eloi, Eloi, lama sabachthani?; ephphatha;* Syriac; *"Talitha koum!"*

Aram, Arameans: The exact location of the land of Aram is somewhat changeable in the Scripture (and at least once, in Ezekiel, it is coupled with Edom). Most likely, however, Aram refers to Syria and its capital, Damascus. The ancient Arameans, as with modern day Syria, were persistent enemies of Israel and Judah. They were repeatedly condemned by the prophets. Still, the Aramean people may encompass a broader ethnic meaning since Abraham was called "a wandering Aramean" (Deut. 26:5) long before Israel became a nation. Certain Jews from the Mesopotamian region who spoke dialects of the Aramaic language were a distinct class in Jerusalem. They were among the first to use Targums as teaching aids to the Scriptures. *See also* Abraham; Eber; Essenes; Hellenism, Hellenization; Herodians; Kir; Padan-aram; Pharisees; Sadducees; Samaritan(s); scribes; Shoa; Syria; Zealots.

Ararat: a mountainous territory north of ancient Assyria. In Jeremiah's time it was a kingdom adjacent to those of Minni and Ashkenaz (Jer. 51:27) in Armenia (2 Ki. 19:37). One of its mountains was supposedly the resting place for Noah's ark after the great flood, probably Mount Masis in modern Turkey, which is the highest peak in the range. *See also* Mount Ararat; Nachidshevan; Noah's ark.

Araunah: a Jebusite who owned a first-rate threshing floor on Mount Moriah. Josephus said Araunah was a particular friend of David (and perhaps the ruler of the fortress) who spared him when Jerusalem was taken by force from the Jebusites. The king purchased Araunah's plot, even though he offered it freely, in order to sacrifice to God and thus end the terrible pestilence brought on by his ill-advised census of the people (1 Chr. 21). It was here that the plague was halted by the angel of death and spared the city. This same piece of ground was the very place where Abraham offered his son Isaac for a potential sacrifice and the location on which David's son Solomon would later build the Temple. *See also* Foundation Stone; Jebusites; Mount Moriah.

Aravat: a word with the possible meaning of "Father of Creation," a name for God who is residing in the tenth heaven, according to *2 Enoch*. *See also* Aravoth; heavens, number of; names (titles) for God.

Aravoth: the tenth heaven, according to *2 Enoch*, the location of God's throne. Descriptions of God's face resemble iron made to glow in the fire. *See also* Aravat; heavens, number of.

Arba: the greatest among the Anakites, according to Joshua 14:7-15. He resided, and apparently ruled, at Hebron which was formerly called Kiriath Arba after him. His people were subdued by the Old Testament hero Caleb. *See also* Caleb; giant(s).

arca: a small box containing the Eucharist kept in the homes of some of the early Christians. *See also* family altar; home stoup.

Arcadia: the Greek or Roman place of paradise. *See also* Abraham's bosom; afterlife; Annwn; Aralu; Asgard; Avalon; Dis; Duat; Elysium; eternal life; future life, doctrine of the; eschatology, eschatological; Gehenna; Hades; happy hunting ground; heaven; hell; Hy-Breasail; Hyperborea; idolatry; intermediate state; Jade Empire, the; Jahannam; Janna; lake of fire; life after death; limbo; *Limbus Puerorum;* Mictlan; new heaven and new earth; Nirvana; Otherworld; Paradise; paradise of God; Pardes; Perdition; philosophy of the Greeks; Promised Land, the; Pure Land, the; purgatory; Shambhala legends; *Sheol;* soul sleep; space doctrine; Summerland; Thule, land of; Tir na nOg; underworld; Upper Gehenna; Utopia; Valhalla; Xibala.

arcanum arcandrum: mysterious and specialized knowledge, usually occultic in nature, known only to certain initiates. *See also* Agrippa Books; alchemy; *Arcanum,* the; *Book of Abramelin, The;* cantrip; *Corpus Hermecticum;* Emerald Tablet of Hermes, the; *Golden Bough, The;* grimoire; Hermeticism; Hermetic wisdom; Hermetic writings; idolatry; magic arts; magic, magick; mana; mantic wisdom; occult, occultic; od; parapsychology; philososphers' stone; *Picatrix;* secret wisdom; spell names; *Spiritas Mundi.*

***Arcanum*, the*:** secret wisdom of the ancient mystery religions, much of which is recorded in the few documents found of that type and era. Such secret societies closely guarded their ritual practices and knowledge, releasing it only step-by-step to the initiates as they progressed through the levels of membership. The *Arcanum* governed the textbook of revelations among the new degrees. *See also* Agrippa Books; alchemy; *arcanum arcandrum; Book of Abramelin, The;* cantrip; *Corpus Hermecticum;* "Dionysian Artificers, The"; Emerald Tablet of Hermes, the; *Golden Bough, The;* grimoire; Hermeticism; Hermetic wisdom; Hermetic writings; idolatry; magic arts; magic, magick; mana; mantic wisdom; occult, occultic; parapsychology; *Picatrix;* sacrament(s); secret wisdom; spell names; *Spiritas Mundi.*

archangel(s): an angel corps of high rank. Scripture does not precisely confirm that the heavenly beings hold such designated degrees of authority, but many extrabiblical sources do, along with long-held popular perception. In some instances, archangels are classed as a distinctive group and ranked accordingly. Usually, when they are so categorized, they fit into the so-called "lower" divisions and positioned just above the last-placed "angels." Even so, angel and archangel are not normally capitalized when writing. According to tradition, there are seven archangels named as Gabriel, Michael, Uriel, Raphael, Raquel, Saraquel, and Phanuel. Pope Gregory I named them as Gabriel, Michael, Raphael, Ariel (Anael), Saniel, Oraphiel, and Zachariel. Other Catholic compilations have alternate names or have been declared secretive. The Jews name ten: Gabriel, Michael, Uriel, Sariel, Raquel, Remiel, Zadkeil, Japhiel, Haniel, and Chamuel. Sometimes Metatron and Lucifer are named as archangels; the latter may be correct in his pre-fallen state as Satan or he may retain his rank since Michael refused to degrade him (Jude 8–10). Other religious expression like Eastern Orthodox, Mormonism, Islam, and others will see variations of the names. It is noteworthy that each name usually ends in "el," a derivative of God's name. Only Michael and Gabriel are mentioned in the Bible but Raphael is in the *Book of Tobit. See also* angel(s); Ariel; Chashmallim; Chayoth; Cherub, Cherubim; El; Gabriel; Lucifer; Metatron; Michael; Michaelmas, Feast of; Ophanim; Phanuel; powers; principalities; Raphael; Raquel; Saraquel; Sarathiel; Seraph, Seraphim; taxiarch; thrones; Uriel; Virtues; voice of the archangel, the.

archbishop(s): authorities of the higher liturgical churches ranking over bishops and usually commanding responsibilities covering a large area and population. The office is not recognized in the New Testament. *See also* bishop(s); Church of England; clergy; Eastern Orthodox Church; ecclesiastic(s); metropolitan; minister(s); monsignor; orders; pastor(s); priest(s); prefect(s); prelate(s); primate; Roman Catholic Church.

archdeacon(s): a High Church position subject to a bishop who supervises the diocesan clergy and holds ecclesiastical courts. *See also* deacon(s), deaconess(es); *deakonos;* orders; Roman Catholic Church.

Archelaus: a Christian bishop and apologist who debated Manes, the founder of Manichaeism. A record of the contest is contained in the *Disputation of Archelaus and Manes. See also* Manes; Roman Catholic Church.

Archelaus (Herod). See Herod Archelaus.

archeology, archeologists: the scientific or scholarly exploration of past civilizations, usually by digging into the earth and studying any finds or artifacts discovered there. The modern method is far removed from earlier digs in which individuals, like the treasure hunters they were, delved into the sites indiscriminately only to recover valuable artifacts. Their destructive methods yielded virtually no helpful historical information and disturbed the sites unnecessarily. Modern archeological protocols have produced much invaluable historical dating data and relic recoveries that have illuminated vital information about past civilizations. The practice of archeology has been crucial to the learning and comprehension of the ancients and invaluable to scholars, both secular and biblical. *See also* Armana Tablets; Babylonian Chronicles; Black Obelisk; *bulla;* carbon dating; Chamber of Parvah; Damascus Document; Dead Sea Scrolls; Ebla Tablets; Emerald Tablets of Hermes, the; *Epic of Gilgamesh, The;* gates of Jerusalem; Genizah Fragment; Gezer calendar; golden plates; Jones, Vendyl Miller; lamassu; Merneptah Stele; Moabite Stone; mushrishu; oops-art; ostraca; ostracon; pottery; pseudo-archeology; "Prayer of Nabonidus"; Rosetta Stone; Sennacherib's Prism; *Sitz im Leben;* Solomon's Stables; Sumerian Tablets; Tablet of Destinies; tell; underground Christian church, the; Wyatt, Ronald Eldon.

archiereus: an Eastern Orthodox and Russian Orthodox term for a bishop, the highest obtainable in the Byzantine rite. *See also* bishop(s); Eastern Orthodox Church; Russian Orthodoxy.

archimandrite: "chief of a sheepfold," a title for celibate priests of the Eastern Orthodox or Eastern Catholic faiths. The position ranks to an honorary title awarded to a monk for exceptional ecclesiastical service. *See also* catholicos; chorepiscope; clergy; Eastern Orthodox Church; ecclesiastic(s); hegymanos; metropolitan; monk(s); patriarch(s); patriarchate(s); priest(s); starets.

Archippus: a co-worker from Colossae with Paul whom the apostle urged to persevere in the Lord's work (Col. 4:17). He was urged by the apostle to complete the mission given him by God, whatever that task may have been. There is speculation that this Archippus received the seemingly left-handed rebuke from Paul because he may have harbored inept or indolent leadership qualities which, in some fashion, brought on Christ's condemnations of the church of Laodicea (Rev. 3:14 – 22) where he was pastor. The allegation is unproven but does seem to hold an element of plausibility. Another Archippus, who may or may not be the same, is mentioned later in the New

Testament in a greeting from Paul and described by him as "our fellow soldier" (Phil. 2:25; 2 Tim. 2:3) and host of a Christian congregation in his home (Phm. 2). *See also* Apphia; missions, missionaries.

Arch of Titus: a Roman imperial monument erected in A.D. 81 to commemorate the victory over the Jewish revolt in A.D. 70. The imagery on the stone represents a menorah and other Jewish prizes, all of which is dedicated to the Roman god of victory, Nike. Titus is being driven in a chariot by the goddess Roma while the goddess Victory crowns his head. *See also* Jewish War; Nike; Roma; Titus.

Archons: a Gnostic description of spirit entities who govern the stars and planets. The Archons also act as a sort of "buffer" between the God of creation (the Demiurge) toward perfection upward, and a corrupt world of evil below. Archons guard the seven heavens, a position some pseudepigraphal writers call "toll collectors." There is some evidence that the term also applied to a Roman official, either civil or military. *See also* Abraxas; Aeons; aerial toll houses; Demiurge; Gnosticism, Gnostic(s); idol(s); Ogdoad; Pleroma.

Area 51: a top-secret military facility in a remote part of Edwards Air Force Base in Nevada, used for highly classified experiments by the Air Force in conjunction with the CIA. The place is a hotbed for UFO conspiracy theories of all descriptions, many of them probably at least partially true. Area 51, along with rumors of an alien space craft crash near Roswell, New Mexico, and the so-called secret Lockheed Martin Skunk Works research facility at Groom Lake, Nevada, are probably the three most cited base theories fueling the UFO controversy in our day. *See also* conspiracy theorists; UFO.

areligious: complete indifference to organized religion. *See also* agnosticism, agnostic(s); antitheism; apatheist; atheism, the new; meta-atheist; scoffers; theism.

Areopagite. See Dionysius.

Areopagus: a hill located near the acropolis in Athens, the equivalent of Mars Hill to the Romans. This place was a usual meeting place of the Greek philosophers and city council and the site to which they brought Paul to hear explanations of the gospel (Acts 17:19). The apostle's message there was not well received, mainly because the Greeks scorned the idea of resurrection. *See also* agora; Parthenon; philosophy of the Greeks; unknown god, an.

Ares: the Greek god of war, son of Zeus and Hera, and love of Aphrodite who was married to Hephaestus. Mars was the Roman equivalent and is often pictured as holding Nike, the goddess of victory. *See also* Aphrodite; Hephaestus; Hera; idol(s); Nike; Olympian pantheon; Zeus.

Aretas IV, King: the father-in-law of Herod the Tetrarch (9 B.C.–A.D. 40). Herod designed to rid himself of Aretas's daughter, who was married to him, in favor of Herodias. The act was taken as an insult that led Aretas to declare war and defeat Herod's army in A.D. 36. The Romans took Herod's side, however, and Vitellius was ordered to punish the rebellion. The death of emperor Tiberius, however, put an end to the campaign. Aretas held Damascus for a short time. Evidently, it was during this occupation that he tried to capture Paul. The apostle escaped by being lowered from the city wall in a basket (2 Cor. 11:32–33). The name "Aretas" became a common one for Arabian kings. *See also* Damascenes, city of the; king(s).

Arethusa: a Greek water nymph, supposedly mentioned by Nostradamus in one of his quatrains. *See also* Andromeda; bugbears; Cassiopeia; Daphne; elemental(s); household deities; idol(s); mythological beasties, elementals, monsters, and spirit animals; nymph(s); Olympian pantheon.

aretology: 1. narratives or hymns about miracles or astonishing deeds accomplished either by a human or the divine. 2. in philosophy, the examination of the nature of virtue and how to obtain it. *See also* miracle(s); music; paranormal; supernatural; virtue(s).

Arguelles, Jose: New Ager, educator, author, and artist (1939 – 2011). Arguelles is known for his interest and expertise of the Mayan calendar and its manipulation, including the Mayan prophecy event of 2012. He was a strong proponent of ecology and human cooperation as well. He conceived the so-called Harmonic Convergence conference in 1987, the first international meditation and prayer event for world peace. His interests also lay in Earth Day events and the annual Whole Earth Festival. Critics have questioned his unabashed combination of Mayan thought with New Age philosophy. *See also* New Age religion; 2012 prophecy, advocates of.

argument of disputation: speech or debate intended to promote one argument over another. The dispute typically includes a premise or thesis to be argued, an alternative premise to be supported, and a discussion designed to demonstrate why the alternate thesis is more valid.

argumentum ad verecundiam: the process of using great men, deeds, institutions, ideas, etc. to argue for truth and rightful justice. Christianity does not support the method because humanity is incapable of true and independent modeling to perfection.

Argus: a multi-eyed giant assigned by the goddess Hera to imprison Io, a human consort of Zeus, in order to prevent further infidelity from her husband. Io had been changed by Zeus into a white heifer in a vain attempt to conceal the betrayal from Hera. Eventually, Hermes was able to hypnotize Argus with his music and storytelling in order to free Io back to human form. Argus's eyes were then presented to the peacock. *See also* giant(s); idol(s); Io; mythological beasties, elementals, monsters, and spirit animals; Olympian pantheon.

Arianism: the doctrine espoused by Arius (A.D. 250–336) purporting that Christ is not co-equal with God. His assertion was that Jesus was human but not divine. According to Arias, the Son did not always exist but was created, thus assuming a lower position in the Trinity. The basic text of Arianism is John 14:28: "If you loved me, you would be glad that I am going to the Father, for the Father is greater than I." The movement brought serious repercussions to Christendom until it was overturned, mainly through the apology of Athanasius. The fact remains that the Arian Church was no small movement within many and various sects of Christendom in that era of controversy. Arius, himself, was declared a heretic by the First Council of Nicea in 325 but exonerated by the First Synod of Tyre in 335, then condemned again by the First Council of Constantinople in 381. *See also* Adoptionism; Anomoeans; appropriation; Arius; Athanasius; Dynamic Monarchianism; dynamism; dyophysitism; eternal subordination of the Son; "four fences of Chalcedon"; Hetrousians; *homoiousios; homoousios;* hypostatic union; incarnation; *kenosis;* kenotic view of Christ; Macedonius; modalism; Monarchianism; monoenergism; monophysitism; Nestorianism; Nestorius; *ousia;* patripassianism; Pelagianism; Pelagius; *perichoresis;* Pneumatomachi; psilanthropism; Sabellianism; Socianism, Socinians; subordinationism; theanthroposophy; *Theophorus;* Trinity; two natures, doctrine of the; unipersonality.

Ariel: 1. the hearth of the altar of burnt offering described as being in Ezekiel's future Temple (Ezk. 43:15–16). It is also a symbolic or poetic name for Jerusalem (Isa. 29:1–7) meaning "hearth of God" or "lioness of God," Isaiah being the prophetic book where the word occurs some five times. The prophetic association means that Jerusalem is under divine judgment despite its holy reputation and will resemble a great bloody altar surrounded by the slain. So, another acceptable translation could read, "the holy city besieged." Woes were pronounced against the holy city at that time. Indications are that the Ariel was a physical object, but its detailed properties are missing; perhaps it was a stone used as a portable altar or some other purpose. The word also occurs in Ezra 8:16 as a name of one of the prominent returning exiles but is of little apocalyptic significance there. 2. an angel, according to Jewish folklore, but the name does not appear in Scripture by this definition. His name means "lion of God" and apparently functions as one of the seven ruling angels of heaven. He may be somehow involved in the combat of the occult and magic. Shakespeare used the name for his servant sprite in *The Tempest*. He is also named as an archangel by some Catholic theologians as directed by Pope Gregory I. *See also* altar; angel(s); city of David; City of God; City of Judah; City of Truth; Daughter of Jerusalem; harg; Holy City, the; Jerusalem as city; magic, magick; occult, occultic; sacred stones; sprite(s); stone(s); woe(s); Zion.

Aries: 1. the sign of the goat in the system of the zodiac. It was considered to be applicable to Israel and the Jews in Roman times and therefore might have been instrumental to the calculations of the Magi. The Exodus of the Israelites from Egypt occurred in the months of the sign of the Aries according to Josephus. Some scholars mention that Jesus was resurrected on the cusp of Taurus and into the Aries rule of constellations. 2. the Greek god of war and bloodshed known to the Romans as Mars. *See also* astrology, astrologers; astronomy, astronomers; constellations; idol(s); Magi; mythological beasties, elementals, monsters, and spirit animals; Olympian pantheon; Pisces; star of Bethlehem; zodiac.

Arioch: 1. the captain of the guard in Nebuchadnezzar's court who was ordered to kill all the wise men of Babylon because they could not interpret the king's dream of the great statue. Instead, Daniel intercepted his deadly mission (Dan. 2:24) and persuaded Arioch to arrange an audience with the king so he could stave off the executions. Interestingly, Arioch tried to curry royal favor as if he alone had been wise enough to discover Daniel's talent for dream analysis and to manage an interpretation. 2. an angelic being mentioned in certain parts of the Book of Enoch. Among his duties he was charged to protect the celestial writings and preserve them from the universal flood. *See also* angel(s); *Book(s) of Enoch*.

Ariosophy: a.k.a. Armanism, a system of Aryan-esoteric theories formulated by Guido von List and Jorg Lanz Liebenfels from 1890 – 1930. The movement was part of an occultic revival in Austria and Germany at the time and came to influence Nazism before World War II. Ariosophy is rather complicated in its concepts and involves manipulation of such materials as Armenian runes, the zodiac, and the gods of the months. *See also* idolatry; Irminism; Norse and Old Germanic pantheon; occult, occultic; rune(s); sect(s); zodiac.

Aristarchus: 1. a disciple and fellow prisoner from Thessalonica who accompanied Paul and Luke to Rome, where they were to be tried before Caesar (Acts 27:2). Earlier, assuming it was the same man, he was caught up in the riot of Ephesus (Acts 19:29) and barely escaped with his life. 2. a Greek astronomer and mathematician of Samos (c. 310 – c. 230 B.C.) who was the true originator of the heliocentric theory though the credit usually goes to Copernicus or Galileo. *See also* astronomy, astronomers; Copernicus, Nicolaus; Cusa, Nicholas; Galilei, Galileo.

Aristides: Greek philosopher who converted to Christianity in the early second century. His writings are among the earliest of all Christian apologetics. *See also* biblical criticism; philosophy of the Greeks.

Aristobulus: a family man whose household were worshipers of the Lord in Rome (Rom. 16:10). Eminent historians suggest he was a brother to Herod Agrippa I. Aristobulus is also a common name for some of Hasmonean descent but are not intended in this reference.

Aristobulus I: a ruler of the Hasmonean line (104–103 B.C.), a son of Simon. He was a cruel and unscrupulous man who killed his own mother and his next older brother Antigonus. It was he who changed the theocracy of Judea into a kingdom, yet retained the high priesthood for himself. He was succeeded by another brother, Alexander Jannaeus, after a brief one-year reign. *See also* Alexandra; Hasmonean dynasty; Jew(s); king(s).

Aristobulus II: Jewish high priest and king of Judea in the Hasmonean dynasty (100 – 49 B.C.) who was captured by the Romans under Pompey in 63 B.C. That event is said to be the fulfillment of Micah's prophecy (Mic. 5:1) spoken centuries before the event. In 67 B.C., Aristobulus substituted a pig for a sheep in an attempt to end the sacrifices in the Temple. This event, and others, precipitated a fratricidal war with his brother Hyrcanus II, prompting Rome to interfere and put an end to Jewish independence in 37 B.C. under his son, Antigonus II. *See also* Antigonus II; Hasmonean dynasty; Jew(s); king(s); Pompey; priest(s).

Aristobulus III: the grandson of Aristobulus II who was made high priest by Herod when only seventeen years of age (40–37 B.C.). Herod shortly killed him by drowning, however, while pretending to horseplay in the swimming pool. This Aristobulus was the very last of the noble Hasmonean line to serve in official capacity. *See also* Hasmonean dynasty; Jew(s); priest(s).

Aristobulus IV: the son of Herod the Great and his second wife Mariamne (31 – 7 B.C.) who married his cousin Berenice (the daughter of Salome). This Hasmonean descendant was destined to succeed Herod the Great but ran afoul of his half brother Antipater III. Herod disposed of Aristobulus before he could rule but he was already unpopular with the Jews. *See also* Herodian dynasty.

Aristo of Pella: early Christian apologist (second century). Only brief excerpts remain of his writing contributions. *See also* Roman Catholic Church.

Aristotle: renowned Greek philosopher, student of Plato, and teacher of Alexander the Great (384–322 B.C.). Many subjects interested Aristotle, not the least of which would include biology, metaphysics, poetry, music, zoology, physics, political science, theater, linguistics, politics, logic, ethics, etc. His works represent the first and only truly great systemized philosophical thinking in the West. His influence on Judaism, Christianity, and Islam has been profound, as it remains so today. Cicero called Aristotle's writing "a river of gold." *See also* philosophy of the Greeks.

Arius: Christian priest at Alexandria (d. A.D. 336) who held that Christ the son was not equal to God the Father. He believed Jesus was human but not divine. Arianism was mainly opposed by Athanasius. Arius's views were seen as heresy, and the man was continuously harried and condemned. Emperor Constantine eventually pardoned him, but he died an ignominious death from dysentery in a public toilet in Constantinople. The Arian controversy almost wrecked the early church as an organization. *See also* Adoptionism; Anomoeans; appropriation; Arianism; Athanasius; complementarianism view of the Trinity; Councils of Nicea; Donatism; dualism; Dynamic Monarchianism; dynamism; eternal subordination of the Son; "four fences of Chalcedon"; *homoiousios; homoousios;* hypostatic union; incarnation; *kenosis;* kenotic view of Christ; modalism; Monarchianism; monoenergism; monophysitism; Nestorianism; Nestorius; *ousia;* patripassianism; Pelagianism; Pelagius; *perichoresis;* psilanthropism; Roman Catholic Church; Sabellianism; Socianism, Socinians; subordinationism; theanthroposophy; Theophorus; Trinity; two natures, doctrine of the; unipersonality.

Arka: in Jewish legend, a subterranean locale to which Cain descended after the Fall (Gen. 4:14). The evil angels Afrira and Kastimon ruled there and, whereas the pair had been in conflict, they reconciled upon Cain's arrival. *See also* Cain; Cainites.

Arkan-ad-din: the Five Pillars of Faith (Five Pillars of Islam) referred to by their Arabic names by all Muslims despite their native language. The five are named as 1) *Shahadah* (confessing the faith)—recited in Arabic as "There is no God but Allah and Muhammed is His messenger [prophet];" 2) *Salat* (prayer)—a set of ritual prayers performed five times a day each day (sometimes combined into three); 3) *Sawm* (fasting)—an annual community event for all Muslims (excepting children, pregnant women, and travelers) that lasts the entire lunar month called Ramadan; 4) *Zakat* (giving of alms)—an obligatory charity giving of 2.5 % of a Muslim's wealth; 5) *Hajj* (pilgrimage to Mecca)—to be performed if possible at least once in a lifetime, providing the believer can afford end endure the trip. *See also* confession(s) of faith; five pillars of Islam; five principles of Islam; Islam; rule of faith.

ark, Noah's. See Noah's ark.

ark of the covenant: the portable Palladium of the Israelites, designed according to God's plan. Inside the ark, or "box," were the Ten Commandments on stone given to Moses. To the Israelites, the ark was their talisman, protection, and most sacred object with special instructions and personnel established for its care and transport. It was carried at least 1,000 yards apart from the traveling tribes at the center of the formation. The ark was the only furniture in the Holy of Holies of the tabernacle and temples. The object was the most cherished talisman for the Israelites during the Exodus and after but is now lost to history. Enigmatically, Scripture does not reveal the fate of the earthly ark. It seems to have simply and suddenly vanished. However, a number of rumors and theories persist as to its possible location and eventual restoration. Some claim it is secure in the deep recesses underneath the former temples (as actually hinted in *2 Maccabees* 2:7-8); others suggest the prophet Jeremiah hid it in the Judean wilderness before the Babylonians could seize it; another legend asserts it was carried to Ethiopia by the son of Solomon and the Queen of Sheba. If this is so, it might help explain the prophecy of Zephaniah 3:9–11, which says that the Ethiopians (the Coptic Church of Ethiopia?) will bring back a holy relic to Jerusalem during the Millennium. Is this relic the ark? If not, perhaps loyal priests and Levites hid it to protect their national treasure from wicked King Manasseh, or by another group who rescued it from the Babylonian rampage of Jerusalem in 586 B.C. Some conspiracists are convinced it lies under Rosslyn Chapel in Scotland. Some even believe the ark is the elusive treasure, or part of it, on Oak Island near Nova Scotia. Evidence for these assertions and others is weak. Rabbis Shlomo Goren (the first to blow the *shofar* when the Temple Mount was retaken by the Jews in 1967) and Yehuda Getz (chief rabbi of Hebrew holy sites) claim to have already found the ark in 1982. It was located beneath the ancient Holy of Holies position and both investigators insisted it can be retrieved when needed. Both men are now dead but instructions were left. They claimed King Josiah had ordered the relic placed there in safety when faced with the threat from Babylon. The Talmud declares that the Urim and Thummin, the ark, the eternal flame, and the holy anointing oil were not in the Second Temple, a condition Rabbi Maimonides said was brought about because the high priests no longer possessed the Holy Spirit. Even so, Revelation 15:5 reveals the prototype ark once more in heaven where it bears its alternate name, "the tabernacle of Testimony." The passage there seems to indicate it may represent the heavenly Temple instead, or in addition to, the ark itself. There may be, then, some strong biblical evidence that the ark and its tabernacle will be rediscovered before the end times. *See also* ark of the Testimony; Axum; Elephantine; furniture and furnishings of the tabernacle, temples, and modern synagogue; Goren, Shlomo; Holy of Holies; Jael and Zarall; Jones, Vendyl Miller; Judaism; *Kebra Nagast;* Kiriath-jearim; Levite(s); Menelik, Prince; mercy seat; Operation Moses; Queen of Sheba; "Raiders of the Lost Ark"; tabernacle, **the**; Temple; Torah Scroll; Wyatt, Ronald Eldon.

History and Mystery

ark of the Testimony: sometimes an alternate name for the ark of the covenant (Ex. 25:10–22). It is possible, furthermore, that the ark of the Testimony is the Decalogue that was placed within the ark. Alternately, the two items may be a single object or they could represent the Temple and its contents as a unit (*e.g.,* Revelation 15:5). *See also* ark of the covenant; tabernacle, the.

Ark, the synagogue: the enclosed space in the synagogue where the Torah Scrolls are kept when not in use. The box, cabinet, or container for storing the Torah scroll is present in every synagogue and normally orientated to Jerusalem. *See also* furniture and furnishings of the tabernacles, temples, and modern synagogue; Judaism.

arm(s): the bodily extension from the trunk to the hands. In Scripture, the arm frequently represents strength or superiority (Ex. 15:16), impotence (when the arm is lost, shriveled, broken, or cited as mere flesh [*i.e.,* Job 31:22; Ps. 10:15]), aid (Ps. 89:21), or comfort (as in an embrace [*i.e.,* Isa. 40:11]). In another direction, arms are weapons.

Armageddon: the region near Jerusalem renowned for its commercial and military significance. It is the site predicted for the final conflict (or much of it) between good and evil, and often but incorrectly referred to as "the battle of Armageddon." Technically, the final eschatological battle will not be limited to the plain but centered in Jerusalem and probably spread worldwide. Armageddon is really the marshalling point for Antichrist's armies. Prophecy indicates the battlefield will stretch from Megiddo in the north (Zech. 12:11; Rev. 16:16) to Edom on the south (Isa. 334:5; 63:1), about 200 miles. Then it is to encompass the Mediterranean Sea on the west to Moab in the east, another100 miles. Millions of fighters will be involved with Jerusalem at the center and probably worldwide. The fiercest fighting seems to occur at the Valley of Decision (the Valley of Jehoshaphat) and in the Kidron Valley—all more or less names for the same place. A few people will survive around the globe, but so few it is said a child can count them. There is no Hebrew word for "Armageddon," so the name is derived from the city and plain of Megiddo (Harmageddon) situated in the western part of the Jezreel Valley near Mount Carmel. Here some of the greatest military victories and defeats have been enacted by the world's armies (*e.g.*, Pharaoh Thutmose III smashed the local Canaanites as early as 1500 B.C., Pharaoh Merneptah fought in 1220 B.C. and Pharaoh Shishak in 924 B.C.); Deborah and Barak overthrew Sisera with his iron chariots (Jud. 5:19-20); Ahaziah died by the arrow of Jehu (2 Ki. 9:27); Gideon defeated the Midianites (Jud. 7); Israel defeated the Syrians under Ben Hadad (if we have located the town of Aphek correctly); King Saul and Jonathan were slain on Mount Gilboah (1 Sam. 31); King Josiah was killed in his attempt to intercept Pharaoh Necho (2 Ki. 23:29); Crusaders fought over the area in 1187 when the Knights of Saint John and the Templars were destroyed by Saladin, at the Horns of Hattin). The Crusaders lost 25,000 men in 1127, the French fought the Turks there in 1799 under Napoleon, and General Allenby duplicated Thutmose's tactics and defeated the Ottoman Turks in World War I. Today, Israel is the scene of numerous conflicts both great and small. When Napoleon first saw Esdraelon, he is reported to have commented that all the armies of the world could be assembled there. One of the clearest prophetic anticipation of the events of Armageddon may be recorded in Zephaniah 3:8–13. The official name for the so-called battle of Armageddon is "the battle of the great day of God Almighty (Rev. 16:14). Other references (with allowances for minor word changes within the various Bible translations) call it: 1. the day of God's vengeance (Isa. 34:8), 2. the winepress of God (Isa. 63:2; Joel 3:13; Rev. 14:19–20), 3. the great and awesome day of the Lord (Joel 2:31), 4. the harvest (Joel 3:13; Rev. 14:15–16), or 5. the day burning like a furnace (Mal. 4:1)

In our day, Armageddon has come to mean "the end of the world" in general terms. *See also* battle of the great day of God Almighty; eschatological, eschatological; Hamon-Gog; Harmageddon; plain of Esdraelon.

Armana Tablets: cuneiform script discovered near Armana in Egypt. Contents reveal that Pharaoh Akhenaton (the single monotheistic pharaoh of Egypt) received several urgent appeals around 1370 B.C. from the Canaanite city-states that asked for protection from the troublesome nomadic tribes known as the *Habiru.* These antagonistic people may have been proto-Israelites. The Armana Tablets, a.k.a. the Armana Letters, were found in 1887 on 375 clay tablets written in Babylonian cuneiform from about 1400 – 1360 B.C. They are mostly diplomatic correspondence addressed to Pharaohs Amenhotep III and Akhenaton from rulers of the Hittites, Mitanni, and Kassites in Babylon plus some other surrounding territories. *See also* Habiru.

Armanenschafft: the high priesthood of Teutonic Wotanism. The term also names a mystical cult dedicated to ancient Wotan worship. *See also* Aesir; Asa; Asatru; blyt; giant(s); idolatry; Norse and Old Germanic pantheon; priest(s); seior; Valupsa; volva; Wotanism.

Armenia: the region (around A.D. 300) just beyond the extremity of the Roman Empire. It, along with Cappadocia and Syria, made up the three main branches of the Christian church in the East. *See also* Cappadocia; Syria.

armies of heaven: an apocalyptic-style term describing a mighty host of angels. Revelation 19:14 suggests the "armies of heaven" are to be resurrected saints who accompany the Second Coming Christ. Some believe angels accompany them but this is not specifically stated in the NIV. *See also* angel(s); spiritual warfare.

Armilus: the Jewish name for the Antichrist. *See also* Antichrist; Black One, the; Islam; stern-faced king, the.

Arminian churches: those religious bodies that may be typed as Arminian in doctrine and church polity. Arminianism (an alternate spelling) is basically the doctrine perfected by Jacob Arminius. The specifics make up partial but important revisions of certain of John Calvin's Protestantism. Those persuasions included might list Methodists, United Brethren, Pentecostals, the Salvation Army, Nazarenes, Churches of Christ, Wesleyans, the Holiness bodies, and certain Scandinavian groups. Arminian eschatology is rather loosely defined in its systemized theology. The United Methodist church, for example, has no doctrinal statement on heaven or hell, except a brief confessional reading: "We believe in the resurrection of the dead, the righteous to life eternal and the wicked to endless condemnation." Arminianism is opposed to the doctrine of predestination, and especially double predestination. The essential theme of the groups is probably the pursuit of perfection of the inner man in Christ, a focus that seems to downplay apocalyptic considerations, except perhaps in specific instances of certain congregational beliefs. *See also* Arminianism; Arminius, Jacobus; Asbury, Francis; Booth, General William; church bodies in America (typed); glossolalia; Pelagianism; Strauss, David Friedrich; Wesleyan Quadrilateral; Wesley, Charles and John; Whitefield, George.

Arminianism: the doctrine accredited primarily to Jacobus Arminius and his supporters (called Remonstrants) that attributes salvation by God's grace as of paramount importance and not human will. The idea runs nearly contrary to Calvinism. *See also* Amyraldism; Arminian churches; Arminius, Jacobus; Calvinism; Calvin, John; Canons of Dort; conditional election; election; fall from grace; Five-Point Calvinism; free will; Grotius, Hugo; monergism; "once saved, always saved"; Pelagianism; perseverance of the saints; predestination; Remonstrants; *Remonstrance,* the; solifidianism; Synod of Dort; total depravity; TULIP.

Arminius, Jacobus: Dutch Protestant and theologian (1560–1609). Jacob Arminius made certain important modifications to the doctrines of John Calvin, especially as they applied to predestination. His theology relieved some of the abject oppositions to free will so prevalent in Calvinism. *See also* Amyraldism; Arminian churches; Arminianism; Calvinism; Calvin, John; Canons of Dort; conditional election; election; fall from grace; Five-Point Calvinism; free will; Grotius, Hugo; monergism; "once saved, always saved"; Pelagianism; perseverance of the saints; predestination; Remonstrants; *Remonstrance,* the; solifidianism; Synod of Dort; total depravity; TULIP.

Armoni: one of the two sons of Rizpah, the concubine of Saul. David delivered him up to the Gibeonites because God was punishing the land by drought resulting from Saul's unjust treatment of that population. Both brothers were later given a decent burial after their mother doggedly guarded their bodies for some time against the wild beasts and the elements. *See also* Mephibosheth, Rizpah.

armor: protective outerwear used in warfare, usually made of metal or hardened leather. In Ephesians 6:11-18, Paul uses the typical armored Roman soldier as a metaphor for defense against evil. Believers are urged to put on the belt of truth, the breastplate of righteousness, the footwear of the gospel, and to take up the shield of faith, the helmet of salvation, and the sword of the Spirit. Thus, we will be fully secured against the devil's schemes. *See also* buckler; shield.

Armstrong, Garner Ted. See Armstrong, Herbert W.

Armstrong, Herbert W.: founder of the Worldwide Church of God, an Anglo-Israel sect that posits that the ten lost tribes are connected to the nations of Great Britain and America. He was followed in leadership by his son, Garner Ted. Both were date setters concerning the end of the age. Armstrong senior predicted the last day in 1936, later revised to somewhere between 1975–1977. Armstrong's ministry lasted some fifty-two years; he died in 1986. *Plain Truth* magazine and *The World Tomorrow* radio program were the main propaganda arms of the sect. *See also* Anglo-Israelism; Ezekiel's lioness and vine allegory; Pack, David C.; sect(s); Weinland, Ronald; Worldwide Church of God.

Arnobius: a pagan teacher of rhetoric in North Africa who converted to Christianity (d. ca. 330). He was required to prove his faith since he had been an outspoken critic of his newly adopted religion. Arnobius's response was a lengthy apologetic work entitled *Against the Pagan*. Its content is orthodox but the writing exposes the fact that Arnobius had a less than complete grasp of Christian doctrine. *See also* Roman Catholic Church.

Arnon: a river, or more accurately a perennial stream, flowing a length of thirty miles in the area of Moab and the Amorites. It terminates in the Dead Sea. The prophets Isaiah and Jeremiah elegized the area in their predictions of the fall of Moab (Isa. 16:2; Jer. 48:20).

aromatherapy: a holistic healing method involving the inhaling of scented steam or fragrance. *See also* holistic; homeopathy; New Age religion; perfumes, ointments, and spices.

arrow(s): ammunition for the archer's bow. There may be significance in the omission of arrows for the rider on the white horse (Antichrist) from the first seal (Rev. 6:2), which would indicate he has no need for military prowess at that point in his career. The omission may be more significant than at first imagined because the bow and arrow, when used in normal conversation, are seldom named as one without the other. In other references, arrows most often represent the barbs of misfortune, wounds resulting in death, or sharp words of reproof, all of which are so often projected on the human race (*e.g.,* Psalm 64:2–3; Proverbs 25:18). Psalm 127:4–5 intends "arrows" in an entirely different meaning: as the blessing of children since happy is the man who has his quiver full of them, or as in Psalm 91:5, as protection from the Lord. *See also* arrows, prophecy of the; belomancy; bow.

arrows, prophecy of the: a prediction of Elisha the prophet. As Elisha lay dying, King Jehoash came to visit the elderly prophet on his deathbed. The diviner told the king to shoot an arrow out of the east window of his sickroom. When this symbolic act was done, the meaning was said to be an assurance that Jehoash would defeat the Syrians. Then Jehoash was told to strike the ground with the remaining bundle of arrows. The king struck three times only, earning Elisha's rebuke for such a paltry number; now, victory over the Arameans would be only three years instead of more that could have been with a bit of additional faith and initiative (2 Ki. 13:14–20). *See also* arrow(s); belomancy; Elisha; Elisha's miracles.

Arsinoe: one of the seven most powerful women who supported the ministry of Jesus, according to the *Apocalypse of James*. No such person is mentioned in the New Testament but the name appears in mythology. *See also* Asclepius.

Artaxerxes I Longimanus: king of Persia (464–424 B.C.) who permitted the rebuilding of the Temple (Ezr. 6:14; 7:7) in 458 B.C. and the walls of Jerusalem under Nehemiah (Neh. 2: 5–11) in 444 B.C. (though some say it was his father, Xerxes, who permitted the building). He was called Longimanus (the long-handed) to distinguish him from others with the same title. Whether that nickname signifies a physical characteristic or denotes the breadth of his dominion is uncertain. Historians agree that he was a powerful ally to both Ezra and Nehemiah on more than one occasion after being initially opposed to their aims (Ezr. 4:7). He is considered to be the last truly efficient Persian king. *See also* Babylonian (and Persian) restoration decrees; Babylonian Captivity, return from; Ezra as scribe; king(s); Nehemiah as governor; restoration of Israel (the Jews); Xerxes I; Zerubbabel; Zerubbabel's Temple.

Artemas: a disciple at Nicopolis whom Paul considered posting to Crete to relieve Titus (Tit. 3:12). If not selected, the choice was to send Tychius instead.

Artemis: in classic mythology, the sister of Apollo, equated with the Roman Diana. She was worshiped heavily at Ephesus (Acts 19:23–41; Rev. 2:1–7) in New Testament times. It was at Ephesus that a riot ensued against Paul and some of his friends led by the silversmith Alexander, a leader in the trade guild that made images of the goddess. *See also* Alexander of Ephesus; Apollo; diva; Ephesus; idol(s); Olympian pantheon; seven wonders of the ancient world.

Arthur, King: one of the most celebrated, and mysterious, characters of Celtic history and folklore. Arthur was a "war chief" fighting the Anglo-Saxon invasion but soon after became embedded firmly in English mythology. But an early reference to him has been found in a poem attributed to Aneirin, written in the sixth century. There is little doubt that he, and his valued wizard Merlin (though they were not likely contemporaries), were both historical characters. Many of their exploits, involving the knights of the Round Table, Camelot, and other stories, are no doubt steeped in mythology and story-telling. *See also* Avalon; Celtic folklore and religion; Excalibur; Holy Grail; king(s); Merlin; Round Table.

Articles of Religion: a 1628 publication by King Charles I of England in which he attempted to build a buffer between the Church of England and predestination Calvinism. He considered it to be so important that when the *Book of Common Prayer* was revised in 1662, it was attached to the articles as a prologue. *See also* Calvinism; Charles I, King; Church of England; confession(s) of faith.

artificial conception: methods other than natural sexual intercourse intended to induce pregnancy in the female cervix or uterus, also called artificial *(in vitro)* insemination. The practice is widespread for lesbian or infertile couples (often using surrogate mothers) and a universal animal breeding technique. Such experiments are generally disfavored for humans by the Roman and Eastern Orthodox Churches and many others who consider the practice a moral issue over a health or scientific one. *See also* contraception; social issues.

Art of Memory: also called the Theatre of Memory or Memory Palace, an ancient mnemonic method used as a recall aid. Many of its aspects are still useful today. As an example of its process: imagine a building, complete with every room within that structure. Each room can then be envisioned as a branch of knowledge and each fact to be stored is further pictured to hold a special place in that room – much like a filing cabinet contains many folders with specific information. The mind can thus be trained to retain large amounts of information, including a multitude of theological concepts. *See also* acrostic poem; ecstasy; "in the spirit."

art, religious: those products of the skill and imagination of artists of all descriptions and talent seen throughout history. Most attempt, and often succeed, to emote profound expressions of devotion and worship as well as exude esthetically pleasing appreciation. No list of artists (professing Christian or not) and their work would be complete without the mention of at least: Fra Angelico (Giovanni da Fiesole) (c. 1395–1455), *The Annunciation* painting; William Blake (1757–1827), *Divine Comedy, The Marriage of Heaven and Hell;* Hieronymus Bosh (c. 1450 – 1516), *The Garden of Earthly Delights, The Temptation of St. Anthony;* Sandro Botticelli (1444 – 1510), *The Birth of Venus, Mystic Nativity;* Peter Brugel the Elder (1525 – 1569), *The Tower of Babel, Fall of the Rebel Angels;* Giacomo Cimabue (c. 1251 – 1302), frescoes; Eugene Delacroix (1798 – 1863), *The Bark of Dante;* Salvador Dali (1904 – 1989), *Crucifixion (Corpus Hypercubus), The Temptation of St. Anthony;* Gustave Dore (1832 – 1883), woodcuts for *Paradise Lost* and *Divine*

Comedy; Albrecht Durer (1471 – 1528), woodcuts of Revelation, *Hands of an Apostle, the Temptation of St. Anthony;* El Greco (c. 1541 – 1614), *The Last Judgment, St. Michael;* Giotto (c. 1266 – 1337), *St. Francis Receiving the Stigmata, Temptation, Ognissanti Madonna;* Benozzo Gozzoli (1420 – 1497), *St. Anthony Between Two Angels, The Procession of the Magi;* Matthias Grunewald (c. 1460 – 1528), *Damnation of Lovers;* Edward Hicks (1780 – 1849), *The Peaceable Kingdom;* Leonardo Da Vinci (1452 – 1519), *Annunciation, The Last Supper, The Virgin of the Rocks;* Michelangelo (1475 – 1564), *David, Moses, Pieta,* the (statues), *The Last Judgment* (fresco); Raphael (Raffaello Sanzio da Urdino) (1483 – 1520), *Virgin and Child with St. Raphael and St. Michael, The School of Athens, Disputation of the Holy Sacraments;* Giovanni Battista Tiepolo (1696 – 1770), *The Sacrifice of Isaac, Three Angels Appearing before Abraham;* Tintoretto (Jocopo Comin) (1519 – 1594), *Paradise, Christ Washing the Disciples' Feet;* Rembrandt Harmenszoon van Rijn (1606 – 1669), *The Angel and the Prophet Balaam, Jacob Wrestling with the Angel, Matthew the Evangelist, The Storm on the Sea of Galilee, Belshazzar's Feast; The Gate of Hell;* Luca Signorelli (1441 – 1523), *The Last Judgment, The Coronation of the Elect;* Diego Velazquez (1599 – 1660), *Crucifixion of Christ, The Coronation of the Virgin.* Choosing the top thirty works of religious art of all time would be subjective and likely impossible. Nevertheless, some of the most often mentioned for the honor include: the *Apocalyptic Tapestry* (1377 – 1382) by John Bondol and Nicholas Bataille, Angers, France; illustrations of the *Book of Kells,* Trinity College, Dublin, Ireland; *The Tower of Babel* painting (1563) by Peter Brugel the Elder, Kunsthistorische Muzeum, Vienna; the Daibutsu statue (Kamakura, Japan, 1252); the Ellora Caves (600 – 1000), Aurangabad, Maharashtra, India; Franciscan Basilica of St. Maria Gloriosa dei Frari, Venice, Italy; Mosaics of the Great Mosque of Damascus (705 –715), Damascus, Syria; *The Procession of the Magi* painting (1459 – 1462) by

Benozzo Gozzoli; *Guan Yin of the South Sea of Sanya* statue (2005), Nanshan Temple of Sanya, China; "Christ the Redeemer" statue by Paul Landowski and Hictor da Silva Costa (Rio de Janeiro, Brazil, 1931); *Last Supper* painting (1495 – 1498) by Leonardo da Vinci, Santa Maria delle Grazie, Milan, Italy; the Ardabil Carpet (1539 – 1540) by Maqsud of Kashan, Victoria and Albert Museum, London; "The Last Judgment" ceiling mural (1508 – 1511) by Michelangelo, Rome, Italy; *Saint Wolfgang Altarpiece* (1471 – 1481) by Michael Pacher, Abersee, Austria; Palazzo Medici-Riccardi, Florence, Italy; *Disputation of the Holy Sacraments* painting (1509 –1511), *The School of Athens* painting (1509 – 1511) by Raphael, Apostolic Palace, Vatican; *Belshazzar's Feast* painting (1635) by Rembrandt, National Gallery, London; Auguste Rodin (1840 – 1917), *The Thinker* (a figure considered to be a philosopher but actually a lost soul contemplating his wasted life) Musee Rodin, Paris; *Holy Trinity* painting (1408 – 1425) by Andrei Rublev, Tretakov Gallery, Moscow; the *Well of Moses* sculpture (1395 – 1425) by Claus Sluter, Chartreuse de Champol, Dijon, France; Spring Temple Buddha statue (2008), Lushan County, Henan, China; *Angels Appearing to Abraham* painting (1724 – 1729) by Giovanni Battista Tiepolo, Palazzo Patriarcale, Udine, Italy; *Paradise* painting (c. 1588) by Tintoretto, Palazzo Ducale, Venice, Italy; *Assumption of the Virgin* painting (1516 – 1518) by Tiziano Vecellio, Santa Maria Gloriosa dei Frari, Venice; *Christ Crucified* painting (1632) by Diego Velazquez, Museo de Prado, Madrid, Spain; *Nozze di Cana* painting (1563) by Paolo Veronese, Louvre, Paris; Voronet Monastery (1488), Voronet, Suceava County, Romania. If one is seeking the world's most vivid or inspiring *apocalyptic* art collection, the list might include: the "Apocalypse of Angers" by Nicholas Bataille (late 14th century); the "Silos Apocalypse" by Beatus of Liebana (Spain, c. 1109);"The Last Judgment" by William Blake (1808); "The Last Judgment" by Hieronymus Bosch (1504); the illustrations of Dante's

Purgatory (14th century); the woodcuts of Albrecht Durer (15th century); the Scivias plates by Hildegard of Bingen (12th century); the illuminated manuscripts of Jerome's commentary on Daniel (12th century); the book covers for the *Left Behind* series by Tim LaHaye and Jerry Jenkins (1995 – 2007); "The Great Day of His Wrath" by John Martin (1851 – 1853); the triptych of Hans Memling (15th century); "The Last Judgment" by Michelangelo (1537 – 1541); the illuminated manuscripts of Revelation (France, 13th century); "The Last Judgment," by Peter Paul Rubens (1617); "The Four Horsemen of the Apocalypse" by Victor Vasnetsov (1887). Artistic expression has definitely influenced theology throughout history, eschatology certainly being no exception. Revelation's visions of heaven and hell permeate literature from Milton's *Paradise Lost* to the poetry of William Butler Yeats and the stories of James Baldwin. Music ranges from African American spirituals and "Battle Hymn of the Republic" to *Quartet for the End of Time* by French composer Olivier Messiaen (first performed in a Nazi prison camp). Moving pictures have capitalized on apocalyptic themes after the static ones by Michelangelo, Picasso, Goya, Bach, and Blake. *See also* Aholiab; apocalyptic themed books and movies; Arguelles, Jose; arts, the; Bazaleel; bestiary; Bible of the poor; book(s); Cellini, Benvenuto; *Book of Kells*, the; Daibutsu, the; diptych; Durer, Albrecht; diptych; Haizmann, Christopher; halo; Michelangelo Buonarotti; Pieta; Spare, Austin Osman.

arts, the: perhaps the highest expression of human emotion and creativity in talents that many claim are divinely animated. Some the finest manifestations of cultural and esthetic endeavor have been produced to the glory of the divine, for worship, and for religious devotion. Styles are many including literature, music, dance, theater, photography, cinematography, drawing, painting, and illustrating, ceramics, staining glass, mosaics, lapidary, sculpting, architecture, (sometimes called the "queen of the sciences"), design, singing, opera, mime; weaving, sewing, and specialties within all the trades. Martial arts and some sports like gymnastics, synchronized swimming, and figure skating may be considered arts or certainly artistic. Even gastronomy is sometimes included. One theory holds that artistic ability is God-given, or at least inspired in its expression. *See also* apocalyptic themed books and movies; art, religious; book(s); cultural mandate; music; worship.

Aryan Nation: a white supremacist organization founded by Richard Butler. Members usually identify themselves as "Christian patriots," but the group is militant, prejudicial, apocalyptic, and thoroughly anti-Semitic. *See also* American Party; anti-Semitic; Christian Identity Movement (CIM); Covenant, The Sword, and Arm of the Lord, The (CSA); cult(s); Fascist millennialism; Fenians; Knights of the Golden Circle; Knights of the White Camellia; Ku Klux Klan; militant domestic organizations; Molly Maguires; Neo-Nazis; Patriot Movement, the; Red Shirts; terrorism; terrorist(s).

Arzareth: or Azareth, an obscure region or event named in *4 Ezra* where the so-called "ten lost tribes of Israel" were detained after their capture by the Assyrians under Hoshea. The journey to exile covered a year and a half, with the refugees being helped along by God's supernatural action in stopping the flow of the Euphrates and performing signs for them. Someday they will emerge from Arzareth via the same process in reverse returning to the fold of God (Isa. 11:15–16). *See also* lost tribes, the ten.

Asa: 1. the third king of Judah (911–870 B.C.). He found himself quickly embroiled in wars with Baasha, king of Israel, and with the Cushites. Asa's rule began well when he initiated religious reform in Judah and he even managed to bribe Ben-Hadad away from his alliance with Israel and join him against Baasha, an act which displeased God. Judah was nevertheless relatively successful in both conflicts, and

Asa was loyal to the God of Israel for most of his reign. His defeat of Zerah the Cushite (2 Chr. 14:9–15) with his vast army was a miraculous deliverance from God. The last years of Asa's reign were bitter as he began to abuse some of the people and imprisoned the seer Hanani. Asa developed a "disease of the feet" (which may be a euphemism for genitals and thus a venereal disease), forcing him to share the rule with his son Jehoshaphat. Even then, Asa sought no aid from God for his illness but depended on his royal physicians only. 2. a Norse collective name for all their early pagan gods. *See also* Alfheimr; Armanenschafft; Asatru; Askr and Embla; blyt; *Edda*, the; Freya; Freyr; Frigg; frost giants; Gefjon; giant(s); harg; Hel; Helm of Awe; king(s); kings of Israel and Judah; kings of Israel and Judah in foreign relations; Loki; Odin; Ragnarok; rune(s); seior; skald(s); Thor; tree of life, the; Valkyries; Valupsa; Vikings; volva; Wotanism.

Asahel: one of David's ablest generals. He was a nephew of the king by one of David's sisters. He was known for his valor and fleetness of foot. Asahel was slain by Abner in self defense but avenged by his brother Joab. *See also* Abishai; Amasa; Benaiah; David; David's generals; Joab.

Asaph: one of three family heads who, along with his four sons, was appointed by King David for the "ministry of prophesying" in the Jerusalem Temple (1 Chr. 25:1). Whether that description names Asaph and his companions as prophets in the normal sense is a bit unclear. We do know, however, that they were skilled musicians and were assigned to that ministry specifically. The appellation appears in a dozen of the Psalms, which we assume to be the same man. Asaph is called a seer in 2 Chronicles 29:30. The name identifies one of the three guilds that conducted the musical services in the Temple (Neh. 7:44) and were the first backbone of the Temple choir. Later, they shared these ministries with the "sons of Korah." Others in Scripture are also named Asaph, including a family of gatekeepers in the Temple and a chronicler or historian in the days of Hezekiah, but they are of secondary importance pertaining to prophecy. *See also* Heman; Jeduthun; music; prophet(s); sons of Korah.

Asatru: or Astaru, the official name for the religion that still worships the ancient Norse gods and a revival of Germanic paganism. The term may also appear as Heathenism, Esetroth, Ostroth, Form Sir, Odinism, or Theodism. The high priest of Asatru and his headquarters are today located at Reykjavik, Iceland, but is now centered mostly in Germany. The revival was supposedly founded by a shepherd-farmer in Iceland named Steinborn Beinteinsson (1929 – 1993) based on the message of the *Edda*. *See also* Alfheimr; Armanenschafft; Asa; Asgard; blyt; *Edda*, the; frost giants; giant(s); harg; Helm of Awe; idolatry; Norse and Old Germanic pantheon; priest(s); Ragnarok; rune(s); sect(s); seior; skald(s); sprite(s); third eye, the; tree of life, the; Valhalla; Valkyries; Valupsa; Vikings; volva; Wotanism.

Asbury, Francis: early American missionary (August 20, 1745– March 31, 1816) and church planter who established the system of "circuit-riding preachers" as tutored by John Wesley. When Asbury arrived in the colonies in 1771, there were about 600 Methodists; forty-five years later, there were 200,000. Asbury accomplished his prophetic and pastoral tasks by riding 6,000 miles a year for forty-four years on horseback, despite ill health and a meager diet consisting mainly of venison jerky. At the close of his career of fifty years, he had recruited over 3,000 ordained ministers, including 700 circuit riders who were almost universally welcomed by the residents. So loyal and tenacious were these itinerant preachers that the common saying in foul weather was, "There's nothing out but crows and Methodist preachers." Asbury was the first bishop of the Methodist Episcopal Church (1785) and established numerous congregations throughout the colonial frontier. *See also* circuit riders; clergy patriots; evangelist(s), evangelism; Methodists; missions, missionaries; revivalism.

Ascended Masters: a New Age identification for spirit beings whose wisdom and guidance is available to those who can contact them in the other world. Some critics identify them with fallen angels or Satan's top lieutenants. Others, both critics and supporters, affirm they may assume corporeal bodies in the new world to come in order to promote evil or mystic knowledge. Both New Age and most Eastern religions admit to some concept that the gurus of the afterlife may interact with our present world via esoteric means. *See also* Bacon, Sir Francis; Bailey, Alice A.; bugbears; idol(s); New Group of World Servers; Saint Germain, Comte de; sect(s).

ascension: the act of rising. Acts 1:9–11 records the ascension of Jesus to heaven from Mount Olivet, the very place to which he will return at the great Second Coming event. Elijah and Enoch are two prophets who ascended and spared the indignity of death. All believers will experience ascension to Christ at some time and in some form. *See also anastasis;* Ascension Day; resurrection(s).

Ascension Day: the date of the formal church calendar celebrating Christ's ascension to heaven. The observance is almost universally forty days after Easter. Liturgical churches name the day the Feast of the Ascension. *See also* ascension; feasts and special days of high liturgy faiths; feasts and special days of Protestantism; liturgical year; liturgy, Christian.

Ascension of Isaiah: an apocryphal compilation of Jewish and Christian works treating the subjects of martyrdom and the events surrounding the ascension to heaven of the prophet Isaiah. The apocalyptic portion (chapters 6–9) is a vision of the seven heavens through which Isaiah is escorted on his journey; the last segment (part of the Christian section) speaks of the coming of Messiah Jesus and containing certain Trinitarian references experienced in the sixth heaven. *See also* Apocryphal Apocalypses.

ascentia: mental assent to a given fact or existence with or without empirical evidence of its reality. Ascentia is essentially a base definition of faith. *See also* faith; fiducia.

ascesis: the desire or need for penance, mortification, or self-denial in order that a penitent may experience forgiveness. *See also* abjuration; *metanoia;* penance; recant; repent, repentance; rogation.

Asch, Sholem: Polish-born Jewish novelist and playwright (1880–1957) who sought to unify the foundations of Judaism and Christianity. His "Christological" series, *The Nazarene* (1939), *The Apostle* (1943), and *Mary* (1947), were praised for their artistry but Asch's efforts in Jewish/Christian ecumenicity scarcely made an impact. At his death, he claimed that he was "a vagabond between two religions." *See also* Jew(s).

Asclepius: in Greek mythology, the god of healing and medicine symbolized by the staff of healing featuring the spiraled serpent. Today, the caduceus (the snake emblem) serves as a medical symbol. The god was heavily worshiped at Pergamum (Rev. 2:12–17), where he was called Aesculapius. Asclepius was an important deity to the ancients, even considered to be one of the "resurrection gods." He was fathered by Apollo and born by a mortal mother Coronis (or Arsinoe) but was considered fully human as well as divine and walked the earth in human form, performing amazing feats of healing and surgery. He was even accredited with resurrection powers. Athena had given him the blood of the Gorgon, which he used to perform his miracles. Zeus, fearing men might learn the healing arts too well and begin to help each other, killed Asclepius with a thunderbolt. This act angered Apollo, who slew the bolt's maker, the Cyclops. Other legends are resident concerning his birth and adolescence, including one which saw him participate in the Trojan War. Another has him succored by animals like Romulus and Remus. He was likewise given power over demons and the elements, and his dignity and nobility were said to keep the universe functioning. Because of his personal similarities to Jesus Christ, Asclepius was probably the most intense rival to Christianity at the time. *See also* Apollo; Hippocratic oath; idol(s); Olympian pantheon; reptilian theory; serpent.

aseity: the doctrine that God is complete within Himself and needs no outside source to be self-sufficient. *See also* omnipotent.

Asenath: sometimes Aseneth, Joseph's Egyptian wife, thus placing her in the early Messianic line (Gen. 41:45). Asenath was the daughter of the priest of Heliopolis (On). Their two sons were Ephraim and Manasseh who became tribal heads (Gen. 46:20).

Asgard: the land of the Norse gods, including Odin, and the location of Valhalla. *See also* Abraham's bosom; Alfheimr; afterlife; Annwn; Aralu; Arcadia; Asa; Asatru; Avalon; Dis; Duat; *Edda,* the; Elysium; eschatology, eschatological; eternal life; future life, doctrine of the; Gehenna; Hades; happy hunting ground; heaven; hell; Hy-Breasail; Hyperborea; idolatry; intermediate state; Jade Empire, the; Jahannam; Janna; lake of fire; life after death; limbo; *Limbus Puerorum;* Mictlan; Nirvana; Norse and Old Germanic pantheon; Otherworld; Paradise; paradise of God; Pardes; Perdition; Promised Land, the; Pure Land, the; Shambhala legends; soul sleep; space doctrine; Summerland; Thule, land of; Tir na nOg; tree of life, the; underworld; Upper Gehenna; Utopia; Valhalla; Vikings; world to come, the; Wotanism; Xibala.

Ashara, Shoko: *nee* Chizno Matsumoto born in 1955 from a poor Japanese family. He became the leader of *Aum Shinri Kyo,* a malicious cult responsible for the subway gassing attack in Tokyo in 1995. For this crime and others, he was sentenced to death. He was hanged by the Japanese government for his crimes in 2018. *See also* Aleph; cult(s).

Ashdod: one of the Philistine pentarchy of cities, perhaps the capital. The city held the ark of the covenant there in the temple of Dagon but was so plagued by God for its presence that they foisted it off on some of the other city-states. The city was conquered by the Assyrians in the eighth century B.C., but Judah under King Uzziah managed it as well (2 Chr. 26:6). *See also* Ashkelon; Ekron; Gath; Gaza; Philistia, Philistines.

Asher: one of the twelve tribes of Israel descended from the patriarch Jacob by his wife Zilpah. Jacob's blessing in Genesis 49:20 states: "Asher's food will be rich; he will provide delicacies fit for a king" (a positive prediction). The tribe is listed in Revelation 7:6 as a representative of the 144,000 servants. *See also* lost tribes, the ten; tribes of Israel, the; twelve tribes.

Asherah: or Ashtoreth, the pagan goddess of Tyre and other cultures. The name means "grove," and she is often named as the mother of Baal and has association with about seventy other gods and goddesses. *See also* Asherah pole(s); Ashtaroth, Ashtoreth(s); high places; idol(s); Levant pantheon; Mount of Corruption.

Asherah pole(s): symbol of the goddess Asherah (Mic. 5:14, *et al.*). Such locations or poles were likely totem-like posts or trees, which served as the core of the pagan ritual. *See also* Asherah; idol(s); Levant pantheon.

ashes. See "ashes to ashes"; sackcloth and ashes.

ashes of the red heifer: an ancient Jewish ceremony in which an unblemished red heifer was sacrificed for the cleansing of the people or a place. The ritual is prominent to eschatological history because the red heifer ritual and associated water of purification are essential to consecrate the ground for rebuilding of the Jewish Temple. So far, a pure red heifer has not been bred in modern times, nor does the moment seem auspicious for the ceremony. Orthodox Jews consider the red heifer consecration to be essential before a new Temple in Jerusalem can be constructed. To qualify, the heifer (the only female species used in Jewish sacrifice) must not only be purely red (a single black hair would disqualify), but she must also be from two to four years old, never have been yoked, and without wounds or blemish. According to Maimonides, only nine were sacrificed between the tabernacle days and the destruction of Herod's Temple. The tenth will be offered before the newly erected third Temple at the end of days. The red heifer is a type of Jesus and his sacrifice on the cross as most Christians advocate. *See also* animals, birds, and insects, symbology of; Temple Mount and Land of Israel Faithful; water of purification.

"ashes to ashes": part of the official burial ceremony for Christians, particularly in English speaking countries. The words are taken from the Anglican *Book of Common Prayer* of 1662 as inspired by passages from Genesis 3:19 and Ecclesiastes 12:7. The full text is as follows: "Forasmuch as it hath pleased almighty God of his great mercy to take unto himself the soul of our dear brother (sister) here departed, we therefore commit his (her) body to the ground, earth to earth, ashes to ashes, dust to dust; in sure and certain hope of the Resurrection to eternal life, through our Lord Jesus Christ; who shall change our vile body, according to the mighty working, whereby he is able to subdue all things to himself." The traditional burial at sea ceremony for the British and American navies is similar, following a prescribed ritual beginning with an order from the Commanding Officer—"All hands bury the dead." Committal words before presenting the body or ashes to the deep are central: "In the sure and certain hope of the resurrection to eternal life through our Lour Jesus Christ, we commend to Almighty God our shipmate _____ and we commit his [her] body to the depths… Ashes to ashes, dust to dust. The Lord bless him and keep him. The Lord make his face to shine upon him and be gracious unto him. The Lord lift up his countenance upon him, and give him peace. Amen." *See also* burial; catacombs; catafalque; cemetery; chaplain(s); death;

dust; funeral; grave; Manes; Martyrium; multiconfessional; sackcloth and ashes.

Ashima: (Ashimah) a false god worshiped by the populations of Hamath and by those refugees who returned to Samaria as part of the Assyrian resettlement campaign (2 Ki. 17:29–30) around 715 B.C. Amos 8:14 calls the idol a "shame" of Samaria. Worship of the deity was somehow combined with the worship of Yahweh by these repatriated Israelites. *See also* idol(s); Levant pantheon.

Ashkelon: a Mediterranean coastal city, one of the five principal Philistine centers. The city, as with all the Philistine pentarchy, was ruled as a sort of city-state and worshiped the god Dagon. It was from Ashkelon that the Philistines returned one of the votive tumors with the ark of the covenant to Israel from where it had lain in state as a spoil of victory (1 Sam. 6:17). *See also* Ashdod; Ekron; Gath; Gaza; Philistia, Philistines.

Ashkenazi: or Ashchenaz, a people descended from the eldest son of Gomer (Gen. 10:3; 1 Chr. 1:6). In the time of Jeremiah, they are represented as inhabiting the region north of Assyria near Minni and Ararat in Armenia (Jer. 51:27). The name has come to identify the Jews of Middle and Eastern European (German and Polish) known as the Ashkenazim. The Ashkenazi community is found today in the Americas, Europe, Australia, South Africa, and Israel. The majority of American Jews are Ashkenazi descended. *See also* Abraham's seed; Gomer; Jew(s); Khazaria; Scythians; seed of Israel; Sephardim; Yiddish.

Ashoka: (or Asoka) great emperor of India (c. 273 – 232 B.C.) who was largely responsible for the conversion of much of the Far East to Buddhism. He sent his son and daughter to Sri Lanka (then Ceylon) as missionaries and even ordered the construction of 84,000 stupas in honor of Buddha. Ashoka became so sickened by war and the struggle for power, he turned to non-violence and is said to have established the first hospitals for the ailing poor. *See also* Buddhism; king(s).

Ashpenaz: a chief official in the court of King Nebuchadnezzar. His responsibilities ran to the care and education of promising Judean captives like Daniel, Hananiah, Mishael, and Azariah. Daniel requested of him to allow him and his three friends to subsist on vegetables and water instead of the rich fare of the king. Ashpenaz feared the king's displeasure, but Daniel's personal guard agreed to the experiment, thus permitting Daniel and his companions to keep *kosher*. The results proved all four of the Hebrew captives to be exceptional in physical appearance and intellect, allowing them to rise to highest rank in the Babylonian regime.

ashram: a Hindu hermitage or monastery. Some specialize in certain rites or studies. *See also* hermitage; Hinduism; monastery; monasticism.

Ashtaroth, Ashtoreth(s): the goddess frequently mentioned in the Old Testament (Ashtaroth or Ashtoreth is a plural form of the name). Variants of the name include Ishtar, Astarte, Venus, Inanna (to the Sumerians), and "the queen of heaven." She is sometimes seen as a consort of Baal. Even Solomon indulged in her worship (1 Ki. 11:5, 33). Her sister goddess, Anath, is not mentioned in Scripture, except as an infusion of the two idols into one, which emerged as Astarte or Ashtaroth (Jud. 10:6; 1 Sam. 7:4). *See also* Anath; Asherah; Eriskegal; high places; idol(s); Isis; Levant pantheon; Mount of Corruption; queen(s); queen of heaven; Sumerian and Babylonian pantheon; Tammuz; Venus.

Ashur. See Asshur.

Ashurbanipal I: or Asnapper/Osnapper/Assurbanipal, an Assyrian monarch (669–627 B.C.), the son of Esarhaddon and last of the strong Assyrian kings. Ashurbanipal was important to the history of Israel and certain of that nation's prophecies. He conquered the mainland fortress of Tyre and all of Egypt as predicted by the prophets. His name is mentioned

History and Mystery

in Ezra 4:9–10, and Nahum 3:8–10 indicating he was the plunderer of Susa and Egypt. He is noted as one who deported conquered Jews and resettled other ethnic people in Samaria. The great library at Nineveh with his name has been unearthed as a major archeological discovery. He was an intellect and his royal library grew to contain the richest cuneiform tablet collection ever assembled, now a part of the British Museum. Like its later production, the Library of Alexandria, it was extensive and well-maintained. But unlike Alexandria, fire does not destroy clay but only made the collection more protected. Ashurbanipal's rule coincided with the reigns of Manasseh, Amon, and Josiah of Judah; the Northern Kingdom had already fallen to Assyrian rule in 722 B.C. He was also contemporary with the ministries of Isaiah, Micah, Nahum, and, possibly Zephaniah. Ashurbanipal is also known as a great scholar, archeologist, and builder. *See also* Assyria, Assyrians; king(s); Library of Alexandria; Nineveh.

Ashurbanipal II: an important and by all accounts a successful early ruler of Assyria (governed 883–858 B.C.). His stated goal for his reign was to convert all peoples to the enlightened faith of the Assyrian god of war Asshur. *See also* Asshur; Assyria, Assyrians; king(s).

Ash Wednesday: the first day of Lent on the Christian calendar. The name derives from the Roman Catholic tradition of placing a smudge of ash from the previous year's burnt palm branches to the forehead of the supplicant in the form of a cross. *See also* Easter; Fat Tuesday; feasts and special days of high liturgy faiths; feasts and special days of Protestantism; Good Friday; Holy Saturday; Holy Week; Lent; liturgical year; liturgy, Christian; Maundy Thursday; Palm Sunday; Shrove Tuesday; Tenebrae.

Asia Minor: a province of the ancient Roman Empire sometimes referred to simply as "Asia" in the New Testament. The territory, with its adjacent islands and lands, held its seat of government in Ephesus. The area is a prominent geographical reference for prophetic pronouncements and biblical writing in general. The area covered the land between the Black Sea and the Mediterranean. The area today is principally the country of Turkey and some immediate surrounding regions but was formerly called Anatolia. *See also* Roman Empire.

Asimov, Isaac: *nee* Isaak Yudovich Ozimov (1920–1992). One of the top trios of science fiction writers with Robert A. Heinlein and Arthur C. Clarke. Asimov was a Jewish atheist but wrote both fiction and nonfiction on Bible themes. He was a humanist and rationalist and deeply intellectual as well as imaginative. *See also* Clarke, Arthur C.; Heinlein, Robert A.; Jew(s).

"asking Jesus into my heart": or "receive Jesus into your heart" or similar phrases that denote a low tech but effective metaphor that attempts to describe one's appeal for Jesus to become his or her personal savior. The phrase is common in many Protestant evangelical denominations, particularly when addressing children. *See also* accept Christ, to; altar call; birth from above; blood of Christ; blood of the Lamb; born again; Christianese; confession(s) of faith; evangelist(s), evangelism; fishers of men; gospel; liturgy, Christian; lost; "nail-scarred hands, the"; "plead the blood"; profession of faith; regeneration; "saved"; soul-winning; "turn your life [heart] over to Jesus"; "walking the aisle"; "washed in the blood."

Aslan: a lion figure representing the allegorical Christ in the novel series *The Chronicles of Narnia* authored by C. S. Lewis. *See also* Harry Potter; Lewis, Clive Staples.

Asmodaeus: a troublesome demon in the apocryphal *Tobit* who preyed on new grooms and killed them on their wedding nights. The angel Raphael bound him before harm could come to Tobias, the son of Tobit. *See also* Abaddon; Abezi-Thibod; Adramelech; Anammelech; Apollyon; Azazel; Azrael; Baal-zebub; demon(s), demonic; devils;

Dibbuk; Dubbi'el; Gadreel; idol(s); Legion; Lilith; Mastema; Pazuzu; Sammael; Sceva; slave girl of Philippi; Syrophoenician woman; *Tobit*; woman of Canaan.

Asmonean. See Hasmonean dynasty.

Asnapper. See Ashurbanipal I.

aspersion: from *asperges*, a method of baptism accomplished by sprinkling the candidate. The method seems to be drawn from Psalm 50:9. Some denominations prefer the term *rantize* in place of aspersion. *See also* affusion; baptism; immersion.

Asphaltitis. See Lake Asphaltitis.

Aspinwall, Deacon William: claimed the Millennium would commence in 1673. He was a leader in the so-called Fifth Monarchy Men organization. *See also* Fifth Monarchy Men.

ass: a long-eared mammal related to the horse—a beast of burden if domesticated but an untamed onager if found in the wild. The animal is also less commonly known as a hermione. The animal was highly useful in ancient times and mentioned often in the Bible. The donkey often symbolizes humility (as when Jesus rode one into Jerusalem epitomized in Mark 11), but today can represent a foolish or uncultured man. *See also* animals, birds, and insects, symbology of; donkey; horse; mule.

assassin(s): one who slays another by stealth, usually for worldly pay, vengeance, political intrigue, or ecclesiastical power. Murder has long been associated with illicit power and is still prevalent today. Perhaps the most notorious of the deadly groups was likely the Hashshashin, which operated around the time of the Crusades. They were for hire to the highest bidder, one of which was none other than King Richard the Lionhearted. Their leader was called the Old Man of the Mountains, a term that stuck to identify the whole band. *See also* Hashshashin; murder; Sicarii; Thug(s); Zealots.

Assemblies of God: officially, the World Assemblies of God Fellowship, an autonomous grouping of churches making up the largest of the Pentecostal denominations. The congregations stress the standard identifying traits of Pentecostalism like tongues speaking and baptism of the Holy Spirit. The fellowship is worldwide in scope. *See also* church bodies in America (typed); denomination(s); denominationalism; full gospel; Pentecostalism; Sixteen Fundamentals of Truth.

Assemblies of the Wise: informal schools of instruction led by rabbis or other learned, usually held out of doors. Education was readily available to any willing participants, and was sorely needed in circumstances like the Babylonian Captivity. It is possible, even likely, that these loose collections of students and teachers were offshoots of the Old Testament "schools of the prophets" and were probably a training ground for such notables as Gamaliel and Paul. *See also* amora; atrahasis; elder(s); ensi; *Hasidim; maskilim;* religious education; religious organizations; sons (schools) of the prophets; wisdom; wise, the; zaddik.

Assembly, the Great. See Great Sanhedrin, the.

Asshur: 1. or Ashur, an early capital city (not mentioned in Scripture) but later to be known as Nineveh. The inhabitants were a people named in the prophecy of Numbers 24:23–24. They were descended from Shem (Gen. 10:22) and are to be identified with Assyria. According to some biblical authorities, Asshur appears to prefigure the Romans who would, centuries later, subdue the Mediterranean. 2. In Assyrian mythology, Asshur was the chief deity and god of war. *See also* Ashurbanipal II; Assyria, Assyrians; idol(s); Nimrud; Nineveh, Ninevites.

Assideans: those Jews of the Maccabean era who defended the Mosaic law against Hellenistic influence. *See also* Jew(s); Judaism.

History and Mystery

Association for Research and Enlightenment: the carefully preserved and studied works of the psychic Edgar Cayce. The center was established in 1931 at Virginia Beach, Virginia. Cayce was reported to have delivered over 14,000 readings during his lifetime, and the ARE possesses thousands of Cayce documentation from which researchers try to ferret out successful prophecies. Critics say that the proof of their failures is in the volume of irrelevant material itself. *See* also Cayce, Edgar; religious organizations; sect(s).

assonance: words that sound alike applicable to any language. In Hebrew, assonance is used in some of the biblical poetry. *See also* accideme; alliteration; apostrophe; apothegm; autograph; Bible; Bible manuscripts; Bible translations; biblical criticism; chiasmus; conflict story; *constructio ad sensum;* context; contextualization; dittography; double sense fulfillment; doublets; doubling; edification; eisegesis; epanadiplosis; epigrammatic statements; etymology; exegesis; figure of speech; folio; form criticism; gattung; gloss; gnomic sayings; grammatical-historical interpretation; *hapax legomena;* haplography; hermeneutic(s); higher criticism; homographs; homonyms; homophones; *homoteleuton;* hyperbole; idiom; *inclusio;* interpolation; interpretation; inverted nun; irony; isagogics; *itture sopherim;* jot and tittle; kere; *kethib;* "L"; liberalist interpretation; literal interpretation; litotes; loan words; lower criticism; "M"; Masoretic Text; minuscule(s); mystery of God; omission; onomastica; onomatopoeia; palimpsest; papyrus; paradigm; parallelism; parchment; *paroimia;* pericope; personification; Peshita; pointing; point of view; polyglot; principles of interpretation; proof texting; pun(s); "Q"; redaction; revelation, theological; rhetorical criticism; rhetorical devices; riddle; satire; *scripto continua;* scriptorium; *sebirin;* simile; similitude; source criticism; sources, primary and secondary; special points; strophe; superscription; symbol(s); synecdoche; syntax; synthetic parallelism; text; textual criticism; *tiggune sopherim;* Time

Texts; Torah; translation; transposition; trope; type(s); typology; uncial(s); vellum; verbicide.

Assumptionist Order of Augustinians: a Roman Catholic anticlerical organization of the 1880s which held a paranoia that the Catholic Church, in league with Freemasonry, was sponsoring a conspiracy against the French Republic. The term "assumptionist" indicates one who supports the church takeover of a secular government or someone who favors an obligation that the federal offices assume the debts of the states (as happened after America's War of Independence). Support for the Assumptionist dissenters came from Jesuits and from promoters of the Shrine of Lourdes who were in sympathy with the French army officer, Alfred Dreyfus, a Jewish soldier wrongly accused of espionage. *See also* religious organizations; Roman Catholic Church.

Assumptionist Orders: a family of some thirteen congregations of Roman Catholic communities (there are some Anglicans also) engaged in various forms of ministry centering in magazine publication, education, ecumenism, pilgrimage, and mission. The original was called the Augustinians of the Assumption which originated in France in 1845with Emmanuel d'Alzon as the first vicar general. Other associations include The Religious Sisters of the Assumption, The Missionary Sisters of the Assumption, Oblates of the Assumption, Little Sisters of the Assumption, and the Orantes of the Assumption. *See also* Augustinian Order; Barnabites; Benedict, Order of; Black Canons; canon(s) of the church; canons regular; Capuchin Order; Carmelites; Carthusians; Celestines; Cistercians; clergy; Dominicans; Franciscans; friar(s); Minim; monasticism; monk(s); orders; Paulist Fathers; Premonstratensian Order; priest(s); religious organizations; Roman Catholic Church; Servite Order; Spirituals of the Franciscan Order; Trappist Order.

Assumption of Mary: the Roman Catholic belief that Mary, the mother of Jesus, was translated directly to heaven, body and soul. The doctrine does not specify if she died first, but the supposition is that she did, and then was immediately raised before corruption. When the pope, using his infallible authority, announced in 1950 that the Assumption of Mary would be official Catholic doctrine, it caused considerable consternation in both the Roman Church and Protestantism across the world. *See also* Assumption of Mary, Feast of the; Dormition of the Theotokos; immaculate conception; liturgical year; Marianists; Mariolatry; Mary; Roman Catholic Church.

Assumption of Mary, Feast of the: Roman Catholic devotional period for the mother of Jesus whom they believe ascended bodily into heaven. *See also* Assumption of Mary; feasts and special days of high liturgy faiths; liturgical year; Marianists; Mariolatry; Mary; Roman Catholic Church.

Assumption of Moses: an interbiblical writing of the first century, sometimes labeled *Ascension of Moses* or *Reception of Moses*. The best version was written between A.D. 7–29. and was made up of two other works—the "Testament of Moses" and "Assumption of Moses." The writer seemed to have been a traditionalist Pharisee appealing to his fellows not to become so intimately involved with politics, a message that went unheeded in later Pharisaism. The text is highly apocalyptic and, it is not unreasonable to state, somewhat frightening in its intensity. All apocalyptic literature of the time was quite popular in the general public and avidly read, including this one. In fact, verse 9 of the epistle of Jude quotes an incident from *The Assumption of Moses*. Josephus recited the Jewish legend that Moses was lifted up in a cloud in view of the people looking on even though the Old Testament clearly states he was buried secretly by God Himself (Deut. 32:48–52. *See also* Apocryphal Apocalypses; Jude.

"as surely as the Lord lives": a common expression in Israel (*i.e.,* Jeremiah 5:2 and many other references) meant to add emphasis to a speaker's words. The saying may be viewed as a sort of sacred pledge that what follows the declaration will be true, important, and dependable. The prophets used the expression frequently, and God Himself, sometimes invoked it in its profundity (Jer. 12:16).

Assyria, Assyrians: ancient empire founded by Babylonian colonists, descendants of Nimrod. Their home territory was present-day northern Iraq. They were an inventive and intelligent people, having inaugurated the 24-hour day, the 60-minute hour, the 60-second minute, the 360 degree circle, and the 12-month year, and they made real contributions in astronomy. They were a fierce, war-loving people, however, and eventually became the conquerors of the Northern Kingdom of Israel in the eighth century B.C. Assyrian cruelty to their subjugated peoples was hardly surpassed in the ancient world. Their kings were apt to boast of the way they flayed, mutilated, impaled, and roasted their captives. They were aided in their military prowess by their invention of the siege tower and battering ram. The Assyrians, it can be argued, invented terrorism as a weapon. The empire is discussed several times by the Hebrew prophets and is repeatedly condemned. The book of Nahum talks of little else. The empire finally fell to Babylon after the capture of Nineveh in 612 B.C. with the aid of the Medes to the east. In a number of references, Assyria is called the land of Nimrod. Some speculate the Antichrist will be an Assyrian. *See also* Akkad; Amorites; Asshur; Ashurbanipal I; Ashurbanipal II; Babylon, Babylonians; Babylonian Chronicles; bees of Assyria, the; cedars of Lebanon; city of blood; Enmeduranki; Esarhaddon; Horites; Jareb; Medes, Media; Mesopotamia; mistress of sorceries; Nimrod-bar-Cush; Nimrud; Nineveh, Ninevites; Ninus; Nisroch; Rabshakeh; razor from beyond the River, a; Sargon of Akkad; Sargon II; Semitic(s); Sennacherib;

History and Mystery

Sennacherib's Prism; Shalman; Shalmaneser; *Story of Ahikar, The;* Sumer; Tablet of Nineveh; Tiglath-pileser I; Tiglath-pileser II; Tiglath-pileser III.

Astara: a New Age or arcane learning sect that claims to be dedicated to elevating human consciousness and health to its highest levels. Since establishment in 1951, the group has used esoteric readings, mystic philosophy, and the like to promote its aims. According to beliefs, life's lessons can be experienced as a Journey Absolute from pre-birth to the afterlife. *See also* idolatry; New Age religion; sect(s).

Astarte. See Ashtoreth(s), Ashtaroth.

Astaru. See Asatru.

astral: an alternate plane of existence, normally invisible and mysterious to most but claimed by some to be enabled to see and travel within it. Other descriptions call it the Akashic Record or the Treasure House of Images. Sometimes the term describes the aura said to surround every living being. *See also* astral body; astral journey; astral plane; astral projection; aura; magic, magick; New Age religion.

astral body: a disincarnate existence capable of life in other dimensions, such as a ghost or spirit or even a person's projection on an astral journey. *See also* apparition; astral; astral journey; astral projection; ghost(s); spirit.

astral journey: a dissociative excursion of the spirit from the body to other dimensions as imagined by some New Age advocates. *See also* astral; astral body; astral projection; New Age religion; otherworldly journeys.

astral plane: a name for the type of heaven perceived by a number of New Age groups. *See also* astral; astral projection; idolatry; New Age religion; Summerland.

astral projection: an occultic practice whereby it is claimed that one can leave the physical body and project (extend) the spirit to another place. *See also* astral; astral body; astral journey; astral plane; Damanhur; near-death experience(s) (NDEs); magic, magick; New Age religion; open heavens; otherworldly journeys; out-of-body experience(s) (OBEs).

astrolabe: a "startaker," an ancient astrological device of varying designs used by astrologers, navigators, and astronomers. Such inventions have been in use since classical antiquity for assorted purposes, some scientific and some not. The astrolabe could locate the positions of the sun, moon, planets, and stars. Other modifications could determine local time and were used to survey, triangulate, and cast horoscopes. *See also* astrology, astrologers; astronomy, astronomers.

astrological megaliths: a rather non-technical designation for any number of huge stone structures of antiquity that may have been used to calculate star data, particularly the time of the winter and spring equinoxes. Such construction has baffled scientists as to their design, method of erection, and purpose (which may have served more than one intent). Stonehenge in Southern England is a famous example (4,000 B.C.?) as is L-Imnajdrasite in Malta (3000 B.C.). The Nabta Stones from 4000 B.C. in the Sahara of Egypt has been designated the oldest discovery. It is common for some to name the pyramids of Egypt and those of Mexico and South America (*e.g.,* Chichen Itza) as observatories, at least as part of their function. *See also* astrology, astrologers; stele.

astrology, astrologers: the arcane art of predicting the future or to discern omens by the study of the stars and their constellations. The Babylonian priests known as Chaldeans were adept at the practice and often came in conflict with the prophet Daniel, as were many cultures in the ancient world. *First Enoch* tells us that the Babylonians were taught astrology by one of the fallen angels. Other ancient cultures were also adept astrologers, including the Celts who may even have preceded them. Even some religious people today still favor astrology for does not Genesis clearly state that

God set the stars in the firmament to *guide* mankind? For the people of God, the practice was forbidden (Deut. 4:19; Jer. 10:2). Even so, some Hebrew intellects were astute astrologers. In that age, no distinction was made between astrology and astronomy, for if one were an astrologer, he was also an astronomer. That attitude managed to persist even to the time of the Protestant Reformation. Philip Melanchthon valued it; John Calvin did not. Most Lutheran pastors of the day sided with Melanchthon because, at least, astrology had a long history whereas humanism did not. The Magi, likely noted only in the Gospel of Matthew, were of this occupation. Astronomy is by no means dead in the modern age. Advocates claim that whereas the record of recorded human history is about 2500 years, God has impressed His actions and counsel in the heavens since creation. Every star and constellation reveals an aspect of God, if we but know how to interpret the message. For evidence, most cite Romans 1:19 and Psalm 19 as relating to the cosmic record, including the message of the gospel and future prophecies. *See also* Age of Aquarius; anthropomancy; apotropaic magic; aretology; Aries; Ariosophy; astral plane; astral projection; astrolabe; astrological megaliths; astronomy, astronomers; athame; audition; augury; automatic writing; bagua; belomancy; Berossus; bibliomancy; black arts; black mirror; black moons; blood moon(s); cartomancy; Celtic folklore and religion; Chaldeans; Chilam-Balam; chiromancy; clairaudience; clairsentience; clairvoyance; cleromancy; chiromancy; cone of power; conjure; constellations; *Corpus Hermecticum;* cosmic cross; cosmology; crop circles; cryptesthesia; crystallomancy; crystal skulls; curious acts; Dark Rift; divination; Draco; dream(s); dreams and visions; eclipse(s); ecstasy; enchantment; enneagram; eschatology, eschatological; esoteric texts; evil eye; extrasensory perception (ESP); Fifth World; Flat Earth Society; foreknowledge; foretelling; Fourth Density; Fulcanelli; galactic alignment; geomancy; grimoire; gris-gris; Halley's

Comet; hepatoscopy; Hercolubus; Hermetic wisdom; hex; hierscopy; horoscope(s); Hydra; hydromancy; idol(s); idolatry; ifa; incarnation; labyrinth walk; lecanomancy; literomancy; locution; magic arts; magic, magick; magic square; magnetism; *mana*; mantic wisdom; mantra; Magi; Maya; medicine wheel; meditation; miracle(s); monition; Muses; mythological beasties, elementals, monsters, and spirit animals; necromancy; New Age religion; Nibiru; Nostradamus; numbers, symbology of; occult, occultic; Olympic spirits; omen; Ompholos Hypothesis; oneiromancy; oracle(s); otherworldy journeys; ouija board; ouroboros; out-of-body experiences (OBEs); paranormal; parapsychology; past life regression; peace pole(s); pentagram; philosophers' stone; pillars of the universe; Pisces; planchette; planetary hours; planets as gods, the; portent; precognition; prediction; prefiguration; premonition; prodigy; prognostication; prophecy, general; psi; psychic(s); psychic healing; psychic reading; psychomancy; psychometry; psychonautics; pyramidology; rebirthing; reincarnation; remote viewing; retrocognition; revelation; rhabdomancy; scrying; séance; secret societies; secret wisdom; sorcery, sorceries; spell; spell names; spiritism; star(s); star of Bethlehem; stigmata; Stoeffler, Johannes; Sumerian and Babylonian pantheon; supermoon; supernatural; superstition; "Sword of God"; talisman(s); tarot; telegnosis; telepathy; teraphim; telesthesia; theugry; third eye, the; totemism; 2012, prophecy of; vision(s); vision quest; visualization; voodoo; Votan, Pacal; voudou; wanga; warlock(s); Web-Bot; witchcraft; wizard(s); *ya sang*; yoga; Zen; zodiac; *zos kia* cultus.

astronomy, astronomers: professionals, both ancient and modern, who study the heavens and attempt to learn the secrets of the universe. In biblical times and before, there was no distinction made between astronomy and astrology; those arts were combined, which resulted in future-telling features added to astrological observations. The Chaldeans of Babylon and Mayans of Mesoamerica were probably the premier astronomers of the ancient world, but the Hebrews had their own. Some 200 men are named in 1 Chronicles 12:32 as coming to David at Hebron who could calculate the seasons, pinpoint astrological dates, and construct calendars for dating the religious festivals and for farming assists. Setting aside the early and often bitter conflict of the Roman Church against the Copernican theory for the moment, a surprising number of innovative scientists produced acceptable astronomical work even though associated with the church. It all started (excepting the imprecise contributions of the early Greek exponents) with the Polish mathematician Nicolaus Copernicus (Niklas Koppernigh, 1473–1543). It was he who set the basics that the earth is not the center of the universe, all the planets revolve around the sun, the sun is the center of the solar system, and that the earth is moving—not the sun. Copernicus became canon of the cathedral at Frauenberg replacing his uncle, Bishop Lucas Watzerlode, who had reared him since boyhood. Tycho Brahe (1546–1601) was a Danish star-gazer patroned by both the king of Denmark and the Holy Roman Emperor Rudolph II. His brash attitude alienated almost everyone but he did bequeath his notes and priceless instruments to Johannes Kepler (1571–1630). Kepler the mathematician, theologian, and astrologer became convinced that he had mapped God's geometric plan of the universe and saw the Trinity represented in the sun (Father), the stellar region (the Son), and intervening space (the Holy Spirit). He personally witnessed the Great Comet of 1577 and a lunar eclipse in 1580. Next came the Italian Giordano Bruno (?1548–1600). Bruno was a mathematician, astrologer, hermeticist, and (amazingly) a Dominican monk. Because of his Copernican support and other eccentricities, he was excommunicated and burned at the stake. The great Galileo arrived a bit later. *See also* adjacent possible; Age of Aquarius; Apophis asteroid; Aries; Aristarchus; astrolabe;

Berossus; celestial disturbances; astrology, astrologers; blazing mountain, a; blazing star; blood moon(s); Blue Star prophecy; *Book of the Hopi;* celestial disturbances; cosmogony; cosmology; comet ISON; constellations; Copernicus, Nicolaus; cosmology; Cusa, Nicholas; cosmic cross; cosmology; Dark Rift; Day of Purification; Day Star; destruction of heaven and earth by fire; Dominic; Draco; eclipse(s); eschatology, eschatological; Fabricius, David; fallen star; Fifth World, the; Flat Earth Society; Fourth Density; four winds of heaven; galactic alignment; galactic superwave; Galilei, Galileo; Gochihr; God Particle, the; Great Change, Prophecy of the; Great Shaking, the; great sign, the; Hale-Bopp comet; Halley's comet; heaven and earth destroyed; heavenly bodies; Hercolubus; hosts of heaven; Hydra; impact event; Jupiter; *Jupiter Effect, The;* Kant, Immanuel; *khemeia;* Magi; Mars; Mercury; moon; Morning Star, the; Nemesis; new heaven and new earth; Nibiru; Olivet Discourse, the; Omphalos Hypothesis; Orion; ouroboros; pillars of the universe; Pisces; Planet 9; planets as gods, the; Pluto; polar shift; procession of the equinoxes; redshift; Saturn; Shekinah glory; Shift, the; signs in heaven; sign of the Son of Man, the; Smyth, Charles Piazzi; star(s); star of Bethlehem; Stoeffler, Johannes; sun; supermoon; "Sword of God"; three levels of heaven; 2012, prophecy of; UFO; Uranus; Venus; Virgo; voice out of heaven; war in heaven; "wonders in the heavens and in the earth"; Wormwood; zodiac.

Astrum Argentum: a fake Satan worshipping group founded by the notorious Aleister Crowley known for its deviant orgies at the Abbey of Theleme in Sicily. Sex and drugs were a huge appeal to its perverse followers. At Crowley's funeral there, the "Hymn to Satan" was sung over the corpse. *See also* Crowley, Aleister; cult(s); idolatry; occult, occultic; Satanism; Thelema.

Asyncritus: a Christian to whom Paul sent greetings (Rom. 16:14).

Atbash: an ancient cipher (from ca. 500 B.C.) and one of the world's most ancient code systems. The technique employed was a rather simple one in which the first letter of a text are substituted with the last, then the second by the next-to-last, and so on. A Jewish version has long been in use by the Qabbalists and some scholars speculate it could have been employed in some of the Dead Sea manuscripts. *See also* Babylon, Babylonians; Leb Kamiah; Qabbala; Sheshack.

Ateret Cohanim: a Jewish yeshiva established (in 1978) in the Muslim quarter of Old East Jerusalem. The name means literally "crown of the priests." The settlers actively encourage fellow Jews to inhabit in the controversial section as they consider it their grant from God before the land was taken from them by Rome and later by the Palestinian population. *See also* Jerusalem, landmarks of; Judaism; religious organizations.

Athaliah: the daughter of wicked Queen Jezebel and Ahab. She became the seventh ruler of Judah—the only female to rule in either the North or South (841–835 B.C.). She gained the throne almost by default because her son Ahaziah was killed during Jehu's purge in Israel. Athaliah nearly succeeded in turning Israel to Baal worship as her mother had wanted. Instead, the faithful priest Jehoiada and his helpers managed to save the young crown Prince Joash from her efforts to exterminate the true kingly line of David. The wicked queen mother even murdered the remainder of her own sons and grandsons to further secure her position. When Joash attained the age of seven, the hated Athaliah was deposed and slain in the Court of the Temple. *See also* Jehoiada; Jehosheba; Joash; kings of Israel and Judah; kings of Israel and Judah in foreign relations; queen(s).

athame: the ceremonial knife used in Wiccan ritual, usually within the magic circle and the possession of a single person. The handle of the blade is either black (for black magic) or white (for white magic). Four other items are central to the

Wicca Sabbat when enacted as a group—the sword, wand, pentacle, and cup (chalice). *See also besom;* boline; idolatry; Sabbat; Wicca; witch(es); witch cake; witchcraft.

Athanasian Creed: the *Quicunque Vult,* a statement of belief popular with Christian churches since the sixth century. Possibly, it was composed as a hymn, a theory borne out by its simplicity and beauty of expression in the Greek language. The Athanasian Creed is Trinitarian based and differs from the Apostolic and Nicene formulas in that it carries a series of *anathemas* for condemnations or those who would disavow its precepts. This statement of faith is somewhat more detailed and of greater length than others equally famous. *See also* Apostle's Creed; confession(s) of faith; liturgical year; Nicene Creed.

Athanasius: bishop of Alexandria (ca. A.D. 293-373). He was the main church father in opposition of Arianism and successfully argued that God the Father and Son are equal and inseparable in their natures. This doctrine, which became standard for the Church, insists that Jesus is of the same essence as God—not merely "like" God. Athanasius was a fiery crusader against Christian heresies of all descriptions but managed to be personally involved with many of them. Athanasius wrote the *Life of Anthony,* supposedly a biography of Antony the mystic who was much respected in the early monastic communities. Actually, the book was a fabrication that helped its author overpower ecclesiastical rivals to his position, continue his battle against Arianism, maintain favor with Emperor Constantine, and establish his canon of the Scriptures. Despite the ascribed name, he was likely not the author of the Athanasian Creed, which was post-Augustinian in composition. Athanasius was then the chief opponent of Arianism. His formulation of the canon included twenty-six books, including the Revelation. *See also* Antony; Arianism; Arius; Cappadocian fathers; Coptic Church; Councils of Nicea; liturgical year.

atheism, atheist(s): a conviction of non-belief in the existence of God and those who adhere to that idea. Such practitioners are considered foolish within the pages of the Bible (Ps. 10:4; Rom. 8:7). Atheism is technically and administratively organized enough to have some influence on the political and religious scenes of our time. They failed in 2014, however, to ban sectarian prayers at public meetings (*Greece vs. Galloway*), to block the arts-and-crafts retailer Holly Lobby in its bid to refuse contraceptives to some employees, to remove "In God We Trust" from currency, to end tax breaks for clergy housing, and to remove a cross-shaped relic from the Ground Zero Memorial and Museum in New York City. Aid from the American Civil Liberties Union to atheist groups is not exceptional. Some theologians declare (probably incorrectly) that there are no true atheists because the human psyche is denied the power to resist the call of God, especially in emergencies. That thought has given birth to the long-quoted military expression, "There are no atheists in foxholes." *See also* agnosticism, agnostic(s); antitheism; apatheist; areligious; atheism, the new; Brights, the; Dawkins, Richard; deism; meta-atheist; O'Hair, Madelyn Murray; Nietzsche, Frederich; possibilianism; Randi, James; Russell, Bertram; scoffers; theism.

atheism, the new: a modern philosophical assumption based on materialism. All that exists is matter, space, energy, or time—and those elements alone. If any other claims can be made that goes beyond those to another domain must be dismissed, or even ridiculed, as superstition. Hardly any theory could more decidedly debunk Christian theology. *See also* atheism, atheist(s); antitheism; areligious; Brights, the; meta-atheist; scoffers; theism.

Athena: in Greek mythology, the goddess of wisdom, skill, the arts, industry, and warfare. The Romans knew her as Minerva. She was worshiped extensively at Pergamum (Rev. 2:12–17) and was the patron goddess of Athens. Images portray her in battle dress sporting a spear and the recognizable Athenian helmet. *See also* Olympian pantheon; idol(s); Parthenon; owl of Minerva.

Athenagoras: a Greek philosopher (second century) who converted to Christianity. His apology for the faith was completed about A.D. 177 and presented to the emperors Marcus Aurelius and Commodus. *See also* philosophy of the Greeks.

Atlantis: mythical island or continent of unknown location first mentioned by Plato in his *Timaeus* and *Critias*. Plato describes in some detail its sinking into the sea in 9600 B.C. after a giant cataclysm of some description. Another reference to the mysterious island is from Berossus, the Babylonian priest contained in a charred fragment from the burned Library of Alexandria who estimated the time between creation and the great flood to be 432,000 years. Other ancient cultures speak of civilizations 11,200 to 13,000 years ago. Aristotle doubted his teacher's claim concerning the lost continent but the theory later gained support from Plutarch, Diodorus of Sicily, Theopompus, and even Josephus. Atlantis was supposedly ruled by ten god-kings or philosopher-kings called "sons of God" and considered the epitome of quality human leadership. Lost continents have been a magnet for the more metaphysical theorists and New Age thinkers. According to a number of New Age mystics and believers of the Mayan doomsday prophecy, ancient Atlantis was destroyed on July 27, 9792 B.C. with only a few surviving priests of the old learning managing to escape. Several New Agers further assert that the destruction was caused by a polar shift, something akin to what some said would again occur on December 21, 2012. The collected knowledge from the survivors was supposedly stored in the labyrinth (the Circle of Gold) in Egypt from where it was later dispersed to future generations and cultures, including the Maya and even as distant as the Far East. The site of the ancient continent, if it exists, is being diligently researched today. The location of Atlantis is a topic of fierce debate among those who believe in its existence. Some claim it can be found in the Mediterranean (Plato said it was near the Pillars of Hercules—the Straits of Gibraltar), somewhere in the Atlantic, the Caribbean, or may even be a belt of interconnected islands around the Equator. It may bear some relationship to other legendary civilizations during or near in time to the existence of the lost continent known as Lemuria (Mu) in the Pacific. In fact, some archeologists are intrigued with the idea that three or four proto-Sumerian cultures of highly advanced civilization have existed even millions of years in the past. They site not only Lemuria but also the Rama in the Indian Ocean (the East) and the Osirian Empire, which was pre-Egyptian located in the Mediterranean Basin and North Africa. There is speculation that these land masses and cultures saw frequent periods of peace and war amongst themselves (perhaps using nuclear weapons and advanced technology) until all were demolished. The huge continents (for that is what they are usually alleged to be) were extant in the far, far distant pre-cataclysmic past and were ruled not by men but the "gods," whoever or whatever they were. The story of Atlantis, whether myth or fact, is an important lesson in prophecy. Here was a people who had everything—political, economic, and military power, advanced technology, global respect, an advanced culture, and unbelievable wealth—but who degraded into moral and abusive depravity, ending in inevitable destruction. The lesson is truly prophetic for it could model or own civilization. *See also* Berossus; Donnelly, Ignatius; giant(s); Hercolubus; idolatry; Ignatius; Lemuria; New Age religion; New Atlantis; orichalc; Plato; polar shift; 2012 prophecy, advocates of; Thule Society; *Titanomachy*.

Atlas: mystical Titan governing the arts of astronomy and navigation. As a loser in the war with the Olympians, Zeus sentenced Atlas to hold up the celestial spheres forever by standing on Gaia and supporting Uranus on his shoulders. Other adventures are ascribed to him but it is the theme of "enduring Atlas" that remains most prominent. Today, an atlas is a world map of some description. *See also* Gaia (Gaea); giant(s); idol(s); Olympian pantheon; Uranus.

Atlia Vendita: the publicized fear of some Roman Catholic leaders that a Masonic conspiracy is afoot to usurp the church. The literal *Atlia Vendita* is a 19th century document from Italy written by a high official of the Carbonari—a secret revolutionary society supposedly associated with Freemasonry. In it lies the blueprint (it is believed) for infiltrating the Vatican to finally elevate naturalism, atheism, deism, and Freemasonry as supreme. *See also* conspiracy theorists; Carbonari; Freemasonry; "Protocols of the Elders of Zion"; Roman Catholic Church; Roman Phalanx; secret societies; *Simonini Letter*.

atone for wickedness, to: one of the six major goals named in Daniel 9:20–24 that God desires to accomplish before final victory over evil is declared. Despite Christ's sacrifice, not all humanity respects God's redemptive measures; instead, they insist on perpetuating wickedness in the world. Someday that atrocity will be ended. Some see the final end time persecution of the Jews as their last sacrifice (of themselves) before the remnant is saved. *See also* atonement; Big Six Clauses, the; anoint the most holy; end sin; finish transgression; inaugurate eternal righteousness; seal up vision and prophecy.

atonement: the act of paying the penalty of the guilty by act of the innocent—reconciliation between adverse parties. Paul asserted that atonement is the cardinal doctrine that Christ had atoned for the sins of humanity via his blood sacrifice as propitiation from sin and death (Rom. 3:25). Popular adaptation sometimes renders the word as at-one-ment. Other terms for the same action include expiation and propitiation. Many theologians, however, see all the atonement ideals to be limited in expression.

They feel there is no real way to make a penal substitution or vicarious punishment, as though the victims were paying a penalty while the sinner goes free. God Himself "expiates" or "atones" for sin by purging or covering it in His own mysterious way in the sacrifice of the Son. *See also* absolution; atone for wickedness, to; Atonement, Day of; Evangelical Alliance; exchange motif; exemplar motif; propitiation; ransom theory of atonement; recapitulation theory of atonement; reconciliation; rector motif; redemption; sacrifice; salvation; satisfaction theory of atonement; shrive; sin(s); TULIP; vicarious atonement; victor motif.

atonement cover. See atoning cover; mercy seat.

Atonement, Day of: officially called *Yom Kippur*, one of the two "high holy days" of Judaism. The holy day begins nine days after the start of Rosh Hashanah. In fact, the Jews consider it the most solemn and fearful of the holidays in which everyone is to "afflict the soul." Luke called the day "the Fast" (Acts 27:9). The observance marked the annual national Day of Atonement for the sins of the priesthood and the nation (Lev. 16; 23:27–32). Leviticus 16:33 clearly states the Israelite religious leaders were obligated to atone for the holy sanctuary, for the tabernacle, for the altar, for the priests, and for the people (the congregation). The date is singular in that the high priest entered the Holy of Holies with incense, the smoke from which was to cover the ark from view so that he might not die. He then returned to sprinkle the blood of the sacrificial bullock on the mercy seat. It was natural then for the Jews to call the festival the Day of Covering. Part of the atonement process during the desert wandering of the Exodus involved the chasing out of the "scapegoat" (the animal called Azazel) represented as carrying the sin of the people far into the wilderness. A second goat selected in the same ceremony, named "for Yahweh," was sacrificed on the altar. Some authorities and historians have calculated that Jesus could have been born on the Day of Atonement and executed at Passover, a not unreasonable if unproven speculation. *See also* atonement; Azazel; book of life; book of death; Days of Awe; feasts and special days of Judaism; High Holy Days; Judaism; ritual defilement; *Rosh Hashanah*; ten days of awe.

atoning cover: the "lid" or heavy cover over the ark of the covenant. That name may be used interchangeably with the *mercy seat*. *See also* ark of the covenant; mercy seat.

Atrahasis. See Utnapishtim.

atrahasis: a technical term meaning "extra wise" or the equivalent. The word could be used to describe the Hebrew prophets, especially Daniel, Solomon, Agur, Job, and Melchizedek. The term can also relate to demi-gods like the Babylonian Utnapishtim. *See also* Ahithophel; Amenemope; amora; Assemblies of the Wise; Azariah as exile; Babylonian Job, the; Chaldea, Chaldeans; Dan'el; Daniel; elder(s); ensi; Ethan; Hananiah the exile; *Hasidim;* Hushai; Jesus ben Sirach; Job as afflicted wise man; Lemuel; Magi; *Maskilim;* Massa; Melchizedek; Mishael; prophet(s); prophetess(es); Solomon; Utnapishtim; wisdom; wise, the; wise woman, a; zaddik.

Attalus: brother to Eumanes, the king of Pergamum during the time of Antiochus IV Epiphanes. Antiochus hired both men to assist him with mercenary troops so that he could usurp the Seleucid throne. The incident is most likely reflected in Daniel 11:21–24. *See also* Eumanes; king(s).

Atta, Mohammed: infamous leader of the nineteen hijackers responsible for the 9/11 attacks on the World Trade Center, the Pentagon, and another unknown target in 2001. *See also* al-Qaeda; anti-Semitic; Islam; terrorism; terrorist(s).

attending spirit(s): a subordinate angelic or demonic agent that supports and serves a higher authority. They are known in Scripture to inspire and influence in both the supernatural and mundane worlds. *See also* angel(s); authorities; banshee;

bogle; brownies; bugbears; clurichauns; daemons; deceiving spirits; demons, demonic; devils; disa; Dogon Nommos; dryad(s); elemental(s); evil (unclean) spirit(s); fairy, fairies; fallen angel(s); familiar spirits; frog(s); Furies; ghost(s); ghoul; gnome(s); Green Man, the; Gregori; hobgoblins; homunculus; household deities; huldafolk; idol(s); Lares; leprechaun(s); Loa Loas; Manes; mythological beasties, elementals, monsters, and spirit animals; nereid; nisse; nymph(s); nyx; Olympian pantheon; Oniropompi; Orisha; Oya; para; paredri; penates; power(s); Robin Goodfellow; satyr; Seelie Court, Unseelie Court; selkie; Sidhe; sirens; sprite(s); sylph(s); spirit guide; spirits in prison; spiritual warfare; sprite(s); Tartarus; teraphim; territorial spirits; thrones; Trickster; Tuatha de Danann; tutelary; undine; wight(s).

Attis: mythical god and consort of Cybele, one of the "resurrection gods." It seems Cybele rejected the sexual overtures of Zeus and in revenge, the chief god spilled his seed on the sleeping Cybele. She birthed a fierce demon named Agdistis; the gods castrated him in order to control his rampages. An almond tree sprang from the blood, the fruit of which was taken by Nana, daughter of the river god Sangarius, and produced Attis. The young man was handsome and desired by Cybele, but she was ignored by him. In jealousy, Cybele drove the young man insane, causing him to castrate himself, an act that became ingrained in the resulting cult. Attis was reborn from the blood in a pine tree (a story with several variations of legend) and a public festival celebrating the life, death, and resurrection sprang up in Greek and Roman society. One distinguishing feature of Attis worship centered on the baptism in blood (*taurobolium*) of a sacrificial bull—a ritual more often attached to Mithraism. The most zealous of devotees, the Galli priests, castrated themselves in devotion, spoke in falsetto, and wore gay women's clothing. The Christian apologist, Origen, did the same.

See also Cybele; idol(s); Mithraism; mythological beasties, elementals, monsters, and spirit animals; "resurrection gods"; Olympian pantheon; *taurobolium;* tauroctony.

attractional church. See church models.

attrition: 1. the beginning of repentance in medieval theology. The fear of God's punishment may lead to contrition. 2. a loss of church membership or enrollment, usually at a slower pace than that caused by a split in the fellowship. 3. imperfect repentance for sin, possibly due to fear of punishment or acute discomfort from the sin itself. Such incomplete measures are usually ascribed as a violation of true contrition.

audition: an auditory revelation from God, presumably without visual cues. Some of the prophets received their instructions in this manner some of the time. *See also* anthropomancy; apotropaic magic; aretology; Ariosophy; astronomy, astronomers; augury; automatic writing; bagua; belomancy; bibliomancy; black arts; cartomancy; chaos magic; chiromancy; clairaudience; clairsentience; clairvoyance; cleromancy; cone of power; conjure; cryptesthesia; crystallomancy; curious acts; divination; dream(s); dreams and visions; ecstasy; enchantment; enneagram; evil eye; extrasensory perception (ESP); foreknowledge; foretelling; geomancy; grimoire; hepatoscopy; Hermetic wisdom; Hermetic writings; hex; hierscopy; horoscope(s); hydromancy; idol(s); ifa; incantation; labyrinth walk; lecanomancy; literomancy; locution; magic arts; magic, magick; magic square; magnetism; mana; mantic wisdom; mantra; miracle(s); monition; mystery religion(s); necromancy; New Age religion; numbers, symbology of; occult, occultic; omen; oneiromancy; oracle(s); otherworldy journeys; ouija board; out-of-body experiences (OBEs); paranormal; parapsychology; peace pole(s); pentagram; Polycarp; portent; precognition; prediction; prefiguration; premonition; prodigy; prognostication; prophecy, general; psi; psychic(s); psychic healing; psychic reading;

psychomancy; psychometry; psychonautics; pyramidology; rebirthing; remote viewing; retrocognition; revelation; rhabdomancy; scrying; séance; secret societies; secret wisdom; sorcery, sorceries; spell; spell names; spiritism; stigmata; supernatural; superstition; tarot; telegnosis; telepathy; telesthesia; theugry; third eye, the; totemism; vision(s); vision quest; visualization; voodoo; voudou; witchcraft; *ya sang*; yoga; Zen; *zos kia* cultus.

Augsburg Confession: a written expression (A.D. 1530) of faith intended to set out the ecumenical orthodoxy of the new evangelical church of the Reformation. The document was authored by Philip Melanchthon (with consultation with Martin Luther) and is considered a fine exposition of the general views of the Protestant Reformation. It was presented to Holy Roman Emperor Charles V at the 1530 meeting of the German Diet. Though rejected by Charles, the Confession became the rallying theme for Lutherans, a status it has retained. The most controversial issue involved faith versus work, a perennial theological problem. Luther considered works a hindrance to faith (even calling the epistle of James a "a book of straw"); Melanchthon was closer to John Calvin and viewed works as desirable to complete ones faith. *See also* confession(s) of faith; Melanchthon, Philip; Protestantism, Protestants; Tetrapolitan Confession.

Augsburg Interim: fully known as the "Declaration of His Roman Imperial Majesty on the Observances of Religion Within the Holy Roman Empire Until Decision of the General Council." The pronouncement was the result of the Roadman Catholic victory over the Protestants in the Schmalkaldic War and signed by both parties on May 15, 1548. The truce allowed some concessions to both sides and allowed the Peace of Augsburg to end the conflict. *See also* Holy Roman Empire; Peace of Augsburg; Protestant Reformation, the; Roman Catholic Church; Schmalkaldic War.

augury: a form of divination or the rite of an augur—a soothsayer and natural sign-reader. Such notables could be readily recognized in the ancient Roman world because they carried a short ceremonial staff with a spiraling top called a *lituus*. The practice was common in ancient Palestine as well (and remains in some circles of our own generation) but was forbidden to the people of Israel. *See also* anthropomancy; apotropaic magic; astrology, astrologers; belomancy; bibliomancy; black arts; black magic; black mirror; cartomancy; chiromancy; cleromancy; cryptesthesia; crystallomancy; curious acts; divination; geomancy; grimoire; hepatoscopy; hierscopy; horoscope(s); hydromancy; lecanomancy; literomancy; magic arts; magic, magick; necromancy; New Age religion; numbers, symbology of; oneiromancy; ouija board; pyramidology; rhabdomancy; tarot; theugry.

Augustan Cohort. See Imperial Regiment, the.

Augustine, Aurelius: one of the great (some say greatest) church "fathers" (354–430 A.D.), also known as Augustine of Hippo. Augustine is renowned for his use of the allegorical method of interpretation (although he began his career as a millennialist), the symbolic interpretive system originally championed by Origen. Early on, he was influenced by Manichaeism and Neoplatonism. Augustine, however, limited allegorism to prophetic Scriptures, a practice that was incorporated into Roman Catholic theology. He is also known as the father of amillennialism, which has undergone some alteration through the years. Augustine's great work is usually considered to be *The City of God*. In youth, Augustine was a profligate and reported that much of his motivation to repentance came from his mother. It was she who patiently prayed for him and was given a vision of herself standing on a ruler—signifying the rule of faith. Her son became a Christian in 387. Thereafter, Augustine ascribed much veracity to authentic prophetic dreams and visions. Though primarily an allegorist, Augustine had a clear vision of the prophets' mental picture of the hereafter. His views on other doctrines, however, including Original Sin, predestination, the Trinity, and others, are not universally received. Augustine seemed to genuinely yearn for the real City of God in heaven to escape a world he considered totally lost and feeble. He said at one point, "How great shall be that felicity, which shall be tainted with no evil, which shall lack no good, and which shall afford leisure for the praises of God, who shall be all in all!" Augustine, along with Gregory, Ambrose, and Jerome, are often named the "Big Four" or the "Latin Doctors" of Catholic theologians. *See also* allegorical interpretation; allegory, allegorism; Ambrose; amillennialism; Augustinian Order; *City of God, The*; Doctors of the Church; federal theory of guilt; friar(s); Gregory I, Pope; idealism; imputation; Jerome; liturgical year; Original Sin; Pelagianism; predestination; Roman Catholic Church; traducianism; Trinity; Tyconius.

Augustine of Canterbury: Roman Catholic monk and missionary (d. 604 A.D.). Augustine was dispatched to England by Pope Gregory to preach Christianity to the Anglo-Saxons. He began work in 597 and was soon designated the first archbishop of Canterbury. *See also* Canterbury; missions, missionaries; monk(s); Roman Catholic Church.

Augustinian Order: a Roman Catholic religious order, named for Augustine of Hippo (354 – 430 A.D.), founded in 1244 in the Tuscany region of Italy. Pope Innocent IV sanctioned the unification of several hermit groups, gave them the Rule of Saint Francis as a guide, and authorized the election of a Prior General to lead. Today, the order is involved with a mixed mission of pastoral care, publication, and evangelism. *See also* Assumptionist Orders; Augustine, Aurelius; Barnabites; Benedict, Order of; Black Canons; canon(s) of the church; canons regular; Capuchin Order; Carmelites; Carthusians; Celestines; Cistercians; clergy; Dominicans; Franciscans; friar(s); Minim; monasticism; monk(s); orders; Paulist Fathers; Premonstratensian Order;

priest(s); religious organizations; Roman Catholic Church; Servite Order; Trappist Order.

Augustus: the designation of the first Roman emperor, Julius Caesar (63 B.C. – A.D. 14). Before 27 B.C., he was known as Octavian. In the New Testament, he is simply called Caesar Augustus (Lk. 2:1). *See also* king(s); Roman Empire.

Aum Shinri Kyo. See Aleph.

aura: also called the "biofield," an energy flux said to be radiated by the human body invisible to all but those endowed with the gift to perceive or "read" it. The shimmering, multi-color pattern emanating from the figure is presumed to indicate personality type, state of mind, spiritual and physical health, etc. *See also* astral; halo; New Age religion.

authenticity: the poignant but, at the same moment, the unattainable goal most Christians' desire in their relationship with Christ. The yearning is to be "real" and honest with God and with others and to represent the faith in the best light. Because of our sinful (though redeemed) state of existence, the intense urge to perfection is ever present but never accomplished in this life. Thus a healthy tension is created and tries to find expression that non-believers simply cannot grasp. *See also* Christianese; "in this place"; on mission; story; walk with God.

author and perfecter (finisher) of our faith: a reference to Christ as the one who initiates faith and sees its nourishment, growth, and fulfillment in blessing at the end of the age (Heb. 12:2). *See also* Abel to Zechariah; alpha; Alpha and Omega; Beginning and the End, the; First and the Last, the; names (titles) for Jesus; omega.

authorities: 1. those in powerful or leadership positions, both secular and celestial. Paul admonished Christians to be respectful and obedient to the governmental authorities (Rom. 13:1–7; Titus 3:1). In this context, he further describes God as supreme over such political entities (Col.

1:16) 2. supernatural beings of whom Paul warns believers to beware. These he called rulers, authorities, dominions, and powers of this dark world, or the spiritual forces of evil in the heavenly realms (Eph. 6:12). At the same moment, Christians are to be respectful of those good forces of heaven (Eph. 3:10). The King James Version translates the passage as "For we wrestle not against flesh and blood, but against principalities, against powers, against the rulers of the darkness of this world, against spiritual wickedness in high places." New Testament authors refer to these unseen forces using a variety of names including "principalities," "powers," "authorities," "rulers," "kings," "angels," "demons," "spirits," "thrones," and "dominions." (Authorities and dominions may be the same order.) Some scholars assert there is (or could be) hierarchies among the evil sects just as there are presumed in the heavenly forces of righteous angels. In any case, these spirit beings have unique intelligence and supernatural abilities (though limited by God's overriding power). *See also* angel(s); archangel(s); attending spirit(s); Bene Elohim; Benefactors; Chashmallim; Chayoth; Cherub, Cherubim; deceiving spirits; demons, demonic; devils; Dionysius the Areopagite; dominions; *elohim;* Erelim; evil (unclean) spirit(s); fallen angel(s); frog(s); Galgallim; Hashmallim; Hayyot; Husk(s); idol(s); Ishim; kingdom; *mal'ak;* Ophanim; powers; principalities; Seraph, Seraphim; spirits in prison; spiritual warfare; things taught by demons; Tartarus; territorial spirits; thrones; tutelary; Virtues.

author of life: or sometimes translated as "prince of life," one of Peter's titles for Jesus (Acts 3:15) stressing his role as Creator both of physical life and the rebirth in faith. *See also* names (titles) for Jesus.

Author of Mighty Deeds: a name for God from the Essene War Scroll. *See also* names (titles) for God; War Scroll.

autocephalous: self-governing, an ecclesiological independence that would refute any religious hierarchy attempting to dominate or control. A church may be independent but still in communion with others of like or similar beliefs, although they are not involved in an organizational structure of hierarchy. *See also* acephali; church, administration of the early; church models; conciliarism; congregational polity; connectional polity; ecclesiology; episcopate; faith and order; Free Church(es); hierarchical polity; indigenous religion; magisterium; plebania; polity; prelacy; presbytery; priesthood of the believer; representative polity; rite; ritual; shepherding (cultic); shepherding (discipleship); shepherding (pastoral); sobornost.

auto-de-fe: the burning of a heretic. The original phrase was of Portuguese derivation with a meaning for "act of faith" but took on its more sinister connotation during the Inquisition. *See also* Conversos; Inquisition, the; Marrano; martyrdom; "pass through the fire"; persecution(s); *relaxado en persona*; Roman Catholic Church.

autograph(s): an original document. The history of the written Word, the Bible, can claim no authentic original manuscripts. All of our Scriptures are copies, or copies of copies. Even such reproductions are rare before the 13th century. *See also* Bible manuscripts; Bible translations; biblical criticism; lower criticism.

automatic writing: a spirit-controlled manipulation of one's writing hand to convey the message the unseen entity wishes to communicate. It is a common occultic practice. *See also* enneagram; idolatry; magic, magick; magic square; New Age religion; ouija board; pentagram; Spare, Austin Osman; occult, occultic; scrying; spirit guide; tarot; *zos kia cultus.*

autosoterism: the belief that a person can gain salvation and heaven through good deeds and works. Such thinking is complete anathema to Orthodox Christianity. *See also* Adam; Adamic Covenant; Cocceius, Johannes; condign merit; congruent merit; covenant of grace; covenant of works; Didache, the; monergism; salvation; solifidianism; stone of stumbling; synergism; works; works, salvation by.

auxiliary ministries: those designated positions (salaried or volunteer) other than pastors who specialize in various fields of skilled ecclesiastical ministry. Most ministers (or just as often called "directors") are trained and professional to some degree and are vital to the on-going administration of churches both ancient and modern. Prime examples include the Minister (Director) of Music, Minister to Youth, Minister of Religious Education, Minster of Family Life, Minister of Church Recreation, and many other sub-clerical duties. *See also* clergy; ecclesiastic(s); *loco tenens;* minister(s); music; religious education; supply clergy.

Avalon: the ancient Celtic paradise, also called the Fortunate Isle, a place of feasting, music, and eternal partying. King Arthur of English legend was said to have been transported there after his death and now awaits the souls of all the righteous to join him. Some Christian writers have used the name as a substitute for heaven. *See also* Abraham's bosom; afterlife; Annwn; Aralu; Arcadia; Arthur, King; Asgard; Celtic folklore and religion; Dis; Duat; Elysium; eschatology, eschatological; eternal life; future life, doctrine of the; Gehenna; Hades; happy hunting ground; heaven; hell; Hy-Breasail; Hyperborea; idolatry; intermediate state; Jade Empire, the; Jahannam; Janna; lake of fire; life after death; limbo; *Limbus Puerorum;* Mictlan; Nirvana; Otherworld; Paradise; paradise of God; Pardes; Perdition; Promised Land, the; Pure Land, the; purgatory; Shambhala legends; *Sheol;* soul sleep; space doctrine; Summerland; Thule, land of; Tir na nOg; underworld; Upper Gehenna; Utopia; Valhalla; world to come, the; Xibala.

avatar: one who descends to earth as a god. The "person" may have died a mortal, but if returning, one would be named a demi-god or incarnated deity. The religious milieus of the West do not normally harbor such beliefs, but some religions of the East, particularly Hinduism and Buddhism, frequently do. In Hindu expression, the Lord Vishnu has already appeared in nine avatar forms: Matsya (the fish), Kurma (the tortoise), Varaha (the boar), Narasimha (the man-lion), Vamana (the dwarf), Parashurama (Rama with an ax), Rama (the perfect man), Krishna (the philosopher king), and Buddha (the preacher of peace). The last will be Kalki (the one on the white horse with flaming sword), the final destroyer who starts the golden age. *See also* apotheosis; Buddhism; henology; Hinduism; idol(s); simulacrum; theogony; theophany.

Ave Maria: also commonly known as the "Hail Mary." The recitation is a prayer of Roman Catholicism, Anglicans, some Lutherans, and other High Church liturgy, a direct result of Mariolatry in those churches. It forms the basis of the discipline of the Rosary and is taken from the quote of Luke 1:28, the angel's pre-nativity greeting to Mary. In the Gospel, however, the name Mary is omitted and was added later to the Western adaptation of the prayer. Orthodox versions and those outside of Roman Catholicism delete any specific appeal to Mary. *See also* centering prayer; Church of England; Eastern Orthodox Church; liturgical year; liturgy, Christian; Mariolatry; music; mysteries of Catholicism, the fifteen; Roman Catholic Church.

avenge. See vengeance.

avenger of blood, the. the ancient Semitic law of vengeance, represented in the Old Testament by Genesis 4:6 and Numbers 35:31. It was expected that the next of kin would castigate the murderer of his relative, or otherwise mete out justice in kind, to the perpetrator. It was a form of primitive justice, of course, but the disadvantage is that there was no end to violence and peace was elusive. Jesus had a more pragmatic and kindly take on the law. *See also* blood feud; kinsman-redeemer; *lex talionis;* two sons and the avenger of blood, the; vengeance.

Avesta: the sacred scriptures of the Zoroastrian faith. Within are outlined the ethics and philosophy of the religion and are commonly recited verbally. *See also* Zoroaster, Zoroastrianism.

Avignon papacy. See Babylonian Captivity of the Church.

awe: an emotion of deeply-felt wonder, humility, and respect. It is a proper attitude for believers toward their God and is the proper understanding of the biblical term "the fear of the Lord" (Ecc. 5:7). *See also* fear(s); fear of the Lord.

axceyous: an Eastern Orthodox term meaning "worthy." The word is repeated often in a number of important Orthodox ceremonies including baptisms, ordinations, and saint recognition services. *See also* Eastern Orthodox Church; worship.

axiom: in theological or prophetic thinking, Bible truths or hermeneutics that appear to be self-evidently ingenuous. As such, they should be understood and accepted as truthful. For example, it is a given in most theologies that God is and that He wants us to know Him and to know our future, at least to some extent.

axios: a term in Greek Orthodoxy (sometimes seen as *axayous* among Coptics) meaning "worthy" or "well done!" The refrain is a suitable acclamation after baptism, for example. *See also* Coptic Church; Eastern Orthodox Church.

axis mundi: the center of the world. Its location varies considerably, depending on who presents the idea. Some claim it is the North Pole, the Garden of Eden, Mount Ararat, Mecca, the Bodhi Tree, the World Tree, the Oracle of Delphi, Mount Zion in Jerusalem, or somewhere else special to the advocate. *See also* Bodhi Tree; cosmic tree; Eden; Jerusalem as city; Mecca; Mount Ararat; Oracle of Delphi; World Tree; Zion.

Axum: the ancient city in Ethiopia, where, the natives insist, the ark of the covenant rests in seclusion. The legend says it was brought to that land by Prince Menelik, the son of Solomon and Sheba. *See also* ark of the covenant; *Kebra Nagast;* Makeda; Menelik, Prince; Queen of Sheba; tabot.

ayatollah: a Muslim leader exerting near supreme control of the Muslim states, especially in Shi'ite regions. Imams also wield considerable influence in the mosques. *See also* clergy; grand mufti; imam; Islam; Khomeini, Grand Ayatollah Ruhollah Musavi; mufti; mullah; vizier.

Ayida Wedo: the snake wife of Dambala, voodoo's high god who is also a serpent. In Haiti she is known as the rainbow snake, and husband and wife rule over waters, lakes, and springs. Both are revered as co-creationists. *See also* bugbears; Dambala; idol(s); mythological beasties, elementals, monsters, and spirit animals; reptilian theory; voudou; voodoo.

ayurvedic medicine: a.k.a. ayurveda, an ancient holistic ("whole body") medical treatment from India. The basic goal is to balance the vibration centers of the body through health, diet, exercise, and various purification techniques. *See also* Chopra Center; holistic; homeopathy; New Age religion.

Ayyavazhi: a religion of Southern India in the Hindu tradition. The faith, which differs from Hinduism in its doctrine of dharma and good and evil, was begun by Ayya Vaikundar, considered to be an avatar. Their symbol is a lotus carrying a flame (representing the soul.) *See also* Hinduism; idolatry; lotus.

Ayyubid dynasty: caliphate rulership of Kurdish origin in the 12th and 13th centuries but which eventually became situated in Egypt as its capital. Its first and most famous leader was Saladin. *See also* Abbasid Caliphate; caliph; caliphate; Islam; Rashidun Caliphate; Saladin; Umayyad Caliphate.

Azal. See Azel.

Azareth. See Arzareth.

Azariah as exile: the Hebrew name for Abednego, one of Daniel's associates in the Babylonian Exile. The term means "God has helped." *See also* Abednego; Belteshazzar; Daniel; Hananiah the exile; Meshach; Shadrach.

Azariah as king. See Uzziah.

Azariah as obstructionist: a bitter political enemy of Jeremiah the prophet (Jer. 43:2 *ff*).

Azariah as priest: the designated priest under the reign of Uzziah. It was he, with eighty priest supporters, who ordered the king to desist from offering sacrifice in the Temple in defiance of priestly privilege. When the king refused, he was struck with leprosy and eventually died out of the favor of all. *See also* priest(s); Uzziah.

Azariah as prophet: a seer during the reign of Asa (2 Chr. 15:1–8), son of the prophet Oded. Azariah admonished the king to disavow idolatry and insisted that Judah and Benjamin would prosper if the king was faithful. The prophet's words seemed to have inspired a reform movement of some brief duration in the land. *See also* Oded; prophet(s).

Azazel: 1. a "scapegoat." During the wilderness wanderings of the Israelites, a goat chosen by lot (named Azazel) was imbued with the sins of the nation by the symbolic laying on of hands by the priest. The act was an important ritual on the Day of Atonement for it helped establish the forgiveness of the people for an entire year (Lev. 16). The animal was then carried in relay far into the desert where it was abandoned or destroyed. The name may be interpreted as "a sending away," something "far removed," or "a getting rid of." Legend has it that the Azazel was carried from the camp by Israel's youngest and swiftest runners, in relay, until dispatched at the end far into the outback. A second goat, designated "for Yahweh," was selected at the same time as the Azazel, but this animal was sacrificed immediately on the altar of burnt offerings. In some interpretations, the Azazel is a type for Christ since

Jesus, too, was a kind of scapegoat for our sins. The importance of atonement or sacrifice is vital to both contemporary and historical apocalyptic theology. 2. in pseudepigraphical writings, Azazel ascribes to the angel of weapons or metallurgy (one of the fallen angels now in the Abyss) or a teacher of unrighteousness. In the pseudepigraphon called *1 Enoch*, Azazel (also called Semyaza) is a fallen angel who is bound and cast into darkness because he led rebellious angels, called the Watchers, to sexual intercourse with human women (Gen. 6:4). He is also charged with teaching men the art of making weapons, metal adornments, cosmetics, dyeing, and lapidary. 3. among the Arabs, Azazel is an evil demon. *See also* Abaddon; Abezi-Thibod; Adramelech; Anammelech; angel(s); Apollyon; Asmodaeus; Atonement, Day of; Baal-zebub; demon(s), demonic; devils; Dibbuk; Dubbi'el; Gadreel; goat; Gregori; idol(s); Legion; Lilith; Mastema; mythological beasties, elementals, Molech; monsters, and spirit animals; Pazuzu; ram; Sammael; Semyaza; scapegoat; underworld; Watchers, the.

Azel: or Azal, the termination point of "my mountain valley" described in Zechariah 14:5. Descriptions seem to hint that the place is, or will be, a gorge but one to be subjected to an end time earthquake when the Mount of Olives will split in two at the Lord's return. Further suggestions could name it in association with the eschatological rescue or refuge of the Jews before the last fall of Jerusalem. *See also* Bozrah; Edom, Edomites; Edom, Moab, and Ammon; eschatology, eschatological; Joktheel; Nabateans; Pella; Petra; remnant; Sele.

Azrael: the angel of death in both Jewish and Muslim folklore. He is described as hideously ugly and, naturally, unwelcome in society. Some denote him as the embodiment of evil. *See also* Abaddon; Abezi-Thibod; Adramelech; Anammelech; Apollyon; Asmodaeus; Baal-zebub; demon(s), demonic; devils; Dibbuk; Dubbi'el; Gadreel; idol(s); Legion; Lilith; Mastema; Pazuzu; Sammael.

Aztecs: a Mesoamerican culture descended from the Toltecs. They thrived early in Mexico around A.D. 800–1200. and were the inventors of one of the world's most remarkable celestial calendars. They were also bloody, cannibalistic, and obsessed with time in an animistic and fatalistic sense. Their legends report that the gods directed the tribes to travel until they came upon an eagle devouring a snake on a cactus plant. That site proved to be present-day Mexico City, where they settled. The snake and cactus image is now incorporated into Mexico's national flag. *See also* Acan; Chilam-Balam; conquistador(s); Cortez, Hernando; *Dresden Codex;* eagle and the condor, the; Eagle Bowl; Inca; Itza-Maya; Itzamna; Katun Prophecies; Maya; Mesoamerica; Maya; Mictlan; Montezuma II; *Popul Unh;* Quetzalcoatl; Sun Stone; Toltecs; Xibala; Xolotl.

Azusa Street revival: an historic outbreak of charismatic revivalism in Los Angeles, California, from about 1906 to 1915. The meetings were organized and led by William Seymour (1870 – 1922), a black American holiness preacher, and featured glossolalia and other demonstrations of the Holy Spirit in action. At the height of the movement, services were held three times a day to a remarkably diverse group of attendees. The episodes are marked today as perhaps the singular catalyst for Pentecostalism in America and elsewhere. *See also* baptism of the Holy Spirit; Brownsville Assembly; charismania; charismatic movement; faith healing; glossolalia; Great Awakenings, the; "Toronto Blessing, the"; Pentecostalism; revivalism.

azymes: unfermented cakes used by the Jews in some of their religious rituals. *See also* Judaism; liturgy, Jewish.

B

Ba. See *Ka*.

Baal: the principal false god in the Canaanite pantheon. The name means "master," "owner," or "husband" and is sometimes paired with his sister consort Anath. Baal became a serious rival to the worship of the true God in Israel and was homaged throughout much of the ancient Near East. The Hebrew prophets were deeply involved in combating idol worship, especially Baalism and its lascivious rites. There are many and varied titles and worship rituals attached to the term "Baal," according to the differing programs and cultures involved with his worship and the adulation of the numerous gods and goddesses related to idolatry in that age. The name "El" seems to equate to Baal, as well as to the Hebrew God in some descriptions. In at least one version of him, Baal is counted among the fertility religions, or so-called "resurrection gods." *See also* Anath; El; fertility gods; idol(s); Levant pantheon; pagan practice; "resurrection gods"; Zaphon.

Baal-berith: (El-Berith) an Ammonite god called "lord of the covenant" (Jud. 9:1–6). He was industriously worshiped by the Israelites after the death of the judge Gideon (Jud. 8:33). A major temple for the idol was located at Shechem, complete with a citadel to protect it. The usurper judge Abimelech, nevertheless, attacked the city and set it afire (Jud. 9:46–49). The deity could also be a local representation of the complex and extensive fertility cult in Canaan. *See also* idol(s); Levant pantheon.

Baalehamin: the sky god of ancient Phoenicia. *See also* idol(s); Levant pantheon.

Baal-Hadad: a god of the Ammonites who replaced the Canaanite prime deity called El from about 2000 B.C. *See also* El; idol(s); Levant pantheon.

Baal-Melqart. See Melqart.

Baal-Peor: or Baal-peor and Baal of Peor, a Moabite and Midianite god ("lord of Mount Peor") cited disreputably in various biblical references (Num. 25:1–5; Deut. 4:3; Ps. 106:28). The prophet Hosea singles out the town or region of Baal-Peor as showing particular wickedness (Hos. 9:10). *See also* idol(s); Levant pantheon.

Baal Shamen. See abomination of desolation, the.

Baal-zebub: the god of the Philistine city of Ekron (2 Ki. 1:2). King Ahaziah of Israel was a patron of this idol. The name "Baal-zebub" is actually a Hebrew pun translated as "Lord of the Flies;" the actual name of the god was Baal-zebul meaning "Baal the prince." His consort was called *mea Domina*, "my lady." Josephus amended that the name "God of Flies" accrued because this deity had power over flies (according to both Philistines and Greeks) so that these pests would not disturb or pollute their sacrifices. It is not unusual to find the name as a stand-in for Satan or the devil. The book of *Jubilees* calls him Mastema. *See also* Abaddon; Abezi-Thibod; accuser of our brothers; Adramelech; Anammelech; angel of light; Anointed Cherub; Apollyon; Apophis; Asmodaeus; Azazel; Azrael; Baphomet; Beelzebub; Belial; Cupay; Day Star; demon(s), demonic; devils; Dibbuk; dragon; Dubbi'el; Evil One, the; father of lies; Gadreel; Ghede; goat; god of this age, the; guardian Cherub; Hahgwehdaetgah; Iblis; idol(s); *Kategor*; kingdom of the air; kingdom of this world; king of Babylon; king of Tyre; Legion; Levant pantheon; Light-Bringer; Lilith; lion; Lucifer; Mastema; Morning Star, the; Pazuzu; prince of demons; prince of the power of the air; prince of this world; red dragon; ruler of the kingdom of the air; Sammael; Sanat Kumar; Satan; seed of the serpent; serpent; Seth; Shaytan; son of the morning, son of the dawn; Typhon.

Baal-zebul. See Baal-zebub.

Baaras: 1. a place near the fortress of Herodion, first built by Alexander Jannaeus and later strengthened by Herod the Great. 2. a rue plant (uncapitalized) of remarkable durability and unusual properties, which grew near the Baaras valley. It was colored flame red and in the evening was known to send out a ray of light like lightning. The plant's root was exceedingly poisonous to the touch and could only be harvested by first coating it with women's urine or menstrual blood. The superstitious used it to drive demons from sick persons and reputedly had association with Solomon's legendary esoteric power over demons. *See also* demonology; flora, fruit, and grain, symbology of; fortresses of Herod the Great; herb(s).

Baasha: third king of Israel (909–886 B.C.) who assumed the throne after assassinating Nadab. He had been an army officer, but that experience did not prevent him from losing Israelite territory to Asa of Judah. The prophet Jehu ben Hanani predicted an end to his new dynasty. *See also* king(s); kings of Israel and Judah; kings of Israel and Judah in foreign relations.

Bab: Siyyid 'Ali Muhammad Shirazi, a Persian merchant (1819–1850) who claimed to be the gateway to the Hidden Imam, Elijah, and John the Baptist according to Baha'i and selected Islamic theology. The term *Bab* means "Gate." His teachings were suppressed by the Iranian government, and the Bab himself was executed by firing squad in Tabriz. *See also* Baha'i International; Baha'u'llah; Birth of the Bab; idol(s); Islam.

Baba Vanga: a Bulgarian prophetess, herbalist, mystic, and seeress (1911–1996). The story of her life reports that she was swept up by a windstorm at age twelve and slammed into the ground, eventually causing blindness because of the dirt in her eyes. From that accident, she developed extraordinary clairvoyance, a mysterious association with aliens and UFOs, an ability to communicate with spirits, and a talent for healing diseases. Her real name was

Vangelia Pandeva Dimitsova (or Vangelia Gushterova after marriage). Someone has estimated that 80 percent of her predictions have proven true, including the break-up of the Soviet Union, the Chernobyl disaster, the death of Princess Diana, Boris Yeltsin's election, the date of Stalin's death (and her own), the sinking of the *Kursk*, and the 9-11 attacks in New York City. Somehow, little written proof of her foreknowledge has surfaced. She was regularly visited by politicians (including Adolf Hitler, who got a cold reception). Sometimes she is listed among the Russian Orthodox notables, but there is no proof she belonged to that church. *See also* idolatry; prophetess(es).

Bab-el: a principal city founded by Nimrod-bar-Cush as described in Genesis 11:1–9. The term means "gate of God" and was intended to represent unrestrained and defiant rebellion against God. That attitude resulted in the city's construction wherein the Tower of Babel was situated. Nimrod's violent nature and actions were direct confrontations to the God who decreed that the post-Noahic population should repopulate the earth and serve Him faithfully. God frustrated further political and religious corruption in that fashion by confusing the language of the builders, thus deriving the name "babble" for incomprehensible speech. *See also* Babel, tower of; Babylon, Babylonians; Babylonia; Enochian; gate of the gods; idolatry; names, symbology of; Nimrod-bar-Cush; ziggurat.

Babel, tower of: a stepped pyramid typical of the religious architecture of the period following the great flood. One of the structures was located in the city of Bab-el, where it stood as the centerpiece of the city designed by Nimrod-bar-Cush and intended to be a symbol of God-defiance and political domination. The intention was to build a structure higher than any flood could reach again and as vengeance on God for sending the first one. Activities performed inside were occultic, idolatrous, and secretive. Those functions caused its destruction by God, thus forcing the migration of the people of the time and disrupting humanity's arrogant bid for independence from the Lord and His commands. God confounded the people's scheme to "build a tower to heaven" by confusing their common language, a reference from which we derive the word "babble." *See also* Bab-el; Christianese; gate of the gods; idolatry; Nimrod-bar-Cush; Semiramis; tower; Zechariah's vision of the four horns and four craftsmen; ziggurat.

Babylon, Babylonians: the capital city of the ancient empire of Babylonia and its predecessor people, known as Sumerians. For nearly 2,000 years, it was the most important city in the ancient world, linking the Orient and Mediterranean lands. Most historians name the Babylon of Nebuchadnezzar II as Neo-Babylon to distinguish it from its antecedents in its region between the Tigris and Euphrates Rivers. The area today is mainly the country of Iraq. Babylon was a magnificent city but has always been considered by the Jews to be an apocalyptic code for a wicked or oppressive institution and an area to be feared. No doubt, this designation sprang from the fact that Judea was captured by the Babylonians in 587 B.C. and endured seventy years of exile there. God Himself described the populace as "that ruthless and impetuous people,… guilty men whose own strength is their god" (Hab. 1:6b, 11b. The prophets predicted that Babylon would be violently overthrown (Isa. 13:19), but since her demise was rather plodding and unspectacular, some apocalypticists believe that a new Babylon will be established in the end time, then radically destroyed in more careful accord with the oracle. An alliance of Medes and Persians under Cyrus facilitated the city's first fall, a situation, incidentally, which some Arabs today attribute to a conspiracy between the Persians and resident Jews. The name reappears in Revelation as "Babylon the Great," representing the corrupt and divisive influences of unnatural religion and politics. Babylon (along with many other enemies of Israel) is often cast as a metaphor for

Israel herself on those occasions when the nation fell into idolatry. In such a usage, the term would be a tag name for Jerusalem (and not a felicitous one) in the same way we refer to our own cities as bywords (*i.e.*, the Big Apple, Motown, Sin City, Hotlanta, Foggy Bottom [Washington, D.C.], etc.). In fact, Babylon is likely the most commonly used sobriquet for this embarrassing purpose. Today, the site is mostly in ruins, except for some few Iraqi renovations started by Saddam Hussein in the 1980s as political propaganda. German excavations from 1899 to 1912 have moved the famous blue glazed bricks of the Ishtar Gate, decorated with fanciful griffons, bulls, and winged lions (called *lamassu* and *mushrishu*), to the Pergamon Museum in Berlin; the great black stones of Hammurabi now rest in the Louvre in Paris. Babylon is important to biblical eschatology; it is the second most often mentioned city in the Bible (after Jerusalem) and is named as an empire over 300 times. *See also* Amytis; angel of Babylon's fall; Assyria, Assyrians; Babylonian (and Persian) restoration decrees; Babylonian Captivity; Babylonian Chronicles; Babylon the Great; Chaldea, Chaldean(s); Ctesiphon; destroying mountain; gadfly; Hanging Gardens of Babylon; head of gold, the; hunched bear; Hussein, Saddam; idolatry; Ishtar Gate; Jerusalem as city; lamassu; Leb Kamai; Medes, Media; merchant(s); Mesopotamia; mushrishu; Nabopolassar; names, symbology of; Nebuchadnezzar II; Nebuzaradan; Neo-Babylon; Procession Street; Religious Babylon; Secular Babylon; Sheshack; Shinar; split of the great city; Sumerian and Babylonian pantheon; Sumer, Sumerian(s); Tablet of Destinies; "Tablets of Faith"; winged lion, the.

Babylonia: the region between the Tigris and Euphrates, along with its associated territories, which became a dominant empire under Nebuchadnezzar II about 500 years before the Common Era. The most important ancient cities of the land were Babel, Erech, and Accad. The land, at one time or another, supported the Ubaidians, Sumerians,

Accadians, Assyrians, Babylonians, and Amorites. The area is a flat alluvial plain which could only support life through the water of the Tigris and Euphrates flowing through for drinking, commerce, and irrigation. Nevertheless, it is the site of one of the two or three earliest civilizations in the world. Babylonia was the conqueror of Judah in 587 B.C. and became a byword for oppression thereafter. The capital city was Babylon, a world marvel of construction and beauty. *See also* Akkadian; Amytis; Arioch; Assyria, Assyrians; astrology, astrologists; Bab–el; Babylon, Babylonians; Babylonian (and Persian) restoration decrees; Babylonian Captivity; Babylonian Chronicles; Babylon the Great; Berossus; Chaldea, Chaldean(s); Ctesiphon; Darius the Mede; daughter of Babylon; destroying mountain; Dura; *Enuma Elish; Epic of Gilgamesh, The;* Euphrates River; Evil-Merodach; gadfly; Hanging Gardens of Babylon; head of gold, the; hunched bear; Hussein, Saddam; idolatry; Jerusalem as city; Kebar; king of Babylon; Kingu; Leb Kamai; Marduk; Medes; Media; merchant(s); Merodach-Baladan; Mesopotamia; mushrishu; Nabonidus; Nabonidus Chronicles; Nabopolassar; names, symbology of; Nebuchadnezzar II; Nebuzaradan; Neo-Babylon; "Prayer of Nabonidus"; prefect(s); Religious Babylon; Secular Babylon; scroll of Babylon's doom; Sheshack; Shinar; split of the great city; Sumer, Sumerian(s); Sumerian and Babylonian pantheon; Tablet of Destinies; "Tablets of Faith"; Tahpanhes; Tigris River; winged lion, the; ziggurat.

Babyloniaca: the epic history or mythology of Babylon composed by the ancient writer Berossus. The book consists of three volumes in Greek and, among other notes, sets the date of the Great Flood. It also contains the account of Oannes who, according to Babylonian mythology, gave the "Tablets of Civilization" to humanity after he emerged from the Persian Gulf to provide them with an alphabet and other marks of civilization. *See also* Aloros I; Berossus; Oannes and the Seven Sages.

Babylonian (and Persian) restoration decrees: a series of four Persian law statutes that allowed the Jews to return to Judah from the Babylonian Captivity. History records the emancipation proclamations as issued by Cyrus in 538 B.C., one by Darius around 519 B.C., one by Artaxerxes I in 458 B.C., and another by Artaxerxes Longimanus in 445 B.C. (or 398 B.C. if the proclamation was by Artaxerxes II instead). The 445 B.C. decree is noted as the most important for it helps to place the starting point for Daniel's seventy weeks prophecy fulfillment in most reliable dating schemes. Each law determined various privileges the Jews were free to employ back home, including when to rebuild the city walls (Neh. 2:5–8, 17–18). *See also* Artaxerxes I Longimanus; Babylonian Captivity; Babylonian Captivity, return from; captivity; Cyrus the Great (Cyrus II); Darius I Hystaspes; Ezra as scribe; Nehemiah as governor; restoration of Israel (the Jews); seventy weeks, prophecy of the; Shealtiel; Sheshbazzar; Zerubbabel; Zerubbabel's Temple.

Babylonian Captivity: the historical designation of that period of history covering the exile of Judea to Babylon in and around 587 B.C. and enduring for seventy years (also called the Babylonian Exile). The banishment was God's punishment of the Israelites for infidelity in worship and national failure. More precisely, the Jews' failure to honor the Sabbath or Jubilee years of the land for 490 years (70 × 7) was the cause for the seventy years of exilic punishment (2 Chr. 36:21; Mt. 18:22). In that case, the idea has implications for the seventy weeks of years explained by the prophet Daniel. The Babylonian displacement has become a hallmark of Jewish history. The prominent prophets of the exile were Daniel and Ezekiel, from whom much of the Bible's apocalyptic writing was produced. The term "Babylon" also became a sort of type casting for oppression from ritual and political corruption as seen in Revelation 17–19:10. *See also* Artaxerxes I Longimanus; Ashpenaz; Babylon, Babylonians; Babylonia; Babylonian Captivity, return from; Babylonian (and Persian) restoration decrees; Babylon the Great; captivity; Cyrus the Great (Cyrus II); Daniel; Darius; Darius I Hystaspes; *Diaspora;* exile; Ezekiel as prophet; Ezra as scribe; *golah*; Nehemiah as governor; Neo-Babylon; restoration of Israel (the Jews); seventy weeks, prophecy of the; seventy years of captivity; Shealtiel; Sheshbazzar; *Tisha b'Av*; Zerubbabel; Zerubbabel's Temple.

Babylonian Captivity of the Church: a period of about seventy years in Roman Catholicism after the inauguration of Pope Clement V (1305–1314). The name is applied by historians (and a relished favorite tag name for Martin Luther) because Clement was appointed through the influence of King Philip the Fair of France, and the pontificate moved from Rome to Avignon, France, in 1309. Since then, the alternate line of popes (usually counted as seven in number) is alternately called the Avignon papacy. There it remained as more or less a puppet of the French monarchy and introduced a series of antipopes that caused serious authoritative discipline within Catholicism for some time. Because the exile matched the seventy years of captivity of the Southern Kingdom of Judah, that period of church history is called the modern-day "Babylonian Captivity of the Church," a catchy phrase originally sourced to the Roman poet Petrarch. *See also* antipope(s); Catherine of Siena; Clement V; papacy; Roman Catholic Church.

Babylonian Captivity, return from: the incidents and time lapse featuring the Jewish return from captive Babylon when their seventy years of exile were completed. Most scholars agree that the repatriation was accomplished in three phases. Perhaps it is easier to view the return from Babylonian Exile in that pattern: the first being under Sheshbazzar (Ezr. 1:1); the second under Ezra eighty years later sponsored by Artaxerxes Longimanus (Ezr. 7:7); and the last, thirteen years later under Nehemiah in 444 B.C. (Neh. 2:1). Even so, exact chronology of the return is not as specific as most scholars would wish. *See also* Artaxerxes

I Longimanus; captivity; Cyrus the Great (Cyrus II); Babylonian Captivity; Babylonian (and Persian) restoration decrees; Darius I Hystaspes; Ezra as scribe; Nehemiah as governor; restoration of Israel (the Jews); Sabbatical year; Shealtiel; Sheshbazzar; Zerubbabel; Zerubbabel's Temple.

Babylonian Chronicles: part of a collection of clay tablets, the inscription of which reports the sacking of Assyrian Nineveh by Mede and Babylonian forces in 612 B.C. A portion of the message reads: "They carried off the vast booty of the city and the temple and turned the city into a ruin heap." The rubble was uncovered and excavated in the 1800s. *See also* Babylon, Babylonians; Babylonia; Nineveh, Ninevites.

Babylonian Exile. See Babylonian Captivity.

Babylonian Job, the: a Babylonian legend that relates the story of a Job-like character similar to that in the Hebrew Bible. It is possible that the tale influenced the biblical rendition to some extent. *See also* Job as afflicted wise man.

Babylonian Noah. See Utnapishtim.

Babylonian pantheon. See Sumerian and Babylonian pantheon.

Babylonian Talmud. See Talmud.

Babylon the Great: Revelation's designation for evil, seductive religious and political power as detailed in Revelation 17–19:10. Suggestively, the name *Babylon* means "confusion." As described there, Babylon the Great seems to be a generic title for an institutional entity of two parts: religious depravity and civil obstruction. Often, the former is called Religious or Mystery Babylon and the latter Secular or Commercial Babylon. No doubt, the depiction of "Babylon the Great" is a tag name for the empire of Babylonia, which was a conqueror and oppressor of Judea in earlier times. The evil institution, both in its capacities as religious and secular degradations, is destined for divine destruction near the end of days. One author has described Babylon the Great as the sum of all evil and the totality of all opposition to God. What of the identity for the final Babylon the Great? Speculation abounds as to whether it referred to pre-Roman Jerusalem and is no longer a player (a preterist belief) or if the city will appear again in the end times. Futurists have tied it to apostate Christendom, the Roman Catholic Church, the United States of America or New York City, the European Union, Rome, or some other modern megatropolis of importance. Others believe Babylon will be literally rebuilt in Iraq, a project feebly began by Saddam Hussein and now underway. Some believe the new site will be in the Saudi Arabian Peninsula or another Muslim center. *See also* Amytis; angel of Babylon's fall; Assyria, Assyrians; Babylon, Babylonians; Babylonia; Babylonian (and Persian) restoration decrees; Babylonian Captivity; Babylonian Chronicles; Chaldea, Chaldean(s); city of power; cup of adulteries; desolate and naked; destroying mountain; Ezekiel's eagles, vine, and cedar allegory; filth of her adulteries; "glorified herself"; great city, this; Hanging Gardens of Babylon; Great Prostitute, the; haunt (prison) for every unclean and detestable bird; head of gold, the; hunched bear; Hussein, Saddam; idolatry; Jerusalem as city; Leb Kamai; Medes, Media; merchant(s); Mesopotamia; mushrishu; Mystery Babylon the Great the Mother of Prostitutes and of the Abominations of the Earth; Nebuchadnezzar II; Neo-Babylon; Nabopolassar; names, symbology of; Religious Babylon; Secular Babylon; Sheshack; Shinar; smoke of her burning; split of the great city; Sumerian and Babylonian pantheon; Sumer, Sumerian(s); Tablet of Destinies; "Tablets of Faith"; whore of Babylon; wine of her adulteries; wine of wrath; winged lion, the.

Bacchus. See Dionysus.

Bach, Johann Sebastian: classical music composer (1685–1750). Bach was a Lutheran with a Pietist background but he preferred to write his music in the formal Latin Catholic style. It was his practice to being each composition with a notation at the top of the score reading *Jesu juva*—"Jesus help!," and end with *soli Deo gloria*—"to God be the glory." Among the major composers of his day, Bach was the only one never to write an opera. *See also* music; *soli Deo gloria*.

back-biting: the habit of spreading gossip or malicious slander concerning a fellow church member with the attempt to keep the victim unaware. *See also* Christianese; church abuse; slurs, religious.

"backbone of biblical prophecy": a common phrase, long in vogue, which describes the book of Daniel. The prophetic insights in Daniel are so precise and thorough that the book has taken on an aura of technical and spiritual superiority approaching a kind of theological awe. *See also* Daniel as Old Testament prophecy.

backmasking: the technique of recording a soundtrack backwards, which, some maintain, emits subliminal messages to the brain, unbeknownst to the listener and of disreputable content. Whether artists and recording companies actually publish such material is highly suspect unless it is an experiment. *See also* subliminal messaging.

backslide: a kind of spiritual apathy that finds the sufferer slowly or quickly falling away from true and strengthening faith or to revert to the sinful nature in action. The malady can inflict individuals, churches, and even nations. The prophets constantly railed against it as an attitude of the undisciplined life (*e.g.*, Hosea 14). *See also* apostasy; Christianese; church abuse; "churn" (religious); doors of evangelism; "falling into sin"; frozen chosen, the; lapsed; slurs, religious.

Backus, Isaac: pioneer for religious freedom in colonial America (1724–1806). Backus denounced the standing ecclesiastical order in Massachusetts, which made Congregationalism the state religion. In that, he preceded Thomas Jefferson and James Madison as champions for the separation of church and state. Backus was of great value to Madison in that president's championship of religious freedom. Backus even opposed George Washington, John Adams, and others with Federalist leanings because he considered them "soft" on religious liberty. The fervor of his convictions can be seen in his quote on matters ecclesiastical and political: "Religious matters are to be separated from the jurisdiction of the state, not because they are beneath the interests of the state, but quite the contrary, because they are too high and holy and thus are beyond the competence of the state." Backus eventually abandoned Congregationalism and became an itinerant Baptist minister on horseback. He favored the revivalism of the Great Awakening style and was cofounder of Brown University. *See also* Baptists; clergy patriots; Edwards, Morgan; Great Awakenings, the; Restoration Movement in America; revivalism.

BACON: a sort of poor man's acronym that spells out the distinctives of the Calvinistic or Reformed doctrines of the faith. It parallels the generally more recognized TULIP illustration (Total depravity; Unconditional election; Limited atonement; Irresistible grace; Perseverance of the saints) by substituting Bad people; Already elected; Completely atoned for; Overwhelmingly called; Never falling away. Some add a further feature by calling the ellipsis "the five strips of bacon." *See also* Calvinism; conditional election; double predestination; election; eternal security; fall from grace; Five-Point Calvinism; free will; grace; "once saved, always saved"; perseverance of the saints; predestination; total depravity; TULIP; Westminster Confession.

Bacon, Roger: Franciscan friar (1214–1294) known as *Doctor Mirabilis* (meaning "wonderful teacher"). He was considered a matchless philosopher and promoter of the controversial but proven scientific method of experimentation and testing, even in the Middle Ages. He envisioned such technical advances as horseless chariots (automobiles), submarines, cranes, and fast oceangoing ships. *See also* clergy scientists; *Doctor Mirabilis;* Franciscans; Roman Catholic Church.

Bacon, Sir Francis: (1561–1626) an accomplished statesman, scientist, jurist, and author quite prominent in the English government at the time. Bacon is often referenced as the "father of modern science" and "the father of Freemasonry." He was almost certainly a Rosicrucian, ranked as a grand master, and deeply interested in a new world order. That earned him the further title of the "guiding light of the Rosicrucian Order" as well. His book, *The New Atlantis*, has become a New Age and conspiracy theorists handbook heralding the New Age of man. It was his intention that America to be the head of the New Atlantis as a model of the great scientific-utopian society. Legend says he eventually faked his own death on Easter Sunday, attended his own funeral, and then departed for the East to become an Ascended Master. Perhaps he is best known as the possible composer of Shakespeare's work, either some or all of it, both as author and actor. Bacon has also been attributed to be the source of the well-know saying, "knowledge is power." What is lesser known is that devotees of Comte de Saint Germain claim that he, Germain, was the reincarnation of Bacon. *See also* Ascended Masters; Donnelly, Ignatius; Freemasonry; Invisible College; history; New Atlantis; Rosicrucianism; Saint Germain, Comte de.

Bactria. See Scythians.

badger: an animal mentioned in Exodus and Numbers as supplying the skin for the outer covering of the tabernacle in some translations. The species was likely intended to name the sea-cow or dugong, or perhaps the dolphin, porpoise, or some other marine mammal. The essential meaning is "skin" from which we know women's shoes and other leather products were also made (Ezk. 16:10). The rock badger mentioned elsewhere is a totally different animal. *See also* animals, birds, and insects, symbology of.

Badimo: an ancestor reverence sect of the Tswana people of Botswana. *See also* ancestor reverence; idolatry; Kirant; sect(s).

Baghdad: the capital of Iraq. In former days, it was the city of influence after Babylon and Ctesiphon. *See also* Babylonia; Ctesiphon.

bagua: a fundamentalist philosophical concept of the East that utilizes an octagonal diagram with eight trigrams on each side. The technique of uses involves application of the graph to several Eastern religious and philosophical processes. The trigrams (related to *yin* and *yang*) are frequently employed in Taoism, geomancy, anatomy, interpretation of the *I Ching*, and any number of other Eastern rituals. *See also* black mirror; enneagram; geomancy; horoscope(s); *I Ching*; idolatry; magic square; ouija board; pentagram; Taoism.

Baha'i International: (frequently shortened to Bahai and spelled without the apostrophe marking) a religious faith expression that seeks to unify mankind into one religious and political kingdom. As such, the doctrine is eclectic and inclusive, but in matters of morality and process, it can be quite *exclusive*. This concept of universal unity conceives religious concord, planetary interdependence, and international government as possible attainments. The Bahai movement began over a century ago, instituted by a businessman named Mirza Ali Muhammed, who claimed he was to be the "gate" or "Bab," the forerunner to the "Promised One." Muhammed's successor, known today as Baha'u'llah, called himself the *Mahdi*, a savior type central to Islamic apocalypticism. Bahai practitioners see themselves as the perfection of Judaism, Islam, Christianity, Hinduism, and Zoroastrianism. Their eschatology consists mainly of the prediction of a socio-economic meltdown soon to occur, which will presage a coming Golden Age for which the Bahai will be the base order. There is to be an imminent catastrophic global calamity that will lead to peace. That blessing is to be produced by a *sulh-al-akbar* (a lesser peace") to be replaced by a *sulh al-a zam* (a "most great peace.") The Bahai sacred number is nine and is represented in the nine sides of their

History and Mystery

temples and the minimum number of worshipers needed to constitute a quorum. *See also* Bab; Baha'u'llah; Birth of the Bab; Church of the Firstborn; idolatry; Islam; sect(s).

Baha'u'llah: *nee* Mirza Husayn Ali-Nuri (1817–1892) or Baha'o'llah, the second international leader of the Bahai faith. He was proclaimed the *Mahdi*, or designated himself as such (a savior type similar to Islamic belief), and operated from the sect public information headquarters in Haifa, Israel. Baha'u'llah, for believers, was the manifestation of God for the current age, just as Moses, Abraham, Christ, Mohammed, and Buddha were to their own eras. *See also* Bab; Baha'i International; Birth of the Bab.

Bailey, Alice A.: *nee* Alice LaTrobe Bateman (1880–1949) but operating under the common moniker AAB. Bailey was a prolific New Age writer whose works (some twenty-four books) were supposedly delivered while in a meditative trance influenced by the Ascended Master Djwhal Khul, whom she called "Master of the Wisdom." She directed the Lucius Trust and Arcane School and is noted among New Agers to be an authoritative teacher of spiritism, the occult, astrology, and related subjects. *See also* Ascended Masters; Great Invocation, the; occult, occultic; psychic(s).

Bakker, Jim and Tammy Faye: husband and wife televangelist team in the 1984–1987 period. Bakker began the popular TV show *"The PTL Club"* (Praise the Lord) and an ambitious entertainment center called Heritage USA. A sex scandal and revelations of financial fraud eventually crashed the empire and ended in a prison term for Jim and a divorce. Bakker was released, remarried, and resumed his telecasting career on a smaller scale. He has since disavowed the pre-Tribulation theological stance once important to him, calling it escapism. Tammy also remarried (to a recently divorced co-conspirator in the scandal), made numerous media appearances, supported gay rights, and retained her fetish for overdone makeup—her defining public persona for years. She died of cancer in 2007. *See also* televangelism, televangelists.

Balaam: an influential or warlock in the days of Moses (Num. 22–24) who personifies any haughty, clever, and occultic oppressor. The Moabite king Balak hired him from his homeland in Mesopotamia to hex the invading Israelites as they prepared to colonize the Promised Land. Balaam pronounced four oracles, three pertaining to Israel and one against his own employer, Balak, and the surrounding nations. Each time he attempted to curse the Israelites, God turned this diviner's haughty utterances into blessings. His primary mission, therefore, failed because of God's direct intervention but Balaam did manage to seduce some of the invading Hebrews into sexual promiscuity and idol worship. Something similar was going on in the church at Pergamum so the name Balaam is a fitting nickname because that fellowship was also lured into some sort of false doctrine or bad behavior (Rev. 2:14–16). The false prophet is mentioned again in Jude 11, once more in an unfavorable light. Balaam has become a type for those who know God but prefer to renounce His ethics and pursue material rewards instead. *See also* Balak, King; False Prophet, the; names, symbology of; star of Bethlehem; warlock(s).

Balak, King: Moabite king in the age of Moses who hired the professional prophet Balaam to curse the Israelites as they approached on their mission to conquer the Promised Land (Num. 22–24). His name again appears in Revelation 2:14 as a type for his devious and unholy actions at that time. *See also* Balaam; king(s).

balance scales: a device used to weigh or balance objects or granules against one another. The third horseman of the Apocalypse carries a scale (the ancient equivalent of a cash register) to symbolize his power to control the Tribulation economy (Rev. 6:5–6). According to the commentary from the heavenly voice speaking of the rider, he will be able to control the financial systems of the Tribulation era. "A quart of wheat for a day's wages, and three quarts of barley for a day's wages, and do not damage the oil and the wine!" seems to imply that necessities for the poor will be difficult to obtain or expensive (less wheat for a day's wage or a bit more of the cheaper quality barley), but luxury goods for the wealthy (oil and wine) will be available to that set. There will likely be shortages and inflation to acerbate the situation. Scales also play prominently in the preaching of the prophets who wanted fair bartering. They figure in the prophecy of the hand writing on the wall in Daniel 5 as well. *See also* four horsemen of the Apocalypse; Maat; *Mene, Mene, Tekel, Parson* (or *Uparsin*).

bald, baldness: the absence of hair on the head. In biblical times, long hair and beards were signs of honor and the shaving of the forehead was forbidden to the Israelites (Deut. 14:1–2). Haircuts for a Nazirite were explicitly denied. A state of natural baldness was rare, and when occurring, it was considered a defect (Isa. 3:24) or a source of embarrassment. It was the duty of the priest to distinguish between natural baldness and that caused by leprosy (Lev. 13:40–44). The taunting address by gangs of youth to Elisha, "Go up, you bald head" (2 Ki. 2:23–24) may have been an allusion to a tonsure worn by the prophets and thus a mockery of his office, for Elisha was not yet an old man. Baldness could be a mark of mourning for both men and women or, in the case of Samson and other Nazirites, a source of their strength and unique calling. At one point, the prophet Micah proposes that parents should shave their heads as bald as a vulture in preparation for the sorrow of the pending exile of their children (Mic. 1:16). *See also* beard; Elisha's miracles; hair; Nazirite(s); Samson; tonsure; white hair.

Baldwin I: second ruler of Jerusalem after it was freed from the Muslims following the first Crusade. He assumed leadership from his brother Godfrey de Bouillon and crowned king by the patriarch of Jerusalem. Successors were Baldwin II, Queen Melisende, Faulk V, Baldwin III, Baldwin IV, and

Baldwin V in the short-lived territories called Outremer. Baldwin's problems were nigh insurmountable when faced with a low Christian population in the city, harassment by Muslim brigands and Bedouins, refugees from Egypt, an influx of Christian pilgrims, and insufficient soldiers to defend his kingdom. *See also* Baldwin IV; Baldwin V; Crusades; Godfrey de Bouillon; king(s); Outremer; Roman Catholic Church.

Baldwin IV: a king in the Jerusalem territories called Outremer following the first Crusade. He was a capable enough leader but suffered from disfiguring leprosy and died in 1185 at the young age of twenty-four, leaving rule to his child nephew, crowned Baldwin V. *See also* Baldwin I; Baldwin V; Crusades; Godfrey de Bouillon; king(s); Outremer; Roman Catholic Church.

Baldwin V: the final king in the Jerusalem kingdom called Outremer, a ruler in title only. He was only nine when he was crowned at the death of his uncle, Baldwin IV, leaving the kingdom in utter disarray and vulnerable to Muslim depredations. Outremer was never secure and its demise quickly followed after 1186. *See also* Baldwin I; Baldwin IV; Crusades; Godfrey de Bouillon; king(s); Outremer; Roman Catholic Church.

Balfour Declaration: a promise by the British government that the Jews would have a "national home" after World War I. The British controlled Palestine at that time and were ostensibly in a position to offer such a pledge. The Jews were to receive Israel, the West Bank, and Jordan. The declaration was the payoff to the work of Chaim Weizman, who invented a synthetic acetone for gunpowder the British needed for World War I. When asked his price, Weizman asked for a national home for his people. The promise was promulgated on November 2, 1017: "His Majesty's Government views with favour the establishment in Palestine of a national home for the Jewish people, and will use their best endeavour to facilitate the achievement of this object." The offer was subsequently modified, denied, and otherwise changed until Israel, through struggle and war, became a nation by act of the United Nations in 1948. Because the United Kingdom reneged the declaration in 1939, persecuted Jews in Nazi occupied territories were prevented from escaping to any sanctuary in Palestine. Many Bible students and historians believe that the Balfour Declaration, the statehood act, and all other important historical events involving the modern nation of Israel are vital to prophetic and apocalyptic interpretation. Other scholars see no connection between today's history and eschatology. *See also* Palestine; termination dates.

Ballou, Hosea: the son of a Baptist minister (1771 – 1852) who became a Universalist in 1794. Ballou, as the most dynamic left-leaning leader of the sect, pushed the denomination to full universalism and closer to the even more radical Unitarianism away from a belief in hell, the Trinity, the divinity of Christ, authority of the Bible, and other fundamental doctrines. *See also apocatastasis;* universalism; Unitarian Universalism; Winchester Platform of 1803.

balm of Gilead: a healing potion from the land of Gilead famous for its medicinal properties. The product was likely turpentine or some substance with a turpentine base. The term is well expressed metaphorically in Jeremiah 8:22 as a cure for spiritual laxness and impurity. The old gospel hymn of the same name also carries the hauntingly beautiful refrain: "There is a balm in Gilead to heal the sin sick soul." *See also* Gilead; gold, frankincense, and myrrh; incense; perfumes, ointments, and spices; salve for the eyes.

Bamah: a name spoken in derision that carries the meaning of "high places" (Ezk. 20:29). The term is a play on two Hebrew syllable—*ba* (go) and *mah* (what). In modern usage of the satirical intent, we might recall the old teenage angst/parental frustration dialogue: "Where did you go?" "Out." "What did you do?" "Nothing." The high places were common enough in Israel and Judah, most of which were devoted to false idol worship. Though some were dedicated to the worship of Yahweh, the altars and shrines there were deemed illegal according to Jewish law because the Temple is the only proper place for worship with sacrifice. After the Babylonian Exile, the Jews were forced to adopt the synagogue for worship, study, and community gatherings but did not sacrifice there. *See also* high places; idolatry; shrine(s).

Bamjan, Ram Bahadur. See Ram Bahadur Bamjan.

ban(s): 1. something or someone made holy – a *cherem* or an *anathema*. At times, God would declare a specific place, person, or article to be sacred or to delineate special instructions regarding them. On those occasions, His children were not to tamper with the designated items, for they are to be separated and considered to be wholly the Lord's possession. Sometimes these sanctified objects were burned to ash in a fiery holocaust. When the Pharisees named such articles or money, they called it "corban." 2. to forbid. In church history, the ban was a method used by Roman Catholic hierarchy (*i.e.*, the papacy) to deputize civil authority and rulers and utilize them to punish or disenfranchise heretics in the name of the Church. The state could then declare certain persons as outlaws and inflict punishments without trial up to and including excommunication and death. *See also* anathema; anti-Semitic; corban; excommunication; *harem;* Holocaust, holocaust; holy; interdict; Roman Catholic Church; sanctification; taboo.

bands. See Zechariah's oracle of the two shepherds and the two shepherd's staffs.

Bangorian Controversy: an ecclesiastical dispute arising during the reign of England's King George I. Benjamin Hoadly, bishop of Bangor in Wales, preached a sermon (1717) before the king declaring the church had no doctrinal or disciplinary authority. The opposition was led by William Law with some fifty pamphleteers eventually wading into the battle. The strife caused King George to suspend the convocation (Church of England assembly) until 1852. *See also* Church of England.

banner(s): small decorative flags used for signaling, theme emphasis, or battle and heraldic standards. In the Bible, a banner served those purposes but is also a metaphor for praise or a sacred memorial. Psalm 20, particularly verse five, references such a recognition; poetically, certain psalms themselves may be labeled a banner. Song of Solomon 2:4 recites "his banner over me is love." Isaiah 13: 2 is a call to worship. Today, banners (labarum) express a form of liturgy or worship as they are represented stationary (in churches and cathedrals) or mobile (in procession). There are hints in Scripture that some memorials and altars were called banners. *See also* furniture and furnishings of the modern church; furniture and furnishings of the tabernacle, temples, and modern synagogue; Labarum; liturgy, Christian; liturgy, Jewish; psalm; Psalms as Old Testament book; sacred stones.

banns: a formal announcement of an impending marriage within a parish. The practice is now associated only with the Church of England since the Catholic persuasions have dropped the requirement and the Protestants were seldom interested. The prior announcement allows time for civil or religious objections to be presented pertaining to the pending marriage as well as opportunity to investigate the legitimacy of the union. In somewhat less legalistic fashion, an engagement announcement in the newspaper, social media, or mailed notice or applying for a marriage license serves the same purpose. *See also* betroth; Church of England; matrimony.

banshee: a woman of the Celtic fairies who wails outside the home of a family to whom she is attached when one inside is near death. The sound of her wailing is said to be one of the most terrifying ever to be experienced. *See also* attending spirits; bogle; brownies; bugbears; Celtic folklore and religion; clurichauns; daemons; deceiving spirits; demons, demonic; devils; dryad(s); disa; elemental(s); fairy, fairies; Furies; ghost(s); ghoul; gnome(s); Green Man, the; Gregori; hobgoblins; household deities; huldafolk; Lares; leprechaun(s); Loa Loas; Manes; mythological beasties, elementals, monsters, and spirit animals; nereid; nisse; nymph(s); nyx; Oniropompi; Orisha; Oya; para; paredri; penates; Robin Goodfellow; satyr; Seelie Court, Unseelie Court; selkie; sirens; spiritual warfare; sprite(s); sylph(s); teraphim; territorial spirits; Trickster; Tuatha de Danann; tutelary; undine; wight(s).

Baphomet: 1. generally believed to be a head or skull supposedly worshiped by the Knights Templar within a dark cave (according to its accusers). It is also called the Mendes Pentacle which may or may not have been contributed as a drawing by Eliphas Levi in 1856. To this ceremonial magician, the symbol combined elements of the occult, the Sabbat, and the Egyptian god Amon in the city of Mendes, Egypt. It was adopted as the logo of the Satanic church by Anton La Vey. The participants allegedly anointed the head with blood or the flesh of unbaptized babies. The Templars were also charged with worshiping the devil as a black cat, urinating or spitting on the cross, and various acts of sexual perversion such as sodomy and bestiality. What the Baphomet actually was remains an unresolved mystery. Sometimes (when not pictured as a head—perhaps that of Jesus, Mohammed, Sophia, a Sufi martyr, or John the Baptist), it is displayed as a bearded horned figure with large female breasts, wings, and cloven hooves. Or it might have been a painted icon, an Egyptian cat, or even a representation of the Antichrist. Some surviving illustrations mark it as a goat-headed figure with androgynous features atop a cube, with a torch blazing between its horns. In Moorish Spain and southern France, the Baphomet is represented as a dog, bull, and goat compilation. Sometimes the forehead carries the pentagram and a third eye. The image can easily be seen as representative of the devil, which it often is in more modern descriptions. It is in no way surprising that the Baphomet is often seen as a Satan symbol. 2. a pentagram within a circle used in demonic or Satanic ritual. Often there is a goat's head drawn within the star. The Baphomet image is commonly used in Satanic worship. *See also* Brotherhood of Satan; chimera; Clement V, Pope; Crowley, Aleister; devils; goat; idol(s); knighted orders; La Vey, Anton Szandor; Luciferans; mythological beasties, elementals, monsters, and spirit animals; New Age religion; occult, occultic; Pan; pentagram; Philip IV, King; Satan; satanic salute; Satanism; satyr; Wicca; witchcraft.

baptism: in Christianity, the act of immersion (or a more superficial contact in some traditions) using water as a sign of one's newly acquired faith in Christ. It can also represent repentance, cleansing, or the infusion of the Holy Spirit on the confirmand. In Judaism, the act of immersion is a ceremonial ritual for a proselyte received into the Jewish faith by the use of the *mikveh* (baptism pool), or to ritually cleanse the priest in preparation for sacral duties. The official Eastern Orthodox typically combines baptism with chrismation. The crossing of the Red (Reed) Sea and the Jordan River often typifies a sort of "baptism" representing cleansing or salvation. The word has prophetic implications because John the Baptist spoke of the act (Lk. 3:16) as a baptism not only of water but also of fire. The Holy Spirit could be active in the baptized person, including Jesus, who was baptized by John, and the "fire" of apocalyptic zeal could sometimes be manifest after the act. Why Jesus would desire baptism (since he was sinless and already in possession of the Holy Spirit) has been a mystery for the Church. Most likely, he allowed the act in deference to the expectation that a religious leader must be baptized (Lev. 8:6; Ex. 29:4; Mt. 3:16) in order for him to assume his position as a priest of Melchizedekian order (Ps. 110:4; Heb. 5:8–10; 6:20) when he attained the age of thirty. For information, the act of pouring water over the baptized person is called affusion; sprinkling is termed aspersion; and complete immersion gains from the Greek word *baptizo,* meaning to "go under" or "sink." Doctrinal splits among various Christian denominations have occurred over these very questions of mode and meaning, along with the perennial dispute as to whether or not baptism grants salvation or is necessary for its saving efficacy. Roman Catholic doctrine (and some of the more liturgical denominations) includes provision for the act of pedobaptism or so-called "infant baptism," which allegedly removes the taint of Original Sin attended to the baby at birth and thus assures no tenure in hell or purgatory for the child. The act was an early cause for the split between Catholics and Protestants, the latter believing baptism is of no consequence if done on behalf of another or before the age of accountability for the candidate. Infant damnation is one of the most vexing and least attractive tenets of dogmatic Christianity. No less is baptism for the dead as routinely practiced by Mormons and certain other sects. Who may administer baptism? Those with authority to enact the rite or ordinance spring from three assertions: 1. only clergy may baptize. This limitation seems to place a distinction between laity and clergy that is not emphasized in the New Testament, 2. any individual Christian may baptize. This invites confusion in the administration and organization of the practice, 3. the Church. The church body, usually interpreted as the local congregation or denomination, may permit baptism in the name of the Christ. The problem here is that theoretically at least, a fellowship can deny baptism to one who deserves it or grant it to one who does not, either from ignorance or prejudice. Liturgical churches prefer reserved dates as appropriate for baptism which are designated the first Sunday after the Epiphany, the Easter Vigil, the Day of Pentecost, and All Saints Day. Baptism is certainly not exclusive to Christianity. The practice is found

History and Mystery

far afield in the ancient world including Manchu, Japan, Mesoamerica, Islam, Hinduism, Buddhism, Jainism, the Hebrews, ancient Rome, Druidism, and other instances. *See also* affusion; alien immersion; aspersion; baptism of desire; baptism of John; baptism of the Holy Spirit; Baptism of the (Our) Lord, Feast of; baptism regeneration; Baptists; burial; covenant(s), biblical; credo-baptism; *exsufflatio;* fire; immersion; liturgical year; liturgy, Christian; liturgy, Jewish; nakedness; Original Sin; pedobaptism; prophetic symbolism; sacrament(s); salvation; seal of God; sign of the covenant; sin of the innocents; vicarious faith.

baptism of desire: a Roman Catholic, Anglican, and Lutheran belief that those desiring baptism but unable to undergo the formal requirements may obtain its benefits with sincere aspiration, confession, and repentance. Eastern Orthodoxy will also accept the doctrine but it is not as rigidly defined. A deathbed confession may serve as a practical example of the baptism of desire if all requirements are ethically honored. Extra importance is ascribed to baptism in those faiths because it is decreed to be necessary for salvation. *See also* baptism; baptism regeneration; Church of England; Eastern Orthodox Church; Lutheran Church; sacrament(s).

baptism of John: an immersion in water by John the Baptist as a sign of repentance and in anticipation of the appearance of the Messiah. Later, John's baptism was superseded by that of the Christ's, which is more closely attuned to the doctrine of salvation and testimony. Those who had received only the baptism of John were edified and rebaptized whenever possible (Acts 18:25,19:1–7), one of whom was the preacher Apollos. John intended his immersions to serve as a sign of repentance and way of welcome for the soon-to-be-revealed Messiah, Jesus, his cousin. Later, the apostle Paul met a number of disciples who had been mentored by John's preaching and penitent baptism still practicing that form of the faith twenty years after John's death. Paul asked them if they had received the Holy Spirit when they believed. The answer was no. Paul then proceeded to rebaptized them not solely to contrition but to carry the name of Jesus in the power of the Holy Ghost. Most high liturgical churches observe the occasion as a holy feast day. *See also* baptism; baptism of the Holy Spirit; fire; John the Baptist; liturgical year; Spirit, the water, and the blood, the.

baptism of the Holy Spirit: 1. the practice of glossolalia according to some Pentecostal type traditions. 2. an immersion ceremony that replaced the pure baptism of repentance introduced and practiced by John the Baptist. The Holy Spirit is said to be within the believer as his or her mark of discipleship following the believer's baptism. It may be the sign by which Tribulation believers are to be identified as well. *See also* Azusa Street revival; baptism; baptism of John; Brownsville Assembly; Baptism of the (Our) Lord, Feast of; enduement; glossolalia; holy laughter; illumination; initial evidence; inspiration; John the Baptist; liturgy, Christian; Pentecostalism; prophetic symbolism; "slain in the Spirit"; Spirit, the water, and the blood, the; theolepsy; "Toronto Assembly, the"; tremendum.

Baptism of the (Our) Lord, Feast of: high liturgy recognition feast day commemorating the baptism of Jesus. *See also* baptism; baptism of the Holy Spirit; feasts and special days of high liturgy faiths; liturgical year; theophany.

baptism regeneration: the belief that the ordinance or sacrament of baptism produces salvation, or at least adds to it for the remission of sin. Sometimes the tenet is termed "saving baptism." The Roman Catholic Church, along with others of similar High Church tradition, holds that the act does impart salvation, but many Protestant denominations insist it is symbolic or an act of obedience and testimony only. Even more see it as more than a mere reenactment but less than salvific. Plenteous New Testament references seem to support both extremes according to how they are interpreted. The issue of the efficacy and purpose of baptism is one of the most complex and decisive doctrines in all of Christendom. *See also* alien immersion; baptism; baptism of desire; grace; pedobaptism; Roman Catholic Church; sacrament(s); salvation.

Baptists: America's largest Protestant denomination, even though Baptist roots are in England and its membership scattered all along the religious spectrum. The many groups (numbering in the 100s) under the Baptist umbrella are somewhat held together (though in many independent and smaller denominations) by a common love for reverence for the Bible, worldwide missionary endeavors, and a pride in local autonomy for every church. Theology is wide-ranging, as would be expected in such a diverse group, but most hold to some form of Calvinism and an insistence on congregational governance. Baptism is by immersion and for believers only. Baptists were persecuted in colonial New England, causing Roger Williams to establish the first Baptist church in Providence, Rhode Island, in 1639 to escape the Puritan theocracy. A group of Baptists were later expelled from Kittery, Maine, to Charleston, South Carolina (ca. 1683), giving them a foothold in the South they would never lose. Baptists were very active in securing religious freedoms as far back as the War for Independence and the Constitutional Convention in 1787. The First Amendment was paramount for them, and religious tests were banned. The denominations received a surge of membership and power during the Great Awakenings, both in receiving new members and preaching their own revivalism message in the South and West. The Baptist affiliations have experienced many divisions and schisms, particularly over the slavery issue before and after the Civil War. The Southern Baptist Convention (SBC) emerged as the most powerful after its start in Atlanta in 1845. Black Baptist churches emerged at the same time but separate from the SBC. In 1814, the so-called "Hardshell" Baptists split over funding for missions and other issues. In the latest episode, more theologically moderate Baptists rebelled against the authoritative and strict fundamentalism of the Southern Baptist Convention. The Cooperative Baptist Fellowship (CBF) was formed in 1991, also in Atlanta, in defiance of the trend in the SBC to a strengthened fundamentalist doctrine, control of the organization from the top down, and restrictions on local freedoms. The CBF can be classed as outside the normal definitions of a denomination since its structure is attuned to networking among its partner organizations, state associations, seminaries and colleges, and missionary outreach to under-recognized ethnic groups with a de-emphasis on conformity and political/administrative regulation. Female participation is emphasized (the third elected executive director is a woman), including ordination for women ministers and chaplains. *See also* Abernathy, Ralph David; American Baptist Churches USA; Backus, Isaac; baptism; Branham, William Marrion; Bunyan, John; Carter, Jimmy; Cary, William and Dorothy; church bodies in America (typed); Clarke, John; congregational polity; Conway, Russell H.; denomination(s), denominationalism; Dunster, Henry; Edwards, Morgan; Falwell, Jerry; Fosdick, Harry Emerson; General Baptists; Graham, William Franklin (Billy); Great Awakenings, the; Helwys, Thomas; Jackson, Jesse Louis; Judson, Adoniram and Ann; King, Martin Luther, Jr.; Landmarkism; Leland, John; Particular Baptists; Philadelphia Confession; Powell, Adam Clayton; Rauschenbusch, Walter; Restoration Movement in America; Rosenthal, Marvin; Sharpton, Charles "Al" Jr.; Smyth, John; Taylor, Charles; Walvoord, John; Westboro Baptist Church; Williams, Roger.

Barabbas: a criminal who was released by Pontius Pilate instead of Jesus (Mk. 15:1–15) prior to the crucifixion in a futile effort to appease the Jews.

Baraitas: individual sayings in the Hebrew Mishna collected from other sources. *See also* Mishna.

Baraminology: a creationist theory that classifies animals into "kinds," or *baramin,* as in Genesis 1:12–24. As such, species not of a kind can neither interbreed nor reproduce. The term was constructed by Frank Lewis Marsh in 1941 from two Hebrew words—*bara* (to create) and *min* (kind) and therefore has a limited true Hebrew connotation. Marsh meant that only members of the same "kind" could replicate themselves which likely disturbs the theory of evolution to some extent. *See also* animals, birds, and insects, symbology of; evolution.

Bar and Bat Mitzvah: a Jewish "coming of age" religious ritual—for boys (bar) at age thirteen and girls (bat) at twelve. *Bar* means "son of" and *bat* is "daughter of" [the Commandment] or "law." The age of the young men and women participating roughly equals the onset of puberty. *See also* age of accountability; Judaism; liturgy, Jewish.

barbarian(s): a term originally coined by Homer to describe the language of the Carians which, to his hearing and other Greeks, sounded like repetitive "bar-bar-bar," or as we might phrase it, "blah-blah-blah." Paul used the term (Rom. 1:14) to denote the whole world population devoid of the gospel by naming them "Greeks and Barbarians" (Greeks and non-Greeks in the New International Version). Later, he used "barbarian and Scythian" (Col. 3:11), along with other classifications of humanity, to emphasize the unanimity of the people of God who worship Him as equals. *See also* pagan, paganism; Scythians.

bar-Cochba (bar Kokhba). See Simon bar-Kokhba.

Bardesanes: a Syrian convert to Christianity who later lapsed into heresy, specifically Gnosticism (ca. A.D. 154-222). *See also* Gnosticism, Gnostic(s).

Bar-Jesus. See Elymas.

Bar-jona: the surname for the apostle Peter. *See also* Peter as apostle.

barley: one of the more important cereal grains cultivated in temperate zones worldwide from ancient times. In the grasses family, barley is a perfect ingredient for bread, malt, and animal fodder for the sustenance of millions. It is generally cheaper than wheat and therefore a more available staple. Barley was an important worship item at Delphi as it was burned on the Adyton altar to Apollo. Possibly the same can be said for Hebrew cereal offerings to Yahweh. Certainly it was central to the Feast of Unleavened Bread. The book of Revelation (Rev. 6:5-6) shows it in reference to the rider on the third seal illustrating predicted economic problems in the Tribulation era. *See also* Delphi, Oracle of; flora, fruit, and grain, symbology of; Unleavened Bread, Feast of.

Barnabas: a Levite from Cyprus who was influential in the early church at Jerusalem. His given name was Joseph (or Joses) but was changed by the other apostles to more carefully indicate his character as a "son of encouragement." He was a generous man (Acts 4:36), an aid to Paul when he was still a new convert and still known as Saul of Tarsus (Acts 9:26 – 27), and an eventual strong companion to him on their missionary journeys as apostles to the Gentiles. The two eventually disagreed in a dispute concerning a proposal that Mark should accompany them on further missionary trips. The two remained friends, however, and were co-supportive (1 Cor. 9:6). Barnabas is numbered among the five special prophets and teachers at the church of Antioch (Acts 13:1–3). *See also* apostle(s); Joseph; Joses; liturgical year; Lucius; Manean; missions, missionaries; Paul; prophet(s); Saul; Simeon.

Barnabas, Epistle of: an anonymous work composed about A.D. 70–100 that claims to be written by Barnabas, the missionary companion of Paul. Most scholars agree he was not the author, but some early Christians, including Clement of Alexandria, considered it canonical. The writing is highly apocalyptic and is said to be supportive of premillennial eschatology and set by most authorities in the Christian Apocrypha. *See also* antilegomena; Apocrypha, the; premillennial, premillennialism.

Barnabites: Roman Catholic priests and brothers formed as the Clerics Regular of Saint Paul, founded in 1530. There is also a lay component to the organization. The founders were Anthony Mary Zaccadria and Jacopo Antonio Morigia in Milan, Italy. Members are required to vow the usual adherence to poverty, chastity, and obedience but added a fourth requisite to never seek public office or position of dignity. Besides the normal charitable and clerical duties of most orders, the Barnabites are dedicated to an intense study of Paul's epistles. *See also* Assumptionist Orders; Augustinian Order; Benedict, Order of; Black Canons; canon(s) of the church; canons regular; Capuchin Order; Carmelites; Carthusians; Celestines; clergy; Dominicans; Franciscans; Minim; orders; Paulist Fathers; Poor Clare Sisters; Premonstratensian Order; priest(s); religious organizations; Roman Catholic Church; Servite Order; Spirituals of the Franciscan Order; Trappist Order.

"barracks emperors": a series of vainglorious emperors of the Roman Empire after Nero (A.D. 69) when the military promoted their own as Caesar. The administrations were marked by dissention, incompetence, corruption, and sometimes persecution. The Roman senate was either defied or ignored. *See also* king(s); Roman Empire.

Barsabbas. See Joseph; Judas.

Barth, Karl: Reformed theologian, (1886–1968) a Swiss by nationality. He was one of the few professing Christians to defy the Nazi regime before and during World War II. He and Dietrich Bonhoeffer formed the "Confessing Church" of Germany as a counterweight to German Lutheranism, which had succumbed to Nazi propaganda or intimidation. Barth's most famous writing was probably his *Commentary on Romans*, a treatise that is pointedly absent of any New Testament advocacy that Christians should submit to repressive national authority. A second book, the *Epistle to the Romans*, presents the Second Coming as an ever-present spiritual concept but insists it will not be a physical reality.

See also analogy of faith; Bonhoeffer, Dietrich; Brunner, Emil Heinrich; Bultmann, Rudolf; dialectic theology; higher criticism; neo-orthodoxy; Reformed Churches.

Bartholomew. See Nathaniel.

Bartimaeus: a blind beggar whose sight was restored by Jesus (Mk. 10:46–52). *See also* miracles of Jesus.

Baruch: a scribe by profession and a friend and close associate of the prophet Jeremiah. His name means "blessed," which fits his character since he acted as Jeremiah's faithful recording amanuensis, among other duties. He even preached when Jeremiah was under house arrest and could not do it himself. There is some historical evidence he was saved from the Babylonians by the personal intervention of Jeremiah and that he accompanied the prophet into exile in Egypt. His name is prominent in some pseudepigraphical writing and many scholars assert that at least some of the apocryphal writings ascribed to him are accurate and perhaps even inspired. *See also Baruch, Book(s) of;* Jeremiah's scroll.

Baruch, Book(s) of: certain writings ranging from *The Apocalypse of Baruch* to those numbered pseudepigraphal works counted one through four. Each claim to be authored by Jeremiah's faithful assistant Baruch or features him as the hero of the stories. *See also* Apocryphal Apocalypses; *Apocalypse of Baruch;* Baruch.

Bashan: a broad, fertile plain east of the Jordan now known as the Golan Heights. The area was originally occupied by the giants known as Rephaim (Num. 21:33; Deut. 3:4) and the last of their kings, Og. Later, it was occupied by the half tribe of Manasseh. The area was famous for its pastureland, oaken forests, and fine cattle and sheep breeding. Many of the prophets and other writers referred to the region by name when they wanted to express fertility or pleasantness (*i.e.,* Micah 7:14). Amos referred to the indulgent women of his times as "cows of Bashan" (Amos 4:1). *See also* giant(s); Og; Rephaim.

Basil: called the Great, archbishop of Caesarea Mazaca in Cappadocia (A.D. 330—1 January 379). As a churchman and Pietist, he advanced asceticism with order, regulation, piety, and community as a Cappadocian monk. Basil was a recognized theologian and humanitarian of the day but is also quoted for his insight into prophetic utterance: "in souls, pure and cleansed from all defilement, the prophetic gift shines clear." He was instrumental in defeating Arianism in the East (via the *homoiousios–homoousios* debate). *See also* Doctors of the Church; Eastern Orthodox Church; Evagrius; *homoousios;* liturgical year; monasticism; monk(s).

basilica(s): 1. a place for public assembly and business or legal transactions in Roman times, often featuring colonnades and arcades. Many Roman cities had them, including Rome, where it was located in the forum. The structures are of interest to Christian history because the architecture contains the germs for the later Christian cathedrals. 2. Roman and Orthodox Catholics picked up on the basilica design and have erected numerous churches for worship and pilgrimage throughout the globe. Some are considered "minor" and others "major" constructs. 3. a Roman Catholic Church with special privileges. *See also* cathedral(s); church; Church of the Holy Sepulcher; liturgical year; Roman Catholic Church; Roman Empire.

Basilideans: followers of the Gnostic teachings from Basilides of Alexandria. They believed that matter and spirit are in conflict (dualism), along with the usual stream of Gnostic ideas. For the Basilideans, however, there exists five Aeons of great energy: Nous (mind), Logos (Word), Phronesis (Intelligence or Prudence), Sophia (Wisdom), and Dynamis (Power). From the union of Sophia and Dynamis, we get 365 heavens (called the Abraxas), the lowest of which is earth. Here we are ruled by the unworthy God of the Hebrews (the Demiurge). A Savior is needed to help us break through the Abraxas. For an answer, we now have

Jesus born from Nous to bring us Gnosis (understanding). *See also* Aeons; Abraxas; Basilides; Demiurge; Gnosticism, Gnostics; idolatry; sect(s); *Sophia*.

Basilides: one of the foremost Gnostic teachers in Alexandria during the first half of the second century. *See also* Basilideans; Gnosticism, Gnostic(s).

Basmala: the designator that begins each sura of the *Qur'an*—"In the name of God, Most Gracious, Most Merciful." When Christians use a similar formula, it emerges as "In the name of the Father, the Son, and the Holy Spirit." However, since Islam and Christianity differ radically concerning an address for God, the term Basmala is not an acceptable Christian expression. *See also* Islam; liturgy, Christian; *Qur'an*.

Bathsheba: the wife of King David whom he stole from Uriah, a sinful act conducted in adultery and murder. Bathsheba is important to prophecy in that she was the mother of Solomon and thus vital to the Davidic and Solomonic Covenants and to the dynastic line of Jesse. *See also* David's wives; queen(s).

battle of the great day of God Almighty, the: the official name for the battle of Armageddon described in Revelation 6:12–17 and Revelation 16:12–21, then to be celebrated as a victory for the returning Christ in Revelation 11:15–19. *See also* Armageddon; eschatology, eschatological; plain of Esdraelon.

battle of White Mountain. See White Mountain, battle of.

Baxter, Michael: an apocalyptic cleric of the Church of England in the 19th century. He predicted the battle of Armageddon in the year 1868. The pamphlet explaining his eschatology is unique for the length of its heading and scope of subject. The title alone is some 116 words long. *See also* Church of England.

Baxter, Richard: Puritan preacher (1615 – 1691) active during the religious wars of his lifetime. He suffered greatly, as did most Puritans of the time, but found the optimism to write *The Saints' Everlasting Rest*, now regrettably not often read. There, Baxter expounded on the value of heaven and even includes a manual on "heavenly meditation" that describes this life as a prelude to the better one. *See also* Puritanism, Puritans.

Bay Psalm Book: one of the earliest and most widely used books in the American colonies during the 17th and 18th centuries. The production was an adaptation of the Psalms in such a way that they could be easily memorized and sung to familiar tunes of the day. The Bay Psalms were composed by three Puritan clergymen—John Eliot, Richard Mather, and Thomas Weld—with the original title of *The Whole Book of Psalms Faithfully Translated into English Metere*. The text appeared in 1640 at Cambridge, Massachusetts, from its printer, Stephen Daye, on a press imported from Europe by Jose Glover. Publication ended in 1773. It contained no music until the 1698 edition. *See also* Eliot, John; Glover, Jose; liturgy, Christian; Mather, Richard; music; New England Primer; psalm; Puritanism, Puritans.

Bazaleel: the chief architect of the ark of the covenant (Ex. 37:1–2) under the direction of Moses. Though undoubtedly personally skilled, most authorities agree he was further inspired and guided by the Holy Spirit for his special tasks. *See also* Aholiab; art, religious.

B.C.: the most current but fading method of dating history from the time before the birth of Jesus *i.e.*, Before Christ). Today's secular timekeeping notation is increasingly named as the "Common Era" in modern society. *See also Anno Domini; Anno Mundi;* calendar; B.C.E.; C.E.

B.C.E.: a method of dating history and its events meant to replace, or at least supplement, the more common B.C. (before Christ). The letters stand for before the Common Era, a system thought to be more politically correct and less offensive to Judaism and to others who do not recognize the divinity of Jesus. Nonbelievers are also supposedly mollified with the system since it excludes any religious elements. The acronym may also be interpreted as "before the Christian Era" or "before the Current Era." *See also* *Anno Domini; Anno Mundi;* B.C.; calendar; C.E.

beadle: a church caretaker or usher. *See also* sexton; usher; verger.

beadsman: a monk or almoner who can be persuaded to pray for a benefactor. *See also* monk(s).

bear: a ferocious land animal greatly feared in ancient times, as it is today. In apocalyptic language, a hunched bear designates Medo-Persia in the book of Daniel, the larger hump evidently representing the stronger alliance of Persia with the weaker Medes. Few indeed are the Bible students who have not puzzled at the words in 2 Kings 2:23–24 describing a pair of sow bears who attacked some forty-two youths in the act of taunting the prophet Elisha. Though we may never know the precise meaning of the passage, it may very well have to do with Elisha's recent experience of viewing his mentor Elijah whisked to heaven in a close encounter chariot—a marvel that should not be disparaged by misguided juveniles. The bear and lion are pictured as lying in wait to ambush us in mayhem (Lam. 3:10). In Revelation, the bear helps describe the beast from the sea (Rev. 13:2). *See also* animals, birds, and insects, symbology of; beast from the sea; hunched bear, the; Medo-Persia.

beard: the growth of hair on a man's face. An untrimmed beard could be a sign of mourning or distress (2 Sam. 19:24), and to mar one's beard was considered a law violation (Lev. 19:27). To shave the beard could be an act of abject humiliation (2 Sam. 10), and to pluck or disfigure the beard demonstrated personal anguish (Ezr. 9:3; Jer. 41:4–5). *See also* bald, baldness; hair.

beast(s): technically, animals. However, beasts in an apocalyptic figure usually denote evil men or oppressive kingdoms. Both Daniel and Revelation use the image extensively. The King

James Version names the angelic beings of Revelation 4 and in Ezekiel's vision as "beasts," which is certainly incorrect to solid interpretive thinking. The KJV, in particular, favored a medieval connotation to some of the animals mentioned in the Bible (*e.g.*, the unicorn has emerged in modern translations as the common cow, the cockatrice—a rooster-headed dragon—is now a plain viper, and the satyr is a goat). Likely, the "snakes" produced by the magicians of Pharaoh and Aaron were probably crocodiles (one of Egypt's gods, which made the miracle even more embarrassing to them in defeat). *See also* Abaddon; abomination of desolation, the; animals, birds, and insects, symbology of; bear; beast from the land; beast from the sea; beast, image of the; Behemoth; bugbears; chimera; crocodile; Crowley, Aleister; Daniel's dream of the kingdom beasts; Daniel's vision of the destroying monster; Daniel's vision of the four beasts; dragon; four living creatures of Revelation; Leviathan; leopard; lion; Lilith; mythological beasties, elementals, monsters, and spirit animals; Nephilim; Rahab; seven-headed beast; terrorism; terrorist(s); wild beasts (animals) of the earth; Wild Man.

beast from the land: Revelation's depiction of the False Prophet (Rev. 13:11–18) who is presented as a two-horned monster like a lamb but speaking like the dragon (Satan). Many Bible students label this chief cohort of the Antichrist as an apostate Jew who will betray his people. It is the task of the False Prophet to be a kind of "public relations" guru for the Antichrist, to regulate the Tribulation economy (using the mark of the beast as collateral), and to promote the worship of his master via the enactment of miracles and coercion. He will be doomed to defeat and banished to the lake of fire by the conquering Christ. *See also* animals, birds, and insects, symbology of; beast from the sea; False Prophet, the; king who exalts himself, the; two-horned ram, the.

beast from the sea: Revelation's depiction of the Antichrist (Rev. 13:1–10) who is presented as a monster with ten horns and seven heads, with ten crowns on his horns and a blasphemous name on each head. One of the heads seems to have been wounded but is partially healed. He is a composite of leopard, bear, and lion. The sea beast is to receive the power of the dragon (Satan) and will be mighty and powerful for much of his Tribulation career—the epitome of mortal evil. He will demand worship of himself and Satan and will war against the saints unmercifully (in partnership with the beast from the land). The Antichrist will be doomed to defeat and banished to the lake of fire by the conquering Christ. *See also* animals, birds, and insects, symbology of; Antichrist; beast from the land; beast, image of the; contemptible person, a; little horn, the; seven-headed beast; 616; 666.

beast, image of the: a dramatization of a statue, hologram, or some other dangerous device to be illegally set in place in the Tribulation Temple (Rev. 13:14–15). The monstrosity is said to be demonically inspired to move, speak, breathe, and even make laws for the days of its existence and otherwise interact but is not quite a living being in our common sense of comprehension. The reproduction is a biblical reference to the strange golem-like construction controlled by the False Prophet in the context of Revelation 13:11–18 and all Satan-followers will eagerly or forcefully worship the idol depiction which is in place to represent the Antichrist. For centuries, theologians had no clue as to what the effigy was. Many thought it was merely a statue that comes to life, a theory of more fantasy than reality. Some speak of the image as being controlled by demonic forces, a supercomputer, a mechanical rendition of the Antichrist, or some other entity constructed to harangue the populace and promote his evil agenda. The most intriguing theory to emerge in our time views the image as a prototype cyborg, defined as part human and part machine, established by the manipulation of DNA from Antichrist or Satan himself. Whatever is the best definition of the image, if we can even conjure one, we know it to be the distillation of Antichrist's charm, power, intellect, and malevolence in solid form. With its aid, the False Prophet demands worship of the Antichrist and Satan and forces compliance to the regime's God-defying demands. The construct may be termed an idol as it represents the Antichrist who, as directed by the False Prophet, insists that the thing be worshiped. The description of the object asserts that the entity can move about and speak and provokes great wonder from the population as they view it bearing the mark of the beast. Perhaps it is the dreaded "abomination of desolation" so central to Antichrist's control in the Tribulation? Daniel and Jesus confirmed the image to be the dreaded abomination of desolation, undoubtedly the precise definition in whatever form it may take. *See also* abomination of desolation, the; Antichrist; beast(s); beast from the land; beast from the sea; Daniel's vision of the destroying monster; demon(s), demonic; False Prophet, the; golem; idol(s); singularity; transhumanism.

beatification: the process in Roman Catholicism whereby an individual is said to achieve sainthood (canonization) and in Eastern Orthodoxy where it is called *veneration*. To qualify, such heroes of the faith must have been credited with at least one miracle or suffered martyrdom, or both. *See also* devil's advocate; Eastern Orthodox Church; patron saint; postulator; Roman Catholic Church; saint(s); veneration of the saints.

beatific vision: an old aphorism, sadly not much in use today, intended to relate some great spiritual experience, epiphany, comprehension, or sacred-like moment with God. The prophets and saints of old must have encountered them often. The phrase is derived from the base meaning of "a happy-making sight," which is no more or less than a glimpse of God. *See also* dreams(s); dreams and visions; *epiphaneia*; theophany; vision(s).

beatitude(s): a somewhat poetic expression of blessing in most contexts (Ps. 1:1). *See also* Beatitudes, the.

Beatitudes, the: a series of admonitions from Christ that summarize the ideal life of the believer (Mt. 5:1–12). Each begins with the preface "Blessed [happy] are…" Jesus cited as worthy: the poor in spirit, the mournful, the meek, those who hunger and thirst for righteousness, the merciful, the pure in heart, the peacemakers, and the persecuted who suffer for him. These select ones are also promised heavenly rewards. The Beatitudes are so stringent that they are likely to elude all of us in their perfection in this earthly life; however, they set the program for the consummate constitution in the Millennium and the afterlife. In fact, there are seven additional beatitudes extant in the book of Revelation (Rev. 1:3; 14:13; 16:15; 19:9; 20:6; 22:7,14). Each pronouncement blesses those who read the Revelation prophecy, the dead in Christ of the Tribulation, those who are spiritually alert, those invited to the wedding supper of the Lamb, those participating in the first resurrection, those who keep the commandments of the prophecy, and those who wash their robes of righteousness and partake of the tree of life and walk the streets of New Jerusalem. *See also* beatitude(s); blessed; blessing(s); Sermon on the Mount, the.

Beatles, the: a highly influential rock-and-roll group from the 1960s. In 1967 they became involved in Transcendental Meditation; later both John Lennon and George Harrison repudiated the association. Harrison then became a devotee of Hare Krishna (ISKCON) and recorded his hit single "My Sweet Lord" as a devotion to Lord Krishna. The Beatles are widely credited with increasing the popularity of Eastern religions in the United States. Furthermore, the band could easily spark religious controversy. John Lennon declared in 1966 that his group was more popular than Jesus and stated Christianity would disappear before rock-and-roll music. His remarks caused barely a ripple in Britain where they originated but anger flared in some Christian circles in America. *See also* Hare Krishna; music; Transcendental Meditation (TM); Yogi, Maharishi Mahesh.

Beatus: a Spanish monk (d. A.D. 798) who believed he would live to see the Antichrist and that the end of the world would occur in A.D. 800. Some of his hearers fasted throughout the night in anticipation of the end, after which Beatus was said to have proclaimed: "Let's eat and drink, so that if we die at least we'll be fed." *See also* Roman Catholic Church.

Beautiful Gate: the most magnificent of the three eastern-facing gates of the Temple and the one most utilized by visitors. As do all the Temple entrances, this one has particular apocalyptic importance. It was also the place where Peter and John healed a lame beggar not identified by name (Acts 3:2,10). Some claim that the Beautiful Gate is the recently excavated Gate of Nicanor since the latter was made entirely of Corinthian bronze. Many are under the incorrect assumption that the Beautiful Gate and the Easter are the same. *See also* beggar at the Beautiful Gate; Eastern Gate; gates of Jerusalem; Jerusalem, landmarks of.

Beautiful Land, the: the name for Judah as noted in the book of Daniel.

Beauty. See Zechariah's oracle of two shepherds and two shepherd's staffs; Union.

beauty: the condition of appearing lovely or handsome. In Scripture, the word more pointedly describes the inward person who is beautiful in spirit, chastity, or purity. Philosophers often term beauty as an emotion.

Becket, Thomas: also known as Saint Thomas of Canterbury and Thomas 'a Becket (ca. 1118–1170). Becket was archbishop of Canterbury when he became embroiled in a dispute with King Henry II concerning the status of the Church of England as opposed to the power of the monarchy. Becket was murdered by agents of the king and is considered a martyr worldwide by both Roman Catholic and Anglican persuasions. Pope Alexander III canonized him. News reports from the year 2016 reveal a partial from Becket's arm bone was returned from Hungary to Canterbury Cathedral; more hearsay claims the assassins' remains were buried in the Dome of Rock as revenge from the Knights Templars. *See also* Anglicanism; *Book of Common Prayer;* Church of England; Dome of the Rock; liturgical year; martyr(s); Protestant Episcopal Church; Roman Catholic Church.

Bede, the Venerable: an exceptional historian, translator, and linguist in early Britain (ca. 672–735). Bede (pronounced "Bead") was from the Northumbrian monastery of Saint Peter, although he had been in one or another of such retreats since age seven. His great work is called the *Historica Ecclesiastic* (the "Ecclesiastical History"), more commonly known as the *Church History of the English People* which helped move his reputation up to his later title of "the father of English history." Most of Bede's writing is objective history but his descriptions of hell are particularly vivid. Bede was an apocalypticist who believed that the unity of humanity's speech would soon be restored from its corruption at Babel. This would bring about Augustine's *City of God,* the book form of which he admired and translated. *See also* liturgical year; near-death experiences (NDEs); Roman Catholic Church.

bed of suffering: a threat from God to the church at Thyatira (Rev. 2:22), which implies divine punishment for moral and ecclesiastical failure if repentance within the fellowship does not become evident. The risk of suffering is made stronger by adding that her children (the individual members of later generations?) will die.

Bedouins: a semi-nomadic Arab (non-Arabs are Berbers) ethnic group common in the Arabian and Syrian deserts, but scattered far and wide in the Middle East. Their culture has little changed from earliest times except there are fewer who seek to roam the wastelands for a lifetime. Bedouins claim descent from the Hebrew Abraham and from Ishmael. The name means "desert dweller" but older Bedouins refer to themselves as "people of the tent." They are prone to raiding and have never paid taxes to any government. Bedouins are Muslim by religion but nominally so. The tribes vary greatly in their religious customs and most of them disregard entirely the Prophet's command to pray five times a day and to make a pilgrimage to Mecca. *See also* Arabia; Berbers; Islam.

Beecher, Edward: fearless abolitionist (1803–1895) and brother to Henry Ward Beecher and Harriet Beecher Stowe (author of *Uncle Tom's Cabin*). Edward was in constant danger for his views, for he was president of Illinois College and a pastor in that state which had a heavy pro-slavery faction. Except for an eleven-year stint as a pastor in Boston, he served unswervingly in Illinois but retired in Brooklyn, New York. *See also* Beecher, Henry Ward; Beecher, Lyman; Congregationalists; slave, slavery.

Beecher, Henry Ward: outspoken Congregationalist minister and pastor of Plymouth Congregationalist Church in Brooklyn, New York (1813–1887), and churches in Indiana. At one point, he was called "the most famous man in America." Beecher was an influential abolitionist so radical in belief that he advocated sending guns instead of Bibles to compatriots of anti-slavery in Kansas and Nebraska. These arms earned the nickname "Beecher's Bibles." He, with others of like mind, advocated a Social Gospel message and sought a philosophical synthesis between Darwinism and Christianity. He even augmented his ministry as a Mugwump politician in 1884 supporting Grover Cleveland for president. Beecher had a reputation as a philanderer, and late in his career, was charged with adultery. The trial ended in a hung jury. *See also* Abbott, Lyman; Beecher, Edward; Beecher, Lyman; Congregationalists; slave, slavery; Social Darwinism; Social Gospel; social issues.

Beecher, Lyman: outspoken Presbyterian evangelist, theological educator, and anti-slavery advocate (1775–1863). Beecher was a firebrand critic of not only slaveholders but also Roman Catholics, drinkers, Unitarians, and his fellow Presbyterians who tried to impeach him for heresy. He was the father of thirteen children, among them the Congregationalist ministers Henry Ward and Edward Beecher and their sisters Catherine Ester and Harriet Beecher Stowe (author of *Uncle Tom's Cabin*). All were active in the abolitionist cause. *See also* Beecher, Edward; Beecher, Henry Ward; evangelist(s), evangelism; Presbyterians; revivalism; slave, slavery; Weld, Theodore Dwight.

Beelzeboul: or Baal-zebub, called the prince of demons meaning "lord of dung." The name is found in some noncanonical apocalyptic literature. It is he who aids destruction with tyrants, causes demon worship, tempts holy men, causes jealousies and murder, and instigates wars. *See also* Apophis; Baal-zebub; Beelzebub; Belial; devils; idol(s); Levant pantheon; prince of demons; prince of the power of the air; prince of this world; Sammael; Satan; Shaytan.

Beelzebub: a disputed New Testament name for Satan (Mt. 10:25; 12:24; Lk. 11:18) or the evil entity who is "prince of demons" or "chief of devils." There appears to be no obvious connection to the idol of similar name, Baal-zebub, nor does there appear to be a direct connection with the name Beelzeboul (a Greek rendering) meaning "lord of dung" "lord of the air," or "master of the house." The Pharisees accused Jesus of being in league with Beelzebub (Mt. 10:25) and even deriving his power of exorcism from him. *See also* accuser of our brothers; angel of light; Anointed Cherub; Baal-zebub; Baphomet; Beelzeboul; Belial; Cupay; Day Star; dragon; Evil One, the; father of lies; Ghede; goat; god of this age, the; guardian Cherub; Hahgwehdaetgah; Iblis; idol(s); *Kategor;* kingdom of the air; kingdom of this world; king of Babylon; king of Tyre; Levant pantheon; Light-Bringer; lion; Lucifer; Mastema; Morning Star, the; prince of demons; prince of the power of the air; prince of this world; prince of demons; prince of the power of the air;

prince of this world; red dragon; ruler of the kingdom of the air; Sanat Kumar; Satan; seed of the serpent; serpent; Shaytan; son of the morning, son of the dawn.

bees: insects noted for their industry and manufacture of honey within their complex hive architecture. In Scripture, they are sometimes emblematic of insight and wisdom (Pro. 34:13–14). They can also be fierce and organized fighters when threatened. The hive is a favored icon of Freemasonry and the Mormon Church and was prominent in the throne scene of King Solomon. *See also* animals, birds, and insects, symbology of; bees of Assyria, the; honey.

bees of Assyria, the: a reference to the opposition of Assyria against Israel (Isa. 7:18). Assyria is described as a formidable, swarming, and stinging enemy. *See also* animals, birds, and insects, symbology of; bee; Assyria, Assyrians.

beggar at the Beautiful Gate: a crippled beggar who was carried daily to the Temple to solicit money before the gate called Beautiful (Acts 3). As Peter and John approached, they had no funds but healed the misfortunate immediately. Peter then used the occasion to utter an evangelistic appeal to the astonished crowd. *See also* Beautiful Gate.

Beghards. See Beguines.

Beginning and the End, the: one of the descriptions of Christ in Revelation meaning Christ is the eternal one. The phrase is similar to the Lord's title of "Alpha and Omega" or "First and the Last." *See also* Abel to Zechariah; alpha; Alpha and Omega; author and perfecter (finisher) of our faith; First and the Last, the; names (titles) for Jesus; omega.

beginning of sorrows: 1. Jesus' name for the trials and hardships, which he would address in Matthew 24 and 25 and Mark 13. Some versions translate his words as "beginning of the birth pains" or similar wording. A number of apocalyptic scholars reserve the phrase for the first half of the seven years of Tribulation while the last half is named "the time of Jacob's trouble." Such a distinction may be permissible but not technically necessary. Jesus specifically mentioned the appearance of false Christs, wars and rumors of wars, nations against nations, famines, and earthquakes around the globe. Such catastrophes have always been with us, of course, but Jesus' point is that they will occur with more frequency and urgency. 2. an essential view of the pre-wrath rapture theorists. The period known as the beginning of sorrows is the first of three parts of the Tribulation, to be followed by "the day of the Lord and "the Great Tribulation." According to the prewrath stance, only the last phase, the Great Tribulation, is to be spared from those loyal to the Lamb (the Church). *See also* birth pains, illustration of; day of the Lord, the; eschatology; eschatological; Great Tribulation, the; pre-wrath rapture; Olivet Discourse, the.

Beguines: devout women of the 12th century living in enclosed cottages but without peculiar monastic rules or vows. They were not nuns. The groups declined in the Middle Ages amid charges of immorality. The male counterparts in similar organizations were called Beghards but also shared a disreputable image. Such charges were undoubtedly false, or at least exaggerated, but there were singled out by Bernard Gui who composed *The Inquisitor's Manual* in 1324. He charged the order with expecting the soon and inevitable end of the Roman Church, of accusing the authorities as being "synagogue of Satan," and other heresies which he "proved" by inquisitional methods. *See also* Brethren of the Free Spirit; na Prous Boneta; oblate; Porete, Marguerite; Poor Sisters of Clare; Roman Catholic Church; Spirituals of the Franciscan Order.

Behaviorism: the school of social science that maintains human behavior is determined by environmental stimuli and not by values or rational thought. American psychologist John Broadus Watson (1878–1958) originated the basic structure of the behaviorist movement from his background as an advertising executive who used behaviorist techniques to influence sales. Watson also taught at Johns Hopkins University from 1908 to 1920. Behaviorism, which is not easily compatible with Christian thinking, became the dominant psychological trend in the 1920s, declined in the 1940s and 1950s, then rebounded in the 1970s spurred by Harvard psychologist B. F. Skinner. *See also* James, William; Porter, Noah; Skinner, Burrhus Fredric (B.F.); Watson, John Broadus.

Behemoth: a land creature (plural *behema*) equivalent of the sea-dwelling Leviathan or Rahab. Perhaps the beast (for the name means "beast") is modeled by the hippopotamus or elephant (*i.e.*, Job 40:15-24). The references in Job strongly suggest something more ferocious than hippopotami or elephants; some creationists see them as dinosaurs. Some of the pseudepigraphal writings note that the animal is male even though the noun is feminine while his counterpart, the Leviathan, is female. It is quite likely that the primeval monsters of chaos in Babylonian mythology, Tiamat and Kingu, are renamed Behemoth and Leviathan in the Old Testament. In the intertestamental period, there arose a belief that these creatures (Leviathan being called "the great sea monsters" in Genesis 1:21) were created by God to exist until the end of days, at which point they would be food for the great banquet of God (Isa. 25:6). *See also* animals, birds, and insects, symbology of; dragon; idol(s); idolatry; Leviathan; mythological beasties, elementals, monsters, and spirit animals; Rahab; Ziz.

Behmenism: a religious movement from the 17th century from the principles of the German mystic Jakob Boehme (157–1624). The expression was not a sect but a general description of Boehme's theosophy. His influence stretched to other mystic organizations like the Quakers, Philadelphians, Woman in the Wilderness, Harmony Society, and others. *See also* communal communities; Gichtelians; mysticism, mystics; New Harmony Community of Equality; Philadelphians; Theosophy; Society of Friends; Woman in the Wilderness.

Bel: a title relating to certain Mesopotamian gods, more acceptable in usage than a name. Most often, the designation refers to Marduk, one of the chief gods of Babylon. *See also Bel and the Dragon;* Belteshazzar; idol(s); Marduk; Sumerian and Babylonian pantheon.

Bela. See Zoar.

Bel and the Dragon: an apocryphal writing of the Persian period of Hebrew history (but considered deuterocanonical by Catholic and Orthodox sources) in which the prophet Daniel outwits the false priests of Bel by proving to the king that their idol is nothing but clay covered in bronze. He scattered ashes on the floor of the pagan temple, then read the footprints of the priests and their families who entered via a secret door in the night to feast on the offerings and clean the idol. To defeat the dragon beast then worshiped, he managed to kill the animal by feeding the creature its favored meal of cakes that were spiked. *See also* Apocrypha, the; Bel; Daniel; dragon; reptilian theory; serpent.

Belgic Confession: a creed favored by the Low Country Reformers (written 1561) that resembled much of the Protestant emphasis then being experienced in Geneva under John Calvin. *See also* confession(s) of faith.

Belial: a Hebrew term meaning "useless," or in contemporary language, a "good-for-nothing." (Beliar is a variant of the name.) *The Testament of the Twelve Patriarchs* refers to Beliar as a "worthless one," a king who embodies evil and will be the end time opponent of Christ. In apocalyptic literature, however, the term may take on a personal or definite meaning as more than simply the absence of good. A person might be "a son [daughter] of Belial" or an object might be "a thing of Belial." The closest contemporary word equivalent might be "iniquity" and is usually suggestive of something satanic in nature, and is sometimes a name for Satan himself. *See also* accuser of our brothers; angel of light; Anointed Cherub; Baal-zebub; Baphomet; Beelzeboul;

Beelzebub; Cupay; Day Star; dragon; eschatology, eschatological; Evil One, the; father of lies; Ghede; goat; god of this age, the; guardian Cherub; Hahgwehdaetgah; Iblis; idol(s); idolatry; *Kategor;* king of Babylon; king of Tyre; Light-Bringer; lion; Lucifer; Mastema; Morning Star, the; prince of demons; prince of the power of the air; prince of this world; red dragon; ruler of the kingdom of the air; Sanat Kumar; Satan; seed of the serpent; serpent; Shaytan; son of the morning, son of the dawn.

believe: to accept as true; to trust; to have faith. Hardly could there be a more important attitude for the acceptance and practice of faith for it is the essence of religion. Without faith (belief) there is no reliability or foundation for trusting God nor our feelings for Him (Mk. 1:15; Jn. 3:18; Acts 16:31). *See also* faith.

Believers' Liturgy: a practice of the early Byzantine churches of locking the gates of the compound so only believers could participate in most of the worship. *See also* Eastern Orthodox Church; Mysteries.

Belkis: the Muslim name for the Queen of Sheba. *See also* Islam; Makeda; queen(s); Queen of Sheba; Queen of the South; Sheba.

bell(s): an upside-down cup-shaped hollow idiophone percussion instrument which produces a voice when struck. The appliance is usually cast from bronze or metal and sound is produced from a clapper on the inside or a hammer from the outside producing vibrations of varying tones and volume, some of which can carry far afield. "Jingle" bells make sound with a free ball inside slotted spheres and chimes are usually tubular in design. The device may be located outside a building, either free-standing or within a campanile (bell tower, cote, or belfry), or inside for smaller sizes and milder tones. Some bells and chimes are digitally programmed to play notes or sound the hours. Inside, handbell choirs can also produce beautiful music while other designs promote the ritual in diverse ways. Bells have a rich history used to warn of community danger, enhance celebrations, and to call an assembly for worship when heard from the outside. Inside, they facilitated worship or augmented it. Their tomes and presence are common in many church settings and set for the same purposes today. Moreover, ringing bells was one of the best ways to chase off demons and evil spirits. *See also* "bells and smells"; bells on the horses; carillon; furniture and furnishings of the modern church; house of Loreta; musical instruments; Sanctus bell.

bell, book, and candle: originally a Roman Catholic ceremony used to excommunicate a church member, certainly in use from the ninth century. The bell was to indicate the ritual was public and open, the book simulated the authority of the church to act and scripture to pursue it, and the candle was to suggest that the ban might later be lifted with repentance. Later, the phrase became associated with the exorcism ritual as well. Most Americans would recognize the phrase in an entirely different perspective. It was the title of a romantic comedy movie from 1958 starring James Steward and Kim Novak who played the character of a beautiful witch. *See also* excommunication; exorcism; Roman Catholic Church.

Bell, George: a sort of erstwhile Protestant prophet of the 18th century who declared that Jesus would return on the night of February 28, 1763. On the night of the event, fellow Methodist evangelist John Wesley was forced to preach all night to calm an anxious and frightened crowd and to prepare them for the inevitable disappointment of the Second Coming delay. *See also* Methodists.

"bells and smells": a colloquial description of the elaborate ritual style of most High Church Anglo-Catholic worship. "Bells" note the frequent ringing at various points and "smells" refer to incense. *See also* bell(s); Christianese; High Church, Low Church; incense; liturgy, Christian.

History and Mystery

bells on the horses: the prophet's pledge that all objects of the Millennium, even the bells of the horses' bridles, will bear the name of the Lord (Zech. 14:20). *See also* animals, birds, and insects, symbology of; bell(s); cooking pot(s); eschatology, eschatological; Holy to the Lord; Millennium; pot(s); sacred bowls.

belly and thighs of bronze: Daniel's description of Greece as an oppressor of Israel depicted in the dream of the great stratified statue (Dan. 2:32). *See also* crushing rock that became a mountain; Greece; stratified man, dream of the.

belomancy: divination by the practice of drawing or casting marked arrows at random. The Babylonians were reported to have used the process at one point to determine if they should first invade Jerusalem of Judah or Rabbah of Ammon (Ezk. 21:21). *See also* anthropomancy; apotropaic magic; arrow(s); arrows, prophecy of the; Ariosophy; arrow(s); arrows, prophecy of the; astral projection; astrology, astrologers; audition; augury; automatic writing; bibliomancy; black arts; black mirror; cartomancy; chaos magic; chiromancy; clairaudience; clairvoyance; cleromancy; cone of power; conjure; cryptesthesia; crystallomancy; curious acts; divination; dream(s); dreams and visions; enchantment; enneagram; evil eye; extrasensory perception (ESP); foreknowledge; foretelling; geomancy; Great Tribulation; grimoire; hepatoscopy; Hermetic wisdom; Hermetic writings; hex; hierscopy; horoscope(s); hydromancy; idolatry; incantation ; labyrinth walk; lecanomancy; literomancy; locution; magic arts; magic, magick; magic square; magnetism; mana; mantic wisdom; mantra; miracle(s); monition; necromancy; New Age religion; numbers, symbology of; occult, occultic; oneiromancy; Olivet Discourse, the; omen; oneiromancy; oracle(s); otherworldly journeys; ouija board; out-of-body experiences (OBEs); paranormal; parapsychology; past life regression; peace pole(s); pentagram; philosophers' stone; portent; precognition; prediction; prefigurement;

premonition; pre-wrath rapture; prodigy; prognostication; prophecy, general; psi; psychic(s); psychic healing; psychic reading; psychomancy; psychonautics; pyramidology; rebirthing; remote viewing; retrogression; revelation; rapture; rhabdomancy; scrying; séance; secret wisdom; secret societies; sorcery, sorceries; spell; spell names; spiritism; stigmata; supernatural; superstition; tarot; telegnosis; telepathy; telesthesia; theugry; third eye, the; totemism; Tribulation ; vision(s); vision quest; visualization; voodoo; voudou; Web-Bot; witchcraft; *ya sang*; yoga; Zen; *zos kia* cultus.

beloved disciple: the apostle John. The Gospels mention Jesus' particular favor with John, the youngest of the disciples. It was he who leaned on Jesus' breast at the Last Supper (Jn. 13:23–25), was present at the crucifixion, and the only disciple not to experience martyrdom. Most scholars assert that he was the author/recipient of the book of Revelation. *See also* John as apostle.

Belshazzar: the Babylonian monarch who witnessed a disembodied hand writing on the wall of his palace in 539 B.C. His name means "may Bel protect the king." Although he is mentioned in Daniel 5 as having Nebuchadnezzar as his father, he was actually the son of a later king named Nabonidus and a grandson of Nebuchadnezzar. *See also* Bel; Daniel's decipher of the hand writing on the wall; hand writing on the wall, vision of the; king(s); *Meme, Meme, Tekel Parsin (or Uparsin);* Nabonidus; Nebuchadnezzar II.

belt: a clothing accessory worn about the waist intended to secure one's garments or to serve as a convenient method of tucking the hem of the long robe for ease of movement in the legs. The article of dress could also hold personal items or weapons. Isaiah the prophet (Isa. 11:5) used the article as a metaphor for the righteousness of the coming Messiah in the Millennium. The strap of leather or cloth, also called a girdle in older Bible translations, is sometimes further used to denote truth, surety, or some other noble concept (as in Ephesians 6:14). *See also* girdle; *Sacra Cintola;* sash.

Beltane: sometimes called "Walpurgasnacht," a Gaelic May Day celebration, probably of Druid origin. The festival was normally held between April 30 and May 1, halfway between the spring equinox and the summer solstice. Rituals were performed to protect the principal cash source—cattle—as well as crops and people. Central to the gala were bonfires, which the people and their cattle circled, leapt over, or passed between a pair of them. Doors, windows, and animals were decorated with May flowers along with a thornbush dressed out in ribbons and shells. Holy wells were visited and the morning dew was considered special for its aid to beauty and youthfulness. As we have learned, all the boys in a township or hamlet met on the moors where they fashioned a round trench capable of holding the entire population. A fire was kindled and a mixture of eggs and milk was concocted as a kind of custard and consumed. A cake of oatmeal was then toasted on the embers and equal portions passed among the attendees. One piece of the cake was blackened in the fire and placed in a receptacle with other unburned pieces numbering one per participant. The people are then blindfolded and each was to draw out a piece, with the holder of the collection taking the last bit. Whoever drew the dreaded black portion was devoted as a sacrifice to Baal. Later, when human sacrifice fell out of fashion, the "winner" was required to jump through the fire three times. Other festivals included Samhain (November 1 for the New Year), Imbolc (February 1 for new birth and planting), Lugnasad (August 1 for harvest), and the marks for all the yearly equinoxes. *See also* Beltane's Eve; bugbears; Celtic folklore and religion; Druidism; Hallowmas; Imbolc; idolatry; Lammas; Lughnasadh; Mayday rites; Midsummer Day; New Age religion; Sabbat; Samhain; Tuatha de Danann; Walpurgis Night; Wicca; witchcraft.

Beltane's Eve: according to legend and folklore, the night of April 30. The day is one of two times a year when moral rules are suspended and supernatural events are common. *See also* Beltane; bugbears; Celtic folklore and religion; idolatry; Wicca; witchcraft.

Belteshazzar: the Babylonian name for Daniel. The new title was undoubtedly intended to advertise one of the Babylonian pantheon, most likely Bel. *See also* Abednego; Azariah as exile; Bel; Daniel; Hananiah the exile; Meshach; Mishael; Shadrach; Sumerian and Babylonian pantheon.

bema: the Greek name for judgment seat. The *bema* was a raised dais from which Roman magistrates and judges passed down rulings in civil and criminal hearings. The name is correct for use as the "the judgment seat of Christ" by which Jesus will reward (or not reward) his heavenly followers according to their service and attitude in their earthly lives. *See also* crown(s); crown of glory; crown of incorruption; crown of life; crown of rejoicing; crown of righteousness; eschatology, eschatological; Gabbatha; judgment(s); judgments, general and particular; judgment on the great Day, the; judgment seat of Christ; Lithostros; marriage supper of the Lamb; Praetorium; reward(s) in heaven; robe, crown, and throne; Roman Empire; welcome, a rich.

Benaiah: commander of the army of Israel under part of David's reign and that of Solomon. He was head of the royal bodyguard under Solomon, and it was he who carried out the king's orders to execute Abiathar the priest (the last of Eli's line) for conspiring with Adonijah to take the throne. He was also ordered to slay Joab for the murders of Abner and Amasa (1 Ki. 2:31–33), then cut down Shimei, who had cursed David during his flight from Absalom (1 Ki. 2:44–46). Benaiah is noted in biblical lore as a valiant man, famous for having descended into a pit to slay a lion and for killing two lion-like men of Moab and an Egyptian giant. *See also* Abishai; Abner; Amasa; Asahel; David; David's generals; giant(s); Joab.

Benedicite Omnia Opera: a canticle of the Christian Church based on the trials of the prophet Daniel. The opening lyrics recite: "O all ye works of the Lord, bless ye the Lord; praise Him and magnify Him forever." *See also* Daniel as prophet; liturgical year; liturgy, Christian; music; Roman Catholic Church.

benediction: a blessing by gesture or speech. The words and actions of grace are normally pronounced on the congregation at the conclusion of worship, but the liturgy is not limited to that occasion. Revelation and other apocalyptic literature use benedictions to express favor to righteous mortals or to God. Perhaps the grandest of the holy sanctions is that found in Numbers 6:22–26, known as the priestly benediction: "The Lord bless you and keep you; the Lord make his face shine upon you and be gracious to you; the Lord turn his face toward you and give you peace." Another of equal beauty is in Jude 24–25. The early Roman liturgy was not lacking in the quality of pronounced benedictions. Around the 13th century, priests would often close the Mass with Thomas Aquinas's *Tantum ergo* ("Down in adoration falling"). The words are the first two verses of a vespers hymn for the Feast of Corpus Christi called *Pange Lingua Gloriosi Mysterium*, which are sung as the sacrament is exposed to the worshipers. A prayer follows, also written by Aquinas: "O God, who under a wonderful sacrament has left us a remembrance of your passion: grant, we beseech you, that we may so venerate the holy mysteries of your body and blood, that we may evermore perceive within ourselves the fruit of your redemption." *See also* blessed; blessing(s); invocation; liturgical year; liturgy, Christian; liturgy, Jewish; *Pange Lingua Gloriosi Mysterium*; postlude; prayer(s).

Benedict of Nursia: an Italian Pietist (ca. A.D. 480–542) who, though active in the church, remained a layman all of his life. He was drawn to the hermit lifestyle early in his career. However, at age fifty he established a monastery at Monte

Cassino and became famous for his developed rules of the monastic life known as the Rule of Benedict. Contrary to popular assumption, he did not establish the Order of Saint Benedict but those associations use his rule of governing. Monte Cassino was bombed to ruin by the Allies in World War II, only the latest in a series of devastations to the site. He believed the monks in community should be pious, self-contained, and active. To aid in this goal, Benedict's orders usually enlisted several offices under the abbots who were to head the organization. Those lesser officials included a prior (provost), deans (over ten monks), a cellarer, the novice-watcher, and a porter (gatekeeper). *See also* Benedict, Rule of; Cistercians; Cluny; dean; desert mystics; liturgical year; provost; Roman Catholic Church.

Benedict, Order of: a series of virtually independent monasteries and other religious institutions using the Rule of Saint Benedict as the structure of their associations. Benedict of Nursia did not formulate the order, however. The monks are alternately known as "Whitecloaks" or White Monks for their white apparel, Trappists, or Bernadines. Their motto of service reads: *pax, ora et labore*—"peace, pray, work." *See also* Assumptionist Orders; Augustinian Order; Barnabites; Black Canons; canon(s) of the church; canons regular; Capuchin Order; Carmelites; Carthusians; Celestines; Cistercians; clergy; Cluny; Dominicans; Franciscans; friar(s); liturgical year; Minim; monasticism; monk(s); orders; Paulist Fathers; Premonstratensian Order; priest(s); religious organizations; Roman Catholic Church; sempect; Servite Order; Spirituals of the Franciscan Order; Trappist Order.

Benedict, Rule of: a system of precepts or rules from the fifth century by which monasteries who adopt them may be governed. Benedict of Nursia was the author and main proponent of administration, widely adopted then and now as the proper way for monks and nuns to live and function. There are over seventy sections covering almost every possible contingency for order, discipline, and productivity

History and Mystery

in the community. A kind of balance seems to have been struck between individual initiative and excessive coercion within the orders. *See also* Benedict of Nursia; Cluny; monasticism; monastic vows; Roman Catholic Church.

Benedict XVI, Pope: the 256th Roman Catholic pope (according to one of the differing lists of historical church heads). Before election he was Cardinal Joseph Alois Ratzinger of Polish descent. He abruptly resigned the office in 2013 citing health reasons and his advanced age. Benedict was the first of the Benedictine Order to assume the high office and often wore the traditional white robes of the institution. Some claim he is the last, or next-to-last, pope in Malachy's "Prophecy of the Popes." *See also* Benedict, Order of; Francis, Pope; pope; "Prophecy of the Popes"; Roman Catholic Church.

Benedictus: one of three great canticles of faith from the Gospel of Luke (Lk. 1:68–79). The poem celebrates the praise of Zacharias, the father of John the Baptist, for the birth of his son and forerunner of the Messiah. There is some speculation the recitation bears resemblance to some of the victory songs of the Maccabees. *See also Cantate Domino;* liturgical year; liturgy, Christian; *Magnificat;* music; *Nunc Dimittis;* Zachariah as priest.

Bene Elohim: an angel class named from early Jewish sources. They are noted for their valiant struggle to undo wrong and promote the right, then praising God for success. In other instances, they may be fallen angels. *See also* angel(s); archangel(s); authorities; Chashmallim; Chayoth; Cherub, Cherubim; dominions; *elohim;* Erelim; Galgallim; Hashmallim; Hayyot; Husk(s); Ishim; *mal'ak;* Ophanim; powers; principalities; Seraph, Seraphim; thrones; Virtues; Watchers, the.

bene esse: a Latin legal term meaning "well being" or something akin. In ecclesiology, it emphasizes the significance of a church doctrine or practice. *Esse* presents the essence or centrality of the action in the life of the church while *bene* indicates it is of benefit to the community as a whole.

Benefactors: a title used by Jesus (Lk. 22:25) to identify Gentile political authority. Unlike them, Jesus said, believers should not be a tyrant expecting subservience but a selfless servant to others. *See also* authorities; tutelary.

benefice: an ecclesiastical office to which revenue or payment is attached. In the corrupt early church, such positions frequently lacked function and required little work. *See also* altarage; benefit of clergy; carrodian; *cathedraticum;* love offering; mensa; papal revenue; pounding; prebend; Roman Catholic Church; stipend.

benefit of clergy: 1. a privilege of the clergy that in some circumstances which places them beyond the jurisdiction of secular courts. The phrase may also refer to clergy discounts on sale items and other gratuities. 2. an older expression for clergy who have performed weddings; those couples not so married were referred to as "without benefit of clergy," a somewhat derogatory appellation describing their common-law living arrangement. *See also* altarage; benefice; carrodian; *cathedraticum;* Christianese; church abuse; clergy; love offering; matrimony; mensa; papal revenue; pounding; prebend; slurs, religious; stipend.

ben Gurion, David: Polish-born as David Green before his name change. Ben Gurion was a fervent Zionist, statesman, and Israeli political leader (1886–1973). He was twice prime minister of Israel and is called the nation's founding father. Ben Gurion was first to sign the Jewish Declaration of Independence and an effective leader helping the new nation gain prominence in the 20th century. According to Hosea 3:4–5, we may imply it prophetically important that he be named David. *See also* Independence Day (Jewish); Jew(s); seven shepherds and eight princes; Zechariah's vision of the four horns and four craftsmen; Zionism.

History and Mystery

Ben-Hadad. See Hadad.

Benjamin: one of the twelve tribes of Israel descended from the patriarch Jacob and his favorite wife, Rachel. Jacob's deathbed blessing of the tribes in Genesis 49:27 named Benjamin a "ravenous wolf," which may explain their fierce fighting nature; one instance (Jud. 20:16) cites a group of 700 left-handed soldiers who could sling a stone at a hair and not miss. The Benjamite tribe holds the dubious distinction as the only one nearly wiped out by their fellow Israelites. The other tribes warred against them because the Benjamites and men of Gilead allowed certain murderers and rapists to go unpunished (Jud. 19–21). The slaughter was so thorough that the victors had to resort to subterfuge to provide wives for the 600 surviving men so the tribe would not perish in Israel. Benjamin is listed among those of the 144,000 servants in Revelation 7:8, and the only one to remain loyal to the line of David when the Northern and Southern kingdoms split. *See also* lost tribes, the ten; tribes of Israel, the; twelve tribes.

Ben Pantheras: the Talmud's identifier for Jesus of Nazareth (son of Pentera), provided we have interpreted correctly. The name is not, as is sometimes thought, the son of a Roman soldier named Pantheras but is a reference to *parthenon*, the Greek reference to "virgin." This Talmudic portion is said to be a recording of earlier oral material telling of an historical person named Jesus, a wonder-worker who died on Passover Eve. Thus, the writing ascribes Jesus' power to magic but scorns him as a heretic. *See also* names (titles) for Jesus.

ben Samuel, Rabbi Judah: a German Talmudic scholar who prophesied (in A.D. 1217) that the Ottoman Turks would occupy Jerusalem for eight Jubilees (400 years). Turkish rule lasted exactly that long ending in 1917. He also predicted the ninth Jubilee would see Jerusalem become a "no-man's" land (1917 – 1967) during which Palestine would be partitioned. He then proclaimed that the tenth

Jubilee year (calculated to be 2017) would see Jerusalem in total control of the territory. If the prophecy holds, the message is a major pronouncement of Messianic times. *See also* Jew(s).

Ben Sira. See Jesus ben Sirach.

Beqa: the name of the great oath in heaven, or the angel who administers it according to *1 Enoch*. *See also* Akae; angel(s); Kesbul; oath(s); secret name, the; "sign, the"; symbalon.

Berbers: the non-Arabic speaking nomadic Muslims of the Sahara Desert of Morocco. *See also* Bedouins; Islam; Moors.

Berea, Bereans: a city near Thessalonica (Acts 17:10–15). The Bereans were said to be of more noble character than their neighbors, the Thessalonians, because they were willing to hear and research the truth of the gospel objectively.

Berenice: daughter of Ptolemy II (ca. 340–81 B.C.). She became the wife of Antiochus II in an arranged marriage with the intent to secure peace between the rival Ptolemies and Seleucids. Berenice was eventually poisoned by the spurned wife of Antiochus, Laodice, whom she had displaced. The incident is likely referenced in the history contained in Daniel 11:6. *See also* queen(s).

Berg, Moses (David): founder of the apocalyptic and exploitive cult known as the Children of God; other names include "The Family," "The Family of Love," and others but is now called the Family International. Berg was born in California in 1919 and died in Portugal in 1994. He was a reclusive leader known to his followers as Moses David and other nicknames who communicated through his periodic "Mo Letters." He was reputedly an anti-Semite and pedophile. Among his many failed apocalyptic predictions was his pronouncement that the comet Kohoutek would devastate the earth in 1973. Berg considered himself to be the reincarnated King David. *See also* cult(s); Family International.

History and Mystery

Bermuda Triangle: the geographical triangular of ocean area in the Gulf of Mexico and North Atlantic with its apexes at Bermuda, Puerto Rico, and west Florida. Some believe the location is supernaturally cursed or haunted because of many unexplained disappearances of ships and planes that occur there regularly. *See also* New Age religion; paranormal.

Bernard of Clairvaux: French abbot (1090 – 11253), a mystic monk who operated the reformed Cistercian Order (he personally established sixty-five of the 300 Cistercian monasteries at the time) under the rule of Saint Benedict. His persona and way of life prompted hundreds, perhaps thousands, to the Cistercian disciplines. His influence was far outside the monastery walls, however. He was able to heal the papal schism between the antipope contender Anacletus II and Innocent II, thus cementing his reputation as the "great peacemaker" and even called "the maker of popes." Bernard was militant and harsh in his methods yet wrote one of the most poignant hymns of Christendom, "Jesus, the Very Thought of Thee" and a number of important theological works including the basic rules for the Knights Templar as well as the controversial theological work called the *Apologia*. A series of sermons on the Song of Songs spiced his nickname as "the honey-tongued doctor." He was a persuasive orator and was instrumental in promoting the Second Crusade and the Knights Templar at the urging of Pope Eugenius III and King Louis VII of France. His austere methods of monastic discipline ruined his health and, as it happened, of his three main tasks—church reform, support of the Knights Templar, and sponsor of the Second Crusade – none were ultimately successful. Bernard was a friend and supporter to both Saint Malachy and Hildegard of Bingham but he was an adversary to Peter Abelard whom he considered ill-informed and heretical because, according to Bernard, Abelard did not pay sufficient attention to the mysteries of God. Bernard was named "Doctor of the Church" by Pope Alexander III in A.D. 1174. *See also* Abelard, Peter; Cistercians; Crusades; desert mystics; Hildegard of Bingham; knighted orders; liturgical year; Malachy; Roman Catholic Church.

Bernice: sister/wife of King Herod Agrippa II (b. A.D. 28). Bernice was the eldest daughter of Herod Agrippa I whose second marriage was to Agrippa's brother, Herod, king of Chalcis (who was her uncle). It is assumed she was in an incestuous relationship with her brother, Herod Agrippa II, when she appears in Acts 25:13, 23 and 26:30. Later she became mistress to both Roman generals Vespasian and Titus. Josephus spoke well of her, however, for her zeal to protect the Jews and Jerusalem against the barbarity of the procurator Florus. *See also* Herod Agrippa II; queen(s).

Berossus: Chaldean astronomer, or perhaps more accurately, an astrologer (second century B.C.) who predicted the end of the world and its renewal for the year 2001 (not far from the Mayan 2012 prophecy). His name is mentioned by Josephus, Eusebius, and others as a representative of the Magian cultures who preached a kind of blend of Greek philosophy, Babylonian esotericism, and Chaldean astrology and dualism. According to Berossus, the Sumerians did not invent civilization, but it was thrust upon them by the gods (ancient astronauts?), the first of whom was called Oannes, who walked in from the Persian Gulf to begin the alien education and rule. Berossus's history of humanity (not extant in the original) spans some 100,000 years. His record from 289 B.C. is written in Greek in which he claims the time between the great flood and the first new king in the land, Aloros I, was 432,000 years. Berossus' account is more than a hundred times longer than the chronology given in the Old Testament but it does match that found in the *Book of Enoch*. His composition, called the *Babyloiniaca*, became the primary historical reference work of his day. Berossus was a contemporary of Alexander the Great. *See also* Aloros I, Ancient Astronaut Theory; astrology, astrologers; astronomy, astronomers; Atlantis; *Babyloniaca*; Chaldea, Chaldeans; Mesopotamia; Oannes and the Seven Sages.

Berrigan, Daniel and Philip: a pair of brothers, Daniel (b. 1921) and Philip (1923–2002) who gained notoriety as counterculture protestors of the Vietnam War. Daniel was a Jesuit and Philip was a Josephite. Philip led a raid on Baltimore's draft board and poured animal blood on the records, then both brothers attacked the Cantonsville, Maryland, board and burned some files. Daniel was even arrested for digging a grave on the White House lawn as an act of political protest, then wrote a commentary on Revelation from his Washington, D. C. jail cell. His comment on Revelation is predictably harsh: "The book of Revelation ought to be burned, it is positively subversive!" He also produced the book *Nightmare of God* in which he compared the Rome of Revelation to America. For a time, both were on the FBI's Ten Most Wanted List. When in prison, Philip was charged with conspiracy to kidnap presidential advisor Henry Kissinger, but the trial resulted in a hung jury. Both men were paroled and they continued their social justice passions. *See also* order(s); Roman Catholic Church; social issues; Society of Jesus.

Besant, Annie: *nee* Annie Wood, born in London but died in India, the second leader of the Theosophical Society (1847–1933) and contemporary with and follow-on leader after the originator, Madame Helena Blavatsky. Besant was the former wife of an Anglican country parson. Shortly after her divorce, she became involved in women's rights and issues of poverty; she held a reputation as a successful orator. Besant furthered the fortunes of the Theosophy sect and established a number of offshoots and associations related to it. *See also* Blavatsky, Madame Helena Petrovna; psychic(s); sect(s); Theosophical Society; Theosophy.

***besom*:** a broom. The name of the article in Hebrew is *besom*, but witches and Wicca adherents use a model of the article to sweep clean a magic circle. The idea of "sweeping up" has even been carried to the navies which may display a broom on a ship's mast to declare that the enemy was swept clean from the sea. *See also* athame; boline; idolatry; Wicca; witch(es); witchcraft.

bestiality. See zoophilia.

bestiary: a compendium of fantastically illustrated animals and commentary popular in the Middle Ages. Dragons, basilisks, griffins, caladriuses, unicorns, and pelicans were particularly favored subjects. Each drawing or painting was usually accompanied by a morality story and helped promote the idea that the world is of God and all of creation has both a practical and a spiritual purpose. One famous bestiary, called the Peridoxion, depicts the world tree over a dragon with doves above. Christ is on one side and the Holy Spirit is on the opposite. Within the tree branches or its shadows, the doves (the people of God) are protected from the dragon (Satan). Another work, called the *Psysiologus*, is a literary and artistic masterpiece of the second century. *See also Animal Apocalypse, The;* animals, birds, and insects, symbology of; art, religious; book(s); bugbears; fable(s); mythological beasties, elementals, monsters, and spirit animals.

Beta Israel. See Falasha Jews.

Bethany: a small town near the Mount of Olives, often paired with Bethphage. Jesus was a frequent visitor because Mary, Martha, and Lazarus lived there. Simon the leper was also a resident in whose home one of Jesus' anointings took place (Mt. 26:6–13; Mk. 14:3). The name means "house of the poor," "house of affliction," or, by some interpretations, "house of unripe figs." *See also* Bethphage.

Beth Arbel: or Beth-arbel, a place of caves located in Galilee, where robbers lurked until rooted out by Herod the Great. The site was originally conquered by Shalman (or Salamanu) of Moab and is identified as imagery (Hos. 10:14) for a warning of destruction. *See also* Shalman; Shalmaneser.

Beth Aven: Hosea's name for Bethel ("house of God") of Judah, a play on words now meaning "house of wickedness." The prophet so named the site because it had become a place of idolatry and sin (Hos. 5:8, 10:5). *See also* Bethel; idolatry.

Beth Eden: as named in Amos 1:5 but simply Eden in other translations from 2 Kings, Isaiah, and Ezekiel. The place was an embroidery market for Tyre, located in northern Mesopotamia and situated on both sides of the Euphrates. Amos is predicting its downfall along with Damascus in Syria.

Bethel: a site originally called Luz in the territory of Benjamin. The new name, Bethel, means "house of God," but Jacob eventually called the locale el-Bethel, "God of Bethel." The place was familiar to Abraham, and Jacob had his dream of the heavenly ladder on that spot. Jacob set a stone in place there and worshiped as an act of remembrance (Gen. 28:19-22). The prophet Hosea charged the place as having become wicked (Hos. 10:15). *See also* Beth Aven; Ebenezer; Jacob, ladder of; Luz; messebas; sacred stones.

bethel: a chapel for sailors or a nonconformist auxiliary worship center of some description. *See also* cella; chapel; chaplain(s); church; sacellum.

Bethesda: a town carrying the meaning of "house of grace." Of more prophetic interest, however, is the pool of Bethesda (actually there were two) located in Jerusalem just north of the Temple near the Sheep Gate. It had five porticoes that could accommodate large crowds (Jn. 5:2–3). Legend held that its waters were periodically stirred by an angel, at which time the first sick or injured to enter the pool would be healed. This section is omitted in the RSV translation as being insufficiently sustained by earlier texts. In any case, Jesus healed an invalid who had waited thirty-eight years in his attempts to be whole. There follows a lengthy story in the Gospel of John accounting for actions in the city after the healing and the man's testimony of how it happened and by whom. Some manuscripts call the place Bethzatha or Bethsaida. *See also* Bethsaida; Jerusalem, landmarks of.

Beth-Ezel: a town of southern Judah named as "a neighboring place." The prophet Micah uses the site as a metaphor for mourning because no help could be expected from "the neighbor" to avoid the punishment of God on the land (Mic. 1:11).

Beth-Horon. See Horon.

Bethlehem: the name of two cities in Israel mentioned in the Bible. The first, a town in the land grant to Zebulun (Josh. 19:15), is not famous. The second, with a meaning of "house of bread," was the birthplace of both David and Jesus. The prophet Micah predicted Bethlehem as the birthplace of the Messiah many centuries before the event (Mic. 5:1–5). It was also home to Rachel and Ruth and Boaz. *See also* Church of the Nativity.

Beth Ophrah: a place name of uncertain origin, though it could be the town of Ophrah where Gideon was born, called to be a judge, fell into idolatry, and died. When used by the prophet Micah (Mic. 1:10), it becomes a pun or by-word meaning "house of dust."

Bethphage: a town somewhere on or adjacent to the Jericho-Jerusalem road near Jerusalem. The place is mentioned in the synoptic Gospels in connection with Jesus and his disciples as they journeyed to Jerusalem on the day of the Triumphal Entry. The little community is often paired with nearby Bethany. Both village names could carry the Aramaic meaning of "house of unripe figs." *See also* Bethany.

Bethsaida: a town mentioned by Jesus in Matthew 11:21. The Lord declared that the Jewish populace who resided there would fare worse on the day of judgment than the pagan cities of Tyre and Sidon because of their refusal to repent or to acknowledge the miracles performed before them. This locale happened to be the hometown of Peter, Andrew, and Philip. *See also* Bethesda.

Beth Shemesh: the name of at least four towns or regions in and around ancient Israel. The name means "house of the sun-god" so we know pagan worship proliferated in some or all. *See also* idolatry.

Beth Togarmah: a future ally of Gog and Magog (along with Cush, Gomer, and Persia) whose precise location or ancestry is not definitely known. Togarmah was the third son of Gomer and related to the Scythian people. The land of Togarmah was a far-flung territory of ancient times but did have contact with the Middle East. *See also* Cush, Cushites; eschatology, eschatological; Gog and (of) Magog; Gomer; Persia, Persians; Put; Rosh, Prince of; Tubal.

betroth: a promise to marry—a formal engagement arranged by a couple or by parental wishes. Mary and Joseph were betrothed when the angel announced to her that she would birth the Messiah. *See also* banns; matrimony.

Beulah: a prophetic name for Palestine following its repopulation by the Jews after the Babylonian Exile (Isa. 62:4). The term "Beulah" means "married," indicating that the land will again be fully inhabited and fruitful. *See also* City No Longer Deserted; Deserted/Desolate, Hebrews as a people; Hephzibah; Holy People, the; Jerusalem as city; Jew(s); Judaism; name, a new; Palestine; Redeemed of the Lord; Sought After.

Beza, Theodore: Calvin's successor to the Geneva theocracy (1519–1605). He expanded and smoothed the theology of Calvinism and made it more suitable for European understanding. *See also* Calvinism; Geneva theocracy of John Calvin; theocracy.

Bhagwan Gita: the "Song of the Lord," Hindu holy writings appearing in the sixth book of the Mahabharata. The story, told in eighteen chapters, concerns the actions of five brothers soon to be engaged in battle (*viz.*, the eighteen-day struggle at Kurukshetra). The leader and hero of the Pandava faction is the third son, Arjuna. Before the conflict, the Hindu god Krishna lectures Arjuna on the morality of war, then expands the record into a full treatise on the essence of Hindu Dharma. *See also* Hinduism; Krishna; *Upanishads;* Vishnu.

Bhagwan Shree Rajneesh: a quasi-Eastern doomsday cult established in America by Chandra Mohan Jain (1931–1990). As leader, Jain was known as "Osho" or Acharya Rajneesh. The order was situated in Oregon, where it quickly became embroiled with the local population who accused the members of poisoning foodstuffs in the community, an apocalyptic act of bioterrorism. The cult members were easily recognized by their orange jumpsuits and the large collection of Rolls Royce automobiles owned by their director. Teachings in the sect consisted of meditation, loose morality, and a sort of contemplative self awareness. Jain was deported from the United States in 1985 but was refused entry in twenty-one other countries. He eventually settled back in India, where he died in 1990. Today, the cult site is called the Osho International Meditation Resort. *See also* communal communities; cult(s); idol(s); terrorism; terrorist(s).

Bhakti: a Hindu religious movement from the medieval period. The Bhaktis believed that *moksha*, liberation from the eternal life cycle, was possible for anyone. The beliefs are similar to Sufism. *See also* Hinduism; idolatry; *moksha;* sect(s); Sufism.

Bible: a.k.a. the Scriptures, the Word of God, the Word, Holy Writ, and any number of other designations. The text is, for most believing Christians and devout Jews, the divinely inspired message of God to His people in written form. As to the matter of the Bible's infallibility, the population seems to divide itself into three categories of belief. The first see the Scripture as absolutely true in every sense of language and meaning. There are no errors or omissions. The second group considers the holy writ as largely reliable and valuable but would hesitate to affirm complete accuracy. The third, predictably, consider the Bible to be largely unreliable, mythical, or irrelevant. They can cite at least 100 erroneous or contradictory statements within the test itself. There were many human authors making up the sixty-six books of the Bible, some known and others unknown. Long periods of time were required to finish the established text (the canon) and its contents emerged from many differing locations. The Hebrew Tanakh (known as the Old Testament) is Judaic in background; the New Testament is the story of the Church centered in Jesus Christ. The work consists of religious history, law, poetry, prophecy, eschatology, ecclesiology; moral instruction, worship technique, practical living application, and narrative in its widest range. It has long been the best-selling publication in the world with about one million sales annually. Most believers are convinced the Word is full, accurate, true, reliable, and useful (2 Tim. 3:16). *See also* Aitken Bible; Aleppo Codex; Bible baseball; Bible belt; Bible Code; Bible divisions; Bible manuscripts; Bible of the poor; Bible societies; Bible translations; *Biblica Hebraica;* biblical criticism; bibliomancy; bibliolatry; book(s); canon of the Scriptures; clay; codex, codices; Devil's Bible; Gutenberg, Johann; higher criticism; inerrancy; *Juxta Hebraica;* King James Version; lower criticism; *norma normans non normata;* parchment; poetry (biblical); Samaritan Pentateuch; scroll(s); *sola Christo, sola fide, sola gratia, sola Scriptura, soli Dei gloria;* stone(s); sword drill; sword of the Lord; Tanakh; Torah; Torah Scroll; vellum; verbal inspiration; Word of God; Wycliffe Bible.

Bible baseball: a Bible trivia game for youngsters. Nine players compete as a team with Bible questions serving as the pitched ball and answers as hits or strikes. Players advance the bases or are called out according to the application of baseball and game detail rules. *See also* Bible; Christianese; religious education; sword drill.

Bible Belt: those areas of the United States whose populations are noted for their favorable to strict evangelistic Christian teaching, belief, and church attendance, particularly the South and part of the Midwest. The term was invented by the writer H. L. Mencken in 1925 while he was reporting the Scopes Trial.

Bible Code: sometimes Torah Code, a recently discovered computer technique whereby hidden messages are allegedly deciphered from the Scripture—a sort of "Bible within the Bible." The system was supposedly discovered by Dr. Eliyahu Rips, a leading expert in group dynamics and a mathematician, along with fellow number crunchers Doran Witztum and Yoab Rosenberg in 1994. However, attempts to find such a cipher had already started as early as the 12th century. The great scientist Isaac Newton spent inordinate amounts of time and effort to find the code that he was convinced existed. Those who advocate the veracity of the process claim that coded references to past and future events of our history can be located by isolating words or phrases searched randomly in the Hebrew Bible. For centuries, some Jewish scholars have claimed that the codes were placed into the Torah when God gave the Word to Moses on Mount Sinai. Yahweh did not simply slip in vital concepts of future history, but dictated each individual letter in a continuous format of characters without spaces or punctuation. Thus, singular persons and isolated events we would call common are included. Paul Couch, an ardent believer in the process, has reportedly found his name, his wife's name, and the name of the media enterprise he founded, Trinity Broadcasting Network. God deliberately concealed these messages, it is said, until a time when technology could reveal them. Everything that has ever happened and all that ever will happen is included somewhere waiting to be uncovered. The messages are now more easily available to us because the computer allows the complex system to be almost fully operative. The process is facilitated by finding words or phrases in a matrix occurring at specific intervals or spacing, a procedure called "equidistant letter sequencing" (ELS), or, simply the "skip" method. The codes may be found written horizontally, vertically, or diagonally, like the find-a-word puzzle in a newspaper, a magazine, or even a child's menu at a restaurant. Even the Bible Code process itself is identified; Genesis 20:2, beginning with the third letter in the fourteenth word, then counting backward five letters at a time, will reveal the phrase "The latticework of equidistant letter sequences for great teaching of the Lord." Nearby is the confirmation, "the great perfection of fluent speech." Statistical odds for a random occurrence are calculated at 100,000,000,000,000 to 1. It is claimed that the assassinations of Anwar Sadat and John and Robert Kennedy were found after the fact; but another, that of Yitzhak Rabin, was discovered *before* it occurred and even named the killer. The incident, obviously, was not averted. Most statisticians and biblical scholars dismiss the practice as unreliable. Almost any ELS process, given space and a pattern, will eventually spell out an "omen" of some sort. Three random ELS results regarding the subject of the rapture may illustrate. In Daniel 12:1-3 we can pick up "sons of God delivered," "in their rapture," and "all upright." There is an association in the collected clips, certainly, but such short and non-specific phrases smacks of forced relevance and can be fitted into many a context. Also, the various Bible translations will not support a uniform ELS signature since the phrasing and spacing are not uniform. The same process "works" for secular books, as well as the Scripture, producing the same phenomenon. Various translations would necessarily produce various results. Confusion might be modified if only the Hebrew language is used but ELS is also applied to the New Testament and other works. Even so, a number of predictions have been presented by Bible coders (or decoders) for the time before and to the year 2012: 1. Earth will be annihilated by a comet striking Canada. 2. The axis of Earth will tilt. 3. Seismic activity will rip Earth apart. 4. Jerusalem to be destroyed in 2010 by a nuclear device to which the Israelis will respond with a massive counterstrike. 5. The years 2007 through 2009 were to see extreme and erratic weather patterns and adverse economic conditions. 6. There will be an asteroid impact. 7. There is to be a huge earthquake in Yellowstone National Park. 8. America will be destroyed. 9. The year 2012 was to be characterized by gloom, terror, and darkness. 10. Massive loss of life will occur (about four billion people by some estimates) by the year 2012. *See also* apocalyptic calculation; Aqiba, Rabbi Joseph ben; Bible; Chamberlain Code; Cheiro; 888; *gematria;* Google Translate message; Haggada; Halakha; *isopseplia;* literomancy; Masseket Hekalot; Newton, Sir Isaac; *notarikon;* numbers, symbology of; Qabbala; *Sefiort;* 616; 666; *temoorah;* Web-Bot; Zevi, Shabbatai; *Zohar.*

Bible divisions: the methods by which the Bible is artificially divided and designed to make research easier. Certainly, the earliest copies had no such sectioning but were added later. Not only is Scripture split into the Old and New Testaments, but it also contains chapters and verses arbitrarily placed within. Paris scholar Frank Stephen Langton installed the chapters for the New Testament in the 1200s. Rabbi Isaac Nathan added verses to the Old Testament about 200 years after Langton. Frenchman Robert Estienne published verses and chapters for the New Testament in 1551, just in time to be included in the King James Version. The Bible has about 31,000 verses. *See also* Bible; Bible manuscripts; biblical criticism.

Bible manuscripts: those copies of the Bible, either New Testament or Old, which have been discovered and now serve as aids to more modern translations. Since there are no autographs, the earlier manuscripts and fragments are precious to Bible lovers and scholars. A list of the important manuscripts would include: 1. Codex Aleppo (ca. A.D. 920), one of the most authoritative and used extensively by the Masoretic translators, 2. Codex Alexandrinus

(A.D. 400-440) with most of the LXX and all of the New Testament, 3. Codex Amiatinus (in Latin) found complete in the eighth century, 4. Codex Bezae (A.D. 400) with most of the Gospels and Acts, 5. Codex Crosby-Schoyen (Coptic) from the third or fourth century A.D., 6. Codex Ephraemi (A.D. 450) with some of the LXX and much of the New Testament, 7. Codex Leningrad (ca. A.D. 1008), the oldest complete Hebrew Bible, 8. Codex Sinaiticus (A.D. 300-100) with about half of the LXX and all of the New Testament, 9. Codex Vaticanus (A.D. 300-100) with most of the LXX and all of the New Testament, 10. the *Codex Leningradensis* (A.D. 1100) as the oldest known Old Testament rendition. The Samaritan Pentateuch is older from around A.D. 200-100. The fortuitous finding of the Chester Beatty Papyri and Codex Porshyianus contributed much to the research as well. The Dead Sea Scrolls pushed all the earlier copies back a full millennium. A number of small but vital fragments have been located, most dated from around 100-200 A.D. Most solid translations of the Scripture use the standard idiom and text available for accurate translations. The most common references are: the Septuagint, Aquila, Symmachus, Theodotion, Vulgate, Syriac Peshitta, the Targums, and the *Juxta Hebraica* for the Psalms. Among the most commonly used fragments are the Bodmer, the Chester-Beatty, the IFIO, the Magdalen, the Oxyrhynchus, the P77, The Rylands, and the Unical. *See also* Aleppo Codex; autograph(s); Bible; Bible divisions; *Biblica Hebraica;* biblical criticism; book(s); canon of the Scriptures; covenant(s), biblical; Copper Scroll; Damascus Document; Dead Sea Scrolls; Elephantine Papyri; folio; Genizah Fragments; Hebrew Bible; Isaiah Scroll; *Juxta Hebraica;* lower criticism; manuscript(s); Masoretic Text; minuscules; Mount Sinai; Nag Hammadi library; New Testament; Old Testament; parchment; Peshita; Saint Catherine's Monastery; Tanakh; testament(s); translation; uncials; vellum; Vulgate; Word of God.

Bible of the poor: a concocted term for a cathedral with its decor, rituals, and furnishings. Since, in former times, most of the population was illiterate the masses could use the art, ritual, architecture, stained glass windows, icons, statuary, etc. to educate themselves somewhat to the faith. They could not understand Latin spoken in the mass so their only acquaintance to the Bible stories consisted of the physical illustrations all around them as they worshiped. *See also* art, religious; Bible; cathedral(s); furniture and furnishings of the modern church; religious education.

Bible societies: organizations planted to print, distribute, and translate the Bible either in whole or partial copies. The largest in the United States, the American Bible Society, was formed in 1816, but earlier groups had been active since 1808. The effort actually began with the Protestant Reformation and never really faded from their purposes. An international organ (United Bible Society) was begun in 1946 and cooperation between the bodies worldwide has been exceptional. Publishers normally print 100 million Bibles annually. *See also* American Bible Society; Bible; Gideons International; Marsh, Jedidiah; religious education; religious organizations; Society for the Propagation of the Faith in Foreign Parts; Society for the Propagation of the Faith in New England.

"Bible thumper": a parody of some fundamentalist or charismatic revivalists who are prone to demonstrate physical antics in the pulpit when preaching. Actions vary including throwing chairs, weeping, gesturing wildly, ranting, shouting, and, of course, thumping the Bible for emphasis. The common saying about such evangelists is "He ain't preached if he's not sweatin' and walkin' on three inches of his britches legs." *See also* Christianese; slurs, religious.

Bible translations: the many renditions of Holy Scripture compiled throughout literate history taken from the earliest transcribings of Greek, Aramaic, and Hebrew manuscripts. Careful research and intuition are necessary disciplines to ensure accuracy of translation and to gain the inherent sense of meaning of every passage. The most popular, most complete, and most recognized are listed, along with dates of publication: American Standard Version (ASV) 1901; Amplified Bible (AMP) 1965; Bishop's Bible 1568; Contemporary English Version (CEV) 1995; Coverdale Bible 1535; Douay-Rheims (NT 1582), (OT 1610); Geneva Bible (NT 1557), (complete 1560); Good News Bible (GNB) 1976; Great Bible 1539; International Standard Version (ISV) 2011; Jerusalem Bible (JB) 1966; King James Version (KJV) 1611; The Living Bible (TLB) 1971; Matthew's Bible 1537; Modern King James Version 1990; Moffatt Translation 1926; New American Bible (NAB) 1970; New American Standard Bible (NASB) 1971; New English Bible (NEB) 1970; New International Version (NIV) 1978; New Jerusalem Bible (NJB) 1985; New King James Version (NKJV) 1982; New Life Version (NLV) 1986; New Revised Standard Version (NRSV) 1989; Orthodox Study Bible (OSB) 2008; Queen James Version (QJV) 2012; Revised Version (RV or ERV) 1952; Revised English Bible (REB) 1989; Today's New International Version (TNIV) 2005; Third Millennium Bible 1998; Tyndale Bible (NT 1526), (Pentateuch 1530); Updated King James Version 2004; Westminster Bible 1936; Wycliffe's Bible 1380 and 1388. The translation of Aquila and the Septuagint are quite early. Additionally, any numbers of paraphrases and Scripture portions have been produced over the years. Unfortunately, some so-called translations have been produced as well that are unscholarly, false, and even profane. *See also* Aleppo Codex; Aquila, translation of; autograph(s); Bible; Bible manuscripts; *Biblica Hebraica;* biblical criticism; Coverdale, Miles; Cranmer, Thomas; Douay-Rheims Bible; dynamic equivalence; folio; Great Bible; Gutenberg, Johann; Hexapla; Hus, John; higher criticism; inspiration; *Juxta Hebraica;* King James Version; King James Only movement; Knox, John; law of first mention; Lollards; lower criticism; Lucian's recension of the Septuagint; Luther, Martin; LXX; manuscript(s); Masoretic Text; Matthew's Bible; miniscule(s); New World Translation; Oahspe Bible; Origen; papyrus; parchment; Peshitta; plenary inspiration; principles of interpretation; Queen James Bible; redaction; revelation, theological; Septuagint, the; seventy, the; source criticism; sources, primary and secondary; Symmachus; Targum(s); textual criticism; translation; Tyndale, William; vellum; Vulgate; Wicked Bible; Wycliffe Bible; Wycliffe, John.

Biblica Hebraica: the best-known critical text of the Hebrew Old Testament based on the oldest complete copy known as the *Codex Leningradensis* (A.D. 1100). It is almost universally used for modern Bible translations, including the New International Version. *See also* Bible; Bible manuscripts; Bible translations; *Juxta Hebraica*.

biblical criticism: or biblical interpretation, the exegesis of the biblical text from a scholarly and intellectual perspective. Usually, a prior assumption is made that the subject material (the Bible in its various renditions, origins, and manuscripts) is of human rather than supernatural origins. The critical process is also important to the quest for the historical Jesus and to trace the early renditions for truth and error. Archeology, folklore, tradition, ancient manuscripts, language, and any available commentaries are tools of the trade. Biblical study in the Hebrew process may derive from the Torah as literal, midrashic, philosophical, or mystical styles. The effort may take on aspects of a number of sub-disciplines when using the critical approach: textual, source, form, tradition, redactive, canonical, rhetorical, narrative, psychological, socio-scientific, postmodernism, or even feminist specialties are extant. Lower criticism is essential base knowledge and any circumstantial evidence is welcome, plus the contributions of higher criticism are vital. *See also* Abbahu, Rabbi; Abelard, Peter; abrogation; accideme; accommodation; alliteration; apostrophe; apothegm; allegorical interpretation; amillennial, amillennialism;

analogical interpretation; ante-Nicene fathers; Aristides; Aristo of Pella; Athenagoras; autograph(s); Barth, Karl; Basil; Bible; Bible divisions; Bible manuscripts; Bible translations; bridal chamber ceremony; Bultmann, Rudolf; Calvin, John; canon of the Scriptures; Cappadocian fathers; cataphatic; chiasmus; Clement of Alexandria; conflict story; *constructio ad sensum;* context; contextualization; covenant theology; criteria of double dissimilarity; Death of God theology; deconstructionism; demythologizing; determinism; Diabolical Mimicry, the; dialectic theology; dialogical critical method; dittography; documentary hypothesis; double sense fulfillment; doublets; doubling; dual hermeneutics; Dwight, Timothy; dynamic equivalence; edification; Edwards, Jonathan; eisegesis; epanadiplosis; epigrammatic statements; eschatology, eschatological; etymology; exegesis; figure of speech; folio; foreshortened prophecy; form criticism; Fourfold Interpretation; gattung; gloss; Gnosticism, Gnostics; *Golden Bough, The;* gloss; gnomic sayings; grammatical-historical interpretation; *hapax legomena;* haplography; Hegesippus; hermeneutic(s); higher criticism; historical Jesus, the; homiletics; homographs; homonyms; homophones; *homoteleuton;* hyperbole; idealism; idiom; illumination; *inclusio;* inspiration; interpolation; interpretation; inverted nun; irony; isagogics; *itture sopherim;* jot and tittle; Jesus Myth, the; Jesus Seminar, the; kere; *kethib;* Kierkegaard, Soren; "L"; law of first mention; liberalist interpretation; literal interpretation; Logos; litotes; loan words; lower criticism; Luther, Martin; "M"; Maimonides, Moses; manuscript(s); Marka; Masoretic Text; Middoth; minuscule(s); mystery of God; mystical interpretation; neo-orthodoxy; Niebuhr, Reinhold; *norma normans non normata;* Origen; omission; onomastica; onomatopoeia; palimpsest; papyrus; paradigm; parallelism; parchment; Pardes; *paroimia;* pericope; personification; Peshita; Philo of Alexandria; plenary inspiration; pointing; point of view polyglot; possibilianism; postmillennial, postmillennialism; postmodernism; premillennial, premillennialism; *preparatio evangelica;* preterism; principles of interpretation; process theology; proof texting; prophecy; "prophetic skip;" pun(s); "Q"; redaction; revelation, theological; rhetorical criticism; rhetorical devices; riddle; satire; *scripto continua;* scriptorium; *sebirin;* simile; similitude; Shammai, Rabbi; Hillel, Rabbi; isagogics; source criticism; sources, primary and secondary; special points; strophe; superscription; symbol(s); synecdoche; syntax; synthetic parallelism; text; textual criticism; theology; Third Quest; threefold sense of interpretation; *tiggune sopherim;* Time Texts; Torah; translation; transmission history; transposition; trope; Tubingen School; type(s); typology; uncial(s); vellum; verbicide.

biblical universalism: also called qualified universalism, a doctrinal position somewhere between eternal torment for the unregenerate and universalism (no punishment for the unsaved). The view may also promote the idea that God assigns irrevocable death to the unsaved but not eternal punishment. *See also* universalism.

bibliolatry: the practice of treating Scripture as if it, in itself, is an object of worship. Some individuals and many Muslims and Orthodox Jews believe that their holy books (Bible and *Qur'an*) are living documents with a soul and worthy of sacrosanct usage. Sometimes even elaborate funerals and burials are arranged when the documents are worn beyond repair. The bibliolatry action is modeled in Sinclair Lewis's 1927 novel, *Elmer Gantry,* when a debate arose among some of the characters as to whether it was permissible to kill a fly with a Bible. *See also* Bible; bibliomancy; idol(s), idolatry.

bibliomancy: divination by random opening of the Bible and favoring the first verse to capture the eye. Such a practice is magical and unscholarly and therefore unacceptable as a means to discern the will of God. *See also* anthropomancy; anthroposophy; apotropaic magic; aretology; Ariosophy; astral plane; astral projection; astrolabe; astrology, astrologers; athame; audition; augury; automatic writing; bagua;

belomancy; *besom;* black arts; black mirror; blood moon(s); cartomancy; chiromancy; clairaudience; clairvoyance; cleromancy; cone of power; conjure; crop circles; cryptesthesia; crystallomancy; curious acts; divination; dream(s); dreams and visions; ecstasy; enchantment; enneagram; esoteric sects; evil eye; extrasensory perception (ESP); foreknowledge; foretelling; geomancy; grimoire; gris-gris; hepatoscopy; Hermetic wisdom; Hermetic writings; hex; hierscopy; horoscope(s); hydromancy; idol(s); idolatry; ifa; incantation; juju; labyrinth walk; lecanomancy; literomancy; locution; magic arts; magic, magick; magic square; magnetism; *mana*; mantic wisdom; mantra; miracle(s); monition; necromancy; New Age religion; numbers, symbology of; oneiromancy; occult, occultic; omen; oneiromancy; oracle(s); otherworldly journeys; ouija board; out-of-body experiences (OBEs); paranormal; parapsychology; peace pole(s); pentagram; philosophers' stone; planchette; planets as gods; portent; precognition; prediction; prefiguration; premonition; prodigy; prognostication; prophecy, general; psi; psychic healing; psychic reading; psychomancy; psychometry; psychonautics; pyramidology; remote viewing; retrocognition; revelation; retrogression; rhabdomancy; scrying; séance; secret wisdom; sorcery, sorceries; spell; spell names; spiritism; stigmata; superstition; tarot; telegnosis; telepathy; telesthesia; theugry; third eye, the; thoughtform; totemism; vision(s); vision quest; visualization; voodoo; voudou; witchcraft; wizard(s); *ya sang*; yoga; Zen; zodiac; *zos kia* cultus.

big bang theory: the cosmological model, widely accepted by some scientists but not proven, that postulates the most popular process by which the universe was created, occurring about fifteen billion years ago. According to the hypothesis, the universe expanded from a dense and hot mass of some description and continues to expand today. Most scientists today are ready to assert by the evidence that the universe came into being in such a manner. Some scientists assert that this expansion creates more space as it continually enlarges.

The big bang continues to bump against creationism, which insists that the universe was created by God *ex nihilo*—out of nothing. The claim is that nothing will produce nothing. Creationists want to know: 1. what mass combustible material was available and where did it originate, 2. what set off the spark, and 3. how could such a magnificent occurrence be dependent on an event outside itself. A common answer to this dilemma is that the big bang was ignited by spontaneous combustion of matter, void, and will. The solution begs the question because matter is something, void is nothing, and will must be God. *See also* analogical day theory; big crunch theory; chaos theory; cosmogony; cosmology; *creatio ex nihilo*; creation; creationism; creation science; Creator; day-age theory; evolution; evolution, theistic; framework hypothesis; gap theory of creation; intelligent design; involution; naturalism; Omphalos Hypothesis; progressive creationism; redshift; "six-day theory, the"; uniformitarianism; Young-Earth Creationist Movement.

bidding prayer: an informal intercessory prayer, normally addressed to general welfare concerns as opposed to distinct individuals in need. A petitioner might, for instance, ask for blessings on "this great nation" rather than a single citizen of the country. *See also* cry to the Lord; impetrate; intercessory prayer; prayer(s).

bier: a stretcher or frame on which a corpse is carried, or a conveyance coffin containing a body, to facilitate the burial rite. *See also* catafalque.

big crunch theory: an opposite scientific option to the big bang theory. The concept surmises that eventually the universe will reverse the big bang of expansion and begin to condense in upon itself due to gravity pressure. At some point, theoretically, there would be another big bang and the process would start again. *See also* analogical day theory; big bang theory; chaos theory; cosmogony; cosmology; *creatio ex nihilo;* creation; creationism; creation science; Creator; day-age theory; evolution; evolution, theistic;

framework hypothesis; gap theory of creation; intelligent design; involution; naturalism; Omphalos Hypothesis; progressive creationism; redshift; "six-day theory, the"; uniformitarianism; Young-Earth Creationist Movement.

Big Six Clauses, the: a contrived name for the six great purposes that God will achieve to announce His ultimate defeat of evil (Dan. 9:20–24). The sextet of prophecies state that there will be an anointing of the most holy, an atonement for wickedness, the end of sin, the end of transgressions, the inauguration of eternal righteousness, and the sealing (ending) vision and prophecy. It may be seen that the first three deal with man's sin; and the next three have to do with God's righteousness. It is surely self-evident that none of these intentions of God have been fully realized in our day and that we are to await a future time of righteousness for their fulfillment. If the Big Six Clauses are addressed to the Jews and not the Church, they could be viewed as blessings forthcoming with their Messiah. *See also* anoint the most holy (or holy one), to; atone for wickedness; end sin; finish transgression; inaugurate eternal righteousness; seal up vision and prophecy; sinful nature.

Bildad: an erstwhile friend of Job who visited the sufferer in his sorrowful condition. Bildad and his companions are sometimes accounted to be prophets but they are more properly called elders who offered Job unworthy counsel at best. *See also* Elihu; Eliphaz; Job as afflicted wise man; Zophar.

Bilderberg Group: an influential association of noted international politicians, financiers, and others whose purposes and agenda are secretive, a position assured by self imposed heavy security. The group's name is derived from the Bilderberg Hotel in Holland where the first meeting occurred in 1954. The society is a magnet for conspiracy theorists everywhere who see sinister motives of all descriptions in the clandestine operations of the members. *See also* Bohemian Grove; conspiracy theorists; fraternal organization(s); Freemasonry; Hashshashin; Illuminati; *Ordo Templi Orientis;* secret societies; sect(s).

Bile: the great sacred oak in Celtic lore from which all the gods and goddesses sprang into the world. Danu, the mother goddess as the "divine waters" is said to have gushed to the earth in the time of primal chaos and nurtured Bile so it could do its creative work. In fact, most Celtic names for their gods and goddesses are derived from the various rivers near their settlements. When considered as a god, Bile is the escort of deceased souls to the Otherworld. *See also* Bodhi Tree; Celtic folklore and religion; cosmic tree; flora, fruit, and grain, symbology of; idol(s); oak; Otherworld; tree(s); tree of life, the; tree of Zaqqum.

Bilhah: a maidservant to Rachel, Jacob's favored wife. She became a secondary wife to Jacob and gave birth to Dan and Naphtali (Gen. 30:1–8). To Israel's shame, she and Reuben (Jacob's eldest) were involved in an incestuous affair (Gen. 35:22). The action caused Jacob's blessing on the tribe of Reuben to be less than ideal (Gen. 49:3–4).

"Billy Graham rule, the": a.k.a. the "Mike Pence rule" (United States vice president in the Donald Trump administration) or the "Modesto Manifesto" (from Modesto, California, where it was formalized by Graham) that states no man is to associate with a woman to whom he is not married. The principle is said to rule out temptation and foil public detractors who may be eager to forward false public accusations for political or personal smear. Some call the prohibition sexist, however. *See also* Graham, William Franklin (Billy).

binary numbers: a system of arithmetic numbering using only the number two as a base. There are only two symbols, one and zero. Moving one space to the left doubles the value. The calculation was ardently supported by the German philosopher and mathematician Gottfried Wilheim von Leibniz (1646 – 1716) because of its simplicity and because he thought it mirrored creation. Unity (1), he surmised, represented God; zero (0) stood for the void from which all things were created. Today, the binary system is the basis for almost all computer calculation.

bind. See binding and loosing; binding of Satan; bound angels; spell.

binding and loosing: the authority given by Jesus to the Church, modeled by Peter, to conduct the missionary affairs of our calling (Mt. 16:19; 18:18). With these "keys" for binding and loosing, Peter opened doors for the gospel to the Jews (Acts 2:14–40), the Samaritans (Acts 8:14–17), and the Gentiles (Acts 10:44–48), thus commencing the Great Commission. It is doubtful that Jesus granted sole church authority to Peter or any other disciple (as insisted by Roman Catholic doctrine) since his theme to them centered on love—not condemnation and control. Nevertheless, the Lord surely intended the apostles—as missionaries, elders, and authority figures—to have some input into the discipline of the church body during their lifetimes, a legacy which has been passed down to us in the norms of Christianity (2 Pe. 2:5). "Binding and loosing" has to do with declaring punishment or absolution of transgressors in the kingdom of God—not determining ecclesiastical actions that are lawful or unlawful. *See also* apostolic succession; binding of Satan; Great Commission, the; keys of the kingdom; loosing of Satan; Peter as apostle; rock(s); Rock (my, the); Roman Catholic Church; stones, living.

binding of Satan: God's constriction of Satan near the end of the Tribulation (Rev. 20:2–3) in which the devil is cast into the Abyss until the duration of the Millennium is completed. After that, he will be briefly released before his final defeat and permanent confinement into the lake of fire. *See also* Abyss, the; binding and loosing; eschatology, eschatological; loosing of Satan; Satan.

binitarianism: the teaching that God exists in only two essential persons—the Father and Son. The Holy Spirit is thus denied personality and a place in the Trinity. *See also* Trinity.

bin Laden, Osama: the major terrorist of the 21st century. He was born into a billionaire family in Saudi Arabia on March 10, 1957, and died in a special operations raid in Pakistan on May 2, 2011. He operated the terrorist organization called al-Qaeda which was responsible for the World Trade Center bombings collectively called 9/11. He was a staunch supporter of Wahhabism Islam and operated mostly from Afghanistan. No doubt, bin Laden was the most prolific and notorious terrorists to date and responsible for thousands of innocent deaths. *See also* al-Qaeda; anti-Semitic; Ibn Abd ul-Wahhab; Islam; terrorism; terrorist(s); Wahhabism.

bio-magnetics: a New Age treatment exposure which is said to balance magnetic forces within the body and thereby promote well-being. *See also* holistic; homeopathy; magnetism; New Age religion.

bird: winged fowl. In apocalyptic language, birds are often descriptive of innocence or simplicity as carrion-eaters, something of small value (since there were numerous common sparrows in the land), or as harbingers of disaster. In the Olivet Discourse, for example, Jesus described his appearing as likened to vultures gathering over a carcass. Revelation and other sources compare Babylon's total divine destruction as carrion food for the birds (*e.g.,* the fall of Babylon the Great). In a sort of atypical theme, ravens once fed Elijah and preserved his life at God's direction (1 Ki. 17:1–6). Birds, usually pigeons and doves, were also important for sacrifice, especially for the poor, and were necessary for some covenant enactments, as in Genesis 15:9–10. Not surprisingly for the science of the age, bats were counted among the birds (Lev. 11:19) but unsuitable for eating. Some wild birds, such as the owl and falcon, were seen as metaphors for the wilderness or desolation, figuratively or literally. *See also* animals, birds, and insects, symbology of; dove; eagle(s); eagle and the condor, the; eagles' wings; haunt (prison) for every unclean and detestable bird; owl; unclean; unclean animals, Peter's vision of the; sparrow; vulture(s).

History and Mystery

birth from above: a description of the radical conversion or change wrought by the Holy Spirit to a new believer. The phrase underscores the fact that regeneration was a miracle of God and not the result of human effort. *See also* accept Christ, to; altar call; "asking Jesus into my heart"; blood of Christ; blood of the Lamb; born again; confession(s) of faith; conversion; firstfruits of the resurrection; firstfruits of the Spirit; "plead the blood"; profession of faith; regeneration; "saved"; "turn your life [heart] over to Jesus; "walking the aisle"; "washed in the blood."

Birth of Baha'u'llah: a Baha'i holy day celebrating the birth of Mirza Husayn 'Ali-Nuri (1817 – 1892), the religion's chief teacher and proclaimed *Mahdi*. The date is one of twin holidays on the Baha'i calendar. The Baha'u'llah celebration occurs on the first day of Muharram of the Islamic calendar with the other set as the Birth of the Bab on the second day. Both dates are movable requiring higher authority within the Baha'i Universal House of Justice to calculate yearly. Distinguishing between the two Baha'i heroes and their birthdays can be confusing to outsiders so a mind process seems to help. To assist, Bab is often compared to John the Baptist (the preparer) while Baha'u'llah is aligned with Jesus. *See also* Bab; Baha'i International; Baha'u'llah; Birth of the Bab; calendar (Islamic).

Birth of the Bab: a Baha'i holy day celebrating the birth of the religion's founder, Siyyid Mirza 'Ali-Muhammed Shirazi (1819 – 1850). The date is one of twin holidays on the Baha'i calendar. The closely associated Baha'u'llah celebration occurs on the first day of Muharram of the Islamic calendar with the other set as the Birth of the Bab on the second day. Both dates are movable requiring higher authority within the Baha'i Universal House of Justice to calculate yearly. Distinguishing between the two Baha'i heroes and their holy days can be confusing to outsiders so a mind process seems to help. To assist, Bab is often compared to John the Baptist (the preparer) while Baha'u'llah is aligned with Jesus. *See also* Bab; Baha'i International; Baha'u'llah; Birth of Baha'u'llah; calendar (Islamic).

birth pains, illustration of: ("beginning of sorrows" in the KJV) an expression used by Jesus to describe the pace of time and events as we near the end of the age. A similar view is presented by Paul in 1 Thessalonians 5:3. The apocryphal books of *Jubilees* (second century) and *Apocalypse of Baruch* (late first century) uses the analogy in much the same manner as do the Gospels. The meaning of the expression is that apocalyptic dealings will become more pronounced and obvious as the time of the end approaches, much like that of a woman experiencing childbirth. The intensity and frequency of prenatal contractions increase steadily and exponentially as the moment of "birth," or advent of the eschaton, advances. Jesus named a number of specific birth pains, mostly from the Olivet Discourse. These certainly include: arrival of false Christs, wars and rumors of war, famines, earthquakes, pestilences, plagues, fearful events and signs from heaven, religious persecution, discord among churches, a falling away from faith, false prophets, increase of lawlessness, love growing cold, and severe oceanic and atmospheric activity. *See also Apocalypse of Baruch;* Apocalypse, the; beginning of sorrows; eschatology, eschatological; *Jubilees, Book of;* little Apocalypse, the; "nation against nation"; Olivet Discourse, the; seven signs, the; "signs of the times"; war on the earth.

bishop(s): in the early Christian church, a pastor, undershepherd, or overseer; the name was certainly in use in the early church to designate exactly such positions. In more recent usage, a bishop in some systems of ecclesiastical authority is a high ranking church official, a prelate. Originally, even the pope of Rome was a bishop but has since increased the prestige of the title and expanded its authority. The term "archbishop" is not biblical, but it sets today as a rank superior to bishop. *See also* Abba; archbishop(s); archiereus; camerlengo; church, administration of the early; chaplain(s); clergy; divine;

Eastern Orthodox Church; ecclesiastic(s); episcopate; *episcopos;* flying bishops; hierophant; man of God; minister(s); orders; pastor(s); patriarch(s); pope; preacher(s); prefect(s); prelate(s); *presbuteros;* priest(s); primate; Protestantism, Protestants; Roman Catholic Church; suffragan.

bitheist: or duotheist, one who believes in two godheads, one of which is usually male and the other female. The designation is common in the more subtle doctrines of Wiccan practice and in Zoroastrianism.

Bithynia: a Roman province of Asia Minor along the Black Sea coast. There were Christians located there in some numbers (*cf.* Acts 16:7 and 1 Peter 1:1). *See also* Roman Empire.

bitter herbs: a serving of potent herbs, such as horseradish, at the Passover meal (Ex. 12:8). The symbolism points up the bitter harshness of the Hebrew slavery in Egypt. *See also* flora, fruit, and grain, symbology of; "four cups, the"; "four questions, the"; "four nights, the"; gall; Haggada; herb(s); Paschal lamb; Passover; bread, unleavened; *Seder;* Unleavened Bread, Feast of.

black: the "color" of no light. When used symbolically, black is often an indicator of calamity, despair, darkness, evil, death, or mental depression. The word as an ethnicity distinction has no theological connection except to specificity of subject.

black arts: magical spells, mantic magic, sorcery, and the like practiced by those who wish to harness evil spirits or occult forces within our natural world. Such actions are forbidden by God's law. *See also* anthropomancy; anthroposophy; apotropaic magic; aretology; Ariosophy; astral plane; astral projection; astrolabe; astrology, astrologers; athame; audition; augury; automatic writing; bagua; belomancy; *besom;* bibliomancy; black arts; black mirror; blood moon(s); cartomancy; chaos magic; chiromancy; clairaudience; clairsentience; clairvoyance; cleromancy; charm(s); conjure; conjure man; crop circles; Crowley, Aleister; cryptesthesia;

crystallomancy; crystal skulls; curious acts; divination; dream(s); dreams and visions; ecstasy; enchantment; enneagram; evil eye; extrasensory perception (ESP); foreknowledge; foretelling; geomancy; grimoire; gris-gris; hepatoscopy; Hermetic wisdom; Hermetic writings; hex; hierscopy; horoscope(s); hydromancy; idol(s); idolatry; ifa; incantation; juju; Key of Solomon; labyrinth walk; La Vey, Anton Szandor; lecanomancy; literomancy; locution; magic arts; magic, magick; magic square; magnetism; *mana*; mantic wisdom; mantra; miracle(s); monition; necromancy; New Age religion; numbers, symbology of; occult, occultic; oneiromancy; oracle(s); otherworldly journeys; ouija board; out-ofbody experiences (OBEs); paranormal; parapsychology; past life regression; peace pole(s); pentagram; philosophers' stone; planchette; planets as gods; portent; precognition; prediction; prefiguration; premonition; prodigy; prognostication; prophecy, general; psi; psychic(s); psychic healing; psychic reading; psychomancy; psychometry; psychonautics; pyramidology; rebirthing; remote viewing; retrocognition; rhabdomancy; Satanism; scrying; séance; secret societies; secret wisdom; sorcery, sorceries; spell; spell names; spiritism; stigmata; supernatural; superstition; tarot; telegnosis; telepathy; telesthesia; theugry; third eye, the; thoughtform; totemism; veve; vision(s); vision quest; visualization; voodoo; voudou; warlock(s); WebBot; witchcraft; wizard(s); *ya sang*; yoga; Zen; zodiac; *zos kia* cultus.

Black Canons: or Austin Canons, a Roman Catholic order of canons regular similar to the Benedictines established in England. The name is derived from the dress of black cassocks and mantles with a white surplice. Those who wear solid white garb are White Canons. *See also* Assumptionist Orders; Augustinian Order; Barnabites; Benedict, Order of; canon(s) of the church; canons regular; Capuchin Order; Carmelites; Carthusians; Celestines; Cistercians; clergy; Dominicans; Franciscans; friar(s); Minim; monasticism; monk(s); orders;

Paulist Fathers; Premonstratensian Order; priest(s); religious organizations; Roman Catholic Church; Servite Order; Spirituals of the Franciscan Order; Trappist Order.

Black Fast, the: the Anglican practice of fasting on the two great fast days, Ash Wednesday and Good Friday. The tradition began in the 19th century, supposedly in imitation of the fasting observance in the early church. *See also* abstinence; Church of England; fast, fasting; Lent; liturgy, Christian.

black horse: the steed used by the rider of the third scal of the Apocalypse (Rev. 6:5). The dark color represents economic failure, famine, disease, poverty, and despair. The accompanying citation states the end times will show a scarcity of life essentials—a quart of wheat will cost a day's wages and three quarts of barley for the same amount. However, there is a call not to damage the oil and wine, as if those luxury items are to be had by the privileged. Another translation, and perhaps a better one, says "Don't waste the wine and oil." All the necessities are parceled out by the black rider who carries a pair of scales as his marker. *See also* animals, birds, and insects, symbology of; eschatology, eschatological; four horsemen of the Apocalypse; horse; pale horse; red horse; white horse.

Black Islam. See Nation of Islam.

black lamb: an animal sacrifice executed to honor the gods of the dead or the underworld in ancient times. Hecate required the present of a black lamb with a dog and Hades demanded them as a sacrificial offering. Today, a black lamb offering is a traditional witch's presentation. *See also* animals, birds, and insects, symbology of; idolatry; underworld; Wicca.

Black Letter Days: some sixty-seven lesser feast days of Anglicanism in the English Prayer Book of 1567. The name derives because the specified print was black whereas the major feasts were in red. *See also* Church of England; liturgy, Christian.

Black Madonnas: depictions of the Virgin Mary, often with the infant Jesus, that are black or deep brown in appearance. Probably the color had little to do with race until recent renditions but there is controversy as to how and why pre-Christian deities may have manifested to a number of of the images. Some Modonnas were black because they were made that way; others assumed the shade because of candle soot through the ages. The icons are favored by both Roman Catholic and Orthodox persuasions and some are reported to have produced miracles. They may be constructed of either wood or stone, of which some are in museums but most reside in liturgical churches across the globe. *See also* Eastern Orthodox Church; Mariolatry; Roman Catholic Church.

black magic. See black arts.

Black Mass. See Satanism.

black mirror: a water-scrying device used in occultic practice. The spell is accomplished by adding ink to a bowl of water and studying its depths. *See also* charm(s); hydromancy; idolatry; juju; magic, magick; New Age religion; occult, occultic.

Black Obelisk: a major archeological find in the ruins of ancient Nineveh at the palace of Shalmaneser. The object was eventually moved to the British Museum. The artifact is a dark stone, seven feet in height, with prolific inscriptions and reliefs on its surface. The second line from the top features Jewish-like figures kneeling in tribute before Shalmaneser with the inscription: "The tribute of Jehu, son of Omri, silver, gold, bowls of gold, chalices of gold, cups of gold, vases of gold, lead, scepter for the king, and spear-shafts, I have received."

Black One, the: the term for the Antichrist used in the pseudepigraphical *Epistle of Barnabas*. *See also* Antichrist; *Armilus;* stern-faced king, the.

Black Road, the. See Dark Rift, the.

History and Mystery

Black Rubric: a tightly composed Protestant explanation of the practice of kneeling for Communion, something John Knox and others disfavored. In response, Archbishop Cranmer inserted the Black Rubric into the second revision of the Anglican Prayer Book, leaving no doubt as to how Anglicans should position themselves for prayer. *See also* Alternative Service Book; Church of England; rubric.

black stone of the United Nations: an icon or worship object placed within the meditation chapel of the United Nations headquarters in New York City when the room was added in the 1970s. Debate centered on what the contemplative focus should be since the United Nations is supposedly neutral to religion. A cross or any other overtly religions symbol or logo simply would not do. The result consists of an unadorned black stone block. The object has been described as a rather gloomy, somber-looking "altar" in the center of the Meditation Room and dimly lit by recessed lighting. The "stone" is actually a chunk of Swedish crystalline ore, the largest of its kind ever mined. It is described as a lodestone, or magnetite, strongly magnetized. It rests upon two narrow cross pieces atop a concrete pillar based on solid bedrock below and weighing in at six and one half tons. It was a gift of Dag Hammarskjold (1905 – 1961) from King Gustaf VI Adolf of Sweden. Entrance to see or utilize the stone and its housing is regulated. *See also* idol(s); idolatry; Meditation Room of the United Nations.

black stones: in opposition to white stones, such pebbles as were considered unlucky. Or they were used as voting symbols to condemn a person on trial. *See also* ephod; idolatry; Urim and Thummin; white stones.

Black Stone, the. See *Ka'aba* Stone.

Blackstone, William Eugene: American evangelist and avid Zionist (1841–1935). His theological views centered on the notion that a Jewish repatriation to Israel was the only sound political and religious ideal that was sensible for the

345

world. He was a dispensationalist and author of the best seller, *Jesus is Coming*. The book has been characterized as the *Left Behind* thriller of his day having sold in the millions of copies over fifty years in forty-eight languages. At one point, Blackstone managed to secure some 431 signatures of prominent Americans to a manifesto regarding his Zionist views. This document, now called the "Blackstone Memorial," was presented to President Benjamin Harrison in March of 1891. Blackstone even sent a copy of the Hebrew Bible, with appropriate passages marked, to Theodore Herzl to encourage the Zionist movement. His actions earned him the title "Father of Zionism" at a Jewish conference in Philadelphia in 1918. Nevertheless, Blackstone never went so far afield as to say Jews are saved without the involvement of Christ as Messiah Because of his genuine humility, Blackstone would permit only the initials W.E.B. to be used for his authorship. *See also* dispensationalist(s); evangelist(s), evangelism; Methodists; revivalism; Zionism; Zionism, Christian.

black sun: the *sonnenrad* (sun wheel), an occultic design of a black circle surrounded by a dark spherical with a swastika graphic. It is sometimes used by German neo-paganism and some white supremacist groups. *See also* Christian Identity Movement (CIM); idol(s); magic, magick; neo-Nazi(s); occultic, occultic; swastika.

black swan event: some grand historical occurrence, usually economically related, affecting the world in a decidedly negative manner. No one can see it developing but, in hindsight, everyone can state it was easy to perceive its approach. A black swan event may also prove to have religious implications as well as political and economic. *See also* social issues.

black theology. See Afro-American theology.

Black Vault: said to be the repository, either real or imagined, of the secret files containing the government's investigations and knowledge about UFOs and related phenomenon. Rumor and published material suggest the "vault" holds the results of Project Bluebook and correlated materials, generally considered to be unavailable to the public. *See also* Alien Disclosure Event; conspiracy theorists; New Age religion; UAP; UFO; Vimanas.

Blair, James: Episcopalian clergyman and educator (1656–1743). Blair was proactive in his position in the colonies, advocating for fair treatment from Britain. In fact, three governors from the crown were sent packing back to England for disagreeing with Blair on political, religious, or educational issues. He founded William and Mary University, the second established in America after Harvard. Late in life he became royal governor of Virginia. *See also* Protestant Episcopal Church.

blasphemy: a contemptuous expression toward God. The root meaning carries the idea of injuring the reputation of another. Revelation 13:1 cites the beast from the sea as having a blasphemous name on each of his seven heads. Under the old Mosaic Law, the punishment for blasphemy was death by stoning (Lev. 24:10–23). To blaspheme is to speak carelessly, falsely, or insultingly toward God or anything holy. Some see the sin of blasphemy as equal to the so-called "unpardonable sin." Such an understanding may be acceptable if the blasphemy is considered a denunciation of the Holy Spirit in matters of salvation. *See also* abomination; abomination of desolation, the; curse(s); profane; sacrilege; sin unto death; social issues; Ten Commandments, the.

Blastus: a personal servant of Herod Agrippa I (Acts 12:20) who assisted the people of Tyre and Sidon to make peace with his master.

Blavatsky, Madame Helena Petrovna: a Russian mystic (1831–1891), the founder of the Theosophical Society and an influential character in her time. Many of her prophecies involve details about continents and islands sinking and rising in the world's oceans. Her most important writings are entitled *Secret Doctrines* and *Isis Unveiled*. The Theosophical Movement was Blavatsky's own invention. It involved a concoction of Judeo-Christian tradition and esoteric Eastern knowledge mixed with crude social Darwinism. Blavatsky has even been suggested as a forerunner of Nazism, due to her introduction of Aryan myth as the superior fifth root race of humankind. "Aryan" is a term for a population of light-skinned giants from the lost continent of Atlantis. According to her, the ancient site called Mu was a harsh and desolate place where native giants dwelt in hardened lava huts who eventually became the ancestors of the aborigines of Australia and other Melanesian peoples. *See also* Besant, Annie; giant(s); Lemuria; psychic(s); sect(s); Theosophical Society; Theosophy.

blazing mountain, a: an issue of the second trumpet of Revelation (Rev. 8:8). The impact of such a large celestial object on the planet causes a third of the oceans to become blood, a third of the fish to die, and a third of the sea traffic to be destroyed. What the object is, precisely, is unknown but seems to resemble a rogue asteroid or other heavenly body. *See also* celestial disturbances; impact event.

blazing star: an issue of the third trumpet of Revelation (Rev. 8:10). The object carries the name "Wormwood," meaning "bitter," and causes a third of the fresh waters of earth to become polluted. The object cannot be precisely identified but seems to resemble a large asteroid or other space object. *See also* celestial disturbances; impact event; Wormwood.

blazon: a love poem praising the beauty and virtue of the beloved being described, sometimes called an "emblematic blazon." The Song of Solomon is replete with the blazon technique. *See also* Canticles; poetry (biblical); psalm; Song of Songs as Old Testament book.

blended worship: any attempt to combine aesthetic and modernized worship styles to either eliminate or modify the traditional worship content and expression. Results have been mostly seen in the type of upbeat (and loud) music presented but the effort has produced a hodgepodge of forms. Most have proven less than satisfactory although some younger audiences have responded positively. *See also* contemporary worship; liturgy, Christian; worship.

blessed: a frequent expression in Scripture, including any positive discussion of eschatological events or the condition of one's life. The meaning holds the idea of "fortunate" or "happy." The Greek is *makarious.* To bless is to make holy, to show favor to, or to ask or ascribe favor to God or another person. *See also* Beatitudes, the; benediction; blessings(s); hallow; initiate.

"Blessed Be": a favored greeting or ritual response common to Wiccan associates and other pagan applications. *See also* pagan practice; Wicca; witchcraft.

blessed hope, the: a New Testament term for the anticipated rapture or resurrection of believers at the Second Coming of Christ. It was a favorite expression used by the early church to communicate their expectation for life in the hereafter. *See also* eschatology, eschatological; hope; rapture; resurrection(s).

blessing(s): a grace or courtesy from God. God's blessings are highly coveted by believers everywhere and throughout Scripture. Such acts of grace are liberally bestowed on the deserving. The absence of divine blessing can only be seen as a spiritual and practical catastrophe. The world's greatest blessings of history might be viewed as the Lord's First and Second Appearances. In some renderings, it is appropriate for persons to bless others or to bless God Himself as an expression of worship. A blessing can also be an alternate name for grace before meals. *See also* antiphon; Beatitudes, the; benediction; blessed; blessings of God; corporate prayer; curse(s); deodate; gestures; "God-shot"; grace; liturgy, Christian; liturgy, Jewish; prayer(s).

blessings of God: receipt of goodness or prosperity from the Father. To the ancient Hebrews, the most important of God's blessings were: 1. a life without undue suffering, 2. children born to the family, 3. living to an old age. Even so, reverence for God (a sign of wisdom) ensures that someone would be blessed in life and after death even if the three great worldly fortunes were hindered or denied. The apocryphal *Ecclesiasticus* is probably the most expansive expression of the theme, the opening pages of which paint a darker picture but ending far more hopefully. *See also* blessing(s).

blindness: the state of being sightless, either in a physical sense or in a metaphorical sense for spiritual darkness. In ancient days, some mistakenly believed that blindness (and other bodily maladies) always signified punishment from God. In Revelation and elsewhere, blindness is a condition of inoperative or false faith (Rev. 3:17). Paul stated that the minds of some believers have been blinded by Satan (2 Cor. 4:4). *See also* blindness of Israel.

blindness of Israel: the theological belief that the nation (or race) of Israel is presently in spiritual darkness because they have refused their Messiah at his first appearance. Inevitably, this doctrine is modified with the hope or assurance that the situation will be reversed and a remnant of Israel will be saved (Isa. 6:9–10; Mk. 4:12; Jn. 12:40; Rom. 11:11–27; 2 Cor. 3:14–15). *See also* blindness; remnant; second Exodus.

blood: an important biblical term centering on sacrifice or redemption (Ex. 24:8), a sign of repentance since the days of Cain and Abel. Without blood sacrifice (animal offerings in the Old Testament and Christ's shed blood in the New), forgiveness and redemption are not effectual. Human martyrdom is recognized as the shed blood of the innocent, especially in apocalyptic literature (*e.g.,* Revelation 6:10). Blood can also be a symbol for violence, death, or punishment (Rev. 14:20). *See also* blazing mountain, a; blood of Christ; blood of the Lamb; "blood of the martyrs"; blood of the saints; blood overflowing;

History and Mystery

grapes; harvest of the earth; libation; martyr(s); names, symbology of; sacrifice; Sangrael; spirit; Spirit, the water, and the blood, the; streets of the city; tauroctony; vicarious atonement; water(s); wine; wine of wrath; winepress.

blood curse: the supposed Jewish willingness to accept liability for the crucifixion of Christ. The meaning points to a passage from the Gospel of Matthew (Mt. 27:24 – 25) wherein Pilate recluses himself from Jesus' capital punishment demand and publically washed his hands of the matter. Rather, he appeared to place the blame on the accusers, the Jewish leaders and people, to which they seemingly readily acquiesced. *See also* blood libel; crucifixion conspiracies; Judaism.

blood feud: an extension of family responsibilities in most of the ancient world that exercised blood-letting and retaliation as a method of protecting familial integrity, justice, and honor. The custom extended to the clan structure as well, or the extended family. An Old Testament example is found in the murder of Abner by David's general Joab (2 Sam. 2:18–23; 3:26–27). *See also* avenger of blood, the; cities of refuge; *lex talionis;* vengeance.

blood libel: the term applied to the disturbing process of accusing a group, particularly a religious group, of kidnapping, ritual abuse, moral turpitude, and sometimes even cannibalism of their victims. Such labels have damaged Jews, Christians, Wiccans, Druids, Roma (Gypsies), and others over the centuries. *See also* anti-Semitic; blood curse; crucifixion conspiracies.

blood moon(s): those instances when the moon appears reddish in color, long considered an ill omen in early folklore. Some theologians describe the events to be signs in heaven (particularly with a lunar eclipse) that occur on the biblical (Hebrew) calendar and thereby important. Genesis 1:14 states that God positioned the heavenly hosts (sun, moon, and stars) for *signals* on His high holy days. The "seasons" mentioned in the verses are not fall, winter, spring, and summer but "signs" relating to the feast days of Israel. Some blood moon promoters claim those same signs are significant to Christianity also. The Christian expression of the Hebrew spring festivals equates the death of Jesus on the cross as having occurred during Passover; his burial at the Feast of Unleavened Bread; his resurrection at Firstfruits; the Spirit poured out at Pentecost. Together, the events make up a kind of "scenic review" of the Messiah's first advent. The Christian expression of the Hebrew fall festivals align with the Tribulation starting on Trumpets; the rapture or resurrection of the dead on Yom Kippur; the Millennium at Tabernacles. Together, the events make up a kind of "dress rehearsal" for the Second Coming. The appearance of a blood moon takes on added eschatological significance only when certain apocalypticists proclaim it to be so. A series of four red moons appearing during the Jewish high holy days of Passover and Tabernacles between April 2004 and October 2015 stirred some interest. Some attributed that this quartet of viewings heralded world-shaking events with prophetic implications since it had occurred only thirty-one times in the past five centuries. As far as can be seen, absolutely no event of prophetic importance happened during the time but speculation persists that blood moons speak of misfortune. Biblical eschatology does, however, discuss the moon turning to blood and similar phenomena as we approach the end times. *See also* celestial disturbances; eclipse(s); eschatology, eschatological; generation; moon; New Moon(s); planets as gods, the; Rogation Days; signs in heaven; sun; supermoon.

blood of Christ: a Christian confessional or metaphor for the spilled blood of Jesus given up on the cross to secure our redemption. The wine of the Communion ritual is also called the blood of Christ because of its mystery substance or symbolic imagery, but always heavy with vital redemptive meaning within the partaker. One of the most extensive discussions of the meaning of Christ's sacrifice with his own blood is found in Hebrews 9:11–15. *See also* accept Christ, to; altar call; "asking Jesus into my heart"; blood; blood of the Lamb; bloodstained robe; body of Christ, the; birth from above; born again; confession(s) of faith; conversion; "plead the blood"; profession of faith; regeneration; sacrifice; "saved"; soul-winning; turn your life [heart] over to Jesus"; "walking the aisle"; "washed in the blood."

blood of the Lamb: the phrase used often in Scripture (including Revelation) as a way to picture the sacrifice of Christ on the cross of salvation. The most common animal sacrifice in biblical times was that of a sheep or lamb. Because of Jesus' substitutionary death and glorious resurrection, salvation for the believer is guaranteed for all of time. Today, the "blood of the Lamb" is popular in conservative and fundamentalist circles to represent the atoning work of Christ in salvation using an easier language. *See also* accept Christ, to; animals, birds, and insects, symbology of; blood; "asking Jesus into my heart"; blood; blood of Christ; bloodstained robe; body of Christ, the; birth from above; born again; confession(s) of faith; conversion; evangelist(s), evangelism; fishers of men; gospel; lost; "nail-scarred hands, the"; "plead the blood"; profession of faith; regeneration; sacrifice; "saved"; soul-winning; "turn your life [heart] over to Jesus"; "walking the aisle"; "washed in the blood."

"blood of the martyrs": part of the oft-quoted phrase, "The blood of the martyrs is the seed of the Church." The expression is attributed to Tertullian and reminds all that martyrdom and sacrifice are the impetus and main ingredients for Christian growth and fidelity. *See also* blood; blood of the saints; martyrdom; Tertullian.

blood of the saints: a sign of martyrdom, especially prevalent in Revelation. Those killed in the Tribulation are often described as saints who have died a martyr's death and await the true justice of God. A famous quote attributed to Tertullian says, "The blood of the martyrs is the seed of the Church." *See also* blood; "blood of the martyrs"; eschatology, eschatological; martyrdom; Tertullian.

blood overflowing: a hyperbolic expression found in Revelation 14:20 wherein the winepress of God's wrath is said to produce blood rising as high as the horses' bridle for a distance of 180 miles. Something similar is found in *2 Esdras* 15:35, recorded as "blood, shed by the sword, will reach as high as a horse's belly, a man's thigh, or a camel's hock." *See also* animals, birds, and insects, symbology of; blood; bridle of the horses; eschatology, eschatological; grapes; harvest of the earth; wine; wine of wrath; winepress.

bloodstained robe: the garment worn by the Second Coming Christ (Rev. 19:13). Whether the blood on the robe signifies the Lord's sacrifice at Calvary or the coming destruction of the armies of the Antichrist (or both) is unclear, but the violent intent of the image is obvious. *See also* blood of Christ; blood of the Lamb; eschatology, eschatological.

blue laws: in America, any statutes restricting or forbidding certain actions on Sunday. Although readily accommodated to the Puritans, the first blue laws were passed in colonial Virginia (1624), prompted mostly by the established Anglican Church. Why the name "blue?" The most probable explanation is that the Puritans recorded their Sabbath edicts on blue paper. In some regions, the blue laws made church attendance mandatory, sometimes including locking the doors against early departure. Restrictions were placed on travel, dress, personal ornamentation, commerce (both public and private), and recreation. There were penalties for non-compliance, and, in certain instances, the militia was authorized to force church attendance. The laws eventually aided such organizations as the Woman's Christian Temperance Union and Anti-Saloon League and led to passage of the Eighteenth Amendment on prohibition (repealed in 1933). There remain today traces of Sunday regulations but most are varied from state to state and city to city, weakly enforced or ignored. *See also* Congregationalists; convectile acts; Davenport, John; Eaton, Theophilus; temperance; Theophilus; Puritanism, Puritans.

Blue Star prophecy: also known as the Blue Kachina or Saquasohuh, the Hopi prophecy that warns of the appearance of the next age of mankind. A certain Blue Star, not clearly defined, is to appear near but not precisely coterminous with the new creation after the year 2012. It is possible we are presently in the Blue Star age or it manifested itself closer to the year 2012. Some claim that the prophecy matches much in Mayan culture, the Web-Bot trials, and Nostradamus. *See also* cosmic cross; eclipse(s); eschatology, eschatological; galactic alignment, the; Great Shaking, the; Great Change, Prophecy of the; Hopi; Maya; Nostradamus; Rainbow Warriors, the; Rattlesnake prophecy; 2012 prophecy, advocates of; 2012, prophecy of; Web-Bot; zodiac.

blyt: a Norse expression for the kinship between themselves and their gods. *See also* Aesir; Alfheimr; Armanenschafft; Asa; Asatru; giant(s); idolatry; Norse and Old Germanic pantheon; rune(s); seior; Valupsa; volva.

B'nai B'rith: a Jewish fraternal and activist organization dedicated to the welfare and progress of Jews around the world. The group was begun in 1843 by twelve wealthy and established New York Jews to aid incoming Jewish immigrants to the United States. Assimilation into the new society was difficult for the arrivals so the philanthropy alleviated some of the stress of resettlement. The name of the association means "sons of the covenant" or "sons of the alliance" but is remarked today for two of its most recognized subsidiaries. The Anti-Defamation League (the most militant arm of B'nai B'rith) fights racial and religious prejudice; the Hillel Foundation attempts to strengthen the religious life of college students. *See also* anti-Semitic; Jewish persecution; Judaism; religious organizations; social issues.

b'nai Noach: Jewish name for Gentiles (the "Noahides") who have agreed to accept Torah under the authority of the Sanhedrin according to Qabbalist Judaism. The proselyte is to appear before a rabbinical court of at least three judges and pledge allegiance to the "the Seven Laws of Torah" (or *mitzvot)* and submit himself or herself to the authority of the Sanhedrin. The seven laws are essentially prohibitions against idolatry, murder, theft, sexual promiscuity, and blasphemy. Additionally, there are certain dietary stipulations, and each candidate must agree to affiliate with courts for the purpose of governing within these select laws. Qabbalists believe that the future one world government will be headed by one of their courts. Their logo is to be the rainbow, each color representing a law of the order. The future great beast of ten horns is called the Council of the Nations; that with seven horns is the Council of the World. *See also* Judaism; *mitzvot;* Qabbalism; Seven Laws of Noah, the.

Boanerges. See sons of thunder.

Boaz: 1. kinsman-redeemer to Naomi and husband to Ruth. He was a prominent farmer and landowner from Bethlehem who became the father of Obed, the father of Jesse, the father of David (Josephus called him "Booz"). Thus, Ruth and Boaz are in the kingly line of Judah and Jesus. Boaz is noted as the son of Rahab, who may have been a prostitute in Jericho (Josh. 2:1; Mt. 1:5). His wife, Ruth, was a Moabitess. Therefore, two generations in succession were Gentiles in the line of King David and Jesus which, in some fashion, makes non-Jews a part of the covenant. 2. one of a pair of fiery pillars erected near the entrance of Solomon's Temple, the other being named Jachin. *See also* Boaz and Jachin; kinsman-redeemer; Naomi; Ruth as Old Testament book; Ruth as Old Testament heroine.

Boaz and Jachin: the two grand free-standing pillars set in place before the Temple of God in Jerusalem. Both featured fiery cressets emitting smoke and fire continuously. Together they symbolized the pillar of fire by night and pillar of cloud by day during the Exodus wanderings. Isaiah (Isa. 4:5) speaks of cloud and smoke that will preside over Jerusalem when the Lord dwells there in the Millennium. The names for the two columns probably accrue from the Hebrew opening words of promise inscribed on them. On the left, Boaz reads: "In the strength (*beaz*) of Yahweh shall the king rejoice." On the right, Jachin records: "Yahweh will establish (*yakin*) thy throne forever." Both quotes seem to be inspired by Psalm 21:1. Another interpretation says that they were named for Boaz, the great-grandfather of David, and a Phoenician word meaning "he will be." The structures were 324 feet high and 18 feet in circumference with capitals beautifully carved in flowering lilies and pomegranates. In the pseudepigraphon called *Lives of the Prophets*, the towers are said to provide sources of illumination for Jews being pursued by the serpent in the latter days. The prophecy suggests a close relationship to Revelation 12:13–14. *See also* Boaz; pillars of the Temple.

Bockelson, Jan: a radical Anabaptist (1509 – 1536) who became an influential prophet in Munster in the German section of the Holy Roman Empire. He established himself as a self-proclaimed king during the rebellion the rebels believed would establish Munster as the New Jerusalem and the site of "a kingdom of a thousand years." Bockelson, or Jan of Leiden as he was also known, paraded proudly in the city in a frenzy, then went mute for three days. When speech was regained, he called upon the population and told them God had told him the city constitution must be replaced with his own. All the gold and silver were to be delivered to him and a strict sexual morality was put in place. Later, Bockelson reversed the code and initiated polygamy; he taking many young women, none of them over twenty. All food and wine went to him even when the city was besieged by reinforcements from surrounding cities and the populace was reduced to eating pets, mice and rats, grass and moss, old shoes and the whitewash on the walls, and even dead bodies. Anyone who defied him was executed. The rebellion was doomed from the start, of course. Along with fellow conspirator Jan Matthys, Bockelson was captured, tortured, and executed. *See also* Anabaptists; Holy Roman Empire; Matthys, Jan; Peasants' Revolt.

Bod: the native name for the people of Tibet, and sometimes referring to their religion or culture. *See also* idolatry; Pure Land, the; sect(s).

Bodhi Tree: known to Buddhist and others as the "Tree of Wisdom." Under one of that species, Buddha reportedly achieved enlightenment. *See also* Bile; Buddhism; cosmic tree; flora, fruit, and grain, symbology of; idol(s); tree(s); tree of life, the; tree of the knowledge of good and evil, the; tree of Zaqqum.

bodily resurrection: the affirmation that believers will resurrect in new and perfected bodies suitable to spend eternity—"when he is revealed, we shall be like him" (1 Jn. 3:2). The belief is patterned on the bodily resurrection of Jesus whose corporeal body could ingest food, bear human touch, pass through walls, etc., but was definitely a new order of being. *See also* body; eschatology, eschatological; glorified body (bodies); resurrection(s); resurrections in Daniel; resurrections in Ezekiel; resurrection, the first.

body: the flesh, blood, bone, and other essential organic matter that constitutes a living person. Theology insists that the spirit of God resides within it when the person is alive. In a more eschatological sense, and in point of deeper understanding, the Bible specifically identifies three types of "body"—not one. Paul explained (1 Cor. 15:40–42) that the creation holds a terrestrial (earthly or natural) body, a celestial (heavenly or spirit) body, as well as implies a third, the resurrection or glorified body, which is examined in more detail in other passages. Perhaps it is correct to say, as some do, that humans are born in an earthly body, carried to Paradise after death in a spiritual one, and raised to heaven in the resurrection body bestowed by Christ at the end of the age. *See also* bodily resurrection; body of Christ, the; carnal; Church; earthly tent; flesh; glorified body (bodies); jars of clay; out of body experiences (OBEs); resurrection(s); temple(s).

body of Christ, the: 1. a New Testament term for the Church (universal) of Jesus Christ. 2. the bread of the Communion ritual is also called "the body of Christ" since it represents his crucified flesh given up in death for our redemption either as a mystery compound or symbolic image. *See also* blood of Christ; body; Christian(s); Christianity; Church; church; Eucharist; Lord's Supper; temple(s); The Way; universal church.

body of Moses, dispute over the: a mysterious reference found in Jude 9 that speaks of a confrontation between Satan and the archangel Michael. The godly archangel is implied to be victorious in the contest, but even in the heat of combat, he did not bring a slanderous accusation against the devil in deference to Satan's high rank. Instead, Michael ordered, "The Lord rebuke you." The incident may or may not be a factor in determining if Moses is one of the two super witnesses described in Revelation 11:1-14. *See also* angelic miracles; Jude as New Testament epistle; Michael; Moses.

bogle: also called a boggart and other names, a goblin-like creature associated with the fairy folk of Druidism. *See also* attending spirit(s); banshee; brownies; bugbears; Celtic folklore and religion; clurichauns; daemons; deceiving spirits; demons, demonic; devils; disa; Druidism; dryad(s); disa; elemental(s); fairy, fairies; familiar spirit; Fomorians; Furies; ghost(s); ghoul; gnome(s); Green Man, the; Gregori; hobgoblins; homunculus; household deities; huldufolk; Lares; leprechaun(s); Loa Loas; Manes; memeton; mythological beasties, elementals, monsters, and spirit animals; nereid; nisse; nymph(s); nyx; Ogham;

Oniropompi; Orisha; Oya; para; paredri; penates; Robin Goodfellow; satyr; Seelie Court, Unseelie Court; selkie; Sidhe; sirens; sylph(s); spiritual warfare; sprite(s); teraphim; territorial spirit; Trickster; Tuatha de Danann; tutelary; undine; wight(s).

Bogomiles. See Cathars.

Bohemian Grove: an exclusive 2,700-acre campground in Monte Rio, California, (and other locations) owned by the all-male Bohemian Club. Some of the most powerful elite of politics and big business meet there regularly to discuss and plan a variety of unknown subjects and projects. It is most famous for its secretive role in the Manhattan Project of World War II which produced the atom bomb. Many conspiracists are convinced Bohemian Grove is a bastion of Illuminati-style organization bent on world domination and manipulation. *See also* Bilderberg Group; conspiracy theorists; fraternal organization(s); Illuminati; secret societies.

boil(s): a skin disease, usually resulting in eruptions of pus or blisters. The product of Revelation's first bowl (Rev. 16:2) was an outbreak of painful sores on the people who carried the mark of the beast and worshiped his image. Boils were a rather frequent punishment from God throughout the history of Israel and other nations and a particularly severe one. The Philistines were afflicted with "tumors" because they had captured and retained the ark of the covenant (1 Sam. 5:1,9–12; 6:11). The King James Version names the latter as hemorrhoids or "emerods" but perhaps they were symptoms of any number of skin diseases; some scholars have even suggested the distress may have been bubonic plague. Boils were one of the major symptoms of Job's discomfort (Job 7:5), and they constituted the sixth plague on pre-Exodus Egypt (Ex. 9:8–12). The Hebrew priests were responsible for examining all skin diseases in the community in order to ascertain if quarantine was necessary. *See also* eschatology, eschatological; leprosy; ritual defilement; sore(s).

boiling pot, vision of the: a vision reported by Jeremiah (Jer. 1:13–16) in which he sees a cauldron boiling and tilting away from the north. God is predicting that He will soon pour out His wrath (*orge*) in disaster on the land of Judah through the enemies from the north (Babylonia). Another metaphor involving a boiling cauldron is found in Ezekiel 24, this one designed for cannibalism of the wicked. *See also* cooking pot(s); cooking pot, prophecy of the; pot(s).

Bokim: or Bochim, an unknown place near Gilgal, where an angel appeared to the Israelites to chastise them for their disobedience of God's commands (Judg. 2:1–5). The apparition pushed the hearers to tears and repentance because of the angel's rebuke so they named the place Bokim, "the place of the weepers."

Boko Haram: a Muslim extremist group operating in Nigeria, Africa's most populous territory. The group has been involved in bombings and assassinations, and it created an international incident when they kidnapped 272 young schoolgirls and threatened to sell them into prostitution and slavery. The linguistic name actually means "education is evil" to highlight its fundamental opposition to learning other than the Wahhabi system, especially for girls. *See also Alluha Akbar;* al-Qaeda; al-Shabab; anti-Semitic; beast(s); Daesh; Fatah; Hamas; Hezbollah; House of War; Intifada; Islam; Islamic State in Iraq and Syria (ISIS or ISIL); *jihad;* Muslim Brotherhood; Nusra Front; Palestinian Islamic Jihad (PIJ); Palestinian Liberation Organization (PLO); radicalized; Salafi; Taliban; terrorism; terrorist(s); Turkistan Islamic Party; Velayat Sinai; Wahhabism; wild animals (beasts) of the earth.

boline: a special knife used by Wiccans and other Neo-Paganists to harvest herbs and other plants for ritual use. *See also* athame; *besom;* idolatry; Wicca; witch(es); witchcraft.

Bolos: the Manichean prison or hell for the undying demons. *See also* Abyss, the; demon(s); demonic; devils; Gehenna;

Hades; hell; Jahannam; lake of fire; Manicheanism; Pardes; Perdition; purgatory; *Sheol;* spirits in prison; Tartarus; Tophet; underworld; Xibala.

Bon: an Asian religion (or perhaps a god) usually considered to be a branch of Tibetan *Vajrayana*. Other researchers claim it to be an offshoot of Buddhism, a synergetic Eastern religion of the tenth and 11th centuries, or even a collection of popular beliefs including fortune-telling, a ritualism that preceded the Dalai Lama. Their religious practice is said to have encompassed animal and human sacrifice, demonology, and witchcraft. Despite its uncertain origins, the followers of Bon were called Bonpos. In any case, the occasion is a festival for Shintoists to honor the souls of their ancestors. In some publications, "Bon" simply names the country of Tibet. *See also* Buddhism; Dalai Lama; idolatry; sect(s).

Bonaparte, Napoleon: French emperor and conqueror (1769–1821) who once fought in the region of Armageddon. He was said to have reported then that all the armies of the world could maneuver in that area. When he visited the conquered area, he was said to have inquired about the cause of the Jews he saw lamenting there before the remaining wall of the Temple. The general was informed that the mourners were remembering their standing Temple which was destroyed 1800 years earlier. He commented then, "A people which weeps and mourns the loss of its homeland 1800 years ago and does not forget—such a people will never be destroyed. Such a people can rest assured that its homeland will be returned to it." Some conspirators who envision a collection of three antichrists in our history usually name Napoleon as the first. The second is habitually asserted to be Adolph Hitler and the third is the fiercest of all—the Tribulation prince of evil called the Antichrist. *See also* Cult of Reason; three antichrists theory.

Bondye: a supreme god of many of the so-called Creole religions (voodoo) of the Caribbean. The deity is beyond human reach so devotees must manipulate lesser entities or spirits (like the Loa) to effect change. *See also* Creole (Caribbean) religions; Dambala; idol(s); Loa Loas; lwa; voodoo, voudou.

bone(s): the skeletal framework of the living body. In Scripture, particularly in the prophecy, the bones of animals and humans were conceived to be primary to strength, stability, and mobility. The bones of the sacrificial lamb or the Paschal lamb must not be broken (Ex. 12:46; Num. 9:12; Ps. 34:20) so, subsequently, the bones of the Lamb of God were not fractured on the cross (Jn. 19:36). In early Western and Eastern Christianity, the bones of saints were considered potent relics. They figure prominently in the vision of the dry bones (Ezk. 37:1–14) as resurrection signs. *See also* Ezekiel's vision of the valley of dry bones; Passover; relic(s); rib(s).

"bonfire of the vanities": a romanticized phrase describing a mob's lack of control, pride, and human fallacy. The most famous outbreak involved an incident in 1497 in Florence, Italy, in which thousands of purely utilitarian articles (cosmetics, toys, dresses, mirrors, art, etc.), along with priceless books and manuscripts from the mid-fifteenth century, were destroyed by Christian zealots in the belief that they led to sin. The city-state of Florence was then under the control of the Dominican Girolamo Savonarola. Later, the tag became the title of a novel by Tom Wolfe and fathered a number of dramas and films. Surely, the words originate with the opening verses of Ecclesiastes (Ecc. 1:2). *See also* Savonarola, Girolamo.

Bonhoeffer, Dietrich: Lutheran pastor during the years of World War II (1906–1945). He and Karl Barth were among the very few to defy the Nazi party, a stance that cost Bonhoeffer his life as a martyr. He was aware of Operation Valkyrie, the plot to kill Hitler in the summer of 1944. Most of Bonheoffer's writings survived only in letters or fragments during his time in German prison camps. His theology showed early glimpses of liberation theology, which was to come along a bit later. Bonhoeffer was the most positive theologian of the 20th century in that he spoke powerfully of the joy, with equal fervor to the suffering and cost, of discipleship (the antithesis of which he called "cheap grace"). *See also* Barth, Karl; Bultmann, Rudolf; cheap grace; higher criticism; liberation theology; Lutheran church; martyr(s); Powell, Adam Clayton.

Boniface: *nee* Winfrid or Wynfrith in England in the seventh century. He became a Roman Catholic missionary to the Franks and is known as the patron saint of Germany. He was killed at Frisia in 754, along with fifty-two companions. Legends grew about him, including the claim he invented the Christmas tree. At one point, he was said to be wandering the forests of northern Germany when he came upon heathen worshipers in ritual around an oak, the symbol of the Teutonic god Thor. They were preparing to sacrifice the son of their king, Prince Asulf, hoping to assure blessings for the race. Boniface was outraged and in one blow with his bare fist knocked down the oak. In its place grew a small evergreen, the first tannenbaum. *See also* liturgical year; martyr(s); missions, missionaries; Roman Catholic Church.

book(s): a convenient designation for the various divisions of the Bible, both Old and New Testament, a name taken from the Greek *biblios* or *biblion* (both have similar meanings). The word *book*, of course, names an enormous variety of printed or written material in both sacred and secular genres but is specialized in theological circles to identify the sections of the Bible, those titles named or referenced within it, and certain early manuscripts rejected from the canon. The term fits even though most of the "books" are actually letters, histories, poems, or other literary compositions. Furthermore, the description is useful even though most early treaties were written on scrolls, not bound codices. Various "books" are present at the great white throne judgment as references for the sentencing action of God

(Rev. 20:11–15), as well as the courtroom scene presided over by the Ancient of Days (Dan. 7:10). There are a number of historical books mentioned in the Old Testament, but none of them reproduced therein. They include: the book of Wars of the Lord (Num. 21:14), the *Book of Jashar* (Josh. 10:13; 2 Sam. 1:18; probably 2 Tim. 3:8), the chronicles of David (1 Chr. 27:24) and of Solomon (1 Ki. 11:41), references to the book of Gad the seer (1 Chr. 29:29), the book of the prophet Iddo (2 Chr. 12:15; 13:22), the book of Nathan (1 Chr. 29:29), the annals of Samuel the Seer (1 Chr. 29:29–30), the book of Ahijah, and the annals of Jehu (2 Chr. 20:34), and the book of Shemaiah the prophet (2 Chr. 12:15). An untitled record from Isaiah is found in 2 Chronicles 26:22, and a lament for Josiah by Jeremiah is set in 2 Chronicles 35:25. There was also a book (scroll) of remembrance listing those faithful to God after the exile (Mal. 3:16), and the official record book of Ahasuerus, which aided the Jews of Persia in the time of Esther and Mordecai bearing the title "the book of the annals of the kings of Media and Persia"(Est. 10:2). There is an additional mention of another collection called "records of the seers" (2 Chr. 33:19), which seems to be a generic reference to various writings of the prophets now unavailable to us. Other accounts name "the annals (chronicles) of the kings of Israel and Judah" as further resources (2 Chr. 36:8; 1 Ki. 14:19; 2 Chr. 20:34; 1 Ki. 14:29; 15:7). Most manuscripts of 2 Chronicles 33:18 note that reference as "the annals of Hozai" (also called *Sayings of the Seers)*. The Book of the Covenant was the written record of God's laws (Ex. 24:7). There are books of history (or pseudo-history): the annals of the kings of Media and Persia, the Seers, the Wars of Yahweh, the books of the Ancient of Days, and probably more. Other umbral works of the type should include the *Book of Songs, Manner of the Kingdom, Acts of Uzziah, Acts and Prayers of Manasseh,* and *Laments for Josiah.* See also Additions to Daniel; *Animal Apocalypse, The; Apocalypse of Adam; Apocalypse of Baruch; Apocalypse of Esdras;*

Apocalypse of Paul; apocalyptic themed books and movies; Apocryphal Acts; Apocryphal Apocalypses; Apocryphal Gospels; Apocrypha, the; movies, art, religious; arts, the; *Ascension of Isaiah; Assumption of Moses;* Baruch, book(s) of; *Bel and the Dragon;* bestiary; Bible; *Book of Abramelin, The; Book of Common Prayer;* Book of Concord; Book of Discipline; *Book(s) of Enoch;* Book of Giants; *Book of Jashar; Book of Kells,* the; book of life; Book of Mormon; Book of Remembrance; Book of Sith; Book of the Covenant; Book of the Law; Books of Adam; books of the kings of Israel and Judah; *Book of Shadows; Book of the Wars of the Lord;* book of works; canon of the Scriptures; codex, codices; cultural mandate; Damascus Document; Dead Sea Scrolls; deuterocanonical books; *Ecclesiasticus; Esdras; 1 and 2 Maccabees; 4 Ezra;* Gebal; *Genesis Apocryphon;* Gospel(s); Hagiographa; Hebrew Bible; Heptateuch; Hexateuch; history and mystery of religious documents and sacred writings; Infancy Gospels; Isaiah Scroll; Jedi Path, The; *Jubilees, Book of;* Judith; *Kormchaia; Kybalion;* Lamb's book of life; letter(s); *Lives of the Prophets; "lots books";* Masoretic Text; New Testament; Octatueuch; Old Testament; outside books; Pentateuch; protoapocalypses; Pseudepigrapha, the; Qur'an; Samaritan Pentateuch; Septuagint; scroll(s); scroll of remembrance; *Sibylline Oracles; Sira;* Susanna; *Tales of the Patriarchs;* Tanakh; *Testament of the Twelve Patriarchs; Tobit;* Torah; *Wisdom of Solomon;* written and oral torah.

Booke of the General Lawes and Libertyes: the common statute (1648) of Puritan Massachusetts granting increased freedoms to the general population who felt disenfranchised from the clergy-dominated colony at that time. The law replaced the earlier Massachusetts Body of Liberties (1641) and was somewhat more generous in granting suffrage and other basic rights despite the opposition of the influential John Winthrop. *See also* Abington School District vs. Schempp; Allegheny County vs. ACLU; antidisestablishmentarianism; caesaropapacy; Caesar cult;

civil religion; collegialism; disestablishmentarianism; Edict of Milan; Edict of Nantes; Edict of Toleration; Emerson vs. Board of Education; emperor worship; Establishment Clause and Free Exercise Clause; Geghan Bill; Government Regulation Index (GRI); idolatry; Johnson Amendment; Lemon vs. Kurtzman; Massachusetts Body of Liberties; *Pontifex Maximus; princeps; principis;* public square; Shubert vs. Verner; state church; ultramontanism; Virginia's Religious Disestablishment law; Toleration Act of 1649; Winthrop, John.

Book of Abramelin, The: a grimoire, said to be the extensive works of an Egyptian sage named Abra-Melin the Mage, then presented to a German Jew called Abraham of Worms; the book's internal dating places the finished product around the year 1458. Various renditions have been produced and its contents have remained popular among occultists to the 20th century. The copy, or some rendition of it, has been particularly tied to the cultic organizations like the Hermetic Order of the Golden Dawn and Aleister Crowley's brand of the occult called Thelema. One of the most unique features of the book is its section on how to contact your own personal guardian angel. *See also* Agrippa Books; alchemy; angel(s); *arcanum arcandrum; Arcanum,* the; books); cantrip; *Corpus Hermecticum*; Crowley, Aleister; "Dionysian Artificers, The"; Emerald Tablet of Hermes, the; *Golden Bough, The;* grimoire; guardian angel(s); Hermeticism; Hermetic wisdom; Hermetic writings; idolatry; magic arts; magic, magick; *mana;* mantic wisdom; occult, occultic; parapsychology; *Picatrix;* spell names; Thelema; *Spiritas Mundi.*

Book of Ahasuerus. See book(s).

Book of Ahijah. See book(s).

Book of Changes. See *I Ching.*

Book of Columba. See *Book of Kells,* the.

Book of Common Prayer: the worship and service manual used by the Anglican communion for centuries. It has undergone numerous changes but remains the basic text of the Church of England and its affiliates. Most of the text is credited to Thomas Cranmer. *See also* Alternative Service Book; Anglicanism; Becket, Thomas; book(s); Church of England; Convergence Movement; Cranmer, Thomas; Henry VIII, King; liturgical year; liturgy, Christian; Protestant Episcopal Church; Thirty-Nine Articles, the; Zebra Book.

Book of Concord: a collection of Reformed belief, much of which was drawn from an earlier prototype called the Formula of Concord (1577), the Augsburg Confession (with Melanchthon's defense of it), and the catechisms of Martin Luther. It became the doctrinal standard of the 17th and 18th centuries for conservative Lutherans. The Book of Concord was as indispensable as the Bible for knowing how to be a Christian of that era because it was said to contain all knowledge. *See also* Augsburg Confession; book(s); confession(s) of faith; Large(r) Catechism, Luther's; confession(s) of faith; Luther, Martin; Reformed Churches; Smalcald Articles; Small(er) Catechism, Luther's.

Book of David. See book(s).

book of death: in Jewish tradition, the record of all the wicked recorded by God on *Rosh Hashanah*. The book of life receives the words, thoughts, and deeds of the righteous at the same moment. Most of the populace will fit neither record so a "Ten Days of Grace" is extended to allow for repentance before the Day of Judgment. *See also* book of life; Book of Remembrance; Day of Atonement, the; Judaism; *Rosh Hashanah*.

Book of Discipline: the tome containing the laws, doctrines, administration procedures, and organization of the United Methodist Church. The Book of Resolution and the Book of Worship are companion volumes. *See also* Book of Worship; confession(s) of faith; Methodists.

Book(s) of Enoch: sometimes called *1 Enoch, Book of Enoch*, or other slight variations of the name, an ancient religious manuscript of antediluvian prophecy ascribed to Enoch, the great-grandson of Noah but probably written later. The book is considered non-canonical by Jews and Christians but was widely read in earlier times. The work is in five distinct sections: a history of the Watchers, the parables of Enoch, astronomical descriptions, dreams and visions, and the epistle of Enoch. *The Book of the Watchers* and *The Animal Apocalypse* make up two of these portions. Other apocalyptic writings in the same collection include *The Astronomical Book, The Book of Dreams,* and *The Apocalypse of Weeks.* All are pseudepigraphical writings and fanciful allegory said to be the record of Enoch's preaching. Each is based on the Torah and the Talmud but all are excluded from the Hebrew canon. Parts of the composition are quoted by Jude (verses 14 and 15 are almost precise speech). Most of the work consists of fantasies touching the secrets of cosmic phenomena. One section discusses rewards and punishments in the hereafter. Perhaps the most interesting portions deal with the fallen angels' appeal to the righteous Enoch to intercede for their forgiveness before God because of their heavenly rebellion and corruption of human flesh. Enoch does so on their behalf, but God refuses to grant a pardon. The writing concludes with Enoch being translated to heaven without experiencing death. In summary, the books of Enoch consists of three related but separate literary productions carrying the themes of the end days, punishment for the wicked and reward for the righteous, the coming Messiah, and other generally accepted apocryphal material written in a quasi-biblical style. The book was in existence during the apostolic period, and portions of it were found among the Dead Sea Scrolls. *See also Animal Apocalypse, The;* Apocryphal Apocalypses; book(s); Book of Giants; Enoch; giant(s); Pseudepigrapha; Semyaza; seventy shepherds; wandering stars; Watchers, the.

Book of Gad. See book(s).

Book of Giants: a portion of the *Book of Enoch* discovered in the 20th century among the Dead Sea Scrolls. Boosted by the Manichaean religion, the work was translated worldwide with ethnic variations added. The book supposedly gives added information about the Nephilim, the Watchers, and some other sources from the Old Testament in the antediluvian era. *See also Book(s) of Enoch*; Enoch; giant(s); Semyaza; Watchers, the.

Book of Hozai. See book(s).

Book of Iddo. See book(s).

Book of Isaiah. See book(s).

Book of Jashar: one of thirteen books of ancient origin mentioned in the Bible (Jashar being named specifically in 2 Samuel 1:18, Joshua 10:13, and probably 2 Timothy 3:8), plus any number of references in the Mishna and Talmud. Of these thirteen, only Jashar is available to us, having survived in reprints some 3500 years. Essentially, the work is a companion to the book of Genesis but covers nearly twice as much material as either Genesis or Exodus. The author's name, simply noted as "Jashar," means "upright" so his book is sometimes called "the Book of the Upright." There are textual corruptions in the manuscripts and the record never attained canonical status. Nevertheless, many historians consider it an accurate record of events from the time of Adam to the conquest of Canaan. The assumption is that the early writers of Scripture trusted it as well. *See also* book(s); *Book of the Wars of the Lord;* Jannes and Jambres; sun stood still.

Book of Jehu. See book(s).

Book of Jeremiah. See book(s).

Book of Kells, **the:** an elaborate copy of the four Gospels and other material considered to be Ireland's most cherished national treasure. The volume was written and drawn by Celtic monks in the early 800s or a bit before and is commonly known as the Book of Columba. The art, calligraphy, illuminations, and craftsmanship of the artifact are likely unsurpassed in any construction of its kind. *See also* art, religious; Columbkille; Gospel(s).

book of life: a calculation and record of all persons born to life, a collection either in God's mind or existing as a heavenly tome of the living. As described in apocalyptic terms, the names recorded there can be removed or lined through if those individuals refuse the sacrificial redemption of Christ. In Revelation, we see the book of life as a promise of inclusion of the names of the faithful in the church at Sardis. We see it again at the great white throne judgment where it is consulted as a reference for those on trial; the names of nonbelievers will not be found therein, thus confirming eternal condemnation. Its presence in the final setting could be stage setting or symbolic. In Jewish tradition, it is believed that God writes every person's words, deeds, and thoughts in His book of life on the holy day called *Rosh Hashanah*; if good deeds outnumber the sinful ones for the year, that person's name will be inscribed in the book of life for another year on *Yom Kippur*; the book of death holds the fate of the wicked. The majority of the population will be contained in neither tome so a ten day period of grace is granted. During *Rosh Hashanah* and the "Ten Days of Repentance," people can be penitent of their sins and perform good deeds to increase their chances of being recorded in the book of life. *See also* Atonement, Day of; book(s); book of death; Book of Remembrance; Book of the Covenant; Book of the Law; book of works; eschatology, eschatological; Judaism; Lamb's book of life; *Rosh Hashanah*; scroll of remembrance.

Book of Mormon: one of the sacred texts, perhaps the central one, of the Church of Jesus Christ of Latter-Day Saints (LDS)—the Mormons. The text supposedly covers history on the North

American continent from about 2200 B.C.—A.D. 421 and records the lives of Jewish tribes who escaped from Palestine and the actions of local Native Americans of the era. The first section of the book concerns the descendants of Jared, who fled from the fall of the Tower of Babel. They eventually became extinct, but other Jews arrived from Jerusalem around 600 B.C. Lehi and his son Nephi became the progenitors of a prosperous people replacing the Jerudites, but they, too, were eventually conquered by the native populations. The record of the Mormon civilization, however, is said to have been inscribed on golden plates and deposited in a hill in present-day Wayne County, New York, by the last prophet, Moroni. In 1827 Moroni returned as an angel to reveal the hiding place to the Mormon prophet Joseph Smith. It was Smith and a few companions who translated the record from "reformed Egyptian" by use of magical spectacles called the Urim and Thummin. The work was published in 1830 and claims to be the inspired story of Jews in America, including the appearance of Jesus Christ to the Nephites. Most certainly, according to reputable historians, the Book of Mormon is a fraud, but it still commands the attention and devotion of faithful Mormons the world over. *See also* Church of Jesus Christ of Latter-Day Saints, the; *Doctrine and Covenants;* golden plates; Moroni; *Pearl of Great Price, The;* Smith, Joseph; Young, Brigham.

Book of Nathan. See book(s).

Book of Remembrance: according to the wisdom literature and Jewish tradition, the heavenly record of a person's good and bad deeds. Malachi 3:16 speaks of a "record [scroll] [that] was written" in the presence of God and Revelation 20:11–15 references a similar tome at the judgment of the great white throne. *See also* book of death; book of life; Judaism.

Book of Samuel the Seer. See book(s).

Book of Shadows: a text for practicing witches, authored by Gerald Gardner. Though there is no universal rule for using the magical chants, rituals, and incantations contained in the guide, many covens follow its guidance. The Sabbat observances are designed to "draw down the moon" to manipulate the elements and fate. *See also* coven(s); "drawing down the moon"; elementals; Gardner, Gerald Brosseau; thoughtform; New Age religion; Wicca; witch(es); witchcraft.

Book of Shemaiah. See book(s).

Book of Sith: the legendary sinister texts serving the "Dark Side" of "the Force" made famous by the *Star Wars* movies and books. It supposedly explains the function and powers of the dark side as practiced by Darth Vader and others on the side of oppression. *See also* Force, the; Jedi Path, The.

Book of Solomon. See book(s).

book of the annals of the kings of Media and Persia. See book(s).

Book of the Covenant: the detailed laws given to Moses from God (Ex. 20:22–24:4). These statutes were far more numerous, precise, and extensive than the basic Ten Commandments. The various rites and laws are most fully explained in the Pentateuch of the Old Testament. God's law was codified by Moses and read to the people accompanied by appropriate sacrifice (Ex. 24:3–8). After the reading, Moses sprinkled some of the blood of the offering on the people to consecrate them to the stipulations of the covenant. Then the people pledged: "We will do everything the Lord has said; we will obey." *See also* Book of the Law; Judaism; Pentateuch; Ten Commandments, the.

Book of the Dead: as depicted in the *Odyssey*, the judgment process in the afterlife overseen by King Minos. The philosophies of Plato, Virgil, and some ancient religions hold associated issues drawn from the event. A manual of the same theme, alternately known as *The Pyramid Texts* (the earliest around 2400 B.C.), was also an Egyptian possession crucial to the burial rites of the ancient kingdom. The Egyptian tome dates from about 1550 – 50 B.C. and was designed to assist the soul of the departed into the underworld and forward to the afterlife. As such, it was called the Dowry of the Dead. Herein were forty-two commandments to be reviewed by Osiris to any who died; then the heart was weighed against an ostrich feather for its purity. These and other Egyptian texts may hold significance for the modern eschatologist in that virtually all of them claim that their god Osiris will rise again, rescued by his son and heir, Horus. These writings (as interpreted by certain apocalypticists today) contain a warning to "the seed of Seth" (humanity) because Osiris, now overseen and protected by Geb (Satan), will resurrect in some form to be assisted then by Thoth (the False Prophet). There are other variations of the *Book of the Dead*, of course, in several major religions. The Tibetan version, for example, the *Bardo Thodol*, contains vivid descriptions of the tortures of hell where the soul can never be destroyed or find relief. *See also* Osiris; philosophy of the Greeks; underworld.

Book of the Hopi: a literary compendium of Native American prophecy that discusses ancient history, the current age, and the future from the prophetic perspective.

Book of the Law: 1. the Mosaic Law and ritual given to Moses as recorded in the Pentateuch. 2. by implication, one of the volumes present at the great white throne judgment to aid in the trial of unbelievers; it seems to be the primary law book defining right from wrong. An early naming of the Torah can be found in Joshua 1:8. *See also* book of life; Book of the Covenant; book of works; Judaism; Lamb's book of life; Pentateuch; Torah.

Book of the Seers. See book(s).

Book of the Wars of Yahweh: probably a collection of songs similar to those found in the *Book of Jashar*. The text is now lost to us but is mentioned in Numbers 21:14 and certain portions are quoted elsewhere. *See also* books(s); *Book of Jashar*.

"Book of Thunder": officially entitled "The Thunder, Perfect Mind," a Gnostic riddling poem written in a paradoxical style of parallel strophes. In the text, a savior type speaks to an audience as if trying to identify himself in a kind of "Who am I?" guessing monologue. The work was originally in Greek but only a Coptic copy has been uncovered at Nag Hammadi in 1945. First impressions hint that the author may be speaking as the goddess Wisdom *(Sophia)* but one passage anticipates the words of Revelation, "I am the first and the last." *See also* Apocryphal Gospels; Gnosticism, Gnostic(s); Nag Hammadi library; riddle; *Sophia*.

Book of Truth: probably the Old Testament in general, or more precisely, the Hebrew Scriptures as named by Daniel (Dan. 10:21). The writing was so designated by the angel addressing the prophet who said it contained the certainty of all prophecy regarding the Jews. Its mention helps accentuate the doctrine of God's control of history and the veracity of Scripture. *See also* Book of the Covenant; Hagiographa; Hebrew Bible; Septuagint, the; Tanakh; Torah; Old Testament.

book of works: by implication, one of the law books opened at the great white throne judgment. Inside are all the deeds and attitudes of those unbelievers under trial and confirming their condemnation. Certainly, God needs no Cliff Notes to remind Himself of our history. Whether then these books and certain others said to be present at the great judgment are literal tomes or not (they could be props or symbols), the purpose of their presence is clear enough. *See also* book of life; Book of the Law; Lamb's book of life.

Book of Worship: the printed procedures for proper worship order in Methodism. *See also* Book of Discipline; liturgical year; liturgy, Christian; Methodists.

books, lot. See "lots books."

Books of Adam: a collection of apocryphal books concerning Adam and Eve. They may be found under a number of titles: *Conflict of Adam and Eve, Contradiction of Adam and Eve, Apocalypse of Adam, Life of Adam and Eve, Testament of Adam, Penitence of Adam, Testament of Our First Parents.* Writings of the Mandean religion are also called the Book of Adam. *See also* Apocrypha, the; Mandaeanism.

books of the Ancient of Days. See book(s).

books of the great white throne. See book(s); great white throne judgment.

books of the kings of Israel and Judah: official histories of the Northern and Southern kingdoms, many of which are unknown to us. Reference to these writings is mentioned in 2 Chronicles 36:8 and elsewhere. First and 2 Kings, 1 and 2 Chronicles, and other portions of the Old Testament with historical value may rightly be identified as part of these records. *See also* book(s); kings of Israel and Judah; kings of Israel and Judah in foreign relations.

Booth, Evangeline Cory: Commanding general of the Salvation Army after her father, William Booth (1865–1950). She arrived from Britain in 1904 and immediately and effectively revitalized the Army in America. Worldwide disaster relief efforts were launched and organizational and financial troubles were righted because of her exceptional leadership. She was awarded the Distinguished Service Medal after World War I. *See also* Booth, General William; Salvation Army.

Booth, General William Bramwell: founder of the Salvation Army (1829–1912). Booth attributes his vision of salvation for the poorer masses to a dream from God. In the experience, he describes a storm-tossed sea in the midst of which was a boulder with a wooden platform surrounding it. Many exhausted souls sought refuge there while a few others secured on the boardwalk tried to help them. Most figures safely on the refuge, however, were totally indifferent to the plight of their fellow victims. Booth's dream fully explains the motto of the Salvation Army: "rescue the perishing." He began his preaching at age fifteen and left his church for the streets where he could see the downtrodden. When asked to predict the greatest danger to the coming generation, Booth replied: "The chief danger that confronts the coming century will be religion without the Holy Ghost, Christianity without Christ, forgiveness without repentance, salvation without regeneration, politics without God, and heaven without hell." Upon Booth's death, his daughter Evangeline Booth became commanding general and her work greatly advanced the denomination with expansion and effectiveness. *See also* Booth, Evangeline Cory; Salvation Army.

Booths, Festival of. See Tabernacles, Feast of.

born again: a rebirth or new birth in a spiritual sense. Since being born physically a second time is impossible, the phrase is both an early and late description of one who has been renewed in the forgiveness of Christ and has begun the Christian walk (Tit. 3:5). The words were likely first spoken in the report of the theological conversation between Christ and Nicodemus (Jn. 3:1–21) but are chiefly used by Southern evangelicals in the United States of the last three centuries. Almost all fundamentalists who take the Bible literally, word for word, concede that the "born again" phrase is a metaphor. There are some few, however, who step far into the theological desert and claim it to be reincarnation. Such thinking is totally foreign to ancient church theology and hermeneutics—something that might be featured in one of those garish newspaper tabloids. *See also* accept Christ, to; altar call; "asking Jesus into my heart"; birth from above; blood of Christ; blood of the Lamb; Christianese; confession(s) of faith; conversion; firstfruits of the resurrection; firstfruits of the Spirit; "plead the blood"; profession of faith; regeneration; reincarnation; "saved"; "turn your life [heart] over to Jesus"; "walking the aisle"; "washed in the blood."

born again virgin: a Christianese notation for one in a fundamentalist sect who, having indulged in sexual intercourse at some point, vows never to do so again until marriage or some other indefinite moment in time. Such abstinence, for whatever moral, practical, or theological reason, is said to value the sanctity of marriage and sexual purity and is considered by many in the group to be legitimate (if technical) virginity. *See also* Christianese; 144,000, the; virgin, virginity.

Bosco, John (Giovanni): an Italian Catholic priest (1815–1888), educator, and writer. Bosco was most famous for his educational system for the young and for founding the missionary group called the Society of Saint Francis de Sales (Salesian Society). He was subject to numerous dreams or visions, many of which were eschatological and not all favorable to the Roman Church. Some contemporaries considered him insane. Nevertheless, he was canonized by Pope Pius XI in 1934. *See also* Francis de Sales; liturgical year; missions, missionaries; Roman Catholic Church.

bosom of Abraham: a poetic term for the Paradise portion or the "good" side of Hades. In a more general aspect, Abraham's bosom can identify the place of sanctity and rest for the beloved after death in *Sheol* awaiting the judgment. The place is named as the poor beggar's refuge in Jesus' parable of the rich man and Lazarus (Lk. 16:19–31). One great emphasis of the story is the idea that there is no transfer or communication from the place of peace (eternity in heaven) and the outer darkness (hell). *See also* afterlife; Annwn; Aralu; Arcadia; Asgard; Avalon; Dis; Dives; Elysium; eschatology, eschatological; eternal life; future life, doctrine of the; Duat; Gehenna; Hades; happy hunting ground; Harrowing of Hell, the; heaven; hell; Hy-Breasail; Hyperborea; intermediate state; Jade Empire, the; Jahannam; Janna; lake of fire; life after death; Lazarus; limbo; *Limbus Puerorum;* Mictlan; new heaven and new earth; Nirvana; Otherworld; parable(s); parables of the New Testament; Paradise; paradise of God; paraeschatology; Pardes; Perdition; Promised Land, the; Pure Land, the; Pardes; purgatory; Shambhala legends;

Sheol; soul sleep; space doctrine; Summerland; Thule, land of; Tir na nOg; underworld; Upper Gehenna; Utopia; Valhalla; world to come, the; Xibala.

bottomless pit, the. See Abyss, the.

bound angels: angelic or demonic beings determined to be so profoundly evil that they were long ago confined by the judgment of God to the Abyss. Peter (2 Pe. 2:4) discusses their imprisonment as does Jude 6. Revelation 9:13–21 details the temporary release of the four angels "bound at the great river Euphrates" who have been kept in waiting for the moment of the unleashing of the sixth trumpet. This act signals the release of 200 million demonic riders from the smoking pit who proceeds to slay a third of the Tribulation population. All are presumed to be the inhabitants of the Abyss permitted to wreck vengeance on the earth for a circumscribed time. *See also* Abyss, the; angel(s); angels of the Euphrates; eschatology, eschatological; fallen angels; spirits in prison; Tartarus.

boundary stones: land markers. Boundary stones were used in Israel to define property lines. To move one was a breach of national law (Deut. 19:14; 27:17) and a violation of personal rights of ownership (Hos. 5:10). Something duplicated or newly designed will likely be necessary for marking the new bounds of millennial Israel.

bow: a weapon for launching arrows. The first horseman of the Apocalypse (Antichrist) is pictured as being armed with a bow (with no mention of arrows for it), which symbolizes his access to military power (Rev. 6:1–2). On other occasions, the bow is figurative of an attack either by a human foe or by God Himself (*e.g.,* Lamentations 3:12-14, Zechariah 10:4). To "unstring" one's bow was to signal loss or helplessness (Job 30:11). A broken bow signs the frustration of plans and actions (Ps. 37:15). The psalmist says that unreliable people are a faulty bow (Ps. 78:57), thereby describing a person or thing as undependable or risky (Hos. 7:16). *See also* arrow(s).

bowing at the name. See name that is above every name, the.

bowl(s): the designation for the last of a sevenfold series of devastations to visit the earth in the time of Tribulation. Some translations call them *plagues*. They constitute painful sores on those bearing the mark of the beast, the sea of blood that kills all marine life, the pollution of fresh water, scorching of the sun, darkness on the kingdom of the beast (Antichrist), preparations for the Armageddon invasion, and the final destruction of Babylon the Great. Some translations use "vials" in place of "bowls." The seven bowls of wrath are unique from the seals and trumpets that precede them. Whereas the earlier sets of maladies in Revelation are devastation to the earth and are associated with natural disasters, the bowls appear to be acts solely of God's hand. They are supernatural and contain no method of alleviation or recovery. It seems the suffers do not even attempt repentance and find no relief. *See also* eschatology, eschatological; plague(s); seal(s); thunder revelations; Tribulation; trumpet(s).

Boxing Day: the traditional day after Christmas when goods are "boxed up" and given to the poor. The occasion also gave the hard-working servants who had no time off during the holidays to enjoy some deserved respite. The charitable donations are observed mainly in England and Canada but elsewhere as well. *See also* Christmas; feasts and special days of Protestantism.

Bozrah: ancient name of Petra located in part of what is now Jordan and the ancient capital city of Edom (about eighty miles south of Jerusalem) carrying a meaning of "sheep pen" or "sheep fold." The name also places another municipality of Moab, which may have been a city of refuge for the tribe of Reuben. The name is mentioned in conjunction with Edom, Moab, Ammon, Teman, and Mount Paran as a plan of safety for Jews trapped in Jerusalem by forces of the Antichrist (Isa. 63:1–6; Mic. 2:12–13). Since the meaning of the name is "sheep pen," it would be apt if the area is truly a place of security and safety since ancient flocks in the tribal days were enclosed and fenced with stones or thatch. The Messiah will deliver some of his people prior to the great battle at Armageddon. The distance from Bozrah to Megiddo (Armageddon) is 176 miles. *See also* Azal; Edom, Edomites; Edom, Moab, and Ammon; eschatology, eschatological; Joktheel; Mount Paran; Nabateans; Pella; Petra; remnant; Sele.

Bradford, William: prominent founder of Plymouth Colony (ca. 1590–1657) and five times its governor. Bradford ruled in typical theocratic fashion according to the strict Puritan ethic. In one instance, he dispatched the local militia under Miles Standish to Wollaston (now Quincy) Massachusetts, to quell a May Day celebration of dancing around the May Pole, drinking, and frivolity then in progress. The town leader of the festival, Thomas Murton, was arrested and Bradford could declare the end of such "basely practices of the madd Bacchanalians." As governor, Bradford hosted Samoset, chief of the Massasoit tribe, even signing a mutual defense pact. His journal, called *Of Plymouth Plantation*, is an invaluable historical document. *See also Mayflower Compact;* Puritanism, Puritans.

Brahma Kumari: an Eastern-style cult who believes that they are destined to rule the world after some catastrophic Armageddon event, leading mankind to a better future based on New Age ideas. *See also* cult(s); idolatry; sects).

Brahmanism: the historic predecessor to Hinduism as initiated in the Vedas. The religion is recognized most readily by the generally novice populations because of its association with the Indian caste system, in which Brahman is the supreme deity and Brahmin is the highest caste. Brahman is viewed as the universal spirit with a meaning of "to grow" or "enlarge." *See also* caste system; Hinduism; idolatry; sect(s); Upanishads; Vedas.

Brainerd, David: an early American missionary to native Delaware tribes in the Northeast (1718–1747). Brainerd traveled over 3,000 miles around the New Jersey area under extreme hardship and suffering from terminal tuberculosis. He was sponsored by the Congregationalists but was officially allied to the evangelical sect called the "New Lights" and became a telling inspiration to a new generation of missionaries. Oddly enough, he was expelled twice from Yale—once for his illness and the second time for his criticism of the faculty. *See also* Congregationalists; missions, missionaries.

brainwashing. See mind control.

Branch Davidians: an apocalyptic group led by David Koresh with dogma far outside orthodox doctrines concerning the Second Coming. Most of the cultists perished in a fiery confrontation with federal agents near Waco, Texas, in April of 1993. *See also* cult(s); Houteff, Florence; Koresh, David.

Branch from (of) Jesse, the: the designation of Christ as one rightfully descended from the line of David (whose father was Jesse) granting him the authority of the kingly line of rule (*cf.* Isaiah 11). The title is also termed "shoot from the stump of Jesse" in parallel language. *See also* Branch of the Lord; names (titles) for Jesus; Root and Offspring of David; Root of Jesse; Tree of Jesse; Zechariah's vision of a crown for Joshua.

branch of an almond tree. See almond tree branch.

Branch of the Lord: the Messiah, spoken of as a harbinger of beauty and glory for Zion. The description (most expansively recorded in Isaiah 4:2–6) is reminiscent of the properties of God's Shekinah glory. *See also* Branch from (of) Jesse, the; names (titles) for Jesus; Root and Offspring of David; Root of Jesse; Shekinah glory; Zechariah's vision of a crown for Joshua.

Branch, the. See Branch from (of) Jesse, the; Branch of the Lord; Zechariah's vision of a crown for Joshua.

History and Mystery

branch theory: a Protestant doctrinal interpretation that the One, Holy, Catholic, and Apostolic Church may encompass other Christian denominations in addition to one's own. The claim of universal unity and authority of the Roman Catholic Church has been strongly and steadily mauled by Protestants since the Reformation and before. The assertion is that the Invisible Church may apply to all believers. *See also* catholic church; Church; church; four marks of the church; One, Holy, Catholic, and Apostolic Church; Protestantism, Protestants; universal Church; visible and invisible church, the.

Branhamism. See Branham, William Marrion.

Branham, William Marrion: a Baptist turned Pentecostal-style preacher (1909–1965) to whom some credit the founding of post-World War II notoriety of the faith healing movement. His particular brand has been labeled Branhamism. Branham was born in a log cabin in Cumberland County, Kentucky, but did most of his work in Texas, Arizona, and Arkansas. Many followers proclaimed Branham a prophet, and it was broadcast that he was the end time prophet to the Bride of Christ (though he never publically verified the title or explained what it meant) and preferred the year 1977 as the end of the age. Branham insisted he experienced visions and heavenly visitations since childhood, and some have testified they saw a halo of light about him on a number of occasions. One of his more significant apocalyptic visions was received as five or six revelations given at a single point in time. His recounting claims he saw: 1) the rise and fall of Benito Mussolini, 2) the establishment of the Siegfried line some two years before its construction and the rise of Adolf Hitler, 3) the appearance of Fascism, Nazism, and Communism—only the last of which would survive on the heels of the others, 4) advanced automobile design including remote steering; also the moral decay of women in the land and, 5) the evolution of a wicked woman coming to power in the United States. Each vision was said to be detailed and specific. Branham's healing gifts and charisma were known worldwide. He was an advocate of the serpent seed doctrine as well. Branham died in Amarillo, Texas, following a head-on car crash. *See also* Baptists; faith healing; revivalism; serpent seed doctrine, the.

Bran mac Feabhail: an 18th century written tale of Bran mac Feabhail's fantastic voyage to distant lands from ancient Ireland. Upon his return, he discovered centuries had passed in Rip van Winkle style. *See also* Celtic folklore and religion; Tuatha de Danann.

Brant, Joseph: a Mohawk war chief (1742–1807), and active Freemason who aided the British cause in both the French and Indian War (1755–1763) and the American Revolution. For his service, the crown awarded a land grant for his people in Ontario, and Brant held the distinction of being commissioned a colonel in the British army. When back in America, the British were prone to hand over their prisoners to the Mohawks for torture but Brant released any identified as Masons. He became a dedicated convert to Christianity and proved to be a proficient scholar. He translated the *Book of Common Prayer* and the Gospel of Mark into the Mohawk language. Brant's ethnic name was Thayendanegea.

brass: a metal named in some Bible translations that probably should have been termed "bronze" in most instances. *See also* bronze; electrum.

Bray, Thomas: Anglican clergyman (1658–1730) and involved missionary among the Native American Indians of the day. He was also active as a contributor to the Society for the Propagation of the Gospel in New England. His greatest legacy, however, may be the thirty libraries he established in Maryland for the edification of his fellow clergy. His work, and that of John Harvard, may be considered the pattern for the free library system in America. *See also* Anglicanism;

Church of England; Dunster, Henry; Glover, Jose; Harvard, John; Mather, Increase; missions, missionaries; "praying Indians"; Society for the Propagation of the Gospel in New England.

bread: the baked produce of ground grain and certain other ingredients. Bread is an important eschatological symbol as it can be said to represent life itself. It is also an important element of New Testament Communion, of Hebrew worship, and as a sign of hospitality. Often the term is paired with wine. Jesus himself is often referred to as "the bread of life." Ritual bread in Israel was never baked using yeast (leaven), for that ingredient was representative of evil or sin. *See also* bread of affliction; bread of despair; Bread of Life; Bread of the Presence; bread, unleavened; "breaking the bread"; elugia; fermentum; fraction; liturgy, Christian; liturgy, Jewish; manna; sacrifice; salt; Unleavened Bread, Feast of; wafer.

bread and cheese test: a rudimentary form of lie detector, popular in the Middle Ages, in which suspected liars were induced to consume a bread and cheese confection during the recitation of a magic formula. Their inability to swallow the concoction was taken as a sign of falsehood. *See also* magic, magick; ordeal(s).

bread of affliction: a metaphor for the suffering of God's people when that state of affairs becomes necessary (Jer. 30:31). *See also* bread; bread of despair; tear(s); thorn in the flesh; trial(s); vale of tears; water of affliction.

bread of despair: the gift of food (*e.g.*, Ezekiel 24:17) brought to the home of one who has died. The kindness was practical since meals could not be prepared in the house of the deceased because of Jewish dietary laws. The custom continues today in many societies. *See also* bread; bread of affliction; tear(s); thorn in the flesh; trial(s); vale of tears; water of affliction.

Bread of Life: a metaphor Jesus gave himself (Jn. 6:35) declaring, he and none other can sustain the faithful believer forever. *See also* bread; names (titles) for Jesus.

bread of [the] angels. See manna.

Bread of the Presence: twelve loaves of sanctified bread placed on the table of showbread within the tabernacle or Temple. Early, it signified food for God but later became a sign of God's provision for the people (Lev. 24:5–9). Sometimes the phrase names the bread of the Communion observance. *See also* bread; Eucharist; Lord's Supper; tabernacle, the; Temple(s).

bread, unleavened: bread baked without yeast since leaven was a symbol of sin. Such a recipe was central to the Passover celebration (Ex. 12:8,15–20; 1 Cor. 5:8). The bread was to be prepared without yeast to remember that Israel had no time for the bread to rise when emancipation from Egyptian slavery was suddenly thrust upon them. *See also* bitter herbs; bread; "four questions, the"; Haggada; leaven; Paschal lamb; Passover; Schism, the Great; *Seder;* Unleavened Bread, Feast of; yeast.

breaker, the: a messianic name, the "one who breaks," found only in Micah 2:13. It pictures the Lord as deliverer in the sense that they would "run interference" for Israel and allow the people to return from the Babylonian Exile.

"breaking the bread": the unofficial action of serving or observing Communion, the Eucharist. *See also* bread; elugia; Eucharist; fraction; fermentum; liturgy, Christian; Lord's Supper; wafer.

breast(s): descriptive of the part of human anatomy prominent in the chest area, most often referring to females but also to males. Scripturally, the word may symbolize grief (Lk. 18:13) as in "beating the breast," sustenance (Isa. 60:16) as a mother suckles her child at the breast, comfort (as one draws another in embrace), or motherhood itself. The breast portion of the Hebrew sacrificial animal was the most prime and belonged exclusively to the priests (Lev. 7:31).

breastplate of the high priest: an adornment made to exact specifications called the *Logion*, worn by Israel's high priest over his chest (Ex. 39:8–21) attached to his ephod. The article was said to be about four inches square (though reason suggests it may have been a bit larger) made of gold with a woven surface of blue, purple, scarlet, and fine linen yarn embroidered with gold figures. Four rows of squares held a unique jewel and a Hebrew letter to designate each of the twelve tribes. Row 1 (at the top) contained a sardius, topaz, and a carbuncle; Row 2 held an emerald, sapphire, and diamond; Row 3 had a ligure, agate, and amethyst; Row 4 sported a beryl, onyx, and jasper. The design takes on new prophetic interest when viewed in conjunction with the walls of the New Jerusalem (Rev. 21). *See also* ephod; furniture and furnishings of the tabernacles, temples, and modern synagogues; gem(s); miter; New Jerusalem; onyx; sapphire; Urim and Thummin.

breath: the respirations of living things so essential to life. Breath is not only physical in biblical usage, for it can also signify the spirit or life-force of a person equally essential to living. The prophet Isaiah uses breath as a metaphor for the Lord's attack to slay the wicked (Isa. 11:4), but he was not the only one to portray the breath of God as creating, sustaining, or punishing throughout the pages of Scripture. At times, it represents the brevity of human life – a mere puff of air (*e.g.,* Psalm 62:9). *See also* Christoplatonism; heart; heart and spirit; heart, soul, spirit; Holy Spirit; insufflation; life; mind; names (titles) for the Holy Spirit; *nephesh; pneuma; psuche;* psyche; *ruach;* soul(s); spirit, strength; wind(s); zoe.

Brehon Laws: the law codes of the Celts, particularly as they were known in Ireland and Britain. The Welsh Laws of Hywel Dda and the Scottish Dal Riada were versions of them. An early complete copy of this legal system was found in the *Book of the Dun Cow* (dated around 1100 A.D.). Some historians date them from the eighth century B.C. and are acknowledged to be particularly fair, broad in scope, and detailed. They, like much of Celtic writing, show similarities with the Vedic Laws of Manu in India. By the end of the 17th century, the Brehon system had been almost erased by the English conquerors. *See also* Celtic folklore and religion; cow.

Brendan of Clonfert: a missionary and explorer (ca. 484 – 577) called "the Navigator," "the Bold," or "the Voyager." Brendan was an early monastic saint who used much of his life in search of the "Isle of the Blessed," which legend says brought him to North America long before the Vikings or Columbus. He considered the place to be the earthly Garden of Eden. Remarkably, Brendan traveled the seas in a currach of wattle and tanned hides. He and Saint Columba were contemporaries. The saint's adventures are recorded in *Saint Brendan's Voyage,* written around the tenth century, which recounts the travels of a boatload of Irish monks. Far out into the Atlantic, they encounter various demons and punished sinners. They even saw Judas, who was sentenced to six days a week in hell but got some Sundays off. The tale features a sort of lighthearted style which may suggest the people of the Middle Ages, like those today, did not always take their hell doctrines too seriously. *See also* Columbkille; missions, missionaries; Roman Catholic Church.

Brethren of the Angels. See Gichtelians.

Brethren of the Common Life: lay organizations with mystical or pietistic inclination about the time of the Reformation founded by Gent Groote. They and other sister groups like them helped dissolve the staid autocratic decrees of the Roman Catholic Church during the Middle Ages. *See also* Friends of God; mysticism, mystics.

Brethren of the Free Spirit: a lay-led Christian movement in northern Europe in the 13th and 14th centuries. They were Antinomian in doctrine, so they were condemned by Pope Clement V and severely persecuted. *See also* Beguines.

Breviary: the Roman Catholic liturgical guide to the rituals, hymns, prayers, canons, and all necessary material for the conduct of the Mass. The term derives from Latin meaning "short" or "concise," a somewhat odd designation since the Mass is not ordinarily brief in duration by most standards. *See also* euchology; furniture and furnishings of the modern church; liturgical year; liturgy, Christian; Mass, *Ordo;* Roman Catholic Church; rubric.

Brewster, William: a non-ordained Puritan in the American colonies (1567–1644). It was he who led the Puritans from Scrooby, England, to Lieden, Holland, and then on to Massachusetts on the *Mayflower.* Though he could not preach or function as clergy for the Puritans, he was an elder and the *de facto* leader of the group. *See also* Puritanism, Puritans.

briars and thorns: plants or shrubs with sharp, pointed barbs. They were often employed to describe eschatological symbols for danger, perplexity, a barrier to progress, punishment, mockery, or injury. *See also* flora, fruit, and grain, symbology of; thorns, thornbush(es).

bribery: an offer of payment or favor to an official to do something or not do something in order that the solicitor may gain illegally. Bribery is severely condemned by almost all the prophets, apostles, and elders in both the Old and New Testaments, and certainly it was forbidden in the Law of God (*e.g.* Deuteronomy 27:25; Amos 5:12). Even so, the practice of buying favors was a normal way of doing business in the ancient world, and still is today. *See also* simony; social issues.

bridal chamber ceremony: an important mystery initiation familiar to some of the ancient religious secret societies. Used primarily by the Gnostics, the ritual dramatized a marriage-like ceremony intended to demonstrate to the initiate the linking of the upper (holy) and the lower (physical) self. It fused the *Sophia* (female/human) with the *Logos* (male/Jesus) to become "one with God." Baptism and anointing were usually accompanying practices. The bridal chamber is referenced in Scripture as well (Matthew 9:15;

Mark 2:19; Luke 5:34) but spoken by Jesus concerning his soon-coming death and resurrection. *See also* anointing; baptism; biblical criticism; covenant ceremony; criteria of double dissimilarity; Diabolical Mimicry, the; Gnosticism, Gnostic(s); *Golden Bough, The;* historical Jesus, the; idolatry; Jesus Myth, the; Jesus Seminar, the; Logos; *logos;* matrimony; pagan practice; *preparatio evangelica; Sophia;* symbalon.

bridegroom of Christ: the Church, but with the emphasis on the Christ as head of that institution, its preeminent partner. In connection with the theme of the bride and the bridegroom, the New Testament teaches ultimate rulership in some capacity of the Church over the new earth as sub-regents with Christ. Revelation also speaks of the joint metaphor of the New Jerusalem "coming down from heaven" prepared as a bride adorned for her husband (Rev. 21:2, 9–10). *See also* bride (wife) of Christ; Church; Crown Rights of the Redeemer; marriage metaphor; marriage supper of the Lamb; New Jerusalem; prayers of Revelation.

bride (wife) of Christ: a description of the Church, one of six or seven metaphors used in that manner. As true believing members of that body, the righteous bride will celebrate the marriage supper of the Lamb described in Revelation 19:7–9 and is anticipated in 2 Corinthians 11:2. Sometimes faithful Israel is called the wife of Yahweh, and the phrase "the wife of the Lamb" is used to describe the New Jerusalem (Rev. 21:9). *See also* bridegroom of Christ; Church; Crown Rights of the Redeemer; marriage metaphor; marriage supper of the Lamb; New Jerusalem; prayers of Revelation.

Bridget of Kildare: a patroness of Ireland (ca. 451–525). She was a nun and abbess with a feast day on February 1. Somehow, she has become associated over the centuries with Brighid, a youthful spring goddess of fertility and nurture honored by the Tuatha de Danann. *See also* Bridget's Cross; Imbolc; liturgical year; nun(s); Roman Catholic Church; Tuatha de Danann.

Bridget of Sweden: a mystic and visionary (1303–1373) who began the Bridgettines nuns and monks of Scandinavia. *See also* liturgical year; near-death experiences (NDEs); nun(s); Roman Catholic Church.

Bridget's Cross: a stylized woven cross said to be the symbol of Bridget of Kildare. Its presence was said to protect the owner from fire and evil. More probably, the legend springs from the pagan Brigid of the Tuatha de Danann, who held the same magical powers. It is an important New Age or Wiccan symbol today. *See also* Bridget of Kildare; idolatry; magic, magick; Roman Catholic Church; Tuatha de Danann; Wicca.

bridle of the horse: in apocalyptic language, the depth of blood (as recorded in Revelation 14:20) issuing from the great winepress of God's anger. The image is intended to denote a large volume and a time of despair. A horse will usually panic at the point in which water reaches its bridle and the rider's control may be lost. *See also* animals, birds, and insects, symbology of; bells on the horses; blood overflowing; eschatology, eschatological; Holy to the Lord.

Bright Monday. See Holy Week.

bright Morning Star, the. See Morning Star.

Bright Monday: an Eastern Orthodox celebration of Easter Monday which members call a "day of joy and laughter." Obviously, they are rejoicing in the resurrection of Christ experienced the day before and anticipating our own. *See also* Bright Sunday; Eastern Orthodox Church; eschatology, eschatological; liturgical year; liturgy, Christian; resurrection of Jesus.

Bright Sunday: an Eastern Orthodox celebration consisting of a nightly apocalyptic vigil. In the observance, the book of Revelation is emphasized with its views of heaven and the last advent. *See also* Bright Monday; Eastern Orthodox Church; eschatology, eschatological; liturgical year;

liturgy, Christian; resurrection of Jesus; Revelation as New Testament prophecy.

Brights, the: a coined title for those persons who hold an exclusive naturalistic world view as opposed to a religious one. They may be an organized group, usually affiliated with the Brights' Network, or individuals choosing the designation. Some consider the name pretentious as promoting themselves as smart but implying that those of religious persuasion are not. The umbrella term encompasses atheists, agnostics, humanists, skeptics, and others of like mind. *See also* agnosticism, agnostic(s); antitheism; apatheist; atheism, the new; areligious; atheism, atheist(s); Christianist(s); meta-atheist; naturalism; scoffers; slurs, religious.

brimstone: literally, burning sulfur or naphtha. The term is a frequent reference to hell, or the lake of fire and the substance burning there and bringing to mind excruciating torment. One popular theory says that Sodom and Gomorrah were destroyed by flaming brimstone from the natural element found around the Dead Sea. One newer theory suggests that the disaster could have been an asteroid strike. *See also* hell; lake of fire; sulfur.

British Empirical Doctrine: the philosophical idea that all knowledge is gained through sensory experience—a thought inherently antithetic to Christianity because it overlooks the concept of faith. The foremost American champion of the movement was Chauncey Wright (1830–1875), who was also favorable to Darwin's evolution theories and a strong influence on his more famous fellow philosopher, William James. *See also* Darwin, Charles; faith; James, William.

British Test Act: English law from 1673 that banned Roman Catholics from public office unless they denounced certain doctrines.

broad and narrow way: also, the "strait gate," the exacting nature of religious practice that is either taken in as easy (broad) or difficult (narrow). Jesus explained the narrow way as leading to the acceptable life while claiming that few will choose to walk it (Mt. 7:14). *See also* straight gate, the; parable(s); parables of the New Testament.

broad church: a polity position of the Church of England that allows for a certain amount of latitude of belief with an expanded range of opinion regarding certain ecclesiastical and social issues. The declaration is really a relaxation of the traditional "high church"/"low church" distinctions prevalent in much of the church hierarchy and laity of some denominations. *See also* Church of England; High Church, Low Church; worship.

bronze: in Bible times, an alloy of copper and tin, called brass in some Bible translations. The word is highly symbolic when not used literally. The metal could refer to strength (Job 40:18; Rev. 1:15), obstinacy (Isa. 48:4), or the unyielding sky or the earth (Deut. 28:23; Lev. 26:19) without rain. Since the compound hardened base metals, it was used extensively both as a practical material (shackles, gates, weapons, coins, mirrors, helmets, household utensils, etc.) and sacred objects (altars, consecrated vessels, etc.). The compound represented judgment when used it its religious sense. Today, the evolution of bronze is an aid to archeological classification as noted in the Early Bronze Age (3100–2100 B.C.), the Middle Bronze Age (2100–1550 B.C.), and the Late Bronze Age (1550–1200 B.C.). *See also* amber; belly and thighs of bronze; brass; bronze feet; bronze serpent; electrum; gold, golden; mountains of bronze; silver.

bronze feet: a feature of the powerful Lamb of God figure as seen in Revelation 1:15. The symbolism portrays Christ's potent ability to stomp evil with his heavy bronze boots yet walk delicately among the seven golden lampstands (the seven Revelation churches). *See also* amber; bronze; eschatology, eschatological.

bronze serpent: a representation of a snake fashioned at the command of Moses. When the Exodus Israelites complained of their hardship in warfare and desert wandering, the Lord sent vipers among them (Num. 21:4–8). To stop the deadly bites, the bronze snake was raised on a pole and all who looked upon it were spared. The lifting up of the serpent is sometimes cited as a sign of the crucifixion of Christ who was also "lifted up" to save. It is at least possible that the fiery serpents were Seraphim, the angels of fire. *See also* idol(s); Nehushtan; Seraph, Seraphim; serpent.

Brook Farm: more accurately, the Brook Farm Institute of Agriculture and Education at West Roxbury, Massachusetts. The community was begun by George and Sophia Ripley under the guiding principles of the French philosopher Charles Fourier. The settlement was in operation from 1841–1847 under the plans of Fourier and administered by the sensationalist newspaper editor Albert Brisbane; it was much favored by many involved in the transcendentalist movement of the 19th century. *See also* communal communities; Fourier, Charles Francois Marie; phalanxes; Ripley, George; transcendentalism.

Brooks, Phillips: an Episcopalian minister and bishop of Massachusetts (1835–1893). Despite his size (6 feet 4 inches and three hundred pounds), Brooks was a gentle man and treasured humanitarian feelings. He wrote the famous Christmas carol "O Little Town of Bethlehem" while on pilgrimage to Israel, mere hours after watching the peaceful town at night. *See also* carol(s); Protestant Episcopal Church.

brother(s): a common address, probably the most common, for men of the faith in both the early and the modern church (in most instances). Paul, for example, uses the term frequently to direct his message and to express affection. Most early writers rarely communicated a similar greeting to women (sisters). In Protestantism, "brother" is a title of affection from a fellow member to another male believer; in Roman

Catholicism and other liturgical realms, the name typically identifies a monk or friar. The early congregations, as did most of ancient society, viewed women as subservient in most occupations, but in the case of Christian writing, the message is clearly intended for the women of the faith as well. Today, politically correct speech (and properly so) attempts to individualize women. Church saints are also called servants (Acts 4:29), prophets (1 Cor. 14:29), those who die in the Lord (2 Cor. 5:8), the Lord's people (2 Cor. 6:16), God's people (Heb. 13:24), the scattered tribes (Jas. 1:1), God's elect (1 Pe. 1:1), dear children (1 Jn. 2:1), dear friends (1 Jn. 2:7), the chosen lady and her children (2 Jn. 1), the called and loved of God (Jude 1), saints (Rom. 1:7), the faithful (Eph. 1:1), the holy and faithful (Col. 1:2), sister (Phm. 2), the churches (Rev. 1:4), and probably others. *See also* adelphopoiesis; fellow servants; friar; monk(s); sister(s).

Brotherhood of Satan: a cult or sect dedicated to Satan that is said to hold a bloodline of existence far into history past, thus making it a generational Satanic worship program. Unlike the more modern Church of Satan promoted by Anton La Vey, the Brotherhood is intense, long-standing, and militant if we are to believe their propaganda. La Vey acknowledged this fact as well. The most recognized and latest leaders that we know about are Daniel De Paul and Keith Shaffer, both regular Freemasons and occultic devotees. De Paul is named the "Grand Magister" of the cult known by his title, Druid Druwydion Pendragon; Shaffer is his assistant, an expert in hypnosis and mind control called Lord Gwydion. Both are linked to the Council of Nine. *See also* Baphomet; Church of Satan; Council of Nine; Crowley, Aleister; idolatry; Luciferans; occult, occultic; Satan; Satanism; sect(s).

Brotherhood of the New Life: a communal community formed at Wassaic, New York, by Thomas Lake Harris (1823–1906). The group duplicated itself in several other locations and operated on some of the principles of spiritualism and Swedenborgianism. *See also* communal communities.

Brotherhood of the Seven Rays: an apocalyptic cult founded by Dorothy Martin. The group believed that the earth would be destroyed by flood on December 21, 1954, because Martin had been warned by extra-terrestrials who gave her knowledge of natural disasters. *See also* cult(s); idolatry; Martin, Dorothy.

Brothers and Sisters of the Red Death: a suicide cult in Russia who expected the end of the world on November 13, 1900. Over 100 members killed themselves on that date. *See also* cult(s); idolatry.

brothers of mine: a reference to the 144,000 servants of Christ in the book of Revelation. They are a special remnant (most say Jewish) to Christ and responsible for proclaiming the gospel in the Tribulation persecutions. *See also* 144,000, the; servants of our Lord, the.

Brothers, Richard: an English sailor who called himself "God's Almighty Nephew" (1793–1824) and predicted the Millennium for 1795. He also expected the ten lost tribes of Israel to reappear and was convinced he would become king of England, thus labeling him as an Anglo-Israelist. He was committed to an insane asylum. *See also* Anglo Israelism.

brother who is praised, the: an unnamed apostle or messenger described as "the brother who is praised by all the churches for his service to the gospel" (2 Cor. 8:18). Later (2 Cor. 8:22), he (or more likely another servant), is introduced with similar explanation. Though neither is named, the task assigned for them was to accompany Titus to Corinth and help him collect and deliver the beneficent offering being gathered there and to convey it to Jerusalem.

brow. See forehead.

Brown, Dan: author of the worldwide best sellers *The Da Vinci Code, Angels and Demons, Digital Fortress,* and *Deception Point.* His works are principally fictional depictions of various conspiracy theories featuring esoteric cults, anti-Christian institutions, and detective thriller themes. *See also* Da Vinci Code, The; Opus Dei.

Browne, Sylvia: a modern-day fortune-teller. She was a regular on the *Montel Williams Show* until the production was cancelled. Few others of her ilk and time have managed to penetrate into the public psyche as did she. *See also* psychic(s).

brownies: or urisk, a Scottish and English fairy described as fur-covered and about two feet in height. They were also known as Tommy-knockers because of their penchant for sabotage in the mines. *See also* attending spirit(s); banshee; bogle; bugbears; Celtic folklore and religion; clurichauns; daemons; deceiving spirits; demons, demonic; devils; disa; dryad(s); elemental(s); fairy, fairies; Fomorians; ghost(s); ghoul; gnome(s); Green Man, the; Gregori; hobgoblins; homunculus; household deities; huldafolk; Lares; leprechaun(s); Loa Loas; Manes; mythological beasties, elementals, monsters, and spirit animals; nereid; nisse; nymph(s); nyx; Oniropompi; Orisha; Oya; para; paredri; penates; Robin Goodfellow; satyr; Seelie Court, Unseelie Court; selkie; Sidhe; sirens; sylph(s); spiritual warfare; sprite(s); teraphim; territorial spirits; Trickster; Tuatha de Danann; tutelary; undine; wight(s).

Brown, John: militant American abolitionist (1800–1859) reviled in the South but considered a martyr by some Northerners. Brown, one of sixteen children, was born of a pious and anti-slavery family in Ohio. His piercing eyes, stern expression, and full gray beard of an adult give him the aspect of an Old Testament prophet. After falling under the sway of radical black preaching, he came to consider himself the avenging arm of God, the one destined to abolish slavery by force. This conviction led him to butcher five proslavery settlers in Kansas. For this and other actions, he called upon God to bless his endeavors. Brown ended up at Harper's Ferry,

Virginia (now in West Virginia), with plans to seize the federal arsenal there. With the secured weapons, he was certain the slaves would rise up in rebellion. A company of Marines under Colonel Robert E. Lee recaptured the arsenal on October 17, 1859, and ten raiders (including two of Brown's sons) were mortally wounded. Brown himself was captured and hanged on December 2, 1859. *See also* slave, slavery; terrorism; terrorist(s).

Brownson, Orestes Augustus: a Presbyterian layman, Universalist minister, and Unitarian minister (1803–1876), all wrapped into one convoluted career. Brownson bounced from cause to cause motivated by his views of social reform and an unsettled theology. Certainly, he was opposed to organized Christianity and helped the Unitarian cause. Finally, however, he ended up a Roman Catholic priest and lost the few followers he had gathered. *See also* Presbyterians; Roman Catholic Church; Unitarian Universalists.

Brownsville Assembly: a church located in the panhandle of Florida famous for birthing the so-called "Brownsville Revival" in 1995. The movement is controversial (some have labeled them cultist) but thrived with recounted miraculous healings, addiction removal, evangelistic fervor, and other outpourings of the Spirit. Multiple services and a full staff were employed to accommodate the large crowds gathered, even on weekdays. As early as 2010, however, the organization has experienced mounting debt, declining attendance, and flagging energy. The spirit-filled exuberance of this experiment in our day may serve, prophetically speaking, as a modern-day model for the time nearing the end when the dynamic of the Holy Spirit is promised to manifest in special ways in much the same way that Pentecost did in early Christianity. *See also* Azusa Street revival; baptism of the Holy Spirit; charismatic movement; denomination(s), denominationalism; glossolalia; holy laughter; Pentecostalism; revivalism; sect(s); "slain in the Spirit"; "Toronto Blessing, the."

Bruderhof Communities: the "place of the brothers," a Christian commune of peace and non-violence with small settlements around the world. At times, the members were also recognized as a German Youth Movement, then the Society of Brothers or Church Communities International; they are casually affiliated with the Hutterites. The movement was begun by Eberhard Arnold after World War I. *See also* communal communities; Hutterites.

Brunner, Emil Heinrich: a Swiss theologian (1889–1966), an associate with Karl Barth. Brunner was of the neo-orthodox school but stressed the incarnation of Christ. Perhaps his most influential work was *The Divine Imperative* published in 1932. *See also* Barth, Karl; dialectic theology; Divine Imperative, the; higher criticism; neo-orthodoxy; Reformed Churches.

Bublas, the: fictional characters of an imaginary Jewish settlement on the planet Venus. They are discovered in the Jewish science fiction novel *On Venus We Got a Rabbi!* by Philip Klass (1974). In the story, the Jews in residence on Venus are holding the first Jewish interstellar Alien Jewish Conference. Among them appear the Bublas, an intelligent species claiming to be Jews who both perplex and trouble the invading colonists because they sport tentacles. During deliberations, it is determined that the Bublas are not really human and can therefore not be Jewish. The writing is a unique and entertaining exploration of the debated question of "Who is a Jew?" *See also* Judaism.

buckler: a small shield (usually round in shape) used for defense in close encounter combat and as a metaphor for divine protection (Ps. 35:2). *See also* armor; shield.

Buddha. See Gautama Buddha.

Buddhism: primarily an Eastern religion, although it has a worldwide following. The movement is indigenous to the subcontinent of India. Most of its rather complex teachings spring from its founder and greatest advocate, Siddhartha

Gautama or *the Buddha*—"the awakened one." Buddha was active at some point between the sixth and fourth centuries, proclaiming that suffering could be eliminated by overcoming ignorance and covetousness. The movement eventually branched into Theravada ("school of the elders,") and Mahayana ("the great vehicle). The former spread easily into Sri Lanka and Southeast Asia, while the latter was favored in the Far East. It is common, especially in Japan, for Buddhism to be syncretized with Shintoism; the largest of the melded religions is probably Soka Gakkai. Estimates of Buddhist population range around 1.6 million. The religion stresses noble living and karma (fate). Reincarnation is emphasized in its eschatology until annihilation of one's essence may be ultimately acquired. The most recognizable Buddhist to Western eyes may be the saffron-robed *bhikhu*. As a mendicant, he is allowed only a begging bowl, a rosary of 108 beads, an umbrella, and a fan as possessions. The Buddhist Lenten season is July—September featuring a three-day festival of feast and almsgiving. The pageantry is elaborate at the annual Water Festival when statues of Buddha are bathed in perfume. Some of the priestesses may "kiss her god"—a fully active cobra. Buddhism may be expressed in a number of forms including Eastern, Japanese, Lamaist Mahayana, Nichiren, Theravada, Tibetan, and Western *See also ahimsa;* Anada; Ashoka; avatar; Bodhi Tree; chakra; Crème, Benjamin; Bon; Daibutsu, the; Dalai Lama; deva(s), devi(s); Dharma; Dhammapada; Eight Adversities of Buddhism, the; Exalted One, the; Five Hindrances of Buddhism, the; Five Hindrances of Buddhism, the; Five Poisons of Buddhism, the; Five Precepts of Buddhism, the; Four Constituents of Buddhism, the; Four Noble Truths of Buddhism, the; Four Precepts of Buddhism, the; Gautama Buddha; idolatry; Indra; Kalachakra Tantra; karma; Kuntia; lotus; Nagarjuna; Nagas; Nichiren Buddhism; Nirvana; pagoda; Pali Canon, the; prayer wheel; Pure Land, the; reincarnation; retrogression; Sangha; *satyagaha;* sect(s); *Skandas;* Soka Gakkai; stupa; Suttanipata; *Sutta Pitaka;*

Tantric Buddhism; *Tao Te Ching*; Theravada Buddhism; thoughtform; Three Jewels of Buddhism, the; Three Marks of Existence of Buddhism, the; Tibetan Book of the Dead; Wheel of Time, the; World Teacher, the; yoga; Zen.

Bugaku: a colorful religious dance performed mostly in Japan. *See also* dance; music.

bugbears: a collection of spirits, fairies, hobgoblins, bogeymen, and like creatures sometimes called "minor spirits." They are not minor because they are unimportant but because they are too numerous to list and are usually subsumed or separated from their more well-known counterparts. They are most readily seen according to "the spirit of the place" which is usually a dreary and deserted region, wild heaths, barren moors, echoing canyons or chasms, places of violence (gallows, scenes of murders), or crossroads. Bugbear is a general term meaning "a frightening thing," or as most Americans would say, a "bugaboo," although it also isolates a particular spirit in some references. To name a few: afrites (or Ifrit, an Islamic demon of the dead), alholdes, barguests, black-bugs, blackmen, bloody bones, boggarts, boggleboos, bogies, boguests, bolls, bomen, Boneless (a bogeyman like the blob in a grade B movie and "Old Bony" who snatches children who are bad), brags, breaknecks, brown-men, buchies, bull-beggars (or bogle, one that "boggles" the mind), bygorns, cacodemons, caddies, calcars, cauld-lads, changelings (fairy child left in place of a stolen human one), chittifaces (an insult to one with a pinched face or a monster who eats patient wives), clabbernappers, cutties, death-hearses, deevs, Dick-a-Tuesdays (will-o'-the-wisps or goblins), doppelganger, dokkaebi, droiches, dudmen, duergars, dunnies, dwarfs (Rumpelstiltskin was a German dwarf), elves, fauns, fays, fetches, fiends, firedrakes (a fiery dragon), flay-boggarts, flibertygibbets, follets, freiths ("to fright" or ghosts), friars' lanterns, Gabriel-hounds, gallytrots, gins, goblins, grants (a kind of bipedal horse), gremlins, gringes, gruagachs; guests (ghosts), gy-carlins, gytrashes, hags (old and ugly witch), harlequins, hell-hounds, the hellwain (a phantom wagon in the night sky), hobbits, hobby-lanthorns, hobhoulards, hodge-poachers, hudskins, Jack-o'-the-wads, jengus, Jenny-burties, jimy-burnt-tails, kitty-witches, Kit-wi-the-Can[dle]stick (Kit as short for Christopher who carried *ignis fatuis* "o" the candlestick), knockers, kobolds, korigans, korreds, kows (cowes), larrs, larves, lemurs, lian-hamshees, lubberkins, madcaps, mami wata; mannikins (little people), mawhins, men-in-the-oak (holdover from the Druids who favored oaks where spirits lived), the mare (nightmares), Meg-with-the-wads, melchdicks, melusine, mermaids and mermen, merrow, miffies, mock-beggars, morgens, mumpokers, nacks, nickers, nickevins, nickies, night bats; nissies, nixies (unfriendly German female water sprite), nokkes, old-shocks, ouphs (from which we get oafs), padfoots, pans, picteens, pigmies, pigwidgeons, pixies (pesky and playful Celtic little people), portunes, puckrels (a witch's familiar or ground-dweller who can "get you in a pickle"), pucks, pygmae (a type of gnome), rawheads, radiant boys, redcaps, redmen, revenants (residents of the Otherworld who like to visit humans from time to time), Robinets (derivative of Robin Goodfellow), rusalka, salamanders (lizards of the fire), scar-bugs, scrags, scrats, shag-foals, shellycoats, snapdragons, the spoorn (or spurns, specters or phantoms), sprets, spunks, swaiths, swarths, the sylens ("Syleham lamps" of Suffolk where the bogs send up lights to lure away travelers), tantarrabobs, thurses, tints, tod-lowries, Tompokers, tomtumblers (imp of which P. T. Barnum's Tom Thumb was a namesake), totems, tritons, troglodytes; trolls, tutgots, urchins (not street-begging kids but a hedgehog, a creature favored by the adepts), vodyanoys, windigoes, wirry-cows (Scottish bugbear, goblin, ghost, ghoul, or scarecrow), waffs (spirit of a dying person), whitewomen (white ladies), wraiths, yeth-hounds. There are plenty more if you'd care to keep on looking. Modern culture doesn't give much play to the minor spirits but for our forefathers they were a central part of daily life. To quote Chaucer, "Now can no man see none elves no mo." *See also* agathodaimon; *Alpha Ovule;* American folklore; ancestor reverence; apparition; Arethusa; Ascended Masters; attending spirit(s); Ayida Wedo; banshee; beast(s); Beltane; Beltane's Eve; bestiary; bogle; brownies; Celtic folklore and religion; clurichauns; Creole (Caribbean) religions; daemons; deceiving spirits; demon(s), demonic; devils; disa; dobbies; dryads; Eblis; elemental(s); evil (unclean) spirit(s); fairy, fairies; familiar; familiar spirit; folklore; folk religion; Formorians; frost giants; Furies; Gargantua; ghost(s); ghoul; giant(s); gnome(s); Green Man, the; Habonde, Dame; Halloween; hobgoblins; homunculus; hound(s) of hell; household deities; huldafolk; idol(s); Kephn; Keres; Lammas; Lares; Legba; leprechaun(s); Loa Loas; Lughnasadh; lwa; magic, magick; Manes; Mesnie Hellequin; Midsummer Day; mythical beasties, elementals, monsters, and spirit animals; *nagual;* nereid; New Age religion; nisse; Norns; nymph(s); nyx; occult, occultic; Oniropompi; Orisha; Oya; para; paredri; penates; poltergeist(s); pooka; *Pytho;* Python, python; *Quashee;* Robin Goodfellow; Samhain; Saracens; satyr; Saturday's child; Seely Court, Unseely Court; selkie; Sidhe; simulacrum; sirens; spirit; spirit guide; spiritual warfare; sprite(s); sylph(s); teraphim; territorial spirits; tiger; Trickster; Tuatha de Danann; tutelary; undine; wight(s); Wild Man; witch(es).

bull: 1. the male species of cattle, still potent in their reproductive capacity. Bulls were often a choice for sacrifice and model for pagan idols because they symbolized virility, power, and strength (*i.e.,* Psalm 22:12). 2. a papal declaration in Roman Catholicism published with the expectation it will be obeyed. The document is traditionally sealed with lead. The word comes from the Latin *bullum,* meaning "seal," thus making it an official decree. *See also* animals, birds, and insects, symbology of; Bull of Heaven; calf, calves; cattle and oxen; concordat; decretal(s); encyclical(s); idol(s); idolatry; lamassu; mythological beasties, elementals, monsters, and spirit animals; Roman Catholic Church; seal(s).

bulla: a lump of clay stamped with a seal while wet and used to authenticate documents and official papers. A *bulla* is considered a prized find when discovered by archeologists. *See also* archeology, archeologists; seal(s); signet ring.

bulletin(s): a printed order of service used in many Protestant denominations. The flyer may also contain a current list of activities, instructions, directions, and other practical information and may even include a special welcome to visitors. *See also* liturgical year; liturgy, Christian; Offertory; order of service.

Bullinger, Heinrich: an active Protestant reformer (1504–1575) and an associate of John Calvin (1504–1575). In fact, Bullinger became John Calvin's replacement in Geneva. Together they wrote the treatise entitled *Consensus Tigurinus* (the "Zurich Agreement"), which tried to satisfy Roman Catholics and Lutherans as to what takes place in the Eucharist regarding Jesus' body. Like most compromises, it pleased no one. *See also* Calvinism; Calvin, John; Geneva theocracy of John Calvin; Protestantism, Protestants; Protestant Reformation, the.

Bull of Heaven: the fierce bull resident in the cosmos named Gugalana. The animal was recruited by a jealous Ishtar to punish Gilgamesh for his disinterest in her. However, Gilgamesh and his friend, Enkidu, killed the beast. The story is one among many of the adventures of Gilgamesh. *See also* animals, birds, and insects, symbology of; bull; *Epic of Gilgamesh, The;* Gilgamesh; idol(s); Mount Nisin; mythological beasties, elementals, monsters, and spirit animals; Sumerian and Babylonian pantheon.

Bultmann, Rudolf: German theologian from a Lutheran and Confessing Church background (August 20, 1884–July

30, 1976). Bultmann's emphases centered on the processes known as "demythologizing" and "form criticism," which tend to call into question the historicity of Jesus. For him, the Gospels are not focused on the incarnate Jesus but are summations of combined early church doctrine, pagan beliefs, myth, and philosophy. His most famous literary contributions were entitled *History of the Synoptic Tradition* (1921) and *Kerygma and Mythos* (1948). *See also* Barth, Karl; Bonhoeffer, Dietrich; closed continuum; demythologizing; dialectic theology;; dispensational hypothesis; form criticism; higher criticism; Lutheran church; neo-orthodoxy.

Bunyan, John: enduring Christian (Baptist) witness and writer (1628–1688 A.D.). His most famous work is the popular *The Pilgrim's Progress,* an allegory of the Christian life symbolized in sufferings and triumphs. Bunyan affirmed that the inspiration and plot for his work came from a dream. He suffered a psychopathic disease showing itself at times as self-loathing, an agitated conscience, and mortification which could not but influence his life and work. *See also* Baptists; *Pilgrim's Progress, The*.

Buraq: Mohammed's horse ("Lightening"). The prophet, according to Muslim tradition, ascended to heaven astride the animal while briefly in Jerusalem. The Buraq is a Mesopotamian hybrid beast with the body of a winged horse and face of a man. It, or something like it, is depicted in Assyrian and Indian art as a *shedu*, a horse body with a crowned head and magnificent beard. See *also* animals, birds, and insects, symbology of; horse; Islam; lamassu; Mohammed; mushrishu; mythological beasties, elementals, monsters, and spirit animals; night journey, the; Pegasus; Sleipnir.

"burden of the word of the Lord, the": a common scriptural phrase used to state the power, danger, or hardship experienced by the prophet. We find its use in Hosea 8:10, Nahum 1:1, Zechariah 9:1 and 12:1, and Malachi 1:1. The New

International Version substitutes other words for "burden" but the meaning remains. Isaiah and Jeremiah used the definition extensively, both as a warning and a rebuke. *See also* mantle; *massa;* oracle; prophecy.

burial: the act of interment of a dead body and—sometimes by implication—for immolation as well. Proper burial, hopefully with the complete body accounted for, is important to Jewish custom. Without it, the memory and honor of the deceased is impugned. Furthermore, leaving dead bodies above ground was a ready source of contamination and pestilence, if noted with exceptions such as Zoroastrianism. A "spiritual" burial is often designated a baptism as the body is immersed. *See also* anointing; "ashes to ashes"; baptism; catacombs; catafalque; cemetery; death; funeral; grave; Manes; martyrium; multiconfessional.

"burned over district," the: certain stretches of western New York State, so-called because the area seemed to be frequently involved in seizures of religious frenzy or enthusiasm from time to time. Whether it be hard-sell evangelism, quirky cults, or excessive religious fervor, the ignition point was, often enough, the Ohio Valley area. The locale was the starting point of the Millerite movement, Mormonism, and episodes of the Great Awakening revivals, to name a few.

Burning Man Festival: an annual celebration of self-expression that began as a modern commemoration of the summer solstice in 1986. The event is staged at Black Rock Desert, Nevada, on Labor Day weekend. The central theme of the festival is the burning of a large human effigy (about 100 feet in height in 2010) on Saturday night. Promoters are usually described as Dadaists who seek to promote the efficacies of the Burning Man (*viz.*, inclusiveness of all attendees (entry via ticket purchase is required)), spontaneous gift exchanging, cashless barter, self-reliance of the individual, self-expression of art, dance, behavior, etc., communal cooperation, civic obedience, environmental consciousness, and encouragement of participation to all who attend. Sometimes the Festival is called "Wicker Man," from a movie of the same name. The Burning Man probably should not be classed as a strictly religious event, although it does have association with New Age. The festival holds uncanny shades of the pagan bonfire rituals. These, originally called "bone fires," were used to predict the favors of the new year. A human or animal was burned in a wicker basket, after which the charred remains of bone could reveal the future for the next twelve months. Julius Caesar reported the wicker figure was stuffed with sacrificial victims collected by the Druids and burned alive. His account may be, and likely is, prejudiced since the Celts vigorously opposed Roman domination. *See also* Celtic folklore and religion; dance; Druidism; Midsummer Day; New Age religion; sect(s).

burning mountain, the. See blazing mountain, the; Wormwood.

burning stick snatched from the fire, a: a description of feeble humanity presented to the prophet Amos (Amos 4:11). The illustration may represent the brevity or fragility of mortal life, which can be rescued by the Lord as someone snatched from the blaze just in time before he is consumed.

burnished man, the: a vision of a mighty angelic figure encountered by Daniel near the Tigris River (Dan. 10). The "man" is described as wearing linen clothing with a golden belt about his waist. His body resembled chrysolite, his face like lightning, his eyes aflame, his arms and legs of burnished bronze, and he was speaking in a penetrating voice. None of Daniel's companions saw the theophany, but they were nevertheless seized with terror and hid themselves. The bright man (assuming he is the same figure) is seen again above the river in Daniel 12. He, or another like him, also appears in Revelation 10:1.

bursary: 1. the treasurer of a monastery or college. 2. a scholarship for a needy student.

Bushnell, Horace: a leading advocate (1802–1876) of liberalization of American theology. He emphasized the social environment in character development. To his thinking, sin is a social evil (and so is virtue a social good) and men are not redeemed in isolation from society. *See also* Social Gospel; social issues; Unitarian Universalists.

Bush, Professor George: a distant relative (June 12, 1796–September 19, 1859) of both Bush presidents of the United States. The ancestral Bush was a gifted student and linguist, a Presbyterian missionary in the American frontier. He returned from the field to New York University to serve as a professor of Hebrew and Oriental literature. In 1844, Professor Bush published *The Valley of Vision* or *The Dry Bones of Israel Revived*. The book was a focused exposition of the dry bones prophecy of Ezekiel 37. The work was an immediate success selling over a million copies—an unheard of event in the 18th century. Therein, Bush revealed his belief that Israel would be restored as part of God's redemptive plan and that Christians had a part to play in that unfolding drama. *See also* Ezekiel's vision of the valley of dry bones; missions, missionaries; Presbyterians.

bush, the burning: a miraculous flaming bush on Mount Sinai that did not consume itself (Ex. 3). From it issued God's plan (given to Moses) for deliverance of the Hebrew slaves from Egypt.

buzzard Christian: any believer who audaciously avoids regular church attendance or activities but will show up for funerals, memorials, and free food. *See also* Christianese; slurs, religious.

Byblos. See Gebal.

Byzantine Church: the Eastern wing (Greek) of Catholicism called Eastern Orthodox, especially as it is intended in the region of ancient Byzantium. The headquarters of the patriarchate was Constantinople at that time. The Eastern brand of religion, in slightly altered forms, quickly spread to Russia and neighboring areas. The Byzantine Empire's power had almost totally collapsed by 1453. *See also* Cappadocian fathers; Constantinople as city; Coptic Church; Eastern Orthodox Church; *Maxims of Duauf*; Melkite; Syrian Orthodox Church; Uniat Church.

C

Cabala. See Qabbala.

Cabrini, Frances Xavier: an Italian-born Roman Catholic nun (1850–1917), the youngest of thirteen children. She was determined to become a missionary, but smallpox in her early twenties impaired her health. Then, at twenty-seven, she finally managed to take her vows and began work with the poor, which earned her the title "Mother" from those she helped. In 1889 Pope Leo XIII sent her to New York to assist the plight of the Italian immigrants. Soon her order had established orphanages, schools, adult education-classes, and hospitals—sixty-seven institutions in all. She became a United States citizen in 1909 and in 1946 was canonized by Pope Pius XII, the first American to be so recognized. *See also* nun(s); Roman Catholic Church.

Cabrius: the Roman god of the working class dear to the subjugated Thessalonians of the first century. The religion, however for some unknown reason, had been usurped by the upper class and incorporated into the state religion. *See also* Olympian pantheon; Roman Empire.

Cadac-Andreas: an Irish scholar (798 – 814 A.D.) in the court of Charlemagne known for his bombastic, tireless, pedantic, and lengthy discourses on theology. He raised the ire of Bishop Theodulphus (Theodulf of Orleans ca. 750 – 821) who grew to detest the man. As it turned out, however, Cadac-Andreas obtained a bishopric from the king but Theodulphus was exiled. So often does it seem that bureaucratic fussiness wins over competence. *See also* Roman Catholic Church.

Cadaver Synod, the: one of the darkest and most bizarre episodes of the Roman Catholic papacy. The incident involved a cleric named Formosus who became bishop of Porta in Portugal in the year 864. During his term, Formosus distinguished himself with exceptional political and diplomatic skills. However, a rival faction sprang up to impede his career and managed to boycott his candidacy for patriarch of Bulgaria. Canon law forbade a bishop from moving from one diocese to another but Formosus was charged with fleeing and was excommunicated from the church. In 878, at the synod of Troyes, Formosus appealed to Pope John VIII and was absolved. The next pope, Marinus I, allowed his return to Porto. In 891, Formosus even became pope himself, at which time he politically allied himself with the German aspirant king, Arnuf of Carinthia, against the dukes of Spoleto for the crown of the Holy Roman Empire. Formosus crowned Arnuf in Rome in 895 but the new king died shortly thereafter. He was quickly followed in death by Formosus himself who was buried in the Basilica of Saint Peter as befitting a sitting pope. Stephen VI was selected in his place, a supporter of the Spoleto faction in Germany. The new pontiff ordered Formosus' body exhumed, dressed it in royal regalia, propped it on a chair and commenced to proceed with a bizarre and macabre trial. A terrified young deacon was forced to be the voice of the "accused." The body was found guilty and the cadaver was then mutilated by cutting out the tongue and the removal of the three fingers used for blessing, then thrown in the Tiber. The grotesque incident set a precedent of shame and even King Philip IV of France used it to further his campaign against the Knights Templar. *See also* Roman Catholic Church; synod.

Caedmon: (c. 657 – 684 A.D) English poet, musician, and monk who claimed to have learned musical composition from a dream. His only surviving work is *Caedmon's Hymn* which honors God in the old English vernacular, marking him as our earliest recorded English poet. *See also* monk(s); music.

Caelum Moor: a private park in Arlington, Texas, (now closed) containing menhirs (standing stones) similar to those at Stonehenge. It is reported trespassers like to use the locale for pagan ceremonies of various descriptions. *See also* Georgia Guidestones; New Age religion; sacred stones; Stonehenge.

Caesar cult: anthropocentric idolatry. Some Roman emperors were decreed, either by themselves or others, to be divine and demanding of worship. One hotbed of Caesar worship was situated in Pergamum (Rev. 2:12–17), but there were many more in the empire. Caesar worship was a simplified ritual and largely politically motivated (merely adding a pinch of incense to fire with a brief pledge of fealty), but the acts were a real and constant consternation to believing Christians who cherished the ideal that there is no God but Jesus Christ. *See also* apotheosis; caesaropapacy; Christianity in the Roman Empire; emperor worship; idol(s); idolatry; *Pontifex Maximus*; *princeps*; *principis*; Roman Empire; state church.

Caesarea: the Palestinian seacoast city built by Herod the Great and dedicated to his patron, Caesar Augustus. No expense was spared so a magnificent seaport in Greek style was constructed with a highly functioning harbor. The place was sometimes called Caesarea by the sea to distinguish it from that city mentioned in the Gospels, Caesarea Philippi. It was at Caesarea where Peter received his vision of the unclean animals, leading to the conversion of the Gentile Cornelius. *See also* Cornelius; unclean animals, Peter's vision of the.

Caesarius of Heisterbach: Cistercian monk (1180–1240) in Cologne, Germany. He is noted as the source quote attributed to Arnauld Almalric's famous order to kill all Cathars and Catholics at Beziers, France, because God could sort them out later. Caesarius predicted a time when the Roman Catholic papacy would be vacant and pestilence would cover the earth. *See also* Almalric, Arnauld; Cathars; Cistercians; Inquisition, the; Roman Catholic Church.

caesaropapacy: a term denoting those instances when the state is politically dominant over the church. *See also* Abington School District vs. Schempp; Allegheny County vs. ACLU; antidisestablishmentarianism; *Booke of the General Lawes and Libertyes*; Caesar cult; civil religion; collegialism;

disestablishmentarianism; divine right of kings; Edict of Milan; Edict of Nantes; Edict of Toleration; Emerson vs. Board of Education; emperor worship; Establishment Clause and Free Exercise Clause; Geghan Bill; Government Regulation Index (GRI); idolatry; Lemon vs. Kurtzman; Massachusetts Body of Liberties; *Pontifex Maximus; princeps; principis;* public square; regalism; Shubert vs. Verner; state church; ultramontanism; Virginia's Religious Disestablishment law.

cafeteria Christians: or café Christianity, a derogatory term for selecting those affirmations or doctrines that are attractive to an individual and rejecting others that are perceived to be uncomfortable or difficult. The label reflects one who is acquiring and practicing faith as if he or she were shopping or dining in a cafeteria buffet, choosing only what is easy or appealing. *See also* carnal Christians; Christianese; "church hopper"; "churn" (religious); denominational mutt; McChurch; nominal Christians; slurs, religious.

Caiaphas: high priest of Israel during the tenure of John the Baptist and Jesus aptly named "a depression." Caiaphas and his father-in-law, Annas (Jn. 18:13–14), were co-ministers, but it was Caiaphas who proposed the death of Jesus. He ruled longer than any priest in the New Testament, and Annas had five sons who held the same office at some point. Caiaphas' words concerning Jesus were more prophetic than he knew: "It is expedient for you that one man should die for the people, and that the whole nation should not perish" (Jn. 11:49–53). Later, Caiaphas also took part in the trial of Peter and John (Acts 4:6). He was eventually dismissed from his position by Vitellius, the Roman governor of Syria. *See also* priest(s); three traitors, the.

Cain: first son of Adam and Eve (Gen. 4:1). He murdered his brother Abel, gaining for himself and his descendants the curse of God. He is mentioned again in Jude 11 as a poor example of faith. For his grievous sin Cain was marked by God and cast from society. Naturally, a frequent question then arises: Whom did Cain marry? No biblical answer is provided so we must resort to speculation. Did he find a pre-history humanoid race in the outer world? One of his sisters? Did he interact with the fallen angels or their offspring? Was he somehow associated with the so-called Cainites? *See also* Abel; Arka; Cainites; land of Nod; mark of Cain.

Cainites: 1. an early Gnostic sect who believed that Cain, Judas, and other ungodly persons were actually spiritual seekers who resisted the evil Creator God. As such, they worshiped the serpent which symbolized their doctrine. 2. a group of men or angels called the daughters of men who are destined to be judged at the end of the age. By some interpretations of Genesis 6, one view identifies the Sethites as a godly and faithful race before the great flood while the Cainites were worldly and rebellious. *See also* Arka; Cain; daughters of men; Gnosticism, Gnostic(s); Sethianism; Sethites; idolatry; Ophites; reptilian theory; sect(s); sons of God; sons of God to be revealed.

Caius: 1. or Gaius, a third century theologian and presbyter of Rome who rejected John the Apostle as author of both the Gospel of John and Revelation. He claimed these two books were instead written by the Gnostic Cerinthus. Caius was an ardent opponent of the Montanist movement. He was strongly challenged by Hippolytus in most of his theological thinking. This Caius may or may not be the person whom some ancient writers accused of being the falsifier of those notes in Josephus referencing Jesus Christ. 2. Roman Catholic pope (A.D. 283–296) who decreed that before any man could attain that high office he first had to be an acolyte, lector, subdeacon, deacon, porter, and exorcist. He may or may not have been a martyr. 3. the Roman emperor called Gaius (whom Josephus called Caius), or Caligula. *See also* Caligula; Eusebius; Josephus, Flavius; liturgical year; martyr(s); pope; Roman Catholic Church; Roman Empire; *Testimonium Flavianum*.

calculation, apocalyptic. See apocalyptic calculation.

Caleb: one of only two faithful spies sent by Moses to scout the Promised Land during the Israelite Exodus from Egypt. Though not a prophet in the strictest sense, he did utter a prophetic-like message in his defense of God's plan of immediate invasion (Num. 14:5–9). He was supported in his appeal by Joshua son of Nun. Caleb also figured prominently in the later conquest of Canaan. *See also* Arba; giant(s); Hebron.

calefactory: a warming room in a monastery where the monks can find temporary warmth on cold days. *See also* chamberlain; Eastern Orthodox Church; monastery; monasticism; Roman Catholic Church.

calendar: a record used to delineate days and years. The word itself comes from the ancient Roman designation "calends" that marked the time as one of three fixed days within a month (named calends, ides, and nones). Calends always fell on the first day of the month. The Christian calendar began with the Julian, but the Gregorian is presently in use, with a year designated as about 365.25 days. The Islamic calendar is totally different and started only in the year A.D. 622 and contains 354–355 days per year. The Jewish calendar has always been lunisolar but has evolved over the years. Its primary purpose is to reckon the Jewish holidays and attempt to date itself from the creation of the world. The modern count loses a full day every 224 years. Subsequent efforts by the League of Nations and United Nations to more precisely adjust the calendar calculation have received scant support. Calendar reckoning is important prophetically and historically because of the warnings of Daniel 7:25, which describe the Antichrist's attempt to manipulate the times. *Second Enoch* describes a solar year of 365 days beginning in March. The difference between the lunar and solar calculation is called an *epact*—an intercalation. Historical study becomes somewhat complicated when exact dates are needed because there have been so many dating methods throughout the centuries.

Besides the Julian, Gregorian, and Hebrew calendars, there were others for the French Revolution, Chinese, the Sun Stone, the Aztec Round and Mayan Round of Mesoamerica, the Phoenix Cycle, the Babylonian, Egyptian, the Gothic Cycle, Greek, and the Roman Republican systems, to name a few. *See also Anno Domini; Anno Mundi;* B.C.; B.C.E.; calendar (Gregorian); calendar (Hebrew); calendar (Islamic); calendar (Julian); carnival; C.E.; Eagle Bowl; embolism; Lord's Day, the; Numa Pompilius; Sunday; Sun Stone; 2012 prophecy, advocates of; 2012, prophecy of.

calendar (Gregorian): the present-day system of time-keeping that replaced the old Julian calendar. The Gregorian system, sponsored by Pope Gregory XIII (A.D. 1502–1585), was adopted in 1582. Gregory devised the new calendar with the aid of the priest/astronomer Christopher Clavius and the astronomer/physician Luigi Lilio Ghiraldi (Aloysius Libius in Latin) in hopes of correcting perceived shortcomings in the Julian system. They added four days to the Julian count and specified that centennial years (those ending in 00) could only be observed as leap years if they were divisible by 400. The new timekeeping was slow to gain acceptance from the general populace, Reformation Protestants, and the Orthodox Church; in some instances around the world, acceptance was still lagging for hundreds of years. The Gregorian effort itself was not free from errors that have yet to be addressed in the modern age. *See also* calendar; calendar (Hebrew); calendar (Islamic); calendar (Julian); *compuctus;* liturgical year; Pascal controversy.

calendar (Hebrew): the Jewish reckoning of time accounted by the lunisolar (primarily lunar) cycle. The Jewish calendar represents a calculation of the number of years reckoned since creation. The dating remains in use even though most people no longer trust the method originated centuries ago. So, in the civil year 2016 the Jewish year is 5777. To determine the Jewish year, simply add 3761 to the western calendar. Bishop Ussher's false dating system of the 1600s is close to that number. The new year begins with Nisan in company with the Gentile dates of March or April. The months in the Jewish year number twelve or thirteen (depending on the leap year count) and each is either twenty-nine or thirty days in length. They are listed in order as: Nisan, Iyar (Iyyar), Sivan, Tammuz, Av (Ab), Elul, Tishri; Cheshvan (Heshvan, Masheshavan), Kislev, Tevet (Tivet, Tebeth), Shevat (Shebat), Adar Rishon (in leap years only), and Adar (Adar Beit in leap years only.) When named along with the feast days associated with each the result is: Nisan (*Pesach, Chag Hamotzi, Yom Habikkurim*), Iyyar, Sivan (*Shavuot*), Tammuz, Ab [Av], Elul, Tishri (*Rosh Hashanah, Yom Kippur, Tisha b'Av, Succoth*), Heshvan [Masheshavan], Kislev (*Hanukkah),* Tevet [Tebeth], Shevat [Shebat], Adar [Adar Beit in leap years] (*Purim*). A leap month must be inserted seven times in every nineteen years cycle. The present reckoning is said to be derived from the action of the Sanhedrin under Rabbi Hillel II in 259 C.E. and holds reference to the Babylonian calendar to which the Jewish captives were exposed in the exile. More likely, the present calendar simply evolved over the years by trial and error. The official Jewish day begins at sunset and continues through the next sunset. The month consists of 30 days, or 360 days per year. The modern Jewish calendar calculations ensure that *Yom Kippur* and *Rosh Hashanah* do not occur on a Friday (a Sabbath) by simply switching days in the previous month; neither will *Rosh Hashanah* fall on a Sunday, Wednesday, or Friday. The rabbis surmise that if these high holy days occur on a Sabbath, the Sabbath rules would prevent Orthodox Jews from performing the needed rituals on that occasion. The religious calendar (cited above) is not to be confused with the civil schedule, which the Jews also utilize. *See also* Adar as calendar month; *Anno Domini; Anno Mundi;* B.C.; B.C.E.; calendar; calendar (Gregorian); calendar (Islamic); calendar (Julian); C.E.; feasts and special days of Judaism; Judaism; liturgy, Jewish; Nisan 17; septa-millennial; six-day theory; Ussher, James.

calendar (Islamic): a calculation of time based on cycles of the moon. There are 354 days and 12 months in the system, half of which have 29 days and the other half 30. Thirty years form a cycle; 11 times in every cycle and extra day is added at the end of the year. Thus, the months and seasons do not correspond; the first day of the Muslim year falls on different seasons in different years. The Islamic reckoning begins with the first day of the flight of Mohammed to Medina. That date in the Gregorian setting or Christian era is July 15, 622. *See also* calendar; calendar (Gregorian); calendar (Hebrew); calendar (Julian); Islam.

calendar (Julian): the older calendar established by Julius Caesar in 46 B.C. and used by Bishop Ussher to determine his "6,000-year" theory for the age of the earth and its end. The Julian is about ten days out of synch from our Gregorian calendar in use today, although it, too, is flawed. *See also* calendar; calendar (Gregorian); calendar (Hebrew); calendar (Islamic); *compuctus;* Paschal controversy; Roman Empire; septa-millennial; "six-day theory, the.

calf: young offspring of cattle. A calf was often a model for pagan idolatry, as seen in the one Aaron fashioned (Ex. 32) or those erected by Jeroboam (1 Ki. 12:25-32). A calf could demonstrate exuberance or joy as it frolics in its youthful energy (Ps. 29:6). Calves were a prominent animal of sacrifice, one of the more expensive and expressive. *See also* animals, birds, and insects, symbology of; bull; cattle and oxen; cow; flocks and herds; golden calf (calves); idol(s); idolatry.

calf and the lion, the. See wolf and the lamb, the.

Caligula: Roman emperor (A.D. 37–41 A.D.) who tried to erect a statue of himself in the Jerusalem Temple. His attempt and subsequent failure then may offer some relevance as a precursor to the abomination of desolation. As a result, Jerusalem found itself in the unique position as the only city in the Roman Empire without a statue of Caligula. His true name was Gaius Julius Caesar Augustus Germanicus, but the title Caligula means "little soldier's boot" taken from his childhood when he accompanied his father, a general of the Roman army fighting the Germanic tribes. The first two years of his reign were tolerable, but he quickly descended into madness. He was known to be among the most cruel of all Roman emperors. He killed at a whim and was given to excesses of all descriptions. His career ended with an assassination brought on by members of the Praetorian Guard and the Senate. *See also* Caius; Christianity in the Roman Empire; idol(s); king(s); Patronius; Roman Empire.

caliph: a Muslim title for a leader considered to be a successor to Mohammed and used as a temporal and sacred title for the ruler of a caliphate (conquered territory annexed by Islamic armies and missionaries). The word means "successor." Only a caliph is entitled to wear a green turban since that color is sacred to Muslims. *See also* Abbasid Caliphate; Ayyubid dynasty; caliphate; Fatimid Caliphate; Islam; king(s); Mameluke(s); Rashidun Caliphate; Umayyad Caliphate.

caliphate: the jurisdiction of an Islamic caliph. The last was held by Ottoman Turks until 1924 but it is generally agreed that militant Islam desires to establish a world caliphate as soon as possible in our era. *See also* Abbasid Caliphate; Ayyubid dynasty; caliph; Daesh; Fatimid Caliphate; Islam; Mameluke(s); Rashidun Caliphate; Umayyad Caliphate.

Calistus: a Gnostic type who formed a commune that practiced fornication, common-law marriages, drug usage for producing sterility, and abortions. *See also* communal communities; Gnosticism, Gnostic(s).

Calixtines. See Ultraquists.

called, chosen, and faithful, the: a reference in Revelation 14:17 naming all godly followers of Christ—the saints in every age.

call(ing): an imperative to communicate or render a service or pursue a vocation. Theologically, a call is an important prophetic action in which God Himself "calls" or commissions certain persons to be prophets or other identified servants for Him. Without such an invitation (or requirement as the case may be) one could not assume the mantle of a prophet of God. Even today, many ecclesiastical denominations insist that their ministers and other leaders profess a "call" from God before assuming their duties or accepting a new post. The commissioning summons of Isaiah (Isa. 6), Ezekiel (Ezk. 1–2), Jeremiah (Jer. 1:4–10), Samuel (1 Sam. 3), Abraham (Gen. 12), Moses (Ex. 3), Gideon (Jud. 6:11–39), David (1 Sam. 16:1–13), and Paul (Acts 9:1–18) are among the most dramatic. Paul listed the five special callings as apostles (now inactive), prophets, evangelists, pastors, and teachers (Eph. 4:11). In a broader but perhaps more universal spirit, the Holy Spirit calls all outside the faith to genuine belief (Rom. 8:29–30) and summons all believers to some type of holy service. *See also* anointing; charge; charisms; commission; ordination; pastor(s); preacher(s); priest(s); *vocare*.

calumny: false statements or gossip that injures the reputation of another, also called a detraction. *See also* liar(s); lie(s); social issues; Ten Commandments, the.

Calvary: the place of Jesus' crucifixion. The site is located somewhere near Jerusalem yet outside the city walls (as stipulated by Jewish law) as they stood at that time. Its exact location is disputed today. The name for the ground comes from the Latin *calvaria* and the Greek *kranion*, both meaning "skull." The Aramaic rendering is Golgotha. *See also* Golgotha; place of the Skull.

Calvary Chapel: a faith group that describes itself as "evangelical, charismatic, and pretribulationist" and prefers the term "association" as opposed to "denomination" as to its identity. The group began in Southern California in 1965 and is pastor-led in polity. Radio and local Bible colleges are emphasized and fellowship units practice expository teaching that follows a chapter by chapter and verse by verse exploration of Scripture. *See also* church bodies in America (typed); denomination(s), denominationalism.

Calvert, Cecilius and George: (George, – ca. 1580–1632) and son (Cecilius, – ca. 1605–1675) team, the First and Second Lords of Baltimore, both British statesmen and colonizers. The elder Calvert hoped to establish an American colony in Maryland that would serve as a profitable investment and as a haven for migrating Roman Catholics. He obtained a charter for that purpose from King Charles I but died before its issue. His son Cecilius accepted the charter and sent his brother Leonard to Maryland in 1634 as the first governor. However, most of the settlers were Protestants and became the majority. Calvert did manage to obtain the Toleration Act from the Maryland Assembly guaranteeing religious freedom for all Christians. Neither George nor Cecilius ever reached Maryland despite the naming of the state's capital city. George, however, had been a member of the Virginia Company (1609–1620) and the New England Company (1622). *See also* Redemptioners; Toleration Act of 1649.

Calvinism: the Protestant doctrines of John Calvin. Calvinism has had deep impact on theology since its inception despite its rather severe philosophy. Protestant denominations in America were particularly affected, especially the Puritans and their follow-on Congregationalists and the Presbyterians of both colonial and modern times. The Massachusetts colonies were essentially theocracies. Calvin promoted the doctrine of predestination, which insists that God has already chosen who will be saved, essentially cutting out the concept of free will. Not until the mid-eighteenth century did Calvinism begin to weaken in the face of the humanistic philosophies of the Enlightenment, which rejected the belief in the natural depravity of man. *See also* Amyraldism; Arminianism; BACON; Beza, Theodore; Bullinger, Heinrich; Calvin, John; Canons of Dort; Chauncy, Charles; conditional election; Consistory, the; double predestination; Edwards, Jonathan; election; eternal security; fall from grace; Five-Point Calvinism; free will; Geneva theocracy of John Calvin; grace; *Institutes of* *the Christian Religion;* Lambeth Articles; Mather, Cotton; Mather, Increase; "once saved, always saved"; perseverance of the saints; Philadelphia Confession; predestination; Protestantism, Protestants; Protestant Reformation, the; Puritanism, Puritans; Remonstrants; reprobation; "Sinners in the Hands of an Angry God"; Synod of Dort; total depravity; TULIP; Westminster Confession.

Calvin, John: Protestant reformer in Geneva in the 16th century (1509–1564). Calvin was a strict moralist, as well as a thorough-going theologian who ruled Geneva with an iron hand (excepting his brief banishment in 1541). He wrote *Institutes of the Christian Religion,* an important and systematic work of Protestant theology. Calvin's Geneva politico-religious government was centered on "presbyters" in leadership positions who controlled the city's welfare and conduct. Calvin proposed John Mark as a possible candidate for the writer of Revelation. In general, Calvin did not favor the Apocalypse and never wrote a commentary on its content. He did, however, espouse that some godly dreams and visions are legitimate sources of prophecy. Calvin would likely be classed as an amillennialist. *See also* Arminius, Jacobus; Beza, Theodore; Bullinger, Heinrich; Calvinism; elect, the; election; Geneva theocracy of John Calvin; *Institutes of the Christian Religion;* predestination; Protestant Reformation, the; Protestant Reformers; Servetus, Michael; TULIP; Westminster Confession.

Cambridge Platonists: an intellectual group of the 17th century, a number of them women, associated with the University of Cambridge. Most of them claimed to be Christian, but were fascinated by the Greek philososphers and felt those teachings should be combined with Christianity to make a perfect "rational" religion for the world. They referred to reason as "the candle of the Lord" and were trying to balance strict Puritan/Calvinistic doctrine with the materialism with the likes of Rene Descartes and Thomas Hobbes. Sometimes they are hardly distinguished from the Latitudinarians. The most active Cambridge Platonist was perhaps Henry More (1614 – 1687) who wrote *Immortality of the Soul* wherein he rejected the concept of a resurrected body and insisted heaven is a purely spiritual state such as philosophers would enjoy. *See also* Caroline Divines, the; Church of England; Latitudinarians.

Cambyses II: second king of Persia (530–522 B.C.) after Cyrus. In that position, he perhaps had some contact with the prophet Daniel. He possessed far less political ability than his father and subsequently failed in his attempted conquest of Northern Africa. He reportedly committed suicide near Mount Carmel upon hearing that he had lost his empire base to the imposter Smerdis, who was posing as Cambyses's brother whom Cambyses claims to have slain earlier. *See also* king(s); Smerdis.

Camisards: the Huguenots of Southern France. Their doctrine held a proposed date for the Second Coming in 1705, 1706, or 1709. *See also* Huguenots; martyr(s); martyrdom; sect(s).

camel: a domesticated pack animal and sometimes war steed for some nations, which was common in biblical times. They are frequently mentioned in Scripture as beasts of burden or wealth, especially when applied to their affinity for desert travel in trade caravans or with nomadic tribes. The animal was an important beast of burden in the ancient world (and today) because it was especially suited to the desert environment, serving their owners in trade, travel, and warfare. The beast is known for its ill-temper and irregular body shape; some have even called the animal a horse designed by committee. *See also* animals, birds, and insects, symbology of; flocks and herds.

camerlengo: a title derived from the Latin for "chamberlain," who is the administrator of the property and revenues of the Roman Catholic Holy See in Rome. The occupant is always a cardinal and will serve in the papacy during any interregnum. *See also* bishop(s); cardinal(s); clergy; divine; ecclesiastic(s); episcopate; interregnum; monsignor; pope; priest(s); primate; Roman Catholic Church; Vatican, the.

Campbell, Alexander: of Scotch-Irish descent, Alexander (1788-1866) and his father Thomas became active in America during the Second Great Awakening. They, in league with Barton W. Stone, were active in the Restoration Movement of the time and favored the frontier style of evangelism. From Alexander sprang the Disciples of Christ denomination even though he was never ordained to the clergy. Campbell was an able speaker and debater; he once did the latter for sixteen hours, with Henry Clay acting as moderator. He also published two journals, the *Christian Baptist* and the *Millennial Harbinger*. *See also* apocalyptic fervor; Campbellites; camp meetings; Christian Church; Churches of Christ; Disciples of Christ; evangelist(s), evangelism; Great Awakenings, the; Restoration Movement in America; revivalism; "sawdust trial, the"; Stone, Barton W.

Campbellites: followers of the camp-meeting revivalist Alexander Campbell, sometimes spoken derisively. The actual name of the denomination was Disciples of Christ. *See also* Campbell, Alexander; denomination(s), denominationalism; Disciples of Christ; slurs, religious.

Camping, Harold: a TV and radio evangelist (1921 – 2013) with a fondness for date-setting the return of Christ. In 1994 he predicted the event for September 6 of that year. It didn't happen so the date was changed on September 29, then October 2, and finally March 31, 1995. When the sensational Camping turned eighty in 2011, his latest prediction (to date) centered on May 21 of that year (at precisely 6:00 p.m. no less). His scenario even tells us where the initiating earthquake would begin and how it was to progress across the earth. Camping's liberties, like all the doomsday prophets who seem to dictate Christ's return, are self-styled and counterproductive to solid apocalyptic thinking, not to mention a direct violation of Christ's command not to indulge in idle speculation about the specific date of his return (Mt. 24:36–51). Unfortunately, much of the mainstream media is unable, or unwilling, to set distinctions between reasonable Christianity and the sensational. Camping apologized for the duplicity before his death. *See also* Reformed Churches; televangelism, televangelists.

camp meetings: a common feature of frontier evangelism during the Great Awakening of the 19th century. The first was held in Logan County, Kentucky, in 1800. By 1810 over a million pioneers, most without religious affiliation and many lacking formal education, were moving westward. The fundamentalist itinerant preachers followed, meeting their constituents in makeshift campgrounds, often with a central tent for meetings and surrounded by hundreds of families in their wagons and on horseback. The gatherings were as much social occasions as religious expression. The assembly began with trumpets at dawn, followed by continuous preaching into the evening, the spokesmen spelling each other throughout the day. The revivals frequently produced bizarre behavior among the listeners, including uncontrolled "holy laughter," shaking, rolling in the dirt, miraculous healings, testimonies, and other emotional outbursts. Evangelists like the Presbyterian James McGready (1758–1817), Alexander Campbell, Barton W. Stone, and others were national figures. American Protestantism prospered from the revivalist style, especially the Christian Church, Disciples of Christ, Baptists, and others. Methodism multiplied their numbers sevenfold. Such evangelistic engagements are rare today, but some account Billy Graham to be the most successful product of the model. *See also* apocalyptic fervor; Cane Creek camp meeting; Great Awakenings, the; liturgy, Christian; Restoration Movement in America; revivalism; "sawdust trail, the."

Campus Crusade for Christ: an international and parachurch Christian organization now (since 2011) known as Cru. The organ was founded in 1951 by Bill and Vonette Bright at the University of California at Los Angeles to evangelize and train college and university students. Since then, the organization has expanded into ministry to athletes, professionals, high schools, inner city outreach, humanitarian networking, publishing, and other programs in 191 countries. One of the most successful projects involved the production and presentation of the highly successful film "Jesus" shown worldwide. *See also* InterVarsity Christian Fellowship; Jesus Movement; Navigators; religious education; religious organizations; youth religious organizations.

Cana: the site of the first recorded miracle of Jesus in which he changed water into wine at a wedding to save embarrassment to the host (Jn. 2:1–11). Some claim this incident may sign the continuing festivities and joy in the Millennium or in heaven. Cana was also the home of the disciple Nathaniel.

Canaan, Canaanites: ancient Palestine. Before the Hebrews possessed the land as a perpetual blessing from God, they called the region the Promised Land or the "land of milk and honey." In Abraham's time, the principal populations were Kenites, Kenizzites, Kadmonites, Hittites, Perizzites, Rephaites, Amorites, Girgashites, and Jebusites (Gen. 15:19). The names of both regions and ethnic inhabitants faded from common use as the original pagan inhabitants were driven out or subdued. The Old Testament views Canaanites with derision, and the prophet pledges there will be no one of that identity in the Millennium (Zech. 14:21), although sometimes the word there is translated "merchant." A better understanding is that a "Canaanite" at this point is a profane person or an enemy of God who is not be found in sanctified Jerusalem. The Canaanites were considered an evil population, and Yahweh ordered the total annihilation of some of them. The Bible books of Leviticus and Romans refer to a sequence of sins ("abominations") laid on the Canaanites including incest, adultery, child sacrifice, homosexuality, and bestiality. Such extreme measures may be tempered if one considers that the inhabitants were tainted with corrupt bloodlines from the fallen angels, as some assert. Others merely see the genocide as a guarantee that the Israelites would not be unduly influenced by their paganism. *See also* Amorites; Araunah; city of David; Foundation Stone; Gibeonites; Girgashites; Hittites; Hobab; hornet; Jael; Jerusalem as city; Jethro; Jonadab; Kadesh, battle of; Kenites; Levant; *Maxims of Duauf;* merchant(s); milk and honey; Mount Zion; Ophel; Palestine; Promised Land; the; Rechabites.

Canaanite woman, the. See Syrophoenician woman.

Candace: a queen of Ethiopia. While returning home after a visit to Jerusalem, a eunuch and proselyte to Judaism in her court was converted to Christianity by the ministrations of Philip the evangelist. He was also baptized by Philip after an angel had directed the missionary to the interview (Acts 8:26–39). It is possible that Candace is a royal title, not the name of the queen so identified with the ruler. Some histories call her Amanitere. Also, it is to be noted that Ethiopia was not the modern state but a kingdom called Meroe of the Upper Nile region where the Blue and White Nile merge. *See also* Cush, Cushites; Ethiopian eunuch, the; queen(s).

C and E Christians: a subdued slang reference to holiday trendy Christians who are prone to attend worship only at Christmas and Easter—the two most celebrated feast days of Christianity. The label is somewhat disparaging because the user may affirm a more committed response to regular attendance is preferable and correct. *See also* Christianese; slurs, religious; Sunday Christians.

candelabra. See lamp, lampstand(s).

Candlemas: a vigil of light held in devotion or memory of a beloved. Vigils in honor of the Virgin Mary or the presentation of the infant Jesus are common enough in Catholicism. The official celebration with blessed candles is February 2. *See also* feasts and special days of high liturgy faiths; Imbolc; Mariolatry; Roman Catholic Church; votive.

candlestick(s). See lamp, lampstand(s).

Candomble: the religion, having its beginnings in Portuguese Brazil, which combines elements of Roman Catholicism and local primitive cults. *See also* Creole (Caribbean) religions; cult(s); idolatry; Kumina; Macumba; Obeah; Orisha; Quimbanda; Rastafarianism; Santeria; Shango; Spiritual Baptists; Umbanda; voodoo; voudou; Yoruba.

Cane Ridge camp meeting: possibly the largest revival-style preaching display of revivalism ever encountered. The assemblies took place in 1801 as part of America's Second Great Awakening at Bourbon County, Kentucky. The meetings were hosted by Barton W. Stone, perhaps the most prominent evangelists of the time, with some 20,000 in attendance over several days. *See also* camp meetings; Christian Church (denomination); evangelist(s), evangelism; Finley, James B.; Great Awakenings, the; Restoration Movement in America; revivalism; "sawdust trail, the"; Stone, Barton W.

Canneh: a city in ancient Syria (Aram). *See also* Syria.

canonical hours: the Divine Office in Christianity, an especially formalized worship in the faith, that enacts the practice of praying at fixed hours in the day at regular intervals. Certain times for prayer are named in the liturgical churches: matins (Office of the Readings at the major morning hour), lauds (morning), terce (mid-morning), sext (midday), nones (mid-afternoon), vespers (evening), and compline (night). The Orthodox versions of praying the day is largely counted by hours and are chronological as such. *See also* Agpeya; compline; Eastern Orthodox Church; lauds; liturgical year; liturgy; liturgy, Christian; matins; nones; prayer(s); prime; Roman Catholic Church; sext; terce; vespers.

canonical penance: penitential discipline practiced in certain periods of history, usually set in duration for days or years for various sins. *See also* church discipline; Roman Catholic Church.

canonical prophets: or writing prophets, those spokespersons of the Old Testament who have left us written histories or preserved works. The list includes (in an educated guess of chronology): Amos, Hosea, Micah, Isaiah, Zephaniah, Nahum, Habakkuk, Jeremiah, Ezekiel, Daniel, Haggai, Zechariah, Obadiah, Malachi, Joel, and Jonah. Sometimes Isaiah is received and recorded as two or three separate individuals and Zechariah as two. *See also* major prophets; minor prophets; prophet(s).

canonization. See beatification.

canon(s) of the church: a common name in ecclesiastical circles both in ancient and modern times. The word could name: 1. laws or a body of laws for a church, particularly in Roman Catholic and Anglican settings, 2. that part of the Mass which follows the Sanctus (offering) in High Church liturgy, 3. a list of saints recognized by the Roman Catholic Church, 4. an official list or catalog (as in "canon law"), 5. a member of a clerical group living according to a canon—a rule, as seen in some religious orders, 6. a clergyman serving in a cathedral or collegiate church, 7. a clergywoman (canoness) in the similar capacities as the male but without the obligated strictures expected of a nun, 8. the uniform of clergy worn when conducting worship services in many types of church bodies, 9. the decree to elevate a person to sainthood (beatification), 10. the seven canonical hours set aside for worship in some High Church bodies (*viz.*, matins nocturne, prime, tierce, sext, nones, vespers, and complin), 11. in Britain, any hour between 8:00 a.m. and 3:00 p.m. in which marriage may be performed in parish churches. *See also* Agpeya; akathist; Antilegoma, Antilegomena; antiphoner; apodictic law; Assumptionist Orders; Augustinian Order; Barnabites; beatification; Benedict, Order of; Black Canons; canon of the Scriptures; canons minor; Canons of Dort; canons regular; canticles; Capitulary; Capuchin Order; Carmelites; Carthusians; Celestines; Cistercians; clergy;

Code of Canon Law; confraternities; consistory; Counter-Reformation; Decretum; Didascalia; Dominicans; Eastern Orthodox Church; ecclesiastic(s); *episcopos;* evensong; faith and order; Franciscans; friar(s); knighted orders; liturgical year; liturgy, Christian; Menologion; Minim; monk(s); Mosaic Law; Muratorian Canon; music; novena; orders; patriarch(s); Paulist Fathers; Premonstratensian Order; priest(s); rede; religious organizations; Roman Catholic Church; Sicilian vespers; statute(s); Ten Commandments, the; Trappist Order; *Triodion.*

canon of the Scriptures: the recognized and traditionally authenticated roll call of books of the Bible. There are sixty-six books in our Scripture—thirty-nine in the Old Testament and twenty-seven in the New. Each has passed a series of popular and ecclesiastical criteria through the centuries to gain acceptance into the current listing. A *canon* was originally a rod or reed of standard measure. Several lists (canons) of the Scripture have arisen in history (*viz.,* from Marcion in A.D. 140, Irenaeus in 180, the Muratorian in 200, and Eusebius in 325). The primary criteria for acceptance of any writing into the canon seem to have been the general recognition and acceptance of the work by conscientious clergy and laypersons in the post-Christian era. See also angels of measurement; Antilegoma, Antilegomena; Bible; Bible manuscripts; biblical criticism; canticles; Council of Carthage; Council of Hippo; Council of Jamnia; Council of Laodicea; Council of Trent (Protestant); measuring rod; Muratorian Canon; rod; Third Council of Constantinople.

canons minor: clergy staff of a collegiate church or cathedral. They are participants in worship leadership (often engaged as singers) but not formally affiliated with the body being served. *See also* canon(s) of the church; dean; don; Roman Catholic Church.

Canons of Dort: five articles of faith (1618 – 1619) by the Reformed Synod of the Dutch Reformed Church defending strict Calvinism. They were promulgated as a direct response to the five points of the Arminian Remonstrants and, in general, disputed Armanism. *See also* Amyraldism; Arminianism; Calvin, John; conditional election; Consistory, the; election; eternal security; fall from grace; Five-Point Calvinism; free will; "once saved, always saved"; perseverance of the saints; predestination; Protestantism, Protestants; Protestant Reformation, the; Reformed Churches; Remonstrants; *Remonstrants*, the; reprobation; Synod of Dort; total depravity; TULIP; Westminster Confession.

canons regular: those orders of priests living in a communal setting usually under the rule of Augustine (*canon* means "rule" or "measure") but are not subject to the Benedictine strictures. They are distinct from monks who live a cloistered, contemplative life nor do they have connection to the monks of Saint Augustine. Canons regular are essentially religious clerics who engage in public ministry and are commonly located within a long list of various orders. Most are classed as either Black or White, depending on the color of their robes. Secular canons, on the other hand, are also affiliated with a church but do not take vows or live communally. *See also* Assumptionist Orders; Augustinian Order; Barnabites; Benedict, Order of; Black Canons; canon(s) of the church; Capuchin Order; Carmelites; Carthusians; Celestines; Cistercians; clergy; Dominicans; ecclesiastic(s); Franciscans; friar(s); Minim; monasticism; monk(s); orders; Paulist Fathers; Premonstratensian Order; priest(s); religious organizations; Roman Catholic Church; Servite Order; Spirituals of the Franciscan Order; Trappist Order.

cantabaptism. See credo-baptism.

Cantate Domino: the liturgical version of Psalm 98 as found in the Episcopal Prayer Book of 1552. It could be used as a substitute for the *Benedictus*, the *Magnificat*, or the *Nunc Dimittis*. *See also* liturgical year; liturgy, Christian.

Cantemus Domino. See Song of Moses.

Canterbury: the headquarters of the archbishop of the Anglican Church of England. The location is in the government district of Kent in the United Kingdom on the River Stour and was the former Kentish royal capital. *See also* Augustine of Canterbury; church; Church of England.

Cantheism: or Kantheism, religions based (at least to some degree) on the use of the cannabis plant from which marijuana is derived. Certain groups have been known to indulge including animist and shamanist practices as well as some sects of Hinduism, Rastafarianism, Satanism, drug cults, Native American religions, and Zoroastrianism. *See also* cult(s); Native American Church; peyote; *pharmakeia.*

Canticles: an alternate name for the Old Testament poetic book named the Song of Solomon or Song of Songs. The main speakers in the dialogue shift suddenly but seem to center on the king himself, his bride (called the Shulammite or Shunammite), and a chorus of palace women called the Daughters of Jerusalem. *See also* canticles; daughter of Jerusalem; poetry (biblical); Song of Songs as Old Testament book.

canticles: "little songs," nonmetrical hymns or chants, drawn chiefly from the Bible but exclusive of the Psalms, and used as worship liturgy in some churches. They are traditionally recited on specified days or evenings of the church calendar. *See also* canon(s) of the church; Canticles; cathisma; chant; hymn(s); liturgical year; liturgy, Christian; invitatory; music; poetry (biblical); praise; sacred music; Song of Songs as Old Testament book; sticheron; theody.

cantor: a term meaning "singer," a worship leader (a common feature of Jewish public worship) who recites and chants the various Jewish rituals where appropriate. Catholic churches also employ cantors on occasion. *See also* chant; chantry; liturgy, Christian; liturgy, Jewish; Judaism; lector; music.

cantrip: a magical spell. *See also* Agrippa Books; alchemy; *arcanum arcandrum; Arcanum,* the; *Book of Abramelin, The; Corpus Hermecticum;* Emerald Tablet of Hermes, the; *Golden Bough, The;* grimoire; Hermeticism; Hermetic wisdom; Hermetic writings; idolatry; magic arts; magic, magick; *mana;* mantic wisdom; occult, occultic; parapsychology; secret wisdom; spell; spell names; *Spiritas Mundi.*

Canute the Great, King: king of Denmark, England, and Norway (A.D 1016 – 1035) in what history calls the North Sea Empire. Canute was Danish and not Briton or Anglo-Saxon but his vast influence at the time was used by the Roman Catholic Church to great advantage. Legend promoted Canute as a deluded monarch who believed he had supernatural powers; he once sat before the sea and challenged its waves to wet his robes. Actually, the original tale denotes just the opposite and claims he was an effective and enlightened leader who gave glory to God for the Sovereign's power. *See also* king(s); Roman Catholic Church.

Caodaism: a.k.a. Dao Cao Dai, a Vietnamese monotheistic religion established in 1926. The group's official title may be translated as The Great Faith for the Third Universal Redemption symbolized by the left eye of God. The sect employs prayer, ancestor worship, vegetarianism, union with God, and a commitment to non-violence with a heavy emphasis on spiritism. *See also* idolatry; sect(s); spiritism.

capernaitic eating: the mistaken impression or belief that Christians literally eat the body and drink the blood of Christ in the Communion setting. The accusation probably springs from pagan belief in the days of early Christianity that asserted believers in the new cult ate the body of their Jesus and has never really disappeared among the uninformed. Cannibalism is assuredly not a Christian practice. *See also* Christianity in the Roman Empire; real presence; theophagy; transubstantiation.

Capernaum: a town mentioned in Matthew 11:23 which is condemned to the depths because of the population's refusal to repent of its evil or acknowledge the miracles done in the city. Jesus said they would fare worse on the day of judgment than the pagan city of Sodom.

Caphtor: the ancient name for Crete as noted by Amos (Amos 9:7). Some ethnologists, most in fact, claim that the Philistines originated from that Mediterranean island or, at least, the general region. *See also* Crete; Kittim (Chittim); Minoan civilizations; Philistia, Philistines.

capital punishment: state-authorized authorization allowing the death sentence for certain crimes and criminals. The judicial practice, or its ban, is a hotly contested debate among ethicists and will likely continue to be. Beheading is the preferred method of execution [murder] among the jihadists and is sanctioned by Sharia law. *See also* crucifixion; Sharia; decapitation; *jihad*; social issues.

Capitulary: a compilation of episcopal or other-type statutes. *See also* apodictic law; canons of the church; rede; statute(s).

Cappadocia: the region near the extreme boundaries of the Roman Empire as of A.D. 300. That area, along with Armenia and Syria, made up the Eastern branch of Christian church following that time. *See also* Anatolia; Armenia; Cappadocian fathers; patriarchate(s); Roman Empire; Syria.

Cappadocian fathers: Greek-speaking church writers of the patristic period. "Cappadocia" defines the area of Asia Minor (modern Turkey), where these theologians were based, and usually associated with Greek Orthodoxy centered at Constantinople. The Big Three in this category of clergy were Basil of Caesarea (called "the Great"), Gregory of Nyssa (Basil's brother), and their friend Gregory of Nazianzus. *See also* Athanasius; Basil; Byzantine Church; Cappadocia; Chrysostom, John; Constantinople as city; Doctors of the Church; Eastern Orthodox Church; Gregory of Nazianzus; patriarchate(s).

capstone. See cornerstone.

captivity: capture, imprisonment, or enslavement. In more eschatological expression, the term defines Satan's actions (Rev. 13:10) involving imprisonment and—by extensio—execution of the faithful as he rampages to and fro on Tribulation earth. The "crime" for such mistreatment is the refusal of the martyrs to worship him or his dictatorial state headed by Antichrist. In an opposite sense, Christ is said to be able to take captivity captive or "lead captives in his train" (Eph. 4:8 referencing Ps. 68:18). The use here seems to mean Christ has ascended with the world's control securely in his providence. From heaven, he can return in complete victory and even assist us to overcome the world in our own conflicted internal and external lives as we experience them today. *See also* Babylonian (and Persian) restoration decrees; Babylonian Captivity; Babylonian Captivity, return from; *Diaspora*; exile; *golah*.

capuchin: the pointed and hooded cloak worn by friar(s). *See also* furniture and furnishings of the modern church; Roman Catholic Church.

Capuchin Order: a strict and autonomous order of reformed Franciscan monks established in 1520. The communities consisted of friars who sought to return to the austere observances of Francis, which they felt had slackened. The female counterparts are the Capuchines or "Poor Clares," who also practice a harsh regulation to the point that they are often called "Sisters of Suffering." Both groups met resistance from 16th century popes and others but eventually found permanence. *See also* Assumptionist Orders; Augustinian Order; Barnabites; Benedict, Order of; Black Canons; canon(s) of the church; canons regular; Carmelites; Carthusians; Celestines; Cistercians; clergy; Dominicans; Franciscans; friar(s); Minim; monasticism; monk(s); orders; Paulist Fathers; Poor Clare sisters; Premonstratensian Order; priest(s); religious organizations; Roman Catholic Church; Servite Order; Spirituals of the Franciscan Order; Trappist Order.

carbon dating: more precisely known as radiocarbon dating. Carbon dating, as it is commonly practiced today, is the scientific method used to estimate the age of any carbon-based material after a portion of it has been burned. The result measures the amount of the inherent radioisotope carbon 14 and is said to be adequately accurate up to about 62,000 years. Some scientists and laypersons are skeptical of the efficiency of the process, but it has become the majority standard for dating archeological and fossil finds everywhere. *See also* archeology, archeologists.

Carchemish: scene of a decisive battle between the Egyptians and the Babylonians on the banks of the Euphrates River in 605 B.C. A Babylonian victory over Pharaoh Necho II assured their dominance. That clash was predicted earlier by the prophet Jeremiah (Jer. 46:2–6, 10–12).

cardinal(s): so-called from the Latin *cardo,* representing "a wedge rammed between two timbers." They are the permanent staff for the benefit of the Roman pope. Such an unusual title accrued from their early practice of injecting themselves into the office and affairs of any local parish, as was their right and directive from higher authority. Those drastic actions broke up the practice of allowing a single priest to pastor in a certain place for life. The power of the cardinals grew rapidly (though there is no precedent in the Scripture for such a position) until they were privileged to select new pontiffs. They prefer to call themselves "princes of the church." Their vestment, a solid and imposing red, also contribute to the name "cardinal." Today's College of Cardinals numbers over 200 and is growing steadily. The average age is about seventy-eight, almost treble Jesus' age of ministry. They form the conclave (limited to 120 in number) who elects new popes and the selection is almost always from their own group. Following the death or departure of a pope, they are allowed nine days of mourning during which they are to appear for the funeral in St. Peter's Basilica and form the conclave.

The College votes four times per day until a two-thirds majority for one candidate is secured. They are forbidden to leave the conclave until the election is completed. If the election exceeds ten days a final vote is taken with any majority accepted as a decision. Smoke is released after each ballot—black for no conclusion and white for an agreement. *See also* camerlengo; clergy; conclave; *Curia;* ecclesiastic(s); Infirmieri; priest(s); religious organizations; Roman Catholic Church.

cardinal virtues: a listing, from various sources, of those behaviors and attitudes that constitute the most important qualities of human interaction and obedience to God. The biblical wisdom writers numbered them as temperance, prudence, justice, and fortitude, but these were expanded in various ways by modern Judaism. These four virtues, and perhaps others, are couched in both Greek philosophy and Christianity. *See also* conscience; deontology; ethics; scruples; social issues; temperance; way to heaven.

Carey, William and Dorothy: husband-and-wife missionary team. William was a self-educated English Baptist shoemaker (1761–1834) and a Calvinist postmillennialist in doctrine. Carey was a sickly youth with a chancy future, but now could rightly be called the greatest exponent of the foreign mission movement worldwide. He was influenced by Andrew Fuller (1754–1815), a Baptist who refuted the hyper-Calvinism of his day and promoted preaching to all peoples. Fuller's published pamphlet, entitled *The Gospel Worthy of All Acceptation*, challenged Carey and helped him establish the Baptist Missionary Society, then the sacrificial mission of he and his wife to India gave him the name "father of modern missions." His work in India saw the death of his son Peter, and his wife experienced a nervous breakdown from which she never recovered. The family suffered unbearably in the subcontinent, and the work went unrewarded for years. Carey is often quoted with his unforgettable pronouncement, "Expect great things from God; attempt great things for God." Meanwhile, Carey translated the Bible into Sanskrit, Bengali, and other dialects. In 1872 he expanded on Fuller's call by his provocative but long-titled book, *An Enquiry into the Obligations of Christians, to Use Means for the Conversion of the Heathens. In Which the Religious State of the Different Nations of the World, the Success of Former Undertakings, and the Practicability of Further Undertakings, are Considered.* The Careys motivated Adoniram and Ann Judson to a similar charge in America. *See also* Baptists; Judson, Adoniram and Ann; missions, missionaries.

cargo cult(s): certain cult-like societies that sometimes form superstitious associations with modern technology. Usually found in isolated cultures, the local natives commonly experience a kind of culture shock upon being introduced to current technological gadgets and manufactured goods, thus "cargo." South Pacific islanders, for example, have been known to invent credulous rituals and beliefs in order to attract more of these devices. To them, an AM/FM radio or a cell phone would be a supernatural wonder worthy to covet and revere. Often enough, especially in more primitive areas, someone would experience a vision of an arriving ship laden with material bounty promising the native's well-being for a lifetime. Hundreds would then destroy their inheritance to await a bonanza of luxury that never came, or came in a form destructive to their culture. *See also* cult(s); Huna; idolatry; John Frum religion; kahuna; Lono; Modekngei; Pele; revitalization movement; Tiki.

carillon: a system of twenty-three or more cast bells for two to six octaves that can be played on a keyboard or automatically. It is a precious musical instrument for many churches. *See also* bell(s); furniture and furnishings of the modern church; musical instruments.

Carmel: a range of hills, about fifteen miles long, in central Palestine near the Mediterranean Sea. It was a fruitful and lush region and often used as a metaphor by the prophets and others in that vein (*i.e.,* Micah 7:14), where it is described as "fertile pasturelands." The Song of Solomon holds the phrase, "Your head crowns you like Carmel," probably referring to the lover's hair which brought to mind the fruit trees of Carmel. The area also locates a city by the same name near the region farmed by the churlish character Nabal (1 Sam. 25:2–40). A colony of Carmelite monks, founded there in the 12th century, now inhabit the mountain. There are also Carmelite nuns of the same order. *See also* Carmelites; Mount Carmel.

Carmelites: a Roman Catholic religious order officially named the Order of the Brothers of the Blessed Virgin Mary of Mount Carmel. The sect was supposedly founded in the 12th century but historical records are surprisingly scarce. Located on Mount Carmel (thus the name), the Carmelites focus primarily on contemplation and prayer and their order is said to be personally protected by the virgin Mary. There are cloistered nuns associated as well as lay postulates. Special inspiration is drawn from the prophet Elijah who was active on Mount Carmel. *See also* Assumptionist Orders; Augustinian Order; Barnabites; Benedict, Order of; Black Canons; canon(s) of the church; canons regular; Capuchin Order; Carthusians; Celestines; Cistercians; clergy; Dominicans; Franciscans; friar(s); liturgical order; Minim; monasticism; monk(s); orders; Paulist Fathers; Premonstratensian Order; priest(s); religious organizations; Roman Catholic Church; Servite Order; Spirituals of the Franciscan Order; Trappist Order.

Carmen Christi: or "hymn of Christ," the title of the hymn recorded in Philippians 2:6-11, which is evidently a very early praise poem. Paul has slightly modified some of the originally text to fit his message in the passage. *See also* hymn(s); liturgical year; liturgy, Christian; music.

carnal: a word to describe flesh or meat. In a religious context, carnal refers to the material, biological, physical, or sexual connections that are implied to be base or iniquitous. The word is most often used as the direct opposite of "spiritual," even though God made the body and the physical world to be good in their fundamental natures. Impulses that mitigate against such wholesomeness are specified as *carnal* and thereby working against the best of human nature and our moral association with the Spirit of God. *See also* after one's own lusts; body; carnal Christians; concupiscence; debauchery; demimondaines; depravity; dissipation; earthly tent; flesh; hedonism; human condition, the; human nature, the; immorality; moral uncleanliness; orgies; sin(s); sinful nature, the; unclean; wicked, wickedness; worldly.

carnal Christians: believers or potential believers sometimes referred to as "babes in Christ," those not attained or attuned to perfection. According to standard theology then, all persons are carnal, for it is our nature and can only be alleviated by the saving action of the sinless Christ. In a more pejorative sense, carnal Christians have come to be known as those who are poor examples of the Christ image and steeped in sinful living. *See also* cafeteria Christians; carnal; Christianese; concupiscence; flesh; human nature, the; McChurch; nominal Christians; sin(s); sinful nature, the; slurs, religious.

carnal nature. See human nature, the.

carnival: usually considered to be a festival of gaiety, celebration, and sometimes near-unbridled frivolity. For religious philologists, however, the term takes on distinct, if not official, ecclesiastical meaning. In theological usage, *carnival* is a bit of an enigma in lexicological circles because of its broad interpretations, its convoluted etymology, and its content. Initially, the word is Italian from the medieval Latin *carnelevare* referring to "meat" (*carne*) and "taking off" (*levare*) or to "begin a fast" or "to abstain from meat." The word has since evolved into a category of calendar entries with certain ecclesiastical rituals attached. The liturgical seasons can then be set to a standard date and enumerated in order. Of greatest interest, however, carnival keeps its past association with pagan mythology and applies Christian principles to it. The carnival events, then, can be said to be both festive and solemn. Every religious festival is both a celebration and a commemoration. *See also* calendar; Christian mythology; fast, fasting; feasts and special days of high liturgy faiths; feasts and special days of Protestantism; liturgical year; liturgy; liturgy, Christian.

carol(s): a musical composition or dance often performed with a festive aire. Today, the carol renditions are familiarly connected to church worship, especially at Christmas or Advent, but their history was equally secular in practice. The word *carol* derives from the Old French *carole*, a circle dance with accompanying singers. Ideally, the circle steps were performed on a bridge. Carols were popular in the Protestant Reformation to aid in bringing music "back to the people" from High Church domination. Any list of most popular or familiar to the West would include: "Angels from the Realms of Glory," (James Montgomery, 1862), [alternately arranged as "Angels We Have Heard on High" which contains the phrase *gloria in excelsis Deo—glory to God in the highest*]," As With Gladness Men of Old," (William Dix, 1867), "Away in a Manger," (disputed authorship, 1885), "Come, Thou Long Expected Jesus," (Charles Wesley, 1749), "Coventry Carol" [Lullay, Thy Tiny Little Child], (Irish traditional, 16th century), "Ding Dong Merrily on High," (Jehan Tabourot and George Woodward), 1924), "Bring a Torch, Jeanette, Isabella," (French traditional, 1553), "The First Noel," (English traditional, 1823), "The Friendly Beasts," (French traditional, 12th century), "Good King Wenceslas," (English traditional, 1853), "God Rest You Merry, Gentlemen," (English traditional, 1833), "Good Christian Men, Rejoice," (Heinrich Seuse, 1328), "Hark, the Herald Angels Sing," (Felix Mendelssohn, George Whitefield, and Martin Madan, 1739), "The Holly and the Ivy," (English traditional, 1823), "I Heard the Bells on Christmas Day," (Henry Wadsworth Longfellow and Johnny Marks, 1863), "I Saw Three Ships," (English traditional, 1833), "In the Bleak Midwinter," (Christina Rossetti and Gustav Holst, 1872), "Infant Holy, Infant Lowly," (Polish traditional, translated into English 1920), "It Came Upon a Midnight Clear," (Edmund Sears and Richard Willis, 1849), "I Wonder as I Wander," (John Jacob Niles, 1934), "Joy to the World," (Isaac Watts, 1719), "O Come All Ye Faithful" [*Adeste Fideles*], (Frederich Oakeley, 1841), "O Come, O Come, Emmanuel" or *Veni, Veni, Emmanuel,* (Advent hymn, 1861), "O Holy Night," (Placide Cappeau de Rouquemaure, 1847), "O Little Town of Bethlehem," (Phillips Brooks, 1865), "Once in Royal David's City," (Cecil Alexander and Henry Gauntlett, 1848), "Silent Night," (Franz Gruber and Joseph Mohr, 1818), "We Three Kings of Orient Are," (John Henry Hopkins, 1863), "What Child Is This?," William Dix, 1865), "While Shepherds Watched Their Flocks," (Nahum Tate, 1700). *See also* Advent; Brooks, Phillips; Christmas; Lessons and Carols; *lithobolia;* liturgical year; liturgy, Christian; music; Noel; Protestant Reformation, the; Watts, Isaac; Yule.

Caroline Divines, the: a collection of 17th century scholars and clergy in England who were considered to be the "Middle Way" between Roman Catholicism and Protestantism. They considered themselves to be neither wholly Catholic nor wholly Protestant, though, in practice, many were aligned for or against some form of faith. They denied the authority of the pope but honored the early church fathers if the dogmatic statements were stripped away. The Divines were said to "hold the mean between two extremes" and to anchor the center of the new Anglican Church. The most important members were Lancelot Andrewes, Thomas Benlow, William Beveridge, John Cosin, Thomas Ken, Thomas Sprat, Herbert Thorndike, John Bramhall, Gilbert Burnet, William Laud, Robert Sanderson, Jeremy

Taylor, John Wilkins, and John Woolton. There is no definitive list on any Divines in any of the countries but some scholars include King Charles I among them. *See also* Cambridge Platonists; Charles I, King; Church of England; Latitudinarians; Laud, William.

Carolingians: the Frankish rulers who reigned in France from 751–987 and in Germany until 911. They were the replacements for the Merovingians in the seventh century. The dynasty produced some noted church supporters and politicians, including Pippin, Charles Martel (Pippin's illegitimate son who blocked the Arab advance into Spain), and Charlemagne. Certain sects ascribe great importance to the Merovingians and Carolingians as they are said to be guardians of the Holy Grail however that object may be described. *See also* Charlemagne; Holy Roman Empire; king(s); Martel, Charles.

Carol, John: first Roman Catholic bishop on American soil (1735–1815). Carroll's self-appointed mission was to attempt to pull American Catholicism away from too much European influence. He was a cousin of Charles Carroll, a signer of the Declaration of Independence. In that connection, he, Benjamin Franklin, and Samuel Chase were dispatched by the Continental Congress to Canada in a failed attempt to enlist French Canadians to the rebel cause. Carroll was the founder of Georgetown University in 1789. *See also* Roman Catholic Church.

Carpocrates: a leading Gnostic teacher in second-century Alexandria. He and his followers claimed that the world and the things in the world were created by angels and thereby greatly inferior to the unbegotten Father. Jesus was born of Joseph and that, although he was born similar to other men, he was more than others. Jesus' soul was able to remember the conversation between him and the unbegotten God. *See also* Carpocratians; Gnosticism, Gnostic(s); icon, iconography.

Carpocratians: the followers of the Gnostic Carpocrates. They were a libertine group who saw no need for any type of moral law, a doctrine that separated them from most belief systems of the time, even including most of Gnosticism. Their work is said to be encapsulated in the pseudo-gospel called *The Secret Gospel of Mark*, which caused somewhat of a stir when it was discovered. The Carpocratians believed in reincarnation and hinted that Jesus was a homosexual. *See also* antinomianism; Carpocrates; Gnosticism, Gnostics; idolatry; Phibionites; sect(s).

Carpus: the keeper of Paul's cloak and other personal items at Troas until they could be reclaimed for him by Timothy (2 Tim. 4:13). Paul asked for certain needed scrolls and parchments in the same request.

carrels: small study niches in the larger libraries and some educational or ecclesiastical buildings. *See also* furniture and furnishings of the modern church.

carrodian: a layperson with retirement benefits from a king or bishop. His stipend or pension is a carrody. *See also* altarage; benefice; benefit of clergy; *cathedraticum;* love offering; mensa; papal revenue; pounding; prebend; Roman Catholic Church; stipend.

Carter, Jimmy: the first president of the United States (1969 election) to inherit the White House after a campaign as an openly "born again" Christian. He was a Southern Baptist who overcame ridicule for his religious stance and fundamental values from a secularly suspicious citizenry. *See also* Baptists.

Cartesian thought: a philosophy influenced by Rene Descartes and his disciples. According to the theory, thought should be based on Descartes' axiom popularized by the phrase, "I think, therefore I am." If one is thinking, a person cannot deny his or her existence. An inability to think is proven non-existence. Descartes considered his conjecture to be basic knowledge that should be fully acceptable to all peoples, faiths, and human processes. *See also* Descartes, Rene.

Carthage: the African city-state defeated by the Romans in 146 B.C. That capitulation represented the final accomplishment of the prophecy in Genesis 9:25–27, which anticipated the full punishment of the Canaanites of whom the Phoenician Carthagenians were the last representatives. *See also* Phoenicia, Phoenicians; Roman Empire; Tyre, Tyrenians.

Carthusians: an austere order of Roman Catholic monks. The order was begun by Saint Bruno in the French Alps in A.D 1984. The group takes its name from their famous place of meeting, the Grand Chartreuse (Charterhouse) in London. Each monk lived in virtual isolation with his own walled cottage and garden, except for times set aside for communal worship and weekly periods for conversation. They were much favored by the popes because they naturally excited almost no controversy. *See also* Assumptionist Orders; Augustinian Order; Barnabites; Benedict, Order of; Black Canons; canon(s) of the church; canons regular; Capuchin Order; Carmelites; Celestines; Cistercians; clergy; Dominicans; Franciscans; friar(s); Minim; monasticism; monk(s); orders; Paulist Fathers; Premonstratensian Order; priest(s); religious organizations; Roman Catholic Church; Servite Order; Spirituals of the Franciscan Order; Trappist Order.

Cart of the Dead: a common Celtic legend in Brittany which revealed an eerie cart carrying souls to their final home. Since it is a November 1 and 2 observance, the appearance is also called the All Saints' funerary cart, sometimes driven by the devil himself. It was considered a practical precaution to avoid the roads on that occasion lest you find yourself wafted along to the Otherworld to join the company of the Wild Hunt. *See also* Celtic folklore and religion; Hallowmas; Otherworld; Wild Hunt.

cartomancy: divination by use of cards. See also anthropomancy; apotropaic magic; arcanum arcandrum; Arcanum, the; aretology; Ariosophy; astral plane; astral projection; astrolabe; astrology, astrologers; athame; audition; augury; automatic writing; bagua; belomancy; besom; bibliomancy; black arts; black mirror; blood moon(s); chaos magic; chiromancy; clairaudience; clairsentience; clairvoyance; cleromancy; cone of power; conjure; crop circles; cryptesthesia; crystallomancy; crystal skulls; curious acts; divination; dream(s); dreams and visions; ecstasy; enchantment; enneagram; esoteric sects; evil eye; extraordinary perception (ESP); foreknowledge; foretelling; geomancy; grimoire; gris-gris; hepatoscopy; Hermetic wisdom; Hermetic writings; hex; hierscopy; horoscope(s); hydromancy; idol(s); ifa; incantation; juju; labyrinth walk; lecanomancy; literomancy; locution; magic arts; magic, magick; magic square; magnetism; *mana*; mantic wisdom; mantra; miracle(s); monition; mystery religion(s); necromancy; New Age religion; numbers, symbology of; occult, occultic; omen; oneiromancy; oracle(s); otherworldly journeys; ouija board; out-of-body experiences (OBEs); paranormal; parapsychology; past life regression; peace pole(s); pentagram; philosophers' stone; planchette; planets as gods; portent; recognition; prediction; prefiguration; premonition; prodigy; prognostication; prophecy, general; psi; psychic(s); psychic healing; psychic reading; psychomancy; psychometry; psychonautics; pyramidology; rebirthing; remote viewing; retrocognition; rhabdomancy; scrying; séance; secret societies; secret wisdom; sorcery, sorceries; spell; spell names; spiritism; stigmata; supernatural; superstition; tarot; telegnosis; telepathy; telesthesia; theugry; third eye, the; thoughtform; totemism; vision(s); vision quest; visualization; voodoo; voudou; wanga; warlock(s); Web-Bot; witchcraft; wizard(s); *ya sang*; yoga; Zen; zodiac; *zos kia* cultus.

cartulary: a keeper of monastic records. *See also* monasticism.

Cartwright, Peter: frontier preacher and politician (1785–1872). Cartwright was arguably the most famous of the western circuit riders of the time even though he was born to a rough-and-tumble life in Rogue's Harbor, Kentucky. After a dramatic camp meeting conversion, he became a Methodist hellfire-and-brimstone preacher in Kentucky, Tennessee, Indiana, Ohio, and Illinois. He was twice elected to the Illinois legislature but beaten in a presidential bid by Abraham Lincoln. By the time of his death, Cartwright had preached nearly 15,000 sermons and baptized some 12,000 people. *See also* apocalyptic fervor; camp meetings; circuit riders; evangelist(s), evangelism; Great Awakenings, the; Methodists; missions, missionaries; Restoration Movement in America; revivalism; "sawdust trail, the."

Carver, John: first governor of the Plymouth Colony (ca. 1576–1621) and strongest financier of the *Mayflower* voyage. This he accomplished by obtaining a grant from the Virginia Colony of London under which the Plymouth Pilgrims would be founded. Carver was a signer of the *Mayflower Compact* and died in office not long after his arrival in America. *See also Mayflower Compact*; Puritanism, Puritans.

case law. See caustic law.

Cassander: the Greek general under Alexander the Great who assumed control of Macedonia after Alexander's death. He had little contact with Palestine in that position. *See also* Diadochi; king(s).

Cassandra: a Greek prophetess, the beautiful daughter of King Priam of Troy. The god Apollo was smitten with her but she shunned him during the Trojan War according to Homer's account. In revenge, Apollo cursed her with the ability to always be accurate in her prophecies but specified that no one would believe her. Cassandra was supposedly raped by Ajax of Locris when Troy fell and was taken prisoner by Agamemnon. She was killed by the king's jealous wife Clytemnestra but was eventually avenged by Athena. Cassandra's life and fate may, in many ways, characterize the Old Testament prophets since they, too, were always accurate and sincere but seldom believed and often abused, even to death. *See also* idol(s); Olympian pantheon; prophetess(es).

Cassandra Prophecy: the notion that attempts to pinpoint the precise day of judgment by combining both biblical and extrabiblical sources; it was popularized by the book of the same name by Ian Gurney. Commonly, the method employs investigation of prophetic issues from the Bible, Nostradamus, the Pseudepigrapha, Saint Malachy, and other future-telling research, whether they are truly reliable or not. *See also* Gurney, Ian.

Cassian of Gaul, John: a monk, mystic, scholar, and ascetic (ca. 360–435) born in France but educated and influential in the Eastern Orthodox tradition. His major writing is *The Institutes and Conferences*, but he is best remembered for his defense of the doctrine of Semi-Pelagianism. *See also* Eastern Orthodox Church; Semi-Pelagianism.

Cassiopeia: the vain wife of King Cephas and mother to Andromeda. When Cassiopeia boasted that her daughter was prettier than the Nereids, or that she herself was fairer than the sea nymphs, the sea god Poseidon chained Andromeda to the rocks and called forth the sea monster Cetus to ravish her. Andromeda was saved by Perseus. One of the northern constellations now carries her name. *See also* Andromeda; idol(s); mythological beasties, elementals, monsters, and spirit animals; nereid; nymph(s); Olympian pantheon; Pegasus; Perseus; queen(s).

caste system: a peculiarity of the culture of India wherein there exists an interdependent yet separate system of social classes. The classifications have a Hindu base, but the country as a whole is quite aware of the understood societal distinctions. One's caste is determined by economics, occupation, social status, and certain other factors. The highest among the ranks, called "varnas," are the Brahmins (teachers, priests), followed by the Kshatriyas (public servants, soldiers), then Vaishyas (merchants and tradespeople), and Shudras (skilled and unskilled laborers). A fifth group is so poor and despised that they are not even assigned a class—the "Untouchables." Such distinctions in modern India are illegal but still recognized. *See also* Brahmanism; Hinduism.

Castle Blanc: an important Knights Templar stronghold in Outremer, also known as Safita. *See also* Acre; Horns of Hattin; Outremer.

Castor and Pollux: astral deities known as "the twin brothers," the children of Zeus and Leda. They were the patron gods of sailors. The ship that sailed from Malta to Puteoli with Paul and his companions aboard carried carvings of Castor and Pollux as her figurehead (Acts 28:11). *See also* idol(s); Olympian pantheon.

castrato: (plural castrati) an adult male singer who has been castrated in prepubescence so his voice would remain in the range of soprano, mezzo-soprano, or alto. The Roman Catholic Church used the procedure from about A.D. 1500. until it was banned by papal decree in 1902. The draconian method was a way to prolong the sweet singing voice of the boys' choirs. *See also* eunuch; music; Roman Catholic Church.

casuistry: a moral theological accounting by Roman Catholic officials for all circumstances relating to the rules and repentance of sinners. A careful analysis is made of both the regulations and the individuals involved before judgment is rendered. The process is a system of applied ethics and jurisprudence exercised by examination of case histories involving rules of conduct (from the Latin *casus* ("cases")). It is claimed by some that moral dilemmas can be solved in such a manner but most agree the approach is close to sophistry and specious thinking. In theology, casuistry is the relation of general ethical principles to particular cases of conduct or conscience but it also often leads to rationalization of actions. *See also* deontology; exemplar motif; rector motif; penance; Roman Catholic Church; sin(s).

catabolic collapse: a theory formulated by John Michael Greer referring to what happens when civilization can no longer produce enough to meet the excessive demands of the population. If the event does, indeed, transpire society will either collapse or somehow adjust its capacities, only to later revert to even more amassing of "stuff." *See also* apocalyptic, apocalypticism; evolution.

catacombs: the vast subterranean chambers and caves underneath the city of Rome. This complex maze of underground passages and spaces became places of refuge for persecuted Christians, who used for assembly, burials, and sketches made on the walls symbolizing their faith. It is probably correct to say that such graffiti were the origins of Christian art. *See also* "ashes to ashes"; burial; catafalque; cemetery; convectile; death; funeral; grave; Manes; martyrium; multiconfessional.

catafalque: a temporary funeral platform for absent coffins. Even though no body may be present, the catafalque is duly honored as if there were. *See also* "ashes to ashes"; bier; burial; catacombs; cemetery; death; funeral; furniture and furnishings of the modern church; grave; Manes; martyrium; multiconfessional.

cataphatic: 1. (kataphatic), a single word evolved from the roots to "descend" and to "speak." The term describes a method of an explanation of theology in simple or noncomplex terms. A simplistic definition or experiment would attempt to "bring God down to speak to (of) Him in ordinary terms." Basically, it is the belief that God can be known to humans both positively and affirmatively. 2. a form of spirituality using meditation with the aid of images. The practice involves both the physical and mystical to achieve a deeper state of devotion. *See also* biblical criticism; icon, iconography.

Catch the Fire Toronto. See "Toronto Blessing, the."

catechism: or catechumen, a system of instruction most common in Roman Catholicism, in which doctrine is drilled to a student with constant repetition. The usual method is via question and answer, both of which are usually spoken by rote. The term grows from the root "instruction" and is often utilized to prepare a candidate for baptism. *See also* catechumen; didactic method; Didascalia; religious education; Roman Catholic Church.

catechumen: those ready or anticipating baptism in the Roman Catholic or Eastern Orthodox faiths. *See also* Eastern Orthodox Church; catechism; Roman Catholic Church.

categorical imperative, the: the lynchpin of the deontological moral concepts of Immanuel Kant. The philosopher believed that humans are special in the creation and morality for they can be summarized in the commandment or duty of reason (the imperative). For him, every action (or inaction) must be necessary in order to be valid. Therefore, humanity has an "impure" freedom of choice; it has led to accusations that Kant's imperative favors the idea that the end justifies the means. *See also* Divine Imperative, the; Kant, Immanuel.

Catharists: those holding the tenet from the Middle Ages that regarded the flesh and the physical world as intrinsically evil. *See also* Cathars; Christoplatonism; sect(s).

Cathars: a radical religious sect active around the 11th century. The name comes from the Greek *cathari*, meaning "pure ones." In Southern France, they were known as the Albigensi and were called Bogomiles in Bulgaria, quite possibly where the movement originated. Their doctrine was basically Gnostic with heavy doses of Zoroastrianism. Unlike the contemporary Catholic Church they opposed, they sought no political or ecclesiastical power, built no buildings, collected no taxes, honored equality (even allowing women to become priests), and refused to own possessions (anything collected beyond their immediate needs they gave to the poor). They possibly believed in the theory of reincarnation and were dualists in that they perceived the world as a battleground between good and evil. In fact, the natural world was but an illusion for them. The priesthood of the group practiced seven degrees of initiation, and performed outdoors dressed in white tunics with a cord about the waist. The Roman Catholic Church accused them of devil worship, human sacrifice, cannibalism, incest, homosexuality (from which we get the word "buggery" from the Bogomiles), and celebrating a black mass with obscene love feasts. Such charges were certainly untrue, but the Catholic Crusaders destroyed them unmercifully; one ruthless knight even gave the infamous order: "Kill them all. God will know his own." In that demand, he did not obligate the persecutors to differentiate between local Catholics and the dissidents. The Cathar Crusade was the most ruthless persecution ever by the established church. The Cathars were said to be the guardians of the Holy Grail, or cup of Christ, which was said to be in their possession when they were annihilated. More likely, the surviving "treasure" consisted of hidden or esoteric documents peculiar to their order. *See also* Albigensi(es); Almalric, Arnauld; Caesarius Heisterbach; Catharist; Inquisition, the; martyr(s); martyrdom; Roman Empire; sect(s).

cathedral(s): a Christian church serving as a seat for a High Church official. The structure is often easily identified by its immense size, elaborate architecture, high spires, and other ornate features. It is frequently the most impressive building in its setting. Those of the Gothic style are perhaps the most grandiose—Burgos, Seville (Spain); Saint Stephens (Austria); Amiens, Reims, Notre Dame, Chartres

(France); Milan, Santa Maria del Fiore (Italy); Cologne, Regensburg (Germany); York Minster, Winchester, Canterbury (England). *See also* basilica(s); bethel; Bible of the poor; cella; chapel; church; furniture and furnishings of the modern church; kirk; sacellum; temple(s).

cathedraticum: a fixed payment made by priests of a parish to their bishop. Many consider such a transaction as bribery. *See also* altarage; benefice; benefit of clergy; carrodian; love offering; mensa; papal revenue; pounding; prebend; Roman Catholic Church; stipend.

Catherine of Siena: an Italian nun and saint, devout from her youth (1347 – 1380), who became a mystic at eighteen. She reported that as the time Jesus asked her to become his betrothed and participated in a kind of celestial wedding. She was highly regarded in her day and was even asked to advise popes from time to time. Her influence was so strong she was able to facilitate the move of Avignon popes back to Rome. *See also* nun(s); Roman Catholic Church.

cathisma: a short hymn used mostly as a responsorial. *See also* canticles; hymn(s); invitatory; liturgical year; liturgy, Christian; music; praise; responsive reading; sacred music; sticheron; theody.

Catholic Apostolic Church: one of the first of the millennial sects that today consists of the Catholic Apostolic Church and the New Apostolic Church of North America. The movement was begun by Edward Irving (1792–1834), who insisted that Jesus would not return until the twelve-fold apostolate would be reestablished on earth. The apostolate idea envisioned a return to first-century Christianity, with a particular emphasis on the charismatic gifts, especially prophecy and preaching. The group numbered themselves among the 144,000 of Revelation 14:1–5, and their sect was modeled after the seven churches of Revelation. *See also* church bodies in America (typed); idolatry; Irving, Edward; Millennial churches; sect(s).

Catholic Church. See Eastern Orthodox Church; Roman Catholic Church.

catholic church: an ecclesiastical body, or group of them, with universal appeal. The worldwide Church of God (not the Roman Catholic Church but the whole body of Christ, which is called his bride) is called "catholic," meaning its oneness is in a purely genetic sense—all of God's people united in Christ but not necessarily uniform in doctrine or practice. The early Christian church of the first three centuries tried desperately to create a cohesive body that would go united into the future. To do so, they stressed three ecclesiastical tools: the canon, the creeds, and a clergy that were shaped and disciplined insofar as possible toward that end. As it turned out, the apparatus of all three "Cs" have been divisive for centuries. *See also* branch theory; Church; church; four marks of the church; One, Holy, Catholic, and Apostolic Church; universal Church; visible and invisible church.

Catholic Church abuse scandal: revelations that have come to light in the 21st century of widespread sexual abuse of children by priests and bishops of the Roman Catholic Church. The resultant exposure and official cover-ups became a national outrage and many feel high church officials have done little to punish offenders or assist the victims. Religious authorities tended to merely move offending priests about to evade censor rather than correct the problem. Evidence was of wrongdoing was presented by investigative journalism in 2002 but, without doubt, the malfeasance existed long before, even as far back as the church's beginnings. As the late William H. Kennedy wrote: "The real 'lunatic fringe' in the Roman Catholic Church consists of cardinals who give safe harbor to child molesters posing as priests (*Law, Egan et al.*), the predatory homosexuals who run and enroll in Roman Catholic seminaries and form bizarre sex cults, and the power brokers who have allied the Vatican's vast financial resources with organized crime. It is the skullduggery of these sorts of Catholics that causes the most harm. The devotional practices and beliefs of Traditional Catholics harm no one." *See also* church abuse; delict; Roman Catholic Church; secularization; shepherding (cultic).

catholic epistles, the: a collective name for the last seven personal missives (excluding Hebrews) of the New Testament—those sent to or from Timothy, Titus, Philemon, James, Peter, John, and Jude. Perhaps this technical identification for those writings was selected because they seem to appeal to readers in general. The classification is also popularly known as the general epistles. *See also* letter(s).

catholicos: (plural catholicoi), the Eastern Orthodox head of an autonomous church. *See also* archimandrite; chorepiscope; clergy; Eastern Orthodox Church; ecclesiastic(s); hegymanos; metropolitan; minister(s); pastor(s); patriarch(s); priest(s); starets.

Catholic Women's League (CWL): one of a number of organizations for Roman Catholic women who are involved in religious education and welfare work for the church. *See also* religious organizations; Roman Catholic Church.

cattle and oxen: livestock vital to the economy and religious ritual of the ancients. Cattle, both bullocks and heifers, were expensive sacrifices; oxen were even more so. The latter were draft animals capable of moving heavy loads. Cattle were frequent representations in the ancient world when an idol was to be fashioned. Possession of quantities of livestock was a sign of wealth or prosperity. *See also* animals, birds, and insects, symbology of; bull; calf, calves; cow; flocks and herds; idolatry; mythological beasties, elementals, monsters, and spirit animals.

cauldron, parable of the fouled. See Ezekiel's fouled cauldron allegory.

caustic law: a.k.a. case law, an authorized agreement in the standard "if—then" legal structure. The contrast of absolute law is significant in that it provides an "if, when, or then" to make it less stringent. "If this is the situation...then the penalty is..." The principle has heavy meaning when considering the admonitions of God to His people and how we obey divine law. The form does have relevance to certain theological admonitions as well. *See also* apodictic law; canon(s) of the church; Capitulary; rede; statute(s).

Cayce, Edgar: "the sleeping prophet" (1877–1945). Cayce was a famous American psychic, perhaps only a bit lesser known than Nostradamus. He reportedly could "read" auras, discern a past life, and see into the future. His works are carefully preserved, documented, and studied today at the Association for Research and Enlightenment (ARE) in Virginia Beach, Virginia (founded 1931). Cayce reportedly could diagnose and cure diseases from a distance as he reclined in a sleep-like trance, a practice which generated his title. He predicted terrible Armageddon-like destruction for North America between 2000 and 2001. *See also* Association for Research and Enlightenment (ARE); psychic(s); pyramid(s); sect(s).

C.E.: the Common Era, a contemporary method of dating in some circles (equivalent to A.D.) but said to be more politically correct in deference to those unfavorable to the Christian timekeeping notations. The initials may also indicate "Christian Era" or "Current Era." *See also Anno Domini; Anno Mundi;* B.C.; B.C.E.; calendar.

Cecilia: a real martyr and saint but also a mixture of legend. She is called the patron saint of music and reportedly sang so beautifully that angels came down to listen. Some say she invented the organ but she was a virtuoso of a smaller version called the viola, not the larger instrument's creator. *See also* music; musical instruments; organ; Roman Catholic.

cedar of Lebanon and a thistle, parable of the: a fable recorded in 2 Kings 14:8–22 and 2 Chronicles 25:17–24. King Jehoash of Israel was militarily threatened by the king of Judah, Amaziah. In response, Jehoash related the parable in which he compared himself to a cedar of Lebanon but Amaziah was cast as nothing but a thistle. The story was a warning which Amaziah ignored to Jehoash's dismay since he was thoroughly defeated by the forces of Israel. *See also* Amaziah; Jehoash; parable(s); parables of the Old Testament.

cedars of Lebanon: a fragrant and precious timber grown mostly in the land of Lebanon. Assyria is described allegorically in Ezekiel 31 as a cedar of Lebanon destined to be brought to ruin. The wood of the cedar was an important building material for Solomon's Temple and kings' palaces. Solomon's palace was actually called "the Forest of Lebanon" because it contained so much cedar and pine. Cedar wood was also used as an article in Hebrew worship (Lev. 14:4). *See also* Ezekiel's eagles, vine, and cedar allegory; flora, fruit, and grain, symbology of; Mount Lebanon; tree(s); Tripoli Prophecy.

Cedars of Lebanon Prophecy. See Tripoli Prophecy.

celebrant: one who officiates at a religious function, such as saying Mass, performing a wedding ceremony, or some other ecclesiastical duty. *See also* clergy; ecclesiastic(s); hierophant; minister; officiant; pastor(s); priest(s).

celestial court, the: Daniel's vision of God's supernal kingdom realm as seen in conjunction with the vision of the rock cut out but not from human hands (Dan. 2:44–45; 7:9–14, 26–27). *See also* angel(s); council of God; crushing rock that became a mountain.

celestial disturbances: unusual and disturbing portents in the heavens, usually descriptive of signs of the end. Among the descriptions, the moon is said to turn to blood and the stars fall from the heavens. Jesus spoke of the phenomena in his Olivet Discourse (Mt. 24:29) as he quoted from Isaiah. Many of Revelation's visions pertain to dynamic flux in the universe. *See also* adjacent possible; Age of Aquarius; apocalyptic, apocalypticism; Apophis asteroid;

Aries; astronomy, astronomers; blazing mountain, a; blazing star; blood moon(s); Blue Star prophecy; *Book of the Hopi;* Comet ISON; cosmic cross; cosmology; Dark Rift; Day of Purification; destruction of heaven and earth by fire; Draco; eclipse(s); eschatology, eschatological; fallen star; Fifth World, the; Fourth Density; four winds of heaven; galactic alignment; galactic superwave; Gochihr; God Particle, the; Great Change, Prophecy of the; Great Shaking, the; great sign, the; Hale-Bopp Comet; Halley's Comet; heaven and earth destroyed; heavenly bodies; Hercolubus; hosts of heaven; Hydra; impact event; Jupiter; *Jupiter Effect, The;* Mars; Mercury; moon; new heaven and new earth; Nemesis; Nibiru; Olivet Discourse, the; Omphalos Hypothesis; Orion; ouroboros; pillars of the universe; Pisces; Pluto; planets as gods, the; polar shift; procession of the equinoxes; redshift; Saturn; Shekinah glory; Shift, the; signs in heaven; sign of the Son of Man, the; star(s); star of Bethlehem; sun; supermoon; three levels of heaven; 2012, prophecy of; UFO; Uranus; Venus; Virgo; voice out of heaven; war in heaven; "wonders in the heavens and in the earth"; Wormwood; zodiac.

Celestine V, Pope: called the *Pastor Angelicus* by various reformers when he assumed the papal throne in A.D. 1294. The College of Cardinals had been deadlocked in its selection process for over two years before his ascension. Celestine was a hermit-monk of the Benedictine order and a venerable and humble priest. He declined to reside in the lavish quarters for his Vatican residence but preferred a modest hut he constructed himself on the palace grounds. Clearly not suited for the politics of the position, he reigned only from July to December before abdicating and eventually became the prisoner of his successor, Pope Boniface VIII. *See also* pope; Roman Catholic Church.

Celestines: a Roman Catholic monastic order, a branch of the Benedictines. The fellowship was founded in 1244 under the original name "Moronites," later assuming their modern identification from Pope Celestine V. The monks were vegetarians and began their strenuous worship practices at 2:00 a.m. They wore a white woolen cassock with a linen band and a white leather belt and a black hood. *See also* Assumptionist Orders; Augustinian Order; Barnabites; Benedict, Order of; Black Canons; canon(s) of the church; canons regular; Capuchin Order; Carmelites; Carthusians; Cistercians; clergy; Dominicans; Franciscans; friar(s); Minim; monasticism; monk(s); orders; Paulist Fathers; Premonstratensian Order; priest(s); religious organizations; Roman Catholic Church; Servite Order; Spirituals of the Franciscan Order; Trappist Order.

celibacy: abstinence from marriage and sexual relations, especially for religious reasons or for a religious calling. In some persuasions, celibacy is required (such as for Roman Catholic priests) while others actually celebrate marriage for all, including the clergy.

cell: a monk's private room in a monastery. Usually the furnishings and comforts are rather Spartan and its use strictly utilitarian. A number of cells are called a *lavra*. *See also* monastery; monk(s).

cella: a small memorial chapel found in early Christian cemeteries. When seen today they usually serve as a commemorative to the dead or as small chapels. *See also* adytum; bethel; cathedral(s); chapel; church; kirk; sacellum; temple(s).

Cellini, Benvenuto: one of the most celebrated Renaissance artists (1500 – 1571), perhaps best remembered for his autobiography praising his rather advanced ego. In it, he records the curious story of how, when he had been imprisoned for stealing the pope's jewelry (yes, your read correctly), he attempted to take his own life. He was prevented from the act by an "invisible power," a most comely youth, who scolded him for contemplating suicide. Unfortunately, the visitation failed because Cellini later became a dabbler in demonology. *See also* art, religious; demon(s), demonic; near death experiences (NDEs).

Celsus: pagan Roman philosopher who wrote a damaging attack on Christianity around A.D. 278. In another fifty years, Origen answered his criticisms quite ably. *See also* Roman Empire.

Celtic folklore and religion: with the more convenient usage *faerie*, the beliefs and religious traditions of the ancient Celtic peoples before the conquest by the Romans. In ordinary works on archeology, the term "Celtic" signifies the pre-Roman period, or, in Ireland and Northern Scotland, the pre-Christian era. The Celts themselves were a numerous Indo-European folk covering land from Britain to Asia Minor but did not survive the Roman conquest despite having been in existence since the sixth century B.C. Their origins may have been in north-central Germany about 4000 years ago but they could also have arisen further south. For certain, they moved west becoming known in the future as Celtiberians in Spain, Gaels in Ireland, Picts in Scotland, Britons in England, Gauls in France, and Belgae in the Low Countries. In Paul's day, they were the Galatians. Some historians have dubbed them the first Europeans. Still, anthropologists are astonished that their language and literature so closely resembles ancient Indian sub-continent culture. British Israelism considered them to be among the ten lost tribes of Israel. Celt society failed quickly after Caesar conquered Gaul in 58 – 51 B.C. They did not, however, completely disappear because many were simply absorbed into their version of Christianity and anchored a continued role in political leadership. The greatest concentration of population was Britain, Ireland, and Wales, with the Druids being one of the earliest representations of their religion, although the Romans never invaded Wales. The Druids were the *de facto* priests of the Celts in Gaul and Britain and highly respected by all classes. Little is known of Celtic history, mainly because early religious taboos prevented their learning from being recorded, but we are certain they treasured a vivid belief in the afterworld and were perhaps the first peoples to develop a doctrine of the immortality of the soul; they buried their dead with food and weapons, often with remains found resting in a chariot. The afterlife, called the Otherworld, was for bliss in the "Isle of the Blest" or a hell called "Isle of the Cold Waves." A chaste system was in place with a structured and efficient society. The Celts, whether continental or in the British Isles, were an advanced culture despite Roman propaganda that promoted them as illiterate barbarians who liked to rush naked into frenzied battle. No doubt they could be fierce, even barbaric in certain circumstances (including warfare and perhaps even human sacrifice), but also generous, practical, and adept with language and writing. Though they were in widely separated societies, the clans and tribes were remarkably cohesive as a race. Primogeniture as a political expedient was not practiced. Women held high social position in all occupations in contrast to the heavily Greek and Roman misogynism; Queen Boudicca of southern Britain being just one of many examples of female prominence. Absolute private ownership of property was not recognized. All the tribes were as proficient, or better, than their contemporaries in metallurgy, agriculture and extensive trade, medicine and surgery, road, bridge, and causeway building, heavy transport (horseback, draught animals, chariots, wagons, and wheelwright expertise), both river craft and a fleet, glass, jewelry, and enamel working, pottery and ceramics, astrology and astronomy, jurisprudence, the arts, fabrics, carpentry, leather-working, and other industrial and cottage skills. They are widely considered the inventors or soap (*sopa*) and the first to benefit from wool weaving and trade. They were exceptionally brave and clever warriors. The Celts saw humans as body, soul, and spirit and the world as animal, vegetable, and mineral and divided into earth, air, and sea. The cardinal colors were red, yellow, and blue and they held the number three to be mystical or magic, along with seven, nine, seventeen, twenty-seven, and thirty-three. Nature (particularly the oak tree and mistletoe), mountains, certain groves, and innumerable sanctified wells were considered sacred. Religion was high-priority, including the extensive practice of augury. With help from the Druids, they were adept at haruspicy, astronomy and astrology, and many methods of presagement. The bull was particularly venerated. Elaborate cauldrons were useful worship items representing purification, inspiration, and plenty. Some actions took place in sacred groves or temples featuring votive tablets and images, with representation of limbs, faces, and body parts hung on the walls or suspended from the trees. One could also find heads of animals and, possibly, bodies of men hung up like trophies of the hunt. Often their mouths would be prized and kept open by sticks of wood. Statues were favored everywhere. There were some 400 known gods and goddesses but only about 100 were more than local deities; we have the recorded names of 374 Celtic deities. Principal among them are the following goddesses: 1. Agrona – a war goddess, 2. Aine – love and fertility, 3. Airmid – healing, 4. Andraste (Britania) – moon, divination, 5. Anu – magic, moon, air, prosperity, in the Morrigan trinity (see Morrigan), 6. Aoibhell – of the Sidhe, 7. Arianrhod – air, reincarnation, time, vengeance, fate, 8. Artio – wildlife, 9. Badb Catha – "The Fury," one of the three-part Morrigan goddess collection who created chaos on the battlefield, (see Morrigan) who prophesied the end of the world; Babd, Erin, and Fodla were also a trinity of goddesses from which Ireland drew its name, 10. Bellona – battlefield goddess, 11. Bellsama – goddess of fire and light, 12. Blodeuwedd – "Flower Face," the goddess of ceremony, agriculture, and lushness, wisdom, and who promoted growth in gardens and children; she was changed into an owl which became her symbol, 13. Boann – consort of The Dagda and named in the River Boyne in Ireland, 14. Branwen – goddess of love and beauty, also known as

History and Mystery

"the lady of the lake," 15. Brid – a great mother goddess of Ireland known for wisdom, knowledge, and the female arts, 16. Brigantia – the "High One," goddess of pastoral scenes and rivers, a Tutelan goddess who came to symbolize Britain itself, 17. Buann – a water goddess, 18. Caer Ibormeith – sleep and dreams, 19. Cailleach – disease and plague, 20. Cerridwen – moon, grain, nature, astrology, 21. Creiddylad – flowers, 22. Cyhiraeth – streams; her banshee-like scream heralded approaching death, 23. The Dagda – three sisters with the same name, Brigid, but with varying functions such as poetry, healing, fertility, or smithing, 24. Danu (Anu) – a mother goddess, – 25. Donn – queen of heaven and goddess of the air and sea, 26. Damona – "divine cow," consort of Borvo, 27. Druanthia – protection, knowledge, creativity, 28. Eostre – goddess of spring from which Christianity got the word "Easter," 29. Eriu – the sovereign goddess, 30. Epona (with any number of alternate names) – an important deity governing horses, 31. Eire, Banba, and Fotla – triune goddesses giving their names to the land of Ireland, 32. Flidais – a shape-shifter, owner of a magic cow that could produce enough milk for 300 men per day, 33. Maeve (Mebd) – earth, fertility, war, one of the Morrigan trinity of the war goddess, prone to eat the heads of her enemies (see Morrigan), 34. Margawse – motherhood, 35. Morrigan – a stand-alone goddess of war or seen as a trinity of fierce goddesses (Anu, Badb, and Macha), 36. Nantosuelta – nature, valleys, streams, consort of Sucellus, 37. Nemain – war, whose name means "panic," 38. Niamh – beauty and brightness, a helper to heroes nearing death, 39. Nostiluca – a witch goddess, 40. Olwen – flowers, springtime, love, rebirth, 41. Scathach – healing, magic, teacher of the fighting arts, and prophecy, 42. Rhiannon – horses and birds, 43. Rosmerta – fertility and wealth whose symbol is a cornucopia, 44. Sabrann – named by the River Lee, 45. Sequana – rivers, health, 46. Sinainn – named by the River Shannon, 47. the important Sheela-na-gig – an Irish mother goddess who creates and destroys with a

Kali-like attitude; representations can be found depicting her as holding open her huge vagina with both hands, 48. Sirona – "star," consort of Grannos, 49. Sulis – goddess of healing, especially concerned with women's health, 50. Tephi – co-founder of tea, 51. The White Lady – mysterious lady of death and destruction, the queen of the dead. The most famous gods are: 1. Addane – a lake monster who created the great deluge, 2. Allathair – an Irish All-Father god of the sky, 3. Apellio – patron of apple trees, 4. Amaethon – agriculture and luck, 5. Angus Og – youth, love, beauty, 6. Arawn – the underworld, 7. Bris – agriculture, prince of the Formorians, 8. Balor – fierce one-eyed god of war who only opened both eyes in battle, 9. Bel – fire and sun, science, crops, 10. Belatucados – a war god, 11. Belenus – the "Fair-Shining One," a sun god, 12. Barinthus – a charioteer of the underworld, 13. Beli – god of death, 14. Bladud – the "Flying King,' a sun-god, 15. Borud – healing, 16. Borvo (Bormo or Bormanus) – Gaulish sacred wells, 17. Bran (Bendigeid Vran or Bran the Blessed) – a giant god or demi-god of prophecy, 18. Camalus – "of the Invisible Sword," overseer of war and sky, 19. Cernunnus (frequently identified as Dagda) – "Father of the Gods," an important horned god who carried a club that could kill with one end and heal with the other, 20. Crom – fire and the winds, 21. Diancecht – healing and medicine (he killed his own son Miach in a jealous rage since the boy was a better physician), 22. Donn – a transporter of the dead to the Otherworld, 23. Dyaus – a sun deity, 24. Dylan – "Son of the Waves," god of the sea, 25. Goibhniu (Gofannon in Wales) – blacksmithing, brewing, 26. Grannus – healing, 27. Gwydion – warrior god and magician, 28. Gwynn Ap Nudd – the underworld, 29. Lebraid – Irish god of the underworld, 30. Lenus – healing, 31. Llew Llan Gyffes (Lugh) – patron of harpers, bards, poets, smiths, sorcerers and water, 32. Llyr – water and the sea, 33. Lodan – Lir's son, an ocean god, 34. Lugh – Irish deity and High King Lamhfhada the long-hand (Lleu in Welsh); Julius Caesar

History and Mystery

called him Dis-Pater, skilled with spear or sling, 35. Manannan Mac Lir – patron of sailors and merchants, 36. Maponus – "Divine Son" who may also be Mabon, 37. Math Mathonwy – magic, enchantment, 38. Mider – the underworld, 39. Mug Ruith – Chief Druid of Ireland and even Chief Druid of the World, a one-eyed sun-god, 40. Myrddin (Merlin) – sorcerer, Druid, wizard, 41. Nechtan – an early water god replaced by The Dagda, 42. Neit – battle, 43. Nuada (with several variations) – healing, harpers, historians, literature, king of the Tuatha de Danann until he lost his hand and had to be replaced with a silver one, then a fleshly one again, 44. Ogmios – eloquence, literature and learning, perhaps related to the Tuatha de Danann Ogma, son of The Dagda who claimed the magic sword called Orna (a weapon that could speak and recount its own deeds) when he slew the Fomorri sea-god Tethra, 45. Luchta (with Goibhaniu and Credhue) – important patrons of wheelwrights and gods of the domestic crafts, 46. Pwyll – cunning, virtue, 47. Sucellus – Gaulish god of the forests, prosperity and domesticity, who carried a hammer in his left hand, husband to Nantosuelta, 48. Taliesin – song, bards, patron of the Druids, 49. Tamanis (Taranis) – the vicious God of Thunder who, with the common triad of Esus and Tautatris, reportedly required human sacrifice for worship, 50. Teutates – war, money, fertility, 51. the mysterious three-horned bulls of power. Many of the deities were associated with local rivers, including Boann and Sionan, but all the gods were considered to be more ancestors of the people than creators. Since the number three was sacred, many of their deities are pictured with three faces, three heads, three horns, etc. They were prone to decapitate fallen enemies and preserve the heads because they believed the soul resided there. The prevailing religious philosophy was that people should live in harmony with nature and themselves, honor truth, do no evil, and worship the gods. Moral salvation was the responsibility of the individual and nothing was preordained. Tales and adventure narratives abound about each if we are to believe heir later chroniclers. The basic eschatological thought, however, is that the tri-part Wiccan goddess Morrigan will create a covering mist to conceal the arrival of Tuatha de Danann from the land of the Fir Bolg. Celtic eschatology links Morrigan with Badb who will overturn the primeval cauldron and destroy everything. Meanwhile the Otherworld serves as the home of ghosts and magic where one may perhaps someday indulge in the favorite pastime there – the mounted and boisterous Wild Ride hunt on the borders and trails between this world and the next. Celtic Christianity eventually gained a permanent foothold in many Celtic lands and became dominant though it was often in conflict with Roman Catholicism practices and beliefs. *See also* American folklore; Anglo-Israelism; Arthur, King; Avalon; banshee; Beltane; Beltane's Eve; Bile; bogle; *Book of Kells*, the; *Bran mac Feabhail*; Brehon Laws; brownies; bugbears; Burning Man Festival; Cart of the Dead; Celtic wheel; Cicero, Marcus Tullius; clurichauns; Columbanus; Coronation Stone; cosmic tree; crane bag; crossfigill; Dagda; Damanhur; Danu; disa; Druidism; dweomer; Easter; Egyptian pantheon; elemental(s); Erigena, John Scotus; Excalibur; fable(s); fairy, fairies; filidh; Fir Bolg; flood; folklore; folk religion; Fomorians; Green Man, the; Habonde, Dame; Hilary of Poitiers; hobgoblins; Imbolc; Lammas; leprechaun(s); Levant pantheon; logos; lost tribes, the ten; Lugh; Lughnasadh; Mabon; Manannan mac Lir; Martin, bishop of Tours; Mayday rites; memeton; Merlin; Morrigan; mythological beasties, elementals, monsters, and spirit animals; New Age religion; nisse; Norse and Old Germanic pantheon; numbers, symbology of; oak; Ogham; Olympian pantheon; pooka; Otherworld; Pelagius; raven; Robin Goodfellow; Round Table; Samhain; Seelie Court, Unseelie Court; selkie; Sidhe; Sumerian and Babylonian pantheon; Synod of Whitby; Tir na nOg; Tuatha de Danann; *Vedas*; Virgil; Wicca; wight(s); Wild Hunt; Wild Man.

Celtic wheel: a chariot wheel of eight spokes made in the form of a votive or amulet. It was the symbol of the god Taranis and a common religious symbol of the ancient Celts. *See also* amulet(s); ankh; Celtic folklore and religion; chariot(s); charm(s); idolatry; Hand of Fatima; Medusa; relic(s); talisman(s); votive.

cemetery: a graveyard, the place of burial for deceased persons or pets. The original refers to a "sleeping place" from the Latin *cemeterium*. The word was widely used by early Christians who viewed such a place as a temporary condition, only a "sleep" from which the faithful would awaken to a home in heaven. *See also* "ashes to ashes"; burial; catacombs; catafalque; charnel ground; death; funeral; grave; Manes; martyrium; multiconfessional.

Cenacle: the site in Jerusalem said to house the hall of the Last Supper and David's tomb. The location of either has not been totally proven. *See also* cenobites; desert mystics; Jerusalem, landmarks of; Upper Room, the monastery; monasticism; monk(s); Therapeutae.

cenobites. See desert mystics; monastery; monasticism; monk(s); Therapeutae.

cenobium: a monastery, especially for Coptic monks. *See also* Coptic Church; monastery; monasticism.

cenoby. See cenobium; monastery.

censer(s): a container (a thurible) for burning coals or incense. The term has apocalyptic significance since angels are sometimes depicted holding censers of fire taken from the altar of God. The seven bowls of Revelation may be described as censers, bowls, or vials containing punishments from God. Isaiah's lips were cleansed by one of the Seraphs who had taken a live coal from the heavenly altar and pressed it to his mouth (Isa. 6:6). *See also* furniture and furnishings of the modern church; furniture and furnishings of the tabernacle, temples, and modern synagogue; incense.

census: an official counting of population. The practice was common in Old and New Testament times, usually as a facility to aid taxation. The census counts of the Exodus immigrants, David's unlawful population count, and that under the governor Quirinius (Lk. 2:1–2) are perhaps the most prominent. In fact, the book of Numbers takes its name from the practice of counting the populace. *See also* Numbers as Old Testament book; Quirinius.

Center for Research on the World Order (CROM): an organization that was, until 2014, a research agency for studies and research of the New World Order (NWO) cults and sects. The organization was led by researcher and author French Joel Labruyere. He and the center were attacked by the occultic elite and, after a measure of success, shut down from further exploration. A new project was begun, called *Nova Polis*, but is purposefully less public in its conduct and findings. *See also* New World Order, the (NWO); religious organizations.

centering prayer: a form of deep meditation (said to originate with the desert mystics) which focuses concentration of a particular aspect of one's faith—a rosary, for example. A more modern aberration of the process is called the contemplative prayer movement. *See also* contemplative prayer movement; rosary; 24/7 Prayer Movement; visualization.

central sanctuary: the place of residence for the tabernacle, or replicas of it, in pre-monarchial Israel. The first, and perhaps the primary one, was at Shiloh and administered by Eli and Samuel. Other sites at various times or for local uses included Bethel, Gilgal, Gibeon, Dan, Hebron, and some few others.

centurion(s): a Roman military official (either officer or enlisted) in command of a century (100 personnel or less). Centurions favorable to Judaism or Christianity are rare, but four who exhibited faith include: one who announced his conviction at the cross (Mt. 27:54); one who sought Jesus' aid for his tormented servant (Mt. 8:5–13), Cornelius, stationed at Caesarea, through whom the Holy Spirit manifested his work among the Gentiles (Acts 10); and Julius who treated Paul kindly on his trip to Rome (Acts 27:1,3, 43). *See also* Cornelius; Imperial Regiment, the; Italian Regiment, the; Julius; legion; Praetorian Guard; Roman Empire; tribune.

cephalophore: a decapitated saint pictured with his severed head under his arm. *See also* decapitation.

Cephas. See Peter as apostle.

Cercle Social: a.k.a. the Society of the Friends of Truth or "the Social Club" established in 1789. The group was a French revolutionary organization founded on a mix of politics, the Masonic Lodge, and a literary salon. Founders, Nicholas Bonneville and Claude Fauchet, aimed to administer a clearing house for international political writings to which all such correspondence was welcome. Publication was managed with a bulletin called the *Mouth of Iron*. Features of the organization expanded and it became focused on the more equitable distribution of wealth and ideals of the French Revolution. *See also* civil religion; fraternal organization(s); Freemasonry; sociology of religion.

Cerdo: a Gnostic type personality who is said to be the originator of modern dualism (that there are two gods, forever in conflict). *See also* dualism; Gnosticism, Gnostic(s); Zoroastrianism.

Ceres: the Roman goddess of agriculture, fertility, and nurturing. She was also the "pig goddess" since she demanded swine entrails as offerings. *See also* idol(s); Olympian pantheon.

Cerinthus: a noted Gnostic from Ephesus near the turn of the first century, thus a contemporary of the apostle John. Often, according to legend, the two came into conflict. Once, so the legend goes, John ran from a bathhouse shouting that the edifice would collapse because that heretic Cerinthus was within. Cerinthus insisted that millennialism was characterized by sensuous pleasure and unsuitable for believers who should be considered more "spiritual" and intellectual in their thinking. The New Testament continually debases Gnosticism as heresy. *See also* Gnosticism, Gnostic(s).

cessationism: the theological belief that the proffered gifts of the Holy Spirit presented to the Apostolic Church (prophecy, exorcism, raising the dead, healing, miracles, etc.) have ceased [stopped by act of God] since the end of the Apostolic age. The most common proof-text used in support of the tenet is 1 Corinthians 13 where the perfection of faith noted there has come and the supernatural gifts are no longer needed or active. What is perhaps missed is that the perfection mentioned in 1 Corinthians 13 refers to the Second Coming—not the present age. Furthermore, the adverse condition of the world today assuredly does not bode to perfection. *See also* charisms; continuationism; five-fold ministry, the.

Chafer, Lewis Sperry: a major exponent of dispensational theology (1871–1952). Chafer was acquainted with C. I. Scofield and became convinced that schools for his friend's dispensational doctrines should be planted. This he did in 1924 with the opening of the Evangelical Theological College, later (in 1936) named the Dallas Theological Seminary. Chafer became the first president and pushed the dispensational views through writing and education. *See also* Congregationalists; Dallas Theological Seminary; Darby; dispensational theology; religious education; Scofield, C. I.

chain(s): linked steel or some other alloy used for securing, lifting, or pulling. In Revelation 20:1–3, an angel is described as binding Satan with a chain. Whether such links are metaphorical or literal is a matter of interpretation. The Lord also uses the term as a symbol of Judah's captivity in Ezekiel 7:23 and is a common metaphor for slavery. *See also* chains of Saint Peter; slave, slavery.

chain letter(s): letters or email messages that attempt to persuade the recipient to forward them to many others. The content often details threats if not continued or the promise of rewards if the chain is unbroken. Actually, the practice is a pyramid scheme and the text often is filled with urban legend or hoaxes. *See also* idolatry; magic, magick; occult, occultic.

chains of Saint Peter: the relic said to be the chain that held Peter (Acts 12:7) but removed by a rescuing angel. The links were presented to Pope Leo I in the fifth century, who then touched them with another set of chains from Peter's earlier incarceration in Mamertine Prison. The touch caused the two sets to meld together seamlessly. *See also* chain(s); liturgical year; relic(s).

chakra: a New Age and Buddhist designation for the seven points of energy concentrations in the human body. The location is specifically positioned with the central nervous system—in the brain and along the spine. *See also* acupuncture and acupressure; Buddhism; Chi; contemplative prayer movement; kundalini; New Age religion; Shakti; third eye, the.

Chaldean rite. See Nestorianism.

Chaldea, Chaldeans: prominent residents of Nebuchadnezzar's Babylonian court, their original home being in modern-day Iraq. They are likely the elite of the Chaldean race of southern Babylonia and are referred to as astrologers and "wise men" in the book of Daniel with whom the prophet often competed. It was they, in particular, who bequeathed to the world the most refined explanations of the arts of divination, astrology, accounting, astronomy, commerce, and other cultural aptitudes. At times, the Chaldeans are equated with the whole of Babylonia, although such a designation is not technically correct. *See also* Babylon, Babylonians; Berossus; Neo-Babylon.

Chalkydri. See Seraphim.

chambering: a more, perhaps, polite way of identifying sexual immorality, fornication, lewdness, wantonness, and the like. The term can be considered dated. *See also* adultery, adulteries; fornication.

chamberlain: a monastic official in charge of beds, linens, bedding, clothing, tools, and other equipment. He also supplies wood for the calefactory. In more secular circumstances, the chamberlain of perhaps a large estate, a king's residence, a castle, and the like held extensive household duties. *See also* calefactory; monasticism; Roman Catholic Church.

Chamberlain Code: or the God Code, a cipher system supposedly presenting empirical evidence that the Hebrew Bible is a far more complex and esoteric text than previously assumed. The code-breaking key to fully understanding the Scripture is available but considered so complex that it could only have been devised by alien intelligence from outside our own dimension. *See also* Bible Code.

Chamber of Parvah: a tunnel under the Second Temple supposedly dug by a magician named Parvah, who wanted to spy on the Jewish high priest in action. Parvah was killed for his defilement of the sacred precincts, but the underground route holds his name as a warning to others who might seek to invade the privacy of the Temple Mount. Such subterranean caverns and passageways are numerous beneath the Mount and may hold necessary treasures and artifacts for archeological study and possible establishment for a future Jewish Temple. Access is nearly impossible, however, because Islamic authorities forbid it and even deny Israel has a history on the Mount.

chambers of imagery. See Ezekiel's four visions of Israel's demise.

chancellor: an administrative official of a government, in academia, or for religious organizations. The latter is typically the chief archivist, notary, and secretary of a region or diocese. *See also* chancery.

chancery: the secretarial office of a bishop or king. *See also* chancellor.

Channing, William Ellery: a Congregationalist turned Unitarian (1780–1842). Channing pastored the Boston Federal Street Church from 1803–1842 but his true calling was to promote Unitarianism nationwide, an involvement that sparked the growing denomination of the time. *See also* Congregationalists; Unitarian Universalists.

chant: a liturgical form utilized by solo voice or choir as an aid to worship, a musical rendition, or reading of sacred text. The melody is usually short and simple, with single notes to which an indefinite number of syllables are intoned. Psalms and canticles are most suitable for chanting. Cantors in the synagogue regularly chant their lessons. Roman Catholic worship is best known for a version called Gregorian, a style named for Pope Gregory I (A.D. 590–604). The vehicle of the chanting is plain-song in a *cantus firmus* (fixed melody) that is free-flowing, monophonic, and lacking in discernible rhythm or harmony. The repertoire consists of around 3,000 melodies and is becoming more popular in the modern age with certain musical tastes and occasions. *See also* antiphony; canticles; cantor; *Carmen Christi;* chantry; death; dirge; funeral; hymn(s); jeremiad; Judaism; *kinah;* kontakion; lament; liturgical year; liturgy, Christian; liturgy, Jewish; mantra; melisma; music; obit; obsequy; plainsong; praise; Requiem; requiescat; Roman Catholic Church; sacred music; sankirtana; threnody; vigil.

chantry: "to sing," an endowment for the maintenance of a priest to chant masses for the soul of the patron in the beginning. A member of the synagogue so gifted fulfills requirements for that faith. Later, the chantry took on the name for the chapels that were inside or outside regular church buildings as self-contained units. *See also* antiphony; cantor; chant; church; liturgy, Christian; liturgy, Jewish; music.

Chanukah. See Hanukkah.

chaos magic: a postmodern phenomenon using esoteric magical principles to promote practical uses. The movement draws from science fiction, hard science, Eastern philosophy, ceremonial magic, neoshamanism, world religions, personal experimentation, and other sources in its attempt to find realistic results. *See also* chaos theory; idolatry; magic, magick; New Age religion; sigil.

chaos theory: the idea that the universe is in a state of perpetual flux. Scientists say that design can be seen in nature despite her inherent chaos; apocalypticists say the same but from differing perceptions. According to the theory, the future can be predicted (albeit on a limited scale and imprecisely) by reference to "chaos patterns" found in our surroundings. Both theologians and scientists can speak of earth's final destiny from their different approaches. The prophet sees the end (usually) in fire and blood; many scientists (not all) envision it as a reversal of the "big bang" theory of creation but the result now being called "the big crunch." *See also* analogical day theory; big bang theory; big crunch theory; cosmogony; cosmology; *creatio ex nihilo;* creationism; creation science; Creator; day-age theory; evolution; evolution, theistic; framework hypothesis; gap theory of creation; intelligent design; involution; naturalism; Omphalos Hypothesis; progressive creationism; redshift; "six-day theory, the"; uniformitarianism; Young-Earth Creationist Movement.

chapel: an alternative or auxiliary site for worship that is generally smaller than the usually recognized church building. The designated area may be an auxiliary of, or sponsored by, a larger church institution or entirely separate and functioning on its own. Frequently, chapels are supervised by chaplains or other selected leadership. *See also* adytum; bethel; cathedral(s); cella; chaplain(s); church; kirk; mission; sacellum; temple(s); Whittenberg Chapel.

chaplain(s): men and women clergy who serve in alternate worship settings as opposed to an established church building, monastery, cathedral, and the like. Their work place, if they have one, is called a chapel and is usually smaller or more specialized in worship than larger ecclesiastical constructions. Chaplains serve from a long line of historical devotion in affiliation with various institutions, including the military, industrial complexes, medical facilities, monasteries, universities, aboard ships, in police departments, in the Civil Air Patrol, and other like organizations. The name "chaplain" derives from a legend of Martin of Tours. The associated incident evolved when Martin cut off half of his military issue cloak to give to a poor beggar who was later revealed in a dream to be Christ himself. This "little cloak," *capella* in Latin, was kept as a relic of the Franks who succeeded the Roman governors of Gaul (France) and was often carried into battle. The small chapels that held such venerated items were called *capellae*. Those early prophets who served in the court of kings were, by implication if not name, chaplains, as were quite likely those militaristic priests called the *Hasidim* during Maccabean times. In 1999, the Pentagon approved endorsement for non-mainstream religions (including Muslims, Wicca, and pagans) which for the first time in American history placed all creeds on an equal footing with Christianity and Judaism for military chaplaincy service. For the time being, atheism has been denied status despite their appeals to be included. *See also* bethel; bishop(s); chapel; clergy; clergy patriots; divine; divine services; ecclesiastic(s); endorsing agency; Hale, Edward Everett; *Hasidim*; imam; Martin, bishop of Tours; man of God; *maskilim*; minister(s); monastery; monasticism; padre; pastor(s); preacher(s); priest(s); rabbi; West, Samuel.

chaplet: a wreath for encircling the head or a short string of prayer beads. *See also* idolatry; rosary; wreath.

Chapman, John: universally known as Johnny Appleseed (1775–1847). Chapman was a small, wiry man with long hair, scraggly beard, and bright eyes. He moved from his birthplace in Massachusetts to western Pennsylvania, where he made a meager living selling apple seeds and saplings. Then in 1800, he set off—wearing cast-off clothing and a tin pot for a hat—down the Ohio River. Along the way, he planted and cultivated apple orchards and educated others in how to do so. Chapman's main interest, however, was not exclusive to apples; he was an active missionary of the small Swedenborgian sect and often spoke of visitations by spirits and angels. *See also* American folklore; missions, missionaries; Swedenborgianism.

charge: 1. one or more churches joined or organized for work or fellowship. 2. a commission from a senior ecclesiastical officer to a clergy candidate before ordination. Instructions, motivational incentives, and encouragement are common themes of the speech. *See also* commission.

chariot(s): a two-wheeled conveyance used chiefly as a weapon of war or official state transportation in many early cultures (from as far back as 2,000 B.C.), as well as a superb platform for hunting and racing. The vehicle was pulled by horses (which may account for the numerous horse-worshiping cults of the day) and carried two or sometimes three personnel. It had a flat bed and light carriage with an excellent spoke wheel and axel design but was generally unsuited for mountainous or swampy terrain. The chariot was also a prestigious platform for persons of dignity and status. The name of the vehicle in Hebrew is *merkabah*, which suggests literature with a theme of ascensions and thrones. That description occurs frequently in *3 Enoch*. There, the chariot is propelled by Seraphim (highest angelic order), the Chayoth (second), and the Ophanim (third), which keep the conveyance in constant motion. The Seraphim control all the others of the triad and are represented as the creature with a human face. In a rather obscure definition, the name "chariot" is occasionally used in connection with the Cherubim (1 Chr. 28:18; 2 Ki. 2:11–12), both of those represented in the Holy of Holies and the angelic hosts who carried Elijah to heaven.

Elisha's exclamation upon seeing Elijah's transport speaks of the mystery of the angelic conveyance: "My father! My father! The chariots and horsemen of Israel!" Whatever association existed between angels and chariots is unclear to us, but it obviously held meaning for the originators. Josephus mentioned certain chariots with their horses, which were evidently idols dedicated to the sun, or perhaps to Moloch. Josiah destroyed these, which he called "chariots of the sun" in his raging purge of idolatry in Judah. Certainly, chariots were more than common conveyances when embroiled in apocalyptic language. Sometimes the word is translated as "shield" in appropriate contexts (*i.e.*, Psalm 46:10). *See also* angel(s); Celtic folklore and religion; chariot of God; Cherub, Cherubim; Cherubim and the departed glory, the; four chariots into the world; four living creatures of Ezekiel; four living creatures of Revelation; horsemen; idol(s); Merkabah; Merkaba mysticism; sea of glass; throne in heaven with someone sitting on it, a; thrones; Vimanas; Zechariah's vision of the four chariots.

chariot of God: Ezekiel's vision of the throne chariot of God powered by the Cherubim in Ezekiel chapters 1 and 10. The vision launched Ezekiel's prophetic ministry in exile. A chariot of God could be the transportable example of God's throne (shown stationary in Revelation 4 and mobile in Ezekiel 1). Not only did Ezekiel see the chariot on at least two occasions, but also Elijah actually rode in one to heaven (2 Ki. 2:11–12) while still in his living body. The chariot of God, as described by Ezekiel, was a wonder in its construct and power. It was introduced by a vision of light, fire, and wind amid an immense cloud. The conveyance seems to be powered by four "wheels," one each associated with the four living creatures who were aboard. Actually, the wheels were designed like "a wheel within a wheel" which suggests a ball or sphere in gyroscope-like control. Each had high rims which were filled with "eyes" (possibly the illusion of images common to fast-moving wheels). The conveyance moved in acute spatial dimensions, rather than curved turnings and at blazing speed, but it could also hover in space. Daniel's account of the great throne of the Ancient of Days features wheels of flame (Dan. 7:9). When a throne chariot of God is encountered, one easily thinks of the ark of the covenant, especially as it was transported part of the way to the Temple Mount via a wheeled cart during the reign of David (2 Sam. 6; 2 Chr. 28:15). There seems to be a definite but uncertain connection between the chariot of God and the throne of God as each is used in Scripture. Certainly, the flaming chariot crossing the heavens is a common image of pagan religious mythology. *See also* chariot(s); four living creatures of Ezekiel; four living creatures of Revelation; Merkabah; Merkabah mysticism; thrones.

Chariots of the Gods?: a book published in 1970 by Erich von Daniken that asserts ancient astronauts once visited Earth. Such "gods" were actually extraterrestrials aboard spaceships of some description. Companion works include *Gods from Outer Space* and *The Gold of the Gods. See also* Ancient Astronaut Theory; Anunnaki; cities of the gods; demigod(s); Enki and Enlil; *Enuma Elish; Epic of Gilgamesh, The;* Igigi; lulu; Mesopotamia; Nibiru; panspermia theory; Sumer, Sumerian(s); Sumerian Tablets; Table of Destinies; Tiamat; transhumanism; UFO; von Daniken, Erich.

charism: 1. a small box or ark for holding aromatic resin and olive oil suitable for anointing in religious functions. 2. an anointing performed by a priest of the Eastern Orthodox Church, usually accompanied by initiatory baptism. The officiate makes the sign of the cross across the candidate's forehead, eyes, ears, nostrils, breast, back, hands, and feet while repeating the formula, "The seal of the gift of the Holy Spirit." *See also* anointing; baptism; furnishings and furniture of the modern church; *ghaliloun*; olive oil.

charisma: a Greek term denoting the social and personal appeal of a charismatic or engaging personality. Almost all the prophets of God exhibited the mark of enthusiasm and purpose, as did the judges, to one degree or another that were so necessary in the proper performance of their duties. Few such gifted people were actually admired by the elite of the land, but all were considered extraordinary in some manner. In essence, *charisma* is associated with the gifts of the Holy Spirit *(charismata)* without which a prophet, nor any Christian, can be truly effective in God's service. The judges of ancient Israel are often called charismatics. *See also* charisms; charm(s); ecstasy.

charismania: a derogatory term for the practices of charismatic religion, similar to "holy roller," "happy clappy," and other expressions. *See also* charismatic movement; Christianese; glossolalia; holy laughter; "holy roller"; names, symbolism of; Pentecostalism; "slain in the Spirit"; slurs, religious.

charismatic movement: an adaptation of Pentecostalism centered in the expression of the Holy Spirit but predominantly within other Protestant denominations. *See also* Assemblies of God; Azusa Street revival; baptism of the Holy Spirit; Brownsville Assembly; charismania; Christian and Missionary Alliance; Church of God in Christ; full gospel; glossolalia; holy laughter; "holy roller"; Pentecostalism; "slain in the Spirit"; tongues, gift of; tongues, interpretation of; "Toronto Blessing, the."

charisms: the gifts of the Holy Spirit that are distributed in some form or measure to all believers. The spiritual gifts are discussed at length by Paul (Rom. 12; 1 Cor. 12; Eph. 4) and briefly by Peter (1 Pe. 4). Such talents and abilities are those charismatic attributes (*charismata*) of the believer imparted by the grace of the Holy Spirit and considered to be supernatural manifestations of the Spirit himself. They are named in Scripture as: prophecy, teaching, serving, exhortation (preaching), giving (charity), helping, compassion, healing, working miracles, tongues, interpretation of tongues, wisdom, knowledge, discernment, apostleship, administration, and evangelism. In Paul's discussion of the gifts (1 Cor. 12:1–13), he names them as wisdom, knowledge (understanding), and faith (that extraordinary faith that allows works for God), plus the charismatic gifts of healing, miracle working, prophecy, discernment of spirits, speaking in tongues (glossolalia), and the interpretation of tongues. Without one or several of the Spirit's bequests, the work of God in the world, including prophecy certainly, would be futile or impossible. Sometimes theologians equate the gift of prophecy to a phrase found in Revelation 19:10 called the "testimony of Jesus" or "spirit of prophecy." All believers possess at least one spiritual gift for use in the kingdom's service. It is helpful to classify the gifts, as imprecise as that may be, because Paul listed them more than once and even tried to rank them as to importance in some instances. The first enumeration is in 1 Corinthians 12:1–12, which we may name as Class I: wisdom, knowledge; Class II: faith, healing, miracles, prophecy, discernment of spirits; Class III: tongues, interpretation of tongues. The second listing (1 Cor. 12:27–30) appears as 1. apostles, 2. prophets, 3. teachers (perhaps those associated with wisdom and knowledge in the first list), 4. miracles, 5. healing, helps, government, diversities of tongues. Yet another grouping appears between the 1 Corinthians 12 passages in verses 6–8 where they are seen as prophecy, ministry, teaching, and exhortation. The last group seems to be those abilities designated particularly for pastors, evangelists, and other clergy. *See also* call(ing); cessationism; *charisma;* church, administration of the early; continuationism; discerning the spirits; enduement; five-fold ministry, the; fruit; fruit of the Spirit; full gospel; glossolalia; Holy Spirit; prophecy; tongues, gift of; tongues, interpretation of; spirit of prophecy.

charity: 1. benevolent acts of sharing abundance from one who has enough to benefit another who does not. 2. The King James Version translates the word to mean "love" (1 Cor. 13) as the greatest of three premier theological virtues—faith, hope, and love. *See also* almsgiving; love.

History and Mystery

charivari: (or Shivaree), a noisy folk custom of frontier America to "serenade" newlyweds on their wedding night. The bride and groom were "entertained" with banging pots and pans, kettles, gunfire, and other noise-makers on their wedding night, sometimes even breaking into the home. The custom probably came from England and France, or even earlier in the Roman Empire as a New Year's celebration called *charivaris*. *See also* American folklore; matrimony.

Charlemagne: the greatest of the Frankish rulers (771–814) who caused the expansion of the Roman Catholic Church, even more than any pope. Because of that influence, he is remembered as an important monarch of the medieval era. Charlemagne was really Charles the Great, the son of Pippin III, whose long reign was destined to last, in one form or another, for 1,000 years. Charlemagne was crowned by Pope Leo III as Holy Roman Emperor on Christmas Day of A.D. 800, anointing him as a Roman emperor. Leo was said to have miraculously recovered from an assassination attempt in which he was blinded and had his tongue cut out. The story is questionable but Leo was nevertheless eager to have the support of the Carolingian monarchs and what was known as the Holy Roman Empire. He was the only pope to ever kneel to a Western emperor. *See also* Carolingians; Holy Roman Empire; king(s); Martel, Charles; Treaty of Verdun.

Charles V, Emperor: Holy Roman emperor who began to reign in his teens (1519) until his abdication in 1556. Charles was the half-Spanish grandson of King Ferdinand of Spain and father of Philip II. He was the ruler who presided over the trial of Martin Luther, and eventually saw the Peace of Augsburg, which officially recognized Lutheranism in 1555. Apocalypticism at the time was running rampant, and many of the day were convinced he was the last world emperor. *See also* Diet of Worms; Gattinara, Cardinal Mercurino di; Holy Roman Empire; king(s); Peace of Augsburg.

Charles I, King: Catholic king of England, Scotland, and Ireland (1600–1649) until his execution. Religious controversy abounded during his reign, which many saw as bringing the Church of England too close to a return to Catholicism. He failed to support the Protestants in the Thirty Years' War and even married a Catholic princess. He was in constant conflict with Parliament and precipitated two English civil wars, the last of which put Oliver Cromwell in power. Charles's appointment of William Laud as archbishop of Canterbury was particularly irksome because Laud was an arch-Catholic in doctrine, if not position. He authored the Articles of Religion as a counter to extreme predestination and supported devotional writing, even authoring some himself. Miracle stories abound about his reign, and he was declared Charles the martyr, then canonized as the first Anglican saint. Afterward, relics were sought out pertaining to his life. *See also* Articles of Religion; *Book of Common Prayer;* Caroline Divines, the; Charles II, King; Church of England; Cromwell, Oliver; king(s); Laud, William; martyr(s); Roman Catholic Church.

Charles II, King: king of England, Scotland, and Ireland (1630–1685), the son of Charles I and first of the restored monarchy after the Protestant rebellion. He was defeated by Oliver Cromwell and forced into exile in France. In 1658, following the death of Cromwell, Charles II was welcomed back, and the kingship was restored. His reign gave him the nickname the "Merry Monarch" because the stiff restrictions of the Puritan Cromwell regime were gone. Charles's parliament enacted laws concerning religion known as the Clarendon Code, which in essence, shored up the ailing Church of England. Charles acquiesced to the policy though he personally favored religious toleration. He dissolved parliament in 1681 and was received into the Roman Catholic Church at his death. *See also* Charles I, King; Cromwell, Oliver; king(s).

charm(s): 1. magical talismans or amulets thought to protect the wearer from evil or to promote worship. Ezekiel (Ezk.

13:17–18) described the practice of certain women who sewed them to their cuffs or veils or wore them as "magic bands" or "charm bracelets." The prophet Ezekiel (Ezk. 13:19–21) warns that God will strip off such ornaments from the arms of the wearers. 2. a spell or hex. In an active sense, a charm (called a "glamour" in earlier days) could theoretically be cast as a spell by magical or occultic means. 3. to infuse rapture or delight in another by the natural or cultivated appeal of a positive personality, personal allure, or other charismatic trait. Even snakes can be "charmed" to a hypnotic effect by a skilled practitioner. *See also* amulet(s); ankh; apotropaic magic; black arts; Celtic wheel; *charisma;* chaplet; *charisma;* crucifix; curse(s); ecstasy; enchantment; evil eye; *geis;* gris-gris; Hand of Fatima; hex; idolatry; juju; Key of Solomon; magic arts; magic, magick; Medusa; mojo; New Age religion; occult, occultic; pow-wow; relic(s); rosary; salt; serpent's egg; sorcery, sorceries; spell; spell names; taboo; talisman(s); teraphim; token; veil(s); wanga; ward; warlock(s); Wicca; witch(es); witchcraft.

charnel ground: any above-ground site set aside for the mummification of the Tibetan dead. The phrase has been extended to include any site where multiple violent deaths may have occurred or for mass disposal of bodies. *See also* cemetery; death; grave.

Charon: the mythological Greek ferryman who transported deceased souls across the rivers Styx and Acheron in hell. The toll was a coin, traditionally placed in or on the mouth of the dead. Failure to pay, or if left unburied, the condemned was forced to wander the shores of hell for 100 years. *See also* Acheron; hell; Olympian pantheon; Styx.

chasmal: a fiery substance (according to *3 Enoch*) that constitutes the illumination from the core of Ezekiel's chariot vision. It is also the building material for the pillars that hold up the earth. Otherwise, the substance cannot be identified. *See also* chariot of God; Chashmallim.

Chashmallim: an angelic order mentioned in *3 Enoch*. See also angel(s); archangel(s); chasmal; Chayoth; Cherub, Cherubim; Galgallim; Ophanim; Seraph, Seraphim; twenty-four elders, the; Watchers, the.

Chauncy, Charles: a Congregationalist minister (1705–1787) who claimed the pulpit of First Church Boston for some sixty years. He was a contemporary, and sharp rival, of his more famous colonial preacher, Jonathan Edwards. Whereas Edwards was a Calvinist and believed an internal transformation was necessary to regeneration, Chauncy championed free will and a more liberal religious stance. Edwards favored the surge of the Great Awakening then taking place in New England but Chauncy was critical of its extravagant emotionalism. Under his leadership, Chauncy fought successfully against his church's adoption of an Anglican system of bishoprics in America. He was well known outside the country and set the stage for the beginnings of Unitarianism in the United States. *See also* Calvinism; Congregationalists; Edwards, Jonathan; Great Awakenings, the; Unitarian Universalists.

Chautauqua Movement, the: an intense and highly popular method of training religious education leaders for adults. The movement sprouted from an experiment sponsored by John Heyl Vincent and businessman Lewis Miller held at Chautauqua Lake, New York. The process involved mostly outdoor seminars enhanced by a blend of invited preachers, teachers, entertainers, motivational speakers, and other experts. The procedure was effective and all the rage until the mid-1920s. Theodore Roosevelt called of the Chautauqua campus "the most American thing in America." The Chautauqua experiment was preceded by the Lyceum Movement in America which emphasized traveling lecturers, seminars for adults, scientific and cultural studies, and even entertainment, but was not primarily religious in content. *See also* religious education; religious organizations; Sunday school(s); Vincent, John Heyl; youth religious organizations.

History and Mystery

Chayoth: name of the heavenly beings who transport the throne of God mentioned in *3 Enoch*. *See also* angel(s); archangel(s); Bene Elohim; Chashmallim; Cherub, Cherubim; dominions; *elohim;* Erelim; Galgallim; Hashmallim; Hayyot; Husk(s); Ishim; *mal'ak;* Ophanim; powers; principalities; Seraph, Seraphim; thrones; twenty-four elders, the; Virtues; Watchers, the.

cheap grace: a profound concept developed by Dietrich Bonhoeffer in his work *The Cost of Discipleship*. Bonhoeffer set forth the true devotion required to follow the precepts of the Sermon on the Mount. Anything less, he said, was to view sin as not accountable, forgiveness as easy, discipleship as not disciplined, and suffering as bypassed. The term "cheap grace" was actually coined by Adam Clayton Powell from the pulpit of Abyssinian Church in Harlem but picked up and made famous by Bonhoeffer. *See also* Bonhoeffer, Dietrich; grace; Powell, Adam Clayton; Sermon on the Mount, the.

Chebar. See Kebar.

cheek(s): the fleshy part of the human face. The cheeks aid in personal recognition of an individual but also invite vulnerability to insult or injury. To strike a person in the face was (and is) contemptuous but Jesus admonished believers to abstain from retaliation in such an instance (Lk. 6:29). Most readers agree that this prohibition applies to "enemies" whom we know or of whom we wish to foster a relationship – not an injunction against the practice of self-defense, to serve one's country in wartime, or to protect others.

Cheiro: a renowned palm reader and psychic living in Ireland from 1866–1936. He was reputed to be a flamboyant individual and is said to have warned a number of his clients of specific disasters in their personal lives, including Grover Cleveland and Oscar Wilde. His other celebrity clientele included Mark Twain, Sarah Bernhardt, Mata Hari, and

Thomas Edison. Known only by the single odd name (though he was born William John Warner but assumed the name Count Louis Hamon), Cheiro was said to have alerted Lord Carnarvon not to open Tutankhamen's tomb, warned Czar Nicholas II that he and his family would be assassinated, and predicted that Edward VIII would abdicate the throne of England. Cheiro (pronounced Ki-Ro as in the capital of Egypt) was also an influential Qabbalist and astrologer. *See also* Aqiba, Rabbi Joseph ben; Bible Code; chiromancy; *gematria;* Haggada; Halakha; *isopseplia;* Masseket Hekalot; *notarikon;* Qabbala; *Sefiort; temoorah;* Zevi, Shabbatai; *Zohar.*

Chemosh: the false god of the Moabites and likely similar to that of the Ammonites who called him Molech or Milcom. Chemosh worship was one of the most abhorrent in the ancient world for it often required child sacrifice. King Solomon built a sanctuary for this false deity, but Josiah destroyed it (1 Ki. 11:7; 2 Ki. 23:13–14). *See also* high places; idol(s); Levant pantheon; Molech/Moloch; Mount of Corruption; "pass through the fire."

Chen Tao: known as The True Way cult and various other titles in a number of countries. The sect is a mix of Buddhism, Taoism, and UFO enthusiasts begun in Taiwan by Chen Hon-Ming (b. 1955). The cult was named God's Salvation Church headquartered in Garland, Texas. Chen believed that the earth has undergone five terrible catastrophes but the people of North America were rescued each time by a space ship from God. His famous failed prediction of the end of the world was well known, announced to be at 12:01 a.m. on March 31, 1998. *See also* cult(s); idolatry.

Cheonodoism: a Korean and Chinese shamanistic-based religion meaning the "Religion of the Heavenly Way." The sect is distinctive in that it adheres to no belief in the afterlife. Early on, the principles of Chenodoism were established by the Chinese founder Ch'oe Che-u (1824–1864) when it was known as the Eastern Learning Movement (Tonghak) that equated God with man. Suwunism is a smaller splinter group. *See also* idolatry; sect(s); shaman, shamanism.

Cherethites. See Kerethites.

Chernobyl: the site in Ukrainian Russia of a nuclear-powered generating plant meltdown in 1986. Some see the disaster as having apocalyptic implications, mainly because the name means "wormwood" or "dark grass." *See also* Wormwood.

Cherokee: a Native American tribe of some considerable power and territory before the westward expansion of white settlers. Some of their seers were among the most important end time prognosticators in North America. *See also* Great Shaking, the.

Cherub, Cherubim: a high rank of angelic creation. This unique order of celestial beings is reported in the books of Ezekiel, Isaiah, and Revelation. In Ezekiel's first encounter with them, and John's in Revelation, they present themselves with four faces but subsequent appearances in Ezekiel show only two faces (that of a human and a lion). Cherubim were depicted in the tapestries of the tabernacle and the temples, and golden statues of them guarded the ark from their perch above the mercy seat. Some theologians of the Middle Ages associated them with knowledge and their companions, the Seraphim, with love. More modern word studies indicated that the latter have reference to fire. Lucifer was named a guardian Cherub in his unfallen state in heaven. *See also* angel(s); archangel(s); authorities; Chashmallim; Chayoth; Dionysius the Areopagite; Ezekiel's call and vision of the Cherubim; dominions; *elohim;* Erelim; Ezekiel's vision of the Cherubim and the departed glory; four living creatures of Ezekiel; four living creatures of Revelation; Galgallim; guardian Cherub; Hashmallim; Hayyot; Husk(s); Ishim; Jael and Zarall; *mal'ak;* Ophanim; powers; principalities; *putti;* Seraph, Seraphim; tears of Michael; thrones; Virtues.

Cherubim and the departed glory. See Ezekiel's vision of the Cherubim and the departed glory.

chest and arms of silver: Daniel's interpretation of Nebuchadnezzar's dream of the stratified statue as being the empire of Medo-Persia (Dan. 2:32). *See also* belly and thighs of bronze; crushing rock that became a mountain; feet and toes of iron and clay; head of gold; hunched bear, the; legs of iron; Medo-Persia; stratified man, dream of the; two-horned ram, the.

Chi: the element in Eastern belief which composes the universe. Chi is also capable of flowing through the chakras of the body. *See also* acupuncture and acupressure; chakra; contemplative prayer movement; kundalini; meridians; Shakti; third eye, the.

chiasmus: or chiasm, a term based on the Greek letter *chi*, which refers to an inverted parallelism or sequence of words or ideas found in many literary forms. If the words, phrases, or text are diagrammed, the resulting pattern evolves into two fundamental elements—inversion and balance—usually graphed as "A to A" and "B to B" in the shape of an X, or the Greek *X* (using its simplest method of expression). The center of the X is a sort of "turning point" or crux for the language where there is usually a change in the trend of thought, and an antithetic idea is immediately introduced. A chiasm is essentially a statement compiled around a center; the "arms" for the *chi* are termed *espanadoses* and are limited only as to how extensive the structure can be diagrammed. The technique fits especially well with the Semitic writing style, often encountered in Hebrew poetry, when seemingly monotonous or repetitious phrases are encountered. According to the chiasm precepts, these passages are not literary defects but a programmable poetic structure used by the best Greek and Roman writers of antiquity. Some theologians insist that the skill of chiasmus is nigh essential to proper exegesis (especially Scripture or any other Semitic work), but the system can become unwieldy and ill-defined in its growing tendency to complexity and manipulation when pursued without the intellect and practice of the user. *See also* accideme; acrostic poem; alliteration; antithetic parallelism; apostrophe; apothegm; assonance; autograph; Bible; Bible manuscripts; Bible translations; biblical criticism; climatic parallelism; colon; conflict story; *constructio ad sensum;* context; contextualization; dittography; double sense fulfillment; doublets; doubling; edification; eisegesis; epanadiplosis; epigrammatic statements; etymology; exegesis; form criticism; gattung; gloss; gnomic sayings; grammatical-historical interpretation; *hapax legomena;* haplography; hermeneutic(s); higher criticism; homographs; homonyms; homophones; *homoteleuton;* hyperbole; idiom; *inclusio;* interpolation; interpretation; inverted nun; irony; isagogics; *itture sopherim;* jot and tittle; kere; *kethib;* "L"; liberalist interpretation; literal interpretation; litotes; loan words; lower criticism; "M"; Masoretic Text; minuscule(s); mystery of God; omission; onomastica; onomatopoeia; paradigm; parallelism; *paroimia; paronomasia;* pericope; personification; Peshita; poetry (biblical); pointing; point of view; polyglot; principles of interpretation; proof texting; psalm; pun(s); "Q"; redaction; revelation, theological; rhetorical criticism; riddle; satire; *scripto continua;* scriptorium; *sebirin;* simile; similitude; source criticism; sources, primary and secondary; special points; strophe; superscription; symbol(s); synecdoche; syntax; synthetic parallelism; text; textual criticism; *tiggune sopherim;* Time Texts; Torah; translation; transposition; trope; type(s); typology; uncial(s); verbicide.

Chicago-Lambeth Quadrilateral: the agreement that officially solidified the Anglican identity as a church. Four important principles of faith were approved: 1. Scripture contains all necessary to salvation, 2. the creeds, especially the Apostles' and Nicene, are sufficient statements of the Christian faith, 3. the sacraments are baptism and Communion, 4. the historic episcopate, locally adapted, is acceptable liturgy. *See also* Anglicanism; confession(s) of faith; episcopate.

Chickamaugan Prophecy. See Rattlesnake Prophecy.

Chief Philip: or King Philip (ca. 1639–1676) as he preferred to be called (but also known as Metacomet and Pemetacom). Philip was a Native American leader of the Wampanoag tribe amid the early colonists of Massachusetts. He was the son of Massasoit, who had aided the Puritans when they landed in New England. By the year 1670, the severe piety of the Puritans had waned and eroded until God seemed to be chastising the settlers with crop failures, illnesses, and the like. It was then that Chief Philip began a series of raids and massacres near Plymouth Colony. The small colonial militias could not cope so Philip continued his attacks and was joined by dissidents from other hostile tribes. The situation was stemmed only by the patriotic preaching of Increase and Cotton Mather with the help of Indian Christians. These believers, known as "praying Indians," emerged of their own volition from imprisonment in Boston Harbor to lead the colonists and eventually kill Chief Philip to end the war. The colonists displayed Philip's bleached skull as a trophy on the Plymouth Green. Effective leadership against the Indians was led by Captain Benjamin Church (1639–1718) of the Plymouth militia, which eventually ended "King Philip's War." *See also* Halfway Covenant; Mather, Cotton and Increase; "praying Indians"; Puritanism, Puritan(s); Society for the Propagation of the Gospel in Foreign Parts.

Chilam-Balam: the most famous seer or prophet of the Itza-Maya peoples of Central Mexico, a people descended from the Toltecs. Chilam-Balam foretold the coming of the white man and warned his nation that the invaders posed a great danger to the New Mayan Empire (A.D. 1000-1350). His stellar prophecies centered on the belief in the return of the feathered serpent god Quetzalcoatl and were based on the Mayan calendar. His pronouncements are recorded in a volume entitled the *Book of the Jaguar Priest*. He also offered a utopian end for his people after the suffering brought

History and Mystery

on by the Europeans. Many Aztec thought Hernando Cortez was a reincarnation of Quetzalcoatl, perhaps due in part to the influence of Chilam-Balam. *See also* Aztecs; conquistadors(s); Cortez, Hernando; *Dresden Codex;* eagle and the condor, the; Eagle Bowl; five stages of the earth, the; Fifth World, the; Great Change, Prophecy of the; Inca; Itza-Maya; jaguar; Katun Prophecies; Maya; Mesoamerica; Montezuma II; precession of the equinoxes; Katun Prophecies; Maya; Quetzalcoatl; Sun Stone; *Papal Unh;* "transition of consciousness"; 2012, prophecy advocates of; 2012, prophecy of; Quetzalcoatl; Votan, Pacal; zodiac.

child, children: offspring of human parents. Children, especially sons, were valued in ancient cultures, including the Hebrews. In fact, having children is considered a religious obligation in Judaism. The New Testament repeats this affection for the young as particularly expressed by Jesus, who loved and blessed the children (Mk. 10:14) and indulged them as recipients of his healing and resurrection miracles. In Scripture, the term "children" may represent infants, small children, young boys or young girls, and surprisingly enough, those in their middle years (thirty-forty?) whom we would consider adults. Perhaps the latter inclusion results from the great longevity of some of the Old Testament personalities. Children frequently represented simplicity of faith and innocence (Lk. 10:21; Mt. 18:2), as they do today. Christians are often called "children of God" or "dear children," and believers are enjoined to be children of light (Eph. 5:1, 8). *See also* abortion; brothers; child prophets; Children's Crusade; chosen lady and her children, the; infanticide; lamb; sons of God to be revealed; "pass through the fire"; saint(s); slaughter of the innocents; Valley of Hinnom.

child prophets: a. k. a. "the small prophets of the Cevennes," boys and girls (some were infants) among the Huguenots who called out Protestants to repentance and resistance to the Roman Church around the years 1688 – 1702. They were active mostly in southern France and subject to the depredations of the Inquisition, as were all dissenters. *See also* child, children; Huguenots; infanticide; Inquisition; prophet(s).

Children of God (COG). See Family International.

children of the resurrection: a title Jesus gave to those people (Lk. 20:36) who will achieve resurrection to eternal life in the future kingdom of God—the so-called immortals. *See also* eschatology, eschatological; resurrection(s).

Children's Crusade: a report, historical or not, in which it is reported a Crusade (some say two migrations) to the Holy Land was instigated in order to peacefully convert Muslims to Christianity. In or around the year 1212 some 30,000 children and youth from France and Germany were persuaded to march to the Mediterranean and were told the sea would miraculously part for their passage. Of course, no such event happened and most of the children were sold into slavery by unscrupulous merchants or perished on the journey. *See also* child, children; Crusades; infanticide.

child sacrifice. See "pass through the fire."

Chilembwe, John: fundamentalist leader of the Nyasaland (Malawi) rebellion in the early 20th century. When his end time predictions failed in 1915, he resorted to violence.

chiliasm: 1. an older name—nowadays not much in vogue—identifying the millennial doctrine. The name is derived from an old term for "thousand." 2. in the arcane art of alchemy, a reference to global change. *See also* global warming; Millennium, millennialism.

Chilmad: the territory the ancients called Media in Iran. *See also* Medes, Media.

chimera: mythological creatures that have mixed animal and human features. The term is important to eschatology since it is so closely related to idol worship, the giant Nephilim, corruptible humans, and what Isaiah called "other lords" (Isa. 26:13). The Greek chimera was a fire-breathing female monster with a lion's head and a snake's tail. The Greeks also produced the centaur with the upper body of a man and the hindquarters of a horse, as well as the satyr with the body of a man and the legs of a goat. The Persians feared the manticore, a creature with the body of a lion, a head of a human with sharp teeth, and perhaps horns, wings, and a scorpion tail that ate its victims, clothes and all. Since then, many cultures have produced representations of them, including the Egyptians, Babylonians, Canaanites, and others. Their gods could be named Baal, Molech, Ishtar, Titans, Anubis, Bastet, Horus, Thoth, Fortune, Marduk, Nibhaz, Nisroch, Raphan, or hundreds of others. Even the famous Sphinx of Egypt is half human and half lion. Those chimeras of the Holy Land called the Nephilim are of most importance to eschatology for our time and religion. *See also* animals, birds, and insects, symbology of; Baphomet; giant(s); Human Animal Hybrid Prohibition Act; idol(s); mythological beasties, elementals, monsters, and spirit animals; Nephilim; reptilian theory; satyr; Sumerian and Babylonian pantheon.

Chinnereth, Sea of. See Galilee, Sea of.

Chinon Parchment: a document—surfaced only in 2001—from the Vatican Secret Archives, which declares the Knights Templar to be innocent of all heresy charges once leveled against them. The paper was likely authored by Pope Clement V but appeared far too late to aid the near extermination of the Templars by King Philip IV of France. *See also* Baphomet; Clement V, Pope; knighted orders; Philip IV, King.

Chintamani Stone: a legendary magic meteorite or stone left behind when "missionaries" from space visited Earth in the distant past. Its origin is said to be the star Sirius (in the constellation *Canis Major*, the Dog Star). The meteorite is said to have properties that promote eternal life and may be the true cup of Christ. Nickolas Roerich reputedly carried a fragment of it to the founders of the now-defunct League of Nations in 1935. *See also* Ancient Astronaut Theory; Holy Grail; idol(s); Roerich, Nickolas K.

Chinvat Bridge: the connection between mortality and the afterlife that the departed souls of Zoroastrian believers must traverse. It is a broad and easy passage for the good and faithful but a shrinking knife edge for the wicked who invariably fall into the abyss of torment. *See also* Zoroaster, Zoroastrianism.

Chi-Rho **symbol:** the Greek letters *chi* and *rho* combined to construct a common sign or "signet" of imperial Christianity. The two characters name the first two letters of Christ's name. To form the design, the *rho* is superimposed atop the *chi*, resulting in a form that resembles a "P" overlaying an "X." The symbol is a universal one but dates from the time Constantine's soldiers emblazoned it on their shields. The device is found today in many churches and other religious institutions, especially the more liturgical bodies. *See also* furniture and furnishings of the modern church; IHS; *In hoc signo vinces;* INRI; Labarum.

chiromancy: palmistry, the pseudo-science of predicting future events of one's life by "reading the palm." Practitioners concentrate on the shape of the hand, the fingers, and the "lines" of the palm, all of which are said to have meaning and expose future happenings as if programmed into the hand since birth. *See also* anthropomancy; anthroposophy; apotropaic magic; Aretology; Ariosophy; astral plane; astral projection; astrolabe; astrology, astrologers; athame; audition; augury; automatic writing; bagua; belomancy; *besom;* bibliomancy; black arts; black mirror; blood moon(s); cartomancy; chaos magic; Cheiro; clairaudience; clairsentience; clairvoyance; cleromancy; cone of power; conjure; crop circles; cryptesthesia; crystallomancy; crystal skulls; curious acts; divination; dream(s); dreams and visions; ecstasy; enchantment; enneagram; esoteric sects; evil eye; extrasensory perception (ESP); foreknowledge; foretelling; geomancy; grimoire; gris-gris; hepatoscopy; Hermetic wisdom; Hermetic writings; hex; hierscopy; horoscope(s); hydromancy; idol(s); ifa; incantation; juju; labyrinth walk; lecanomancy; literomancy; locution; magic arts; magic, magick; magic square; magnetism; *mana*; mantic wisdom; mantra; miracle(s); monition; mystery religion(s); necromancy; New Age religion; numbers, symbology of; occult, occultic; omen; oneiromancy; oracles; otherworldly journeys; ouija board; out-of-body experiences (OBEs); paranormal; parapsychology; past life regression; peace pole(s); pentagram; philosophers' stone; planchette; planets as gods; portent; precognition; prediction; prefiguration; premonition; prodigy; prognostication; prophecy; psi; psychic(s); psychic healing; psychic reading; psychomancy; psychometry; psychonautics; pyramidology; rebirthing; remote viewing; retrocognition; revelation; rhabdomancy; scrying; séance; secret societies; secret wisdom; sorcery, sorceries; spell; spell names; spiritism; stigmata; superstition; tarot; telesthesia; telepathy; telesthesia; theugry; third eye, the; thoughtform; totemism; vision(s); vision quest; visualization; voodoo; voudou; wanga; warlock(s); Web-Bot; witchcraft; wizard(s); *ya sang*; yoga; Zen; zodiac; *zos kia* cultus.

Chittim. See Kittim.

Chiun. See Rephan, star of.

Chloe: a female family head from whom Paul learned that the Corinthians were becoming fractious—some devoting themselves exclusively to Paul, some to Peter, others to Apollos, and yet others to Christ (1 Cor. 1:11–12). The information was a primary cause for Paul to send his first letter to the Corinthian church.

choir: a group of singers, a common sight in most churches that are large enough to support one. Choirs play an important role in worship and other special occasions, *cf.* Neh. 12:27-43, when Nehemiah used two of them to celebrate the rebuilding of Jerusalem's walls. Choirs and orchestras are prominent elsewhere in biblical worship as well. Some name grouped church singers a *schola*. *See also* chorus; Jubilee Singers; liturgy, Christian; music; Zinzendorf, Count Nicholas Ludwig von.

Chondogwan: a distinctive Korean religion developed by PakT'aeson in the 1950s. The leader was a former Presbyterian who claimed to possess special spiritual powers and the movement eventually prospered. Strangely enough, the sect is also called "the olive tree" movement. *See also* idolatry; sect(s).

Chopra Center: a religious experiment founded by the Indian-born American physician Deepak Chopra (b. 1947). Beliefs center in the health and happiness of the individual through Ayurvedic medicine, including yoga and mind-body integration techniques. *See also* ayurvedic medicine; sect(s).

chorepiscope: an Eastern Orthodox bishop with jurisdiction in rural areas. *See also* archimandrite; catholicos; clergy; Eastern Orthodox Church; hegymanos; metropolitan; patriarch(s); priest(s); starets.

chorus: 1. grouped voices used for singing or chanting. Choral performances are prominent in Scripture as praise from humans, nature, or angels. They are particularly prevalent in Revelation. 2. the phrases of a song or hymn repeated after each verse, perhaps as a refrain. *See also* choir; liturgical year; liturgy, Christian; music.

chosen lady and her children, the: someone and/or a local congregation of believers to whom John addressed his epistle of 2 John (2 Jn. 1). Which was intended, the single person or numbers of them, is not clear. *See also* child, children; chosen sister, your; woman (women).

Chosen One, the: a favored title for the Son of God, but one spoken in derision by the rulers of the people at the time of Jesus' crucifixion (Lk. 23:35). The pseudepigraphon of *2 Baruch* names the Messiah as the Chosen One or the elect one.

chosen people: God's chosen, the Jews. The title may also be legitimately applied to the Church as God's chosen for the age of the Gentiles in other contexts. Peter (1 Pe. 2:9) spoke of the Church as a royal priesthood, a holy nation, and a chosen people. *See also* Jew(s); Judaism.

chosen sister, your: an unnamed female helper noted by John (2 Jn. 13) whose "children" sent along greetings to the church. Or perhaps the "chosen sister" represents a congregation. *See also* chosen lady and her children, the; elect lady, the; elect sister, your; woman (women).

Chozeh: a Hebrew term for "prophet." It is used twenty-two times in the Old Testament with the base meaning of "gazer." *See also* interpreter; *Kohen; Lewi;* man of God; man of the Spirit; messenger of Yahweh; *Nabhi;* prophet(s); *Ro'eh;* servant of Yahweh; servants, my; *Shamar;* watchman.

chrestus/Crestos: a confusion of terms, often mispronounced or misspelled from the first century and the subsequent source of much controversy. *Chrestus* can mean "slave" while *Crestos* is Greek for the Christian Messiah Jesus. *See also* names (titles) for Jesus; slave, slavery.

Chrislam: the futile attempt to merge or synergize Islam and Christianity promoted by some today. *See also* Christianity; Islam; sect(s).

Chrismation: the Eastern Orthodox of promoting a faith candidate to full acceptance, the equivalent of Confirmation in Roman Orthodoxy. *See also* Confirmation; liturgy, Christian; Eastern Orthodox Church.

chrismon(s): a small Christian symbol representing Christ of some part of his ministry. Traditionally, they decorate the tree during Advent and Christmas in many homes and churches. *See also* Christmas; Christmas tree; Christingle; crèche; symbol(s).

chrisom: a white garment for dressing newly baptized children. *See also* pedobaptism.

Christ. See Jesus Christ.

Christadelphians: or Thomasites, a movement or sect that some class as a religious denomination originating from the theology of John Thomas around 1844. The term is from the Greek meaning "Brethren in Christ." Thomas based his beliefs on the ideal that the Bible alone is sufficient as guide to all Christian behavior, belief, and polity and became a worldwide movement. The group teaches that there is no heaven or hell, that the Jews will return to Zion, and that Jesus was a created being. They reject Trinitarianism, immortality of the soul, and a personal devil. They refer to themselves as "ecclesains" rather than a church because, like so many other New Testament doctrines, this one has also become corrupted. Christadelphians also allow for conscientious objection or alternate service in the military. *See also* idolatry; sect(s).

Christ-consciousness: the belief, mostly attractive to New Age religion, that a divine potential is available for everyone. Few, however, are aware of this inbred capability. The use of "Christ" as the motivating name within the movement is intended more as a model figure than a personal savior. *See also* actualization; Christ within; idolatry; New Age religion.

"christened on a Sunday": a Medieval proverb implying that someone is feeble-minded or brainless, because *sale* (salt but also "mother wit") could not be bought on a Sunday. *See also* Christianese; slurs, religious.

Christ hymn. See *Carmen Christi*.

Christian(s): a disciple or servant of Christ who has undergone personal and real redemption with faith and accountability in him. The name was first attached to the fledgling sect of

Jesus' followers (formerly known as "The Way") at Antioch (Acts 11:26). At that time, the label was intended to be an insult, but since then, it has become a badge of honor. *See also* Advent; body of Christ; Christianity; Church; church; *koinonia;* universal church; Way, The.

Christian and Missionary Alliance: a generally orthodox alliance of churches that began as a parachurch of two persuasions in 1877. The originator was A.B. Simpson, who steered the association along general Protestant doctrinal lines but with an emphasis on faith healing. *See also* charismatic movement; church bodies in America (typed); denomination(s), denominationalism; missions, missionaries; Simpson, Albert Benjamin.

Christian Apocrypha: also known as the New Testament Apocrypha—a non-canonical collection of writings purportedly containing information regarding the life of Jesus and certain first-century leaders. Almost all have a Gnostic slant in theology. *See also* Gnosticism, Gnostic(s).

Christian Atheism. See Death of God theology.

Christian Catholic Apostolic Church: a communal-type cult founded by John Alexander Dowie at Zion, Illinois, in 1896. The group numbered some 6,000 followers, called "Zionites," at its height but floundered because Dowie was a con artist and stock manipulator who fleeced his flock regularly. Some historians declare the church as a forerunner of Pentecostalism. Though Dowie never went to Africa, some of his followers started missions in South Africa. *See also* communal communities; cult(s); Dowie, John Alexander.

Christian Church (body of Christ). See Church; church.

Christian Church (denomination): a church denomination born from the Great Awakening movements in the United States. Central to the tenets of the organization lies in the conviction that the New Testament is the only spiritual guide necessary for the believer to function. The movement grew from earlier rebellions from established denominations, which eventually flowed into one stream. James O'Kelly of Virginia left the Methodists in disputes about bishoprics, Abner Jones split from the Baptists in Vermont, and Barton W. Stone departed the Presbyterians. The three groups joined in 1820 and called themselves simply "Christians." Some later affiliated with the Disciples of Christ, but more remained unified. A merger occurred in 1931 with the Congregational Church, then (1857) they became the Evangelical and Reformed Church and labeled itself the United Church of Christ. *See also* Campbell, Alexander; Churches of Christ; church bodies in America (typed); denomination(s), denominationalism; Disciples of Christ; Great Awakenings, the; Reformed Churches; Restoration Movement in America; Stone, Barton W.

Christian Church underground. See underground Christian Church, the.

Christian Coalition: the successor organization to the Moral Majority led by Ralph Reed (b. 1961). At its peak, the association held 1.6 million members, mostly white evangelicals and Catholics. The group has since toned down its political rhetoric and is now called the Christian Coalition of America. *See also* Moral Majority; public square; Religious Left, the; religious organizations; Religious Right, the.

Christianese: a modern invented word or phrase intended as a parody of some Christian terms, generally outside the purvey of official theological language. As examples, a *baby Christian* is one new to the faith, *ultravangelism* is excessive salesmanship in sharing the gospel, *bragimizing* is talking about one's self more than Jesus when witnessing the faith, a *liturginist* is one who focuses on one aspect of his/her denomination or practice, etc. Sometimes reference is made to "God talk" or "Bible talk" with the same intent which can be meaningless to another person. Other kinds of shop talk may or may not be recognized and understood:

"Covered by the blood," (I'm saved), "falling under the power" (caught up in religious ecstasy), using the plan of salvation is "witnessing" in personal evangelism, "Christian walk," (daily living in morality and obedience), "I've been convicted," (the person feels strongly drawn to a salvation experience), "hedge of protection" (a wall of perceived divine defense), "feel at peace" or "not at peace" (I am content in the circumstance—or not), "What's your life verse?" (a favorite Bible passage), "sweet fellowship," (joy of companionship with other believers), "driving religion into the ground" (someone is taking faith far too intensely or personally), "get into the word," (study your Bible), "God is moving," (a strong spiritual atmosphere is present), "reach the lost," (be a witness in evangelism), etc. "Bless your heart" (best said with three heaping lumps of Southern sweetness) can open the door to say anything meaningless or even hurtful. A "mountaintop experience" is an exciting spiritual experience or reflecting on a good hair day. Then there is the old standby that almost everyone, Christian or not, has said at one time or another, "thoughts and prayers" (surely that one has just about become satiated). To "go home to be with the Lord" is to die. "See the fruit" means the good results of our work are obvious. "Doing church" or "church stuff" names all the activities and business of a given congregation as there is opportunity, desire, and resources and may include "evangelistic outreaches" (programs aimed at salvation and recruitment). "Come to Jesus" has a dual meaning, depending on the context. The phrase may be an evangelistic appeal to find salvation in Christ or it may refer to an intense and possibly contentious or adversarial conversation. An age old favorite leaps up as if it is a sacred Bible text—"God helps those who help themselves" is neither chapter nor verse. To assert "only God can judge me," or its twin, "I cannot judge others" is an impossible code. As is often the case with language, however, religious expression can become jargon or lingo that, to all appearances, is normal and sensitive but can be given or received as insult or injury. "Sow a seed" or "you can't outgive God" means "give us your money." More examples may be in order: "God laid it on my heart" (I need an excuse to speak bluntly and I will because the words are from God), "love up on" (I want to show you special attention or let you see my kindness but it sounds creepy), "I have been given a word from the Lord" (listen to me as I have divine authority), "I'll pray for you" (a dismissal–let's stop this complaint or conversation now and get over yourself and, all too often, we neglect to do precisely what we pledged), "bathe it in prayer" (your problem will go away if you just pray about it, and you can go away too), "God moved me" (I can do or say this because God gave me permission), "Can I get an amen to that?" (from preachers who seek frequent affirmation when speaking, especially if they think the insight is either profound or dubious), "fire burning in my heart" (intends zeal but may covey "I need to say this no matter what the results may be"), "my quiet time" (I spend time in disciplined devotion, do you?), "a lost sheep straying from the fold" (she's not as spiritual or moral as we are), "we're taking prayer requests now" can be a opening to reveal publically what should be private, or to gossip, "to give a testimony" can be a bragging opportunity, "let me share my testimony with you" (I want you to hear my story so you'll be moved to my version of faith), "let me share my burden with you" (I have troubles and want to talk about them), "I found the Lord" (I know Jesus but you don't), "Lord willing" (yes, I should do that but if I don't it just wasn't God's will), "my walk with God" (I have a closer relationship with God than you do), "I need to stop striving and start thriving" (I'm not okay today but it may get better if you sympathize), "you've committed a grave sin" (your action was deplorable compared to mine), "I covet your prayers" (see, I have real troubles and you should feel sorry for me), "I see that hand!" or "with every head bowed and every eye closed" (evangelists' public effort to evoke or manipulate emotion and audience response), "we missed you at church" (why were you not where you should have been…again?), "ministerially speaking" (code from pastors who desire to talk to other preachers about attendance numbers or finances, etc. in order to brag or complain), "God said it, I believe it, that settles it" (I'm right, you're wrong, this conversation is ended), "I don't drink, smoke, or chew or go out with girls that do" (I'm a better man than you are). "Name it and claim it" promotes the prosperity gospel as God answers prayer for any reason. Sometimes when we seek to comfort, we automatically spout what we've heard before—words that may be theologically sound but inadvertently add injury to a deeply hurting and confused friend. "Let me see that smile again" is downright cruel; I just lost my child and you want me to *smile* in the face of it? "Everything happens for a reason" and "God won't give you more than you can handle" really implies God inflicts us with tests, pain, and grief just because He can. "God is good, all the time" is catchy but not helpful. "It gets better" or "when God shuts a door He opens a window" are true enough sayings perhaps but it doesn't seem that way at the moment. "Don't worry. God is in charge" says your pain is overrated so you should just be able get over it really quickly. "Maybe it happened for a reason" sounds like "take your medicine and grow up" or "maybe you somehow deserved what you got?" The simple query, "How are you doing?" is practically empty; how do you *think* I'm doing? And there is that old favorite: "Call me if you need anything." I'm incapable of lifting the phone so I won't. Perhaps we could get up and go *see* if anything is needed? What is said may emerge as good and helpful or hurtful and selfish, depending on one's attitude and intent. We don't mean to be insensitive. In fact, we intend just the opposite. But genuine condolence is difficult because, deep inside, we might think grief is somehow "catching" or it hurts us to share another's pain on some level. How can we sweeten our church-speech? Perhaps we might ask ourselves a few pertinent questions. Does what I am about to say make sense? Will the hearer "get it" because it is, after all, religious shorthand and not common language? Am I saying what I really mean? Are my words self-centered? Am I disguising my true feelings? Can I choose more commonly understood words to be clearer? Most of the time our words are the least effective way to communicate feelings, anyway; my physical presence and taking out the garbage might be more tangible. Using high-value theological and technical religious terms can, and usually does, confuse hearers as well. *See also* accept Christ, to; Acts 29; Alka-Seltzer Christians; already not yet; altar call; apostasy; "asking Jesus into my heart"; authenticity; Babel, tower of; back-biting; backslide; "bells and smells"; benefit of clergy; Bible baseball; "Bible thumper"; blood of Christ; blood of the Lamb; born again; born again virgin; buzzard Christian; cafeteria Christians; C and E Christians; carnal Christians; charismania; "christened on a Sunday"; Christianist(s); Christ within; church abuse; church discipline; church field; "church hopper"; churchianity; churching; church key; church models; "churn" (religious); "clobber passages"; confession(s) of faith; conversion; Creeping Jesus; defrocking; denominational mutt; dial-a-prayer; disfellowshiping; "dones"; doors of evangelism; doubting Thomas; drive-by evangelism; Evana; excommunication; "falling into sin"; family life center; fanatic; fire insurance; frozen chosen, the; "God shot"; God talk; hardening the heart; "here, there, or in the air"; "holy roller"; hyper-grace; "I just want to love Jesus"; in-fighting; "in this place"; "itchy ears"; "Jesus freak"; Jesus junk; "led to"; lost; "love the sinner, hate the sin"; McChurch; missional; "nail-scarred hands"; "nickels and noses"; nominal Christians; "nones"; "no-shows"; offense, to give; "once saved, always saved"; on mission; parody religions; Pharisaism; plan of salvation; "plead the blood"; "popery"; pot luck; pounding; "prayed up"; "prayer warrior"; "praying around the world"; preacher's kid(s); "preaching to the choir"; profession of faith;

prosperity religion(s); pulpit theft; purpling; "putting out the fleece"; right hand of Christian fellowship, the; ritual abuse; rice Christians; "Roman Road, the"; "saved"; "sawdust trail, the"; servant's heart; 7-11 songs; "sheep stealing"; shunning; sinner's prayer; "slain in the Spirit"; slurs, religious; soul-winning; "souper"; spreading the gospel; "stews"; story; "sugar stick"; Sunday Christians; Sunday school answer; "sweet Jesus"; sword drill; televangelism, televangelists; testimony; theology; "three points and a poem"; throne of grace; traveling mercies; "turn or burn"; "turn your life [heart] over to Jesus"; *usus loquindi;* "waiting on the Lord"; "walking the aisle"; walk with God; "washed in the blood"; WASP; Way of the Cross; "wearable tech"; What would Jesus do?; wildfire; will of God; witness(es).

Christian Identity Movement (CIM): a quasi-secretive white supremacist movement extant in any number of related organizations but only loosely organized. The association commonly promotes racism, violence, and radical religious beliefs. The eschatology of CIM is heavily apocalyptic, insisting that the federal government (which is under Jewish control) must be overthrown in a race war (Armageddon), out of which a new Aryan nation will emerge. Recent growth of the system may be attributed to defections from conservative religious groups since 1940. The Aryan Nation white brotherhood is one of the most populous and violent gangs, many of whom are organized in prisons across the country. Since the movement is but loosely organized, the groups are usually named by the most active individuals or churches (*e.g.,* the Church of Jesus Christ Christian, Aryan Nation under Wesley A. Swift in the 1950s [a Klu Klux Klan organization)], the Christian Conservative Churches of America with John R. Harrell [1959], and the Church of Israel, a Mormon splinter group led by Daniel Gayman in 1972). *See also* Alt-right; American Party; anti-Semitic; Aryan Nation; black sun; Brown,

John; Coughlin, Charles E.; Covenant, The Sword, and the Arm of the Lord, The (CSA); Creativity Movement; cult(s); Fascist millennialism; Fenians; Knights of the Golden Circle; Knights of the White Camellia; Ku Klux Klan; militant domestic organizations; Molly Maguires; Neo-Nazis; Patriot Movement, the; Red Shirts; religious organizations; sect(s); Smith, Gerald Lyman Kenneth; terrorism; terrorist(s); Turner, Nat; Vesey, Denmark.

Christian Israelite Church: the bizarre sect of England formed by the radical John Wroe in 1822. The doctrines of the group are a mix of Hebrew religion and Christianity, with heavy influence from the predictions of Joanna Southcott and British Israelism. In heaven, only 144,000 select of the people of Abraham will be immortal and rule. These are to be identified today by their peculiar dress and uncut hair, earning them the nickname "beardies." The church is alive today and most active in Australia and the United States. *See also* idolatry; sect(s); Wroe, John.

Christianist(s): a somewhat degrading term for religious fundamentalists or right-wing Christian adherents, one coined by blogger Andrew Sullivan in 2003. *See also* Brights, the; Christianese; fundamentalism, fundamentalist(s); slurs, religious.

Christianity: the popular name for the followers of Jesus Christ or those tenets and beliefs derived from him. Central doctrines include: 1. expiation for sin brought about solely by the death and resurrection of Christ, 2. creation and history are in God's control, 3. the particulars of the Trinity, 4. Christ will come again to manage the world according to prophecy and, 5. evangelism, righteous living, and sincere faith are requisite values. The influence of Christianity has varied throughout the ages, either in favor (as in the optimistic 19th century) or disfavor (as in the Middle Ages). The philosopher Irving Babbitt (1865-1933) once wrote, "At the heart of genuine Christianity are certain truths which have already once saved Western civilization and, judiciously employed, may save it again." Such thinking is perhaps more generous to the institution of Christianity, but there is no doubt that the Savior for whom it is named, Jesus Christ, will certainly prevail according to apocalyptic Christian theology. *See also* Basmala; body of Christ, the; Chrislam; Christian(s); Christianity in the Roman Empire; Christian mythology; Church; church; *Golden Ass, The;* history of the Church; saint(s); universal church; Way, the.

Christianity in the Roman Empire: the early Christian church in conformity or conflict with the Roman Empire. Christianity in the Roman Empire began after the resurrection of Jesus and since then spread rapidly in the known world. Almost immediately it came into conflict with Roman authority, particularly certain emperors and their magistrates throughout the occupied lands. Roman religion only lightly touched on faith, dogma, or morality; it was pointed instead to the proper performance of ritual and how the beliefs contributed to the unity and continued success of the empire. Religion and politics were definitely intertwined. The authorities and the citizens were basically tolerant of foreign practices and values because the empire was so diverse. As long as Jupiter was at least minimally recognized, differing beliefs were basically ignored or tolerated. Periodically, however, many Christians and Jews suffered persecution to one degree or another, especially after emperor worship was introduced. These absolutely refused to acknowledge any god not their own and often they would not participate in the festivals, daily life habits that hinted of ritual defilement, or to give even minimal pretended devotion to Jupiter Olympus. Roman authority and Roman citizenry mistrusted or despised the Christian movement in particular for a number of reasons: 1. plagiarism. Romans viewed the Christians as having usurped and changed their revered customs and writings, not as a new religion, but as copiers and corrupters of ancient traditions. 2. exclusivity. Christians had little in common with what they viewed as a pagan and corrupt society, so they tended to exclude themselves from most public intercourse and in private life, and conduct themselves as a distinct entity with differing morals and beliefs. 3. pacifism. Most Christians were not necessarily opposed to warfare when it was necessary but objected strongly to the Roman army and navy in their militaristic worship, which they considered idolatry. (Roman soldiers even worshiped their weapons at times.) 4. perplexity. Christianity and its identified lifestyle were markedly different from Roman expression, which caused confusion about who these people actually were. 5. secretiveness. Christian worship and ritual were not generally practiced in the public square. Some believers were conscientiously trying not to purchase meat sacrificed to idols in the marketplace. Many of their actions seemed furtive and suspicious. Certainly, some Christians tried to hide themselves during times of severe persecution. Else, like the famous churchman Origen, they openly sought martyrdom as a sure path to sainthood and heaven. 6. use of the codex instead of the scroll. Christians soon learned to use a codex (book) form for devotional study and community worship. It was a practical move since the book could be handled more easily than the cumbersome scrolls. 7. incest. The Christian concept of love within the community fostered rumors of unsavory sexual practices in the meetings or because of the Christian admonition for "brothers and sisters" to "love one another." The love feasts (separate from the Communion ritual) were construed as an opportunity for the practice of some sort of erotic magic. 8. cannibalism. The Christian enactment of the Lord's Supper was suspected to be the actual eating of flesh. 9. troublemakers. The Christian presence could easily (and often did) incite the populace to riot and violence in protest against the movement. 10. self-confidence. Many Christians tended to be brave (not a universal axiom by any means) and assertive about their preaching and evangelism. Romans were accustomed to the opposite—cowering before the authorities. 11. sedition.

Christian nonconformity was often recognized, or blamed, as rebellious citizenship throughout the empire. 12. doctrine and atheism. Christian beliefs held little affinity with paganism. The Roman gods were ridiculed and abandoned, and Roman ritual (including the rather modest pinch of incense offered to the emperor) was resisted. After the time of Constantine, fortunes reversed for the Church, and it found itself in a favored status. This development brought its own tension and stress with the Roman way of life. Although foreign religions were rather grudgingly accepted there were strict limits placed on some practices besides Judaism and Christianity. Certain astrologers and magicians were watched. Any attempt to foretell the time or manner of someone's death was forbidden. Similarly, use of love potions and incantations were subject to punishment. Any rite involving human sacrifice was forcibly proscribed. The Romans of the upper class, especially, considered imported religions as superstitious and reprehensibly crude. *See also* Acts as New Testament history; Caesar cult; Caius; Caligula; Christianity; Church; church, administration of the early; church, divisions of the early; Claudius; Claudius Lysias; Colosseum, the Roman; Constantine I; Diocletian; Domitian; Edict of Milan; Edict of Toleration; emperor worship; Felix; Festus, Porcius; Florus; Galerius; Gratian; Hadrian; Herod Agrippa I; Herod Agrippa II; Herod Antipas; Herod Antipater II; Herod Archelaus; Herod Philip I; Herod Philip II; Herod the Great; history of the Church; Julian the Apostate; Lysanias; Nero; persecution(s); Pilate, Pontius; Pliny the Younger; Quirinius; Roman Empire; Septimus Severus; Tertullus; Titus; Trajan; Vespasian.

Christian mythology: the study or practice of intermixing or reinventing orthodox Christian doctrine with rudiments of paganism. The concept is not universally defined but is normally interpreted to assume certain elements of Christianity have been superimposed, negated, or allied in some fashion to ancient myth and religions. By assuming the old superstitions, or at least adapting those beliefs to the spirit of evangelical revelation, the early church offered a message the newly converted believers could understand. Old pagan gods and ceremonies die slowly and reluctantly. To the church hierarchy, this was the penalty that had to be paid to convert the pagans. For example, the Roman Catholic Church did not try to abolish the Roman ritual of Saturnalia because it was far more practical to simply adopt the dates and copy some of the rituals and call it Christmas. Almost every Christian feast day or holiday has experienced some of the same manipulation. Any more modern holdovers to the practice might be seen today as folk religion or folklore from the past. What, really, do Santa Clause and the Easter bunny and a Halloween ghoul have to do with pure Christian faith? Trying to align myth and orthodoxy is a way of understanding the way time, death, and the sacred were conceived in antiquity, then adapting that to the present. The process may be expiring today, or it may simply be transforming yet again. *See also* Christianity; deconstructionism; demythologizing; Diabolical Mimicry, the; euhemerism; festival; folklore; folk religion; godless myths; heterodoxy; higher criticism; meta-narrative; myth; mythos; myths universally duplicated in the Bible; turned to fables; unsound doctrine.

Christian Reconstructionism. See Reconstructionism.

Christian Science. See Church of Christ, Scientist.

Christian Zionism. See Zionism.

Christingle: a religious object intended to focus attention of the worshiper on Jesus as the central figure of Advent. The artifact may be a lighted candle, an orange, an egg, a ribbon, cereal or fruit, or any object with symbolic Advent implications in the inner eye of the viewer. *See also* Advent; Advent wreath; Christmas; Christmas tree; chrismon; icon, iconography; relic(s); symbol(s).

Christmas: the traditional holiday observed as the celebration of Christ's birth. The New Testament does not record the actual day of Jesus' nativity so one had to be found. The term actually means "Christ's mass," reflecting its Roman Catholic origins. Most likely, the church simply incorporated and adapted the Roman Saturnalia festival which celebrated the pagan New Year, since the wild festivities of that gala could not be sufficiently countered or subdued by the Christian authorities at that time. The official determination that this particular holy day would be celebrated annually on December 25 was made only in the mid-fourth century. Pope Liberius decided it would be smart to align that date with Saturnalia which invariably took place on the winter solstice, the shortest day of the year and a most unlikely time for Jesus' birth. It was a clever move that proved highly successful. Though a Christian holiday, many non-Christians celebrate the days with gift giving, cards, Santa Claus, music, parties, and many other traditions of the season. Prophetically speaking, Revelation 12 records another version of the Christmas story in a rather bleak and cosmic language. There are no shepherds, Magi, or manger, but the theme there harkens back to the intrigues of King Herod and his intent to destroy Jesus by killing all infants under the age of two. A related term, Yule, seems to carry a more pagan sense, especially from Druidism. *See also* Advent; Advent wreath; Boxing Day; carol(s); Christingle; Christmas tree; chrismon(s); crèche; Druidism; Epiphany; feasts and special days of high liturgy faiths; feasts and special days of Protestantism; First Advent; holiday(s); innocents, slaughter of; Lessons and Carols; liturgical year; liturgy, Christian; Magi; Nicolas; Noel; Saturnalia; Twelfth Night; Yule.

Christmas tree: a brightly decorated evergreen conifer (fir, pine, spruce, or artificial) commonly seen in homes at Christmastime worldwide. Worldwide the Christmas "tree" may be evergreen boughs, spruce branches, spruce trees decorated with red apples, or the hawthorn as in early England, or even a tree trunk with thorns. The tree is traditionally adorned with lights, bulbs, chrismons, ornaments of many descriptions, and capped with a star, an angel figure, or other special symbolic object. Presents may be placed underneath, phrased as "on" the tree. Origins of the tradition are surely pre-Christian, especially from Druidism, but Christianity (and almost all non-Christians) have embraced the festivity wholeheartedly. Even Jews have been known to erect a "Hanukkah bush" to join in the celebration. The true Christmas-centered tree probably began in early modern Germany and the ancient Estonia/Latvia regions but became highly popular in Lutheran lands. One legend says Martin Luther was taken one clear night by the sight of an evergreen with stars shining through the branches. He attempted to duplicate the event for his family by substituting candles for the stars. The tree is usually the center of the family or community celebration of Advent and Christmas, along with a crèche and other sacred and festive objects. *See also* Advent; Christmas; chrismon(s); Christingle; crèche; Druidism; floral, fruit, and grain, symbology of; symbol(s); Yule.

Christ of Bourages: a false Messiah of the sixth century whose true name may never be known. He was a working man who ventured one day into the forest where he was stung by a swarm of flies, an act that drove him crazy for two years. Afterward, he claimed not only to be Christ but also exhibited the power to heal by touch. His preaching emphasized the Millennium, causing thousands to flock to him. Finally, on a march to the palace of the bishop of Le Puy, he was intercepted by the bishop's mercenaries and killed with the sword. Even after his death, his followers persisted for a time.

Christ of God, the: a favored name for Jesus Christ (Lk. 23:35), but one offered in derision from the rulers of the people at the time of Jesus' crucifixion. *See also* names (titles) for Jesus.

Christophany: a stylized appearance of Christ—a theophany. *See also* angel of the Lord, angel of Yahweh; theophany.

Christoplatonism: a more or less manufactured but useful word (naming credit should probably accord to Randy Alcorn) displaying the insistence that those in heaven have no body nor will we obtain one. Not all agree but the majority through the ages has preferred to believe the existence there is spirit only. The philosopher Plato believed that material things, encompassing earth and all that is on it, including the human body, are evil while anything immaterial like the soul and heaven are good. Since the early church was attuned to Plato, it adopted his reasoning called Platonism. The teachings of Origen (185 – 254 A.D.) and Philo (20 B.C. – 50 A.D.) embraced and promoted the "spiritual" view that the immaterial is better and even Scripture should be read allegorically. Modern theology in some circles is slowly evolving that heaven is, or certainly could be, a truly physical realm of some description. *See also* allegorical interpretation; breath; Catharists; empyreanism; heart; heart and spirit; heart, soul, mind; heaven; humanism; life; life after death; mind; Philo of Alexandria; Plato; *psuche;* psyche; scholasticism; soul(s); spirit; strength; *zoe.*

Christos Kurios: Greek for "Jesus is Lord," the basic confession of faith in the early Christian church. The testimony mocked and directly repudiated the artificial title of the emperor, *Kaiser Kurios,* which promoted Caesar's false claim to deity. *See also kurios*; Lord; names (titles) for Jesus.

*Christotokos***:** an Eastern Orthodox term meaning "birth giver of Christ," Mary the mother of Jesus. The word supports Nestorianism which asserts that Jesus was both human and divine but these natures are joined or mixed and not a single solid entity. *See also* Eastern Orthodox Church; Mary; Nestorianism; *Theophorus; Theotokos.*

Christ the King, Feast day of: a celebration on the Western Latin calendar commemorating Jesus Christ as king of the universe. The official name is the Solemnity of Our Lord Jesus Christ, King of the Universe. The recognition was set in 1925 by Pope Pius XII in response to growing secularism and nationality worldwide. The date chosen makes it a moveable feast day observed on the last Sunday of October, immediately following the Feast of All Saints and the Sunday before Advent. *See also* feasts and special days of high liturgy faiths; liturgical year; Roman Catholic Church; Stir-up Sunday.

Christ within: a base expression for the inner being of a believer that can be "felt" and even displayed in public life. The intent of the phrase is a reaching for some description that emphasizes the actions of the Holy Spirit in fellowship with the holy. The statement affirms that the spirit of God interacts with the spirit of the accepting person to produce a worthy and joyful life. The Society of Friends often refers to the sensation as "the Inner Light" and the idiom is popular with Pentecostals and many other spiritual Christians of all persuasions. *See also* Christ-consciousness; Christianese; ecstasy; Inner Light; Pentecostalism; "river, the"; Society of Friends.

Chronicles of David. See book(s).

Chronicles of the Kings of Israel. See book(s).

Chronicles of the Kings of Israel and Judah. See book(s).

chronological approach to Revelation: the manner of interpreting the events of Revelation as occurring in the sequence in which they are recorded. The system has difficulties since the narrative of Revelation appears to be nonprogressive or convoluted at points within the account. *See also* contrapuntal approach to Revelation; pre-wrath rapture; progressive/complimentary approach to Revelation; recapitulation approach to Revelation.

Chronos: a serpentine-shaped god with three heads—a man, a bull, and a lion. He was noted as the personification of Time in pre-Socratic philosophy who, with his consort, moved about the heavens dividing the seasons. In Greco-Roman times, he turned the wheel of the zodiac. *See also* idol(s); Olympian pantheon; reptilian theory; zodiac.

chronos. See kronos.

Chrysostom, John: (Saint John of Antioch), influential church father of the Antiochian School (A.D. 354–407) and archbishop of Constantinople. His name was acquired, meaning "the golden-mouthed," because of his oratory abilities. Chrysostom's piety, liberality, and eloquence were renowned, and he was much beloved by his many followers. He condemned false clergy and corrupt courts, thus making certain enemies in high places. While still bishop, he ran afoul of Queen Eudoxia who threatened to banish him from Byzantium. The churchman's reply was simple but profound: "You can't banish me for this world is my Father's house." Despite the thesis of the Antioch school as exponents of literal interpretation, Chrysostom does not mention millennialism. *See also* Doctors of the Church; Eastern Orthodox Church; liturgical year.

Church: the universal totality of believers who are counted as being in the body of Christ, the Church universal, usually designated with a capital "C." It is a human institution with a divine purpose and destiny. Also called "the body of Christ," the followers function as the mode by which the gospel is promulgated in the world and Christians are supported and matured. It is an institution that will always occupy special attention from Christ both now and in the hereafter. Its divine operation and purpose may be difficult to define in its entirety except to quote, "The mission of the Church is to *be* the Church." *See also* body; body of Christ, the; branch theory; bride of Christ; bride (wife) of Christ; catholic church; chosen people; Christian(s); Christianity; Christianity in the Roman Empire; church; church abuse; church, administration of the early; church age theory; church decline; church discipline; churching; church planting; Church Triumphant, Church Militant; communion of the saints; denominations, denominationalism; ecclesiology; *ekklesia;* four marks of the church; great high priest; history of the Church; marriage metaphor; marriage supper of the Lamb; New Israel, the; One, Holy, Catholic, and Apostolic Church; Third Church, the; underground church; universal church; universal church; visible and invisible church, the; Way, the; worship.

church: the body of Christ described locally. When designated with the small "c," the church referenced is the local congregation or denomination (*ecclesia*) within the larger universal Christian Church (large C). The name allows a special church "building" for worship and education, but the proper emphasis is on the believers who constitute the congregation. Worship is sometimes referred to as simply "going to church." The local body must be a collection of believers working together for praise and service to God because Christianity is a team sport. Much of today's culture views our churches as either dull and irrelevant or hypocritically corrupt. Christ and the New Testament, however, see them as pitons in the cliff of the kingdom of God. *See also* Anastasis; basilica(s); bethel; Canterbury; cathedral(s); cella; chantry; chapel; Church; church, administration of the early; church age theory; church bodies in America (typed); church decline; church, divisions of the early; Churches of Christ; church models; Church of the Holy Sepulcher; Church of the Nativity; Corinthian Church; denomination(s), denominationalism; ecclesiology; Edicule; *ekklesia;* elder(s); Ephesus; episcopate; *episcopos;* faith and order; family life center; fold; furniture and furnishings of the modern church; Guadalupe, Our Lady of; history of the Church; house churches; House of Loreta; house of prayer; Jerusalem Church; katholikon; kirk; *koinonia;* Laodicea; megachurch; minister(s); mission; parachurch(es); Patrick's Purgatory; sacellum; temple(s);

Pergamum; Philadelphia; sacellum; sanctuary; Sardis; seven churches of Asia Minor; Smyrna; temple(s); Thyatira; Thessalonian Church; underground Christian church, the; Westminster Abbey; Whittenberg Chapel; World Church of Peace; zeta.

church abuse: or religious abuse, any deliberate or sly action or speech intended to unjustly criticize or condemn another of faith or a particular faith community. Harmful actions can be self-evident but words can also damage the personhood or reputation of another. Common congregational labels illustrate the practice clearly: 1. to "hold accountable" may be an excuse to force compliance to established polity or leadership, 2. a "bad attitude" tends to shame those who disagree or for exercising their free will, 3. a "black sheep" is one who is deemed consistently contrary to the established pattern of belief and practice—a conconfomist, 4. a "critical spirit" casts one as unwilling to compromise or is critical of a given practice of the church, 5. a "family matter" is some secret agenda or failing of the congregation which the members do not desire to be made public knowledge, 6. a "Jezebel spirit" is a woman who refuses to be conventional, usually to clergy, a governing council, or male dominance, 7. a "doctrine of man" can be any belief that is painted to be inconsistent with the established rules and doctrines of a given congregation, 8. one who is "unteachable" is a dissenter who should be shunned or removed. *See also* apostasy; back-biting; backslide; benefit of clergy; Catholic Church abuse scandal; charismania; Christianese; Christianist(s); Church; church; church discipline; "church hopper"; churching; "clobber passages"; defrocking; delict; disfellowshiping; excommunication; "holy roller"; in-fighting; Inquisition, The; *Inquisitor's Manual, The;* "Jesus freak"; *Malleus Malefiracum;* McChurch; Nicolaitans; offense, to give; persecution(s); ritual abuse; parody religions; shepherding (cultic); shunning; slurs, religious; televangelism, televangelists.

church, administration of the early: the early church (described most cogently in the book of Acts) as it learned to govern itself and fulfill its mission. The infant church began as a democratic organization that loosely recognized both leadership and laity in a number of capacities. In truth, there is no mortal leader of any Christian fellowship because Christ is the undisputed head. However, each administrative duty within the organization carried specific responsibilities in which gifts of the Spirit were to be used to the benefit of the entire church body as expressed in its earlier existence. Elders, or presbyters, were usually older men who were fully experienced and carried the respect of most of the younger members, especially the young men. The younger women tended to look to the older ladies. An elder may or may not have held other distinctions of service in addition to his honorary title, which seems to have been carried over from the Old Testament. They were termed *presbuteros*. The function and usefulness of elders is described in 1 Timothy 6. It was not a church office according to careful reading and interpretation of relevant usages. Nevertheless, some present-day denominations administer their polity by the use of leaders called elders. Pastors, or shepherds/undershepherds, were called *episcopos* and responsible for spiritual guardianship and guidance of the congregation. Equivalent terms for pastor *(poimen)* include bishop, overseer, or the more modern "minister." "Reverend" is a purely honorific and modern title. Their main tasks were preaching and teaching when accepted to do so by the members and in general offered oversight and guardianship for the membership. The qualifications for pastor are enumerated in 1 Timothy 3:1–7 and Titus 1:5–9. Deacons *(deakonos* for males and *deakones* for females) were singular servants chosen for specialized tasks by the congregation. The first of them were seven in number, selected in Acts 6:1-7, and were specifically instructed to administer the distribution of funds for the needy widows in order to "free up" the *episcopos* for needed time and attention to their primary callings to preaching, evangelism, and prayer. Deacons were not "leaders" in the traditional sense. The *oikonomo* were a generalized body of servants or "stewards" of which treasurers were a prime example. They were trustee types with whom the members placed great confidence, and all the membership shared in this responsibility to one degree or another. The so-called "minor orders" refers to ministerial positions below those of bishop, presbyter, and deacon. One of a minor order could be a subdeacon, reader, acolyte, etc. Otherwise, the early church made little distinction between "clergy" and "laity." The calling of prophet was distinct from other positions, although an evangelist or pastor could certainly preach "prophetically" in pursuit of his or her mandate. The pyramid pattern of church authority did not arise until A.D. 606 when Pope Boniface III asserted papal supremacy. The early church certainly had no hierarchy but one was snugly in place by the late second century. In fact, the first monarchial bishop of Rome was likely not Peter, as Roman Catholicism contends, but a leader named Victor (A.D. 189-199). If the Church is to fulfill its mandated task of preaching, prophecy, and philanthropy, it needs the best organizational platform and motivation possible, even a divine plan or structure, which God ordained for His people. *See also* acephali; autocephalous; bishop(s); call(ing); charisms; Christianity in the Roman Empire; Church; church; church, divisions of the early; church models; clergy; congregational polity; connectional polity; deacon(s), deaconess(es); *deakonos;* ecclesiology; elder(s); episcopate; *episcopos;* faith and order; Free Church(es); history of the Church; hierarchical polity; laity; magisterium; megachurch; minister(s); *oikonomo;* papacy; pastor(s); plebania; polity; preacher(s); prelacy; *presbuteros;* presbytery; priest(s); representative polity; rite; ritual; shepherding (cultic); shepherding (discipleship); shepherding (pastoral); sobornost.

church age theory: the concept that all of church history may be arbitrarily divided into segments of history in accord with how God has dealt, or will deal, with each age. It is a primary tenet of dispensational theology. *See also* Church; dispensation(s); dispensational theology; economy; Great Week, the; history of the Church; *oikonomo;* seven churches of Asia Minor, the; "six-day theory, the"; six (or seven) ages of the world.

church bodies in America (typed): the classification of church affiliates in America according to general theological beliefs and congregational organization. A complete listing of denominations would be impossible since there are 41,000 or more in North America alone. Church historians and theologians have managed to class the prominent religious bodies in the United States by use of general doctrinal beliefs and church polity. One of the more recognized systems lists the groupings as: 1. Lutheran, 2. Reformed, 3. Arminian, 4. United, 5. Inner Light, 6. Millennial, 7. Anthropocentric and Anti-Trinitarian, 8. egocentric cults, and 9. esoteric sects or mystics. Each alignment has its individual doctrines, polity, and eschatology, but the bundling of similar bodies is an aid to research toward individual similarities and differences. *See also* African Independent Churches; African Methodist Episcopal Church; African American Episcopal Zion Church; American Baptist Churches USA; Anthropocentric and Anti-Trinitarian churches; Arminian churches; Assemblies of God; Baptists; Calvary Chapel; Christian Church (denomination); Christian and Missionary Alliance; church; Churches of Christ; Church of God; Church of God in Christ; Church of the Brethren; Church of the Nazarene; Church of the United Brethren; communal communities; communion; Congregationalists; Covenant Churches; cult(s); denomination(s), denominationalism; Disciples of Christ; Dunkards; Eastern Orthodox Church; egocentric cults; esoteric sects; European Free Church; Evangelical Free Church in America; Exclusive

Brethren; Free Church(es); full gospel; Inner Light churches; International Church of the Foursquare Gospel (ICFG); Lutheran Church; McChurch; Methodists; Millennial churches; Moravian Church; mysticism, mystics; National Baptist Convention; Native American Church; Pennsylvania Dutch; Pentecostalism; Plymouth Brethren; Presbyterians; Protestant Episcopal Church; Protestantism, Protestants; Protestant Reformation, the; Reformed Churches; Reformed Church in America; River Brethren; Roman Catholic Church; Salvation Army; Schwarzenau Brethren; sect(s); Society of Friends; United churches; Vineyard Ministries International; Waldenses; Wesleyan Church; World Council of Churches; Unitarian Universalists; Wesleyan Church; Westboro Baptist Church.

church decline: the generally accepted theory that today's church, as it has been traditionally recognized, is falling from public favor and at risk of feeble response to today's spirituality—or even its demise. Attendance, financial support, enthusiasm, and purpose are said to be in dissolution worldwide, especially in Europe. Causes range from competitive modern entertainment and commercial pressure, a shortage of priests and ministers, the challenge of alternative religions, a tolerance for liberal theology, issues of disagreement concerning morals and ethics, the adversity of science, physical and political obstruction or persecution, an unfavorable reaction to religious authority, and many other considerations. Some observers claim the rejection is due to the three "I's" of church malady—Isolation, Ingrowth, and Invisibility. What is too often overlooked, however, is that the Church (defined as the body of Christ even in its varying expressions) may be challenged or changed but it will not be defeated according to the prophecy of Christ (Mt. 16:18). *See also* Church; church; churchianity; church models; dispensational theology; humanism; secular humanism; secularism; modernism; postmodernism; "post-secularists"; rescuers of the Church; social issues.

church discipline: those actions of a church or cultic body that are designed to punish or remove a member from the organization. The range of psychological weapons available is extensive, from friendly admonition to outright persecution. Some violent cults do no stop at murder. The pattern of disciplining may be individual action or consensus of the group, and is pursued until the accused recalcitrant is reformed or dismissed. *See also* canonical penance; Church; church abuse; churching; defrocking; disfellowshiping; excommunication; ritual abuse; shepherding (cultic); shunning.

church, divisions of the early: the practical and theological state of affairs during Christianity's formative years. Christianity began its spread after the resurrection of Jesus Christ in obedience to the Great Commission. Difficulties were immediately apparent, both before and after the era of Constantine the Great. Persecution was common enough from both pagans and Jews in the early years. The real problem, however, was sprouting within the growing church itself. The institution quickly began to separate or "split" into three differing doctrinal bases and three geographical regions. The first group, centered in the Middle East at Jerusalem (and later Antioch), were influential early on, a not surprising actuality because it was the cradle of faith where Jesus actually walked and talked. It became an intellectual center for conservatism, especially at Antioch in Syria. Jerusalem, strangely, was rather ignored and the Temple site almost totally neglected. The population spoke a common dialect akin to Aramaic, the language of Jesus and his contemporaries. The region was home to Miaphysites and Dyophysites alike, so there was some dynamism in the population. Despite the opposing doctrines among the believers, the Syrian Christians were energetic and missionary minded until the Islamic incursion nearly halted all of the church's efforts. Some missionaries had even managed to push the gospel successfully into lands as far away as Sri Lanka (Ceylon) and China. Antiochian influence slowly faded, however, in the face of its opposing neighbors, Rome and Constantinople, even before the Islamic assault. The second region of influence was Western—the Latin-speaking church. By design and undisguised power politics, the bishops of Rome made concerted efforts, often with fraudulent strategy, to dominate the Christian world. Here was, after all, the center of the old Roman Empire, and, as they insisted, the seat of Peter. The popes developed their authority and eventually succeeded in becoming master of all things theological and doctrinal. Despite the collapse of Rome to the Barbarians, the Western section never faltered in its drive to be the imperial church. The third of the ecclesiastical divisions was east, toward the core of Eastern Orthodoxy centered at Constantinople. Here was the "new" Rome, transplanted there by Constantine himself and already flowering as the greatest cultural center of the known world. The Eastern Church, however, hindered itself by indulging in grievous (and often meaningless) debates concerning orthodoxy. All three sections fought long and hard for supremacy, simultaneously trying to chock up a real worldwide unified Christianity. The maddening internecine disputes dragged on, with bishops excommunicating each other, slandering, enlisting government aid to the cause, and differing on just about every theological question. Today's manner is perhaps more genteel, but Christian unity is still elusive and will likely remain so. *See also* bishop(s); Christianity in the Roman Empire; church; church, administration of the early; history of the Church; deacon(s); deaconess(es); elder(s); episcopate; *episcopos; oikonomia; presbuteros;* preacher(s); presbytery.

Churches of Christ: 1. a New Testament identification for those local congregations that made up the body of Christ in the first century and retained afterwards. 2. American denominations that sprang from disenfranchised Christians after the Civil War during the Second Great Awakening. Members claim that their doctrines are rooted in history from Pentecost and are deeply fundamentalist in belief. The group eventually split to form a newer organization, the Disciples of Christ, under Alexander Campbell. Worship consists of weekly observance of Communion, immersion baptism, local church polity led by elders, and some singing without musical accompaniment. The denomination is also known as the United Churches of Christ since a merger in 1961 between the Evangelical and Reformed Church and the Congregational Christian Churches was completed. Unification has been rocky with numerous disputes and lawsuits along the way. When the unification was announced in 1957, some 300 churches withdrew to form the Association of Congregational Churches. *See also* Campbell, Alexander; Christian Church (denomination); church; church bodies in America (typed); denomination(s), denominationalism; Disciples of Christ; Great Awakenings, the; Niebuhr, Reinhold; Restoration Movement in America; United Churches.

churches of Revelation, the seven. See seven churches of Asia Minor, the.

church field: a common reference among many Protestant ministers or missionaries to name their areas of ministerial responsibility, both urban and rural. The districts and populations indicated may be large or small. *See also* Christianese; cure; diocese; eparchy; episcopate; fold; katholikon; ministry; missions, missionaries; parish; patriarch(s); patriarchate(s); pentarchy; presbytery; see.

church furnishings. See furniture and furnishings of the modern church.

"church hopper": a colloquial term for one who regularly visit churches from time to time and place to place. As suggested by the name, church hoppers are usually seeking a casual worship location but are adverse to regular attendance or membership because of the duties or doctrine expressed by any given body. *See also* cafeteria Christians; carnal Christians; Christianese; "churn" (religious); denominational mutt; McChurch; slurs, religious.

churchianity: Christianese for a dull, lukewarm, or slothful approach to church membership and loyalty. The attitude produces little or no zeal of spirit, worship, or morality in the congregation but is of the style so aptly typified in Revelation's church at Laodicea (Rev. 3: 14 – 22). *See also* Christianese; church decline; church models; lukewarm; slurs, religious.

churching: 1. a ceremony in some denominations for women who have given birth. 2. a disciplinary action available to some denominations which may be leveled against a member whom the administration sees as a moral deviant or non-conformist. *See also* canonical penance; church abuse; church discipline; defrocking; disfellowshiping; excommunication; feasts and special days of high liturgy faiths; liturgy, Christian; Christianese; Church; church; fencing the table; ritual abuse; shepherding (cultic); shunning.

church key: one of the oldest slang phrases in American tradition. A church key is nothing more than a hand-held device for puncturing holes in cans or to pop off bottle tops, especially those containing alcoholic beverages. *See also* Christianese.

church models: a short series of contemporary methodologies in play in contemporary America that modern innovators are exploring in an to attempt to reverse the trend to church decline in the nation. In essence, there are three basic paradigms in operation meant to investigate processes by which millennials and related age groups are rejecting church attendance, the traditional concepts of religion, and the relevance of morality and service while testing ways to correct the refutation. They are recognized under the labels traditional, attractional, and missional. 1. the traditional (also called the Constantinian or conservative) church

is the style commonly associated with the 50s and 60s familiar to our parents and grandparents. It flourished in the day when the church was an honored institution with a respected place in society where the members serve the body and does what the church is doing. Most attendees are present by geographical preference—they participate where they live and choose a denomination because their parents did. By far, the traditional approach is the most numerous in the land but is also universally acknowledged as failing rapidly. At its best, the traditional model exhibits honor to the scriptures, is worship centered, is countercultural in embodying God's values (though often presented as obligated morality), is evangelical by holding standardized worship services, targets the unchurched with varying degrees of evangelistic appeal, and retains most of the best from the glory days of the church past. It is the church of the *status quo* although some have made gestures toward a more contemporary worship style, lively (and loud) music, or some other token adjustment. At its worst, the traditional church strongly resists change and is unwilling to adapt to a shifting culture, it is "country club" oriented (if you come and fit in we might accept you), is mistrustful of modern cultural habits and therefore defensive, insular, and self-protective. It expects visitors to come to them rather than seeking out prospects (the sign outside says everyone is welcome), fails to articulate a dedicated mission statement, and communicates in religious jargon ("God talk" or "Christianese") no one but the initiates fully comprehend.
2. the attractional church perceives the traditional model as irrelevant and borrows from contemporary business and marketing strategies to become pertinent. Robert Schuller's Crystal Cathedral was the first of its type and Willow Creek, Saddleback, and hundreds of others were quick to follow. Often the theology, if any is articulated, resembles the reconstituted philosophy of Normal Vincent Peale. The congregations are characterized by giving the people what they want, preaching simple sermons, lessening stress in a

difficult and complex world, and acting as a sort of religious mall that use the resources of the church as a supplier of religious goods and services. At its best, an attractional church is creative and purpose-focused, it reaches people who would never consider a traditional church, enjoys superb programming, is responsive to change and favors user-friendly contemporary language. At its worst, it degrades the urgency of sin, judgment, and the lordship of Christ to almost nothing; the offerings and infrastructure (building, resources, programs, music, leadership, etc.) are exceptional but invariably expensive and some of them produce only pure novelty. Success is measured in the number of attendees, the gospel is a product instead of a sustenance, and consumerism is reinforced. The true call to discipleship and denial of self is seldom considered as practical. Many attractional churches have recognized their long-term ineffectiveness and closed their doors or were forced to do so for economic reasons. Still others were too cultic and centered about a charismatic leader no longer present. 3. the third model, and surely the most dynamic, is the missional (sometimes called the apostolic). The main dramatic difference in the paradigm is that it sees North America as a mission field and approaches "doing" church like a missionary would. Basically, it embraces apostolic or early church teachings and values, acknowledges that it is marginal in today's society, and sees itself with a mission to change the world (or at least the local community where it is situated). It tries to practice unobtrusive but real evangelism, stresses discipleship learning, Bible teaching, church distinctiveness, accountability, love for one another, reconciliation, worship, hospitality, and views the kingdom of God as larger than itself. It typically uses social media extensively and may or may not be innovative in its worship style. Work is centered in the membership and not the pastor or elders. The rejuvenating task is a difficult one for all types and few churches today are fully missional because change is largely unwelcome, because paradigm shifts can be awkward, and because, once a church has been established ("planted"), the members tend to absorb much of the group energy and turn inward. Christianity as we have known it is in flux today and it remains to be seen how God will salvage or redesign His Church to faithful service and purpose in the new era. There are ways to monitor or measure a church's methodologies and goals. *See also* acephali; autocephalous; Christianese; church; church, administration of the early; church decline; churchianity; church planting; conciliarism; congregational polity; connectional polity; conservative(s); ecclesiology; episcopate; faith and order; Free Church(es); fundamentalism, fundamentalist(s); hierarchical polity; magisterium; missional; missions, missionaries; moderate(s); Peale, Norman Vincent; plebania; polity; prelacy; presbytery; representative polity; rescuers of the church; shepherding (cultic); shepherding (discipleship); shepherding (pastoral); sobornost; traditionalism; Transformational Church Assessment Tool (TCAT); worship.

Church of Bible Understanding: a modern cult, formerly known as the Forever Family. The sect was begun in 1961 by Canadian Stewart Traill (b. 1936). Traill was a former vacuum cleaner repairman and son of a Presbyterian minister who recruited a group of disenfranchised youth (some as young as thirteen) which existed solely for purposes of personal power and profit. As much as 90 percent of the group's income (which could be substantial in some ventures) went directly to the leader. *See also* cult(s); idolatry; Traill, Stewart.

Church of Christ. See Churches of Christ.

Church of Christ, Scientist: the sectarian beliefs originated by Mary Baker Eddy (founded as a church body in 1879) that essentially deny the reality of the material world. The main publication of the organization, which is central to the group's beliefs and practices, is entitled *Science and Health with Key to the Scriptures*. Mrs. Eddy subscribed to

History and Mystery

a dualistic idea that matter is opposed to spirit. Dramatic healing, which is the pillar purpose of the sect, could be attained by a sort of mental denial of anything negative and to treat illness as an illusion. The "myths" of Christianity must be eradicated. She called the process "divine science" and declared it the only way to heaven. Eddy was closely associated with the mesmerist Phineas P. Quimby of Maine from whom she borrowed many techniques and doctrines. The Second Coming is surely the advent of the Divine Mind that Jesus had attained. Worship in the sect is simple—one reader speaks passages from the King James Bible and another reads excerpts from *Science and Health*. Every congregation maintains a reading room to encourage self-study. In 1908 the organization established the *Christian Science Monitor* newspaper, which is recognized today for good journalism. The doctrines of the sect are so foreign to orthodox belief that some pundits have ridiculed that the sect is neither Christian nor science. In Christian Science theology, God is infinite Mind, human beings are reflections of that Mind, and angels are nothing more than the thoughts of God that reach human beings. Matter does not truly exist and neither does evil. *See also* Eddy, Mary Baker; faith healing; idolatry; magnetism; New Thought Movement; Quimby, Phineas Parkhurst; sect(s).

Church of Christ, Temple Lot: an offspring of Mormonism but not associated with the Utah group. The Temple Lot is a splinter group of the former Reorganized Church of Jesus Christ of Latter-Day Saints (now Community of Christ). The Temple Lot group is located in Independence, Missouri. *See also* church bodies in America (typed); Church of Jesus Christ of Latter-Day Saints, the; idolatry; sect(s).

Church of England: the form of Catholicism established by Henry VIII in England. The king's action suited the era of Reformation then in full swing. Its creation allowed Henry to divorce Catherine of Aragon and marry Anne

Boleyn. The faith is known as Episcopalian in America and is frequently cast as Protestant despite perceived technical refutations of that classification. *See also* Act of Conformity; Act of Supremacy; advowson; Alternative Service Book; Anglicanism; Articles of Religion; Bangorian Controversy; baptism of desire; banns; Baxter, Michael; Becket, Thomas; Black Fast, the; Black Letter Days; Black Rubric; *Book of Common Prayer;* Bray, Thomas; broad church; Clapham sect; Canterbury; cardinal(s); Caroline Divines, the; Charles I, King; Chicago-Lambeth Quadrilateral; church bodies in America (typed); Church of England; coadjutor; consistory; Cranmer, Thomas; Cromwell, Thomas; Cross, Feasts of the; curate; diocese; *episcopi vaganti;* epistoler; flying bishop(s); Hales, Stephen; Hampton Court Conference; Henry VIII, King; High Church, Low Church; Jones, Hugh; Jurieu, Peter; Ken, Thomas; Latimer, Hugh; Latitudinarians; Laud, William; Law, William; Lewis, Clive Staples; Low Sunday; Malthus, Thomas Robert; Mass; metropolitan; monstrance; More, Thomas; Newman, John Henry; Newton, John; Newton, Thomas; normative principle; Oxford martyrs; Oxford Movement; parish; Payne, J. Barton; Philadelphians; pram service; prelacy; primate; Pole, Cardinal Reginald; Pratt, John Henry; Protestant Episcopal Church; Protestant Reformation, the; Raikes, Robert; rector; Reformed Churches; Ridley, Nicholas; Robinson, John A. T.; Seabury, Samuel; see; Society for the Promulgation of the Gospel in Foreign Parts; sodality; Stir-up Sunday; *Te Deum Laudamus;* Thirty-Nine Articles, the; three cornerstones of Anglicanism, the; tippet; Tractarianism; Triumph of the Cross, Feasts of the; verger; vestry; vicar; vicar general; warden; Weems, Mason Locke; White, Gilbert; William and Mary; Wolsey, Thomas.

Church of God: Protestant denomination formed in 1886 on the principles of evangelism, missions, and Reformation tenets. Most are charismatic and Pentecostal with about seven million members in nearly 180 countries. Polity is cooperative among the laity, bishops, and exhorters that meet annually in a General Assembly. *See also* church bodies in America (typed); denomination(s), denominationalism; Weinland, Ronald.

Church of God in Christ: the largest charismatic Pentecostal church in America. The membership is mostly African-American. *See also* Afro-American theology; church bodies in America (typed); denomination(s), denominationalism.

Church of Jerusalem. See Jerusalem Church.

Church of Jesus Christ of Latter-Day Saints, the: the sect more popularly called Mormonism or LDS. Some insiders might call the church "Reformed Christianity" since they see themselves are the true church in the world. Mormons are universalists in their eschatology (all persons will be spared hell) even though trials and punishments are to be expected in this life and the next. They practice baptism for the dead and perpetual marriage sealing in anticipation of the new age. Salvation is possible for the dead. Independence, Missouri, is to be the New Jerusalem and was the site of the original Garden of Eden. Among the sect's most controversial issues, polygamy ranked high (the founder, Joseph Smith, had at least twenty-seven wives.) Terrestrial, telestial, or celestial governance among the planets may be possible for some—granted in accord with church fidelity—for many in the new era. Mormonism also identifies many more Old Testament personalities as prophets than those offered by orthodox beliefs, some of whom are quite obscure. The religion centers on the history of various Indian tribes supposedly descended from exiled Israelites that were said to exist from 600 B.C. to A.D 420. Their story is recorded on golden plates delivered by the angel Moroni that Smith and some friends translated from obscure Egyptian hieroglyphics by the use of magic spectacles. Joseph Smith and Brigham Young were

Freemasons, and much of Mormon theology is centered in Masonic ritual and symbolism. The sect is guided by the three great writings of the faith: *The Book of Mormon, Doctrine and Covenants,* and *The Pearl of Great Price.* The sect even had its own newspaper, *The Morning and Evening Star.* Certain high-ranking officers of the church are called "prophets." Smith's lieutenants were labeled "elders" and the title has stuck as a generalized leader designation. The chief prophet is the president of the church who is assisted by two associates to make up the First Presidency. The president of the LDS still bears the titles of Prophet, Seer, and Revelator. Next are twelve apostles constituting the "Quorum" who are in turn augmented by the "seventies" to aid missionary activity and charitable work (which is extensive and aggressive). Local leadership is headed by a bishop but unpaid laypersons are the backbone of all church functions. Local congregations are situated as stakes and wards. The Utah household of Brigham Young held some nineteen members. The church did not officially reverse itself on the practice until 1890, and not all conformed then, nor do they now. Also, blacks were not admitted to the Mormon priesthood until 1978. Women still are not. Some breakaway cults of Mormonism are downright violent and exploitative while others struggle to survive. Mormons claim to be the fourth largest Christian denomination, although most mainline churches would dispute the name "Christian" in that pronouncement. Most membership is outside the United States. They number about two percent of the American population. More recent examinations seem to indicate that Mormon history and doctrine have finally run afoul of logic and the Church is experiencing an epidemic of lost membership. *See also anima sola;* Book of Mormon; church bodies in America (typed); Church of Christ, Temple Lot; Church of the Firstborn; Community Church (Mormon); *Doctrine and Covenants;* elder(s); exaltation; Freemasonry; golden plates; idolatry; Moroni; Millennial churches; Mountain Meadows Massacre; *Pearl of Great Price*, the; Pioneer Day; prayer(s) for the dead; priest(s); restorationism; Romney, Mitt; sect(s); Smith, Joseph Jr.; space doctrine; stake; Urim and Thummin; ward; white horse prophecy; Young, Brigham.

Church of Satan: organized worship (to some degree or other) of Satan or, at a minimum, the facilitation of evil. The most recognized organization for the purpose was instituted at the "Black House" (its literal color) in San Francisco, California, on Walpurgasnacht April 30, 1966, by Anton Szandor La Vey. Occultic ritual and direction of the Satanic Bible were sacrosanct. La Vey retained the position of high priest until his death in 1997. The church's headquarters is now in Hell's Kitchen in New York City but is reputedly not nearly so active. Many associated with the cult would insist the groups do not literally believe in the devil except in an interpretation of his persona as a metaphor for "adversary" of the enlightened human spirit. Nevertheless, the objectives and ritual of the diverse individuals and congregants can only dispute that assertion. Despite its 20th century developed structure, diverse persons and peoples have dedicated themselves to Satanic devotion for centuries but yet remain an aberration. *See also* Brotherhood of Satan; La Vey, Anton Szandor; Luciferans; occult, occultic; Satan, Satanic Bible; Satanism; sect(s); Walpurgis Night; Warnke, Alfred "Mike."

Church of the Brethren: a small Pietist fellowship began in Germany by Alexander Mack in 1708. The group formed with pietistic leanings and some Anabaptist beliefs, then moved to America, where they were known as the German Baptist Brethren. One of their more famous branches is called the Dunkards. The Church of the Brethren is of Inner Light grouping known for their baptism practice of immersing the candidate three times face-first. Other beliefs center to particular practices, such as foot-washing, "love feasts" (Communion), and the holy kiss. They are pacifists and abstain from alcohol, tobacco, oaths, legal arrangements, frivolous amusements, etc. *See also* church bodies of America (typed); denomination(s); denominationalism; Dunkards; holy kiss; Inner Light churches.

Church of the Firstborn: (the Morrisites), a splinter group of the Mormon Church formed in 1861. One Joseph Morris claimed to have had revelations naming him as the seventh angel in the book of Revelation. He wrote Brigham Young a number of times seeking recognition of his new church but received no answers. They were excommunicated by the latter-day saints instead. Morris told his followers not to plant crops at their colony in Kingston Fort, Utah, since Jesus was soon to return. By 1862 they were facing starvation so Morris extended his predicted end date, losing members at each failure. In an incident known as the Morrisite War, three disenchanted followers seized a load of wheat destined for the community. Morris regained the food with violence and imprisoned the perpetrators. The Utah militia was called out, and Morris and many of his flock were arrested; six were charged with murder, and Morris himself was killed in a skirmish. The territorial governor pardoned everyone, however, and the church began to regather at Deer Lodge, Montana, under the leadership of George Williams. Williams claimed that the Second Coming was to occur in Deer Lodge County. The Bahai religionists became involved at this point, and yet another sect formed under Leland Jensen. Jensen declared that the Montana State Prison, where he was once incarcerated, was actually Ezekiel's Temple and began to make more radical Second Coming announcements. *See also* Baha'i International; Church of Jesus Christ of Latter-Day Saints, the; idolatry; sect(s); Young, Brigham.

Church of the Holy Sepulcher: the Christian worship center over the supposed site of the burial tomb of Jesus. The church is a complex attraction that terminates the *Via Dolorosa*. Inside are: 1) the Anointing Stone, or Stone of Unction, where Jesus was laid after his crucifixion to be prepared for a hasty burial; 2) the Tomb itself, or the Aedicule, a two-room artificial excavation at the center of the Anastasis. The first, called the Chapel of the Angel, contains a cube of marble on which the angel was seated when the women came to anoint the body of Jesus; the second room is the mortuary chamber with a slab of white marble about two yards long covering the resting place of Jesus. Above are forty-three hanging lamps—four belonging to the Copts and the remainder equally divided among the Latins, Greeks, and Armenians; 3) the Katholikon [Catholicon], the main body of the Basilica, containing an iconostasis (the decorated partition separating the altar from the congregation) and the omphalos dome of the Rotunda above the transept. Some consider this location to be the center of the world; 4) the Holy Prison, a narrow space said to hold the incarcerated Christ until his mock trial; 5) the Chapel of Saint Helena, a lower-level worship center off the main structure. She was the mother of Constantine who did much to locate and preserve the holy relics of the region; 6) the Tomb of Joseph of Arimathea, the only part of the Holy Sepulcher belonging to the Ethiopian community. It is a small rock-hewn tomb within the Rotunda. Joseph of Arimathea was the wealthy donor of the space of Jesus' burial, an unused excavation at the time; 7) the Altar of the Crucifixion, the place of Christ's torture, flanked by a Roman Catholic and a Greek Orthodox edifice. The remaining features of the Holy Sepulcher include: 1. the entrance hall, 2. station for the Muslim guards (doorkeepers), 3. the Chapel of Adam, 4. Altar of the Nails of the Cross, 5. Altar of *Sabat Mater* (portraying the suffering of Jesus' mother), 6. the Place of Mourning, 7. the Rotunda (as the main body of the sanctuary), 8. a Jacobite chapel, 9. a Coptic chapel, 10. the Altar of Mary Magdalene, 11. the Franciscan Church, 12. Arches of the Virgin Mary, 13. Chapel of Longinus, 14. Chapel of the Division of the Holy Robes, 15. Chapel of Derision and,

16. the Latin choir loft. *See also* Anastasis; church; Edicule; Golgotha; Helena; Jerusalem, landmarks of; Martyrium; Via Dolorosa.

Church of the Last Testament: the cult founded by Russian-born Sergey Anatolyevich Torop ("Vissarion"). The church is headquartered in Siberia and claims to hold over 10,000 followers worldwide. *See also* cult(s); idolatry; Vissarion.

Church of the Nativity: the site and Christian worship center revered in Bethlehem as the place of Jesus' birth. The location was commissioned by Constantine and his mother Helena in A.D. 327. It is considered an Islamic holy site as well. *See also* Bethlehem; church; Islam; Martyrium.

Church of the Nazarene: a denominational organ splintered from Methodism after the Civil War. Members wanted what they determined to be a need to restore the simplicity and piety of John Wesley. The organized church began with Dr. P.F. Bresee in 1895, then thirteen years later reformed itself at Pilot Point, Texas, in union with the Association of Pentecostal Churches in America. They called themselves the Pentecostal Church of the Nazarene but later dropped "Pentecostal" to distinguish themselves from others of the same or similar names. The worshiping community regularly engages in glossolalia (tongue speaking), choose their own ministers, and practice local church polity. *See also* church bodies in America (typed); denomination(s), denominationalism; Pentecostalism.

Church of the New Jerusalem. See Swedenborgianism.

Church of the United Brethren: an evangelical denomination formed among German emigrants to Pennsylvania as a refuge from the less tolerant Puritan colonies of New England. Bishop Martin Boehm, a Mennonite, was one of those settlers but was an ardent evangelist. He, in partnership with the German Reformed Philip William Otterbein, established the Church of the United Brethren in 1800. Later, in 1946, the movement merged with the

Evangelical Church (also originated among German-speaking settlers). Later, the church spread to English-speaking congregations and by 1968 both were aligned with the United Methodists. *See also* church bodies in America (typed); denominations, denominationalism; Otterbein, Philip William.

church planting: the process of starting a new church, a practice most often associated with Protestant ecclesiology. For best results, and for legal purposes, any new fellowship should have a constitution, by-laws, statement of purpose, goals, certain legal documents, a statement of faith, and arrangements for worship. New churches are continually started nationally and abroad. *See also* Church; church; church models; missions, missionaries.

Church Triumphant, Church Militant: frequently called the two categories of the faithful designated as the Church Triumphant (the saints in heaven) and the Church Militant (the population of earthly believers.) Sometimes the phrases *Church Expectant, Church Penitent,* and *Church Suffering* are added to the classic formula as well. *See also* Church.

Church Universal and Triumphant: doomsday cult led by Elizabeth Clare Prophet, now known sometimes as the Summit Lighthouse. The sect emphasizes plagues (such as AIDS), which are prominent signs that we are living in the last days. *See also* cult(s); idolatry; Millennial churches; mind science; Prophet, Elizabeth Clare.

"churn" (religious): contemporary religious jargon for people leaving their childhood faith for another faith or none at all. *See also* backslide; cafeteria Christians; carnal Christians; Christianese, "church hopper"; denominational mutt; McChurch; slurs, religious.

Cicero, Marcus Tullius: renowned Roman author and statesman (106 – 43 B.C.) who, unlike many Romans of his day, believed in a real afterlife. Many Christians followed his readings because he saw a joyous reunion with loved ones and eternal life after death. Some considered him a sort of "pre-Christian Christian," an enlightened pagan who beliefs were close to their own. Cicero claimed to be a Celtic Druid and was heavily into Roman politics. Many credit him as the first to accurately ascribe the broad variety of ways prophecy was practiced in antiquity by placing it into two categories. The first he called inspiration received directly through divine revelation, dreams, visions, trances, and the like; the second he named as basically divination or the careful examination of natural signs. *See also* divination; prophecy; prophecy types; Roman Empire.

cilice. See hairshirt.

cinnamon: a sweet-smelling plant and its by-products used as spice or oil. It was part of the precious cargo of Commercial Babylon noted in Revelation 18 and an ingredient in some incense compounds. There is evidence it was imported all the way from China. *See also* flora, fruit, and grain, symbology of; incense; perfumes, ointments, and spices.

circatore: in many abbeys, a low-ranking official subordinate to the prior or prioress in charge. Their labors are varied but in the past they were prone to circulate outside after dark looking for parishioners who might be loitering about. *See also* monasticism; Roman Catholic Church.

Circle of Necessity. See Wheel of Existence.

circuit(s): small collections of Methodist congregations acting in a more or less cooperative spirit but absent any hierarchal authority. *See also* circuit riders; connection polity; Holy Fool(s), the; Great Awakenings; Methodists; missions, missionaries; revivalism; Wesley, Charles and John; Whitefield, George.

circuit riders: preachers on horseback who regularly traveled place to place in the barely settled frontiers of America from as far back in history as colonial America. At first, the riders concentrated on New England and the South, then entered the frontier West where few churches were established. Most practiced a "revivalist" style of preaching that was more entertaining than that offered at local saloons. They were welcomed almost everywhere; new denominations sprang up, and religion reached to the limits of the country. Efforts of the circuit riders, though successful, were strenuous and debilitating to the evangelists who seldom stopped their movements and barely survived despite the hospitality of the frontier. *See also* Asbury, Francis; camp meetings; Cartwright, Peter; circuit(s); clergy; connection polity; Great Awakenings, the; Holy Fool(s), the; Methodists; missions, missionaries; revivalism; Wesley, Charles and John; Whitefield, George.

circumcision: the process of surgically severing the foreskin of the penis. In the Old Testament, circumcision was the prime identifier of the Israelites and was performed on every boy baby eight days after birth. It was the seal of the Abrahamic Covenant and essential to maintain fidelity and inclusion into the fellowship of God's chosen people; women were counted within the community via the inclusive circumcision practice of the men. Jews have been known as "the circumcised." On occasion in history, some Jews reversed the mark via a surgical operation so they could deny their heritage, a process hinted at by Paul (1 Cor. 7:18). Such an action in the time of the Maccabees, for example, allowed them to participate in the Greek gymnasium exercises (which were ordinarily practiced in the nude). Circumcision is still practiced today by observing Jews and is a medical procedure favored by many males for health or cosmetic reasons. A number of other ancient peoples also practiced circumcision—Egyptian priests, the Edomites, the Ammonites, the Moabites, and certain desert dwellers. *See also* Abrahamic Covenant; Circumcision, Feast of the; covenant(s), biblical; female genital mutilation; Judaism; *mohel;* Prepuce, the Holy; sign of the covenant; uncircumcised.

Circumcision, Feast of the: High Church special recognition of the circumcision of Jesus. *See also* circumcision; feasts and special days of high liturgy faiths; Feast of Fools; liturgical year; Prepuce, the Holy.

circumincession. See perichorisis.

Cistercians: an early Roman Catholic order active between the 11th and 13th centuries. Its most prominent supporter was probably Bernard of Clairvaux, who joined in 1113. Cistercians could claim to be the prototype of other maturing monastic orders. The monks were also quite instrumental in founding and supporting the Knights Templar. *See also* Assumptionist Orders; Augustinian Order; Barnabites; Benedict, Order of; Benedict of Clairvaux; Black Canons; canon(s) of the church; canons regular; clergy; Capuchin Order; Carmelites; Carthusians; Celestines; Dominicans; Franciscans; friar(s); Minim; monasticism; monk(s); orders; Paulist Fathers; Premonstratensian Order; religious organizations; Roman Catholic Church; Servite Order; Spirituals of the Franciscan Order; Trappist Order.

cities of refuge: a series of towns in Israel designated as "safe houses" for the protection of persons accused of murder or manslaughter. Particularly, if the perpetrator killed accidently, he could be safeguarded until a proper trial could be arranged or until the death of the presiding high priest. The presence of such refugees temporally isolated the accused from the law of *lex talionis*. *See also* blood feud; *lex talionis;* vengeance.

cities of the gods: a phrase sometimes used to identify those Sumerian settlements of early civilization which legend states, were ruled by gods and demi-gods in prediluvian days. Lower Mesopotamia boasted the city-states or regions of Sippar, Babylon, Akkad, Kish, Nippur, Adab, Agade, Umma, Isin, Shuruppak, Lagash, Uruk, Larsa, Ur, El-Ubald, and Eridu. The capital and cult center of the gods apparently moved from place to place as normal or crisis events dictated. Abraham's origin was in Ur. *See also* Anunnaki; *Chariots of the Gods?;* cuneiform; demi-god(s); Enki and Enlil; *Enuma Elish; Epic of Gilgamesh, The;* Igigi; idolatry; lulu; Mesopotamia; Nibiru; panspermia theory; Sumerian and Babylonian pantheon; Sumer, Sumerian(s); Sumerian Tablets; Table of Destinies; Tiamat.

cities of the plain: that collection of five cities near the Dead Sea, including Sodom and Gomorrah, which were destroyed by God as punishment for their excessive wickedness during the time of Abraham and Lot. Two theories exist as to where exactly the cities were located. The oldest, originated by W.F. Albright, claims the five locales were on the southeastern edge of the Dead Sea and included Sodom, Gomorrah, Zeboiim, Admah, and Bela (Zoar). All but Zoar were destroyed by fire, and all the ruins were subsequently submerged (Gen. 10:19; 13:10, 12; 14:2,8; 19:24–25,29). A later theory (since 1973) places the five cities on the southwestern edge of the Dead Sea and included Bab-edth-Dhur (Sodom), Numeria (Gomorrah), Safi, Feifah, and Khanazir. Three of the five were burned, but some archeologists claim the evidence suggests that destruction may have happened 300 years before Abraham. *See also* Admah; Gomorrah; Pentapolis; Sodom; Sodom and Gomorrah; Zeboiim; Zoar.

citron wood: a type of wood mentioned in Revelation 18:12 named among the many costly trade goods of Secular Babylon. It is also mentioned as building material for the tabernacle and temples. Scholars differ slightly in defining this woody tree and call it either the bitter apple or simply "goodly trees." The Greek name *thyine* (meaning "to sacrifice") was highly desirable as an aromatic timber certainly suitable for burning in the sacrifice ritual, so perhaps the Babylon treasure was of that nature. By whatever name, the wood was probably fragrant, rare, and much desired. *See also* flora, fruit, and grain, symbology of.

City No Longer Deserted: a name for righteous Israel, most likely reserved specifically for the millennial age, in which Jerusalem will prosper in population and beauty (Isa. 62:12). *See also* Beulah; Deserted/Desolate; Hebrews as a people; Hephzibah; Holy People, the; Jerusalem as city; Jew(s); Judaism; name, a new; Redeemed of the Lord, the; Sought After.

city of blood: the prophet Nahum's designation for wicked Nineveh (Nahum 3:1). Ezekiel 22:1–4 names Jerusalem as a city of bloodshed because of her own wickedness and violence. *See also* Assyria, Assyrians; city of oppressors; Jerusalem as city; mistress of sorceries; Nineveh, Ninevites.

city of chaos: the locale mentioned in Isaiah chapter 24 (according to some translations) or "ruins" in other renditions. The place identifies either Nineveh or Babylon, depending on when the Isaiah scribe penned the words. In a larger apocalyptic sense, however, a city in ruined chaos applies to any metropolis that defies God and thereby sets itself up for divine judgment.

city of David: Jerusalem. The city was founded by David, and his seat of government was there during the United Kingdom era (1 Ki. 2:10; 3:1; 8:1; Neh. 3:15). David was able to wrest Mount Zion from the Jebusites early in his reign (2 Sam. 5:6–10) and establish it as not only his capital but also the pride of the nation. Isaiah calls the place "the city where David settled" (Isa. 29:1). *See also* Ariel; City of God; city of Judah; City of Truth; Daughter of Jerusalem; Holy City, the; Jebusites; Jerusalem as city; Jerusalem, landmarks of; Zion.

City of Destruction: a prophetic name for a city in Egypt, probably Heliopolis (Isa. 19:16–18), known by some as Leontopolis. Historical accounts relate that the high priest of Jerusalem, Onias III (reigned 187–185 B.C.), solicited permission from King Ptolemy VI and Queen Cleopatra in Alexandria to construct a rival temple in the area of the

Upper Nile near Memphis. That such a glaringly unsavory name, "City of Destruction," should be used for such a sanctified purpose has fueled the suspicion that Heliopolis was the real site under consideration. Onias did eventually succeed in building an inferior copy of the Jerusalem Temple there. The high priest's motivation to do so, taken from the writings of Isaiah (Isa. 19:16–25), led him to the conviction that the prophecy and its related details applied to him whereas most scholars see the oracle as reserved for the Millennium. This substitute Temple in Egypt (which Josephus named oddly as the "Onion") lasted 343 years until it was shut down by the Romans. The occasion for its closing at the time was due to the mistrust of those surviving Jews who had managed to flee there after the loss of the Jewish War. Josephus described the structure as similar in design to the one at Jerusalem but in another place called it a tower. The discrepancy has not been satisfactorily resolved. The city's relationship to prophecy is dynamic. The expectation is that in the end days, Egypt will be in terror of God and the Jews. Five of her cities will learn to speak the Hebrew language, and seven will pledge allegiance to the Lord, one of which will be the "City of Destruction." In the Six-Day War, Israel controlled five cities in the Sinai Peninsula, one of which was the vital port city of El Arish (*arish* in Arabic means "destruction"). *See also* Heliopolis; Egypt, Egyptians; Onias III; Onias IV; Onion, Temple of.

City of God: a term used to denote Jerusalem, the place chosen by God for His dwelling among the tribes of Israel. It also describes the New Jerusalem of the future (Rev. 3:12; 21; 22) in appropriate context. *See also* city of David; City of Truth; Daughter of Jerusalem; Jerusalem as city; New Jerusalem; Zion.

City of God, The: Augustine's great work that (in its most eschatological content) compares the New Jerusalem with man-made cities. The purpose of the book was to defend Christianity against pagan charges that Rome's considerable calamities at that time were the result of the citizenry's turning away from the ancient gods. *See also* Augustine, Aurelius.

city of Judah: Jerusalem. *See also* city of David; City of God; City of Truth; Holy City, the; Jerusalem as city; Zion.

city of oppressors: a derogatory name for Jerusalem in her defiance of God, especially her rulers, as pronounced by the prophet Zephaniah (Zeph. 3:1). *See also* city of blood; Jerusalem as city.

City of Palms: the ancient city of Jericho, so named because palm trees were profuse there. *See also* Jericho; palm.

city of peace. See Jerusalem as city.

city of power: a cryptic reference to facinorous Babylon the Great. The name here seems to be applied somewhat facetiously as the city is already doomed before its destruction is portrayed in the text (Rev. 18:10). *See also* angel of Babylon's fall; Babylon the Great; desolate and naked; filth of her adulteries; "glorified herself"; great city, this; Great Prostitute, the; haunt (prison) for every unclean and detestable bird; idolatry; merchant(s); Mystery Babylon the Great the Mother of Prostitutes and of the Abominations of the Earth; Religious Babylon; Secular Babylon; smoke of her burning; whore of Babylon; wine of her adulteries.

City of Righteousness, The: a millennial name for Jerusalem (Isa. 1:26). *See also* Faithful City, the; Holy City, the; mother of us all; New Jerusalem.

city of the Great King: Jerusalem (Ps. 48:2; Mt. 5:35). *See also* Great King, the.

City of Truth: Jerusalem, as cited in Zechariah 8:3. *See also* city of David; City of God; Daughter of Jerusalem; Holy City, the; Jerusalem as city; Zion.

civil religion: the supposed generic faith of a nation's religio-political concept of history and destiny of the native country. Practice may range from outright devotion to the nation to "watering down" orthodox religious faith to suit a wide range of civil acceptance. In America, Jean-Jacques Rousseau coined the phrase "God's New Israel" in his book *Social Contract* in 1762. In essence, the thought is that a given country is secure in God's favor (however God is defined) even though the practice of civil religion may be minimal and unparticular at best. *See also* Abington School District vs. Schempp; Alleghany County vs. ACLU; antidisestablishmentarianism; *Booke of the General Lawes and Libertyes;* caesaropapacy; Cercle Social; collegialism; Cult of the Supreme Being; disestablishmentarianism; divine right of kings; ecumenism; Edict of Milan; Edict of Nantes; Edict of Toleration; Establishment Clause and Free Exercise Clause; Geghan Bill; Government Regulation Index (GRI); *homo religiosus;* inclusive language; Lemon vs. Kurtzman; Massachusetts Body of Liberties; National Day of Prayer; PC; *princeps; principis;* public square; regalism; Shubert vs. Verner; social issues; sociology of religion; state church; ultramontanism; Virginia's Disestablishment law.

civil unions: or "domestic partnerships," the marriage of same-sex couples. Religious and political controversy swelled concerning the issue as in no other time in history. In June of 2015 the Supreme Court declared legal bans on same-sex marriages in the states to be unconstitutional. *See also* adelphopoiesis; "clobber passages"; end time world conditions; LGBTQ; matrimony; Rainbow Coalition; Rainbow Family; postmodernism; social issues.

clairaudience: hearing voices in the prophetic or clairvoyant mode originating supernaturally. *See also* anthropomancy; anthroposophy; apotropaic magic; aretology; Ariosophy; astral plane; astral projection; astrolabe; astrology, astrologers; athame; audition; augury; automatic writing; bagua; belomancy; bibliomancy; black arts; black magic; black mirror; blood moon(s); cartomancy; chiromancy; clairaudience; clairvoyance; cleromancy; cone of power;

conjure; crop circles; cryptesthesia; crystallomancy; crystal skulls; curious acts; divination; dream(s); dreams and visions; ecstasy; enchantment; enneagram; esoteric sects; evil eye; extrasensory perception (ESP); foreknowledge; foretelling; geomancy; grimoire; gris-gris; hepatoscopy; Hermetic wisdom; Hermetic writings; hex; hierscopy; horoscope(s); hydromancy; idol(s); ifa; incantation; juju; labyrinth walk; lecanomancy; literomancy; locution; magic arts; magic, magick; magic square; magnetism; *mana*; mantic wisdom; mantra; miracle(s); monition; necromancy; New Age religion; numbers, symbology of; occult, occultic; omen; oneiromancy; oracle(s); otherworldy journeys; ouija board; out-of-body perception (ESP); paranormal; parapsychology; peace pole(s); pentagram; philosophers' stone; planchette; planets as gods; portent; precognition; prediction; prefiguration; premonition; prodigy; prognostication; psychic(s); psychic healing; psychic reading; psychomancy; psychometry; psychonautics; pyramidology; remote viewing; retrocognition; revelation; rhabdomancy; scrying; séance; secret wisdom; sorcery, sorceries; spell; spell names; spiritism; stigmata; superstition; tarot; telegnosis; telesthesia; theurgy; third eye, the; thoughtform; totemism; vision quest; visions; visualization; voodoo; voudou; wanga; warlock(s); web-bot; wizard(s); witchcraft; *ya sang*; yoga; Zen; zodiac; *zos kia* cultus.

clairsentience: the ability to obtain occult knowledge by touching an object. *See also* anthropomancy; anthroposophy; apotropaic magic; aretology; Ariosophy; astral plane; astral projection; astrolabe; astrology, astrologers; athame; audition; augury; automatic writing; bagua; belomancy; bibliomancy; black arts black mirror; blood moon(s); cartomancy; chaos magic; chiromancy; clairaudience; clairvoyance; cleromancy; cone of power; conjure; crop circles; cryptesthesia; crystallomancy; crystal skulls; curious acts; divination; dream(s); dreams and visions; ecstasy; enchantment; enneagram; esoteric sects; evil eye;

History and Mystery

extrasensory perception (ESP); foreknowledge; foretelling; geomancy; grimoire; gris-gris; hepatoscopy; Hermetic wisdom; Hermetic writings; hex; hierscopy; horoscope(s); hydromancy; idol(s); ifa; incantation; juju; labyrinth walk; lecanomancy; literomancy; locution; magic arts; magic, magick; magic square; magnetism; *mana*; mantic wisdom; mantra; miracle(s); monition; mystery religion(s); necromancy; New Age religion; numbers, symbology of; occult, occultic; omen; oneiromancy; oracle(s); otherworldy journeys; ouija board; out-of-body perception (ESP); paranormal; parapsychology; past life regression; peace pole(s); pentagram; philosophers' stone; planchette; planets as gods; portent; precognition; prediction; prefiguration; premonition; prodigy; prognostication; psychic(s); psychic healing; psychic reading; psychomancy; psychometry; psychonautics; pyramidology; rebirthing; remote viewing; retrocognition; revelation; rhabdomancy; scrying; séance; secret societies; secret wisdom; sorcery, sorceries; spell; spell names; spiritism; stigmata; supernatural; superstition; tarot; telegnosis; telesthesia; theugry; third eye, the; thoughtform; totemism; vision(s); vision quest; visualization; voodoo; voudou; wanga; warlock(s); WebBot; wizard(s); witchcraft; *ya sang*; yoga; Zen; zodiac; *zos kia* cultus.

clairvoyance: unusual imagery in the prophetic or mediumistic mode originating supernaturally. *See also* anthropomancy; anthroposophy; apotropaic magic; aretology; Ariosophy; astral plane; astral projection; astrolabe; astrology, astrologers; athame; audition; augury; automatic writing; bagua; belomancy; bibliomancy; black arts; black mirror; blood moon(s); cartomancy; chaos magic; chiromancy; clairaudience; clairsentience; cleromancy; cone of power; conjure; crop circles; cryptesthesia; crystallomancy; crystal skulls; curious acts; divination; dream(s); dreams and visions; ecstasy; enchantment; enneagram; esoteric sects; evil eye; extrasensory perception (ESP); foreknowledge; foretelling; geomancy; grimoire; gris-gris; hepatoscopy;

Hermetic wisdom; Hermetic writings; hex; hierscopy; horoscope(s); hydromancy; ifa; incantation; juju; labyrinth walk; lecanomancy; literomancy; locution; magic arts; magic, magick; magic square; magnetism; *mana*; mantic wisdom; mantra; miracle(s); monition; mystery religion(s); necromancy; New Age religion; numbers, symbology of; occult, occultic; omen; oneiromancy; oracle(s); otherworldy journeys; ouija board; out-of-body perception (ESP); paranormal; parapsychology; past life regression; peace pole(s); pentagram; philosophers' stone; planchette; planets as gods; portent; precognition; prediction; prefiguration; premonition; prodigy; prognostication; psychic(s); psychic healing; psychic reading; psychomancy; psychometry; psychonautics; pyramidology; rebirthing; remote viewing; retrocognition; revelation; rhabdomancy; scrying; séance; secret societies; secret wisdom; sorcery, sorceries; spell; spell names; spiritism; stigmata; supernatural; superstition; tarot; telegnosis; telesthesia; theurgy; third eye, the; thoughtform; totemism; vision(s); vision quest; visualization; voodoo; voudou; wanga; warlock(s); Web-Bot; wizard(s); witchcraft; *ya sang*; yoga; Zen; zodiac; *zos kia* cultus.

Clapham sect: a notable group of English reformers (ca. 1790–1830) meeting in the homes of Henry Thornton and William Wilberforce. Most were evangelical Anglicans (called "saints" at the time) who worked for abolition of slavery, prison reform, foreign missions, and other worthy causes. *See also* missions, missionaries; religious organizations; slave, slavery; Wilberforce, William.

clapping hands and stomping feet: an action by the prophet Ezekiel (Ezk. 6:11–14). Such a display was not intended as applause or glee as it might be interpreted today. Rather, the striking of the hands and stomping of the feet indicated displeasure or distress. The prophet performed those actions to accent his prediction of the certain doom of Judah. Later, in Ezekiel 25:6, the phrase denounces the attitude of Ammon, which celebrated with malice the troubles of the land of Israel. The prophet Nahum expresses the same sentiments in his ridicule of Nineveh (Nah. 3:10). Balak performed the same action (Num. 24:10) to express his anger at Balaam. Poetically, clapping the hands could denote scorn (Job 34:37), whereas today it would be counted as applause. *See also* Aha!; gestures; striking hands and striking the thigh.

Clarke, Arthur C.: renowned science fiction writer (1917–2008) who suggested that our world populations will someday learn telepathy and other sci-fi fantasies that will become all too real in the future. He is quoted as saying, "The doctrine of man made in the image of God is ticking like a time bomb at Christianity's base, set to explode if other intelligent creatures are discovered." He also formulated the so-called "third law" which states: "Any sufficiently advanced technology is indistinguishable from magic." Perhaps this author can be stood up as representative of all those writers in the future-telling genre dealing with eschatological subject matter in company with Robert Heinlein and Isaac Asimov. Clarke was adamant that UFOs do not exist. *See also* Asimov, Isaac; Heinlein, Robert A.; UFO.

Clarke, James Freeman: clergy in the Disciples of Christ (1810–1888). Clarke was an influential transcendentalist but remembered for his inspired history called *Ten Great Religions* published in two volumes. *See also* Disciples of Christ; transcendentalism.

Clarke, John: English-born clergyman with Baptist leanings (1609–1676) and an early advocate of religious liberty in the American colonies. He assisted Roger Williams in opening Rhode Island to seekers of religious freedom and helped settle Newport. There he became pastor for the city and a member of the colony's general assembly and three times deputy governor. *See also* Baptists; Coddington, William; Hutchinson, Anne; Williams, Roger.

classes of humanity in the Apocalypse: those peoples addressed directly in the book of Revelation. Excepting angels, Revelation primarily pushes its words to select groups—Jews, Gentiles, and saints. Their classes are more carefully distinguished by noting the Greek words used to name them: *laos* (people in general), *hagios* (saints), *doulos* (servants, slaves), *Ioudaios* (Jews), and *oikos* (other people of God). *See also* Gentile(s); Jew(s); saint(s); slave, slavery.

classic premillennialism. See historic premillennialism.

classis: the governing body of the Reformed Church denomination. *See also* Reformed Churches.

Claudia: a fellow disciple who joined Paul in sending along greetings to Timothy from Rome (2 Tim. 4:21).

Claudius: the fourth Roman emperor who reigned from A.D. 41 – 54, a nephew of Tiberius. He was a weak and disinterested ruler but did favor the Jews for a time. Eventually, he chased that entire race from Rome (Acts 18:2), however. It was he who was emperor when Agabus prophesied famine in the land (Acts. 11:28). Claudius turned over most of Palestine to Herod Agrippa I as a political favor. *See also* Christianity in the Roman Empire; king(s); Roman Empire.

Claudius Lysias: the Roman garrison commander in Jerusalem who protected Paul against the Jewish mob, which threatened to kill Paul, thinking the apostle had desecrated the Temple (Acts 23:26). Lysias also arranged an audience with Governor Felix to hear Paul's defense. *See also* Christianity in the Roman Empire; Roman Empire.

clay: malleable earthen material from which a potter can throw jugs, ewers, vases, or other useful and decorative vessels. Such ware was fragile and because of this property it is often cited in Scripture as a prophetic device. Jeremiah was told by God to purchase a clay jar, and then smash it before the elders at the entrance to the Potsherd's Gate to vividly demonstrate His anger against Jerusalem. The apostle

Paul referred to the potter's skill in Romans 9:19–22 when speaking of the sovereignty of God. Again, in 2 Corinthians 4:7, he declares the power of the gospel as being present in earthen vessels (our bodies). The commentary of Revelation 2:27 pictures Christ's rod of iron as smashing the nations like pottery. The latter image is a pointed feature of his millennial reign emphasizing his authority. Pots and their shards (called ostraca) are vital clues to archaeology in this day, and the abundant pieces were convenient and cheap writing material for the ancients. *See also* jars of clay; ostraca; ostracon; papyrus; parchment; potter's house; pottery; stone(s); vellum.

clean clothes for Joshua. See Zechariah's vision of garments for the high priest.

Clement V, Pope: the Roman Catholic pope (1264–1314) who, under pressure from Philip of France, condemned and outlawed the order of the Knights Templar. He was also the first pope to remove the See from Rome to France. *See also* Babylonian Captivity of the Church; Chinon Parchment; knighted orders; Philip IV, King; pope; Roman Catholic Church.

Clement of Alexandria: truly named Titus Flavius Clemens, one of the earliest Christian apologists (defenders) and philosophers of the church (ca. A.D. 155–220). His center of operations was Alexandria, but prior to his conversion, he was an extensive traveler, was initiated into the mysteries of some of the pagan cults (including Gnosticism), and a lover of Greek philosophy. The latter he incorporated into much of his Christian thought. *Logos* (the Word) was the central theme of his teaching, not Christ or God. He even promised pagans deification if they adopted the Christian faith. Clement was more of a moralist than a true theologian. He may be credited as the practical initiative for a number of the so-called extreme Roman Catholic doctrines to be developed later. For example,

Clement had theories of purgatory and demanded that sex be used for procreation only. Like most of the church fathers at Alexandria, he espoused the allegorical method of interpreting the Bible, which naturally influenced this theologian's eschatological thesis; his influence in the early church was tremendous. He accepted John as the author of Revelation. He was Origen's teacher and mentor. *See also* idealism; Roman Catholic Church.

Clement of Philippi: a Christian worker known and praised by Paul in the church of that town (Phil. 4:3).

Clement of Rome: or Clement I, an early church leader (ca. A.D. 30–100) who believed in an imminent return of Christ. Roman Catholic authorities assert he was an early pope, the third after Peter, but the age of his ministry was likely before a true papal authority was established. Additionally, history does not sustain the assertion that Peter was the first of that office for the same reason. Clement was, nevertheless, the first of the "Apostolic Fathers" and today carries the title of Clement I. His most famous writing is probably the *Epistle to the Corinthians*, which contains valuable historical data and glimpses of the structure of the early church. Clement's name also appears in *The Shepherd of Hermas*. The following quote perhaps explains his central concerns for the Second Coming of Christ. He says that every apocalyptic event is necessary and urgent because "men had formerly perverted both the positive law, and that of nature; and had cast out of their mind the memory of the Flood, the burning of Sodom, the plagues of the Egyptians, and the slaughter of the inhabitants of Palestine [Canaan]." *See also* anchor; Roman Catholic Church.

Cleopas. See Clopas.

Cleopatra of Egypt: queen of Egypt (47–30 B.C.). She preserved her kingdom by charming Julius Caesar and Mark Antony, but was overcome by Octavian. History testifies that despite her allure and exceptional beauty, she was covetous for land

and riches and of a flagitious nature. Josephus called her "this wicked creature." Cleopatra's dalliance with Herod the Great caused him to mistrust her, and he even seriously considered assassinating her when she visited Judea. He was dissuaded and instead grudgingly offered tribute to protect his kingdom. After her death by suicide, Egypt became a Roman province. *See also* Egypt, Egyptians; Hathor; Ptolemaic, Ptolemies; queen(s); Roman Empire.

Cleopatra of Syria: daughter of Antiochus the Great. She most likely represents the "daughter of women" (as translated in some editions) of Daniel 11:17–19. Antiochus intended to use her to unbalance his Southern rival, the Ptolemies, but Cleopatra chose to remain loyal to her new husband, Ptolemy V. She is not to be confused with the more well-known Cleopatra of Egypt, nor the mother of Cleopatra of Jerusalem who was a wife of Herod the Great and became the mother of Herod the Tetrarch. *See also* Antiochus III the Great; Herod Philip II; queen(s).

clergy: those officially ordained to a number of "called" ecclesiastical ministries, essentially priests, rabbis, imams, ministers, and other clerics. Those who serve the Church not so directed are called laity or laypersons. *See also* abbot; ablegate; agapetae; archbishop(s); archimandrite; auxiliary ministries; ayatollah; benefit of clergy; bishop(s); Black Canons; camerlengo; canon(s) of the church; Cohanin; church, administration of the early; call(ing); canons regular; cardinal(s); catholicos; celebrant; chaplain(s); chorepiscope; circuit riders; clergy patriots; clergy scientists; clerical collar; clericus; coadjutor; curate; dean; divine; ecclesiastic(s); "eight inch nails"; elder(s); episcopate; *episcopos;* evangelist(s), evangelism; flying bishop(s); friar(s); grand mufti; hegymanos; hierophant; imam; laity; laying on of hands; lay minister(s); *loco tenens;* man of God; metropolitan; minister(s); monk(s); monsignor; mufti; mullah; mystagogue; mystagogy; nuncio; *oikonomo;* officiant; orders; ordination; padre; parson(s); parsonages, vicarages, and manses; pastor(s); patriarch(s);

patriot ministers; pope; preacher(s); prefect(s); prelate(s); *presbuteros;* presbytery; priest(s); primate; *princeps; principis;* prior, prioress; prophet(s); prophet, priest, and king; provost; rabbi; rector; Reverend; starets; suffragan; supply clergy; vestry; vicar general; vicar of Christ; vice god; viceroy; vizier.

clergy patriots: a list of American clergy, highly influential in their day but under-recognized, active in the Revolutionary War, as well as both before and after the conflict. Before General George Washington opted for a chaplain corps for his armies, ministers in support of the rebellion were effective recruiters, cheerleaders, and actual leaders in battle and were used by both sides. The rebel preachers simply picked up muskets and fought as they taught and preached. The British were well aware of their effectiveness and treated them harshly if captured. The British called the fighting parsons (and those who inflamed the revolution) the "Black Robed Regiment" and blamed them as the primary cause of the revolt. Reportedly, the specter of George Whitefield (a close friend of the worldly Benjamin Franklin) once appeared over a regiment of British soldiers leading to panic in the ranks. Washington, too, was aware of the benefits of clergy in uniform and even submitted (it is reported) to being baptized in support of his effort to incorporate a chaplain corps in the Continental Army. The officiant was Reverend John Gano, "the fighting chaplain," who was also a talented officer in combat. Samuel West sermonized on "that terrible denunciation of divine wrath against the worshippers of the beast and his image." He was not referring to the seven-headed beast of Revelation but to the British lion. The ministers were not above labeling their British opponents as beasts, savages, haughty tyrants, and the whore of Babylon. Other prominent clergy combatants included David Jones, Samuel Sherwood, Jacob Cushing, Abraham Keteltas, Peter Gabriel Muhlenberg, Samuel Eaton, Elder McClanahan, William Henry Drayton, William Tennent,

Oliver Hart, Samuel Doak, James Caldwell, Jonas Clark, David Grosvenor, Thomas Reed, John Steele, Isaac Lewis, Joseph Willard, James Latta, William Graham, John Craighead, John Blair Smith, James Hall, Phillips Payson, Benjamin Balch, David Avery, Stephen Farrar, Naphtali Daggett, John Wise, Jacob Green, Samuel Stillman, Robert Treat Paine, and scores of others. Of the fifty-six signers of the Declaration of Independence, two were ordained clergy. Actually, just one was counted as Lyman Hall had left the ministry to pursue a career in medicine leaving only John Witherspoon. Of all the signers of the Declaration, at least twenty-nine were educated in colleges designed to train ministers. Charles Carroll of Maryland was the only Roman Catholic. Ministers and active lay persons during and after the war contributed to the running of the government and formation of the Constitution. Prominent among these individuals were Abraham Baldwin, Rufus King, William Trent Payne, Charles Pickney, John Langdon, James McHenry, Benjamin Rush, John Witherspoon, Jonathan Mayhew, Jeremy Belknap, Samuel Stanhope Smith, James Manning, Abiel Foster, Benjamin Contee, and Paine Wingate. *See also* Asbury, Francis; Backus, Isaac; chaplain(s); clergy; clergy scientists; Cutler, Manasseh; Dwight, Timothy; Founding Fathers; Muhlenberg, Frederick Augustus Conrad; Muhlenberg, John Peter Gabriel; Seabury, Samuel; Tennent, Gilbert; Washington, George; West, Samuel; Whitefield, George; Witherspoon, John.

clergy scientists: those ordained individuals who were interested in science both as amateurs and serious investigators. Their numbers are in the hundreds and all have made significant contributions to scientific learning and recording. A few representatives would include John Ray (1627 – 1705), Gilbert White (1720 – 1793), Octavius Picard-Cambridge (1828 – 1917), Henry Baker Tristram (1822 – 1906), Julian Tenison Woods (1832 – 1889), Stephen Joseph Perry

(1833 – 1889), Paul A. McNally (1890 – 1955), Robert Joseph Boscovich (1711 – 1787), Nicholas Copernicus (1473 – 1543), Francisco J. Ayala (b. 1934), Edward Hitchcock (1793 – 1864), John Polkinghorne (b. 1930), Arthur Peacocke (1924 – 2006), Alister Edgar McGrath (b. 1953), David Wilkinson (b. 1963), Angelo Secchi (1818 – 1878), Michael Reiss (b. 1960), and many others. *See also* Albertus Magnus; Bacon, Roger; clergy; clergy patriots; creation science; creationism; Copernicus, Nicolaus; Cusa, Nicholas; Cutler, Manasseh; de Chardin, Pierre Teilhard; de Lamarck, Chevalier Jean-Baptiste Pierre Antoine de Monet; Draper, John Williams; evolution; evolution, theistic; Fabricius, David; Hales, Stephen; Kant, Immanuel; Knapp, Seaman Asahel; Malthus, Thomas Robert; Mendel, Gregor Johann; Omphalos Hypothesis; Polkinghorne, John; Pratt, John Henry; progressive creationism; Ricci, Matteo; Scopes trial; Steno, Nicholas; Stiles, Ezra; Sumner, William Graham; Swedenborg, Emanuel; White, Gilbert; William of Ockham; Winthrop, John; Young-Earth Creationist Movement.

clerical collar: a stiff starched strip of white linen or plastic worn about the neck as a collar by many liturgical priests and pastors when in public. "Roman collar" is an alternate designation for the article. The fashion identifies the wearer as clergy for instant recognition when it is desirable to do so. *See also* clergy, furniture and furnishings of the modern church.

clericus: a local gathering of clergy. *See also* clergy.

cleromancy: the practice of divination via casting small objects such as pebbles, beans, shells, sticks, knuckle bones, or either common or specially designed dice. Despite their size and numbers, all the magical tokens were generically known as *sortes* in the Roman world, from which we get the modern word *sortilege*. The Wiccans call the ritual "casting the bones" but sortilege and astragalomancy are alternate names for the practice. *See also* anthropomancy;

anthroposophy; apotropaic magic; aretology; Ariosophy; astral plane; astral projection; astrolabe; astrology, astrologers; athame; audition; augury; automatic writing; bagua; belomancy; bibliomancy; black arts; black mirror; blood moon(s); cartomancy; chaos magic; chiromancy; clairaudience; clairsentience; clairvoyance; cone of power; conjure; crop circles; cryptesthesia; crystallomancy; crystal skulls; curious acts; divination; dream(s); dreams and visions; ecstasy; enchantment; enneagram; esoteric sects; evil eye; extrasensory perception (ESP); foreknowledge; foretelling; geomancy; grimoire; gris-gris; hepatoscopy; Hermetic wisdom; Hermetic writings; hex; hierscopy; horoscope(s); hydromancy; ifa; incantation; juju; labyrinth walk; lecanomancy; literomancy; locution; magic arts; magic, magick; magic square; magnetism; *mana*; mantic wisdom; mantra; miracle(s); monition; mystery religion(s); necromancy; New Age religion; numbers, symbology of; occult, occultic; omen; oneiromancy; oracle(s); otherworldy journeys; ouija board; out-of-body hic(s); psychic healing; psychic reading; psychomancy; psychometry; psychonautics; pyramidology; rebirthing eye, the; thoughtform; totemism; vision(s); vision quest; visualization; voodoo; voudou; wanga; warlock(s); Web-Bot; wizard(s); witchcraft; *ya sang*; yoga; Zen; zodiac; *zos kia* cultus.

climatic parallelism: two or more parallel lines of poetry in which the first is incomplete in meaning until the second or those lines following repeat parts of the first and add understanding. Often, especially in biblical psalms, the stanza will end with a praise phrase such as: "Ascribe to the Lord, O heavenly beings,/ascribe to the Lord glory and strength" (Ps. 29:1). *See also* acrostic poem; antithetic parallelism; chiasmus; colon; doubling; poetry (biblical); psalm; synthetic parallelism.

"clobber passages": or "clobber texts," a series of Bible references which seem to disavow homosexuality and same-sex marriages. Advocates claim such conditions undermine

God's view of the sanctity of marriage and constitute crimes against nature. The four most often recounted paradigms so as to "clobber" the opposition include Genesis 19:1–5, Leviticus 18:22, Romans 1:18–32, and 1 Corinthians 6:9–10. Four more are supplemental: Leviticus 20:13, Deuteronomy 23:17, 1 Timothy 1:9–10, and Jude 6–7. As with most religious debates, believers adhere to the veracity and universal authority of Scripture as they interpret it; secularists do not. *See also* Christianese; civil unions; end time world conditions; LGBTQ; matrimony; postmodernism; Rainbow Coalition; Rainbow Family.

cloister: private or living quarters in a monastery or convent. *See also* abba; abbess; abbot; agapetae; convent; Eastern Orthodox Church; hegumene; monastery; monasticism; monk(s); mother superior; nun(s); priory; Roman Catholic Church.

Clopas: (also spelled Cleopas or Cleophas), the husband of one of the Gospel references to Mary, and father to the disciples James the Less and Joses. He is mentioned only once or twice in the Bible (Jn. 19:25) but some historians name him a brother of Joseph, Mary's husband and Jesus' mother. He may also be the same man identified as one of two travelers on the road from Jerusalem to the village of Emmaus shortly after the resurrection of Jesus (Lk. 24:13–35). In that post-Easter incident, he and his companion were prevented from recognizing Jesus when the Lord joined them on their walk until they broke bread together later that evening. Both men returned immediately to Jerusalem to testify to the authenticity of the resurrection. Other scholars insist this Cleopas (a Greek name) is evidently not the same individual who was husband to one of the Marys who stood near the cross of Christ, nor is he likely the same man called Alphaeus, the father of James the Apostle. Those who see no connection one to the others seem to be the majority opinion. *See also* Alphaeus; Emmaus; James; Joseph; Joses; Mary.

close: the grounds or campus of a cathedral.

close Communion, open Communion: distinctions as to who is welcome to the table of Communion for participation in the Lord's Supper enactment. "Close" Communion prohibits all non-believers, those outside of one's denomination, or even those of a particular church fellowship (Roman Catholicism, certain fundamentalist groups). "Open" Communion allows any who profess Christ to share in the ritual (usually Methodism and similar persuasions). *See also* alien immersion; Eucharist; Exclusive Brethren; fencing the table; liturgical year; liturgy, Christian; Lord's Supper.

closed continuum: Rudolf Bultmann's theory that God does not intervene in human history. The concept essentially murders faith in a personal, caring, involved, and omnipotent Creator. *See also* Bultmann, Rudolf; controlled continuum.

cloud(s): visible water or ice particles in the atmosphere. In apocalyptic usage, clouds are often vehicles for the divine, both in a poetic and a literal sense (Ps. 68:4). Often, the clouds are a metaphor for the glory of God in the Bible (Ex. 13:21; 40:34; Job 37:15–16; Mt. 26:64; Rev. 14:4). The image is intended as an accomplice to the self-realization of God. Jesus is pictured as rising heavenward on one (Acts 1:9) and is predicted to return with the clouds of heaven (Dan. 7:13; Mt. 24:30; Rev. 1:7). During the Israelite Exodus, God appeared in theophany form as a pillar of cloud in daylight and one of fire at night. In essence, clouds symbolize both transportation for the deity and his glorification, often taken together with both meanings. *See also* eschatology, eschatological; pillar of cloud; Shekinah glory; smoke.

"cloud nine": a more or less slang phrase meaning "a wonderful place to be." The words seem to have hung on after Dante wrote of heaven having nine levels (in opposition to the standard seven). *See also* heaven; heavens, number of; seven levels of heaven.

cloud of witnesses. See witnesses, great cloud of.

clouds and darkness, a day of: a metaphor for great distress and calamity when the people of God will be harassed (Ezk. 34:12). In such times, according to the commentary by Ezekiel, God will shepherd His people and see that they are protected and prospered. The passage is easily transmuted into an eschatological paradigm. *See also* advents(s) of Christ; age of lawlessness; "all these things"; apocalyptic, apocalypticism; apocalyptic calculation; apocalyptics; apocalyptic time; appearing, the; appointed time, the; coming ages, the; consummation, the final; darkness; darkness at the crucifixion; darkness in earth and sky; day he visits us, the; day of evil; day of God, the; day of (our Lord Jesus) Christ; day of Revenge; day of the Lord, the; day of [their] visitation; day of the Lamb's wrath, the; day of trumpet and battle, a; day of vengeance of our God; "days of Elijah"; "days of Noah"; Day, that (the); due time, in; *elthnen;* end of all things, the; end of the age, the; End, the; end, the; end time; *en takhei;* eschatology, eschatological; eschaton; fullness of time; Glorious Appearing; great and dreadful day, that; "here, there, or in the air"; *kairos;* Second Coming; Second Coming procession; rapture; secret rapture; TEOTWAWKI; termination dates; time; time is near, the; time of fulfillment; times and the seasons, the; "until he comes"; wrath, the coming.

Clovis: first king of the Franks who assumed rule in 481. Clovis was born an Arian Christian but converted to Roman Catholicism to match the faith of his wife. Facing defeat by the Huns, Clovis asked his spouse, Clothilda (d. 545), to pray for his army. The results were positive and Clovis was baptized (in the nude) during which angels descended from heaven with three lilies to be given to Clothilda. These flowers, the *fleur-de-les* of course, became the symbol of France through all the following centuries. As a result of Clovis' diligence and the help of three great Catholic saints – Dionysius, Martin of Tours, and Genevieve—he ensured Europe would become Roman and not Arian. Clovis was the epitome of what history calls a "Holy Roman

Emperor." As an aside, the latter notable, Genevieve, was a valued counselor to the Merovingian kings of the 15th century and a model for a later maid of France, Joan of Arc. *See also* Arianism; king(s); lilies; Martin, bishop of Tours; Merovingian; nakedness; Roman Catholic Church.

Club of Rome: an international think tank of the world's finest minds organized in Rome in 1968. The group states as its mission: "to act as a global catalyst for change through the identification and analysis of the crucial problems facing humanity and the communication of such problems to the most important public and private decision makers as well as to the general public." The collection is now headquartered in Winterthur, Switzerland. Many prophecy conspiracists see this organization as a model for the coming one world government of the Antichrist. *See also* conspiracy theorists; ten nation confederacy.

Club 27: an unsubstantiated esoteric rumor or belief that some people, most of them in the entertainment industry (especially rock stars), will suffer an early death if one double-crosses the devil or if one earns the disfavor of the British royalty or British Intelligence. You might, for instance, suffer a heart attack at age 27. The death of Mick Jagger's girlfriend, Wren Scott, is often put forward as the most used analogy.

Cluny: a town in eastern France and the center of monastic reform and practice in the 12th century. A monastery was established there in 910 A.D. by William I of Aquitaine that took on a decidedly Benedictine flavor and was tightly governed under the Rule of Saint Benedict. It promoted ascetic reforms with such success that by the middle of the century there were over 1000 monasteries of its stripe around the continent. The abbey was sacked by Huguenots in 1562. *See also* Benedict of Nursia; Benedict, Order of; Benedict, Rule of; Huguenots; monastery; monasticism; monk(s); Roman Catholic Church.

clurichauns: small, mischievous poltergeist-like spirits of ancient Ireland sometimes called "the older folk." The beings may be the Leprechauns or something like them who, legend says, dominated the Emerald Isle before the Tuatha de Danann gained control. Many fairy legends describe them as rather surly creatures much too fond of drink. If one does not trouble them, they will not pester you. If, however, you mistreat them they will wreck your home, especially the wine cellar. *See also* attending spirits; banshee; bogle; brownies; bugbears; Celtic folklore and religion; daemons; deceiving spirits; disa; dryad(s); elemental(s); familiar spirit; fairy, fairies; filidh; Fomorians; Furies; ghost(s); gnome(s); Green Man, the; hobgoblins; homunculus; household deities; huldufolk; Lares; leprechaun(s); Loa Loas; Manes; mythological beasties, elementals, monsters, and spirit animals; nereid; nisse; nymph(s); nyx; Oniropompi; Orisha; Oya; para; paredri; penates; Robin Goodfellow; satyr; Seelie Court, Unseelie Court; selkie; Sidhe; sirens; spiritual warfare; sprite(s); sylph(s); teraphim; territorial spirits; Trickster; Tuatha de Danann; tutelary; undine; wight(s).

Clutterbuck, Dorothy: a wealthy woman resident near the New Forest of England (1880–1951) before and during the Second World War. She proclaimed herself a witch, and was commonly known as "Old Dorothy." She reportedly mentored Gerald Gardner, a British patriot who claimed to be in charge of promoting occultic or psychic powers to prevent the invasion of England by the Nazis. The British government reputedly accepted Gardner's efforts and verified his success on several occasions, along with that of his witchcraft assembly—"the witches of New Forest." *See* Fortune, Dion; Gardner, Gerald Brosseau; psychic(s); Wicca; witch(es); "witches of New Forest, the."

coadjutor: a bishop attending another bishop who is in charge of a diocese. The coadjutor holds the right of succession. *See also* Church of England; Roman Catholic Church; vicar general.

Cocceius, Johannes: the Dutch theologian (1603–1669) who first advanced the basics of the theory of the "covenant of works" and the "covenant of grace." His work acts as a modification of strict Calvinistic doctrine, especially concerning double predestination (the impelling decrees of election and reprobation). He was able to see glimpses of Jesus throughout the Old Testament in one form or another. *See also* Adamic Covenant; autosoterism; covenant of works; Reformed Churches; works; works, salvation by.

cock(s). See rooster.

Coddington, William: a religious dissenter who fled Puritan Massachusetts to a sanctuary in Rhode Island. He followed Anne Hutchinson into banishment, but later the two had a falling out. Coddington bought Aquidneck Island from the Narragansett Indians in 1638 and established the towns of Portsmouth and Newport (with John Clarke). He became governor in 1674 and died in office, having become affiliated with the Society of Friends since he was a disenfranchised Puritan. His son, William Coddington, Jr. succeeded him as governor. *See also* Clarke, John; Hutchinson, Anne; Society of Friends; Williams, Roger.

Code of Canon Law: the official "rule book" of the Roman Catholic Church stating its laws and procedures in condensed form. The project was completed in 1917 (since revised) and remains in effect today. *See also* canon(s) of the church; Roman Catholic Church.

Code of Hammurabi: the written laws by which King Hammurabi managed to set forth a unified Mesopotamia. Earlier codified statutes were in evidence before him, but they lacked the depth and breadth of Hammurabi's code of rules and covenants between the people and their king. No doubt the code had a positive influence on the Hebrew sense of justice, or at least, the culture milieu of the ancient Near East. *See also* Hammurabi.

codex, codices: a bound book. Codices replaced the ancient scrolls, which were difficult to peruse rapidly and were too bulky for convenient use. To constitute a codex, papyrus or other material was made from sheets folded and sewn together, sometimes with a cover. They were used more often than scrolls after 1 – 100 A.D. *See also* book(s); folio; papyrus; parchment; scroll(s); lower criticism; vellum.

Cohanin: Jewish priests descended directly from the sons of Aaron. Naturally, such a lineage is essential to any future reestablishment of the Temple and its leadership since only Aaron's descendants qualify for the high priesthood in the tribe of Levi. *See also* Jew(s); Judaism; Levite(s); Levitical Covenant; priest(s).

Coinneach Odhar: a Scottish prophet (d. 1577?) who used a blue stone with a hole in it to envision the future. He offered several predictions about his country, some of which actually transpired. The most severe was his announcement that his homeland was doomed.

Colet, John: brilliant English Renaissance humanist, scholar, and master teacher (1467–1519). Colet was among the very first to attempt to present the Bible in English to everyone, in direct defiance of Pope Innocent VIII who had banned the practice (in 1487) on penalty of death. He translated the Scriptures from Greek and began covertly reading them to his students in the quasi-privacy of the classroom. The few public Bibles available then were to be found in huge bound Latin volumes chained to church altars here and there. Shortly thereafter, William Tyndale produced the first printed New Testament. *See also* Innocent VIII, Pope; Roman Catholic Church.

collar. See **clerical** collar.

Collect: a specific prayer for a particular day of worship. In liturgical rites, especially Roman Catholicism, the Collect is usually recited at the end of the entrance ritual and before the day's Bible reading. *See also* liturgical year; liturgy, Christian; prayer(s); Roman Catholic Church.

collective unconscious, the: a psychological term meant to show that below the conscience mind, there lurks a deep layer of hidden, inborn forces with an uncontrollable universal will. The theory has theological implications, for it bolsters the New Testament idea that sin is not only individual (which is surely is) but is also mysteriously intuitive to our empirical way of thinking. As social humanity, we share in the origin and participation in sin as a natural order of living. Our collective sins interlock, something Augustine called the "sinful mass."

College of Cardinals. See cardinal(s).

collegialism: the belief that the church is independent but equal to the state. *See also* antidisestablishmentarianism; *Booke of the General Lawes and Libertyes;* Caesar cult; caesaropapacy; civil religion; disestablishmentarianism; divine right of kings; Edict of Milan, Edict of Nantes; Edict of Toleration; emperor worship; Establishment Clause and Free Exercise Clause; Geghan Bill; Massachusetts Body of Libertyes; *Pontifex Maximus; princeps; principis;* regalism; state church; Toleration Act of 1649; ultramontanism; Virginia's Religious Disestablishment law.

colon: a single line of poetry, also called a stich or stichos. *See also* acrostic poem; antithetic parallelism; climatic parallelism; doubling; poetry (biblical); psalm; stichometry; synthetic parallelism.

colophon: a literary protection or signature at the end of a writing, often accompanied by a curse on those who would tamper with the original text. The book of Revelation contains a colophon as recorded in Revelation 22:18–19, which promises a blessing on those who read it along with a warning to those who would abuse it.

colored prophecy: a nonliteral method of biblical interpretation that relies on "Jewish coloration" (reading with a Jewish bias) or other nonspecific writing styles that tend to favor an allegorical system of understanding. *See also* idealism; Judaism.

colors, liturgical: the required colors for vestments, hangings, altar cloths, and related articles specified by the rubrics of Roman Catholicism and a few Protestant denominations. Each color represents a particular liturgical season and is regularly changed to match the themes of the year—violet or blue, white, green, red, gold, black, rose, or other hues for special occasions. The main colors stand out as red (for the Feast of the Holy Innocents with alternate white for circumcision) after Epiphany through Septuagesima, Passion Sunday, Ascension (except Low Sunday and Assumption), and for apostles and martyrs; blue is for Advent, Saint John's Day (or white), and Septuagesima to Passion Sunday; green is for confessor days (alternate blue); white is used at Christmas, Epiphany, and for virgins who are not martyrs; black is for funerals. *See also* Advent wreath; colors, symbology of; liturgical year; liturgy, Christian; ordinary time; Roman Catholic Church; white.

colors, symbology of: an irregular descriptive style within apocalyptic writing wherein colors may take on symbolic meaning beyond the normal usage of naming the hues of the spectrum. The most obvious examples are in Revelation where "white" (righteousness and purity) and "black" (sin or death) are in use. Revelation 4:3 describes a circular emerald rainbow, which surely has symbolic value. Colors named elsewhere may or may not indicate esoteric meaning, depending on the context and intended usage. *See also* black; colors, liturgical; flowers of red and white; horse; Islam; liturgical year; onyx; rainbow; Roman Catholic Church; sapphire; white.

Colosseum, the Roman: originally, the Flavian Amphitheater. The name "Colosseum" is perhaps derived from its great size, or perchance for the great statue of Nero situated nearby. Christians and Romans knew it, of course, as the site of the barbaric practices of the gladiatorial combats and massacre of thousands of the faithful and the helpless, both human and animal. *See also* Christianity in the Roman Empire; martyrdom; Roman Empire.

Colossians as New Testament epistle: Paul's letter to the Colossian church. Its most prominent eschatological theme is the assurance that believers will share in the glories of the returning Christ and that they will receive rewards for their fidelity and good works. *See also* Paul as apostle.

Colossus of Rhodes: a huge statue (over 105 feet high) straddling the harbor of Rhodes. The Greeks built the edifice to celebrate the city's victory over the Cyrus invasion in 280 B.C. and was dedicated to the Titan god Helios. It is named as one of the seven wonders of the ancient world but was destroyed by earthquake in 226 B.C. *See also* Helios; seven wonders of the ancient world.

colportage, colporteur: distribution of Bibles, tracts, religious publications, and similar printings using a variety of methods available, legal or not. The bearer of the material is called a colporteur. *See also* Andrew van der Bijl; Gideons International; missions, missionaries.

Columbanus: early Gaelic Celtic missionary (A.D. 540–615) and monastic starter. His name translates to "the white dove." One of Columbanus's most famous journeys took him to Bregnez in Austria. It was there, so the legend goes, that he encountered some devotees of the fierce god Wotan preparing a huge barrel of beer to honor their deity. Columbanus had no problem with alcohol but hated to see good beer offered to a false god. In fury, he blew on the barrel, causing it to explode, and Woten lost his offering. Other legends claim he conversed with wolves and bears. Oddly enough, he is the patron saint of motorcyclists with a Catholic feast day of November 23 (November 24 in Ireland). *See also* missions, missionaries; Odin; Roman Catholic Church.

Columbine: a sort of generalized or popular recognition label for school shootings in America. Columbine High School in Littleton, Colorado, was the scene of one of America's first mass shootings in a church or educational facility on April 20, 1999. Some of the fifteen murders that day were precipitated by anti-Christian fervor that has led to an unofficial recognition of, or reference to, crimes against religious victims, particularly the young and innocent. *See also* "hate crimes"; persecution(s); slaughter of the Innocents; social issues; terrorism; xenophobia.

columbine: a lovely blossom of the buttercup family that flowers into blooms of red, white, yellow, blue, or purple with sweet spurs on the petals. Early Christians chose it as a symbol of their faith because its flower resembles a grouping of doves. *See also* dove; flower(s); flora, fruit, and grain, symbology of; grass; herb(s); Holy Spirit; hyssop; lilies; lotus; papyrus.

Columbkille: commonly known as Saint Columba (521–546). Columba was born in Dublin, Ireland (a contemporary of Brendan of Clonfert), but was soon exiled to Scotland where he worked feverously as a spiritual leader and innovator. Perhaps his most famous prophecy states that Ireland would be inundated by water seven years before the Second Coming (Saint Patrick said the same). Somehow, Columbkille's name became associated with the famous *Book of Kells*. *See also Book of Kells*, the; Brendan of Clonfert; Roman Catholic Church.

Columbus, Christopher: b. Cristoforo Colombo in Genoa, Italy (ca. 1451-1506), acknowledged as the most persistent (not the first) explorer to the New World in the 15th century. Though not well acknowledged, the "Admiral of the Ocean Seas" was an unabashed Roman Catholic apocalypticist. Most are unaware that he claimed to have spotted a UFO during his maiden voyage to the New World in the waters of the Bermuda Triangle. There, he claimed his compass became erratic and soon after he and Pedro Gutierrez observed a brilliant light from the deck of the *Santa Maria*. This "glimmering at a great distance" Columbus attributed his discovery of land four hours later. He believed himself to be the Messiah announced by Joachim of Fiore and that he was to lead the Christian armies into the last Crusade. No doubt he intended to use the captured resources of the New World he discovered to finance another Crusade to the Holy Land and to reconstruct the Temple in Jerusalem. Some historians suggest he and many of his ships' crew were Jews. He and his patron, Ferdinand of Aragon, saw the victory of Spain over the Moors of the Iberian Peninsula as a sign of the approaching Millennium. Columbus even authored a book entitled *The Book of Prophecies* in support of his position. His personal prediction for the end of the world was the year 1656 (some records say 1658). *See also* Roman Catholic Church; UFO.

Comet ISON: a spectacular comet (scientifically named C/2012 S1) which appeared in 2012. Due to the proximity to the sun, its brightest manifestation was November 28 and was expected to continue its visibility. It faded quickly, however, after rounding the sun's far side and was torn apart on Thanksgiving Day by space gravity. As with the appearance of comets throughout history, this one generated the usual intensified apocalyptic interest. *See also* apocalyptic, apocalypticism; astronomy, astronomers; celestial disturbances; cosmology; Hale-Bopp Comet; Halley's Comet.

"Come up here": the only recognized calling formula recorded for us of God's command to usher His followers from earth to heaven. The phrase is used in Revelation 4:1 and 11:12. *See also* eschatology, eschatological; door(s) of Revelation; "in the Spirit"; rapture; sounds of the rapture; voice of God; voice out of heaven; voices of Revelation.

Comforter, my: a reference in Jeremiah (Jer. 8:18), a probable indicator of Yahweh as Counselor for the nation of Israel. The meaning in Hebrew, however, is somewhat ambiguous. The New International Version translates the word and its modifiers as "O my Comforter in sorrow." *See also* names (titles) for God.

coming ages, the: Paul's indication of the eschatological future, expressed as gratitude to God for His grace in the kindness of Christ (Eph. 2:6–7). "The coming ages" seems to express a rather long time on the earth, a thought that would be contrary to Paul's usual expectation that our time here will be short. There is the idea then, that "the coming ages" includes the future time with Christ as well. *See also* advents(s) of Christ; age of lawlessness; "all these things"; apocalyptic, apocalypticism; apocalyptic calculation; apocalyptics; apocalyptic time; appearing, the; appointed time, the; clouds and darkness, a day of; coming of the salvation, the; consummation, the final; day he visits us, the; day of evil; day of God, the; day of (our Lord Jesus) Christ; day of Revenge; day of the Lord, the; day of [their] visitation; day of the Lamb's wrath, the; day of trumpet and battle, a; day of vengeance of our God; "days of Elijah"; "days of Noah"; Day, that (the); due time, in; *elthnen;* end of all things, the; end of the age, the; End, the; end, the; end time; *en takhei;* eschatology, eschatological; eschaton; fullness of time; Glorious Appearing; great and dreadful day, that; "here, there, or in the air"; *kairos;* Second Coming; Second Coming procession; rapture; secret rapture; TEOTWAWKI; termination dates; time; time is near, the; time of fulfillment; times and the seasons, the; "until he comes"; wrath, the coming.

coming of the salvation, the: Peter's description of the promise of Christ's return (1 Pe. 1:5). He concludes his brief description by adding "that is ready to be revealed in the last time." *See also* advents(s) of Christ; age of lawlessness; "all these things"; apocalyptic, apocalypticism; apocalyptic calculation; apocalyptics; apocalyptic time; appearing, the; appointed time, the; clouds and darkness, a day of; coming ages, the; coming consummation, the final; day he visits us, the; day of evil; day of God, the; day of (our Lord Jesus) Christ; day of Revenge; day of the Lord, the; day of [their] visitation; day of the Lamb's wrath, the; day of trumpet and battle, a; day of vengeance of our God; "days

History and Mystery

of Elijah"; "days of Noah"; Day, that (the); due time, in; *elthnen;* end of all things, the; end of the age, the; End, the; end, the; end time; *en takhei;* eschatology, eschatological; eschaton; fullness of time; Glorious Appearing; great and dreadful day, that; "here, there, or in the air"; *kairos;* Second Coming; Second Coming procession; rapture; secret rapture; TEOTWAWKI; termination dates; time; time is near, the; time of fulfillment; times and the seasons, the; "until he comes"; wrath, the coming.

coming one, the. See coming prince (ruler), the.

coming prince (ruler), the: typical title of the Messiah, who is called *the Prince* of the Jewish people. He is named in conjunction with the first great division of Daniel's seventy weeks prophecy and is usually equated with the Anointed One (Dan. 9:25). For Christians, the title could anticipate the Second Coming Christ. In Daniel, the Coming One is the very Anointed One of Israel and the ruler who will appear according to the divine timing of the prophecy. Some scholars claim that the Coming One was the historical Cyrus, Zerubbabel, or Joshua the priest in a departure of opinion from traditional belief. The identity is further complicated in that another ruler is addressed in the same context (Dan. 9:26) who is obviously *not* a Messiah figure. *See also* Anointed One, the; eschatology, eschatological; Jew(s); Messiah; ruler (prince) who will (is to) come, the.

Commandments of God. See Ten Commandments, the; torah.

commemoration(s): acts or ceremony designed to memorialize or remember important events or persons of history. The rituals are common enough in civic society but have special significance in church life, especially those of high liturgy form. There the commemoratives may take the form of recognitions of saints and are emphasized in most liturgical formats throughout the church year. *See also* feasts and special days of high liturgy faiths; liturgical year; liturgy; memorial(s).

commentary: a Bible study aid that offers scholarly explanations of the Scripture paradigms. The text usually reads in verse-by-verse explorations and attempts to clarify or instruct the reader on both familiar and obscure biblical passages. *See also* concordance.

Commercial Babylon. See Secular Babylon.

commercial theory of atonement. See satisfaction theory of atonement.

comminate: to threaten with divine punishment or vengeance. *See also* vengeance.

commination: a worship rite of the seven psalms, common to Roman Catholicism, after which ashes are applied to the forehead of the communicant with the words, "Remember, O man, that thou art ashes, and unto ashes shalt thou return." *See also* liturgical year; liturgy, Christian; seven psalms, the; Roman Catholic Church.

commission: an official authorization or mandate to do something. Christians are commissioned to fulfill certain tasks or pursue specific callings in service to the kingdom of God and clerics and missionaries are subject to the same, usually performed via a special ceremony. *See also* call(ing); charge; charisms; Great Commission, the; liturgical year; mantle; ordination.

Committee of Triers: a means by which Oliver Cromwell filled clerical vacancies after the purge by the Committees of Ejectors because they the office-holders would not conform to Puritan standards. Replacements were mostly Presbyterians, Baptists, and Independents. *See also* Committees of Ejectors; Cromwell, Oliver.

Committees of Ejectors: a means devised by Oliver Cromwell to dismiss those clergy who would not support his Puritan policies as Lord Protector of England. Over 6,000 lost their positions and had to be replaced by the Committee of Triers. *See also* Committee of Triers; Cromwell, Oliver.

Commodianus: Christian poet and theologian dated to around the middle of the third century. He was probably the first to detail a millennial program and predicted some actions of the Antichrist. His theology turned toward the millennial Sabbath theory. *See also* Roman Catholic Church.

common readings: in liturgical circles, any grouping of readings appropriate for a type of generalized worship celebration as opposed to mandated selections for special events called "propers." Most Protestant services also attempt to select passages of Scripture appropriate to the theme of worship being practiced at the moment. *See also* feasts and special days of high liturgical faiths; liturgical year; liturgy; liturgy, Christian; liturgy, Jewish; proper readings; Propers.

communal communities: those sects or associations that attempt to live in a closed society wherein all work and produce is shared either for religious or secular reasons. Almost all such types of devotion have failed throughout history, including political Communism. Possible exceptions may name the Amish, Mennonites, and some of the monasteries developed by various religions. Even the Church's early experiment with the process fizzled (Acts 4:32–37). *See also* abbey; Adelphi Organization; Agapemone; agapetae; Ahmad, Mirza Ghulam; Amana Community; Amish; Applewhite, Marshall; Assemblies of the Wise; Behmenism; Bhagwan Shree Rajneesh; Branch Davidians; Brook Farm; Brotherhood of the New Life; Bruderhof Communities; Calistus; Christian Catholic Apostolic Church; church bodies in America (typed); cloister; communion; Communistic millennialism; Community of Christ; convent; Cotton, John; cult(s); Davenport, James; de Laudonniere, Rene Gaulaine; Dowie, John Alexander; Dukhobors; Eaton, Theophilus; Ephrata Cloister; Essenes; Familists; Feraferia; Findhorn Foundation; Fourier, Charles Francois Marie; Fruitlands Community; Heaven's Gate; Helicon Home Colony; Holzhauser, Venerable Bartholomew; Hopedale Community; House of David;

Houteff, Florence; Hubbard, Elbert Green; Feraferia; Findhorn Foundation; Focolare Movement; Hutterites; Icarian Communities; Inner Light churches; Jeffs, Warren; Jones, Jim; Jonestown; Jouret, Luc; Keith, George; Kieninger, Richard; Koinonia Farm; Koresh, David; Labadie, Jean de; Labadists; Ladd, William; Lama Foundation; Mennonites; Modern Times; monastery; monasticism; monk(s); Mount Tabor; Myrtle Hill commune; Nettles, Bonnie; New Harmony Community of Equality; New Haven Colony; Nob; Noyes, John Humphrey; nun(s); Oneida Community; Owen, Robert; Owen, Robert Dale; Pennsylvania Dutch; Peoples Temple; phalanxes; prophetic associations; Purnell, Benjamin; Qumran; Rapp, Father Johann Georg; religious organizations; Ripley, George; sect(s); Schafer, Paul; Socinianism, Socinians; Solar Temple, the; sons (school) of the prophets; Taborites; theocracy; theocratic kingdom; United Society of Believers; Villa Baviera; Vissarion; Zinzendorf, Count Nikolaus Ludwig von; Zionites; Zoar Society.

commune(s). See communal communities.

communicable attributes: those quality traits of God that He chooses to impart, at least to some degree, to humanity. Some measure of love, for example, or justice, insight, kindness, and the like are gained through the Father's benevolence and desire to distribute.

communicatio idiomaum: the widely held patristic concept wherein there is an intentional interchange of characteristics between body and spirit in the human person.

Communion. See "breaking the bread"; Eucharist; Lord's Supper; sacrament(s).

communion: when pertaining to ecclesiological structure, a body of believers sharing a common belief system – a fellowship or denomination. *See also* church; church bodies of America (typed); communal communities; communion of the saints; denomination(s), denominationalism; fellow servants.

communion of the saints: a doctrine primarily basic to Roman Catholicism having to do with heaven and purgatory. "Communion," in this sense, refers to the commonality the living may have with the deceased in that prayers and good deeds may benefit those souls already departed (exclusive of hell). The doctrine essentially incorporates the unity in Christ for the living and the dead. *See also* Church; communion; Roman Catholic Church.

Communistic millennialism: the view that the oppression of church and state should be eliminated and replaced with Marxist ideals. Many religious commune sects may be declared to have a similar agenda but usually unconnected to any abject political interest. *See also* communal communities; Lenin, Vladimir; Marx, Karl; Millennial churches.

Community of Christ (cultic): a contemporary cultic group in the United States with a minor following led by Jeffery Lundgren. The group has been accused of murder and other various internal punishments of dissidents within the congregation. *See also* Church of Jesus Christ of Latter-Day Saints, the; cult(s); idolatry; Lundgren, Jeffery.

Community of Christ (Mormon): followers of Joseph Smith III, originally called the Reorganized Church of Jesus Christ of Latter-Day Saints (name changed in 2001). The group, located at Independence, Missouri, represents the descendants of the Joseph Smith who declined to follow Brigham Young into exile in Utah. The Independence group differs from the larger component in several ways. They use variations of the Book of Mormon and *Doctrine and Covenants* and outright reject the Pearl of Great Price. *See also* Church of Jesus Christ of Latter-Day Saints, the; idolatry; sect(s).

Community Rule. See Manual of Discipline.

Compactata: the formal agreement that reconciled the aftermath of the bloody conflict between the Calixtines, led by Jan Rokycane, and the Roman Catholic Church. The document was signed at Prague in 1436. The Calixtines (a.k.a. the Ultraquists) were less radical than most Hussites to whom they were affiliated but the more stringent group, the Taborites, refused to surrender. *See also* Roman Catholic Church; Taborites; Ultraquists; White Mountain, battle of.

Companions: early converts who lived in the presence of Muhammed. *See also* Islam.

comparative religion: the systematic study of the commonalities and differences among the religions of the world. The subject is commonly addressed in seminaries and Bible colleges as an academic discipline.

comparative theology. See systematic theology.

compass rose depiction: the emblem or logo brand of the Anglican Communion. The design is by Canon Edward West of New York City consisting of a stylized compass with a centered cross of Saint George, surrounded by the inscription, "The truth shall make you free." *See also* Anglicanism.

compenetration: a contrived hermeneutical method whereby an oracle, prophecy, or any given Scripture passage is stated to have *primary* meaning to the events of the time it was uttered, but could hold *future* implications as well. The concept was conceived by the Roman Catholic expositor Cuthbert Latty, who was attempting to liberalize Old Testament prophecy yet still maintain the Roman Catholic tradition of literalism, particularly as it applied to the doctrines of the virgin birth stories related in Isaiah 7:14 and Matthew 1:18–24.

complementarianism: the view of many fundamentalist Jews, Christians, Muslims, and others that women have specific (and almost always subservient) roles in marriage. Paradoxically, the view is often stated with a preliminary caveat that men and women are supposedly equal. *See also* egalitarian view of authority; feminist theology.

complementarian view of the Trinity: the thesis that all three members of the Trinity are equal in power and in all other attributes. Nevertheless, the implication is that, as the divine collective, the Father has a greater authority. The view becomes complementarian when it is construed further to the relationships between men and women, in that men have authority over women. *See also* Adoptionism; Anomoeans; Arianism; Arius; Donatism; dualism; Dynamic Monarchianism; dynamism; egalitarian view of authority; eternal subordination of the Son; feminist theology; "four fences of Chalcedon"; *homoiousios; homoousios;* hypostatic union; incarnation; *kenosis;* kenotic view of Christ; modalism; Monarchianism; monoenergism; monophysitism; Nestorianism; Nestorius; *ousia;* patripassianism; Pelagianism; Pelagius; *perichoresis;* psilanthropism; Socianism, Socinians; subordinationism; theanthroposophy; *Theophorus;* Trinity; two natures, doctrine of the; unipersonality.

compline: prayer service for late night in the liturgical canonical hours of the Divine Office. *See also* Agpeya; canonical hours; lauds; liturgical year; liturgy; liturgy, Christian; matins; nones; prayer(s); prime; sext; terce; vespers.

comprecation: a prayer meeting. *See also* prayer(s).

Compromising Church: a contrived name for the historical period of A.D 313–630 according to dispensational theology. The time is represented by the church at Pergamum (Rev. 2:12–17) and pertains to the era when that congregation was accommodating itself to worldly standards. The period in question was a self-indulgent age and saw the beginnings of persecution of its own numbers. A ritualistic style of worship developed with limited spirituality. *See also* dispensation(s); dispensational theology; Pergamum.'

compuctus: a Latin derivative used to describe the internal mechanizations for determining the proper date for Easter. As it stands today, in the West Easter is dated to the first Sunday after the first full moon following the vernal equinox, allowing it to occur anywhere between March 2 and April 25 (though it could delay even to May). The East uses the Julian calendar instead of the Gregorian so Easter is dated somewhere between April 4 and May 8. *See also* calendar (Gregorian); calendar (Julian); Easter; Paschal controversy; supermoon.

compunction: a pronounced twinge of conscience that may accrue to the sensitive believer for wrongdoing. Compunction is considered a positive emotion in that it may lead to confession, repentance, forgiveness, and even reconciliation between God and the individual sinner. Unremitting guilt or debilitating worry after confession and repentance, however, is spiritually and physically unhealthy.

compurgation: the ecclesiastical equivalent of a sworn oath taken before testimony in a trial. The oath-taker swears solemnly that his or her speech will be truthful. *See also* oath(s); promise; Roman Catholic Church.

conceptualism. See nominalism, nominalist(s).

Concerned Christians: a rather macabre religion that, ironically, began as a Christian ministry to expose cults and false teachings. Monte Kim Miller was its founder in the 1980s which grew more bizarre as time passed. Mind control became his method of operation, so much so that in 1998 some fifty of the group mysteriously disappeared in Colorado. Miller had predicted that Armageddon would begin in Denver near that time. He further claimed to be one of the two end time witnesses in Revelation 11. *See also* cult(s); idolatry.

conciliarism: an emphasis on ecumenical councils as a source of doctrine and church fidelity. The tendency runs strong in Catholicism but has limited value for most Protestants. *See also* acephali; autocephalous; church, administration of the early; councils, church; church models; congregational polity; connectional polity; ecclesiology; episcopate; faith and order; Free Church(es); hierarchical polity; magisterium; plebania; polity; prelacy; presbytery; representative polity; rite; ritual; shepherding (cultic); shepherding (discipleship); shepherding (pastoral); sobornost.

conclave: the body of cardinals who elect new popes to the Roman Catholic papacy as needed. Although there are over 200 in the College of Cardinals of the church at this time, an election quorum is limited to 120, each of whom is selected by the pope. *See also* cardinal(s); *Curia;* Infirmieri; religious organizations; Roman Catholic Church.

concomitance: Eucharistic doctrine that affirms the simultaneous presence of Christ's body and blood in each sacramental element, the bread and wine. The doctrine opposes the view that the body is in the bread and the blood is in the drink. It would also, of course, counter the notion that the body of Christ is not present in any but a metaphysical presence. *See also* consubstantiation; Eucharist; Eucharistic theory of the Reformers; invination; real presence; sacrament(s); scaring; theophagy; transubstantiation.

concordance: a Bible study aid that lists names, subjects, and topics to allow quick and detailed identification. Definitions are brief but thorough, which make the work slightly different from Bible dictionaries. *See also* commentary.

concordat(s): an agreement between the papal authority and a secular nation to work cooperatively. Roman Catholicism and European nations made them often, including Pope Pius XII's liaison with Adolf Hitler. Supposedly, the main objective of an issued concordat is to guarantee religious freedom to Roman Catholics. *See also* Concordant of Collaboration; Roman Catholic Church.

Concordant of Collaboration: a document or statement of virtual capitulation of Pope Pius XII to Adolf Hitler in 1933 that seemed to validate much of Nazism, especially in its opposition to the Jewish race. The action earned him the title "Hitler's Pope" from John Cromwell's 1999 bestseller of the same name. Six years earlier Pope Pius XI had secured the Roman See to Mussolini. *See also Adversus Judaeos;* anti-Semitism; concordat(s); Day of Pardon; Lateran Treaty; Roman Catholic Church.

concreated holiness: the tenet that Adam was created sinless and with an eternal inclination to righteousness and holiness.

concubine: a female who voluntarily enslaves herself to a man, primarily for sexual pleasure. In patriarchal times, concubines did not enjoy equal status with a wife but were better treated among the Hebrews than in many other cultures. Often the concubine served as a surrogate mother for barren wives (as it was with Sarah and Hagar and Rachel and Bilhah) and shared many common rights with other women of the time. In Old Testament days, King Solomon was notorious for keeping a large harem of concubines, some 300 of them plus 700 wives. *See also* Abishag; David's wives; prostitute, prostitution.

concupiscence: from the Latin *concupiscentia* – the natural inclination or innate tendency for humans to gravitate to or do evil. *See also* after one's own lusts; body; carnal; carnal Christians; debauchery; depravity; dissipation; flesh; hedonism; human condition, the; human nature, the; immorality; moral uncleanliness; sin(s); sinful nature, the; social issues; unclean; wicked, wickedness; worldly.

concursive inspiration: a theory of grasping knowledge of God that assumes revelation (God's impartation of Himself to us) and inspiration (the capability to understand) are one and the same process. *See also* inspiration; revelation, theological.

condemnation: to pronounce guilty or give out punishment. In standard Christianity, condemnation is the unavoidable state of being for all unrepentant and all those untrusting to the salvation in Christ, including assignment to eternal punishment.

condign merit: a distinction of some religious faith bodies of medieval origin between certain good works or merits. A condign merit tabs the work as that being performed with divine assistance—that is Spirit-motivated—and that is done in a state of grace. *See also* autosoterism; congruent merit; solifidianism; works.

conditional covenant(s): a type of treaty or covenant in which fidelity to the agreement depends on each party's loyalty to the stipulations of the contract. Most biblical covenants appear to be unconditional, in that God will honor them in spite of humanity's violation of the terms. Two examples of conditional covenants might be the Adamic and the Mosaic. *See also* Adamic Covenant; covenant(s), biblical; conditional election; conditional prophecy; Mosaic Covenant; suzerainty treaty; unconditional covenant(s).

conditional election: the Armenian belief that God chooses (for salvation) those whom he knows will find faith. The faith article then emphasizes human free will in matters of faith. The opposite view is Calvinistic and called unconditional election because God chooses whom He will without consideration of human intellect, faith, or desires. *See also* Arminianism; BACON; Calvinism; conditional covenant(s); double predestination; election; eternal security; fall from grace; Five-Point Calvinism; free will; grace; "once saved, always saved"; perseverance of the saints; predestination; Remonstrants; total depravity; TULIP; Westminster Confession.

conditional immortality. See annihilationism; soul sleep.

conditional prophecy: a proposal from God, usually in the form of a forthcoming curse or blessing, the fulfillment of which was dependent on Israel's faithfulness (*cf.* 2 Kings 21:7–8 and 2 Chronicles 33:8). Both of these references refer to the Law of Moses. Such prophecies make up a special class of certain God-given predictions whose fulfillment is contingent upon the actions of later generations, which were not God ordained. All too often, the people refused to meet the conditions and were denied the blessing being readied. The idea is that God may choose to produce or deny fulfillment of a given prediction if certain criteria are not met by future generations who might otherwise attain it. For example, the punishment predicted by Jeremiah (Jer. 26:12–13) could be rescinded if the people repented. Application of the conditional principle is usually necessarily restricted in prophetic utterance but is, nevertheless, legitimate. *See also* conditional covenant(s); prophecy types.

cone of power: a visualization technique used by witches to raise energy from the environment for practical use. The power is focused from the earth up when called upon by certain preparations and specified ceremonies are enacted. The traditional cone-shaped hat associated with witches and wizards, in fact, historically channeled such energy. *See also* idol(s); idolatry; New Age religion; visualization; Wicca; witchcraft.

confederation of ten kings. See ten-nation confederacy.

confession: 1. the act of professing one's guilt for sin with a view to forgiveness. Most Protestant believers aver that confession to God and to others is best accomplished one-on-one to the offended Deity or person. Roman Catholic practice is more centered on the confessor's auricular ("in the ear) admission to a priest who is authorized to assign penance and offer restitution. Both confessor and mentor are normally screened inside a sealed structure called the "confessional." Catholic authorities claim there are three steps to the perfect confession: candid expression (involving the whole person), mournful contrition, and burning gratitude for God's mercy. Protestants stress honesty in confession followed by a genuine attempt to remedy wrongs done whenever possible but usually abjure the need of any intermediary except the Holy Spirit. 2. the act of articulating one's faith tenets, either verbally or in writing (*e.g.* 2 Corinthians 9:13) as a testimony or witness to faith. *See also* Act of Contrition; confession(s) of faith; confessor(s); Confiteor; liturgical year; liturgy, Christian; liturgy, Jewish; Roman Catholic Church; seated at the feet; *sigillum*; testimony; witness.

confession(s) of faith: 1. those statements of doctrine that attempt to delineate and clarify certain common beliefs of a religious system. They are usually, but not always,

History and Mystery

associated with Protestantism. Among the more famous doctrinal statements must be included: 1) of the 16th and 17th centuries or earlier—Apostle's Creed; Athanasian Creed, Augsburg Confession (Luther and Melanchthon, 1530), Belgic Confession (de Bres, 1561), Book of Concord (Lutheran), Canons of Dort; Confessions of 1560, Five Pillars of Islam, Formula of Concord (German, 1577), Gallic Confession (French, 1559), Guanabara Confession of Faith (Huguenots in America, 1558), Heidelberg Confession, Helvic Consensus, Irish Articles (1615), Nicene Creed, Schleitheim Confession (Swiss Anabaptist, 1527), Scots Confession (Knox, 1560), Sixty-Seven Articles (Zwingli, 1523), Smalcald Articles (Luther, 1537), Tetrapolitan Confession (German Reformed, 1530), Thirty-Nine Articles (Church of England, 1562), the Westminster Confession of Faith (1647), and the Savoy Declaration (1658), which modified the Westminster to suit Congregationalist favor. 2) additional Presbyterian persuasions—Book of Confessions (Presbyterian USA, 1983), Confessions of 1967 (Presbyterian USA), Westminster Larger Catechism (1649), Westminster Shorter Catechism (1649). 3) Baptists—London Baptist Confession of Faith (1689), Philadelphia Confession (1688), Baptist Confession (1689), A Declaration of Faith of English People Remaining at Amsterdam in Holland (Helwys, *et al.* 1611), [Baptists have generally mistrusted written creedal statements.] 4) Reformed churches—Belhar Confession (South Africa, 1986), Canons of Dordt (1619), Conclusions of Utrect (Netherlands, 1905), First Helvetic Confession (Swiss Reformed, 1530), Harmonia Confession Fielei (Swiss Protestants, 1581), Heidelberg Catechism (Reformed, 1563), Helvic Consensus (Reformed, 1675), Second Helvetic Confession (Reformed, 1562), Tetrapolis Confession (Bucer, 1530), Theological Declaration of Barmen (German under Hitler, 1934). One of the most expressive confessions of faith can be found in the New Testament itself: "He [God] appeared in a body, was vindicated by the Spirit, was seen by angels, was preached among the nations, was believed on in the world, was taken up to glory" (1 Tim. 3:16). Non-Christian movements often hold their own statements of faith as well. 2. an expression of many Protestant persuasions that proclaims one's acceptance of salvation in Christ and offered as a testimony of that faith. *See also* accept Christ, to; altar call; Apostle's Creed; *Arkan-ad-din;* Articles of Religion; "asking Jesus into my heart"; Athanasian Creed; Augsburg Confession; Belgic Confession; birth from above; Book of Concord; Book of Discipline; born again; Chicago-Lambeth Quadrilateral; Confessions of 1560; conversion; Credo; creed(s); Five Hindrances to Buddhism, the; Five Pillars of Islam; Five-Point Calvinism; Five Poisons of Buddhism, the; Five Precepts of Buddhism, the; Five Ways, the; Four Noble Truths of Buddhism, the; Gallic Confession; Half-Way Covenant; Heidelberg Catechism; Helvetic Consensus; Lambeth Articles; Large(r) Catechism, Luther's; liturgy, Christian; Philadelphia Confession; Tetrapolitan Confession; Nicene Creed; Pittsburg Platform of 1885; "plead the blood"; profession of faith; Reformed Churches; regeneration; religious education; *Remonstrants*, the; rule of faith; "saved"; Saybrook Platform; Savoy Confession; Smalcald Articles; Three Jewels of Buddhism, the; Three Marks of the Existence of Buddhism, the; Small(er) Catechism, Luther's; Thirteen Principles of Faith, the; Thirty-Nine Articles, the; three cornerstones of Anglicanism, the; "turn your life [heart] over to Jesus"; "walking the aisle"; "washed in the blood"; Wesleyan Quadrilateral; Westminster Confession.

Confession of 1560: creed of the Scottish faith primarily authored by John Knox. It was the standard of faith and practice until adoption of the Westminster Confession in 1647. *See also* confession(s) of faith; Knox, John; rule of faith; Westminster Confession.

confessor(s): one who endured imprisonment, personal loss, torture, or other form of suffering (short of martyrdom) from the early Catholic Church because he or she publicly professed the name of Christ. Often, confessors were later martyred. In a more liturgical sense, a confessor is one who hears a verbal repentance or utters one individually, silently or aloud. It is the Roman Catholic Church, however, that is most recognized for the sealed confessional and strict privacy owned by the listening priest. *See also* confession; Roman Catholic Church; seated at the feet; *sigillum*.

Confirmation: the occasion in which an inexperienced convert (the confirmand) has received adequate education in the faith and can express himself or herself articulately concerning a religious stance. Usually the event is recognized with an appropriate ceremony or announcement. For many Protestant denominations, the rite of believer's baptism marks the confirmation implications but Roman Catholicism views the act as a sacrament. *See also* age of accountability; baptism; Chrismation; liturgical year; liturgy, Christian; Roman Catholic Church; sacrament(s).

Confiteor: a general confession of sins often used in the Mass from the literal translation "I confess." As a ritual, the *Confiteor* is a prayer recited at the beginning of the Mass and other church rituals acting as an appeal for God's forgiveness for the congregation as a whole without mention of specific wrongdoing. It was even heard to be recited by Cardinal Gregory at the Council of Clermont who dropped to his knees begging to be included in the first Crusade at the appeal of Pope Urban II. *See also* Anamnesis; Angelus; confession; liturgical year; liturgy, Christian; prayer(s); Roman Catholic Church; seated at the feet.

conflation: creating a new text by fusing two or more separate paradigms. Such practice is risky exegesis, which could put forward a linguistic or theological error.

conflict story: a technique of form criticism proposed by Vincent Taylor in 1933. Scholars in the 1920s had discovered a literary style in the Gospels (extensively used by Rudolf Bultmann) in which a "dialogical controversy" or "scholastic dialogue" [the *conflict*] could be discerned. The narrative consists of an inquiry (either hostile or accommodating) that is presented by some character in search of knowledge. The question, along with Jesus' response, resulted in a "bibliographal apothegm" characterizing Jesus as wise and authoritative. *See also* accideme; alliteration; antithetic parallelism; apostrophe; apothegm; assonance; autograph; Bible; Bible manuscripts; Bible translations; biblical criticism; Bultmann, Rudolf; climatic parallelism; *constructio ad sensum;* context; contextualization; dittography; double sense fulfillment; doublets; doubling; edification; eisegesis; epanadiplosis; epigrammatic statements; etymology; exegesis; form criticism; gattung; gloss; gnomic sayings; grammatical-historical interpretation; *hapax legomena;* haplography; hermeneutic(s); higher criticism; homographs; homonyms; homophones; *homoteleuton;* hyperbole; idiom; illumination; *inclusio;* inspiration; interpolation; interpretation; inverted nun; irony; isagogics; *itture sopherim;* jot and tittle; kere; *kethib;* "L"; liberalist interpretation; literal interpretation; litotes; loan words; lower criticism; "M"; Masoretic Text; minuscule(s); mystery of God; omission; onomastica; onomatopoeia; paradigm; parallelism; *paroimia; paronomasia;* pericope; personification; Peshita; plenary inspiration; poetry (biblical); plenary inspiration; pointing; point of view; polyglot; principles of interpretation; proof texting; psalm; pun(s); "Q"; redaction; revelation, theological; rhetorical criticism; riddle; satire; *scripto continua;* scriptorium; *sebirin;* simile; similitude; source criticism; sources, primary and secondary; special points; strophe; superscription; symbol(s); synecdoche; syntax; synthetic parallelism; text; textual criticism; *tiggune sopherim;* Time Texts; Torah; translation; transposition; trope; type(s); typology; uncial(s); verbicide.

confraternities: distinctive Catholic orders that sprang up during the Roman Catholic Counter-Reformation, also called guilds or "oratories." In fact, the musical composition called "oratory" comes from the public appreciation of music because the common people could find a place of service like the confraternities were offering. The majority emerged in Italy, the seat of the Vatican itself. They were unwavering in their support of the pope and few had any love for the Reformers. Nevertheless, some Catholics did rush north to join the dissidents. Some of the brotherhoods were harsh and bleak in their approach to service (called the *Zelanti*), while others were more brooding and contemplative in the energy of the Holy Spirit (the *Spirituali*). Many (perhaps the majority) were lay led, not a few of which were headed by women. Others consisted of clergy under special vows called "clerks regular," a take on earlier "canons regular." Confraternities were also common among the conquered peoples of the New World because of a critical shortage of trained priests and ministers from Europe. *See* also canons regular; Counter-Reformation; Innocent III, Pope; monk(s); religious organizations; Roman Catholic Church; tertiary.

Confucius, Confucianism: Chinese philosopher and teacher (557?–479 B.C.). His given name was Kong Fu-Zi; the identification as Confucius having been bestowed by the Jesuits then in China as missionaries. There is some dispute today as to whether the legacy of Confucius should be considered a religion or pure philosophy. The emperors of the Han dynasty (206 B.C. – A.D. 220) declared Confucianism to be the state religion of China. His eschatological leanings were seldom mentioned, although he did invent the fortune cookie. *See also* Analects; *Li*; sect(s); *Tao Te Ching*.

Congregationalists: Protestant Christians with roots to early reformers like John Wycliffe and Jan Hus. They become more formalized under the influence of Robert Browne in 1592 in England. There they were called Separatists to distance themselves from the established Church of England and Calvinistic Presbyterianism. Congregationalists, unlike the

Pilgrims of Plymouth Colony (1620) and the Massachusetts Bay Company (1629), were not desirous to break from the Church of England but to reform it. They were readily accepted in the Plymouth and Massachusetts Bay Colonies in colonial America but moved rapidly west where they lost much, but certainly not all, of their strict Puritan features. They were self-governing and refused bishops or other church hierarchy. By doctrine, they were Calvinists who approved the melding of church and state. The Cambridge Platform of 1648 essentially made them the established church in New England. Most Congregationalists were abolitionists, teetotalers, and favored women's suffrage. In 1931 Congregationalists joined the Christian Church to form the Congregational Christian denomination, then in 1957, allied with the Evangelical and Reformed Church to constitute the United Church of Christ. Modern Congregationalism has split into three branches: the United Church of Christ, the National Association of Congregational Churches, and the Conservative Christian Conference. *See also* Abbott, Lyman; Beecher, Edward; Beecher, Henry Ward; Brainerd, David; Chafer, Lewis Sperry; Chancy, Charles; church bodies in America (typed); Cotton, John; Cutler, Manasseh; Davenport, James; denomination(s), denominationalism; Dowie, John Alexander; Channing, William Ellery; Chauncy, Charles; Dwight, Timothy; Finney, Charles Grandison; Gladden, Washington; Herron, George Davis; Ladd, William; Livingston, David; Lovejoy, Owen; Marsh, James; Marsh, Jedidiah; Mather, Richard; Mayhew, Jonathan; Millikan, Robert Andrews; Nee, Watchman; Pilgrim(s); Porter, Noah; Prince, Thomas; Puritanism, Puritans; Reformed Churches; Saybrook Platform; Separatists; Sheldon, Charles Monroe; slave, slavery; Stiles, Ezra; Stoddard, Solomon; Strong, Josiah; Unitarian Universalists; United Churches; Weld, Theodore Dwight; Wheelock, Eleazar; Williams, John; Wines, Enoch Cobb; Wise, John.

congregational polity: the ecclesiastical policy of organizations that allow the local membership of a given church body to govern itself with little or no oversight from higher authority. No doubt the practice, or one close to it, was begun early among the historical Christian bodies but has largely lost its impendence to some form of overseeing church structure. Not all groups, however, have abandoned self-governing principles and continue to cling to their autonomy from both church and state. Baptists, Bible churches, various Free Churches, and many independents are the best models for congregational polity. *See also* acephali; autocephalous; church, administration of the early; church models; conciliarism; connectional polity; ecclesiology; episcopate; faith and order; Free Church(es); hierarchical polity; magisterium; plebania; polity; prelacy; presbytery; representative polity; rite; ritual; shepherding (cultic); shepherding (discipleship); shepherding (pastoral); sobornost.

Congregation for the Propagation of the Doctrine of the Faith: the Roman Catholic agency charged with maintaining the purity of church doctrine. It can be named as the modern arm of the Inquisition, but without the overt persecution of earlier days, and has been set in place to assure conformity to Roman Catholic doctrine insofar as possible. *See also* Inquisition, the; religious organizations; Roman Catholic Church.

congruent merit: a distinction of some religious faith bodies of medieval origin between certain good works or merits. Congruent works were said to be those lacking intrinsic value, which God may or may not honor. *See also* Adamic Covenant; autosoterism; condign merit; solifidianism; works.

Coniah. See Jehoiachin.

conjure: to enchant by magic or sorcery or to summon by bewitching, charming, spell casting, or hexing. The formula is usually a set pattern of prayers, incantations, or magical rites to achieve the desired effect. *See also* black arts; conjure man; hungan; idolatry; magic, magick; mambo; shaman, shamanism; sorcery, sorceries; veve; voudou; voodoo; witch(es); witchcraft; wizard(s).

conjure man: a witch doctor or shaman, especially associated with the voodoo-type religions. *See also* conjure; cult(s); hierophant; hungan; idolatry; mambo; medium; meonenim; mystagogue; shaman, shamanism; spirit guide; tutelary; voodoo; voudou; witch(es); witchcraft; witch of Endor.

connectional polity: a loose confederation of some Methodist denominations that eschew episcopal-type church hierarchy in favor of cooperation between small groups, called *circuits*. *See also* acephali; autocephalous; church, administration of the early; church models; circuit(s); circuit riders; conciliarism; congregational polity; ecclesiology; ecclesiology; episcopate; faith and order; Free Church(es); hierarchical polity; magisterium; Methodists; plebania; polity; prelacy; presbytery; representative polity; rite; ritual; shepherding (cultic); shepherding (discipleship); shepherding (pastoral); sobornost.

conqueror(s): one who triumphs over another or overcomes an adverse situation. A conqueror may be good or evil depending on who is victorious at the moment and the true motive of the action. In Revelation 6:2, the rider on the white horse is granted the ability to overcome all opposition and triumph in the eschaton. The Revelation saints are often called names, such as conquerors, overcomers, or similar nouns to signify their victory in the Lamb; Jesus himself bears the title. Paul affirmed (Rom. 8:37) that believers are even more than conquerors. Revelation relates that the Tribulation saints will conquer in two ways: "by the blood of the Lamb" and "by the word of their testimony" (Rev. 12:11). Even though many are martyred (Rev. 11:7), the saints will succeed to eternity. *See also* conquest motif; martyrdom; overcomer(s).

conquest motif: or conquest metaphor, an apocalyptic writing that speaks of conquest and subjugation, a common theme in such discourses. When unscrupulous humans or demons attempt to exercise power and control, it inevitably plays to dispense suffering for all. When the Lamb (Jesus) conquers (Rev. 5:1–5), he will do so with his own blood of sacrifice and his great power. When God judges wickedness, He does so with justice and thoroughness. *See also* conqueror(s); deliverance motif; endurance motif; exchange motif; exemplar motif; rector motif; salvation; victor motif.

conquistador(s): rapacious and ruthless conquerors (the meaning of the name) from Spain and Portugal who ravaged and annexed much of Mesoamerica and South America for gold, glory, and the gospel. The most recognizable is perhaps Hernando Cortez, who subdued Mexico, but other invaders include Vasco de Balboa in Panama, Cabeza de Vaca in Texas and the Southwest, Francisco Pizarro against the Incas, Pedro de Valdivia in Chile, Gonzalo de Quesada in Columbia, and others. They were almost always accompanied and aided by the Jesuits. *See also* Aztecs; Chilam-Balam; Cortez, Hernando; eagle and the condor, the; Inca; Maya; Mesoamerica; Montezuma II; Quetzalcoatl; Society of Jesus.

conscience: that imperceptible, often unconscious, "voice" of the mind in most of us that alerts us to moral and ethical behavior or the violation of them. Some Christians assert that the conscience is generated by the Holy Spirit, but clearly all persons do not experience the same reaction to a prompt of conscience. In fact, it may even be so dulled as to be absent. Perhaps the old Indian proverb fits the definition best: "a three-cornered thing in my heart that stands still when I am good, but when I am bad, it turns around and the corners hurt a lot. If I keep doing wrong, the corners wear off and I do not hurt anymore." According to Scripture (but not necessarily psychology), the conscience may be clean (Deut. 20:5–6), troubled (1 Sam. 25:31), or weak (1 Cor. 8:7). *See also* cardinal virtues; deontology; ethics; scruples; social issues; way to heaven.

conscientious objectors: those who refuse military service on moral or religious grounds (as generally interpreted today). Groups like the Amish, Quakers, Jehovah's Witnesses, certain communal cults, and others are considered conscientious objectors by default. The Selective Service Commission recognized only religious dissenters in 1917. Later, World War II officials alleviated the "religion only" practice and provided opportunity for alternative service. Only once was an American inductee court-martialed for his objective stance. Henry Weber was convicted and sentenced to death around the time of World War II. Public outcry reduced the sentence to five years imprisonment. Since then the Supreme Court has wrestled with the interpretation of what genuinely constitutes a conscientious objection.

consecrate: to ordain or make holy. Each worship item and process of the ancient Jewish system of sacrifice required consecration to make all acceptable to God. Persons can also be consecrated or commissioned to religious service. In some religious ritual, the bread and wine of the Eucharist is said to be capable of being consecrated into the body and blood of Christ. *See also* epiccesis; epiclesis; epidesis; Eucharist; ordination; sacrament(s); sacrifice; sanctification; words of institution.

conservative(s): one who clings to historic Christian faith doctrine inasmuch as he or she can discern it. Such conservatism is usually presumed to be somewhat more moderate than fundamentalism but far to the right from liberals. *See also* church models; fundamentalism, fundamentalist(s); moderate(s).

consistent preterism. See radical preterism.

consistory: an organization or functionary with a number of applications to both civilian and ecclesiastical life. 1. the original consistory constituted an individual or a committee in the administrative organs of the Roman Empire (the *comites consistorials*). They were responsible for certain imperial duties at court, in the military, in the judiciary, or any area of government needing specific attention. 2. in Roman Catholicism, the consistory is an official meeting of the Sacred College of Cardinals. 3. for Protestantism, the name denotes a separate governing office in Europe. 4. the Church of England uses the name to identify a type of ecclesiastical court. 5. Scandinavian usage defines a "chapter" (either as a place or body) called into session to administer certain affairs of the church. The term *chapter* likely evolved from a "chapter" in the church rule book that guided the discussions. 6. In Judaism, the consistory is a body of governors over districts, provinces, or countries. 7. for Reformed Churches, the consistory is government at the local level (the equivalent of the session in Presbyterian circles). *See also* canon(s) of the church; canons regular; Church of England; confraternities; Consistory, the; Judaism; Reformed Churches; religious organizations; Roman Catholic Church; Roman Empire; session.

Consistory, the: a group of laypersons and clergy (with lay domination) of Calvinistic Protestants in the city of Geneva, Switzerland. This group was responsible for supervision of the corporate life of the city and held considerable sway as to public direction and theocratic policy. Calvin's Geneva experiment also used the Ministry of the Word, a group of clergy with pastoral duties, and the Court of Discipline to enforce the Calvinistic approach to the gospel, whether willing or not. *See also* Calvin, John; Calvinism; consistory; Geneva theocracy of John Calvin; religious organizations; Servetus, Michael.

conspiracy theorists: radical, and sometimes racist, individuals or groups who attribute ulterior motives and false identities to persons or organizations they perceive to be a threat to cherished Christian or democratic values wherever they are encountered. Many political institutions have been accused of such subterfuge including: the Council on Foreign Relations, the Trilateral Commission, the Central

Intelligence Agency (CIA), the United Nations (UN), the Russian KGB, the World Bank, British Intelligence, Scotland Yard, the Israeli Mossad, the International Monetary Fund (IMF), the North Atlantic Treaty Organization (NATO), the World Constitution and Parliament Association (WCPA), the North Atlantic Free Trade Agreement (NAFTA), the European Union (EU), the World Trade Organization (WTO), the United Nations Commission on Global Governance, the International Criminal Court (ICC), the Organization of Economic Development (OEDC), the Royal Institute of International Affairs, the Council of Europe, the French Secret Service, the Vatican, Zionism, the British monarchy, the Jesuits, the World Jewish Congress, the National Conference of Christians and Jews, B'nai B'rith, Freemasonry, the Brookings Institution, Interpol, and even the World Health Organization (WHO). Secret or fraternal societies of many descriptions are fair game wherever they are including the Illuminati, Freemasonry, and the Bilderberg Group, which are perennial favorites. Arguably, the Skull and Bones fraternity at Yale University could be named as the most consistent conspiracy group because it has produced and favored so many powerful political and economic figures. To illustrate the popularity and extent of conspiracy theories (according to a 2013 poll of registered voters), 6 percent of all Americans believe Osama bin Laden is still alive, 7 percent say the moon landing was faked, 11 percent judge the government allowed 9/11 to transpire, 14 percent believe in Bigfoot, 21 percent claim a UFO crashed at Roswell in 1947, 28 percent believe Saddam Hussein was involved in the 9/11 attacks, 29 percent are certain aliens exist, and 51 percent maintain there was a larger cabal involved in the assassination of JFK. Humanists, atheists, feminists, homosexuals, liberal politicians, "international bankers," and a host of industrial or special interest groups are always suspect. Freemasonry is a frequent and ready target always. Religious institutions are not exempt and include the Roman Catholic Church, the World Council of Churches, the National Council of Churches, Vatican II, the United Religious Center, the United Religious Initiative, Evangelicals and Catholics Together (ECT), and the Anti-Defamation League of B'nai B'rith. Conspiracy theories invariably range from the ridiculous to the sublime (*e.g.*, the United Nations and NATO are Illuminati fronts dedicated to world domination; the British royal family is intimately involved in the occult and witchcraft; the World Trade Center represented the pillars before Solomon's Temple and/or the tower of Babel, which made them targets for terrorists; the Great Seal of the United States is of occultic or Masonic design; the Jews are a race dedicated to the dominance of the world's financial markets; the European Union is the precursor to a one world government; and on and on). Many of the conspiracy theories involve apocalypticism in one form or another. See also *Adversus Judaeos;* Alien Disclosure Event; Area 51; *Atlia Vendita;* Bilderberg Group; Black Vault; Bohemian Grove; Club of Rome; crucifixion conspiracies; Damanhur; Freemasonry; Georgia Guidestones; Hashshashin; Icke, David Vaughan; Illuminati; Illuminati network; Knights of the Golden Circle; Knights of the White Camellia; Ku Klux Klan; New World Order, the (NWO); *Ordo Templi Orientis;* "Protocols of the Elders of Zion"; Roman Phalanx; secret societies; *Simonini Letter;* Skull and Bones Society; Taxil, Leo; TGAOTU.

Constantine I: called "the Great." He was the Roman emperor (A.D. 324–337) who built and ruled from the city of Constantinople. This monarch made Christianity legal throughout the empire and secured munificent favors for the church. Constantine claims to have seen the sign of the cross in the heavens during his struggle for dominance in Italy with the words "in this, conquer." From that moment at the battle of Milvian Bridge, he assumed God was directing his path to the emperor's throne and subsequent rule. His

Edict of Milan (A.D. 313) ended Christian persecution and proclaimed the new faith as the official state religion of the empire. Constantine's favor proved a mixed blessing as the church soon fell into legalism and internecine dissent once the spur of persecution was removed. For him, Christianity was a political expediency more than a life choice of good behavior, proper theology, and holy ethics. In practice, Constantine was the typical bloody tyrant and hardly the highest example of Christian virtue, even delaying his baptism until the last possible moment before death. *See also* Christianity in the Roman Empire; Constantinople as city; Edict of Milan; Helena; *In hoc signo vinces;* king(s); Labarum; Lactantius; patriarchate(s); Roman Empire.

Constantinople as city: the city occupied and beautified by Constantine the Great in A.D. 330 as the new seat of the Roman Empire and base for the emerging Eastern branch of Christianity. The site was in Byzantium on the Bosporus, where it became a magnificent metropolis. Besides Constantine, Justinian and Theodosius were perhaps its greatest rulers. By the turn of the first millennium, Constantinople was the largest city in the known world with 600,000 inhabitants. The beauty and culture of the place was so refined and famous that the populations of the day merely called it "The City." Constantinople held out against hostile forces for many years but finally fell to Crusaders in 1203 and 1204, then the Ottoman Turks in 1453 (after having been so recently saved from the invading Vandals). Today the place is Istanbul, Turkey. The city was and is the center of Eastern Orthodox Christianity. *See also* Byzantine Church; Eastern Orthodox Church; Roman Empire.

Constantinople as patriarchate. See patriarchate(s).

constellations: groups of stars that fill the night sky, of which there are eighty-eight in the zodiac. Every star belongs to its own constellation and the constellations do not overlap. Since earliest time, humans have imagined that these star collections outline various mythical animals, objects, and heroes associated with primitive religion and to which they ascribed personal and national destiny. The same is true today but on a lesser scale, excepting certain New Age and occultic beliefs where they are central. Among the constellations, the brightest is the Southern Cross and the largest (with 101 stars) is Centaurus. *See also* Age of Aquarius; angels of the heavens; Aries; astrology, astrologers; astronomy, astronomers; Cassiopeia; horoscope(s); hosts of heaven; idolatry; moon; mythological beasties, elementals, monsters, and spirit animals; New Age religion; occult, occultic; Pisces; planets as gods, the; Rahati'el; star(s); sun; zodiac.

constructio ad sensum: in grammar, to "construct according to sense"— to read or translate with common sense or most practical application. *See also* accideme; alliteration; apostrophe; apothegm; assonance; autograph; Bible; Bible manuscripts; Bible translations; biblical criticism; chiasmus; conflict story; context; contextualization; dittography; double sense fulfillment; doublets; doubling; edification; eisegesis; epanadiplosis; epigrammatic statements; etymology; exegesis; folio; form criticism; gattung; gloss; gnomic sayings; grammatical-historical interpretation; *hapax legomena;* haplography; hermeneutic(s); higher criticism; homographs; homonyms; homophones; *homoteleuton;* hyperbole; idiom; *inclusio;* interpolation; interpretation; inverted nun; irony; isagogics; *itture sopherim;* jot and tittle; kere; *kethib;* "L"; liberalist interpretation; literal interpretation; litotes; loan words; lower criticism; "M"; Masoretic Text; minuscule(s); mystery of God; omission; onomastica; onomatopoeia; palimpsest; papyrus; paradigm; parallelism; parchment; *paroimia; paronomasia;* pericope; personification; Peshita; pointing; point of view; polyglot; principles of interpretation; proof texting; pun(s); "Q"; redaction; revelation, theological; rhetorical criticism; riddle; satire; *scripto continua;* scriptorium; *sebirin;* simile;

similitude; source criticism; sources, primary and secondary; special points; strophe; superscription; symbol(s); synecdoche; syntax; synthetic parallelism; text; textual criticism; *tiggune sopherim;* Time Texts; Torah; translation; transposition; trope; type(s); typology; uncial(s); vellum; verbicide.

consubstantiation: a concept of the Eucharist by which adherents believe the bread and wine of the sacrament somehow truly hold within them the actual body and blood of Jesus. The process of change may best be described as the presence of Christ "hovering around" or somehow inherent in the bread and wine via some mysterious sense but does not actually invade the elements to accidentally change the substance. The concept is most often identified with Ulrich Zwingli and to some extent Martin Luther. *See also* Anaphora; Calvin, John; concomitance; ecumenism; elevation; epiclesis; Eucharist; Eucharistic theory of the Reformers; invination; liturgy, Christian; Lord's Supper; Marburg Conference; monstrance; Protestant Reformation, the; sacrament(s); theophagy; transubstantiation; sacrament(s); sacring; Zwingli, Ulrich (Huldrych); wafer; wine.

consummation, the final: eschatological language for the end of days when all will be made new in the power of Christ. The phrase, or others like it, is most discernible in the pastoral epistles of John. *See also* advents(s) of Christ; age of lawlessness; "all these things"; apocalyptic, apocalypticism; apocalyptic calculation; apocalyptics; apocalyptic time; appearing, the; appointed time, the; clouds and darkness, a day of; coming ages, the; consummation, the final; day he visits us, the; day of evil; day of God, the; day of (our Lord Jesus) Christ; day of Revenge; day of the Lord, the; day of [their] visitation; day of the Lamb's wrath, the; day of trumpet and battle, a; day of vengeance of our God; "days of Elijah"; "days of Noah"; Day, that (the); due time, in; *elthnen;* end of all things, the; end of the age, the; End, the; end, the; end time; *en takhei;* eschatology, eschatological;

eschaton; fullness of time; Glorious Appearing; great and dreadful day, that; "here, there, or in the air"; *kairos;* Second Coming; Second Coming procession; rapture; secret rapture; TEOTWAWKI; termination dates; time; time is near, the; time of fulfillment; times and the seasons, the; "until he comes"; wrath, the coming.

contemplative prayer movement: a cult bloc of the 21st century wherein meditation can be used to form the opinion that the practitioner is divine and allows a more concentrated prayer process. Alternate names for some factions are labeled the kundalini meditation or serpent meditation. Others name the practices as *lectio divina,* Christian yoga, "breath prayer," "entering the silence," mantra chanting, or even "Christian meditation." A less esoteric type of Christian meditation is called "centering prayer" and springs from the early church mystics. Criticism from Christian commentators usually focuses on the contemplative prayer movement which they believe to be based in the occult or Eastern religion practices. *See also* centering prayer; chakra; Chi; kundalini; latter rain, the; mantra; occult, occultic; sect(s); Shakti; 24/7 Prayer Movement; sect(s); visualization.

contemporary worship: an attempt to modernize the traditional style of church worship into a more relevant, up-to-date, or dynamic presentation. The desire is to achieve a program that more closely conforms to societal norms in music and audience participation and thereby has produced many styles and expressions. The intent, of course, is to appeal to a wider and more youthful audience but results in most cases have been mixed at best and probably less than spectacular. *See also* blended worship; liturgy, Christian; worship.

contemptible person, a: a "vile person" in some translations, and one of several titles for Antiochus Epiphanes as presented in the book of Daniel (Dan. 11:21). As such, Antiochus is a type for the Antichrist who fits the description of a "vile" person unsuited to royalty. The phrase describes anyone who is morally degraded but the Daniel reference is specifically addressed to Antiochus. Revelation 22:10 suggests an aura of resignation for those depraved persons who will not repent, allowing them to continue in their sin and eternally absent themselves from the rewards of heaven. *See also* Antichrist; Antiochus IV Epiphanes; king who exalts himself, the; little horn, the; willful king, the.

contemptus mundi: Latin phrase meaning "contempt of the world." It describes a form of Christian literature of the Middle Ages in which the earth is pictured as a place of unhappiness, suffering, and selfishness with only fleeting pleasures. It is a common attitude of monks and other religious isolationists. Even compared to the blessings of heaven, such an attitude does not truly effect the biblical view of our present lives.

context: the immediate narrative surrounding a literary thought or subject matter being examined. Attention to the context is a crucial technique when interpreting Bible texts. The process makes examination of the immediate words and thoughts important because they inevitably impinge on the meaning of specific verses. Often, the context will explain or suggest the most logical meaning of any given thought or word that might be in doubt. Context can also apply to other ideas not necessarily written near the subject but still pertinent to the investigation. If an idea of interpretation does not agree in context to its neighbors, or to biblical truth as a whole, it is probably incorrect. The practice is of particular importance when dealing with apocalyptic literature. *See also* biblical criticism; contextualization; eisegesis; exegesis; form criticism; grammatical-historical interpretation; hermeneutics; higher criticism; interpretation; liberalist interpretation; literal interpretation; lower criticism; paradigm; parallel passage; pericope; point of view; principles of interpretation; revelation, theological; source criticism; syntax; text; textual criticism; translation; typology.

contextualization: a hermeneutical alert that reminds the Bible student that the meaning of a given passage of Scripture may differ today from its meaning when first written. In more recent theology theory, contextualization infers the interpretation of the Bible with a view to how it relates today. The admonition from Paul, for example, to "slaves, obey your masters" (Eph. 6:5), seems unrelated and dated today. *See also* biblical criticism; context; eisegesis; exegesis; form criticism; grammatical-historical interpretation; hermeneutics; higher criticism; interpretation; liberalist interpretation; literal interpretation; lower criticism; paradigm; pericope; point of view; principles of interpretation; revelation, theological; source criticism; syntax; text; textual criticism; translation; typology.

continuationism: the theological belief that the proffered gifts of the Holy Spirit presented to the Apostolic Church (prophecy, exorcism, raising the dead, healing, miracles, etc.) are still in effect since the age of the early church. *See also* cessationism; charisms; five-fold ministry, the.

contraception: methods of birth control (fertility control) considered to be anathema by Roman Catholic officials (arguably the world's most vocal critics) and some other groups and individuals. The various pharmaceuticals, forms, and devices available for the purpose are intended for prevention of conception by means other than the biological or natural. *See also* abortion; artificial conception; Roman Catholic Church; Sanger, Margaret Higgins; social issues.

contrapuntal approach to Revelation: the method of systemization of the sequence of Revelation whereby the events can be said to occur in an other than chronological manner. In music theory, contrapuntal pertains to counterpoint in which two or more relatively independent melodies can be sounded together. Similarly, certain events in Revelation can be viewed as happening nonsequentially yet supportive and expansive of one another. To exemplify: the seals can be said to commence the Tribulation action and continue their calamities to the end. The trumpets start later and also function to the end. The bowls occur latest and they too are active to the end. More precisely, the seventh seal begins the seven trumpets, and the seventh trumpet complements the seven bowls. Some have claimed that the seventh seal *is* the seven trumpets, and the seventh trumpet *is* the seven bowls. *See also* chronological approach to Revelation; progressive/complementary approach to Revelation; recapitulation approach to Revelation; silence in heaven.

contrition: a state of the mind and heart described as sorrow for sin and a desire for repentance. Often, remorse is the first step toward godly reconciliation or conversion.

controlled continuum: a theological reply to Rudolf Bultmann's "closed continuum" that assumes there is order in the universe, allows for miracles, that control is exercised by God, and that there are areas of life in which God and man can interact. *See also* closed continuum.

convent: a community of some religious order, priests, or nuns (though more commonly reserved for females); also their residence and workplace. *See also* abba; abbess; abbot; agapetae; cloister; Eastern Orthodox Church; hegumene; monastery; monasticism; mother superior; nun(s); priory; religious organizations; Roman Catholic Church; sister(s).

conventicle: a secret or illegal church meeting. Many of the early Christian communities used secretive meeting places as do some persecuted Christian bodies today. *See also* catacombs; religious organizations.

convectile acts: any civil or ecclesiastical law aimed at forcing people to attend religious services. Perhaps the first recognized was initiated by the Church of England in 1593, but it had not been the last. *See also* blue laws; Congregationalists; Puritanism, Puritans.

Conventuals. See Spirituals of the Franciscan Order.

Convergence Movement: a rather recent trend among some revisionists to combine charismatic expression with the voice of the *Book of Common Prayer*. *See also Book of Common Prayer;* sect(s).

conversae: or *conversi,* either a lay brother or sister or those who have turned novices at a later-than-normal age. The latter often lack the liturgical skills of other officials and may even be illiterate. *See also* initiate; neophyte; novitiate; postulant; Roman Catholic Church.

conversion: a secular noun referring to a switch or change from one position to another or one affiliation to another. In the vocabulary of the psychology of religion, however, conversion is an act of contrition and repentance that affects the individual with a sense of forgiveness from God and the assurance of His presence in the Holy Spirit. The commitment conveys an act of abrupt change toward an enthusiastic attitude, usually with the heightened emotional features being conspicuous, whether long lasting or not. The experience may be public or private, but its result is almost always irrepressible. A common vernacular term is "born again" but carries the technical name "regeneration." Modern evangelical experiences are most commonly brought to mind when the miracle transpires as a drastic (though not always traumatic) occurrence, which is expressed as the acceptance of Jesus Christ as personal savior. The prophets of Israel usually demanded repentance from the people when necessary but the God of the Jews was already known, both personally and nationally. It should be noted, however, that the early church expression of conversion is not the same. Then, the experience was more group orientated than individual. People were brought into a state of obedience on order from royalty or an overlord who simply decreed his people to be Christians. With it went the whole package of doctrine as just another kingly decree. "Mass conversions" were the norm. Catholic priests were known to baptize newly "converted" Roman soldiers as they crossed a river by sprinkling them with branches. It is not surprising then that missionaries usually went "straight to the top" when spreading the gospel, so a larger harvest of souls could come about with a single response to the missionary appeal. That is not to say, however, that any noble or commoner is not genuinely moved and conscientious about their faith when it had been established. *See also* accept Christ, to; altar call; "asking Jesus into my heart"; birth from above; blood of Christ; blood of the Lamb; born again; Christianese; confession(s) of faith; convert; firstfruits of the resurrection; firstfruits of the Spirit; liturgy, Christian; *metanoia;* "plead the blood"; profession of faith; recant; regeneration; repent; "saved"; sinner's prayer; "turn your life [heart] over to Jesus"; "walking the aisle"; "washed in the blood."

Conversos: Jews of the 14th and 15th centuries who converted to Roman Catholicism to escape persecution. Most were in Spain during the Inquisition. *See also* Alhambra Decree; anti-Semitic; Anusim; Inquisition, the; Jew(s); Judaism; Marrano; persecution(s); *relax ado en personas*; slurs, religious.

convert: 1. one who has changed from one belief system to another, or one who professes faith after possessing none. 2. as a verb, an overt profession of faith brought on by a conscious act of will. *See also* conversion.

conviction: 1. a strong and nearly unshakable belief (1 Th. 1:5). Conviction is a mark of loyalty to orthodoxy but should not exclude openness of dialogue and study. 2. in some circles, to be "under conviction" is to experience the call of the Holy Spirit to repentance and acceptance of the gospel. A number of Protestant denominations claim that a person who is agitated and seeking faith is said to be "under conviction" of the Holy Spirit. 3. a resolution of "guilty" in a court of law or ecclesiastical hearing. *See also* core beliefs.

Convolution of Aries: a charismatic/healing phenomenon originating in France and Belgium. It was rumored that the grave of a young Jansenist priest named Francois de Paris caused miraculous healings. Multitudes flocked to the cemetery Saint-Medard near Paris where many experienced agitated charismatic bodily contortions, falling to the ground, shouting, and other spiritually induced extremes. *See also* idolatry; Jansenism; sect(s).

Conway, Russell H.: a Baptist minister (1843–1925) and crusader for the general acceptance of capitalism and wealth as a religious virtue. His trademark lecture, "Acres of Diamonds," was presented over 6,000 times, the revenue going to the education of young men. With the zeal of a former atheist—which he certainly was—Conway was called to Philadelphia's Grace Baptist Church, which he grew into the prodigious Grace Temple, then organized Temple University, where he was president until his death. Conway's message might be credited as incipient activity toward the Social Gospel and prosperity religion movements. *See also* Baptists; prosperity religion; revivalism; Social Gospel; social issues.

cooking pot(s): a practical household item for food storage, preparation, and serving. Domestic use tended to the cheapest material available, usually clay, to more durable and expensive (bronze, etc.). Scripture records that the Millennium will see even common cooking vessels inscribed with Christ's name. *See also* bells on the horses; boiling pot, vision of the; cooking pot, prophecy of the; eschatology, eschatological; Millennium; pot(s); sacred bowls.

cooking pot, prophecy of the: 1. a vision of Ezekiel (Ezk. 11:3; 24:1–14). The prophet is shown a cooking pot (a kettle), which is destined to hold the flesh of twenty-five unworthy Jewish elders on the very eve of Babylon's siege. Their boiling tissue is a detestable stew that symbolizes God's displeasure with Israel's leadership and her people at the time. The prophet describes how the Sovereign Lord will obtain the container, add water and the grisly ingredients with the bones and spices, and then heat the stew. The leftover blood will be poured on a rock, not into the earth where it will be absorbed from view. Even when the recipe is done, God will not extinguish the flame but continue to heat the vessel in the hot coals until all its impurities are burned away and all the encrustations of unfaithful Israel are sloughed away. 2. a more positive follow-up comes from

Zechariah as a counterweight to Ezekiel. This prophets states that in the Millennium, even ordinary cooking pots will be sacred to the Lord (Zech. 14:20). *See also* bells on the horses; boiling pot, prophecy of the; cooking pot(s); eschatology, eschatological; Holy to the Lord; Millennium; pot(s); sacred bowls.

Copernicus, Nicolaus: Polish (Prussian) mathematician and astronomer (A.D. 1473 – 1543) credited with establishing the model that the earth revolves around the sun. He was also a Roman Catholic canon of the church. *See also* Aristarchus; astronomy, astronomers; clergy scientists; Cusa, Nicholas; Galilei, Galileo; Roman Catholic Church.

Copper Scroll: a unique find among the Dead Sea Scrolls, officially known as 3Q15, named for the cave where it was located. Unlike other discoveries in the area, this artifact was made of rolled copper so fragile it had to be cut into strips to be examined. The scroll contains, among other things, detailed revelations of where certain Temple treasures were secreted by the Essenes. Thousands of intervening years have made it difficult to identify the topological features noted in the text to trace even a few of the remains of the Temple artifacts, if there are any still extant. *See also* Bible manuscripts; Dead Sea Scrolls; Essenes; Isaiah Scroll; Manual of Discipline; Qumran; Shrine of the Book; *War of the Sons of Light Against the Sons of Darkness;* War Scroll.

Coptic Church: native Egyptian Christians. The name (meaning "Egyptian") identifies their Demotic traditional formal language as well. With them, there are three more Orthodox patriarchs in the Holy Land—Greek, Armenian, and Syrian. The Copts claim their origin from the missionary activities of Mark, the author of the second Gospel, with the early church headquartered in Alexandria. They were disenfranchised by the Council of Chalcedon on the accusation they were monophites—a claim they deny to this day. The Ethiopian Orthodox Tweahedo Church and its offspring, the Eriteran Orthodox, are considered within the Coptic tradition. Orthodox ritual provides for seven major feasts (Annunciation, Nativity, Epiphany, Palm Sunday, Easter, Ascension, and Pentecost) plus seven minor feasts (circumcision of our Lord, Christ's Temple entrance, escape of the Holy Family, first miracle – Cana, the transfiguration, Maundy Thursday, and Saint Thomas Sunday). Coptic heroes of the faith include Saints Basil, Gregory the Theologian, and Cyril. *See also* abba; Agpeya; apathela; apothegm; Athanasius; axios; Byzantine Church; coenobium; Coptic ritual paraphernalia; Council of Chalcedon; Eastern Orthodox Church; Defnar; Didascalia; Egypt, Egyptians; El-Nayrouz Feast; elugia; epidesis; Epsalmodia; Exaltation of the Cross; gathliek; hoos; holy kiss; Holy Light, ceremony of the; hyten; Meatfare Sunday; Melkite; metanyia; Monophysitism; "old man"; ostrich eggs; paramone; "seven and four" ritual; Syria; Tasbeha; theotekons; three kneelings; virgins' house.

Coptic ritual paraphernalia: those unique items of the Coptic Christian tradition useful or necessary to the practice of the faith. Articles include the: elugia (a bit of bread of the Eucharist displayed for veneration), eskeem (a leather belt or habit for monks considered to hold a high level of spirituality, faragia (a black tunic for monks and priests with its color to indicate death to the secular world), ghaliloun (boiled oil applied to baptized persons), laqqan (a small basin of holy water sunken in the floor of a Coptic church), melote (a sheepskin cloak also serving as a carrier for personal items or a sleeping mat), myron (a Coptic chrism), tonya (a white tunic for Coptic priests at Mass), zinnar (a sacred ribbon tied to the shoulder of a baptized person or a gown symbolizing union with Christ), lamb (a name for the bread of the Eucharist or a miniature cross), wrapper (sewn cloth holding the lamb), spoon (silver with a cross atop used to dip the holy blood). *See also* Coptic Church; furniture and furnishings of the modern church.

Coracion: a supporter of millennial doctrine (ca. A.D. 230–280) who drew his beliefs from his teacher, Nepos of Egypt. However, he later became thoroughly converted to the amillennial views of Dionysius and an ardent opponent of any view smacking of millennialism. *See also* Nepos; Roman Catholic Church.

corban: 1. the Judaic practice of declaring something holy or dedicated to God. The Pharisees were notorious for using the rule to hoard their assets instead of using some of them to care for their elderly parents. Jesus naturally condemned such hypocrisy (Mk. 7:9–13). 2. the daily morning and evening sacrificial system practiced religiously by Temple attendants. *See also* ban; evenings mornings, prophecy of the; Holocaust, holocaust; morning and evening sacrifices; oblation; sacrifice; sacrifice, the daily; 2,300 evenings and mornings.

core beliefs: those religious convictions held by believers which supposedly are so basic, ingrained, immutable, enduring, and essential that they cannot be shaken. *See also* conviction.

co-redemptrix: Mary, the mother of Jesus, who is named a cooperative (or even superior) assistant to Christ in the mission to redeem humanity according to one aspect of Roman Catholic belief in Mariolatry. *See also* Marianist; Mariolatry; Mary; Mary Mother of God, Feast of; Our Lady of the Angels; queen of heaven; Roman Catholic Church; Second Eve, the.

Corinthian Church: believers in the city of Corinth on the narrow isthmus between the Peloponnesus and Greek mainland. The first settlers were Phoenicians, and the town grew into a people that were commercialized, luxury-loving, and licentious. Paul's time in Greece was spent there, followed by Apollos. Two of the apostle's letters to the church there are printed in the New Testament. Their eschatological theology revolved around four questions concerning the resurrection for which they desired a response from the founder. First, did Jesus *really* rise from the dead? Second, would Christians also participate in a resurrection since the one for Jesus was so unique? Third, would their already deceased family members know resurrection? And last, what kind of body does one inherit in the resurrected state? *See also* church.

cormemuse: a kind of bagpipe played in the Middle Ages, perhaps even in church ritual or open air religious festivals. *See also* musical instruments.

Cornelius: the first recorded Gentile convert to Christianity (Acts 10). Cornelius was a centurion of the Italian Regiment (Cohort) stationed at Caesarea. He was a God-fearing Gentile who experienced a heavenly vision, as did Peter, to the effect that he was to become the first Gentile believer. Subsequently, and in obedience to the vision, Peter presented the gospel to him and baptized the man with his entire household. *See also* Caesarea; centurion(s); Italian Regiment, the; liturgical year; unclean animals, Peter's vision of the.

cornerstone: (capstone) a foundation block of a new construction, the basis for building. In Zechariah 4:7–10 the capstone represents the proposed foundation for the new Temple of Zerubbabel. In Ephesians 2:20, Paul described Jesus Christ as the chief cornerstone of the household of God. Isaiah 28:16 discusses the cornerstone that undoubtedly references the Messiah. Peter (1 Pe. 2:4–8) quoted from Isaiah 8:14, 28:16, and Psalm 118:22 to describe in some detail how Jesus Christ is the capstone, or the living Stone, of the Church. The biblical metaphor, then, has been in place before time began. We, as members of that body, are also called living stones. Jesus declared that the same capstone of faith that sustains the believer could also crush those who fall against it (Lk. 20:18–19). As such, it can be stated that what is chosen and precious to believers (Jesus) is a disaster to dissenters because his righteousness and power will overwhelm disbelief and opposition. Even the Pharisees understood that this parable was pronounced against them specifically. At least one messianic group in Israel today is said to have possession of a literal cornerstone ready to be installed when the apocalyptic time is right for rebuilding the Temple. They periodically exhibit this foundation publically. Thus, a cornerstone can be a physical block for building or a metaphor for living beings strengthening the fellowship of believers. A capstone can also be a keystone, that section which bridges two sides of an arch. Without the keystone, the structure would collapse. *See also* living stones; parable(s); parables of the New Testament; rock(s); Stone, the living; temple(s); Temple Institute; Temple Mount and Land of Israel Faithful Movement.

Coronation Stone: a.k.a. *Lia Fail* (Irish), Stone of Scone (Scottish), Stone of Destiny (Gaelic), Jacob's Pillow, or Jacob's Stone. The Coronation Stone is an English designation from the time it resided at Guildhall near Kingston upon Thames, London. The Saxon kings were crowned on it since 1296. The origin, however, is not English since the Irish and Scots have a claim to it as well. According to Celtic legend and related religions, the Stone is the very one the patriarch Jacob used to rest his head at Bethel and preserved by the Hebrews. Reportedly, it accompanied the Exodus Israelites from Egypt and supplied them water in the desert. From there, the article found its way to Sicily, Spain, and finally Ireland in 583 B.C. The Irish insist it was delivered by the prophet Jeremiah and was personally blessed by Saint Patrick. Subsequently, it was taken by the Scots, who lost it to England, who returned it to Scotland as a gesture of good will. The Stone, at some stages of its history, was reputed to have magical powers and could speak, shout, or roar when a coronation was in progress. The artifact itself is about six feet and seven inches in height, thirty-two inches in length, and twenty-four inches in depth. It weighs 336 pounds and its only adornment is a Latin cross and the names of some crowned heads. *See also* Celtic folklore and religion; Excalibur.

corporate guilt: an instance in which the punishment for the sin of one person or group may be continued upon those who follow. While it is true that every person is responsible for his or her own poor choices, it is also true that God may prolong that discipline into the next generation. Nations are judged as well as individuals, as are groups over single persons. Such a perspective appears in the Ten Commandments (Ex. 20:5–6) when God declares punishment to the third and fourth generations of those who reject the Lord. Another example is the kingdom of Israel, which was punished because Jeroboam set up the golden calf idols, or that of Judah, which was destroyed mainly through the sins of Manasseh. In the case of Achan (Josh. 7), an entire family was destroyed for the sins of the father. That is not to say, however, that God *always* extends punishment for the sins of the one to the sins of the many. Other passages affirm the individuality of personal sin. *See also* social issues; sour grapes, proverb of the.

corporate prayer: a prayer spoken aloud by one person on behalf of a group of others. *See also* blessing(s); Oremus; prayer(s).

corporeal presence. See real presence.

Corpus Christi, Feast of: a special feast day of Roman Catholicism dedicated solely to the enjoyment of the Eucharist. Its modern title is the Solemnity of the Holy Body and Blood of Christ. Juliana, a nun at Mount Comillon near Liege, wanted a unique festival on this one occasion, which was celebrated but once a year in the liturgy of the times. Her efforts were successful and the day has become a joyous one for worshipers who spend it in festivities and as a welcome "break" for the laity. *See also* feasts and special days of high liturgy faiths; liturgical year; *Pange Lingua Corporis Mysterium*; Roman Catholic Church.

Corpus Hermecticum: collected works, real or fake, claiming to mark the knowledge of ancient occultism, which has influenced a variety of esoteric practices. Its touch is said to be evident in Qabbala, alchemy, numerology, astrology, Gnosticism, the mystery religions, and tarot reading, to name a few. *See also* Agrippa Books; alchemy; *arcanum arcandrum; Arcanum, the; Book of Abramelin, The;* cantrip; "Dionysian Artificers, The"; Emerald Tablet of Hermes, the; *Golden Bough, The;* grimoire; Hermes Trismegistus; Hermeticism; Hermetic wisdom; Hermetic writings; idolatry; magic arts; magic, magick; *mana;* mantic wisdom; occult, occultic; parapsychology; *Picatrix;* secret wisdom; spell names; *Spiritas Mundi;* Tablet of Hermes.

corroboree: a festival of dance indigenous to the Australian Aborigines. The ritual goes by many names and some of the rites are sacred. The spear dance, for one, is performed by both men and women, the meaning of which is unknown to any but the inner circle. The corroboree is performed with painted bodies, music, and costume. *See also* dance; music.

corruption: that which is spoiled or made impure, especially having to do with religious ritual or purity of the worshiper and/or ecclesiastical equipment in use. The prophets preached against this failure unceasingly. Cadavers are considered corrupt following death, especially in some religious circles, but according to Christian belief, the body will be raised *incorruptible* at the end of the age (1 Cor. 15:42–54). Outside a religious context, corruption is dishonest behavior in many fields, including politics and business. *See also* Mount of Corruption; social issues.

Cortez, Hernando: Spanish conquistador and explorer who conquered Mexico (1485–1547). Many Mesoamerican peoples thought Cortez to be the reincarnation of the feathered serpent god Quetzalcoatl when he invaded Mexico in 1519, a prophecy that perhaps aided his decisive invasion. *See also* Aztecs; Chilam-Balam; conquistador(s); eagle and the condor, the; Inca; Itza-Maya; Maya; Mesoamerica; Montezuma II; Quetzalcoatl; Toltecs.

corvee: conscripted labor. King Solomon used corvee workers to complete his many building and taxation projects in Judah. The burden of assessments and forced labor was a major factor causing the split of the Northern and Southern Kingdoms after the inauguration of Rehoboam of Judah. *See also* slave, slavery.

Cosmerism: a religious philosophy mixing Christianity and Buddhism. Most other religions, however, are said to contain truth as well. *See also* sect(s).

cosmic cross, the: according to John Major Jenkins and others, the exact point where the elliptic will cross over the Milky Way and is to have a significant impact on our world at that time. The cosmic cross (also called the sacred tree by the Maya) was to occur at the same time as the winter solstice of 2012. Such an alignment occurs only once every 25,800 years, an astrological fact known to the ancient Mayans. *See also* cosmology; Dark Rift; eclipse(s); galactic alignment; impact event; *Jupiter Effect, The;* Maya; Mesoamerica; precession of the equinoxes; 2012 prophecy, advocates of; 2012, prophecy of; zodiac.

cosmic ladder: any mystical progression, hierarchy, step, or degree that is said to enhance spiritual understanding and advancement. The concept is prominent in Jewish mysticism and certain esoteric religions or philosophies.

cosmic tree: often labeled the "tree of life" or "world tree" for many preliterate religious populations. They venerated a tree that they believed was the center of the universe connecting heaven and earth and (through its roots) the underworld. Some could bear the offspring of the gods, while others were the homes of gods and fairies so they served divination purposes as well. In Norse mythology, the Celts, the Finns, Slavics, Druids and others worshiped the oak (which they knew as the Tree of the World) for those reasons. The great tree is known by many names around the globe: *Agac Ana* to the Turks, *Ashvattha* for Hindus, *Kalpa Vriksha* for Brahmas,

Kien-Mu to the Chinese, *Modun* in Mongolia, *Vilagfa* in Hungarian lands, and *Yggdrasil* to the German and Norse regions. The Celtic tree of life was called a *crann bethadh*. The Lithuanians associated their thunder god, Perkunas, with the oak. Estonians smeared the sacrificial blood of animals on the oaks for the god Taara and the Slaves revered the tree for their god Perun. Ancient Germanic peoples worshiped the oak as connected to their thunder god Thunor (Thor). Greece and Rome had their own oaken cults, including the Greek goddess Leto (Latona to the Latins). Leto was the Titan mother of Apollo and Artemis who haunted the sacred groves. The Hindus considered the papal tree to be sacred because the god Brahma dwelt there with Vishnu inhabiting the twigs and one of the deities on every leaf. Every Indian village was positioned by a sacred grove (a *sarna*). Even Shiva dwelt in a bel tree. Cosmic tree legends are also prominent in Greek, Latvian, Asian, Mesoamerican, and other lore as well. *See also* Bodhi Tree; Celtic folklore and religion; Druidism; *Edda*, the; enneagram; fairy, fairies; idolatry; Norns; Norse and Old Germanic pantheon; tree of life, the; tree of the knowledge of good and evil, the; tree of Zaqqum; underworld.

cosmogony: beliefs concerning the origin of the universe. Ninety-five per cent of scientists believe the earth is billions of years old but some conservatives say it is less than 10,000. *See also* analogical day theory; big bang theory; big crunch theory; chaos theory; cosmology; *creatio ex nihilo;* creation ; creationism; creation science; Creator; day-age theory; evolution; evolution, theistic; framework hypothesis; gap theory of creation; intelligent design; involution; naturalism; Omphalos Hypothesis; progressive creationism; Scopes Trial; "six-day theory, the"; uniformitarianism; Young-Earth Creationist Movement.

cosmology: the study of the universe that deals with its possible origins and its ultimate fate. Scientific and religious thinking about the matter seem to run in one of two patterns. First, most western cultures and Christianity view history as linear – moving along in a straight path from the unknown beginning of time to an infinite end. Excuse the oxymoron. The East and many oriental religions see history a cyclical – time revolving in upon itself in a never-ending circle of existence repeated over and over. There is no relief or release except for the very few who escape the circle of death and rebirth into non-existence. Christian eschatology is important to our theology since it touches upon our lives in the present and into the mysterious future. The book of Revelation speaks of a theological cosmology consisting of three realms – that of the home of God (heaven), the earth and those who dwell here, and the Abyss or hell, where nefarious creatures are or will be imprisoned. Ancient concepts regarding cosmology of the sky sometimes speak of seven or more heavens and even a compartmentalized Hades. Despite an accumulation of myth and knowledge, we cannot yet know the secrets of the universe. Believers can only glimpse it as parts are slowly revealed by divine revelation. *See also* analogical day theory; Apophis asteroid; astrology, astrologists; astronomy, astronomers; big bang theory; big crunch theory; celestial disturbances; chaos theory; Comet ISON; cosmic cross; cosmogony; *creation ex nihilo;* creation; creationism; creation science; Creator; Dark Rift; day-age theory; eclipse(s); end, the; evolution; evolution, theistic; framework hypothesis; galactic alignment; galactic superwave; gap theory of creation; Hale-Bopp Comet; Halley's Comet; impact event; intelligent design; involution; *Jupiter Effect, The*; Maya; naturalism; Nemesis; Nibiru; Omphalos Hypothesis; pillars of the universe; precession of the equinoxes; progressive creationism; "six-day theory, the"; space doctrine; 2012 prophecy, advocates of; 2012 prophecy; zodiac; uniformitarianism; Young-Earth Creationist Movement.

cosmophobia: fear of the universe, especially as it associates with the eschatological ending of existence in our human experience. *See also* apocalyptic fervor; eschatophobia.

Cotton, John: an early New England Congregationalist minister (1595–1652). He acted as pastor to a federation of parishes in the Reformed tradition and was a passionate apocalypticist. He and Cotton Mather are credited with producing the first published literature for children in America, both steeply moralistic in tone. Cotton strongly believed that his Congregationalist form of Puritanism was the true church and was not shy to persecute those who differed. In fact, he was instrumental in the expulsion of Roger Williams and Anne Hutchinson from the Massachusetts Bay Colony, where he had pastored since his flight from England in 1633. Cotton claimed that Puritan New England was "The Heav'n on Earth, if any be." Eventually, even English Puritans began to suspect Cotton's authoritarian writings and actions, which lacked any sign of religious toleration. *See also* Congregationalists; Hutchinson, Anne; Mather, Cotton; Mather, Increase; New Haven Colony; Williams, Roger.

Coughlin, Charles E.: a Roman Catholic priest (born 1861 in Canada) who became a famous host of a talk radio show which, at its height, had more listeners than any broadcast of any personality on the air. At first a supporter of Franklin D. Roosevelt (he once called the New Deal "Christ's Deal"), Coughlin changed sides radically before World War II. He then became an attack leader against the government, against Jews, and a strong opponent of American's entry into the war. His influence eclipsed to nothing after Pearl Harbor. *See also* anti-Semitic; Roman Catholic Church; Smith, Gerald Lyman Kenneth.

Council, Heavenly. See Heavenly Council.

Council of Carthage: a church assembly (A.D. 397) that reconfirmed the present-day canon of the New Testament as the correct list. Augustine was influential in the deliberations. *See also* Council of Hippo; councils, church; Roman Catholic Church.

Council of Chalcedon: church doctrinal meeting of A.D 451 that officially defeated Monophysitism as a legitimate church doctrine. This convocation was called ecumenical but perhaps did more to solidify the Roman Catholic patriarchate over all others as supreme; however, it by no means ended the fierce conflict of the parties divided over the composition and essence of Jesus Christ. Protestants generally consider it the final legitimate pronouncement of doctrine about the nature of Christ, provided any of the councils are accepted as authorative. One Eutychus, presbyter at Constantinople, declared that Christ was "a fusion of human and divine elements." The church was confused as to when this occurred. Furthermore, the Apollinarian concept, which states that Jesus did not have a human mind but only the body and soul of a man, was still prevalent. The Roman pope Leo the Great, attacked the diversity, causing the council to conclude that Jesus held two natures but they are to be regarded as one. The transcript wording is: "one and the same Christ, Son, Lord, only begotten, to be acknowledged in two natures, without confusion, without change, without divisions, without separation." The declaration appeared in all caps. The wording of the four "withouts" caused them to be labeled the "four fences of Chalcedon." Some historians class the meeting as the fourth ecumenical council. *See also* councils, church; Councils of Ephesus; diphysitism; Eastern Orthodox Church; "four fences of Chalcedon"; hypostatic union; Justinian I; miaphysitism; Monophysitism; Roman Catholic Church; Theodora.

Council of Churches. See National Council of Churches; World Council of Churches.

Council of Constance: a quasi-ecumenical convocation sanctioned by the Roman Catholic Church meeting in Constance, Germany, from A.D. 1414 – 1418. The meeting was said to have healed the so-called Western schism which had plagued the Roman Church, then consisting of several rival popes and internal disarray. Old claimants to the throne were deposed and Pope Martin V was elected. The attendees (some say there were up to a thousand present) did more than work on internal strife, however. They dug up the bones of John Wycliffe, burned them, and threw the ashes in the river. Then they burned John Hus and many of his followers. The council may have repaired the intrastructure of the Vatican but it did nothing to curb its deadly inquisitorial pursuits. *See also* antipope(s); councils, church; Hus, John; Roman Catholic Church; Wycliffe, John.

Council of Ephesus. See Councils of Ephesus.

council of God: the realm of the prophet or seeker who "stands" or solicits a message from the Divine. Conversely, God Himself is said to preside over a council of heaven, either in the intimacy of the Trinity or in conjunction with the angels. The results can be described as a *counsel* from God directed to His angels or to us. The Word of God is then given as a trust or instruction in righteousness. A magnificent heavenly council is detailed in Daniel 7:9–10 and other locales. To be in the council of God, essentially, is an awesome honor to those invited to view or participate. Prophets were often assumed to be in such a relationship. *See also* angel(s); council of heaven; council, the heavenly; court of heaven; divine council; Heavenly Council; heavenly court.

council of heaven: a standing committee, according to *3 Enoch*, populated by two sets of twins in heaven. The first, *Irin*, decrees the will of God and the second, *Qaddishin*, pronounces His sentence as they preside in a kind of heavenly court. Some sources call them "Watchers and Holy Ones," but we assume they are not numbered among the fallen angels. The Jews might label the council as the Sanhedrin of heaven. *See also* angel(s); council of God; council, the heavenly; court of heaven; divine council; Heavenly Council; heavenly court.

Council of Hippo: a church convocation (A.D. 393), perhaps the earliest, which helped set the current New Testament canon for all of Rome, Gaul, Asia Minor, and North Africa. The meeting was heavily influenced by Augustine, and the list of accepted books was the same drawn up by Athanasius in 367. *See also* Council of Carthage; councils, church; Roman Catholic Church.

Council of Jamnia: a hypothetical Jewish convocation occurring in the latter years of the first century at Jamnia (Yavne) in Israel. As legend records, the canon of the Hebrew Scriptures was officially affirmed at that time. Since 1960, however, most scholars do not see the Jamnian canonical work as plausible; rather, they affirm the Hebrew canon as developing gradually over the years. It appears, however, that there was a Jewish council in A.D 90. At the time, some historians assert, the leaders decreed in writing that any Jew who accepted Jesus as the Messiah was to be excommunicated. The meeting then would have taken place near the time of the writing of Revelation. *See also* Judaism.

Council of Jerusalem. See Jerusalem Council.

Council of Laodicea: the official church assembly (held A.D. 367) that named all twenty-seven books of the New Testament and declared them legitimate. The action did not, however, eradicate all doubt of the value of Revelation nor disrupt the allegorical method of interpretation. *See also* councils, church; Roman Catholic Church.

Council of Nine: a dangerous sect created in the mid-1970s by Dr. Michael Aquino. Its function is to appoint the high priest of the Temple of Set and its executive director. The Temple of Set is a highly-organized organization with a secret membership. "Set" is another name for Satan. They are devotees of black magic. *See also* Brotherhood of Satan; idolatry; Satan; Satanism; sect(s).

Council of Trent (Protestant): a Protestant gathering of the Reform Movement (A.D. 1643). In session, the Protestant canon was established in the form we have today. *See also* councils, church; Protestantism, Protestant.

Council of Trent (Roman Catholic): a Roman Catholic convocation that met intermittently from 1545 to 1563. Among other actions, the attendees condemned the Protestant Reformation and further formulated Roman Catholic church doctrine. It did, however, agree in principle to the Protestant insistence on justification but added that human freedom and merit are inherent in life and faith. Those foremost with an apocalyptic agenda were Francisco Ribera, Luis de Alcazar, and Cardinal Bellarmine. The delegates particularly affirmed that transubstantiation and not consubstantiation constituted the sacrament of the Eucharist, that giving the wine to laity was unnecessary since all they needed was in the bread, and that only priests and bishops have the power to forgive sin or retain them. Invocation of the saints and the veneration of relics and icons were decreed permissible. As part of the Catholic Counter-Reformation, a uniform catechism and liturgy (in Latin only) was confirmed, celibacy of priests was reaffirmed, and the thorny problem of church authority was attempted but soft-pedaled. The Apocrypha was declared to be sacred Scripture and pronounced damnation on any who thought otherwise. The Vatican Council of 1870 finally made the papal primacy the official line of the Church; the one in 1546 certified the Vulgate as the official Bible of Catholicism. In essence, the purpose of the Trent councils was to formulate a new "game plan" to combat the growing popularity of Protestantism. The Inquisition was insufficient and a new intellectual approach was needed. In this, the Jesuits were invaluable. *See also* consubstantiation; councils, church; Counter-Reformation; Pius V, Pope; Roman Catholic Church; sacerdotalism; sacrament(s); Society of Jesus; Tridentine; Tridentine Mass; transubstantiation; Vatican I and Vatican II.

councils, church: any convocation of ranking prelates of the church meeting to discuss and decide matters of doctrine, discipline, and practice in the name of unity and ecumenism.

History and Mystery

The first seven called councils were recognized by Roman Catholicism and Eastern Christianity (from A.D. 325 to 787) but the Great Schism precluded further cooperation after. All international councils are considered infallible and binding. The first seven include the: First Council of Nicaea of 325 producing the Nicene Creed, First Council of Constantinople of 381 discussing Macedonianism, Council of Ephesus in 431 considering the status of Mary and Pelagianism, Council of Chalcedon in 451 debating the nature of Christ, Second Council of Constantinople of 553 (also called the Fifth Ecumenical) which condemned Origen, Third Council of Constantinople in 680-681 (the Sixth Ecumenical) that condemned Montanism, and Second Council of Nicaea in 787 that refuted iconoclasm. *See also* conciliarism; Council of Carthage; Council of Chalcedon; Council of Constance; Council of Hippo; Council of Laodicea; Council of Trent (Protestant); Council of Trent (Roman Catholic); Councils of Constantinople; Councils of Ephesus; Councils of Nicaea; Eastern Orthodox Church; Ecumenical Council of A.D. 999; Protestant, Protestantism; religious organizations; Roman Catholic Church.

Councils of Constantinople: a series of seven convocations attended by representatives of the entire major orthodox patriarchies at one time or another, only the second and third of which are considered to be ecumenical. The first convened as the First Council of Nicaea in A.D. 325 and concluded with the Second Council of Nicaea in 787. Some were ecumenical synods and others a forum for debate, ecclesiastical trials, or other church matters. The humanity and divinity of Jesus, for once, was a hot topic for debate. By the sixth, most of the debate concerning the sustenance of Christ's body had been resolved and a major stumbling block of theology had been overcome after it was decided that Christ had two natures, both working in perfect harmony. The Councils of Hippo and Third Council of Carthage had done the same in the West. The third council

(A.D. 680) finally fixed the canon of the Eastern Church in conformance to the modern list. The meetings continued until the 14th century. *See also* councils, church; Councils of Nicaea; Eastern Orthodox Church; four marks of the Church, the; Gregory of Nazianzus; One, Holy, Catholic, and Apostolic Church; Roman Catholic Church; Second Ecumenical Council.

Councils of Ephesus: three so-called ecumenical councils transpiring in the Christian Roman Empire, each pondering certain theological sticking points in the Church. There were a series of three church councils meeting at Ephesus in A.D. 431, 449, and A.D. 475. The first was perhaps the most vigorous for it vilified Nestorianism and perhaps hastened the split of the Eastern and Western branches of Catholicism. The meeting was chaired by Cyril of Alexandria, a bishop not noted for his ecumenical spirit. The "heresy" of Nestorius (patriarch of Constantinople) was on the rise, declaring Jesus had two separate natures—human and divine. He could be called *Christotokos* (Christ) but not *Theotokos* (as the son of Mary). Also, Pelagianism was debated, which denied that divine aid was necessary to perform good works (thus nullifying the doctrine of Original Sin). Both Nestorius and Pelagian were defeated and condemned. The second Ephesian Council took place in 449 as ordered by Emperor Theodosius II and meant to be conciliatory. Fewer than 200 bishops responded so its impact was muted. Politics intervened in the convocation, however, to such an extent that the findings were just short of outrageous. It was called "the Robber Synod" and all its actions were rescinded by the Council of Chalcedon in 451. The last, in 475, was attended by some 500 – 700 bishops led by Pope Timothy II, and may have been among the most partisan. Among other acts, it condemned the actions of the Council of Chalcedon and ascribed the patriarchy of Constantinople to be above all others (except Rome). *See also* councils, church; Cyril of Alexandria; Council of Chalcedon; Eastern Orthodox Church; hypostatic union; incarnation; *kenosis*; miaphysitism; Nestorianism; Nestorius; Pelagian; Pelagianism; Roman Catholic Church; two natures, doctrine of.

Councils of Nicaea: or Council of Nicea, which was convened twice in Turkey. The first, called by Constantine I in A.D. 323, was to settle the Arian controversy. In the dispute, Bishop Athanasius was vindicated over Arias and set the standard view of the nature of Christ's divinity. The vote was 218 to 2. As incidental work, they also established the official date for Easter, prohibited self-castration (evidently and extreme still practiced), and prohibited kneeling for prayer. The second, in 787, restored the veneration of icons. Both convocations are considered acceptably ecumenical. *See also* aniconism; Arianism; Athanasius; councils, church; Councils of Constantinople; Easter; Eastern Orthodox Church; Iconoclasts, War of the; Roman Catholic Church.

council, the heavenly: a model conference between the prophet and God, with the divine court of heaven sometimes in attendance. Amos uses the Hebrew word *Sodh* to name this holy assembly and the prophet Micaiah (and others) relate its experiences (1 Ki. 22:19–23). *See also* council of God; court of heaven; divine council.

Counselor. See Wonderful Counselor.

Counter Cult Movement: an advertising campaign to raise awareness of the dangers and methodology of damaging cults. *See also* cult(s); Cult Awareness Network; deprogramming; exit counseling; religious organizations.

Counter-Reformation: the actions of the Roman Catholic Church during, and for some time after, the launch of the Protestant Reformation. Those actions, led most vigorously by the Society of Jesus (the Jesuits), were the Church's response to, and reaction against, Martin Luther and other dissidents from Roman Catholic ecclesiology and doctrine. The movement capitalized on the theological direction of Thomas Aquinas and those procedures developed from the series of convocations called the Council of Trent. The stimulus and redefinition of Catholicism to prevent Protestant dominance may well be better termed a "Roman Catholic revival," which likely saved it from the inner decay and provincialism so prevalent in that day. The revitalization of the Roman Church assumed many forms besides the efforts of the Jesuits, all combined to make the results positive if not thorough. Catholic orders began to reform and new ones sprang up, notably the "confraternities," certain guilds or "oratories" as they were called. The majority emerged in Italy, the seat of the Vatican itself. They were unwavering in their support of the pope and few had any love for the Reformers. Nevertheless, some Catholics did rush north to join the dissidents. Other Counter-Reformation organizations consisted of clergy under special vows called "clerks regular," a take on earlier "canons regular." *See also* canon(s) of the Church; confraternities; Desmond Rebellions; Innocent III, Pope; Loyola, Ignatius; Council of Trent; Protestant Reformation, the; Roman Catholic Church; Society of Jesus.

counting the omer: a Jewish religious day called *Lag B'Omer*. The process undertaken by Orthodox Jews for determining the proper time for Pentecost (*Shavot*). Each day is counted from the seventeenth of Nisan until the fiftieth day is reached (Silvan 6), marking the day Moses came down from Mount Sinai with the Ten Commandments. An "omer" is about one to two quarts of a dry measure, such as grain. The "counting" (*Sefirat HaOmer*) is reminiscent of the omer of barley that was brought to the Temple for offering until Pentecost when wheat replaced it. The time then is forty-nine days between the omer offering and Pentecost. The time is a solemn period, but on the thirty-third day, known as *Lag B'Omer*, the mourning ceases for weddings, picnics, bonfires, and other celebrations. *See also* feasts and special days of Judaism; Judaism; Pentecost.

course of this world. See spirit of the age.

Court of Discipline. See Consistory, the; Geneva theocracy of John Calvin.

court of heaven: often, especially in apocalyptic literature, the rulership of God portrayed in heaven as a royal court scene. Typically, one may see a throne, magnificent scenery, angelic attendants, kingly pageantry, and other common throne room accouterments. The most vivid in Scripture are probably to be found in Ezekiel (Ezk. 1:25–28), Daniel (Dan. 7:26–27), and Revelation (Rev. 1:12–16; 4). *See also* angel(s); council of God; council of heaven; council, the heavenly; divine council; heaven; Heavenly Council; heavenly court; thrones; throne in heaven with someone sitting on it, a.

Court of the Gentiles: the outermost boundary of the Jerusalem Temple, also called the Outer Court. Here, non-Jews were allowed to venture. Between it and the adjacent area was a balustrade with signs warning that any Gentile to pass the barricade would be subject to death. In Revelation 11:1–2, John is told to measure the entire Temple with the exception of the Court of the Gentiles. This section has been given over to the nations and is not to be afforded protection during the Tribulation. The meaning implied is that not all Jews will be spared from persecution and death instigated by the "Gentiles"; in fact, few will. *See also* Court of the Israelites; Court of the Priests; Court of the Women; middle (dividing) wall of partition; Temple(s).

Court of the Israelites: that portion of the Temple three flights of steps down from the Court of the Priests, sometimes called Solomon's Porticoes. It was divided east and west, the former for women and the latter for men. Only Jewish men could enter, a special privilege because it was the only position from which the sacrifices could be observed. *See also* Court of the Gentiles; Court of the Priests; Court of the Women; Temple(s).

Court of the Priests: the section of the Temple wherein only the priests could enter and perform their duties. It was located just below the Holy Place. *See also* Court of the Gentiles; Court of the Israelites; Court of the Women; Heikhal; Temple(s).

Court of the Women: the portion of the Temple for the women, as far as they were allowed to venture. Their section was the east side of the Court of the Israelites. *See also* Court of the Gentiles; Court of the Israelites; Court of the Priests; Temple(s).

coven(s): a local group of Wiccans (witches) or other neo-pagans. Members can number any size and either sex but usually number about half a dozen. In ritual formation, the group seeks to "draw down the moon" by manipulation of the elements and rites, many of which are often drawn from the *Book of Shadows*. *See also Book of Shadows;* elementals; esbat; idolatry; Sabbat; thoughtform; Wicca; witch(es); witchcraft.

covenant(s), biblical: any one of a number of promises made by people to God (as a vow or pledge to obey – technically termed a conditional covenant) or from God to people (a suzerainty treaty). The term is used 272 times in the Old Testament with a meaning of "to divide" or "to cut in two." Such "cutting" may involve carving words into a stone or clay tablet but more likely it centers in the dismemberment of animals. Those covenants named in the Bible include (not counting the many secular or ordinary commercial treaties made in the course of normal human interaction): 1. the Edenic, which outlined God's plan for the human race in relationship to the earth (Gen. 1:26–30; 2:15–17), 2. the Adamic, which proposed the manner of relationship between humanity and the divine as relayed to Adam and Eve (Gen. 3:14–19), 3. the Mosaic, the agreement between God's chosen people and the Lord in which the Israelites were to obey the Law of Moses to guarantee blessings and social and religious stability (Ex. 19:5–8), 4. the Abrahamic, in which the Jews and the nations of the world were to be blessed (Gen. 13:14–17), 5. the Noahic, in which God pledged the world would never again be destroyed by water (Gen. 8:21–9:17), 6. the New Covenant, whereby the law of God will someday be written on the heart (Jer. 31:31–34; Heb. 8:6–13), 7. the Palestinian (or Land) Covenant, in which the Jews were guaranteed a place of residence in the Holy Land forever (Deut. 30:1–9), 8. the Aaronic, which gave the Jews a perpetual priesthood and worship method (Num. 17; Ps. 115:12, *et al.*), and 9. the Davidic, which granted the Jews a theocratic government and nation in perpetuity. The pledge to Solomon can be considered a subsidiary of the Davidic Covenant (2 Sam. 7:4–17; 1 Chr. 17:3–15), and the Aaronic is sometimes viewed as ancillary to the Mosaic. Joshua 24:1-28 provides an example of how a covenant could be enacted or renewed. In the commitment at Shechem, at least two copies were made and witnesses were called – human, divine, or even an object to bear testimony. Additionally, punishments and blessings were spelled out. There is no question that the early covenants were made between God and the Jews. As Paul reports, "Theirs is the adoption as sons; theirs the divine glory, the covenants, the receiving of the Law, the temple worship and the promises" (Rom. 9:4). A covenant of God can be violated; it cannot be escaped. *See also* Aaronic Covenant; Abrahamic Covenant; Adamic Covenant; angel of the covenant; baptism; *berith;* Bible manuscripts; circumcision; conditional covenant(s); covenant ceremony; covenant of salt; covenant theology; Davidic Covenant; Edenic Covenant; eternal covenant; everlasting covenant, a (the Land Covenant); Levitical Covenant; Mosaic Covenant; New Covenant, the; New Testament; Noahic Covenant; Old Testament; Phinehas; seven years covenant with Israel; sign of the covenant; Solomonic Covenant; suzerainty treaty; tabernacle, the; testament(s); unconditional covenant(s); vassal treaty.

covenant ceremony: a formalized ritual, evidently a common practice in the ancient world, whereby people ceremonially ratified various treaties or agreements. A variation of such a ritual took place between God and Abraham (Genesis 15 and referenced again in Jeremiah 34:18–20). The process involved laying out bifurcated animals on the ground between which the Spirit of God passed. Such a formalized procedure was meant to certify the validity of the covenant and to renew its promise with enacted legal rites, a process that is still practiced today in some less complex ceremony and by alternate means. It is important to note that when God performed the ritual to seal the Abrahamic Covenant that Abram did not walk through the sacrifices; God alone moved from beginning to end, which affirms that the covenant is unconditional. Today's Methodist Church, as one example, still celebrates the covenantal doctrine with a special rite and recognition day. *See also* Abrahamic Covenant; bridal chamber ceremony; conditional covenant(s); covenant(s), biblical; covenant of salt; covenant theology; unconditional covenant(s).

Covenant Churches: any group or denomination that forms itself into a covenant agreement as to doctrine and faith practice. Many today are independent congregations that may or may not have the name "Covenant" in its title. An exception would be the Evangelical Covenant Church began by Swedish immigrants in 1885 with a Lutheran type theology. The Puritans of Plymouth could be called a Covenant Church. *See also* church bodies in America (typed); denomination(s); denominationalism; Puritanism, Puritan(s).

Covenanters: Scottish Presbyterians of the 16th and 17th centuries. The name is derived from the covenants or "bands" formed in Scottish history and agreed upon in order that the doctrines and polity of the groups would remain united. The more famous of the written agreements were entitled *The Natural Covenant* and *Solemn League and Covenant*. The key figures in the movement were Prophet Pedan and John Wishart. *See also* Presbyterians.

Covenant Name for God, the. See Yahweh.

covenant of death: a phrase (from Isaiah 28:14–22) used frequently by prewrath rapturists that signals the beginning of Daniel's seventieth week. The start of the time period is the signing of a deceptive false treaty between Antichrist and the nation of Israel. For most dispensational premillennialists, the conclusion of the dreaded treaty signals the rapture of believers and start of the Tribulation's seven years. *See also* Antichrist; covenant theology; Palestinians; seven years covenant with Israel; seventy weeks, prophecy of the.

covenant of grace: one of a pair of doctrinal elements essential to covenant theology. It teaches that humanity is now governed by the "covenant of grace," providing salvation through Jesus Christ since the earlier "covenant of works" initiated with Adam was a failure. *See also* covenant of redemption; covenant of works; covenant theology; grace; monergism; salvation; solifidianism; stone of stumbling; works, salvation by.

covenant of redemption: a doctrinal element of some theologians inherent to covenant theology. It professes that God and the Son have made a pact in the past to provide salvation for the human race through sacrifice on the cross by the Son while the Father agreed that his death would redeem believers. Sometimes the covenant of redemption is simply infused with the covenant of grace and counted together. *See also* covenant of grace; covenant of works; covenant theology; redemption; salvation.

covenant of salt: an agreement or contract between individuals that was generally ratified by sharing a meal (*i.e.*, Exodus 24:9–11). Salt was used as seasoning or preservation of food, but more importantly, it served a more esoteric purpose. The salt signified the permanence or inviolability of the terms of the contract (2 Chr. 13:5). Nomads today still eat bread with salt with the same significance. If the covenant was with God and not exclusively with other persons, the salt was present in the appropriate sacrifice (Lev. 2:13; Num. 18:19; Ezk. 43:24). *See also* covenant(s), biblical; covenant ceremony; covenant theology; salt.

covenant of works: one of a pair of doctrinal elements essential to covenant theology. It teaches that God entered into such an agreement with Adam, promising eternal life for obedience but death for disobedience. Mankind was thereby put on probation, but Adam failed to honor his part of the bargain. Since Adam is the federal head of the human race, the covenant of works was made null and void. We are now governed by the "covenant of grace," which brings salvation through Jesus Christ. Many sects, cults, and religious bodies (perhaps including the Roman Catholic) have a works-based doctrinal core or primary peripheral law of redemption. More Protestant Christianity base belief on the covenant of grace exclusively. *See also* Adamic Covenant; autosoterism; Cocceius, Johannes; condign merit; congruent merit; covenant of grace; covenant of redemption; covenant theology; Didache, the; monergism; salvation; solifidianism; stone of stumbling; synergism; works; works, salvation by.

covenant premillennialism. See historical premillennialism.

covenant theology: a system of interpretation of Scripture on the basis of two covenants (sometimes counted as three) powered by basic pronouncements instituted by God for the redemption of humanity from the beginning to the end of time. The concept originated in Europe around the 16th and 17th centuries and teaches that God made a covenant (called the covenant of works), with Adam delineating eternal life for obedience but death for disobedience. Adam failed and death subsequently ensued for the human race. However, God then instituted the covenant of grace by which Christ became the ultimate mediator for man's salvation. The treaty of grace originated with either Adam or Abraham (depending on the theologian consulted) and will continue in effect until Christ's return. A third covenant is sometimes discussed, called the covenant of redemption, but it is often simply equated with the covenant of grace. The theological importance of covenants, both Jewish and Christian, cannot be overemphasized. New England Puritanism and other early congregational groups were so-called Covenant Churches. *See also* biblical criticism; covenant(s), biblical; covenant of death; covenant of grace; covenant of redemption; covenant of works; dual covenant theology; eternal covenant; everlasting covenant(s), an (the); Ezekiel's pledge to the Jewish remnant; Judaism; Land Covenant; Levitical Covenant; Mosaic Covenant; New Covenant, the; New Testament; Noahic Covenant; Old Testament; Phinehas; seven years covenant with Israel; Solomonic Covenant; suzerainty treaty; testament(s); theology; unconditional covenant(s); vassal treaty.

Covenant, The Sword, and the Arm of the Lord, The (CSA): a United States militant domestic organization holding the stated purpose to ignite a race war that will ultimately lead to the Second Coming of Christ. It is not, however, just another quirky religious cult but a union of violence whose members believe they are God's chosen people destined to dominate all others. The group was started by Jim Ellison and aided by his disciple Richard Wayne Snell. The two met in 1983 at a CSA conference in Ft. Worth, Texas, to discuss means and methods by which the Alfred P. Murrah Federal Building in Oklahoma City, Oklahoma, could be destroyed. Snell was soon diverted by his stronger desire to murder Jews and African-Americans elsewhere so the Oklahoma assignment fell to two of his recruits, Timothy McVeigh and Terry Nichols. The attack on April 19, 1995 resulted in the deaths of 168 persons, including nineteen children in the second-story daycare facility, and injured more than 680. *See also* American Party; anti-Semitic; Aryan Nation; Christian Identity Movement (CIM); cult(s); Fascist Millennialism; Fenians; Knights of the

Golden Circle; Knights of the White Camellia; Ku Klux Klan; militant domestic organizations; Molly Maguires; Neo-Nazi(s); Patriot Movement, the; Red Shirts; terrorism; terrorist(s).

Coverdale, Miles: a disciple of John Wycliffe, the first scholar to translate the complete Bible into English (in the year 1535). He was an Augustinian friar but changed to become an early Puritan as his translation work progressed. *See also* Bible translations; Puritanism, Puritans.

covet: to yearn to possess something with lust, jealousy, or some other lessthan-ethical feelings. Coveting is forbidden by the ninth Commandment. *See also* social issues; Ten Commandments, the.

cow: livestock for the production of milk, hides, meat, and other agricultural purposes necessary to human development. Sometimes we symbolize the animal as contented, predictable, or inoffensive. For Hindus, the cow is shown deference for its service, stateliness, and *ahimsa* and representative of the attitude that all animals should be honored. Also, Lord Krishna sported a cow-head which supposedly adds dignity. *See also ahimsa;* animals, birds, and insects, symbology of; Brehon Laws; calf; cattle and oxen.

cowan(s): a laborer capable of simple construction skills but far inferior to those of a master mason. The latter was designated a *majister* or *maite*–a "master of the works." The distinction between the proficiencies of the two talents came to distinguish the progressive ranks of Freemasonry. *See also* Freemasonry.

cow and the bear, the. See wolf will live with the lamb, the.

Cradle of Civilization. See Fertile Crescent.

crane bag: a container used to further the work of a practicing Druid. The sack or purse may be of any size and constructed of leather, cloth, or any other suitable material and used to carry sacred objects—his "tools of the trade."

Modern occultic or New Age users prefer to describe the object as more of a concept enabling them to more fully accommodate the environment in order to live in balance, harmony, and peace. *See also* Celtic folklore and religion; Druidism; idolatry; magic, magick; New Age religion.

Cranmer, Thomas: Church of England supporter of Henry VIII (1480–1556) and archbishop of Canterbury in 1539 when he produced the so-called "Great Bible." He also produced the much favored *Book of Common Prayer* (revised in 1662). His translation was intended for use by the general public but got its special name because the finished volume was some fourteen inches in height. Cranmer was quite active in the political and ecclesiastical activities of the Church of England and a major factor in its formation. He was a victim of Queen Mary's purge and eventually burned at the stake after a trial conducted not in England, but in Rome. Cranmer is counted as one of the Oxford martyrs, along with Nicholas Ridley and Hugh Latimer. Only six months earlier, he had been forced to witness the burning of his two friends. Cranmer's death was perhaps delayed because he made several recantations, and, to repudiate them, stretched his hand into the flames calling, "This unworthy hand." *See also* Bible translations; *Book of Common Prayer;* Church of England; Henry VIII; Latimer, Hugh; martyr(s); Mary, Queen of Scots; Oxford martyrs; Ridley, Nicholas.

Crassus, Peter: Roman historian Catholic layman and jurist (11th century) whose famous quote expresses well the Christian concept of separation of church and state: "Render unto Caesar the things that are Caesar's, but not unto Tiberius the things that are Tiberius'; for Caesar is good but Tiberius is bad." The thought echoes the pronouncement of Jesus in Matthew 22:21. *See also* Roman Catholic Church; Roman Empire.

creatio ex nihilo: the Latin phrase most often used by theologians to describe the method of God used in creation—that is, "creation out of nothing." Many researchers insist that whoever wrote the opening verses of Genesis did so considerably later than many other biblical writings – as much as 400 years after. So these writers or redactors knew the creation stories of the Babylonians and others wherein Marduk, for example, fought against a sea monster to establish the world. He did so by blowing wind into Tiamat, distending her belly until she split into sky and earth. Psalm 74 praises God for vanquishing Leviathan. Then, creation was not "from nothing" as many Jewish and Christian observers believed, but from a formless void, chaos, wind, and "deep waters." "In the beginning, when God created the heavens and the earth, the ground was a formless void and darkness covered the surface of the deep waters, while a wind from God swept over the waters" (Gen. 1:1-2). Most modern science scoffs at the idea of creation out of nothing so advocates need such "substances" as wind and water for base materials. No effort is expended to explain where these basic ingredients originated; even "voids" and "chaos" are, in some ways, "something." *See also* analogical day theory; Behemoth; big bang theory; big crunch theory; chaos theory; cosmogony; cosmology; creation; creationism; creation science; Creator; day-age theory; *Epic of Gilgamesh, The;* evolution; evolution, theistic; framework hypothesis; gap theory of creation; intelligent design; involution; Leviathan; Marduk; naturalism; Omphalos Hypothesis; progressive creationism; "six-day theory, the"; Sumerian and Babylonian pantheon; uniformitarianism; Young-Earth Creationist Movement.

creation: the mighty acts of God that established the universe (Gen. 1). In eschatological prophecy, the Lord is destined to redo His creative act by destruction or refurbishment of the present earth and sky because it, like humanity, has been tainted by sin's defilement. Nature, now in its corrupt or imperfect form, is to be replaced by a new heaven and new earth (Rev. 21:1). Prophets and other proclaimers often prefaced or referenced the great creation as part of their sundry prophetic admonishments. The Egyptians, Mesopotamians, Syrians, and many other ancient cultures had their own particular explanations for formation of the universe. In Jewish thinking, before God created the heavens and the earth, He made repentance and torah, hell and heaven, the celestial temple and the divine throne, and the name of the messiah. *See also* analogical day theory; big bang theory; big crunch theory; chaos theory; cosmogony; cosmology; *creatio ex nihilo* creation; creationism; creation science; Creator; day-age theory; destruction of heaven and earth; evolution; evolution, theistic; framework hypothesis; gap theory of creation; intelligent design; involution; new heaven and new earth; naturalism; Omphalos Hypothesis; "post-secularists"; prayers of Revelation; progressive creationism; Scopes Trial; "six-day theory, the"; uniformitarianism; Young-Earth Creationist Movement.

Creation Hymn: a contrived but descriptive title for the praise song of Revelation 4:11 as enacted by the twenty-four elders as they lay their crowns before the Creator God. *See also* music; praise paradigms of Revelation, the.

creationism: the conservative belief that the universe and all in it were created solely by the will and power of God. According to most adherents (like the Christian Young-Earth Creationists) the earth is relatively young – about 6,000 years old. The idea is almost always employed to controvert the theory of evolution and seems to be regaining some of its lost legitimacy to the scientific method promoted by Darwin, Spencer, and Huxley. The Scopes Trial, adjudged in Dayton, Tennessee, in 1925, became a national focus of evolution versus science. The case was argued by William Jennings Bryan and Clarence Darrow. Bryan won the case for the fundamentalists, but the verdict only stirred further controversy. Many experts in any number of disciplines, including theology, believe that creationism will continue its modification theories, but we will likely never know the full extent of God's creative genius and purpose for starting and ending our world. *See also* agnosticism, agnostic(s); all-encompassing theory; analogical day theory; big bang theory; big crunch theory; chaos theory; cosmogony; cosmology; *creatio ex nihilo;* creation; creation science; Creator; day-age theory; emanations, doctrine of; evolution; evolution, theistic; framework hypothesis; gap theory of creation; God gene, the; God particle, the; intelligent design; involution; Millikan, Robert Andrews; naturalism; Omphalos Hypothesis; progressive creationism; redshift; Scopes Trial; "six-day theory, the"; theory of everything, the; uniformitarianism; Young-Earth Creationist Movement; *yugas.*

creation psalm: any biblical psalm celebrating the creation of the world at the hand of God, *e.g.,* Psalm 104. *See also* enthronement psalm; historical psalm; imprecatory psalm; messianic psalm; penitential psalm; psalm; psalm of judgment; psalm of lament; Psalms as Old Testament book; royal psalm; supplication psalm; thanksgiving psalm; wisdom psalm; worship psalm.

creation science: the theories of a group of persons (made up of both scientists and theologians) who assert that, properly understood, the biblical account of creation from Genesis 1 and the scientific method are basically compatible. Genesis contains pure science but the scientific process, as it is generally understood, holds insufficient raw data to make the earth's creation and time to do it (about 20,000 years) a genuine approach. *See also* agnosticism; agnostic(s); analogical day theory; big bang theory; big crunch theory; chaos theory; clergy scientists; cosmogony; cosmology; *creatio ex nihilo;* creation; creationism; Creator; day-age theory; evolution; evolution, theistic; framework hypothesis; gap theory of creation; intelligent design; involution; naturalism; Omphalos Hypothesis; progressive creationism; Scopes Trial; "six-day theory, the"; uniformitarianism; Young-Earth Creationist Movement.

History and Mystery

Creativity Movement: the rise of a racist religious expression in the United States organized by Ben Klassen in 1973. Also known as the Church of the Creator or World Church of the Creator, the sect is deeply into white supremacy. There is no belief in the supernatural or standard church doctrine but does observe some sixteen commandments to govern the group. *See also* American Party; anti-Semitic; Aryan Nation; Christian Identity Movement (CIM); Covenant, The Sword, and the Arm of the Lord, The (CSA); cult(s); Fascist millennium; Fenians; Knights of the Golden Circle; Knights of the White Camellia; Ku Klux Klan; militant domestic organizations; Molly Maguires; Neo-Nazi(s); Patriot Movement, the; Red Shirts; religious organizations; sect(s).

Creator: a common name for God emphasizing His power of initiating and sustaining the universe (*i.e.*, 1 Peter 4:19). Perhaps it can be considered the basic name of the deity, in use even by some non-believers. *See also* analogical day theory; big bang theory; big crunch theory; chaos theory; cosmogony; cosmology; *creatio ex nihilo;* creation; creationism; creation science; day-age theory; evolution; evolution, theistic; framework hypothesis; gap theory of creation; intelligent design; involution; Maker of All Things; Maker, the; Name of the Lord, the; names (titles) for God; naturalism; Omphalos Hypothesis; prime mover; Possessor (Creator) of Heaven and Earth; progressive creationism; Scopes Trial; "six-day theory, the"; uniformitarianism; Young-Earth Creationist Movement.

creatures crawling on the wall. See Ezekiel's four visions of Israel's demise.

crèche: a display representing the birth of Jesus, often called a "manger scene." Crèche is a French word for "cradle." The representation may be any size, with or without live participants, and fashioned by the imagination of the creators. In this politically correct age, the reproductions may be illegal on public property. *See also* Advent; chrismon(s); Christmas; Christmas tree; Francis of Assisi.

Credo: 1. a concise statement of doctrine that may be recited or printed. In Christian liturgy, the Latin "I Believe" is the opening phrase of most Christian creeds. 2. a section of the Catholic mass following the offering. *See also* confession(s) of faith; Athanasian Creed; Augsburg Confession; Belgic Confession; confession(s) of faith; Confession of 1560; creed(s); Heidelberg Confession; Helvetic Confession; liturgical year; Large(r) Confession, Luther's; liturgy, Christian; Nicene Creed; Philadelphia Confession; Pittsburg Platform of 1885; profession of faith; Roman Catholic Church; rule of faith; Savoy Confession; Smalcald Articles; Small(er) Catechism, Luther's; Tetrapolitan Confession; Wesleyan Quadrilateral; Westminster Confession.

credo-baptism: or cantabaptism, the conviction that only true believers should be allowed to undergo the ritual act of baptism. Thus, children and non-believers are denied on doctrinal grounds. *See also* age of accountability; alien immersion; baptism; liturgy, Christian; pedobaptism; sin of the innocents; vicarious faith.

creed(s): a basic statement of belief or doctrine, usually in written format. A number of creeds have been promulgated over the history of the Christian Church and in other religions. Perhaps 1 Timothy 3:16 is an early one: "He appeared in a body, was vindicated by the Spirit, was seen by angels, was preached among the nations, was believed on in the world, was taken up to glory." *See also* confession(s) of faith; rule of faith.

Creeping Jesus: a religious slur for a person, normally intended for a Roman Catholic, who seeks to make an ostentatious display of his or her piety in a hypocritical manner. *See also* Christianese; Jesus freak; Roman Catholic Church; slurs, religious; Sunday Christians.

Creme, Benjamin: (b. 1922) one who could perhaps be described as the "poster child" for the future Maitreya, whom Creme designates as the supreme messiah for Christians, Jews, Muslims, Hindus, and Buddhists. The claim is that this

History and Mystery

coming Maitreya is the "Avatar for the Aquarian Age." Creme governed a religious association called Share International and may also be identified under the name "Tara Centers" in its various outlets worldwide. He perceived the end of the age to be on June 21, 1982. *See also* Exalted One, the; World Teacher, the.

Creole (Caribbean) religions: a grouping of the multitudinous animistic religions of the Caribbean region. Some of the cults reach into other countries but most are centered within those islands and in parts of South America. The listing includes Alabua Secret Society, Batuque, bugbears; Candomoble, Dahomery, Daome, Dereal, Espiritism, Hoodoo, Ibo, Konngo, Kulam, Kumina, Macumba, Mami Wata, Manding, Myral, Nago, Obeah, Orisha, Oyotunji, Petwo, Quimbanda, Quimbois, Rada, Rastafarianism (the largest), *Regla de Palo,* Santeria, Shango, Spiritual Baptists; Umbanda, voodoo, Yoruba, and others. *See also* animism; Ayida Wedo; Bondye; Candomoble; conjure, conjure man; Dambala; execration; Ghede; gris-gris; hungan; idolatry; juju; Kumina; Legba; Lao Loas; lwa; Macumba; magic, magick; mojo; Obeah; occult, occultic; Orisha; Oya; poppets; Quimbanda; Rastafarianism; Santeria; sect(s); shaman, shamanism; Shango; spiritism; spell; Spiritual Baptists; Umbanda; veve; voodoo; voudou; wanga; Yoruba.

Crescendo of the Universe: a contrived but descriptive title for the praise section of Revelation 5:13–14 in which all of heaven, all upon the earth and under the earth, and all in the sea voice an exultant song of praise to God. *See also* music; praise paradigms of Revelation, the.

Crescens: a disciple whom Paul noted as being on mission to Galatia (2 Tim. 4:10). *See also* missions, missionaries.

Crete: an island in the Peloponnesus, the fourth largest in the Mediterranean. The land was the cradle of the Minoan civilization in the second century B.C., and the race known as the Philistines possibly originated there or another

Mediterranean island. Legend says it was the birthplace of the mythical Zeus. Paul had some unintentional contact with the island during his sea voyage to Rome (Acts 27:7,13). Rome conquered the area in 68 B.C. and made it a province of the empire. Paul dispatched Titus to the island to establish and discipline the church there (Tit. 1:5). The Cretans did not enjoy a favorable reputation in the ancient world; Paul even quoted one of their philosophers, Epimenides (ca. 600 B.C.), who said, "Cretans are always liars, evil brutes, lazy gluttons" (Tit. 1:12). *See also* Caphtor; Kittim (Chittim); Minoan civilizations; Philistia, Philistines; Zeus.

Crimean War: conflict between the Russian Empire and an alliance of France, England, the Ottoman Empire, and Sardinia (1853–1856). Many people of the day thought the clash of these nations precluded the end of days. Although this is true of all wars, the Crimean was pointedly apocalyptic because the Russian intent was to seize the Middle Eastern Ottoman Empire and the seat of Jerusalem much as the Crusaders attempted to do.

crimson: the color red or reddish-purple. The word, especially describing its red pigment, is frequently a metaphor for sin or blood; more notably in its purple cast, the word symbolizes royalty. By contrast, the prophets of God generally dressed plainly, and sometimes in outlandish costume (such as John the Baptist, who wore skins and a large leather belt). Both blood and sin are important apocalyptic concepts, along with associated colors and dress to symbolize them. *See also* colors, symbology of; purple; purple and scarlet.

Crispus: the synagogue ruler in Corinth who became a believer upon hearing the preaching of Paul (Acts 18:8). He was one of the few whom Paul personally baptized (1 Cor. 1:14).

criteria of double dissimilarity: or criterion of double standards, one of the more critical tests used by scholars of the historical Jesus movement to determine the true foundations of the Christian record. According to the standard, the Bible must be searched for ideas that could not be traced to Judaism or even the early church but must have sprung up historically whole as something new. Only the earliest form of a synoptic expression can be regarded as authentic, if it can be demonstrated as dissimilar from Judaism and turned into a distinctly Christian theology. *See also* biblical criticism; bridal chamber ceremony; Diabolical Mimicry, the; Gnosticism, Gnostics; *Golden Bough, The;* historical Jesus, the; Jesus Myth, the; Jesus Seminar, the; *preparatio evangelica*.

crocodile: aquatic reptiles found in Africa, Asia, the Americas, and northern Australia. The species is greatly feared by most native human populations but were revered in ancient Egypt. There, they were tamed, kept in tanks in the pagan temples, worshiped as gods, and embalmed with the notables to survive in the afterlife. *See also* animals, birds, and insects, symbology of; beast(s); Egyptian pantheon; Jannes and Jambres; Leviathan; mythological beasties, elementals, monsters, and spirit animals; reptilian theory.

Cromwell, Oliver: military and political leader in the Protestant revolt of the English Civil War (1599–1658). He and his supporters, the "Roundheads," defeated the royalist and ended the monarchy of Charles I, a task which he devoutly believed was accomplished because he was an agent of God. Cromwell was an ardent Puritan tolerant of any Protestant group, but certainly not Catholics. He preferred to rule a commonwealth, not as a king but more of a governor ruling under martial law and was titled "Lord Protector of England, Scotland, and Ireland." In actuality, hardly a more repressive government could be named. Academic learning proceeded underground in secret societies. After Cromwell's death, the government fell apart and the royalist regained power in 1660. As an apocalypticist, Cromwell believed the world ending would commence when the Jews were converted, possibly in his own lifetime. His followers saw the conflict between parliamentary and loyalist forces as a struggle between Christ and the Antichrist, and regarded the defeat of King Charles I as a sign that the millennial kingdom was at hand. To that end, he readmitted Jews into England following their forced *Diaspora*. As an historical footnote, Jews banished from Catholic Spain were never officially welcomed back. *See also* Charles I, King; Charles II, King; Committee of Triers; Committees of Ejectors; Fifth Monarchy Men; Laud, William; Separatists.

Cromwell, Thomas: first Earl of Essex and chief minister to Henry VIII (1485–1540). Cromwell was a strong supporter of the Reformation and helped his king secure the desired annulment from Catherine of Aragon so he could marry Anne Boleyn. His hand was easily felt in the formation of the Church of England even though he was born the son of an alehouse keeper. Cromwell was a shrewd politician but that did not prevent his execution for treason and heresy in 1540, much to the disappointment of Henry. *See also* Church of England; Henry VIII; Puritanism, Puritans.

Cronus: son of the Greek deities Uranus (the sky god) and Gaia (the earth goddess). He was prone to devour any offspring by his wife Rhea, eventually consuming three daughters (Demeter, Hera, and Hestia) and two sons (Poseidon and Hades). Zeus, the last son, was saved by Rhea, who hid him with the aid of Uranus and Gaia. The mother presented Cronus with a stone wrapped in swaddling clothes, which the god ate without hesitation. Later, Cronus was forced to vomit out those who were eaten to become living deities themselves. The Babylonian chronicler Berossus claims Cronus is to be equated with Marduk. *See also* Gaia (Gaea); idol(s); Marduk; Olympian pantheon; Rhea; Titans; Uranus; Zeus.

crop circles: strange geometric designs found in many places but mostly in England's standing grain fields. Some figures are small but others quite complex yet always formed in the characteristic geometric-patterned shape. Most are proven hoaxes, but many people are convinced there are some designs that remain unexplained or represent the work of extraterrestrials. *See also* idolatry; New Age religion.

Crosby, Francis Jane Van Alstyne: a popular Methodist hymn writer (1820–1915). Blind at age five, she was composing by the time she was eight. Despite her blindness and eventual advanced age, she composed some 8,000 hymns and gospel songs while attending to her other ministries of preaching, teaching, and various mission works. She is affectionately known internationally as "Fanny." In 2015 over 2,000 of her unpublished works were found in the archives of Wheaton College. *See also* Methodists; music.

crosier: or "crook," a bishop's pastoral staff in the shape of a shepherd's crook. Despite popular understanding, the shape is not intended to symbolize the cross. *See also* Crosier of Saint Patrick; Roman Catholic Church.

Crosier of Saint Patrick: the *Bachal Isu* or "staff of Jesus" wielded by Patrick. A certain volume called the *Book of Gospels* says that possession of the item identified and secured the true archbishopric of Armagh, Ireland. *See also* crosier; Malachy; Roman Catholic Church; Patrick.

cross: an instrument of torture consisting of crossed wooden beams to which a victim was impaled via the extremities. The gruesome punishment is an ancient practice, but the Romans perfected the technique and used it most extensively. It was the device on which Jesus was crucified and has become a universal symbol for Christianity. The Christian cross is predominately pictured as a vertical beam crossed by shorter one near the shoulders of the victim. The term for "cross" is derived from the Latin *cruciare* – "to torture." The arms of the condemned were nailed to the horizontal board and the feet to the vertical. Other cross configurations were just as effective, and the same method of punishment was used. A cross may be assembled via various designs but there are common features. The upright is called the *stipes crucis*. The *sedecula* is a small plank fastened to the upright below the main crossbeam. It provided the victim, whose torso had been twisted to the side because the feet were spiked laterally through the heel, sufficient support to prolong the agony of death – which sometimes extended to days. A *pablibulum* formed the crosspiece for the arms and shoulders. Whipping wielded by a *lictor* with the *flagellum* (flagrum) was a requirement before crucifixion. Beatings for religious offenses were no small matter, whether administered by whips or rods, the number of stripes determined by custom or legal code. For the Jews, thirty-nine lashes were required – one less the prescribed forty in Deuteronomy 25:3 lest there be a mistake in the counting. Most Romanesque and Gothic abbeys and churches were designed in the shape of the cross, with a long center aisle leading to the altar called the nave. The word springs from *navis*, or "ship," probably because the vaulted ceiling resembles the keel of a boat as viewed from underneath. If the entryway has a space, it is termed the narthex; side rooms (if any) are vestibules. The chancel contains the high altar and the "arms" to the side are transepts. *See also* anchor; crucifix; crucifixion; "Dream of the Rood, The"; flagrum; Holy Rood; *Lux;* names, symbology of; relic(s); rod; rood; saltire; whip.

Cross, Feasts of the: a commemorative feast day in many liturgical denominations recognized by a variety of names. Each honors the crucifixion of Christ. In Eastern Orthodoxy, for example, the day is one of twelve feasts of the Byzantine liturgy known as the Exaltation of the Cross. In Roman Catholicism, it is the Triumph of the Cross. Other persuasions know the time as Elevation of the Cross, Holy Cross Day, Holy Rood Day, Roodmas, Veneration of the Cross, or some similar designation. To Anglicans it is Holy Cross Day. *See also* Church of England; Coptic Church; Eastern Orthodox Church; Exaltation of the Cross; feasts and special days of high liturgy faiths; liturgical year; liturgy, Christian; Roman Catholic Church.

crossfigill: an ascetic exercise by ancient Celtic monks who stood long hours in prayer with arms outstretched to form a cross. *See also* gestures.

cross of Nero: a basic design or peace symbol (also known as "the witches' foot") that traces its origin to the most vicious of Christian killers, the Roman emperor Nero. Even earlier it was a Pythagorean sign for life but a Teutonic rune of death. The central design looks like an inverted Y with the vertical stem extending below the cantered arms. Clearly, it is the foundational form of the modern peace symbol. Also called the "broken cross" or a "stipe," the contorted cross is now recognized as a blasphemous symbol and used in the Church of Satan. Further, it is considered historically to be a sign of despair, the death of man or an unborn child, and a replica of the Anglo-Saxon "sign of the great bustard," a phallic symbol linked to eternity; the imprint of the giant bird's foot left on sand was its inspiration. Occult organizations consider it a sign of total emancipation from God. *See also* Nero; peace symbol; swastika; symbol(s).

crow: birds seen by the ancients as harbingers of death, alienation, or solitude. They portray a spirit message from darkness to bring humiliation. Crows were especially favored by the god Apollo. *See also* animals, birds, and insects, symbology of; idolatry; Morrigan; mythological beasties, elementals, monsters, and spirit animals; owl; raven.

Crowley, Aleister: World War II spy, occultist, and magician (d. 1947). Crowley has been dubbed by the press as "the most wicked man on earth" and even called himself (as did others) "the Beast **of** 666" (even his own mother called him that). He personally preferred his magic name "Baphomet." Crowley established modern schools of sorcery and magic and was an expert of the occultic and evil arts. His rituals were called his "workings." Crowley's ultimate goal was to facilitate the transformation of the Age of Osiris to the Age of Horus, then subsequently to conquer the Judeo-Christian God and His Messiah. Crowley's book, entitled *The Book of the Law*, explicitly states his vengeful nature, his killer instinct, and his vow: "With my Hawk's head [Horus] I peck at the eyes of Jesus as he hangs on the cross." He was also a thirty-third degree

Mason and at one time a leader of the notorious *Ordo Templi Orientas* society and founder of Thelema and the Hermetic Order of the Golden Dawn. Perhaps Crowley's greatest project was an attempt to open a gateway in a "dimensional vortex" that would allow evil entities into the earthly realms. It has been reported that Jack Parsons (co-founder of the Jet Propulsion Laboratory) and the New Age guru L. Ron Hubbard tried to recreate Crowley's experiments. *See also Astrum Argentum;* Baphomet; *Book of Abramelin, The;* cult(s); gate of the gods; goetia; Horus; Hubbard, L. Ron; occult, occultic; Satanism; thaumaturgy; Thelema.

crown(s): a sign of distinction, honor, or authority especially for royalty. Crowns are common symbols in apocalyptic language. There, a crown may be a mark of victory, rulership, or rewards. A diadem and tiara are variations of the royal headpiece and Jesus was mockingly crowned with one constructed of woven thorns before his crucifixion. 1. the New Testament lists a number of crowns, which are to be heavenly rewards from the judgment seat of Christ. 2. the twenty-four elders of Revelation 4 and elsewhere are shown with crowns, which they periodically cast before the throne of God in reverence. If we could identify which coronets are in use here, we could perhaps better distinguish this group as mortal representatives or as angels. If their crowns are symbols of victory, they are most likely mortal because they have overcome the world; if they are ruling crowns, they are probably angelic. Paul compared the perishable fillet of laurel leaves given the victorious Roman or Greek athlete with the solid crown of salvation for the believer (1 Cor. 9:25). 3. kings and queens are readily recognized by the crowns they wear. Many are found in the Old and New Testaments with that sign of authority. The woman of the sun in Revelation 12 wears a tiara of twelve stars, most likely representing the twelve tribes of Israel. Many evil entities in apocalyptic literature wear temporary ruling crowns as well, including the Antichrist beast of Revelation 13. 4. as redeemed believers and heirs to the eternal kingdom, the saints are to rule in the Millennium and after as regents of Christ. Because of that honor and responsibility, we should be diligently practicing the needed skills now. 5. crowns were sometimes used as tribute payment by the ancients of a subjected nation to its overlord. *See also bema;* crown of glory; crown of incorruption; crown of life; crown of rejoicing; crown of righteousness; Crown Rights of the Redeemer; judgment seat of Christ; king(s); names, symbology of; queen(s); reward(s) in heaven; robe, crown, and throne; twelve-starred crown; welcome, a rich; Zechariah's vision of a crown for Joshua.

crown for Joshua, a. See Zechariah's vision of a crown for Joshua.

crown of beauty: an expression found in Isaiah 61:3 by which the prophet intends a blessing for those found in God's favor during a brighter age. The phrase is intended as opposition to the alternative—ashes of bereavement. *See also* crown(s); garment of praise; oaks of righteousness; oil of gladness; year of the Lord's favor.

crown of glory: a believer's reward announced in 1 Peter 5:4. The crown is described as having properties that never fade away and is reserved for church leaders of any description. Often, the tasks of ordained and volunteer workers in church administration or worship leadership are overly difficult and not adequately compensated by the world's measure. God sees the hardship and plans the special glory crown for those who serve Him faithfully in management or specialized servant positions. Paul told the Thessalonians: "For what is our hope, our joy, or the crown in which we will glory in the presence of our Lord Jesus when he comes? Is it not you?" *See also bema;* crown(s); crown of incorruption; crown of life; crown of rejoicing; crown of righteousness; judgment seat of Christ; reward(s) in heaven; welcome, a rich.

crown of incorruption: a believer's reward noted in 1 Corinthians 9:25 (also called the imperishable crown). Those believers who struggle greatly in the cause of Christ despite unrelenting opposition will not go unnoticed by Christ. Our endurance and discipline in the faith will gain us an honorable crown at the judgment seat of Christ. Those who earn it are masters of temperance and self-control. *See also bema;* crown(s); crown of glory; crown of life; crown of rejoicing; crown of righteousness; judgment seat of Christ; reward(s) in heaven; welcome, a rich.

crown of life: a believer's reward promised in James 1:12 and repeated for the church at Smyrna in Revelation 2:10. Those who suffer for the faith of Christ, even to a martyr's death, will not go unrecognized in the hereafter. Jesus forgets no trial we encounter or a single tear we shed. He will honor those who endure temptation and oppression, even to the point where we can (even now) see such hardship as joy. *See also bema;* crown(s); crown of glory; crown of incorruption; crown of rejoicing; crown of righteousness; judgment seat of Christ; martyr(s); martyrdom; reward(s) in heaven; welcome, a rich.

crown of rejoicing: a believer's reward recorded in 1 Thessalonians 2:19. This crown is reserved for those who are not ashamed of the gospel and proclaim it boldly. Witnessing evangelists, whether activated in word or deed, are pleasing to God and will be recognized for their testimony. Paul celebrated with the Philippians by saying: "Therefore, my brothers, you whom I love and long for, my joy and crown,…" *See also bema;* crown(s); crown of glory; crown of incorruption; crown of life; crown of righteousness; judgment seat of Christ; reward(s) in heaven; welcome, a rich.

crown of righteousness: a believer's accolade as announced in 2 Timothy 4:8. The apostle Paul described this award as one he anticipated for himself as he approached the end of life. Believers often endure much, some even "wearing themselves out," for the sake of the gospel. The reward sustains those who are centered on the soon-coming Jesus. The righteous crown is for those who look with joy and anticipation for the coming of the Lord and will not be embarrassed or terrified by his appearing. The book of Revelation closes with an endorsement for such an attitude of expectancy: "Behold, I am coming soon! Blessed is he who keeps the words of the prophecy in this book" (Rev. 22:7). *See also bema;* crown(s); crown of glory; crown of incorruption; crown of life; crown of rejoicing; judgment seat of Christ; reward(s) in heaven; "waiting for the Lord"; welcome, a rich.

crown of twelve stars. See twelve-starred crown.

Crown Rights of the Redeemer: the understanding common to orthodox Christian doctrine, that the Church belongs to Christ, her invisible and universal head. Our ecclesiastical differences aside, we are one as all of humanity is one. *See also* bride of Christ; bride (wife) of Christ.

Cru. See Campus Crusade for Christ.

crucifix: jewelry in the shape of a cross typically worn as adornment or in some instances as a charm for favor and protection (an encolpion). Larger images of the crucifix are universally depicted, mainly in liturgical worship especially in Roman Catholic and Eastern Orthodox churches. Most Protestant denominations prefer to display an unadorned cross (with no image or representation of Christ's tortured body) to emphasize the empty cross and victorious Easter resurrection rather than the crucifixion and death of Good Friday. *See also* amulet(s); charm(s); cross; crucifixion; gris-gris; Hand of Fatima; Holy Rood; idol(s); juju; liturgy, Christian; magic, magick; rood; talisman(s); wanga.

crucifixion: a method of torture and slow execution whereby a living body was nailed to a "T" shaped wooden cross. Though common in many cultures, it was a particular favorite of the Romans as a form of excruciating capital punishment. Death was usually caused by asphyxiation, blood loss, congestive heart failure, and the filling of the pericardium with bodily fluid. If life lingered, the victim's legs were sometimes broken to hasten death. The Roman philosopher Marcus Tullius Cicero mused of the barbaric practice: "To bind a Roman citizen is a crime, to flog him an abomination, to kill him is almost an act of murder: to crucify him—What? There is no fitting word that can possibly describe so horrid a deed." Jesus' mode of execution was by crucifixion, thereby fulfilling some thirty-two individual Old Testament prophecies. His legs, however, were not broken—also a fulfillment of prophecy. Who killed Jesus? Some say the Romans were responsible, as indeed they were the direct cause of Christ's torment and death. The Jews, however, were the impelling cause by their accusations and riotous actions before Pilate. A common understanding is that the subjugated Jews could not authorize an execution without Roman acquiescence. However, some thirty years later, the Jerusalem high priest killed Jesus' brother James. Either the rules were relaxed as time passed or, there was a difference between condemnation at criminal trials and ordinary murder. The real answer to the poignant question of who killed Jesus is nearer than we think. We, the race of humanity, are responsible. Our sin and ignorance have demanded the sacrifice of the Son of God, ordained since the foundation of the world. *See also* capital punishment; Church of the Holy Sepulcher; cross; crucifix; crucifixion conspiracies; "Dream of the Rood, The"; "*Eloi, Eloi, lama sabachthani?*"; Holy Rood; "It is done"; rood; sacred wounds, five; saltire; seven words from the cross, the; *Via Dolorosa*.

crucifixion conspiracies: any number of accusations that deny Jesus died on the cross and the fact of his resurrection. The most common presented may be listed: 1. bribery theory (the Roman guards were paid to ignore tampering with the tomb), 2. conspiracy theory (the disciples and others conspired to concoct the stories), 3. drugged theory (the sponge lifted for Jesus to drink contained a pain-killer or knock-out concoction), 4. escape theory (Jesus and his family escaped to France or elsewhere), 5. hallucination theory (the disciples and other witnesses were victims of mass hysteria or a public hallucination of what they were watching), 6. spiritual theory (the entire crucifixion story and resurrection are to be taken in a spiritualized or symbolic understanding, not literal), 7. stolen body theory (the disciples stole the body of Jesus and faked the empty tomb), 8. substitution theory (God managed somehow to substitute someone else on the cross—mostly a Gnostic idea), 9. swoon theory (Jesus did not die on the cross but awakened from a faint when entering the cool tomb). *See also* blood curse; blood libel; conspiracy theorists; crucifixion; *Da Vinci Code, The;* Gnosticism, Gnostics; *Holy Blood, Holy Grail;* Holy Grail; Jesus Myth, the.

Crusader States. See Outremer.

Crusades: a series of military or paramilitary expeditions, some nine in number by some reckonings, promoted by the established church (Roman Catholic), with some involvement by the Byzantine establishment on occasion, and certain Christian kingdoms in Europe during the 11th through the 13th centuries. Oddly, the adventures were called Pilgrim Invasions or more benign names, for the name "Crusade" did not appear until many years later. Most honest historians will admit that the real purpose of the attacks was a papal plan for the reestablishment of the Mediterranean Christian empire under the leadership of the pope. For many commoners, however, the Crusades were a calling from God and a chance to personally participate in some of the prophecies of Revelation. A number of incursion campaigns were mounted from Western Europe into the Muslim-held Middle East under the conviction that the Holy Land should be liberated from Islamic control and reclaimed for Christianity. Popes Gregory VII and (especially) Urban II were the main church promoters, but they were not alone in the furor to gain the Middle East. An alternative motivation prompted a preemptive strike to prevent a Muslim invasion of the West, which most Europeans were convinced was inevitable. Apocalyptic fever was aflame off and on during those decades. Further, Caliph al-Hakim of Egypt had foolishly ordered the total destruction of Constantine's Basilica of the Holy Sepulcher in Jerusalem, an action that infuriated Christians. Only the first official Crusade managed to offer any form of real success for the West, and some were colossal failures. Christians did manage to set up a Latin Kingdom in Jerusalem called Outremer, but it was never strong and had collapsed by 1291. It was then that the Temple area became a Christian worship site, the *al-Aqsa* Mosque was a church, and the Dome of the Rock was a cathedral. One disastrous expedition consisted almost entirely of children; another enlisted the poor and impoverished of the continent only. The latter invasion (called the Peoples Crusade), led by Peter the Hermit, was a colossal failure as the Seljuk Turks destroyed them by the thousands when they reached Asia Minor. Participation in a crusade would guarantee the salvation of one's soul, as promised by the church. Commitment was called "taking the cross." In a secular side effect, Europeans were exposed to the liberal ideas and wealth of the Orient through the various campaigns. The conflicts are still contentious for both Christianity and Islam and may have apocalyptic implications contained within their sad history. Crusades were also regularly launched against so-called dissidents who were either in open or silent defiance of the Roman Catholic hierarchy but usually called the Inquisition. Resentment is still present in Islam today by which they view the Crusades as an insult to their religion and culture but Christians are equally incensed that the Holy Land is held in defiance of either Jewish or Christian sensitivities. *See also* Acre; Baldwin I; Baldwin IV; Baldwin V; Bernard of Clairvaux; Castle Blanc; Children's Crusade; Church of the Nativity; *Deus Volt!;* Eastern Orthodox Church; Frederick II; Godfrey de Bouillon; Horns of Hattin; Islam; *Jerusalem Journey;* Judaism; knighted orders; Louis VII,

King and Queen Eleanor; Northern Crusades; Outremer; Peter the Hermit; *Reconquista;* Richard the Lionheart; Roman Catholic Church; Roman Empire; Saladin; Tafurs; Tenth Crusade, the; Tortosa; Urban II, Pope.

crushing rock that became a mountain: the ending scene of Nebuchadnezzar's dream of the stratified statue (Dan. 2:44–45). God's eternal kingdom is being forecast: the theocracy that will crush all human government and instigate the divine rule of peace and justice. The prophecy is repeated in Daniel 7:9–10 under different symbolism. *See also* Babylonia; belly and thighs of bronze; celestial court, the; chest and arms of silver; Daniel's vision of end time; Daniel's visions of the mighty kingdom; election; elect, the; eternal kingdom, the; Ezekiel's pledge to the Jewish remnant; Ezekiel's vision of the restored theocracy; feet and toes of iron and clay; head of gold, the; Greece; heavenly court; kingdom of God; legs of iron; kingdom of God; Medo-Persia; messianic age, the; millennial geography; millennial Sabbath; millennial sacramentalism; millennial Temple; millennial worship; Millennium, millennial; New Covenant, the; New Eden; rebuilding the Temple; remnant; restoration of all things; restoration of Israel (the Jews); restoration Temple (and land); rock(s); rod of iron; Roman Empire; Sabbath rest; Son of Man; stratified man, dream of the; times of refreshing.

cryptesthesia: the alleged ability for paranormal perception. See also anthropomancy; anthroposophy; apotropaic magic; aretology; Ariosophy; astral plane; astral projection; astrolabe; astrology, astrologers; athame; audition; augury; automatic writing; bagua; belomancy; besom; bibliomancy; black arts; black mirror; blood moon(s); cartomancy; chaos magic; chiromancy; clairaudience; clairsentience; clairvoyance; cleromancy; cone of power; conjure; crop circles; crystallomancy; crystal skulls; curious acts; divination; dream(s); dreams and visions; ecstasy; enchantment; enneagram; esoteric sects; evil eye; extrasensory perception

(ESP); foreknowledge; foretelling; geomancy; grimoire; gris-gris; hepatoscopy; Hermetic wisdom; Hermetic writings; hex; hierscopy; horoscope(s); hydromancy; idol(s); idolatry; ifa; incantation; juju; labyrinth walk; lecanomancy; literomancy; locution; magic arts; magic, magick; magic square; magnetism; *mana*; mantic wisdom; mantra; miracles(s); monition; mystery religion(s); necromancy; New Age religion; numbers, symbology of; occult, occultic; omen; oneiromancy; oracle(s); otherworldly journeys; ouija board; out-of-body experiences (OBEs); past life regression; pentagram; philosophers' stone; planchette; planets as gods; portent; precognition; prediction; premonition; prodigy; prognostication; prophecy, general; psi; psychic(s); psychic healing; psychic reading; psychometry; psychonautics; prognostication; prophecy; pyramidology; rebirthing; remote viewing; retrocognition; revelation; rhabdomancy; scrying; séance; secret societies; secret wisdom; sorcery, sorceries; spell; spell names; spiritism; supernatural; superstition; tarot; telegnosis; telepathy; telesthesia; theugry; third eye, the; thoughtform; totemism; vision(s); vision quest; visualization; voodoo; voudou; wanga; warlock(s); Web-Bot; witchcraft; wizard(s); *ya sang*; yoga; Zen; zodiac; *zos kia* cultus.

crypto-Jew: an adherent of Judaism who pretends to be of another faith. Concealing one's Jewish heritage reached a peak during the Nazi regime in Germany but is still practiced to some degree today. *See also* anti-Semitic; Jew(s); Judaism.

Crystal, Ellie: twenty-first century New Age mystic, author, and Internet and broadcast guru. Her writings and appearances are prolific, with topics formed from the broadest range of metaphysical beliefs. She has even commented on the "Prophecy of the Popes." *See also* New Age religion; psychic(s).

crystallomancy: attempted foretelling of the future via means of a crystal ball or similar object. *See also* anthropomancy; anthroposophy; apotropaic magic; aretology; Ariosophy;

astrolabe; astrology, astrologists; audition; augury; automatic writing; bagua; belomancy; bibliomancy; black arts; black mirror; blood moon(s); cartomancy; chaos magic; chiromancy; clairaudience; clairsentience; cone of power; conjure; crop circles; cryptesthesia; crystal skulls; curious acts; divination; dream(s); dreams and visions; evil eye; extrasensory perception (ESP); foreknowledge; foretelling; geomancy; gris-gris; hepatoscopy; Hermetic wisdom; Hermetic writings; hex; hierscopy; horoscope(s); hydromancy; lecanomancy; literomancy; locution; magnetism; magic arts; magic, magick; *mana*; mantra; monition; necromancy; New Age religion; numbers, symbology of; occult, occultic; oneiromancy; otherworldly journeys; ouija board; premonition; prodigy; prognostication; psychic healing; psychic healing; psychomancy; psychometry; psychonautics; pyramidology; rebirthing; remote viewing; rhabdomancy; scrying; séance; sorcery, sorceries; spell names; spiritism; tarot; telesthesia; theugry; vision(s); voodoo; voudou; voodoo; vodou; witchcraft; *ya sang*.

crystal skull(s): one or more human skull artifacts made of clear or milky quartz. The skulls are claimed by some to be Mesoamerican objects with mysterious powers. Most scientific investigators, however, date their origins to Europe of the mid-nineteenth century or later. The crystal craniums do not figure in genuine pre-Columbian or Native American history or their mythologies (unless smaller forms of the head used in ritualism are counted). The most famous crystal of the group is probably that belonging to Anna La Gullion Mitchell-Hodges, who claimed to have discovered it in Belize as a young woman accompanying her adopted father. She also reported that a Mayan descendant insisted it was used by their high priest to cause death—thus the object became known as the "skull of doom." All sorts of magical and paranormal powers are attached to each skull so far discovered (the total number when all are found is said to be thirteen). Richard Hoagland attempted to link the skulls to life on Mars. David Hatcher Childress assigned their origin to Atlantis where they held anti-gravitational properties. Perhaps the most fascinating legend propounds that the reuniting of all thirteen skulls will forestall the catastrophes alleged to define the Mayan doomsday of December 21, 2012. The crystal skull legend is a hot button topic today for many New Age and occult enthusiasts. Hollywood has cashed in with the filming of *Indiana Jones and the Kingdom of the Crystal Skull*. *See also* crystallomancy; idolatry; Mesoamerica; New Age religion.

cry to the Lord: a familiar Old Testament admonition to "pray fervently," often from a state of anguish. *See also* bidding prayer; impetrate; intercessory prayer; payer(s); supplication psalm.

Ctesiphon: a replacement capital for Babylon after that city declined in influence, except as a pagan religious center. It was also at one time the capital of the Parthian Empire and the political and commercial center of Seleucia. *See also* Babylon, Babylonians; Babylonia; Bagdad.

Cub: also Chub, Ludim, or Lud, a people mentioned (by their Hebrew name) probably referring to the land of Lydia (Ezk. 30:1–9). Cush (the upper Nile region or Ethiopia), Put (Libya), Arabia, Egypt, Migdol, and Aswan (in Egypt), and the people of the covenant land (Judah) are mentioned in the same paradigm as being subject to destruction. Little is known about the peoples of Lydia, except that they were frequently employed as mercenaries and probably lived between the upper Tigris and Euphrates. Isaiah (Isa. 66:19) put them in the area from the Aegean to the Caspian Seas.

cubit(s): an ancient measurement of length. The actual distance was measured from the middle finger to the elbow, approximately eighteen inches (called the "common" cubit). Some noted authorities claim that exact measurement is 18.74 inches. If this standard is acceptable, without any variations that could have easily crept in over time, the giant Goliath would have been almost nine and a half feet tall, as one example of height. A slightly longer unit, used in Ezekiel 40:5, was about a handbreadth larger and called the "long" cubit. Most of the shorter measurements used in Scripture are noted in cubits. Revelation 21:15 says the walls of New Jerusalem are 144 cubits thick (about 200 feet or 65 meters). *See also* span.

Culleton, R. Gerald: author of the 20th century whom some claim to be an expert on the Antichrist. He has predicted much but is most noted for his belief that a German antipope will be set up in the near future in the Roman Catholic church and Rome will be destroyed. The recently resigned Pope Benedict XVI is of German descent and still retains his title as pope which, in the thinking of some, makes him an antipope. *See also* antipope(s); Benedict XVI, Pope; Roman Catholic Church.

cult(s): 1. a deviant or strange religious group often laced with apocalyptic rhetoric. Many or all of any cult's tenets are nonorthodox when compared to traditional Christian belief and may even be described as bizarre or violent. Usually, such groups are relatively small in number, leading some sociologists and theologians to distinguish them from a sect, because the latter group often has a more substantial history and membership. Cults also trend to cruelty and subjugation of mind and body. At least one published estimate, however, claims there are some 7,000,000 cultists among about 5,000 cults identified in the United States alone. In contrast, there are only about fifty "legitimate" religions. Almost without exception, cults present heretical views of Jesus Christ—his person, words, works, and especially his resurrection. Scientific pollsters, presumably unbiased, have issued a list of the "Top Ten" most bizarre cults in America. Results name them as: (1) Peoples Temple, (2) *Am Shinri Kyo* (Aleph), (3) Heaven's Gate, (4) Manson Family cult, (5) Branch Davidians, (6) Bhagwan Shree Rajneesh Commune, (7) Solar Temple, (8) Villa Baviera,

(9) cargo cults, (10) Raelians. A companion list offers the most dangerous groups: (1) Scientology, (2) Unification Church ("Moonies"), (3) Klu Klux Klan, (4) Movement for the Restoration of the Ten Commandments of God, (5) *Am Shinri Kyo* (Aleph), (6) Children of God (COG) now Family International, (7) Solar Temple, (8) Branch Davidians, (9) Peoples Temple, (10) Heaven's Gate. There is certainly a consideration that the groups cannot truly be classed as bizarre or violent since they are habitually both. Often, the terms *cult* and *sect* are used interchangeably, or one is subsumed under the other, and considered acceptable form. Mormons, Jehovah's Witnesses, and Seventh-Day Adventists, for example, are often called both. Even so, since the term "cult" seems to connote a more pejorative image, many reserve its use for those groups that are truly weird, dangerous, or radically outside a traditional belief system. By some standards, cults also seem to have more coercive rules of obedience, a cohesiveness of fear, and are frequently led by charismatic or unscrupulous leaders. Often their existence is confined to a certain locale or exclusive conclave. 2. a secular definition is also extant, such as a "cult following" of a celebrity, a social fad, or the like. 3. a cult (or cultus) may also be a ritual practiced by a specified religious grouping. *See also* Adamites; Ahmad, Mirza Ghulam; Aleph; alien Jesus; Amicale; Anglo-Israelism; Armanenschafft; Applewhite, Marshall; Ashara Shoko; *Astrum Argentum;* Berg, Moses (David); Bhagwan Shree Rajneesh; Branch Davidians; Brotherhood of the Seven Rays, the; Brothers and Sisters of the Red Death; Brothers, Richard; Caesar cult; Cantheism; cargo cult(s); Christian Catholic Apostolic Church; Church of Bible Understanding; Church of the Last Testament; Church Universal and Triumphant; Community of Christ (cultic); Concerned Christians; Counter Cult Movement; Crowley, Aleister; Cult Awareness Network; cult of the dead; deprogramming; Discordianism; Divine Light Mission; Divine Science, Church of; doomsday cult(s); Dowie, John

Alexander; Dungeons and Dragons; Eckankar; egocentric cults; Eleusian Mysteries; emperor worship; esoteric sects; exit counseling; Family International; Fascist millennialism; Father Divine; fertility gods; Filippovich, Daniil; Fillmore, Myrtle and Charles; ghost dance cult; Gnosticism, Gnostic(s); Great White Brotherhood, the; Hare Krishna; Hashshashin; Hawkins, Yisrayl "Buffalo Bill"; Heaven's Gate; Hermeticism; House of David; House of Yahweh; Heaven's Gate; Houteff, Florence; Hubbard L. Ron; Hulon, Mitchell Jr.; Human Enhancement Revolution (HER); Human Potential Movement; *Hyoo-go;* idolatry; Irminism; Jeffs, Warren; Jones, Jim; Jonestown; Jouret, Luc; Khlysty, the; Kieninger, Richard; Koresh, David; Le Vey, Anton Szandor; Living Word Fellowship, the; Luciferans; Lundgren, Jeffery; Manson, Charles; Martin, Dorothy; Matsoua, Andre; Messiah Foundation International; militant domestic organizations; mind control; Moon, Sun Myung; Movement for the Restoration of the Ten Commandments of God; Muntzer, Thomas; mystery religion(s); nature cult(s); Nettles, Bonnie; New Group of World Servers; New Message from God; new religious movements; Nidle, Sheldon; Nxivm; *Ordo Templi Orientis;* Patriot Movement, the; Peoples Temple; Phibionites; Philadelphians; *Pontifex Maximus;* Priory of Sion; Process Church of the Final Judgment; Prophet, Elizabeth Clare; Psychiana; Purcell, Benjamin; Quiboloy, Apollo; Raelism; Rainbow Coalition; Rainbow Family; Ram Bahadur Bamjan; Religious Science; revitalization movement; Roerich, Nickolas K.; Roman Phalanx; Samothrace; Sanat Kumar; Satanism; Sathya Sai Baba; Savonarola, Girolamo; Schafer, Paul; Scientology, Church of; Sea of Faith; sect(s); Select Followers, the; Selivanov, Kondrati; Shango; shepherding (cultic); Sicarii; Silva Mind Control; Skoptsy, the; Solar Temple, the; Spare, Austin Osman; Spiritualist churches; Stevens, John Robert; sun worshipers; Sword of God Brotherhood; Temple of the Psychedelic Light and the Church or Realized Fantasy; *Templi Orientis;* Thelema;

The Way International; things taught by demons; Traill, Stewart; Triads; Twelve Tribes; UFO; Unification Church; Unity Church; Villa Baviera; Vissarion; Vorilhorn, Claud; Way, the; Weor, Samael Aun; White, Ellen G. (Harmon); Whittenberg prophets, the; Wicca; Woman in the Wilderness; Word-Faith Movement; Word of Faith Fellowship; Wroe, John; Yahweh ben Yahweh; Zimmerman, Johann Jacob; Zealots.

Cult Awareness Network: an organization that began as an anti-cult rescue effort. The group went bankrupt, however, due to legal and ethical issues regarding their methods of kidnapping and reprogramming. All assets were purchased by the Foundation for Religious Freedom which, ironically, promotes religious liberty. *See also* Counter Cult Movement; cult(s); deprogramming; exit counseling; religious organizations; sect(s).

Cult of Reason: one result of the French Revolution in 1789 that was hostile to established Christianity. Thousands of Catholics and some Protestant clergy were executed. Ten years later the French invaded Rome and took Pope Pius VI prisoner to France. The same happened to Pope Pius VII in 1801 under Napoleon. *See also* Bonaparte, Napoleon.

cult of the dead: the age-old religious practice of veneration or glorifying the dead and dying. Some of the ritual rites were, and are, grisly dramas and blood and food reminiscent of ancient ancestor worship. The ancient Egyptians were the most advanced in the arts of the death cult. *See also* ancestor reverence; cult(s); Day of the Dead; Guadalupe, Our Lady of; idolatry; necrolatry; necromancy; veneration of the saints.

Cult of the Supreme Being: a sort of civil religion developed by Maximilien Robespierre (1758 – 1794) in the intended French Republic following the great rebellion. The structure of belief seems to be a kind of civic-minded system of virtues with a bit of basic theology mixed in. *See also* civil religion; sect(s).

History and Mystery

cultural mandate: the expression best promoting God's imperative to Adam and Eve and humanity's future progress: the command to rule over the earth and develop a God-glorifying culture. Genesis explains the mandate and shows interests in the arts, crafts, music, metallurgy, farming, and many other pursuits capable to human creativity. The same motivation was directed to Noah after the great flood. Such is our obligation to the world and to God. *See also* arts, the; book(s); dance; music; sociology of religion.

cultural relativism: the sense that every culture's ethics, moral sense, and social customs are right or suitable for that group. The concept is central to secular anthropology but could be a hindrance, even a threat, for religious missionary activity. *See also* culture war; human condition, the; missions, missionaries; relativism; secular humanism; social issues; sociology of religion.

culture war: known as *Kulturkampf,* a clash of ideals or societal values of one culture or set of beliefs in conflict with another. Topics of disagreement may range far and wide into religion, politics, race, mores, fashion, and many other norms of society as disputes occur, are acted upon, and (rarely) compromised. History provides many examples of *Kulturkampf* such as the Jewish/Hellenist divide of the Maccabean era, the Allied/Nazi conflict of the 1940s, and the Cold War differences after. Today's hot topics, at least in America, would likely be listed as abortion, gun control, church/state relations, racial equality, censorship and privacy, public morality, immigration, recreational drug use, entitlement, homosexuality, feminism, and political correctness. Few of these issues are new, of course, but never in American history has the culture wars appeared to be so deeply ingrained in uncivil word and action. *See also* cultural relativism; human condition, the; relativism; secular humanism; social issues; sociology of religion.

cumin: a medicinal herb with aromatic seeds, said to be effective in passing bodily gas. People of the Middle Ages used it both in this manner and as a food flavoring. *See also* flora, fruit, and grain, symbology of; herb(s).

cuneiform: an early alphabet system developed in Mesopotamia. The writing was exacted by pressing wedge-shaped stems of the papyrus reed into wet clay, then dried. In fact, the word "cuneiform" derives from Latin meaning "wedge-shaped." Cuneiform script enabled much of our understanding of the ancient Near East and its relationship to the Hebrew alphabetical characters. The writing uses the pictograph method and was developed as early as the fourth millennium B.C. *See also* alphabet; element(s).

cup: a small drinking vessel or chalice. In symbolic language, the cup sometimes represents that which falls to one's lot in life, either good or ill (*e.g.*, Psalm 23:5; Lamentations 4:21). We "drink from the cup" of our own destiny. Jesus once challenged the disciples to drink from the cup of suffering pattered on the agony he was to endure on the cross and in the preliminary events of Passion Week (Mk. 10:38). Jesus prayed to the Father that the cup of death might be spared for him but, nevertheless, that God's will should prevail (Mk. 14:36; Lk. 22:42). Jesus once accused the Pharisees of cleaning the outside of the cup while filthy corruption remained inside untouched (Mt. 23:25). The cup of wine is prominent in the Last Supper enactment for it signed Christ's shed blood (Lk. 22:20; 1 Cor. 11:25). Throughout history, adventurers have sought after the Holy Grail, whether defined as the Communion cup or Jesus or some other definition. *See also* cup of adulteries; cup of blessing; cup of fury (wrath); cup of suffering; Holy Grail; relic(s).

Cupay: the designation for the devil of the ancient Incas, the god of death. *See also* Apophis; Beelzebub; Evil One, the; Ghede; Hahgwehdaetgah; Iblis; idol(s); *Kategor;* lion; Mastema; Sammael; Sanat Kumar; Satan; Shaytan.

Cupid: the Roman god of love, the Greek equivalent being Eros. According to myth, he was the son of Venus and Mercury who sometimes appeared as a winged infant carrying a magical bow and quiver of arrows. When targeted, the arrow

History and Mystery

struck its victim with awe and love for which there was no recovery. *See also* Eros; Olympian pantheon; Valentine's Day.

cupio dissolui: a Latin form of the message of Philippians 1:23–24 when Paul spoke of his yearning for heaven. The phrase means "I wish to be dissolved" and may even carry connotations of suicide.

cup of adulteries: one of the accouterments of the woman on the beast (false religion or the whore of Babylon), which is described as golden yet filled with abominable things and the filth of her infidelities (Rev. 17:4). *See also* Babylon the Great; desolate and naked; filth of her adulteries; "glorifies herself"; Great Prostitute, the; idolatry; prostitute, prostitution; Religious Babylon; whore of Babylon; wine of her adulteries; wine of wrath.

cup of blessing: or cup of thanksgiving, the promise that drinking the Lord's cup at Communion will produce God's favor in some manner (1 Cor. 10:16). *See also* liturgy, Christian.

cup of fury (wrath): an apocalyptic phrase to denote God's anger. God's justice will manifest in that evildoers will be forced to drink the wine cup of His fury, even to the dregs (Ps. 75:8). A thorough discussion of the phrase is found in Jeremiah 25:15–38 where God's anger spills over onto His people. The phrase is also seen as earth's cup of iniquity. *See also* eschatology, eschatological; great signs, the; wine of wrath; wrath of the Lamb.

cup of reeling: a prophetic metaphor (Zech. 12:2–3) that pictures Jerusalem as a consternation to all the world's peoples. The prophet amplifies his description by adding that God would also make the city a heavy stone causing injury to all who molest her; while certifying that all the nations of the earth would, nevertheless, surely harass its inhabitants throughout her history.

cup of suffering: figurative language for suffering of the saints, usually to death. James and John rashly proclaimed that they were capable of "drinking" it with their Lord (Mk. 10:38–39), though they had no true concept of Christ's heavy burden for the sin of the world and his pending torture on the cross, nor even the pending pain of their own persecutions. Jeremiah reports that the cup of God's wrath will be poured out on unfaithful Judah (Jer. 25:15–38). *See also* vicarious suffering.

curate: an Anglican or Roman Catholic assistant pastor. The title generally refers to his job as the "cure" or care of souls. *See also* canon(s) of the church; Church of England; clergy; cure; diocese; ecclesiastic(s); parish.

cure: the spiritual charge (inferior in rank to the parish priest) of an Anglican or Roman Catholic parish, or the parish itself. *See also* church field; Church of England; clergy; curate; diocese; ecclesiastic(s); eparchy; episcopate; fold; katholikon; ministry; missions, missionaries; parish; patriarchate(s); pastor(s); pentarchy; presbytery; priest(s); rector; Roman Catholic Church; see.

Curia: a Roman Catholic "court" or administrative and political staff established by Pope Urban II in 1090. The system was modeled on almost any secular monarchy extant at the time and allowed the pope a more readily available, dependent, and personal support group in defiance of the growing power of the cardinals and other officials already in place with their own agendas. *See also* cardinal(s); conclave; Infirmieri; religious organizations; Roman Catholic Church.

curious acts: a description of magical practices in some Bible translations, or sorceries in others, as noted in Acts 19:19 *See also* anthropomancy; anthroposophy; apotropaic magic; aretology; Ariosophy; astral plane; astral projection; astrolabe; astrology, astrologers; athame; audition; augury; automatic writing; bagua; belomancy; *besom;* bibliomancy; black arts; black mirror; blood moon(s); cartomancy; chaos magic; chiromancy; clairaudience; clairsentience; clairvoyance; cleromancy; cone of power; conjure; crop circles;

History and Mystery

crystallomancy; cryptesthesia; crystal skulls; divination; dream(s); dreams and visions; ecstasy; enchantment; enneagram; esoteric sects; evil eye; extrasensory perception (ESP); foreknowledge; foretelling; geomancy; grimoire; gris-gris; hepatoscopy; Hermetic wisdom; Hermetic writings; hex; hierscopy; horoscope(s); hydromancy; idol(s); idolatry; ifa; incantation; juju; labyrinth walk; lecanomancy; literomancy; locution; magic arts; magic, magick; magic square; magnetism; *mana*; mantic wisdom; mantra; miracles(s); monition; mystery religion(s); necromancy; New Age religion; numbers, symbology of; occult, occultic; omen; oneiromancy; oracle(s); otherworldly journeys; ouija board; out-of-body experiences (OBEs); past life regression; pentagram; philosophers' stone; planchette; planets as gods; portent; precognition; prediction; premonition; prodigy; prognostication; prophecy, general; psi; physic(s); psychic healing; psychic reading; psychometry; psychonautics; prognostication; prophecy; psychomancy; psychometry; pyramidology; rebirthing; reincarnation; remote viewing; retrocognition; revelation; rhabdomancy; scrying; séance; secret societies; secret wisdom; sorcery, sorceries; spell; spell names; spiritism; supernatural; superstition; tarot; telegnosis; telepathy; telesthesia; theugry; third eye, the; thoughtform; totemism; vision(s); vision quest; visualization; voodoo; voudou; wanga; warlock(s); Web-Bot; witchcraft; wizard(s); *ya sang*; yoga; Zen; zodiac; *zos kia* cultus.

curse(s): 1. a pronouncement of ill will directed from one person to another or from God—or man to God. 2. an expression of contempt voiced usually in anger or derision. Apocalyptic expression is filled with curses, along with their opposite—blessings. Several lengthy chapters beginning in Ezekiel 25 spell out curses for Israel's enemies. Many other Bible references discuss the power and meaning of curses of all types and almost all the prophets dealt with them in one fashion or another. Those curses of immediate prophetic import named in the Bible include those upon: the serpent (Gen.3:14–15), the earth (Gen. 3:17–18, 5:29, 8:21), Cain

(Gen. 4:11), Canaan (Gen. 9:23), the enemies of Israel (Gen. 12:3), recalcitrant Israel (Deut. 28:15), Jehoiakim (Jer. 22:18-23, 36:30), Jehoiachin (Jer. 22:24-30), unbelievers (Mt. 25:41), the fruitless fig tree (Mk. 11:21), nature (Rom. 8:19-22), false preachers (Gal. 1:8), those who remain under the Law of Moses only (Gal. 3:10), and Christ, for our sin (Gal. 3:13). It is interesting that the last English word in the Old Testament is "curse." *See also* antiphon; apotropaic magic; blasphemy; blessing(s); charm(s); curse on the line of Jehoiachin; curses of Amos; curses of Daniel; curses of Ezekiel; curses of Habakkuk; curses of Haggai; curses of Hosea; curses of Isaiah; curses of Jeremiah; curses of Joel; curses of Jonah; curses of Malachi; curses of Micah; curses of Nahum; curses Obadiah; curses of Zechariah; curses of Zephaniah; evil eye; Fall, the; *geis;* hex; idolatry; imprecation; New Age religion; poppets; pow-wow; profane; spell; spell names; taboo; ward; warlock(s); Wicca; witch(es); woe(s).

curse on the line of Jehoiachin: a pronouncement of doom on the dynasty of King Jehoiachin most pointedly recorded in Jeremiah 22:24-30. God condemned the kingly line of Jehoiachin (Coniah) of Judah because his father, Jehoiakim, had burned the parchment containing the Word of God delivered to him from Jeremiah (Jer. 36:30-31). As Jehoiakim's son, Jehoiachin actually reigned a short term after his father but had no descendants to sit on the throne of David. The rendition of 1 Chronicles 2:17 in some Bibles (but not later versions) mentions one Assir as a possible son of Jehoiachin who was born in captivity at Babylon. He did not, however, succeed to the royal title; that position fell to Shealtiel. The curse on his royal family then necessitated that the messianic line of Jesus be traced through David's son Nathan in the messianic sense (as recorded in Luke—through the genealogy of Mary) but in a legalistic sense through David's son Solomon (as recorded in Matthew—through the genealogy of Joseph). *See also* curse(s); Davidic Covenant; genealogy of Jesus; Jehoiachin.

curses of Amos: the prophet's condemnation of Damascus, Beth Eden, Gaza, Ekron, Tyre, Sidon, Edom, Ammon, Moab, Judah, and Israel. Amos also prophesied concerning the final judgment of all the nations. In particular, he cursed the elders and priests of the land who were far from the righteous leaders they ought to be. *See also* curse(s); Amos as Old Testament prophecy.

curses of Christ. See woe(s).

curses of Daniel: Daniel's invective and pronouncements of doom against Babylon, Medo-Persia, Greece, Syrian Greece, and, by inference and prophetic interpretation, the Roman Empire and the kingdom of the future Antichrist. *See also* curse(s); Daniel as Old Testament prophecy; Daniel's description of the hand writing on the wall; Roman Empire.

curses of Ezekiel: the prophet's condemnation of Ammon, Moab, Edom, Babylon, Cush, Put, Lydia, Arabia, Libya, Gog, the "mountains of Israel," Tyre, Sidon, Philistia, Egypt, Jerusalem, and Assyria. Some nations mentioned by Ezekiel are singled out for special rebuke, naming them as occupants of *Sheol* (hell) who lie dead among the godless uncircumcised: Egypt, Assyria, Elam, Meshech and Tubal, Edom, and Sidon. His pointed condemnations of false prophets, false leaders, idolaters, and the king of Tyre are particularly telling. *See also* curse(s); Ezekiel as Old Testament prophecy; idolatry; mountains of Israel, prophecy against the; Jerusalem, siege of (pantomime).

curses of Habakkuk: Habakkuk's condemnation of those who practice violence, fraud, injustice, prideful acts, arrogance, oppression, and other sordid social ills. *See also* curse(s); Habakkuk as Old Testament prophecy.

curses of Haggai: Haggai's invective against postexilic Judea for their reluctance to build the restoration Temple. *See also* curse(s); Haggai as Old Testament prophecy.

curses of Hosea: Hosea's indictment of Israel, an extensive narrative of condemnation for that nation. *See also* curse(s); Hosea as Old Testament prophecy.

curses of Isaiah: pronouncements of disfavor from the prophet Isaiah. Much of Isaiah's prophecy is concerned with God's displeasure with Israel and long passages record the nation's intended punishment, frequently at the hand of contentious nations surrounding Jerusalem. One unique condemnation, however, concerns "the nations," those peoples in a generic sense who are not of the house of Israel (Isa. 34); another generally censures "the wicked," those who are bent to evil (Isa. 56:9–12). Specific condemnations are reserved for Babylon, Assyria, Philistia, Moab, Damascus, Cush, Egypt, Edom, Tyre, Arabia, Jerusalem, and even the earth itself at one point. In conjunction with Assyria's demise (the country named as "the rod of His anger") Isaiah cited the locales of Calno, Carchemish, Hamath, and Arpad as being under direct threat. The prophet seemed to reserve rather pointed denunciations against Babylon since he named that land first and mentioned it twice in one of his condemnations. Blessings also, nonetheless, are prominent in the book of Isaiah from place to place as God promises redemption for the remnant of God's people. *See also* curse(s); Isaiah as Old Testament prophecy; remnant; king of Babylon; second Exodus; song of the vineyard; whip.

curses of Jeremiah: the prophet's condemnations of Israel's neighbors (Jer. 44 and several chapters following). Jeremiah pronounced God's judgment on Egypt, Babylon, Philistia, Moab, Ammon, Elam, Hazor, Edom, Damascus, Kedar, and, of course, Jerusalem. Like his predecessor, Isaiah, Jeremiah seemed to emphasize Babylon's punishment. In another paradigm, he condemned Egypt, Judah, Edom, Ammon, Moab, and all who live in the desert places (Jer. 9:25–26). Jeremiah's composition of Lamentations can be considered an extended condemnation and grief of his peoples' failures. *See also* curse(s); Jeremiah as Old Testament prophecy.

curses of Joel: the prophet's condemnation of Tyre and Sidon. Much of Joel's condemnations sound much like the descriptions of the battle of Armageddon. *See also* curse(s); Joel as Old Testament prophecy.

curses of Jonah: Jonah's prolonged indictments against Nineveh. *See also* curse(s); Jonah as Old Testament prophecy.

curses of Malachi: the prophet's condemnation of Esau (Edom), unfaithful Levites, false priests, and unfaithful Judah. The curses also extend to sorcerers, cheaters over wages and tithes, and oppressors of the poor and aliens in the land. *See also* curse(s); Malachi as Old Testament prophecy.

curses of Micah: the prophet's condemnation of Samaria and Jerusalem. *See also* curse(s); Micah as Old Testament prophecy.

curses of Nahum: the prophet's condemnation of Nineveh and all things Assyrian. *See also* curse(s); Nahum as Old Testament prophecy.

curses of Obadiah: the prophet's condemnation of Edom (also called Esau). *See also* curse(s); Obadiah as Old Testament prophecy.

curses of Zechariah: the prophet's condemnation of Damascus, Hamath, and Hadrach, Tyre and Sidon, Gaza and Ashkelon, Ekron and Ashdod, Assyria and Egypt, Lebanon and Jordan, Greece and Philistia, Judah and Jerusalem, idols and diviners, Geba and Rimmon, and wicked shepherds (princes). *See also* curse(s); Zechariah as Old Testament prophecy; Zechariah's oracle of Jerusalem's destruction; Zechariah's oracle of two shepherds and two shepherd's staffs; Zechariah's vision of the flying scroll; Zechariah's vision of the four horns and four craftsmen.

curses of Zephaniah: the prophet's condemnation of Judah, Philistia, Moab, Ammon, Cush, Assyria, and Egypt under the Ethiopians. *See also* curse(s); Zephaniah as Old Testament prophecy.

Curse, the. See Fall, the.

cursillo: the Roman Catholic practice (normally lasting over a three-day weekend) for prayer, study, and mission outreach. *See also* religious education; retreat; Roman Catholic Church.

curtain(s): a screen, usually fabric, that provides some measure of privacy when separating spaces or that embellishes the decor, as with a tapestry. Both uses were employed by the ancients, and the Israelites provided them extensively in the tabernacle and Temples. At one point, the writer of Hebrews used the article metaphorically to represent the sacrificed body of Christ as our way to salvation (Heb. 10:20) as it mimicked the high priest's actions on the Day of Atonement. *See also* curtain of the Temple; Curtain of the Throne, the; veil(s).

curtain of the Temple: the covering or veil between the Holy Place and the Holy of Holies in the Jerusalem Temple. The New Testament record recounts the rending of the partition on the occasion of Jesus' death on the cross. The veil was torn from top the bottom following the miracle of darkness prevailing at the crucifixion, thus causing the public to see inside the Holy Places which had been a strict religious taboo and never done. Most scholars see the event as the act of God ripping the barrier of mystery that partially hid the Father's glory and distanced Himself from His people because of their uncovered sins. The sacrifice of Jesus, however, forever removed the hindrance. Now the Holy Place, representing the most sublime and secretive recesses of God's relationship with His creation, is now exposed and we may have a personal relationship to the Father through Christ's victory over sin and death. *See also* accommodation; curtain(s); veil(s).

Curtain of the Throne, the: a curtain or veil, according to *3 Enoch*, hiding the divine majesty before the great throne of God. On it is written the history of all generations, past and present, represented by all those in responsible positions. Major classes of the ancient world are also present, named as rulers, leaders, shepherds (clergy or civic authorities), oppressors, keepers, punishers, counselors, teachers, supporters, bosses, presidents of academies, magistrates, princes (political leaders), advisors, noblemen, warriors, and elders and guides from all generations from Adam to Gog and Magog. The record speaks of two Messiahs – one of peace, who is to be killed, and the other of vengeance who will triumph. Christians would read of the Curtain and consider it an unacceptable duality instead of the one Jesus. *Third Enoch* seems to be replete with the doctrine of predestination and foreknowledge. *See also* curtain(s).

Cusa, Nicholas: an Italian polymath turned liberal cardinal (1401–1464). Cusa was interested in mathematics, astronomy, physics, and calendar reform. He came to believe, either from his faith or science (or both) that the earth moves and that the universe is boundless. *See also* Aristarchus; astronomy, astronomers; clergy scientists; Copernicus, Nicolaus; Galilei, Galileo; Roman Catholic Church.

Cush, Cushites: 1. a son of Ham and grandson of Noah who fathered the mighty Nimrod. 2. a locale first designated as a place in Genesis 2:13. Its location was the Fertile Crescent, thus placing it in ancient Babylon or another land mentioned in Genesis at the River Gihon (location unknown). 3. a country bordering Egypt and Sudan (the upper Nile). In most Bible literature, Cush is named as the Upper Nile region, possibly present-day Sudan or Nubia, if not Ethiopia proper (2 Ki. 19:9; Esth. 1:1; Ezk. 29:10). Josephus noted that they supported the national economy by the sale of slaves and monkeys. That land may have prophetic significance because of persistent claims that some of the more modern line of kings in Ethiopia sprang from Solomon and the Queen of Sheba and that the ark of the covenant resides in the ancient city of Aksum. Both assertions are unproven at this time, and good evidence is lacking for every version of the legend. 4. in other passages, the Cushites were in central and southern Arabia. Certainly, that is the place mentioned in Habakkuk 3:7 called Cushan, then associated with the Midianites. 5. a future ally of Gog and Magog, along with Beth Togarmah, Gomer, Persia, and Put. 6. a certain Cush, a Benjamite and foe of David, to whom he sang a *shiggaion* (Ps. 7). Particulars of this rendition are unavailable. 7. some authorities claim that the female object of desire in the Song of Solomon may be a Cushite. *See also* Arabia; ark of the covenant; Beth Togarmah; Candace; Ebed-Melech; Elephantine; Ethiopian eunuch, the; Falasha Jews; Gog and (of) Magog; Gomer; *Kebra Nagast;* Makeda; Menelik, Prince; Meshech; Nubia; Operation Moses; Persia, Persians; Put; Queen of Sheba, Queen of the South; Rosh, Prince of; Seba, Sabeans; tabot; Tubal; Zera.

Cutheans: a people of Samaria imported by the Assyrians to replace some of the ten tribes expelled from the area after the Northern Kingdom was conquered (2 Ki. 17:24–41). The Cutheans were professing Jews, but their sincerity was disbelieved by pure-blooded Hebrews. The name "Cutheans" became a by-word for any idolater, whether of that particular race or not, much like the Hebrew terms *goy* or *nokhri*. These people also obstructed Nehemiah in his reconstruction efforts in Jerusalem. Josephus said there was a copy of the Jerusalem Temple in the land but he could have been referring to the Temple of Samaria. *See also* lion.

Cutler, Manasseh: a Congregational clergyman (1747–1823) and chaplain to the Massachusetts colony militia in the Revolutionary War. Besides being an effective minister, Cutler was also a physician, lawyer, educator, scientist, botanist, mathematician, and astronomer. He helped establish the town of Marietta, Ohio and served as that state's senator. Cutler's contributions to American history were immense. *See also* clergy patriots; clergy scientists; Congregationalists.

Cyaxares: a Median king (ca. 614 B.C.) who advanced against Nineveh as predicted by the prophet Nahum. He was allied with Nabopolassar of Babylon and the Scythians. *See also* king(s).

Cybele: a deity of Phrygian mythology, a nature goddess adopted by the Romans as Rhea Silvia. She was known as a vestal virgin and the mother of Romulus and Remus by the god Mars. She was strongly worshiped at Smyrna (Rev. 2:8–11). To the Greeks, she was known as a daughter of Uranus and Gaia (Gaea), the wife of Cronus, and mother of Zeus and other major deities. She was also the consort of Attis in Greco-Roman lore. She was called "mother of the gods" in some cultures. *See also* Attis; Gaia (Gaea); idol(s); *Magna Mater*; Olympian pantheon.

cycle of history: the idea that world history may occur in cycles, with some events repeating themselves in duplicate or in similar fashion. The idea is opposite the general Western assumption that history is linear – moving in a straight line and never repeating. If biblical historical events are indeed circular, they can usually be predicted to be in cycles of years numbering forty, fifty, seventy, or 100 and thus useful to prophecy. *See also* cycle of prophecies; cyclorama; numbers, symbology of; prophecy.

cycle of prophecies: a progressive series of predictions that are paralleled by a corresponding collection in another but similar context. *See also* cycle of history; prophecy.

Cyclopes: a fierce race of one-eyed giants. We meet them in the *Odyssey* when Odysseus and his fellow Achaeans became trapped in the cave inhabited by one of them named Polyphemus. The monster began to devour members of the crew as the giant gulped down huge portions of torso and limbs amid slurps of blood until Odysseus' crew was threatened with extinction. Finally, Odysseus managed to get Polyphemus drunk and the crew gouged out his one eye while in a stupor. *See also* Anak; Anunnaki; Fir Bolg; Fomorians; frost giants; giant(s); Laestrygonians;

mythological beasties, elementals, monsters, and spirit animals; Nephilim; Titans; Watchers, the.

cyclorama: a story or pageant told in pictorial technique one scene at a time until completed. The description fits the style of Revelation and is sometimes used to express its apocalyptic narrative flow. *See also* cycle of history; harvest of the earth.

Cynics: an offshoot of the Stoicism system of Greek philosophy. The sect derived from Antiahenes (fifth century B.C.), who derided all forms of worldly living and any form of normal social interaction. The most famous of the group was Diogenes, who lived a life of unorthodox protest, all the while carrying a lamp and claiming to be looking for an honest man. *See also* Diogenes; philosophy of the Greeks.

Cyprian: a student of Tertullian (ca. A.D. 200–258) who succeeded his teacher as bishop of Carthage. He was a supporter of millennial doctrine. Cyprian also believed that the Second Coming was at hand, perhaps because he was living under the vicious persecution of the emperor Decius. Martyrdom was common then and continued under Gallus (251–253) and Valerian (253–260). He is quoted: "The kingdom of God, beloved brethren, is beginning to be at hand." Cyprian joined the martyrs in A.D. 258 while expressing thanks to God for releasing him from the "chains of the body." *See also* liturgical year; martyr(s); Roman Catholic Church.

Cyprus: a Mediterranean island off the coast of Syria. There were Christians connected with it before the martyrdom of Stephen, and the place was visited by Paul, Barnabas, and Mark (Acts 13:4; 15:39). Its ancient name was Kittim. *See also* Kittim (Chittim); Minoan civilizations.

Cyril of Alexandria: patriarch of Alexandria (412-444). Cyril was a leader in the Council of Ephesus of 451, which managed to outlaw the Nestorians. He is most remembered, however, for expelling the Novatians (Christians who refused forgiveness to other believers who betrayed the faith under the persecution of Decius—the *Lapsi*—in A.D. 250) and all Jews from Alexandria. More notoriously, he was implicated in the abduction and lynching of the respected Greek philosopher (a woman in a man's world at the time) named Hypatia. *See also* anti-Semitic; Councils of Ephesus; Hypatia; liturgical year; Roman Catholic Church.

Cyrus Cylinder: a barrel-shaped record of the liberating laws of Cyrus the Great, some of which are reproduced in 2 Chronicles 36:23 and Ezra 1:2–4. The cuneiform text, discovered in 1879, was pressed into the clay records. This documentation showed the decree of the Persian king Cyrus that dictated religious toleration and the reestablishment of any sanctuaries destroyed by the Babylonians. *See also* Cyrus the Great (Cyrus II).

Cyrus the Great (Cyrus II): founder of the Persian Empire (559–530 B.C.). Isaiah prophesied of him as one anointed by God to free the Jews from Babylonian Captivity and named him personally 200 years before he was born, which proved to be the case. He is thought by most scholars to be the subject of Daniel's vision of the ram with two horns, representing the Median and Persian divisions of his empire (Dan. 8:3–4, 20). The name Cyrus is distinctive in Scripture for it marks a rare reference to a pagan monarch who was literally "anointed" by the Lord to be a savior type (Isa. 44:28) and is actually named in prophecy. Some historians, including Josephus, assert that Cyrus decreed the return of the Jews to Jerusalem and the rebuilding because he had personally read, and marveled, at the words of Isaiah spoken some 140 years before the destruction of the Temple, including the details that he was to conquer Babylon, free the Jews, and return their Temple treasures. Cyrus was succeeded to the throne by Cambyses II, Smerdis, and Darius I. *See also* Anointed One, the; anointing; Babylonian (and Persian) restoration decrees; Cyrus Cylinder; Ezra as scribe; king(s); Koresh, David; Nehemiah as governor; restoration of Israel (the Jews).

D

da Casale, Umbertino: a radical monk (c. 1259 – c. 1330) who claimed the two ravening beasts of Revelation (one from the sea and the other from land) were representative of two of Catholicism's most notorious popes—Boniface VIII and Benedict XI. Both pontiffs were sworn persecutors of their opposers both inside and outside of the established church. *See also* monk(s); Roman Catholic Church.

Daejonggyo: or Taechongyeo, a Korean religion of rather recent origin promoting the worship of Dagun (or Tangun), a legendary founder of Gotoseon, an early kingdom-state. Bocheonism is a splinter group. *See also* idolatry; sect(s).

daemons: a class collective of nature spirits, either benign, benevolent, or hateful, fed with essence from the forces of nature or from the gods themselves. The Greeks called them *daimones* and the Roman Church referred to them as *genii*. Both Greek and Roman myth held a vital place for them, mostly as spirit guides or guardian beings assigned to persons for protection or conveyance to the hereafter. Hesoid, Plato, and Pindar speak of them. The Greeks perceived such ghost-like beings to be agents of Zeus, about 30,000 in number, surrounding us but unseen by mortals. It did not take long for the Christian Church to turn daemons into demons. *See also agathodaimon;* attending spirit(s); authorities; bugbears; deceiving spirits; demons, demonic; devils; disa; dryad(s); elemental(s); evil (unclean) spirit(s); fairy, fairies; familiar spirits; Furies; ghost(s); homunculus; household deities; idol(s); Lares; Loa Loas; Manes; mythological beasties, elementals, monsters, and spirit animals; Olympian pantheon; Oniropompi; Orisha; Oya; para; paredri; penates; power(s); spirit guide; spirits in prison; spiritual warfare; sprite(s); sylph(s); Tartarus; teraphim; territorial spirits; thrones; Trickster; Tuatha de Danann; tutelary; undine; wight(s).

History and Mystery

Daesh: a rather new acronym Muslims have applied to a proposed bloodthirsty Islamic state to be ruled by Sharia law. The term is derived from Arabic (*Al-Dawla alIslamiya fi al-Iraq wa al-Sham*) which roughly translates as: "to trample down and crush" or "a bigot who imposes his view on others." *See also* Alluha Akbar; al-Qaeda; al-Shabab; anti-Semitic; beast(s); Boko Haram; caliphate; *harem;* House of War; Fatah; Hamas; Hezbollah; Islam; Islamic State in Iraq and Syria (ISIS or ISIL); *jihad;* Muslim Brotherhood; Nusra Front; Palestinian Islamic Jihad (PIJ); Palestinian Liberation Organization (PLO); Salafi; Sharia; radicalized; Taliban; Tenth Crusade, the; terrorism; Turkistan Islamic Party; Velayat Sinai; Wahhabism; wild animals (beasts) of the earth.

Daesun Jinrihoe: a Taoist-derived religion of Korea founded in 1969 by Park Hangyeong (1918–1996). The sect called Jeung San Do is an offshoot and both are splinter groups of an earlier syncretic movement based on similar themes. *See also* idolatry; sect(s); Taoism.

Dagda: sometimes identified as the horned god Cernunnus, a respected leader or chief or god of the ancient Irish Tuatha de Danann and Druidism. He was viewed as a father-figure competent in agriculture, wisdom, manliness, and personal combat. His weapon of choice was a huge club with could kill nine man with a blow from one end, then restore them to life with the other end. In other sources, Dagda is a set of tri-goddesses, all named Brigit, each with various talents and responsibilities. *See also* Celtic folklore and religion; Danu; Druidism; idol(s); Tuatha de Danann.

Dagon: the god of the Philistines and some other communities, a vegetation or grain idol. As that may be, some authorities assert Dagon sported the head of a fish, perhaps reminiscent of the origins of the Philistines as mariners and colonists. When the Philistines captured the Jewish ark of the covenant, Dagon's statue toppled before it and broke into pieces. Alexander the Great spared Dagon's temple but the Maccabees destroyed it. *See also* idol(s); "Keeper of the Bridge"; Levant pantheon; threshold, not stepping on the.

Daibutsu, the: "the great Buddha," a huge statue in Kamakura, Japan. The giant and awe-inspiring figure, made mostly of bronze, was cast in A.D. 1252 and stands at forty-two feet in height with a base ninety-seven feet in circumference. The sculpture weighs some 550 tons. *See also* Buddhism.

Dajjal: the Muslim Antichrist. Some Muslims see him as a one-eyed monster, the king or leader of the Jews of the future who will descend on them in war. *See also* Ahmadinejad, Mahmoud; Antichrist as a Muslim; Islam; *jihad; Ka'bah;* Koran, the, madrassa(s); Mohammed; *Qur'an;* Sharia, third eye, the; Wahhabism.

Dalai Lama: the spiritual leader of Tibetan Buddhism known as Lamaist Mahayana. The title descends for the Mongolic word for "ocean" and the Tibetan "teacher," or guru. The Dalai Lama (now the fourteenth of the line) has been in exile from the Chinese Communist since 1959. It is said, in some traditions, that one of Tibet's Dalai Lama will show the way to Shambhala, the land of Paradise. The Dalai Lama form of Buddhism sees their leader as a kind of god-king espousing a type of "secular ethics," formed into a comparatively benevolent or easy belief system. Devotees commonly strive for trances of the mind in order to encourage spirit action or visions. *See also* Bon; Buddhism; Shambhala legends.

Dallas Theological Seminary: the educational anchor of dispensational theology. The school was started by Lewis Sperry Chafer as the Evangelical Theological College in 1924 but assumed its present name in 1936. *See also* Chafer, Lewis Sperry; dispensational theology; religious education; religious organizations; Walvoord, John.

Dalmanutha: a rather bleak spot on the western side of Lake Galilee. It was here Jesus fed the 4,000 according to

Mark (Mk. 8:1–13). Most likely the area is in the vicinity of Magdala (or Magadan in Matthew) which was the hometown of Mary Magdalene.

Damanhur: perhaps the largest (over 500 residents) of the surviving communal communities in the world. In addition, they are reported to have thousands of supporters worldwide but not in residence. The settlements were started in the Alpine foothills of northern Italy by the founder, Oberto Airaudi (1950 – 1975) where it is today. The establishment has their own flag, constitution, currency, schools, newspaper, and civil administration. Beliefs, however, are rather odd. Esoteric doctrine is borrowed from Celtic paganism, New Age, Gnosticism, the Illuminati, ancient Egyptian and Greek religions, and Theosophy. Damanhur means "city of light" but, oddly enough, much of the community is underground in elaborate work and living spaces. The purposes are said to be dedicated to the Egyptian god Horus and to the religion of Aleister Crowley called Thelema. In Honor of Horus (depicted with a falcon head) the founder Airaudi is nicknamed "Falco." Conspiracy theories abound concerning the group and their agenda, some or much of which might be true. For example, the members are said to be active in astral travel, magical technology to produce and capture psychic energy ("ether"), equipping for the coming Age of Aquarius, time travel (or their version of it), and intense ecological pursuits. *See also* Age of Aquarius; astral projection; Celtic folklore and religion; communal communities; conspiracy theories; Crowley, Aleister; Gnosticism, Gnostic(s); Horus; Illuminati network; New Age religion; New World Order, the (NWO); secret societies; sect(s); Thelema; Theosophy.

Damaris: a female convert to Christianity, one of the few positively influenced by Paul during his mission to Greece (Acts 17:34).

Damascenes, city of the: the residents of Damascus, the principal municipality of Syria whom Paul mentioned in 2 Corinthians 11:32. *See also* Aretas IV, King; Damascus; Syria.

Damascus: a city of Syria familiarly designated the capital and bearing the title "Pearl of the Desert." The settlement is ancient, being noted as extant in the time of Abraham (Gen. 14:15) and was situated on the crossroads of two principal trade routes of the Middle East. It may very well be the world's oldest continuously inhabited city. The land and city were harsh enemies of Israel, especially during the reign of David and the later kings, but eventually fell to the Romans after surviving many triumphs and defeats on the battlefield. The city was Paul's destination as he journeyed to persecute the Christians before his conversion and later became a first century Christian strongpoint in nearby Antioch. Damascus also maintains the site of the Mausoleum of Saladin and a tomb with a richly carpeted 400-foot-long hall of prayers which, according to legend, holds the head of John the Baptist. It is here that the street called "Straight" mentioned in Acts 9:11 is located; the avenue is, however, very crooked and narrow. *See also* Damascenes, city of the; Syria; Valley of Aven.

Damascus Document: or Damascus Rule, an archaeological discovery at Cairo in 1896 dated from the Middle Ages. It (also called the Zadokite Document) was uncovered in Cairo and parts of it resided among the Dead Sea Scrolls. The document consists of two parts: the first being an exhortation to the Dead Sea community and the second consisting of the several legal statutes and organizational structure of the brothers. There are similarities to Daniel within its content. The treatise speaks of an age of wrath to fall on the Jews 390 years following the fall of Jerusalem in 587 B.C. (about 196 B.C.), or near the time of Antiochus Epiphanes. The work is similar to, but not the same as, the Dead Sea Manual of Discipline. *See also* Bible manuscripts; Dead Sea Scrolls; Manual of Discipline.

Damascus Rule. See Damascus Document.

Damasus I, Pope: (A.D. 366–384), headed the papacy during the rule of the Roman emperor Gratian following the influence of Constantine I. The celebrated Vulgate translator Jerome was his personal secretary whom he encouraged to complete the work. Under Damascus's guidance, Catholic Christianity gained rapid prominence in the empire. He also presided over the Council of Rome in 382 to set the biblical canon and actively promoted the veneration of the saints. *See also* liturgical year; pope; Roman Catholic Church.

Dambala: voodoo's high god who, with his wife Ayida Wedo, rules over water and is considered a creation deity. *See also* Ayida Wedo; Bondye; idol(s); voodoo; voudou.

Dame Folly: the caricature of one of two types of women encountered in the book of Proverbs. Dame (Lady) Wisdom is contrasted to Madam (Dame) Folly with obvious distinctions. Over the years, the term Dame Folly has emerged as a general personification of foolishness. *See also* fool; Lady Wisdom; Proverbs as Old Testament book; Raca; wisdom.

Dames, Ed: a remote viewer who predicted a time of barren earth, 200–300 mph winds, and the death of 80 percent of the world's population. The problem is that he made his forecasts in 1996 and pronounced their fulfillment within three and a half years. He also claims to have had a remote viewing of Satan. *See also* psychic(s).

Damian, Peter: a dynamic reformer, Benedictine monk, and cardinal (c. 1007 – 1072) active in the 11th century who is highlighted in history, not for his preaching or radical apocalypticism, but for his condemnation of women. His vitriol for the gender can hardly be matched in any era. Damian viewed all women as sisters of the Great Whore of Babylon in Revelation and labeled them bitches, sows, screech-owls, night-owls, blood suckers, she-wolves, harlots, prostitutes, provocateurs of lascivious kisses, wallowers for fat pigs, couches of unclean spirits, companions of the very stuff of sin, and other less genteel terms. *See also* liturgical year; monk(s); Roman Catholic Church.

Dan: one of the twelve tribes of Israel descended from the patriarch Jacob by his wife Bilhah. Jacob's blessing in Genesis 49:16–18 states: "Dan will provide justice for his people as one of the tribes of Israel. Dan will be a viper along the path that bites the horse's heels so that its rider tumbles backward. I look for your deliverance, O Lord." The prophecy seems to be a mixed message indicating that Dan will not be totally faithful to its heritage (which, indeed, was the case) yet appears to express hope for the tribe's recovery. It is conspicuously absent in the tribal listing of the 144,000 servant grouping in Revelation 7:1–8. Legend states that the omission was intentional because Dan was to be the tribe of the Antichrist. A more likely proposition, if the lore is creditable, is that the tribe will spawn the False Prophet since Antichrist is not Jewish. The False Prophet is believed to be of that race. *See also* Falasha Jews; False Prophet, the; Hippolytus; lost tribes, the ten; tribes of Israel, the; twelve tribes.

dance: movement of the body in rhythmic fashion, whether accompanied by music or not. Religious expression in dance is common to most faith forms, usually seen as interpretive movement. Among the many styles, a general grouping might include ballet, ballroom, Caribbean, clog, contra, country/western; dancehall, disco (electronic), folk, freestyle, historic, Latin (rhythm), line, modern, rock and roll, square/round, street, swing, tap, traditional, and dozens of variations. Dancing, including the religiously interpretive sort, may be performed singly, in pairs, or in groups. Liturgical dance is specifically choreographed for worship expression. Dancing in some religious circles did not, however, engender much support as it was considered obscene. Reuben Torrey, for example, conceded that dancing was not a sin as long as men and women did not do it together. Another Christian observer opined that "many of the couples performing these dances should have a marriage license before stepping onto the ballroom floor, and if they had a marriage license, there would be no excuse for committing such acts in public." One fundamentalist sect promoted the saying that it never promoted sexual action while standing lest someone think they were dancing. *See also* arts, the; Bugaku; Burning Man Festival; corroboree; cultural mandate; David; dirge; Dogrib; ghost dance cult; liturgy, Christian; liturgy, Jewish; Miriam; Muses; music; *perichoresis;* prophetic ditty; Salome; Santeria; shaman, shamanism; Solara; Song of Moses; Song of Moses and the Lamb; Tenrikyo; United Society of Believers; veve; Whirling Dervishes; Wovoka.

Dan'el: 1. a sort of demi-god or ancient hero of legend not to be confused with the prophet of the Old Testament book of Daniel. The name was prominent in the religion of ancient Ugarit. 2. there is reputed to have been a Canaanite figure named Dan-El, a wise and righteous man who intercedes with the gods for the life of his son, Aqhat, in the Ugaritic legend of Aqhat. 3. a potentate among the fallen angels according to some apocalyptic literature. *See also* atrahasis; Daniel; demons, demonic; devils; idol(s); nephilim; prefect(s); satyr; sirens.

Daniel: 1. the most significant apocalyptic prophet of the Old Testament. There is some theological dispute about who he was and when he wrote, and questions regarding the details of the many dreams and visions he reported. There is no doubt, however, that the utterances and recordings in the book of Daniel are central to prophetic understanding and are unparalleled in their preciseness and prominence. This man's prophetic accomplishments are made unique in at least two ways. First, Daniel was respected and even beloved by many of his contemporaries, and second, many of his predictions carried with them the exact date of their fulfillment. Few, if any, of Israel's prophets enjoyed such a working environment. Jesus also spoke of him in connection to the abomination of desolation discourse (Mt. 24:15). Daniel's Hebrew name, meaning "God is my judge," was changed to Belteshazzar when he was taken captive to Babylon to honor one of the gods of the Babylonian pantheon, most likely Bel. 2. a Daniel is mentioned by Ezekiel (Ezk. 14:12–18), along with Noah and Job, as heroes of the faith. However, this Daniel may be Dan'el, a sort of demi-god or ancient hero of legend and not the prophet of the Old Testament book of Daniel. The name was prominent in the religion of ancient Ugarit. There is reputed to have been a Canaanite figure named Dan-El, a wise and righteous man who intercedes with the gods for the life of his son, Aqhat, in the Ugaritic legend of Aqhat. 3. another Daniel is mentioned in Ezra 8:2 and Nehemiah 10:6 as a descendant of the priest Ithamar who returned from Babylon to Judea by permission of Artaxerxes. 4. a fourth Daniel (1 Chr. 3:1) is named as David's second son by his wife Abigail, formerly the spouse of Nabal the Carmelite. This Daniel is also called Chileab in 2 Samuel 3:3 and was born in Hebron. The assumption is that he died young. *See also* Abednego; atrahasis; Azariah as exile; *Bel and the Dragon;* Belteshazzar; *Benedicite Omnia Opera;* Dan'el; Daniel as Old Testament prophecy; Hananiah the exile; Hagiographa; Meshach; Mishael; prophet(s); Shadrach.

Daniel as Old Testament prophecy: the only truly apocalyptic book of the Old Testament. The treatise of Daniel is often described as "the backbone of biblical prophecy" because of its detailed and astounding predictive material. Within its pages is the first mention of such important apocalyptic subjects as the abomination of desolation, the preliminary descriptions of the Antichrist, and numerous dreams and visions defining the fate of the Jews and peoples of many nations. The early rabbis placed the book in the Hagiographa. Why Daniel, which is clearly a prophetic and apocalyptic book, would be listed in the Writings is something of an anomaly. Perhaps the Jewish scholars classed it as such because they recognized its unique apocalyptic style and desired to somehow tone down its rather dynamic message. Otherwise, it might tend to unduly influence the other prophecies as well, which they considered an unacceptable risk. The official reasons given by the rabbis is that Daniel is not named among the prophets (whom they number as fifty-five) because his message reveals the future and was not intended to be broadcast like the preaching of other prophets. In any case, the rabbis considered Daniel to be a dangerous book which must be carefully handled even though they never doubted its inspiration. Young men under thirty were not allowed to read it. The Septuagint (LXX) translators removed Daniel from the Writings and placed it with the Prophets, a more logical arrangement. When the book was written is a controversy, some insisting it was in the sixth century under Babylonian rule as the context indicates; others insist it was well into the second century under the Maccabean leadership; still more see it as parts composed in both eras. Both premises hold strong indicators but no definitive proof. If the composition was late, the book is not prophecy at all but history. The Qumran Jews possessed and studied Daniel which was *before* the time claimed following the Babylonian Captivity. Daniel's dreams and visions within the book are significant. Many scholars logically see the first (Nebuchadnezzar's dream) as a prophecy of nations from man's perspective but the remainder from the viewpoint of heaven. The early vision was interpreted by Daniel (a man), but the others used angels for instruction. *See also* Additions to Daniel; "backbone of biblical prophecy"; *Bel and the Dragon;* curses of Daniel; Daniel; Dura; furnace; God of Daniel; God of Shadrach, Meshach, and Abednego, the; Nebuchadnezzar II; son of the gods, a; statue erected by Nebuchadnezzar; Susanna.

Daniel's account of the image of gold and the fiery furnace: the recitation of Nebuchadnezzar's construct of a statue of himself, which he set up on the plains of Dura (Dan. 3).

His subjects were ordered to prostrate themselves before it in worship, something the loyal Jews Shadrach, Meshach, and Abednego refused to do. The three were summarily thrown into a fiery furnace but were miraculously rescued from the flames by a messenger of God. *See also* Abednego; Daniel; Daniel as Old Testament prophecy; furnace; God of Daniel; God of Shadrach, Meshach, and Abednego, the; Meshach; oven; prefect(s); Shadrach; son of the gods, a; statue erected by Nebuchadnezzar.

Daniel's capture and training in Babylon: the history of Daniel's forced removal to Babylon with his compatriots Hananiah, Mishael, and Azariah (Dan. 1). The account is a record of his training for service with King Nebuchadnezzar, his testing, and his start to rise in influence. *See also* Abednego; Akkadian; Alexander the Great; Azariah; Cyrus the Great (Cyrus II); Daniel; Daniel as Old Testament prophecy; Hananiah the exile; *kosher;* Meshach; Mishael; O God of my Fathers; Shadrach.

Daniel's decipher of the hand writing on the wall: the insipid Babylonian king Belshazzar's vision of a disembodied hand writing the destiny of his failed kingdom on his banquet room wall (Dan. 5). Only the prophet Daniel could interpret the message. The phrase has become a familiar expression implying some doom or fate has been prescribed from which there will be no reprieve (*i.e.,* "the handwriting is on the wall)." *See also* apocalyptics; Belshazzar; curses of Daniel; Daniel; Daniel as Old Testament prophecy; hand writing on the wall, vision of the; *Mene, Mene, Tekel Parsin* (or *Uparsin*); riddle.

Daniel's dream of the kingdom beasts: a revelation from God to the prophet Daniel concerning Judah and certain nations or kingdoms yet to arise during the time of Babylon and after (Dan. 7–8). The kingdoms are in symbolic forms of stylized (duly interpreted) animals—a lion, a bear, a leopard, a monster of unimaginable fierceness, a little horn, a ram, and a goat. Eventually, all the evil kingdoms were overthrown by the Ancient of Days—God's great future kingdom. *See also* Ancient of Days; animals, birds, and insects, symbology of; Antichrist; Antiochus IV Epiphanes; apocalyptic, apocalypticism; apocalyptics; beast(s); celestial court; Daniel; Daniel as Old Testament prophecy; Daniel's vision of the destroying monster; Daniel's vision of the four beasts; flying goat, the; four winds of earth; Heavenly Council; heavenly court; horn(s); hunched bear, the; kingdom of the world; winged leopard, the; winged lion, the; little horn, the; prince of the host; ram and the goat, the; Roman Empire; sacrifice, the daily; saints of the Most High; stern-faced king, the; ten-nation confederacy; thrones; two-horned ram, the; 2,300 evenings and mornings; Ulai; winged leopard, the; winged lion, the.

Daniel's experience in the lions' den: the revelation of Daniel's ordeal in the den of lions (Dan. 6). Falsely accused by his enemies, the prophet was condemned to death as a traitor under King Darius. He was miraculously rescued and his accusers were fed to the beasts instead. *See also* angelic miracles; Daniel; Daniel as Old Testament prophecy; Darius the Mede; God, your; law of the Medes and the Persians; living God, the; names, symbology of; sacrifice, the daily; satrap(s).

Daniel's interpretation of Nebuchadnezzar's statue dream: the first major dream revelation by Daniel in exile (Dan. 2). The prophet and his friends were able to unravel, not only the meaning of the dream of the king's great statue but also the dream itself. The statue of various metals making up the image proved to be that of Babylon and the future empires of Medo-Persia, Greece, Rome (Western and Eastern Empires), and the Antichrist (the ten toes). All were demolished by the overpowering kingdom of heaven. *See also* apocalyptic, apocalypticism; apocalyptics; belly and thighs of bronze, the; celestial court; chest and arms of silver; council of heaven; crushing rock that became a mountain; Daniel; Daniel as Old Testament prophecy;

eternal kingdom, the; feet and toes of iron and clay; head of gold, the; Heavenly Council; Hesoid; kingdom of God; legs of iron; Lord of kings; Rock (my, the); Roman Empire; stratified man, dream of the.

Daniel's interpretation of Nebuchadnezzar's tree dream: Nebuchadnezzar's dream of a splendid tree (Dan. 4) displaying that king as a superb ruler but soon coming to a bad end. The nocturnal vision not only showed a magnificent tree depicting Nebuchadnezzar's powerful personality and rule, but also predicted his approaching downfall when the great tree failed and was cut down. Daniel interpreted the symbols for him so that the king could learn humility and remind all of Who the King of the universe truly is. The king's overweening pride precipitated a temporary madness brought on by God (Dan. 4) that ended only when the needed attitude adjustment was complete. *See also* apocalyptic, apocalypticism; apocalyptics; Daniel; Daniel as Old Testament prophecy; golden head, the; holy ones; King of heaven the; Lord (King) of heaven, the; Most High God, the; "Prayer of Nabonidus"; Roman Empire; tree(s); winged lion, the.

Daniel's prayer for the exiles: Daniel's poignant appeal to God as his people approached liberation from the Babylonian Exile (Dan. 9:1–19). The prophet seemed to be at the top of his game on this occasion as he sought to prepare his own heart and that of the other Jews for their return home. He knew from his fellow prophet Jeremiah that the enslavement would last seventy years. Such a prophecy prompted him to appeal to God to make them more spiritually ready for the event, which appeared to be imminent. Daniel did not accompany the exiles in return. *See also* Daniel; Daniel as Old Testament prophecy; God of (in) heaven; God of my fathers; God the great and awesome; Holy One, the; Lord my God, the; Most Holy Place (One); my God; Name, you; seventy years of captivity.

Daniel's vision from the revealing angel: a series of visions concerning the future of the Jews and the global nations (Dan. 10–11). The prophecies are introduced by a shining angel dressed in bright linen, then proceeded to discuss the intrigues of the Ptolemaic-Seleucid wars, and finally evolve into a description of the rise and rule of Antichrist. *See also* abomination of desolation, the; angel(s); apocalyptic, apocalypticism; apocalyptics; burnished man, the; contemptible person, a; Daniel; Daniel as Old Testament prophecy; eschatology, eschatological; foreign god, a; four winds of earth; god of fortresses; God of gods; guardian angel(s); Kebar; king of the North; king of the South; king who exalts himself; laying on of hands; prince of Greece; prince of Persia; Prince of princes; prince of the covenant (testament); your prince; Tribulation, the.

Daniel's vision of end time: the closing revelations of the book of Daniel in which events and circumstances of end time events are recorded (Dan. 12). The narrative speaks of resurrection, Jewish worship in the days to come, eternal punishment of evil, rewards for the righteous, the abomination of desolation, the sealing of his prophecies, and other eschatological matters. *See also* abomination of desolation, the; apocalyptic, apocalypticism; apocalyptics; Big Six Clauses, the; celestial court, the; cloud(s); coming prince (ruler), the; council of heaven; court of heaven; crushing rock that became a mountain; Daniel; Daniel as Old Testament prophecy; Daniel's visions of the mighty kingdom; Daniel's vision of the seventy "sevens"; day of the Lord; end of the age, the; End, the; end, the; end time; end time world conditions; eschatology, eschatological; eternal kingdom, the; "extra days" prophecy of; Ezekiel's pledge to the Jewish remnant; Ezekiel's vision of the restored theocracy; False Prophet, the; "going here and there"; heaven, war in; kingdom of God; New Covenant, the; Son of Man; 1,290 and 1,335 days, the; sealed words of Daniel.

Daniel's vision of the destroying monster: a generic description of the fantastic beast vision recorded in Daniel 7:7–14 from which sprang the little horn (Antiochus Epiphanes or the Antichrist). The monster is depicted as terrifying in its rampage and frightening in appearance, trampling everything underfoot in its rage. It was unique from the other beasts previously seen in the context and decidedly more ferocious. The terrifying monster is usually considered to be Rome as Antiochus' sponsor, although Antiochus himself was Greek. The final representation of the little horn is undoubtedly Antichrist. The ogre in this guise seems to have more of a mechanical structure, which fits better in a modern context perhaps more akin to the image of the beast statue in Revelation 13:14 – 16). The image is also called "the fourth beast" and described as emerging from the portrayal of the winged leopard. The entity is declared to be unstoppable and powerful with iron teeth, stomping feet, and ten horns (Dan. 7:7) of power. *See also* abomination of desolation, the; Antichrist; apocalyptics; beast(s); Daniel; Daniel as Old Testament prophecy; Daniel's dream of the kingdom beasts; Daniel's vision of the four beasts; horn(s); kingdom of this world; little horn, the; prince of the host; Roman Empire; sacrifice, the daily; saints of the Most High; saints, the host of the; stern-faced king, the; ten horns; ten-nation confederacy; thrones; 2,300 evenings and mornings; Ulai.

Daniel's vision of the four beasts: a vision in Daniel 7:1-8 which revealed the trail of empires from the lion of Babylon to the single horn replacing three others on the head of the great monster. The appearance of the "little horn" from the fourth beast is an important depiction of Antiochus Epiphanes and typically the coming Antichrist. The four horns sprouting from the last beast (Greece) may represent Alexander's divided empire after his death—the provinces of Greece, Turkey, Syria, and Egypt. These could also eventually constitute part of the Antichrist's ten-nation confederacy in the latter days. *See also* animals, birds, and insects, symbology of; Antichrist; apocalyptics; beast(s); Daniel; Daniel as Old Testament prophecy; Daniel's vision of the destroying monster; Daniel's dream of the kingdom beasts; flying goat, the; hunched bear, the; Roman Empire; winged leopard, the; winged lion, the.

Daniel's visions of the mighty kingdom: a number of view shifts from the earthly powers to the heavenly reign of glory as detailed in the book of Daniel. When taken in conjunction with the dream of the crushing rock (Dan. 2: 34–35; 44 – 45), the prophet sees the annihilation of the feeble kingdoms of men (Dan. 7:11-14) to be replaced by the eternal and indestructible kingdom of God at the end of this age. The account is central to apocalyptic learning and prophecy. *See also* apocalyptic, apocalypticism; apocalyptics; crushing rock that became a mountain; Daniel's vision of end time; eschatology, eschatological; eternal kingdom, the; Ezekiel's pledge to the Jewish remnant; Ezekiel's vision of the restored theocracy; kingdom of God; New Covenant, the; Son of Man.

Daniel's vision of the seventy "sevens": a significant recounting to the prophet Daniel concerning the conundrum of the seventy weeks of years which predicts the fortunes of the world from the end of the Babylonian Exile to the end of the age (Dan. 9:20–27). Hardly a more detailed nor exacting prophecy can be found in Scripture. *See also* age of grace; age of the Gentiles; apocalyptic, apocalypticism; apocalyptics; backbone of biblical prophecy, the; Daniel; Daniel as Old Testament prophecy; Daniel's vision of end time; eschatology, eschatological; fullness of the Gentiles; Gentiles; "great parenthesis," the; heptad; Lord our God, the; prophetic postponement; ruler (prince) who will (is) to come, the; seventy weeks, prophecy of the; times of the Gentiles.

Dante. See Alighieri, Dante.

Danu: or Dana and Anu, the mother goddess of the Tuatha de Danann. She was connected to the earth and its fertility and represents the Tuatha's namesake. Danu also exists in Hindu mythology and appears in an early Indian deluge story. *See also* Bile; Celtic folklore and religion; Dagda; idol(s); Tuatha de Danann.

Daoism. See Taoism.

Daphne: in Greek mythology, a nymph who escaped Apollo's advances by changing into a laurel tree. It is reported that Berenice, the second wife of Antiochus II, sought sanctuary from the vengeful Laodice in the temple of Daphne with her young son. Both were executed, nevertheless. The story is likely alluded to in Daniel 11:6. *See also* Andromeda; Apollo; Arethusa; Cassiopeia; elemental(s); idol(s); laurel; mythological beasties, elementals, monsters, and spirit animals; nymph(s); Olympian pantheon.

dar-al-Islam. See House of Islam.

Darbyism: the description by some—rather unacceptable to most dispensationalists—for those persuaded of the prolific distinct actions of dispensational theology supposedly formulated first by J. N. Darby. *See also* Darby, John Nelson; dispensational theology.

Darby, John Nelson: perhaps the earliest modern, and certainly the most original, exponent of dispensational theology (1800–1882). He was a lawyer, then ordained as a Church of England priest and authored over fifty theological books. Eventually, he associated with the Plymouth Brethren church in England in the early 1800s and later used much of their doctrine, with large doses of futurism attached, to formulate many of his theories. Whether or not he drew any or many of his ideas from the teen mystic Margaret MacDonald is a controversial subject. His biography reveals he formulated the doctrine of dispensationalism while recovering from a fall from a horse in 1827. After this, his conviction was confirmed that the church was "in ruins" and needed a new theology. Even today, dispensationalists are sometimes called "Darbyists" but the title is usually considered somewhat slanderous by those so named. Darby made several trips to North America, where his system found fertile ground in post-Civil War America. His work was carried on and promoted by such men as James Inglis (author of the Dispensational journal *Waymarks in the Wilderness),* Paul and Timothy Loizeaux, the Presbyterian James H. Brooks (central to the founding of the Niagra Conferences), the Jew Arno C. Gaebelein, Lewis Sperry Chafer, and, of course, C. I. Scofield. Today's greatest exponents are Tim LaHaye and Hal Lindsey. *See also* Apostolic Brethren; Chafer, Lewis Sperry; Dallas Theological Seminary; Darbyism; dispensational theology; Edwards, Morgan; Irving, Edward; Jurieu, Peter; Lacunza, Emmanuel; MacDonald, Margaret; Niagara Bible Conferences; Plymouth Brethren; Scofield, C. I.

dar-e-mehr: a term in North American Zoroastrianism for a house of worship—"a portal to all that is good: charity, devotion, kindness, and love." *See also* Zoroaster, Zoroastrianism.

Darius I Hystaspes: king of Persia (521–486 B.C.). Darius was not in line for the kingship but managed to gain it by overpowering the pretender Gautama (Pseudo-Smerdis). During his rather distinguished reign of thirty-six years, the Jewish Temple construction was completed after being temporarily halted by opposition in Palestine. The prophets Haggai and Zechariah were operative during his tenure (Hag. 1:1, 2:1; Zech. 1:1, 7). Darius campaigned successfully in Thrace, Macedonia, and managed to control the Aegean Sea with his navy. However, in two subsequent expeditions into Greece, he lost heavily, one of the engagements being the stand of the Athenians at Marathon in 490 B.C. With Darius I, the family of Cyrus became extinct in the politics of Persia. *See also* Babylonian (and Persian) restoration decrees; king(s); Persia, Persians; Smerdis; Zerubbabel; Zerubbabel's Temple.

Darius the Mede: the ruler of Babylon under Cyrus the Great immediately following the death of the last designated Babylonian ruler, Belshazzar (Dan. 5:30–31). Many historians, including Josephus, claim that he was king of the Medes who were allied by purpose and kinship to Cyrus and the Persians. Darius is noted as the monarch whose decree forced Daniel into the den of lions (Dan. 6). This Darius is not to be confused with the later Persian dictator, Darius I Hystaspes (521–486 B.C.) whose son and heir was Xerxes (Ahasuerus) and who had connections to Esther (Dan. 9:1). Some scholars assert that Darius is the same as Cyrus the Great himself but the conjecture is unlikely. The strongest historical probability is that this Darius (the one associated with the lions' den) is Gubaru, a Cyrus appointee in Babylon after its fall in 539 B.C. There appears to be some confusion in the book of Daniel as to which Darius is intended when the names are mentioned at certain points. *See also* Darius the Persian; Gobryas; Gubaru; king(s); Persia, Persians; Ugbaru.

Darius the Persian: evidently a ruler to be located somewhere in the lists of Persian kings or governors, but his true identity is disputed. There is a "Darius the Persian" mentioned in Nehemiah 12:22, but it is unknown with certainty if this king is Nothus (423–404 B.C.), Darius II (423–404 B.C.), or Darius III (336–331 B.C.). *See also* Darius I Hystaspes; Darius III Codomannus; Darius the Mede; king(s); Persia, Persians.

Darius III Codomannus: the last king of Persia (336–331 B.C.). He was defeated by Alexander the Great and lost both his kingdom and his life at the time. *See also* Darius the Persian; king(s); Persia, Persians.

darkness: the absence of light. In apocalyptic usage, darkness is usually pointing to secrecy, distress, or despair—a place where evil can lurk and flourish. Theological illustrations commonly contrast darkness to light as a kind of "evil vs. goodness" allusion. One of the most picturesque is from Paul who describes the kingdom of light in opposition to the dominion of darkness (Col. 1:12-13). *See also* clouds and darkness, a day of; darkness at the crucifixion; darkness in earth and sky; light; night; outer darkness; three days of darkness.

darkness at the crucifixion: a reference to the episode in the Gospels in which the day became dark during the crucifixion of Jesus. The nighttime conditions lasted approximately three hours from noon to 3:00 p. m. (the "ninth hour") and were followed immediately at Jesus' death by the rending of the Temple curtain from top to bottom. Some scholars offer a natural explanation for the absence of light, perhaps a sandstorm or an eclipse, or some other celestial anomaly. But others consider it a miracle showing the power of God and the Father's wrath for the death of His son. Given the apocalyptic meaning of darkness, it is highly likely they are right. Tertullian called the event a portent. *See also* clouds and darkness, a day of; darkness; darkness in earth and sky; ninth hour, the.

darkness in earth and sky: an apocalyptic description of part of the turmoil to be expected near the end of time. The fourth trumpet of Revelation (Rev. 8:12) reduces ambient light on the earth by a third; the fifth bowl (Rev. 16:10) casts the headquarters of the Antichrist into total darkness. At various times, God has caused diminishing light to manifest a sign of His displeasure or to dramatize certain of His works, not the least of which occasioned at Christ's crucifixion (Lk. 23:44–45). In contrast, He has also lengthened the day for His own purposes (*e.g.,* Joshua 10:12–15). *See also* advents(s) of Christ; age of lawlessness; "all these things"; apocalyptic, apocalypticism; apocalyptic calculation; apocalyptics; apocalyptic time; appearing, the; appointed time, the; clouds and darkness, a day of; coming ages, the; consummation, the final; darkness; darkness at the crucifixion; day he visits us, the; day of evil; day of God, the; day of (our Lord Jesus) Christ; day of Revenge; day of [their] visitation; day of the Lamb's wrath, the; day of the

Lord, the; day of trumpet and battle, a; day of vengeance of our God; "days of Elijah"; "days of Noah"; Day, that (the); due time, in; *elthnen;* end of all things, the; end of the age, the; End, the; end, the; end time; *en takhei;* eschatology, eschatological; eschaton; fullness of time; Glorious Appearing; great and dreadful day, that; "here, there, or in the air"; *kairos;* night; outer darkness; rapture; Second Coming; Second Coming procession; secret rapture; TEOTWAWKI; termination dates; three days of darkness; time; time is near, the; time of fulfillment; times and the seasons, the; "until he comes"; wrath, the coming.

Dark Rift, the: also called the Great Rift, the overlapping but non-luminous dust clouds at the center of the Milky Way galaxy. The naked eye sees the Rift as dividing the brighter band of the Milky Way lengthwise through about one-third of its extent forming a dark lane bordered by numerous stars. The Rift has significant import to 2012 prophecy believers who presumed it would be the locale of the sun at that time. The Maya believed that the site was the navel of the universe and thereby the source of all creation. They called the Rift the Black Road and knew it as the site for the new age "birth of Venus." *See also* cosmic cross; cosmology; eclipse(s); galactic alignment; impact event; *Jupiter Effect, The;* Maya; precession of the equinoxes; 2012 prophecy, advocates of; 2012, prophecy of; zodiac.

dark sayings: puzzling or enigmatic parables. The interpretation of such riddles was considered a valuable talent for prophets, soothsayers, and others who were attempting to interpret divine will or esoteric theology (including Christianity) in certain circumstances. *See also* deep, the; deep secrets, so-called; deep things of God; *disciplina arcane;* idolatry; mystery; mystery of God; occult, occultic; parable(s); riddle; Satan's so-called deep secrets; secret wisdom; things taught by demons.

Darwin, Charles: explorer and scientific investigator who is generally credited with the discovery of the concept of evolution. Darwin (1809–1882) and his theory have not met universal favor outside much of the scientific community but is still prevalent among most (not all) scientists. His explosive theories on the origin and evolution of life, something he called the "mystery of mysteries," were developed simultaneously and often in collaboration with Alfred Russell Wallace (1823 – 1913). Darwin himself seemed reluctant to abandon his early religious convictions until late in life (he once considered training for the ministry), and then only when pressed. His friend and more outspoken advocate, Thomas Huxley, was not so reticent. Darwin's first publication, one among many, was entitled *The Origin of the Species by Natural Selection*. At its initial official debate held at Oxford, the principal opponent was bishop of the university Samuel Wilberforce (1805 – 1873), a son of William Wilberforce. The advocacy was led by Huxley. The controversy the two generated has scarcely subsided over the decades. *See also* evolution; evolution, theistic; Fiske, John; Huxley, Aldous Leonard; Huxley, Thomas Henry; names, symbology of; naturalism; progressive creationism; Scopes Trial; Social Darwinism.

Dasa Laksana: a Jain holy day to contemplate the principles and purposes of Jainism. *See also Divali;* Jainism.

date-setting: a colloquial term describing the futile and unlawful practice of attempting to predict the exact time of Jesus' return to earth. The Lord has forbidden the tendency and even spoke of himself as not knowing the day and hour of his appearing—only the Father is privy to the knowledge of this profound secret of the universe. Those who persist in trying are usually numbered among the sensationalists, the cultists, doomsayers, or loyalists to certain apocalyptic sects. The action has caused, or should have caused, embarrassment to many who have attempted such a prediction, and to legitimate eschatology in general. *See also* apocalyptic calculation; appointed time, the; "forcing the time"; Great Disappointment, the; investigative judgment;

Jehovah's Witnesses; Millerites; Miller, William; Russell, Charles Taze; Rutherford, Joseph Franklin; seventy weeks, prophecy of the; Seventh-Day Adventism; White, Ellen G. (Harmon).

dates of termination. See termination dates.

Dathan: an Israelite who, along with Abiram, was swallowed into the earth (Num. 16:25–30) because he was a participant in the rebellion of Korah. Even as Moses was pronouncing his prophecy against the pair, they and their families were consumed to the depths. The rebels involved in that incident were destroyed for opposing the leadership of Moses and Aaron and in violation of the covenants. *See also* Abiram; Korah.

Daughter of Babylon: a title from Zechariah 2:7, which likely names the capital city of Babylonia from which the Jews were destined to be rescued from their exile.

Daughter of Jerusalem: the name used to describe the city of Jerusalem, a suburb of a city in Israel, or the population of any municipality in Judea (such as encountered in Micah 4:8). As such, the word "Daughter" is capitalized. *See also* Daughter of Judah; Daughter of Zion; Jerusalem as city; Jerusalem, landmarks of.

daughter of Jerusalem: a female worshiper of Yahweh if the word "daughter" is not capitalized. *See also* daughter of Zion.

Daughter of Judah: a poetic name for Jerusalem (*i.e.*, Lamentations 2:2). *See also* Daughter of Jerusalem; Daughter of Zion; Jerusalem as city; Jerusalem, landmarks of.

Daughter of Zion: a name used to designate the city of Jerusalem or a suburb of any city in Judah. *See also* Daughter of Jerusalem; Daughter of Judah; Jerusalem as city; Jerusalem as city; Jerusalem, landmarks of; Virgin Daughter of Zion.

daughter of Zion: a Jewess, a female worshiper of Yahweh. *See also* daughter of Jerusalem.

daughters (four) of Philip: four unmarried daughters of Philip the evangelist (Acts 21:7–9) who had the gift of prophecy. *See also* Philip; prophet(s); prophetess(es).

Daughters of Jerusalem: a group of female mourners addressed by Jesus during his cross-bearing struggle to Golgotha. His words to them were prophetic: "Daughters of Jerusalem, do not weep for me; weep for yourselves and for your children. For the time will come when you will say, 'Blessed are the barren women, the wombs that never bore and the breasts that never nursed'" (Lk. 23:28–29). Certainly Christ's prediction found fruitage at the destruction of Jerusalem by the Romans in A.D. 70 but there is a clear possibility he envisioned an end time catastrophe as well.

daughters of men: a group of men or angels, known only extrabiblically, called Cainites who are to be judged at the end of the age. *See also* Cainites; Sethites; sons of God; sons of God to be revealed.

Davenport, James: Congregationalist revival preacher (1716–1757) active in the First Great Awakening. He was heavily influenced by George Whitefield but with great fervor in his actions. Davenport could preach all-day sermons, often sang madly in the streets, and was known to burn books and possessions of his followers. He pointedly attacked Increase Mather and other "elitist" ministers in New England. *See also* Congregationalists; evangelist(s), evangelism; Great Awakenings, the; Mather, Cotton; Mather, Increase; Restoration Movement in America; revivalism.

Davenport, John: Puritan clergyman (1597–1670) who, with Theophilus Eaton, helped establish New Haven, Connecticut (in 1638), where he and Eaton were known as the "Moses and Aaron" of the colony. Davenport was Calvinist in doctrine and the partners controlled New Haven like a theocracy and much disfavored religious liberty of conscience. Davenport's notable writing is an epic poem entitled *Discourse About Civil Government in a*

New Plantation Whose Design is Religion (published 1633). Davenport and Eaton wrote the strict Puritan code of conduct into the colony's "blue laws" and enforced them to the utmost. *See also* blue laws; Eaton, Theophilus; New Haven Colony; Puritanism, Puritans.

David: first king of the united Israel and described as "a man after God's own heart" carrying a base meaning of "beloved." He was one from whom Jesus Christ was descended in the tribe of Judah. It is at least possible that the name is a title (*Davidum*) meaning "the commander," according to some research, and that he was called something else as a child. Peter named him both a patriarch and a prophet (Acts 2:29–30). Perhaps the most frightening moment in David's career occurred when he saw an angel of the Lord standing in midair with a drawn sword over Jerusalem (1 Chr. 21:16). The king's acts of repentance and careful following of the angel's instructions preserved the city in that instance, and in many another crisis moment of that king's career. He was associated with the history of Israel at an early age, having been anointed by Samuel to be king after Saul, having slain the giant Goliath, and performing other heroic deeds. David is centered as the core of the Davidic Covenant, which assures Israel she will have a perpetual kingship, physical evidence that endured through the kingdom of his son Solomon. This millennial leadership is destined to be either as a resurrected *type* of David or with David himself as a mortal ruler in the Millennium, as is suggested in Jeremiah 30:8–9 and Ezekiel 34:24. David was certainly not free from indiscretion or sin (*cf.* the adulterous and murderous incident involving Bathsheba and Uriah). For that violation, the prophet Nathan brought God's accusation to the king and pronounced the divine judgment that war, familial upheaval, and the death of the firstborn son of David and Bathsheba would be the consequences of his sin. Even so, David was highly favored by God and generally beloved by the people of Israel. *See also*

Bathsheba; Davidic Covenant; Davidic kingdom; David's generals; David's wives; giant(s); Goliath; king(s); kings of Israel and Judah; kings of Israel and Judah in foreign relations; names, symbology of; Nathan; psalm; Psalms as Old Testament book; Solomon; Tower of David; Uriah.

Davidic Covenant: described in 2 Samuel 7:10–17 and 1 Chronicles 17:7–15. The covenant provides for an eternal ruling house for David and guarantees that the seed of the Messiah would come from David's lineage. Other provisions dealt with particulars of his earthly reign, and that of his sons Solomon and Nathan especially, in all its colorful events. Matthew and Luke list the genealogy of Jesus, each with a different perspective. *See also* covenant(s), biblical; covenant theology; curse of the line of Jehoiachin; David; Davidic kingdom; genealogy of Jesus; Judaism; Nathan; Solomon; Solomonic Covenant; unconditional covenant(s).

Davidic kingdom: the earthly Messianic kingdom promised to David to be fully realized in the Millennium according to the Davidic Covenant. *See also* David; Davidic Covenant; Judaism.

David's generals: those most prominent in David's army and among his closest advisors. They can be named as Abishai, Abner, Amasa, Asahel, Benaiah, and Joab. Joab was a nephew of David by his sister Zeruiah as were Abishai and Asahel. Amasa was also the king's nephew by his other sister Abigail. Benaiah was a Levite, the son of one of the priests who helped David assume the reign over all of Israel. Abner was the son of Ner, King Saul's uncle. *See also* Abishai; Abner; Amasa; Asahel; Benaiah; David; Joab.

David's wives: the marriage alliances of David. King David had a number of Hebrew and foreign wives, a common occurrence of his time for royalty, though not sanctioned by the Law of Moses. He also held at least ten concubines. Together, with their prominent offspring, they may be listed as: Michal (childless and taken from David early and given to another), Abigail (Chileab [Daniel]), Ahinoam of Jezreel (firstborn son Ammon), Haggith (Adonijah), Abital (Shephatatiah), Eglah (Ithream), Maacah (Absalom), and Bathsheba (Solomon). There were others but we cannot identify them or their histories. *See also* Bathsheba; concubine; David; Geshur, Geshurites; Michal; Nabal; queen(s); woman (women).

Da Vinci Code, The: a popular detective novel written by Dan Brown in 2003. The theme of the mystery story derives from the alternate religious history that claims Jesus married Mary Magdalene. It is said that the Merovingian kings of France hold the bloodline of Jesus, so there are mortal descendants of Jesus and Mary Magdalene alive today. Speculation is that the Holy Grail was not so much a mythical quest for the cup of Christ but a code for the womb of Mary. *Angels and Demons* is a prequel that thrives on the conspiracy theory that the Illuminati are bent on destroying the Vatican. *See also* Brown, Dan; crucifixion conspiracies; *Holy Blood, Holy Grail;* Holy Grail; Illuminati; Merovingians; *Opus Dei;* Order of the Rosy Cross; Priory of Sion; secret societies.

Davis, Samuel: Presbyterian clergyman (1723–1761) and a leader in the First Great Awakening. He was a close associate of Gilbert Tennent and a dynamic preacher. Davis became an active president of the College of New Jersey (now Princeton) and recognized as an enlightened educator, as well as minister. *See also* evangelist(s), evangelism; Great Awakenings, the; Presbyterians; Restoration Movement in America; revivalism; Tennent, Gilbert.

Dawkins, Richard: evolutionary biologist and avowed atheist (b. 1941), virulent opponent of creationism and its advocacy in schools. For Dawkins, any form of faith is unreliable and "not in the sense of faith as meaning belief in something for which there is no evidence." His pronouncements, published in such books as *The Blind Watchmaker* and *The God Delusion*, have prompted response from the other side with published variations of pronouncements like "to debase belief in the divine and the unexplained mysteries that surround us simply because they are not definable by science, is to display utter arrogance at best and total stupidity at worst." *See also* atheism, atheist(s); evolution.

day-age theory: a stratagem to interpret the word "day" used in the Genesis creation story to equate to a long period of time, not a literal twenty-four hours. The idea might fit the theistic evolution and progressive evolution theories but not the big bang favored by many scientists. *See also* analogical day theory; big bang theory; big crunch theory; chaos theory; cosmogony; cosmology; *creatio ex nihilo;* creation; creationism; creation science; Creator; evolution; evolution, theistic; framework hypothesis; gap theory of creation; intelligent design; involution; Omphalos Hypothesis; progressive creationism; "six-day theory, the"; theistic evolution; uniformitarianism; Young Earth Creationist Movement.

Dayan, General Moshe: former leader of the Israeli Defense Forces (1915–1981) whose military genius was instrumental in defeating the Egyptians and Syrians and capturing the Temple Mount during the Six-Day War. He subsequently met with Arab officials in the *al-Aqsa* Mosque and returned governance of the area to the Muslim Waqf, which had been under Jordanian control for nearly twenty years. He also relinquished control of the captured sacred ground (despite pleas from his chief of chaplains) in hopes the act would demonstrate good faith. Rather, the Arabs considered it a show of weakness. Dayan ordered the Jewish flag to be lowered from the Dome of the Rock, agreed to restrictions of Jewish presence on the Temple Mount, and prohibited prayer or reading of the Scriptures by Jews or Christians in the vicinity. As a non-religious Jew, perhaps Dayan did not appreciate the apocalyptic significance of the Jewish victory, nor the eschatological opportunity before him. Nevertheless, he considered his actions to be practical and politically expedient at the time, and Dayan rose to high governmental offices in his later life. *See also* Goren, Shlomo; Jew(s); seven shepherds and eight princes.

day he visits us, the: a reference from Peter (1 Pe. 2:12), noting the special time of Christ's appearing. The apostle urges all Christians to so conduct themselves in the acceptable counterculture way of the faith so as to cause unbelievers to praise God when that day comes. *See also* advents(s) of Christ; age of lawlessness; "all these things"; apocalyptic, apocalypticism; apocalyptic calculation; apocalyptics; apocalyptic time; appearing, the; appointed time, the; clouds and darkness, a day of; coming ages, the; consummation, the final; day of evil; day of God, the; day of (our Lord Jesus) Christ; day of Revenge; day of [their] visitation; day of the Lamb's wrath, the; day of the Lord, the; day of trumpet and battle, a; day of vengeance of our God; "days of Elijah"; "days of Noah"; Day, that (the); due time, in; *elthnen;* end of all things, the; end of the age, the; End, the; end, the; end time; *en takhei;* eschatology, eschatological; eschaton; fullness of time; Glorious Appearing; great and dreadful day, that; "here, there, or in the air"; *kairos;* rapture; Second Coming; Second Coming procession; secret rapture; TEOTWAWKI; termination dates; time; time is near, the; time of fulfillment; times and the seasons, the; "until he comes"; wrath, the coming.

Day of Atonement. See Atonement, Day of.

day of Christ. See day of the Lord.

day of clouds and darkness, a. See clouds and darkness, a day of.

day of evil: one of Paul's varied descriptions of the end of the age and the immediate days preceding it (Eph. 6:13), certainly including our own time. In the text associated with the phrase is the apostle's plea for all believers to "put on" the full armor of God. Each virtue he desired for them was patterned or illustrated after the uniform of the Roman soldier of his day, one or more of whom could have been guarding him even as he wrote to the Ephesian church. Those accouterments included the belt, breastplate, boots, shield, helmet, and sword. The spiritual equivalents for each item of dress and weapon are: truth, righteousness, readiness, faith, salvation, and prayer. With this godly equipment in place, we will be able to defeat the evil one and lead a devoted life to the end of our days. With a second but conjoint usage, the "day of evil" is that time of God's great vengeance either in Israel's history or the end of the age (Eph. 6:13). The prophet Amos accused Samaria of "putting off" or indulging in mental denial that the evil day was coming, thereby effectively dismissing it from their minds (Amos 6:3). *See also* advents(s) of Christ; age of lawlessness; "all these things"; apocalyptic, apocalypticism; apocalyptic calculation; apocalyptics; apocalyptic time; appearing, the; appointed time, the; clouds and darkness, a day of; coming ages, the; consummation, the final; day he visits us, the; day of evil; day of God, the; day of (our Lord Jesus) Christ; day of Revenge; day of [their] visitation; day of the Lamb's wrath, the; day of the Lord, the; day of trumpet and battle, a; day of vengeance of our God; "days of Elijah"; "days of Noah"; Day, that (the); due time, in; *elthnen;* end of all things, the; end of the age, the; End, the; end, the; end time; *en takhei;* escapism; eschatology, eschatological; eschaton; fullness of time; Glorious Appearing; great and dreadful day, that; "here, there, or in the air"; *kairos;* rapture; Second Coming; Second Coming procession; secret rapture; TEOTWAWKI; termination dates; time; time is near, the; time of fulfillment; times and the seasons, the; "until he comes"; wrath, the coming.

day of God, the: an expression found only in 2 Peter 3:12 wherein the prediction that the heavens and the elements will dissolve in fire at the end of the age is written. It is an equivalent phrase to the day of the Lord. *See also* advents(s) of Christ; age of lawlessness; "all these things"; apocalyptic, apocalypticism;

apocalyptic calculation; apocalyptics; apocalyptic time; appearing, the; appointed time, the; clouds and darkness, a day of; coming ages, the; consummation, the final; day he visits us, the; day of evil; day of God, the; day of (our Lord Jesus) Christ; day of Revenge; day of [their] visitation; day of the Lamb's wrath, the; day of the Lord; day of trumpet and battle, a; day of vengeance of our God; "days of Elijah"; "days of Noah"; Day, that (the); due time, in; element(s); *elthnen;* end of all things, the; end of the age, the; End, the; end, the; end time; *en takhei;* eschatology, eschatological; eschaton; fullness of time; Glorious Appearing; great and dreadful day, that; "here, there, or in the air"; *kairos;* rapture; Second Coming; Second Coming procession; secret rapture; TEOTWAWKI; termination dates; time; time is near, the; time of fulfillment; times and the seasons, the; "until he comes"; wrath, the coming.

day of grace: the church age in which we now live. In this period, between Old Testament Judaism and the Second Coming, God seems to have chosen to deal with His creation in temperance and mercy. The Almighty isn't confronting sin in individuals and society inasmuch as His authority and power could achieve. Rather, He prefers to use this era to draw people to Him by exhibiting mercy and love. That is not to say, however, that God does not preempt human malfeasance from time to time and confront specific sin and sinners, including their nations, through divine justice. The unleashed wrath of God, however, is reserved for the Tribulation.

day of Jehovah. See day of the Lord.

day of (our Lord Jesus) Christ: a New Testament term for the time believers will meet their Lord (1 Cor. 1:8, Phil. 1:10, *et al.*). *See also* advents(s) of Christ; age of lawlessness; "all these things"; apocalyptic, apocalypticism; apocalyptic calculation; apocalyptics; apocalyptic time; appearing, the; appointed time, the; clouds and darkness, a day of; coming ages, the; consummation, the final; day he visits us, the; day of evil; day of God, the; day of (our Lord Jesus) Christ; day of Revenge; day of [their] visitation; day of the Lamb's wrath, the; day of the Lord; day of trumpet and battle, a; day of vengeance of our God; "days of Elijah"; "days of Noah"; Day, that (the); due time, in; *elthnen;* end of all things, the; end of the age, the; End, the; end, the; end time; *en takhei;* eschatology, eschatological; eschaton; fullness of time; Glorious Appearing; great and dreadful day, that; "here, there, or in the air"; *kairos;* rapture; Second Coming; Second Coming procession; secret rapture; Sunday; TEOTWAWKI; termination dates; time; time is near, the; time of fulfillment; times and the seasons, the; "until he comes"; wrath, the coming.

Day of Pardon: a formal reconciliation between Roman Catholicism and Judaism promoted by Pope John Paul II. Repentance for anti-Semiticism, recognition of the state of Israel, and moralization of the Holocaust were recognized by the Vatican. The official date for the Pardon is normally set for the first day of Lent, March 12, 2000. *See also Adversus Judaeos;* Concordant of Collaboration; Judaism; Roman Catholic Church.

day of Purification: the Hopi and Onondaga peoples' reference to a future day when they will be sanctified following the eschaton. That end is predicted for the time Sirius (the Blue Star) initiates the Fifth World. World War III will presumably be a conflict between spiritual and materialistic forces from which only the Hopi will emerge unscathed. The Hopi word *koyanisquatsi* carries a meaning of "life out of balance" which describes, for them, the chaotic world in which we now live. *See also* Blue Star prophecy; Fifth World, the; Great Change, Prophecy of the; Great Purification, the; Great Shaking, the; Hopi; Onondaga; Quetzalcoatl; Rattlesnake Prophecy; 2012 prophecy, advocates of; 2012, prophecy of; Rainbow Warriors, the; Wheel of Time; World War III.

day of Reckoning. See day of the Lord.

day of Revenge: the final engagement and victory of the Sons of Light over the Sons of Darkness according to some of the Dead Sea manuscripts. *See also* advents(s) of Christ; age of lawlessness; "all these things"; apocalyptic, apocalypticism; apocalyptic calculation; apocalyptics; apocalyptic time; appearing, the; appointed time, the; clouds and darkness, a day of; coming ages, the; consummation, the final; day he visits us, the; day of evil; day of God, the; day of (our Lord Jesus) Christ; day of [their] visitation; day of the Lamb's wrath, the; day of the Lord; day of trumpet and battle, a; day of vengeance of our God; "days of Elijah"; "days of Noah"; Day, that (the); due time, in; *elthnen;* end of all things, the; end of the age, the; End, the; end, the; end time; *en takhei;* eschatology, eschatological; eschaton; fullness of time; Glorious Appearing; great and dreadful day, that; "here, there, or in the air"; *kairos;* rapture; Second Coming; Second Coming procession; secret rapture; TEOTWAWKI; termination dates; time; time is near, the; time of fulfillment; times and the seasons, the; "until he comes"; wrath, the coming.

Day of the Dead: (*Dia de Muertos* in Spanish) the traditional annual celebration for Mexico's reverence to loved ones now departed. Activities consist of erecting special altars at gravesides with food, blankets, and incense offered, usually dated at the Allhallowstide observances of October 31 and November 1 and 2. The October 2014 commemoration set a Guinness' Book of World Records for the altar unveiled at the *Fiesta Gala de Veras*. It measured 558 meters as the largest Day of the Dead offering ever. Similar festivities are recognized worldwide featuring grotesque statuary of skeletons and skulls, along with body painting and costuming and other bizarre décor. There are indications that the genesis of the Day of the Dead festivals began from ancient Aztec custom but clearly a Roman Catholic ritual and theological parody has intervened. Today, perhaps the largest and fastest growing Day of the Dead fringe movements is Mexico's dedication to *Santa Muerte* (Saint Death) which has accumulated some five million worshipers across the globe. The cult is led by a diminutive but flamboyant Mexican grandmother named Enriqueta Romero, now in her 70s, from her modest home in Morelos. The group is opposed by both the Mexican government and the Roman Catholic Church. *Santa Muerte* is now the second largest saint following in Mexico, second only to the Virgin of Guadalupe. *See also* ancestor reverence; cult of the dead; death; Guadalupe, Our Lady of; idolatry; Roman Catholic Church; sect(s); veneration of the saints.

day of [their] visitation: a phrase, perhaps somewhat dated, which refers to the Second Coming of Christ. The words seem to convey something more than a quiet passage to earth; rather, vengeance and justice are more pronounced than is other less strident terms. The phrase may also refer to the first advent of Christ when the Messiah was manifest but unrecognized as such. *See also* advents(s) of Christ; age of lawlessness; "all these things"; apocalyptic, apocalypticism; apocalyptic calculation; apocalyptics; apocalyptic time; appearing, the; appointed time, the; beginning of sorrows; clouds and darkness, a day of; coming ages, the; consummation, the final; day he visits us, the; day of evil; day of God, the; day of (our Lord Jesus) Christ; day of Revenge; day of the Lamb's wrath, the; day of the Lord; day of trumpet and battle, a; day of vengeance of our God; "days of Elijah"; "days of Noah"; Day, that (the); due time, in; *elthnen;* end of all things, the; end of the age, the; End, the; end, the; end time; *en takhei;* eschatology, eschatological; eschaton; fullness of time; Glorious Appearing; great and dreadful day, that; "here, there, or in the air"; *kairos;* rapture; Second Coming; Second Coming procession; secret rapture; TEOTWAWKI; termination dates; time; time is near, the; time of fulfillment; times and the seasons, the; "until he comes"; wrath, the coming.

day of the Lamb's Wrath, the: the expression voiced by the victims of the sixth seal (at the Second Coming of Christ) who cry for the rocks and mountains to fall upon them rather than face the anger of the Lord at his appearing (Rev. 6:16–17). One does not normally associate rage and aggression with a lamb's disposition, but in this instance, the loving savior and the adversary of sin are one and the same personality. *See also* advents(s) of Christ; age of lawlessness; "all these things"; apocalyptic, apocalypticism; apocalyptic calculation; apocalyptics; apocalyptic time; appearing, the; appointed time, the; clouds and darkness, a day of; coming ages, the; consummation, the final; day he visits us, the; day of evil; day of God, the; day of (our Lord Jesus) Christ; day of Revenge; day of [their] visitation; day of the Lord; day of trumpet and battle, a; day of vengeance of our God; "days of Elijah"; "days of Noah"; Day, that (the); *Dies Irae*; due time, in; *elthnen;* end of all things, the; end of the age, the; End, the; end, the; end time; *en takhei;* eschatology, eschatological; eschaton; fullness of time; Glorious Appearing; great and dreadful day, that; "here, there, or in the air"; *kairos;* rapture; Second Coming; Second Coming procession; secret rapture; TEOTWAWKI; termination dates; time; time is near, the; time of fulfillment; times and the seasons, the; "until he comes"; wrath, the coming.

day of the Lord: or "the day of Christ," an expression (*aharit ha-yamim*), usually seen in the Old Testament, as "the time of Jacob's trouble," the Great Tribulation, "the end of days," the period of Daniel's seventieth week, the Day of Reckoning, or any number of other identifiers. The precise phrase appears some twenty-four times at least. A few of the more prominent descriptions for such a time include: 1. the time of Jacob's trouble (Jer. 30:7), 2. his strange work [alien task] (Isa. 28:21), 3. day of Israel's calamity [doom, disaster] (Deut. 32:35), 4. the indignation [wrath] (Isa. 26:20; Dan. 11:36), 5. the overwhelming scourge (Isa. 28:15, 18), 6. the year of retribution [time of vengeance]

(Isa. 34:8; 35:4; 61:2), 7. time of wrath [distress, anguish, trouble, ruin, darkness, gloom, clouds, blackness, trumpet and battle cry] (Zeph. 1:15–16; Joel 2:2), 8. hour of trial (Rev. 3;10), 9. the coming wrath (1 Th. 1:10), 10. the wrath (1 Th. 5:9), 11. the hour of his judgment (Rev. 14:7) or simply 12. "that day" (Isa. 2:11, 17; 2:20; 4:2; Joel 3:18; Mk. 13:32; Lk. 21:34; 2 Tim. 1:12, 18; 4:8). More variations include: the day of Christ, day of God, day of the Lord Jesus, day of our Lord Jesus Christ, that great and dreadful day of the Lord, the great day of God Almighty, and the great day of God's wrath, plus related phrases like day of calamity, battle, disaster, reckoning, his burning anger, salvation, clouds and darkness, your watchman, his coming, judgment, God's wrath, redemption, slaughter, the great day of [their] wrath, and more. Many commentators merely call the time "that day" or "the day" so study of the context of the words is important. "Judgment Day" and "Day of the Lord" are synonymous to all the others. The phrase and its synonyms are prominent in Amos, Ezekiel, Isaiah, Obadiah, and Joel. In fact, the oracle in Ezekiel 7:5–9 can even betoken fear by shouting, "Behold the day! Behold it comes!" In the New Testament, the day of the Lord is pictured as coming like a thief in the night and will be preceded by signs of the end (Mt. 24:2; 1 Th. 5:1–2; 2 Th. 2:1–2). Thus, the day of the Lord includes the Tribulation period and/or the Millennium. According to prewrath theology, the day of the Lord is the second phase of the Tribulation to be endured by the saints. The other stages are the beginning of sorrows and the Great Tribulation. Some commentators see the day of the Lord in three phases: 1. the wrath of God, 2. the peace of God, and 3. the judgment of God, each occurring in order. Another, perhaps clearer, presentation of the three stages may be: 1. Christ's lordship (the rapture and rewards of believers, 2. the judgment of Christ (the Tribulation and wrath of the Lamb), and 3. the kingship of Christ (the Millennium and New Jerusalem). Some Israelites believed the traditional interpretation that they and the Gentiles would suffer on the day of the Lord, but from another viewpoint, most preferred to think God would take vengeance on their enemies alone. In a very simplistic sense, "the day of the Lord" carries little or no eschatological freight; it is merely any day God may choose to act in some manner or basically rule His creation normally. Even so, most of the context surrounding the phrase clearly point to an eschatological emphasis. "Woe to you who long for the day of the Lord! Why do you long for the day of the Lord? That day will be darkness, not light. It will be as though a man fled from a lion only to meet a bear, as though he entered a house and rested his hand on the wall only to have a snake bite him. Will not the day of the Lord be darkness, not light—pitch-dark, without a ray of brightness?" (Amos 5:18–20). *See also* advents(s) of Christ; age of lawlessness; "all these things"; apocalyptic, apocalypticism; apocalyptic calculation; apocalyptics; apocalyptic time; appearing, the; appointed time, the; beginning of sorrows; clouds and darkness, a day of; coming ages, the; coming of the salvation, the; consummation, the final; darkness in earth and sky; day he visits us, the; day of evil; day of God, the; day of (our Lord Jesus) Christ; day of Revenge; day of [their] visitation; day of the Lamb's wrath, the; day of trumpet and battle, a; day of vengeance of our God; Days of Awe; "days of Elijah"; "days of Noah"; Day, that (the); due time, in; Desolation, day of; *elthnen;* end of all things, the; end of the age, the; End, the; end, the; end time; *en takhei;* eschatology, eschatological; eschaton; fullness of time; Glorious Appearing; great and dreadful day, that; Great Tribulation; "here, there, or in the air"; hour of testing; hour of trial; *kairos;* rapture; Second Coming; Second Coming procession; secret rapture; seventy weeks, prophecy of the; TEOTWAWKI; termination dates; three stages of judgment; time; time is near, the; time of fulfillment; time of Jacob's trouble; times and the seasons, the; Tribulation; "until he comes"; wrath, the coming.

day of trumpet and battle, a: Zephaniah's description of the turmoil at end of days (Zeph. 1:14–16). *See also* advents(s) of Christ; age of lawlessness; "all these things"; apocalyptic, apocalypticism; apocalyptic calculation; apocalyptics; apocalyptic time; appearing, the; appointed time, the; clouds and darkness, a day of; coming ages, the consummation, the final; day he visits us, the; day of evil; day of God, the; day of (our Lord Jesus) Christ; day of Revenge; day of [their] visitation; day of the Lamb's wrath, the; day of the Lord; day of vengeance of our God; "days of Elijah"; "days of Noah"; Day, that (the); due time, in; *elthnen;* end of all things, the; end of the age, the; End, the; end, the; end time; *en takhei;* eschatology, eschatological; eschaton; fullness of time; Glorious Appearing; great and dreadful day, that; "here, there, or in the air"; *kairos;* rapture; Second Coming; Second Coming procession; secret rapture; TEOTWAWKI; termination dates; three days of darkness; time; time is near, the; time of fulfillment; times and the seasons, the; "until he comes"; wrath, the coming.

day of vengeance of our God: Isaiah's identification of the date of the Messiah's triumph, the *Dies irae,* in its eschatological sense (Isa. 61:2). *See also* advents(s) of Christ; age of lawlessness; "all these things"; apocalyptic, apocalypticism; apocalyptic calculation; apocalyptics; apocalyptic time; appearing, the; appointed time, the; clouds and darkness, a day of; coming ages, the; consummation, the final; day he visits us, the; day of evil; day of God, the; day of (our Lord Jesus) Christ; day of Revenge; day of [their] visitation; day of the Lamb's wrath, the; day of the Lord; "days of Elijah"; "days of Noah"; Day, that (the); due time, in; *elthnen;* end of all things, the; end of the age, the; End, the; end, the; end time; *en takhei;* eschatology, eschatological; eschaton; fullness of time; Glorious Appearing; great and dreadful day, that; "here, there, or in the air"; *kairos;* rapture; Second Coming; Second Coming procession; secret rapture; TEOTWAWKI; termination dates; three days of darkness;

time; time is near, the; time of fulfillment; times and the seasons, the; "until he comes"; wrath, the coming; year of the Lord's favor, the.

day of vengeance of our Lord. See day of vengeance of our God.

day of Yahweh. See day of the Lord.

daysman: a judge, administrator, or mediator of earlier times. Jesus is displayed in that character in 1 Timothy 2:5. *See also* judge(s).

Days of Awe: *yamin noraim,* or "the terrible days" of Judaism. The Days of Awe are the seven days (or years or hours in some elements of prophetic thinking) between *Rosh Hashanah* and *Yom Kippur.* The ancient rabbis chose the name from Joel 2:11, which speaks of the day of the Lord or the time of Jacob's trouble. Christian theology would name this period the Tribulation; pre-Tribulationalists would assert that the rapture of the Church will transpire just prior on what the Jews call *Yom Teruah,* the "day of the awakening blast" to start the New Jewish Year. *See also* day of the Lord; eschatology, eschatological; feasts and special days of Judaism; Great Tribulation; High Holy Days; hour of testing; hour of trial; Judaism; *Rosh Hashanah;* ten days of awe; time of Jacob's trouble; Tribulation; *Yom Kippur*.

"days of Elijah": a rather contemporary and lyrical expression spoken or sung as, "These are the days of Elijah [and/or Ezekiel and/or Moses]." The message is intended to project the hubris and hope of our age relating to what appears to the senses to be the approach of the end of the age—a time of mixed excitement, trepidation, wonder, and anticipation as suspected to have existed in the careers of the prophets Elijah, Moses, David, Ezekiel, and probably others. The phrase is not, however, intended to copy the "days of Noah" reference in?" (Amos 5:18–20). *See also* advents(s) of Christ; age of lawlessness; "all these things"; apocalyptic, apocalypticism; apocalyptic calculation;

apocalyptics; apocalyptic time; appearing, the; appointed time, the; beginning of sorrows; clouds and darkness, a day of; coming ages, the; consummation, the final; day he visits us, the; day of evil; day of God, the; day of (our Lord Jesus) Christ; day of Revenge; day of [their] visitation; day of the Lamb's wrath, the; day of the Lord; day of trumpet and battle, a; day of vengeance of our God; Days of Awe; "days of Noah"; Day, that; due time, in; Desolation, day of; *elthnen;* end of all things, the; end of the age, the; End, the; end, the; end time; *en takhei;* eschatology, eschatological; eschaton; fullness of time; Glorious Appearing; great and dreadful day, that; Great Tribulation; "here, there, or in the air"; *kairos;* rapture; Second Coming; Second Coming procession; secret rapture; seventy weeks, prophecy of the; TEOTWAWKI; termination dates; three stages of judgment; time; time is near, the; time of fulfillment; time of Jacob's trouble; times and the seasons, the; Tribulation; "until he comes"; wrath, the coming.

"days of Noah": Jesus' illustration of the world's attitude at his Second Coming. The description is an apt one, for Noah's generation was characterized by unpreparedness, enjoying the routine of life, and sensing no urgency or eschatological danger (Mt. 24:36-39). The Lord declares that conditions will be similar in the last days. According to more radical modern theories, it is possible that the Lord had in mind a reference to the wicked Nephilim as well, the evil breed of giants living at that time, which would imply an "alien" type population on earth in the last days intent to no good end. *See also* advents(s) of Christ; age of lawlessness; "all these things"; apocalyptic, apocalypticism; apocalyptic calculation; apocalyptics; apocalyptic time; appearing, the; appointed time, the; beginning of sorrows; clouds and darkness, a day of; coming ages, the; consummation, the final; day he visits us, the; day of evil; day of God, the; day of (our Lord Jesus) Christ; day of Revenge; day of [their] visitation; day of the Lamb's wrath, the; day of the Lord, the; day of trumpet and battle, a; day of vengeance of our God; Days of Awe; "days of Elijah"; Day, that (the); due time, in; Desolation, day of; *elthnen;* end of all things, the; end of the age, the; End, the; end, the; end time; *en takhei;* eschatology, eschatological; eschaton; fullness of time; Glorious Appearing; great and dreadful day, that; Great Tribulation; "here, there, or in the air"; *kairos;* rapture; Second Coming; Second Coming procession; secret rapture; seventy weeks, prophecy of the; TEOTWAWKI; termination dates; three stages of judgment; time; time is near, the; time of fulfillment; time of Jacob's trouble; times and the seasons, the; Tribulation; "until he comes"; wrath, the coming.

Dayspring. See Day Star; Morning Star, the.

Day Star: the Revised Standard Version translation of "son of the morning" or Dayspring, a reference to the king of Babylon (Isa. 14:12). Most scholars assert that this passage is a veiled reference to Lucifer, "the bright one," in his pre-fallen angelic state. The term is drawn from the appearance of the planet Venus, the brightest object in the sky other than the sun and moon, and the harbinger of dawn. A star to come out of Jacob is predicted in one of Balaam's oracles (Num. 24:17) referencing the future. *See also* accuser of our brothers; angel of light; Anointed Cherub; Baal-zebub; Baphomet; Beelzebub; Belial; dragon; Evil One, the; father of lies; Ghede; goat; god of this age, the; guardian cherub; Hahgwehdaetgah; Iblis; idol(s); *Kategor;* kingdom of the air; kingdom of this world; king of Babylon; king of Tyre; Levant pantheon; Light-Bringer; lion; Lucifer; Mastema; Morning Star, the; planets as gods, the; prince of demons; prince of the power of the air; prince of this world; red dragon; ruler of the kingdom of the air; Sammael; Sanat Kumar; Satan; seed of the serpent; serpent; Shaytan; son of the morning, son of the dawn; Sumerian and Babylonian pantheon; Venus.

Day, that (the): a designation of the time of the Lord's Second Coming from Hebrews 10:25, Zephaniah 3:11, and 2 Peter 1:19. *See also* eschatology, eschatological; Second Coming.

day-year principle. See "six-day theory, the."

deacon(s), deaconess(es): men (deacons) or women (deaconesses) selected in most Protestant churches for specialized service. Roman Catholic deacons are solely men with somewhat different responsibilities. The early church (Acts 6:1–7) chose and ordained seven to relieve the apostles from mundane but essential services such as care of the widows in their midst. Many of the deacons were evangelists, prophets, and teachers, and they practiced other gifts as the Holy Spirit gave them calling and ability in addition to their serving duties. The original seven were named as Stephen (described as "a man full of faith and the Holy Spirit"), Philip (a dynamic evangelist), Procorus, Nicanor, Timon, Parmenas, and Nicolas (a covert to Judaism from Antioch). Qualifications for deacons are discovered in 1 Timothy 3:8–13. *See also* archdeacon(s); church, administration of the early; daughters (four) of Philip; *deakonos;* Eastern Orthodox Church; ecclesiastic(s); elder(s); *episcopos;* Nicanor; Nicolas; *oikonomo;* orders; Parmenas; pastor(s); Philip; Phoebe; *presbuteros*; Procorus; Protestantism, Protestants; Roman Catholic Church; Seven, the; Stephen of Jerusalem; Timon.

Dead Sea: also called the Eastern Sea (Zech. 14:8), Sea of the Arabah (with its surrounding desert lands), or Salt Sea (Deut. 3:17). Josephus called it Lake Asphalitis. This body of water, located south of Jerusalem, receives its inflow from the Jordan but has no outlet. Thus, the lake is composed mostly of salt and is classed as geologically "dead." The salt composition of the water is about 250 parts per 1000. Somewhere along its shoreline, it is believed that the cities of Sodom and Gomorrah once thrived. It has apocalyptic significance, however, in that the Millennium will see its waters purified and productive for growth and maritime shipping. *See also* Dead Sea Scrolls; Essenes; Lake Asphalitis; Qumran.

Dead Sea Scrolls: a collection of some 2500 ancient biblical manuscripts, fragments, and religious scrolls whose dating is somewhat narrowly disputed. Nevertheless, they are early, from near the turn of the first century—a full millennium before any medieval copies previously available. Discovery was first made in late 1946 or early 1947 when Bedouin tribal members began to sell them to antiquities dealers. Credit for the first discovery likely should go to a young Bedouin named Muhammad adh-Dhib in one of the region's caves. The earliest theory is that the scrolls were probably composed and collected by the desert-dwelling conservative scholars known as the Essenes and those ascetics like them. More modern forensic, archeological, and scholarly evidence may suggest, however, that various groups hid a number of them in a fervent effort to preserve them from Roman ridicule and destruction. Perhaps some patriots were simply trying to rescue their precious texts from the Temple, while others—perhaps dissident priests, Zealots, or scribes—hurried to save their diligent work. Most of our present Old Testament is included in the caches uncovered, along with several noncanonical writings. A complete text of Isaiah (actually a replica) is now on display at the home of the Scrolls—the Shrine of the Book in Jerusalem. Many eschatological and apocalyptic manuscripts are numbered in the finds, including Daniel. The Essenes, particularly, were keen apocalypticists and even centered their ascetic lifestyle on those beliefs to a large extent. It is reasonable to assume that more ancient scrolls will be located and even Temple artifacts and treasures, which some of the manuscripts describe, may surface. Besides almost all of the Hebrew Bible, the scrolls contained eclectic Jewish religious literature and works produced by the communities themselves. They wrote commentaries, hymns, extensive eschatological texts, and their own constitution for being. The major eschatological surprise is that they expected the coming of an apocalyptic prophet and two Messiahs, as did other Qumran and Jewish apocalyptic works. *See also* Angel of Darkness; Angel of Light; archeology, archeologists; Bible manuscripts; *Book(s) of Enoch;* Copper Scroll; Damascus Document; Dead Sea;

Essenes; *Genesis Apocryphon;* Isaiah Scroll; Manual of Discipline; Qumran; Renewal, the; scriptorium; Sons of Darkness; Sons of Light; Shrine of the Book; Teacher of Righteousness; *War of the Sons of Light Against the Sons of Darkness;* War Scroll.

deakonos: a masculine term for "deacon," the female equivalent being *deakones*. The term relates to the position of a servant, or even a bondslave. Their service was specialized and limited to practical matters as opposed to more specialized callings such as church leadership. *See also* archdeacon(s); church, administration of the early; deacon(s), deaconess(es); ecclesiastic(s); elder(s); *episcopos; oikonomo;* orders; pastor(s); *presbuteros.*

dean: an assistant to a bishop in charge of a cathedral or an administrative facilitator of a college or university. A dean may be a priest of the Roman Catholic Church titled as a *vicar forane* if he is appointed by a bishop to administer a specified division of a parish. In an academic setting, a dean is in charge of certain faculty or student affairs such as administration, admissions, discipline, and the like. *See also* canons minor; ecclesiastic(s); don; provost; religious education; Roman Catholic Church.

Death: the end of life when it is personified. The rider on the fourth horse of the fourth seal (Rev. 6:7–8) is named Death. In *The Testament of Abraham,* Death is also called the Shameless Face and the Pitiless One. Death himself, so personified, is made to describe his fearsome duties there with the words: "I approach the righteous in beauty, and very quietly, and with gentle guile; but sinners I approach, stinking of corruption, with the greatest possible ferocity and asperity, and an expression that is both savage and without mercy." He (Death) also told Abraham within these writings that he arrives in one of seventy-two forms, including the singular passing of the righteous at the appointed hour. *See also* angel of death; death; four horsemen of the Apocalypse; Grim Reaper.

death: the cessation of physical life. In Scripture, the term generally holds a negative or fearful aspect, as when unbelievers are condemned to the "second death" with no hope of redemption, or when life ends with no act of contrition or acceptance of salvation. The term can, and often does, refer to spiritual morbidity, as well as physical demise. The punishment for the transgression of Adam and Eve was a pronouncement from God that *death* would result from their discretion. Did He mean physical or spiritual death? Did Adam or Eve know exactly what it is? God intended both, of course, and we have had our lesson. In the fourth seal of Revelation, Death is seen riding astride a pale horse, with Hades following close behind. "Sleep," or the phrase "slept with the fathers" is a frequently used euphemism for death. Whereas the experience of death can be, and invariably is, a source of fear for almost everyone, for the believer it is absent of despair (*e.g.* Job 26:6). As testimony to such hope, Psalm 116:15 declares: "Precious in the sight of the Lord is the death of his saints." *See also* Abaddon; Abraham's bosom; afterlife; angel of death; Annwn; Aralu; Arcadia; Asgard; "ashes to ashes"; Avalon; Bolos; burial; catacombs; catafalque; cemetery; chant; charnel ground; Day of the Dead; Death; Death and Destruction; death, the first; death, the second; dirge; Dis; Duat; eternal life; exequy; funeral; future life, doctrine of the; Gehenna; "gone west"; grave; Hades; happy hunting ground; heaven; hell; Hy-Breasail; Hyperborea; Jade Empire, the; Jahannam; Janna; jeremiad; kontakion; Kidron Valley; *kinah;* lake of fire; lament; life; life after death; limbo; *Limbus Puerorum;* Manes; martyrium; Mictlan; multiconfessional; Nirvana; obit; obsequy; Otherworld; Paradise; paradise of God; Pardes; Perdition; Promised Land, the; Pure Land, the; purgatory; Requiem; requiescat; Shambhala legends; *Sheol;* sin unto death; sleep; soul sleep; space doctrine; Summerland; Tartarus; threnody; Thule, land of; Tir na nOg; Tophet; Tyropoeon Valley; underworld; Upper Gehenna; Utopia; Valhalla; Valley of Decision; Valley of Hinnom; Valley of Jehoshaphat; Valley of Slaughter; vigil; world to come, the; Xibala.

Death and Destruction: a phrase from Proverbs 15:11 describing the fierce and punishing potential reserve of power within God's nature. The same sentence notes a similar potential within the human race as well which is not, in contrast, always displayed in righteousness. The key Hebrew words rendered in English are from the familiar apocalyptic language *Sheol* and *Abaddon*. *See also* Abaddon; death; *Sheol.*

death angel. See angel of death.

Death of God theology: also called Christian Atheism (popularized beginning in the 1960s) which asserts that the God of traditional Christianity is outdated and "dead." The most influential promoter of the theory was Bishop J.A.T. Robinson of the Church of England drawn from his book *Honest to God. See also* biblical criticism; deicide; Robinson, John A. T.; theology.

Death Star. See Nemesis.

death stroke. See wounded head of the beast.

death, the first: according to theological usage, the ending of physical life. *See also* death; death, the second.

death, the second: the dreaded fate of all unbelievers (also called the second resurrection). Those souls condemned before the great white throne judgment who have been called forth for that purpose and are to be sentenced to the lake of fire. The Scripture states that the second death has no impact on any believer in Christ (Rev. 2:11; 20:14; 21:8). As applied to theology, the spiritual death and residence in hell for unbelievers describes the fate of unbelievers before the final judgment. Christians need not fear this eventuality since eternal life in heaven is assured for those claimed by Jesus in response to one's personal profession of faith. *See also* death, the first; eschatology, eschatological; great white throne judgment; last judgment; resurrection(s); resurrection, the first; resurrection, the second.

debauchery: unabashed and boorish behavior, often involving drunkenness and unbridled immorality. Naturally, all of

Scripture condemns such behavior (1 Pe. 4:3). *See also* after one's own lusts; body; carnal; concupiscence; depravity; dissipation; flesh; harmartiology; hedonism; human condition, the; human nature, the; immorality; moral uncleanliness; moral relativism; orgies; sin(s); social issues; unclean; wicked, wickedness; worldly.

Debir. See Kiriath-sepher.

Deborah: a prophetess of rare and special charismatic gifts during the period of the judges (Jud. 4–5). Her name means "bee." She was well respected as an arbiter (the people called her a "mother in Israel") and loyal to Yahweh. However, she is probably best remembered for her ability to unite some of the uncooperative tribes of Israel into a fighting force against the Canaanites. She, with her general Barak, defeated King Jabin of Hazor and his commander Sisera. By act of God, Sisera's imposing force of 900 iron chariots became bogged in the lowlands of Megiddo near the Kishon River and his army was destroyed. Sisera himself escaped but was killed by another woman, Jael the Kenite. Deborah's victory song (Jud. 5:2–31) celebrates Israel's triumph in exquisite poetry. The rhapsody praises those who helped—Jael plus the tribes of Issachar, Benjamin, Ephraim, Zebulun, and Naphtali. But shames those who were pusillanimous—Asher, Reuben, and Dan. Deborah is named the fourth judge in the land who ruled about forty years. *See also* Jael; judge(s); Judges as Old Testament book; prophet(s); prophetess(es); Sisera.

de Brebeuf, Jean. See Lalemant, Gabriel; North American Martyrs, Feast of the.

Decalogue, the. See Ten Commandments, the.

Decameron, The: a collection of novellas told in a style reminiscent of *Canterbury Tales* or Dante's *Inferno*, subtitled *Prencipe Galeotto* ("Prince Galehaut") or *Umana Comedia* ("Human Comedy"). The author was the Renaissance humanist Giovanni Boccaccio (1313 – 1375) who was probably inspired to write by the Black Dead epidemic of 1349 – 1353. The stories imamate from seven young women and three men sheltering from the disease in a villa outside Florence, each of whom is charged to relate a story per night to the company. Allowing for time for chores and the holy days being exempt, the group recites 100 tales over the two weeks of their seclusion. Besides the stories, the book consists of drawings, poems, and the like and much of the theme is apocalyptic in tone, carries a hint of numerology, and is a bit bawdy. *See also* book(s); apocryphally themed books and movies.

decapitation: severing the head from the body, often as a form of capital punishment. It was the legal method of executions in the Roman Empire and the fate of Paul the apostle because he was a Roman citizen. Traitors to the Islamic faith, or other perceived enemies of it, are often beheaded by fundamentalist or terrorist Muslims. *See also* capital punishment; cephalophore; Islam; *jihad;* Roman Empire; Sharia; terrorism.

Decapolis: ten cities of the Levant region strung out in Israel, Jordan, and Syria. The Gospels name part of the area as the Gerasenes where Jesus healed the demon-possessed man called Legion. Individually, the ten were named by Pliny's *Natural History* as Damascus, Canatha, Capitolias, Philadelphia, Pella, Gadera, Hippos, Raphana, Scythopolis, and Gerasa. Another ancient writer called them Damascus, Abila, Scythopolis, Hippos, Raphana, Gadara, Pella, Dion, Philadelphia, and Gerasa. Differences may be because some counted Damascus in Syria as an "honorary" member and disagreement as to changeable alliances. The collection maintained its Hellenistic influences more firmly than their Semitic neighbors. *See also* Pella.

deceit: deception. Treachery is a shortcoming of morality and fair play strongly condemned by the prophets and others (Hos. 10:2). God is not deceived by His creation even though we may try from time to time. Satan, however, can readily deceive humanity if given the opportunity. Deceitfulness and betrayal are prophesied to increase exponentially as the end days approach. *See also* deceiving spirits; deception; social issues.

deceiving spirits: an eschatological prediction from Paul and John asserting that an evil age is imminent in which hypocritical liars will propagate occultic messages from Satan and his minions (deceiving spirits) rather than the true Word of God (1 Tim. 4:1; 1 Jn. 4:1–3). *See also* attending spirit(s); authorities; bugbears; daemons; demon(s), demonic; demonology; devils; disa; dryad(s); elemental(s); evil (unclean) spirit(s); fallen angel(s); familiar spirit(s); frog(s); Furies; ghost(s); Gregori; Husk(s); idol(s); Lares; lwa; Manes; Oniropompi; Orisha; Oya; para; paredri; penates; power(s); spirit guide; spiritual warfare; sprite(s); territorial spirits; things taught by demons; thrones; tutelary.

de Chardin, Pierre Teilhard: French paleontologist and geologist (1881 – 1955) and a Jesuit priest. He conceived the omega point theory which posits that the entire universe is evolving towards a point of divine unification. Teilhard interpreted the universe as an ever-evolving process in which the divine unfolds Himself. According to his thinking, the Logos (Christ) draws all things to himself which interprets Jesus' name for himself in the book of Revelation as Alpha and Omega. He and his writings were censored by the Roman Catholic Church, mainly because of his view of Original Sin, nor was he popular with evolutionary scientists. Much of his work was done in China. Because of his rather modernistic thinking, Teilhard did gain a following among some intellectuals, humanists, and naturalists. *See also* evolution; Alpha and Omega; clergy scientists; omega point; Roman Catholic Church; Society of Jesus.

de Cisneros, Francisco Ximenes: a Castilian who relinquished a promising career in the Catholic hierarchy to become an Observant Franciscan, one of the more rigorous orders of the Roman church. Despite his best intentions, however, he seemed to find himself in influential positions he'd once spurned—confessor to Queen Isabella in 1492, archbishop of Toledo (Spain's largest see), regent for the young Charles Habsburg, and other positions. At times, he appeared to be a noble reformer in the mold of Zwingli or Luther, but at other moments, his austerity reared and he could be a tyrant along the lines of an Inquisitor. *See also* Roman Catholic Church.

Declaration of a Global Ethic, The. See Parliament of the World's Religions.

deconstructionism: a process of modern theology whereby critics attempt to overcome any arbitrariness, manipulation, or bias that may have crept in when copying, translating, or interpreting the Bible or church history. *See also* biblical criticism; Christian mythology; demythologizing; higher criticism.

deconversion: a term used by atheists, agnostics, and others to name one who has abandoned personal faith.

decretal(s): an announcement from the Roman Catholic pope regarding matters of faith which he expects to be heeded. *See also* bull; Decretum; Roman Catholic Church.

decretive will: that conviction by which God ponders and decrees that which will come in future history. God's omnipotent will is to come to pass either because He acts to accomplish it or because He permits it to transpire through His unrestrained agency of creative circumstance. *See also historia salutis;* plan of salvation; will; will of God.

Decretum: a collection of canon laws arranged thematically and dating from the 11th century. *See also* canon(s) of the church; decretal(s); Roman Catholic Church.

Dedan: territory of the Arabian peoples south of Israel in the central regions of the Arabian Peninsula or at Rhodes. *See also* Arabia.

dedication: 1. absolute loyalty to a person or cause, including a religious one. 2. a ceremony in which an object (typically a new building such as a church or church auxiliary construction) is sanctified for specific use and publically recognized as an asset to the people who will use it. In many Protestant settings, children also (mostly infants) are ceremonially presented by their parents before the congregation with mutual pledges that all will cooperate in the growing welfare of the new member and strive to positively influence the new religious life. Often, such childhood dedications are in lieu of pedobaptism which is not a strong doctrine in most conservative Protestant denominations. *See also* feasts and special days of Protestantism; installation.

Dedication, Feast of. See *Hanukkah*.

deductive reasoning: thinking or logic that is derived by starting from a perceived truth to logical particulars. The method has been a positive for theology, philosophy, and related disciplines. *See also* inductive reasoning.

Dee, John: noted Welsh mathematician, navigator, astrologist, Rosicrucian occultist, and counsel to Queen Elizabeth I (1527–1609), as well as her personal astrologer. Dee claims to have uncovered the alphabet code for the prediluvian language called Enochian with the help of a scryer named Edward Kelley in the year 1582. He called the alphabet "Angelical." According to common belief of the time, if one could speak with angels, they could be known and set to tasks on behalf of humanity. Dee reportedly used a series of chants with a complex phonetic stream labeled "Angelic Calls" to manipulate the exotic alphabet. He also claimed to have found or created the necessary mystery grains to make a philosophers" stone. Dee was a secret agent in the Elizabethan court (incredulously with the code number 007), causing some supporters to assert that the Enochian ciphers dealt with espionage and not occultic practice. *See also* alphabet; angelic language; attending spirit(s); chaos magic; divination; Enochian; goetia; occult, occultic; Oniropompi; Order of the Rosy Cross; paredri; philosophers' stone; Rosicarian Manifestos; sorcery, sorceries; spirit guide; tutelary.

deep secrets, so-called: esoteric knowledge or action, often contrary to the spirit of prophecy. Praise is presented by Christ for the church at Thyatira because they did not indulge in Satan's so-called deep secrets (Rev. 2:24). Evidently, the "deep secrets" and "deep things of Satan" were occultic or sectarian in nature and tied to false doctrine, which many in the fellowship of Thyatira were resisting. *See also* chaos magic; dark sayings; deep, the; deep things of God; *disciplina arcane;* idolatry; mystagogue; mystery; mystery of God; occult, occultic; riddle; Satan's so-called deep secrets; secret wisdom; things taught by demons.

deep, the: a word, described in a number of Hebrew terms, referring to a great depth either physically or figuratively. According to the specific language, the deep may refer to the Sea of Galilee, the great primeval watery mass at creation, the underworld or realm of the dead, or the oceans. The great deep may also represent the unfathomable mysteries of God. *See also* Abyss; deep secrets, so-called; deep things of God; mystery; mystery of God; primeval ocean; secret wisdom; underworld.

deep things of God: a phrase from 1 Corinthians 2:10 by which Paul implied the great mysteries of God—truths taught by the Holy Spirit for the benefit of the believer. The expression holds prolific eschatological import. *See also* deep secrets, so-called; deep, the; *disciplina arcane;* esotericism; mystery; mystery of God; mystery religion(s); mystical; secret wisdom.

deep things of Satan. See Satan's so-called deep secrets.

deer: the hind, a fleet and graceful land animal representing surefootedness, beauty, grace, innocence, or agility (Ps. 18:33), and sometimes vulnerability. *See also* animals, birds, and insects, symbology of.

de Escalante, Silvestre Velez and Dominguez, Francisco Atanasio: Spanish Franciscan friars, missionaries to the Southwest of America (dates of birth and death unknown). The pair were trailblazers who hoped to open an all-weather route from Santa Fe, New Mexico, to Monterey, California, in 1776. The party failed but the explorer's maps and experiences assured later success. *See also* Franciscans; friar(s); missions, missionaries; Roman Catholic Church.

Defamation of Religious Resolution, the: a United Nations resolution described as an effort "to promote and encourage universal respect for and observance of all human rights and fundamental freedoms without distinction as to race, sex, language, or religion." Despite its high-sounding explanation, the resolution was originally called "Combating Defamation of Islam" and was sponsored by Muslim nations in the general assembly. The purpose is clearly to limit freedom of speech and to sanction the brutality of Sharia law. Since the general assembly has only declaratory powers, the resolution can be vetoed by the Security Council as long as that process is effective. *See also* anti-Semitic; Islam.

Defender of the Faith. See Henry VIII, King.

Defnar: the Antiphonarium, a collection of short stories or saint's biographies read in Coptic monasteries during midnight praise. *See also* antiphoner; Coptic Church; liturgical year; liturgy, Christian.

defrocking: an ecclesiastical action that removes a clergyperson from his or her occupation. Dismissal may be due to misconduct, crimes, incompetence, noncompliance to church doctrine, or some other reason. The name accrues from the early church practice of denying the accused the right to wear the habits of the organization. *See also* church discipline; disfellowshiping; excommunication.

Degandawida: a prophet and seer of Native American heritage known as "the Great Peacemaker" dating from the 12th or 13th century. Legends of his person and deeds present

Degandawida as a respected hero who traveled about in a stone boat carrying wampum, a peace sign of his mission; some even declare he was born of a virgin mother. Degandawida's mission was to unite the Indian peoples from among the five tribes of present-day New York State. He proclaimed his revelation or vision that the blood feud so long engulfing the nations of the Huron-Iroquois stock could be ended. Hiawatha (Iroquois leader immortalized by Henry Wadsworth Longfellow's epic poem of 1855) took up the cause and managed to unite the Mohawks, Oneida, Cayuga, Seneca, and Onondaga tribes. They were later joined by the Tuscarora and established a workable "Great Peace." *See also* Hiawatha; missions, missionaries; prophet(s).

deicide: the death of a god. Most modern Christians, until the mid-twentieth century, held the Jews responsible for the death of Jesus. Since then, Roman Catholicism has partially downplayed the accusation and most Protestants have abandoned it. In any case, the God of Christianity is incapable of dying and is ever-living according to the most orthodox views. *See also* Death of God theology.

deism: belief in God wherein He may be recognized as Creator and the Supreme Being, but that Someone basically is uninterested in human affairs or in personal faith and worship. Deism was a product of the 15th century Enlightenment movement which assumes the mind can know truth through its unaided reason. As such, it was more a philosophy than a religion which reached it apogee in America with strong sponsors like Thomas Jefferson, Thomas Paine, and Benjamin Franklin. Some, like the famous contemporary George Whitefield, equated deism with atheism as do many theologians today. Most of America's Founding Fathers were Deists. For example, Thomas Jefferson was interested in religion but considered most current theology, especially the doctrine of the Trinity and the divinity of Christ as absurd. He even excised much of the elements of the New Testament Gospels that he did not account as creditable. Benjamin Franklin seldom attended any church but when he did he preferred to use the Anglican *Book of Common Prayer* as a devotional guide. George Washington never received Communion and spoke of the deity in monarchial, not personal, terms. Many, if not most, leaders for American independence were Freemasons. Established denominations in the Revolutionary War were not lacking, however. Anglicans and Methodists were mostly Tories but Presbyterians were ardent rebels. Baptists were a bit ambivalent because they felt stung by the rebuke they took from the Continental Congress when they reversed the cry of the patriots, "No taxation without representation," by reminding the delegates that they had to pay a tax to support Congregationalism in the colonies. Quakers were pacifists and suffered for it. The United States motto, "In God we trust," did not appear on coinage until the Civil War—an entirely different era—and was not seen on paper currency until 1864. The Constitution does not mention God or Christianity, with the exception of the dating note, "the Year of our Lord." The Great Seal of the union has no religious emblem except the all-seeing eye of Providence, which is more akin to Freemasonry or Egyptian iconoclasm than religion. Finally, deism has no creed, articles of faith, or holy script; neither Satan nor hell exist; those are only symbols of evil which can be overcome by man's own enlightened reasoning. *See also* acosmism; atheism, atheist(s); Jefferson Bible; possibilianism; theism.

de Labadie, Jean: a French mystic (1610 – 1674) credited with the establishments of failed communal societies in Amsterdam, Holland, and Maryland in the United States around 1683. His followers were known a Labadists. See also communal communities; Labadists.

de Lamarck, Chevalier Jean-Baptiste Pierre Antoine de Monet: mostly simply known as Lamarck, an impoverished, and eventually blind, evolution scientist (1744 – 1829) who initially trained for the priesthood. Lamarck was an established academic, soldier, biologist, and scientist but his most enduring work was in the realm of evolution of the natural order. His most recognized published work, *Zoological Philosophy*, was published in 1809 and outlined his belief that biology acts "as an intermediary between God and the various parts of the physical universe for the fulfilling of the divine will." Most scientists today claim de Lamark's main errors were that animal bodies are shaped by the environment and that these characteristics are passed to their offspring. *See also* clergy scientists; evolution.

de las Casas, Bartolome: called "Apostle to the Indies" (1474 – 1566). Las Casas was a Spaniard and the son of one of Christopher Columbus's crew to the New World. His first trip was intended to set his fortune, but he was soon caught up in the plight of the natives under abusive Spanish rule. Las Casas became a Roman Catholic priest in 1512 and served his life trying to foster colonial reforms from his bishoprics in Venezuela, Santo Domingo, and Guatemala. His efforts were diluted and of little effect, but he did write the definitive *History of the Indies* before his death. *See also* missions, missionaries; Roman Catholic Church.

de Laudonniere, Rene Gaulaine: a French Huguenot (1562 – 1582) who founded a colony called Fort Caroline in Florida. The site was to be a haven for persecuted Huguenots and a counter to the Spanish influence in that region. There were 300 colonists to begin the work, but the planting failed miserably. Aristocrats would not work, the Indians became hostile, and some of the members became pirates and began raiding the rich Spanish galleons in nearby waters. The Spanish authorities destroyed the settlement in 1565 and slaughtered most of the colonists. Laudonniere escaped to write his account of the adventure in 1586. *See also* communal communities; Huguenots; Ribaut, Jean.

delict: the Catholic ecclesiastical term for a crime. Church crimes for reference appear in the *Code of Canon Law* for Roman Catholicism and in *Code of Canons for the Eastern Churches* for Orthodox churches. *See also* Catholic Church abuse scandal; church abuse; Eastern Orthodox Church; *Inquisitor's Manual, The; Malleus Malefiracum;* persecution(s); ritual abuse; Roman Catholic Church.

Delilah: the Philistine coquette who seduced the Israelite judge Samson, eventually causing his imprisonment and death (Judg. 16). She may be a type for betrayal and deceit. *See also* Samson.

deliverance ministry. See exorcism.

deliverance motif: the scriptural ideal and pledge that God will rescue the faithful from evil, hardship, and persecution. The need for succor is no strange feeling to Christians who are sometimes called upon to persevere while awaiting temporal or eternal relief from suffering in its many forms. When it happens, deliverance feels like a victory and calls for celebration, as modeled in Revelation 15. *See also* conquest motif; endurance motif; exemplar motif; exchange motif; rector motif; salvation; Song of Moses and the Lamb; victor motif.

Delphi, Oracle of: the cult center in Greece active for a thousand years of recorded Greek and Roman history. The cult was established when the stone vomited up by Cronus (which he thought was the last son of Rhea) was sanctified by Zeus at Delphi in southern Greece, then appointed the first Pythoness. Inquirers sought the prophetess of Apollo, the Pythia, who was seated on her tripod in the temple of Delphi. She was consulted on any matter, great or small, for the shrine enjoyed a long and universal reputation for future telling. Delphi was the most ancient sanctuary in Greece and was regarded as the center of the earth with its *Omphalos* or navel-stone in Apollo's temple, where the Pythia voiced her oracles. The oracle was said to have her position on that spot also known as "the Whispering Stone." It was the most sacred object in Apollo's temple.

How she (or they, as there may have been as many as three on active occasions) functioned is somewhat conjecture. Typically, however, when a reading was needed, she dressed in a long robe and a wreath of laurel leaves, drank from the sacred spring Kassolis, and breathed a mysterious underground vapor. In some accounts, she ingested hallucinogens, particularly absinthe. Surely, most of her ecstasy was self-induced. Her services cost about two days' wages for a commoner but ten times that for the nobles, rulers, or military leaders. The host town then became a wealthy city and subject to frequent plundering, the most vicious of which was perpetrated by the troops of Emperor Constantine, the first Christian ruler of the Roman Empire. Perhaps the Pythia did possess some sort of *mana* (a generalized supernatural force) somewhere in her psyche. Her pronouncements were invariably vague, even unintelligible, and depended on the resident priests to convey the message of Zeus through Apollo. Her pronouncements were made, not personally to the public, but related by the shrine priests who released them in Homeric hexameters (thus making them even more opaque). Even Socrates did not disdain to heed the Pythia, who had named him the wisest of men. Legend says the Pythia was asked the question, "Is anyone wiser than Socrates?" When the great philosopher heard her answer was a simple and unexpected No he said, "I wonder what she meant by that?" This lack of preciseness undoubtedly contributed to the eventual downfall of Delphi despite one or two revivals. The shrine was also associated with the ecstatic worship of Dionysus and the Olympic games, held there in the city in honor of the gods It is inconceivable to think that the Oracle at Delphi held no influence whatsoever in Israel's history, particularly under Roman occupation. *See also* Apollo; barley; Chronos; idolatry; laurel; *mana*; Mount Parnassus; Olympian pantheon; oracle(s); Plutarch; *Pytho;* Python, python; shrine(s); Sibyl(s); Sibylline Oracles, the.

delusion: a perception of the mind identifying something as real when in actuality it is not. The term has important ramifications for eschatology in that a vital end time prediction states the world can expect a spirit of strong delusion to saturate the population as the ages close (2 Th. 2:11–12). In this instance, the deception is said to originate with God Himself as judgment upon the wicked. The noun modifier "strong" emphasizes that the delusion is supernatural. Satan, called the father of lies, also uses falsehood and evil seduction to draw away anyone who allows him access to the core of being. *See also* deception; lie(s).

Demas: a proclaimed follower of The Way (Christianity) who is praised in Colossians 4:14 but later condemned as a traitor to the faith in 2 Timothy 4:10.

Demeter: the Greek mother-goddess of the harvest, sponsoring fertility, law and order, marriage, and life after death (her major contribution to the fertility religions). She was the mother of Persephone, who was abducted by Hades when still a virgin to become queen of the underworld. In grief, Demeter periodically halted grain production into seasonal sections. She was honored yearly, along with Persephone, at the celebrations of the Eleusian Mysteries. *See also* Eleusian Mysteries; Eriskegal; Hecate; idol(s); Olympian pantheon; Persephone; queen(s); "resurrection gods"; underworld.

Demetrius the Christian: a friend to the apostle John who was noted (3 Jn. 12) as one holding a good reputation. A fellow member called Gaius was the recipient of John's third letter and also praised. Demetrius's opposite in character would be Diotrephes, who was unfavorably mentioned in the same letter (3 Jn. 9). *See also* Diotrephes; Gaius.

Demetrius the silversmith: a precious-metal silversmith of Ephesus who made votives to the goddess Artemis (Acts 19:23–41). Because his business and others of the trade were threatened and supposedly because the goddess was being blasphemed by the Christian gospel, Demetrius incited a riot in the city that could have brought disaster on the apostles and citizens of the town. The city officials finally calmed the mob with few negative consequences.

Demetrius the Syrian: an heir to the Seleucid throne who was overthrown by Antiochus IV. The history is likely contained in Daniel 11:21–24. *See also* Syria.

demi-god(s): (and goddesses) part human and part god as defined by ancient astronaut theorists. A demi-god was a human who was partly divine (an offspring of the gods). As such, the demi-gods were allowed some access to the greater gods and were permitted to claim the *dingir,* a small written "d" before their names. Or, they could bear the prefix or suffix "Mes" or "Mesh" to the same effect. The prefix "Nin" indicated a true god or goddess. Some of the demi-gods were born with the aid of artificial insemination from semen donated by the male gods. After the great deluge, the earthborn goddesses gained more prominence than her male companions whereas, in the prediluvian era, the males were more essential. *See also* Anunnaki; *Chariots of the Gods?;* cities of the gods; Enki and Enlil; *Enuma Elish; Epic of Gilgamesh, The;* idol(s); Igigi; lulu; Mesopotamia; mythological beasties, elementals, monsters, and spirit animals; Nibiru; panspermia theory; Sumer; Sumerian Tablets; Table of Destinies; Tiamat; UFO.

demimondaines: those living a hedonist lifestyle, usually in a flagrant or exhibitionist manner. The name springs from a French comedy called *Le Demi-Monde,* by Alexander Dumas. The term eventually became a tag for prostitutes and courtesans. *See also* after one's own lusts; antinomianism; carnal; dissipation; hedonism; immorality; prostitute, prostitution; social issues; worldly.

Demiurge: the Gnostic concept of the Creator God of the Old Testament. The term carries a base meaning of "public craftsman," a word borrowed from Plato's identification of the Creator. Since the Demiurge made an imperfect world, humanity must possess secret knowledge in order for the soul to find its way back to heaven. The seven heavens are spheres called Aeons which are guarded by Archons. The Supreme Father is the "good" God far remote from the earth and its inherent sin. In *The Apocalypse of John*, the writer goes further and claims that the people who follow the Demiurge are the descendants of Seth. Only the Gnostics, in whom rests the secret knowledge, will become immortal. *See also* Aeons; Archons; Gnosticism, Gnostic(s); Hebdomad; idol(s); Pleroma; Sakla; Seth; Sethianism.

de Molay, Jacques: last grand master of the Order of the Knights Templar. His organization, probably the most powerful religious order in history, was accused, condemned, and nearly destroyed on charges of heresy after a long and prosperous existence in the fourteenth century. Accusations included the worship of the Baphomet, conspiracy with the Saracens during the Crusades, sexual perversions among the warrior monks, and various sacrilegious acts. The promoters of the abolishment were France's King Philip IV, who was heavily indebted to the Knights, and Pope Clement V. Jacques de Molay himself was arrested on October 13, 1307, and sentenced to death after extensive torture. Since the day was a Friday, the thirteenth day of the week has taken on a superstitious association as being unlucky. He was burned at the stake in March of 1314, still professing his innocence. Just before his death, de Molay was said to have prophesied that his enemies, both the pope and the king, would die—the secular within twelve months and the religious within forty days. His omen, if the story is true, proved to be 100 percent accurate. Philip died on November 29 and Clement on April 20. *See also* Baphomet; knighted orders; Roman Catholic Church.

demon(s), demonic: 1. sometimes called fallen angels. Disgraced and displaced angels are assumed to be celestial beings created by God but who rebelled against His authority at some point in eternity past. The worst of their lot are confined to the Abyss but others are active in our world today. Their defeat, along with their master Satan, is assured in eschatological certainty. The New International Version of Romans 8:38 uses "heavenly rulers" as an alternate translation for demons. Paul warned believers (1 Cor. 10:20–21) that knowingly partaking of proscribed ritual events, such as banquets on behalf of idols, are really participation in demon worship. A myth, based on Genesis 6:1–4, and used by *1 Enoch* and *Jubilees*, reveals that demons originated when the angels of heaven looked upon the daughters of men and lusted after them. These, numbering 200 and led by Semyaza, initiated intercourse with women from whom giants and other monsters were born into the world. 2. an alternate definition presents the notion of those who do not view the demonic as authentic fallen angels. Rather, they may be the spirits of the Nephilim, the half-breed giants of Genesis 6. When human and angel DNA became mixed, the offspring became soulless entities. Once the Nephilim monsters died, their spirits somehow attached themselves to earth, looking for flesh to inhabit. *See also* Abaddon; Abezi-Thibod; abomination of desolation, the; Abyss, the; Adramelech; *agathodaimon;* Agrippa Books; alukah; Anammelech; angel(s); Apollyon; Apophis; Asclepius; Asmodaeus; attending spirit(s); Attis; authorities; Azazel; Azrael; Baal-zebub; banshee; Baphomet; Behemoth; Belial; bogle; Bon; Bolos; bound angels; brownies; bugbears; chimera; clurichauns; Cupay; daemons; deceiving spirits; demonology; demon possession; devils; Dibbuk; disa; discerning the spirits; dryad(s); Dubbi'el; elemental(s); energumen; enneagram; evil (unclean) spirit(s); exorcism; fairy, fairies; fallen angel(s); familiar spirits; four living creatures of Ezekiel; frog(s); Furies; Gadreel; ghost(s); ghoul; gnome(s); Green Man, the; Gregori; giant(s); goetia; grimoire; guardian Cherub; Hahgwehdaetgah; haunt (prison) for every unclean and detestable bird; hobgoblins; homunculus; household deities;

huldafolk; Husk(s); Iblis; idol(s); idolatry; Igigi; incubus; Jannes and Jambres; James I, King; *Kategor*; Kephn; key of Solomon; king of Babylon; king of Tyre; Lares; Legion; leprechaun(s); Leviathan; Lilith; lion; Loa Loas; locusts; lulu; magic arts; Manes; Mastema; Mephistopheles; *misophaes;* nereid; Nibiru; nisse; Nephilim; nymph(s); nyx; Oannes and the Seven Sages; Oniropompi; Orisha; Oya; pandemonium; panspermia theory; para; paredri; Pazuzu; penates; pentagram; power(s); prefect(s); prince of demons; prince of Greece; prince of Persia; prince of the power of the air; psychopathology; *Pytho;* Quashee; Rahab; Robin Goodfellow; Sammael; Sanat Kumar; Satan; satyr; Sceva; scorpion; seed of the serpent; Seelie Court, Unseelie Court; selkie; serpent seed doctrine, the; Seth; Shaytan; Shiva; Sidhe; sigil; sirens; slave girl of Philippi; Solomon; sylph(s); spirit; spirit guide; spiritual warfare; spell names; spirits in prison; spiritual warfare; sprite(s); succubus; Syrophoenician woman; Tartarus; teraphim; territorial spirits; theolepsy; things taught by demons; three traitors, the; thrones; *Tobit;* transhumanism; Trickster; Tuatha de Danann; tutelary; Typhon; unclean; underworld; undine; war in heaven; Watchers, the; wight(s); woman of Canaan; Xibala; Yama.

demonology: the study of demons and their influence. In earlier times, the term also described the practice of calling and manipulating demons, including the spells and rituals involved. Is the practice dangerous? Certainly the Bible and its most keen interpreters would say Yes. In any case, following the Chinese proverb on the subject is decidedly best: "Be in awe of supernatural beings but have nothing to do with them." *See also* Agrippa Books; alukah; attending spirit(s); authorities; Baaras; deceiving spirits; demon(s), demonic; demon possession; devils; devils of Loudon, the; discerning the spirits; evil (unclean) spirits; energumen; exorcism; fallen angel(s); goetia; grimoire; Human Animal Hybrid Prohibition Act; Human Enhancement Revolution

(HER); Igigi; incubus; James I, King; lulu; magic arts; misophaes; Oannes and the Seven Sages; pandemonium; panspermia theory; psychopathology; *Pytho;* sigil; spell names; spiritual warfare; succubus; theolepsy; things taught by demons; transhumanism; unclean; war in heaven.

demon possession: a condition (held as absolute truth by some but by others as an altered mental state rooted in psychotic behavior) in which the personality, body, and mind of a person may be "possessed," or controlled by a demonic entity. The Bible, especially the New Testament, reports the condition with frequency (*i.e.,* Luke 9:37–45; Mark 5:1–20; Acts 19:15). In each instance, the victims suffered intently thereby prompting Jesus or another to exorcise, or "cast out," the evil spirit (or a number of them) said to inhabit the body. Many people are convinced that Judas Iscariot, the Antichrist, and the False Prophet were or are to be crazed by Satan in the same manner. Healing, usually via exorcism, can only be accomplished by Christ or in the authority of his holy name. Whether so-called demon possession is caused by fiendish activity or is a description of some known or unknown mental aberration will likely remain in debate. What is certain is that Jesus and those who purged the afflicted in his name treated the symptoms as a malevolent spiritual condition in accord with the general beliefs of the time. There seems to be enough distinction within the reports, both ancient and modern, to somehow differentiate some aspects of possession from typical mental illness. Some analysts assert that nominal believers can be demon "influenced" as opposed to total possession. A debate also rages as to whether or not a Christian can be demon possessed. Most answer negatively but do claim that a believer can be influenced by demons if the psyche allows it. It may be possible to distinguish some mental illness from demon possession by looking at the symptoms of the latter. Those possessed may 1) possess unusual physical strength, 2) exhibit fits of rage, 3) display a disintegration or splitting of personality, 4) show resistance to spiritual matters, 5) demonstrate supernatural powers such as clairvoyance or speaking an unknown language, and 6) sound out an alteration of the voice. Mentally disturbed persons may show one or more of the symptoms but seldom all of them. *See also* Antony; authorities; demon(s), demonic; demonology; devils; devils of Loudon, the; energumen; evil (unclean) spirits; exorcism; *exsufflatio;* fallen angel(s); Hitler, Adolf; incubus; Legion; Marx, Karl; psychopathology; Puritanism, Puritans; *Pytho;* Sceva; Simon Magus; slave girl of Philippi; spirit; spiritual warfare; succubus; Syrophoenician woman; theolepsy; war in heaven; woman of Canaan.

demotic millennialism: an egalitarian ideal of the new age that can be brought about by human goodness without reference to religion. The model foresees a new world based on individual freedom, judicious living, and a sort of holy anarchy in which the "saved" behave justly from love and not fear. ("Demotic" refers to what is popular or to the common public culture.) The precepts resemble the Zealot enthusiasm of New Testament times who cried "No king but God" or the more recent writings of Karl Marx. Realistically, the concept is almost surely a phantasm because human sin is pervasive in this world and will remain so until the new age. *See also* dominion theology; idealist eschatology; Millennium, millennial; postmillennial, postmillennialism; Reconstructionism.

demythologizing: a modern hermeneutical method that tries to reverse the so-called "myths" of the Bible. Popularized by Rudolf Bultmann in 1941, the process dismisses any theory contrary to the scientific world view. To demythologize, then, is an effort to clarify the myth to usable human philosophy. For instance, the cross and resurrection show judgment that opens up for people the "possibility of an authentic life." Eschatology is especially suspect to the method since few miracles in the Bible are not contrary to the scientific method whether applied to literature or the physical world. The essence of Bultmann's views is that Scripture is nestled into the reader's encounter with the Word and his own experience while neglecting weightier matters in the plain language or historical context. *See also* Bultmann, Rudolf; biblical criticism; Christian mythology; deconstructionism; form criticism.

denarius: the most common currency of exchange mentioned in Scripture. The amount was a silver coin, the price of a normal day's wages for a laborer, sometimes called a penny or a cent. Revelation's third seal says that a denarius will buy a quart of wheat or three quarts of the inferior barley in the Tribulation. Today, the value would be about fifteen cents, but what its value will be in the eschaton is unknown. *See also* gold, golden; kondrantes; lepta; mammon; shekel; silver; talent.

Dendayn: in pseudepigraphal literature (*i.e.*, *1 Enoch*, an immense parcel of land or desert located east of the Garden of Eden where the chosen righteous dwell), including Adam, the great grandfather of Enoch. In other references the place is called the Garden of Righteousness.

denial. See escapism.

denomination(s), denominationalism: larger religious bodies or organizations to which congregations may be affiliated. Ordinarily, church member status is secured by a common faith tradition or theology usually exists to make maximum use of resources, for educational and faith guidance, as well as for national or regional unanimity. Those churches with no denominational identity are called non-denominational or "independent." Research has identified over 40,000 Christian denominations, many with similar-sounding names or uncertain doctrine. *See also* African Independent Churches; African Methodist Episcopal Church; African Methodist Episcopal Zion Church; American Baptist Churches USA; Assemblies of God; Baptists; Brownsville Assembly;

Calvary Chapel; Campbellites; Christian and Missionary Alliance; Christian Church (denomination); church; church bodies in America (typed); Churches of Christ; Church of God; Church of God in Christ; Church of the Brethren; Church of the Nazarene; Church of the United Brethren; communion; communal communities; Congregationalists; Covenant Churches; denominational mutt; Disciples of Christ; Dunkards; Evangelical Free Church in America; Exclusive Brethren; faith; "I just want to love Jesus"; Inner Light Churches; Landmarkism; Lutheran Church; mainline Protestantism; Methodists; Millennial Churches; Moravian Church; National Baptist Convention; Pentecostalism; Plymouth Brethren; Presbyterians; Protestant Episcopal Church; Protestantism, Protestants; Reformed Churches; Reformed Church in America; Salvation Army; Schwenkfelders; Society of Friends; Unitarian Universalists; United Churches; Vineyard Ministries International; Waldenses; Wesleyan Church; Westboro Baptist Church.

denominational mutt: one who wanders from denomination to denomination or seems to harbor a kind of blended pseudo-theology or religious credence. Like dogs of mixed breed, they are often lovable and compliant companions but impossible to identify as to true stock and class of core beliefs. *See also* cafeteria Christians; Christianese; "church hopper"; "churn" (religious); denomination(s), denominationalism; McChurch; nominal Christians; slurs, religious.

deodate: a gift to or from God. *See also* blessing(s); "God-shot."

Deo gratias: the typical response by the worshipers at the dismissal of the Tridentine Mass, the servers at Low Mass, or the choir in the Roman and Lutheran rites. The Latin translates simply as "Thanks be to God." *See also* liturgical week; Mass; Roman Catholic Church; Tridentine Mass.

deontology: an ethical system based on principles in which codified rules are to be followed so that one can be morally justified in her decisions and actions. Christianity rejects the deontological concept because the authentic life cannot be maintained exclusively by rules, regulations, laws, and principles no matter how noble. The sinful nature of man disrupts good lawmaking and positive law observance, even if the deontologically based Ten Commandments are allowed to be paramount. *See also* casuistry; ethics; Judeo-Christian ethic; metathesis; Protestant ethic; orthopraxy; refined gold; scruples.

deosil: clockwise, or the appearance of the sun rise from east to west. The direction has some application to certain pagan rituals. *See also* pagan practice; prayer wheel; widdershins.

de Payens, Hughes: one counted as the founder and first grand master of the Knights Templar, which was established in 1118. There was, however, a membership of sorts already present in Jerusalem when they were organized, including the "poor" seven Frenchmen who constituted the core of its formation. De Payens and his companions took their vows to knighthood on Christmas Day of 1119 and began the stirring career of the Knights Templar. *See also* knighted orders; Roman Catholic Church.

deposition: in canon law, to dismiss a church official from the ordained ministry in some liturgical churches.

deposit of faith: the attitude, knowledge, and provision from Christ to his followers that delivers to them all that is needed for salvation. The content of the gift resides, according to most liturgical churches, in Scripture, in tradition, and in the magisterium of the institution. Less liturgical denominations would likely not use the term but would embrace the source of the salvation provision to be the Holy Spirit working in the dynamic of an individual. The latter would particularly eschew any reference to tradition or ecclesiology. *See also* faith; *fideo qua creditur* and *fides quae creditur*; magisterium; rule of faith.

depravity: behavior that is abhorrent to cultivated conscience. In more theological terms, the term may encompass "total depravity," the complete hopelessness of mankind who is born into sin. There is no escape from such a defeat unless the Savior intervenes. *See also* debauchery, immorality; orgies; Phibionites; social issues.

deprecation: a prayer for deliverance. *See also* prayer(s).

deprogramming: procedures used to force another into abandonment of a faith, usually into a cult, in which the deprogrammer attempts to cleanse the effects of the possessive and destructive cultic mind-set. The techniques of deprogramming, however, are often as severe as the initiation into the sect (*i.e.,* kidnapping, sleep deprivation, psychological pressures, physical restraint, and the like). Many family members and cult specialists consider deprogramming as an acceptable substitute, however, for the alternative of continued debasement inside the cult environment. *See also* Counter-Cult Movement; cult(s); Cult Awareness Network; exit counseling; exorcism.

Derbe. See Iconium, Lystra, and Derbe.

descant: harmony in music with a fixed theme. The tune produced is usually sung by a soprano to complement one or more verses of a hymn or psalm. *See also* music.

desecrate: to treat without respect or reverence.

Descartes, Rene: devout Roman Catholic and radical philosopher (1596 – 1650). From the year 1628, he began to teach that human personality is of two natures—material and immaterial. The problem his philosophy tried to solve was how these two halves could be combined. His philosophical thrust is called Cartesianism and insists the known and the unknown are to be considered separate and that the individual self is the proper starting point for philosophical discussion. Descartes was also a mathematician, the discoverer of analytic geometry who claimed the idea came to him in a dream. The presentation of his math theories appeared in *Discourse on Method* (1637). The famous x

and *y* references typically used are even called *Cartesian co-ordinates,* from the adjective form of "Descartes." Descartes lived in fear of the Catholic Church since he had knowledge of what happened to Galileo. *See also* Cartesian thought; dichotomy; Roman Catholic Church.

descent into hell (Hades), Christ's. See Harrowing of Hell, the.

desert. See wilderness.

Deserted/Desolate: Jerusalem's unfortunate name, which God decreed will be changed to Hephzibah ("my delight is in her") and Beulah ("married") when the city is again in favor (Isa. 62:4). *See also* Beulah; City No Longer Deserted; Hebrews as a people; Hephzibah; Holy People, the; Jerusalem as city; Jew(s); Judaism; name, a new; Redeemed of the Lord, the; Sought After.

desert mystics: or desert fathers [mothers], Christian hermits (anchorites) who prefer to practice the faith in contemplation either alone or in communities, often pitched in austere surroundings such as inhospitable desert lands. The movement began around A.D 270 under St. Anthony (Antony) and continues today. Most historians agree the earliest hermits were in Egypt. Eremitical recluses are individuals; cenobics live in orders or communities. A less-than-comprehensive list of the most famous might include Anthony (255–345), Palladius (368–431), Saint Benedict (480–543), Saint Gregory I (540–604), Bernard of Clairvaux (1090–1153), Francis of Assisi (1181–1226), Thomas Aquinas (1225–1274), Meister Eckhart (1260–1328), Thomas a' Kempis (1380–1471), Ignatius Loyola (1491–1556), Teresa of Avila (1515–1582), John of the Cross (1542–1591), Thomas Merton (1915–1968). *See also* ancress; Antony; Aquinas, Thomas; Benedict of Nursia; Bernard of Clairvaux; Essenes; Francis of Assisi; John of the Cross; Loyola, Ignatius; monasticism; monk(s); mysticism, mystics; oblate; orders; Pachomius; Telemachus; Teresa of Avila; Therapeutae; Thomas a' Kempis.

desired of all nations, the: a prophecy of Haggai 2:7, which declares that the blessings of the Messiah, or the treasury of all nations, will flow to the millennial Temple on some future day. The millennial Jerusalem will be the premier city during the 1,000 years of Christ's reign on the earth (*cf.* Isa. 60:5, 11; 61:6). Ezra encouraged the builders of the replacement Temple with similar speech. The phrase could also equally anticipate the arrival of "good things"—the tribute of the nations due at all times to the messianic king. *See also* names (titles) for Jesus; New Jerusalem.

desire of Israel: a "royal person" (1 Sam. 9:20) who is, or will be, friendly to the Jews. The phrase may be recited in a messianic sense or someone affiliated with government. *See also* Judaism; Messiah; names (titles) for Jesus.

desire of women: an uncertain phrase from Daniel 11:37 which may refer to a divine being or a human of unknown temperament. The context describes an evil one antagonistic to the Jews so if this personality is the Messiah (or someone like him) he is portrayed in opposition to the one who exalts himself. *See also* Judaism; Messiah; names (titles) for Jesus.

De Smet, Pierre Jean: Jesuit missionary (1801–1873) to the Plains Indians who knew him he was known as "Blackrobe." Eventually, De Smet traveled to the Pacific dealing with the various tribes to present the gospel and promote peace between them and the whites. He is known to have parlayed successfully with Sitting Bull at least twice. *See also* missions, missionaries; Roman Catholic Church; Society of Jesus.

Desmond Rebellions: a pair of abortive attempts by the Irish Catholics of Munster to oust the English feudal lords then in control of their land. The motivations for the wars were primarily political, but there was an important religious element. Since Pope Pius V had excommunicated Elizabeth I of England in 1570, most Irish Catholics felt no loyalty to the crown. The first uprising (1569 – 1573) saw James

Fitzmaurice Fitzgerald, the Earl of Desmond and head of the Fitzgerald dynasty in Ireland, try to thwart further control by the English. The royalists managed to contain the revolt by splitting loyalties among the Irish clans and the use of superior military tactics. The second rebellion (1579 – 1583) was a repeat performance of the first but even more devastating. Fitzgerald returned from European exile and attacked Munster with his able brother John, who by then considered themselves Counter-Reformationists and enjoying Vatican support. Papal mercenaries from Spain and Italy were supplied to invade Ireland and vacate the country of the Protestants there. The landing force of 600 attacked at Smerwich Harbor, led by the staunch English Catholic Nicholas Sanders (called "Dr. Slander" because of his opposition to Protestantism). The campaign did not succeed, and Slanders died of exposure while hiding out as an outlaw. Slanders is one of several suspects in the alleged forgery of the "Prophecy of the Popes." The Second Desmond rebellion resulted in 30,000 deaths due to war, famine, and plague after five years of fighting. *See also* Counter-Reformation; "Prophecy of the Popes"; Roman Catholic Church.

desolate and naked: a phrase common in many of the early translations of the Bible indicating the fate of Babylon the Great in Revelation 17:16 and 18:19. The great city will be brought to ruin, burned, devoured, and abandoned. *See also* angel of Babylon's fall; Babylon the Great; city of power; cup of adulteries; desolate and naked; Desolation, day of; filth of her adulteries; "glorified herself"; great city, this; Great Prostitute, the; haunt (prison) for every unclean and detestable bird; Mystery Babylon the Great the Mother of Prostitutes and Abominations of the Earth; nakedness; Religious Babylon; Secular Babylon; smoke of her burning; whore of Babylon; wine of her adulteries.

Desolation, day of: an end time description of tragedy described clearly by the prophet Zephaniah. *See also* day of the Lord; desolate and naked; eschatology, eschatological.

desponsyni: a reference to the blood relations to Jesus, especially his brothers and (presumably) sisters. Eusebius may have coined the term. Of the siblings named in the Bible we know of James, Joseph (Joses), Judas (Jude), and Simon – all of whom assumed high honor and provided immense service for the church. Roman Catholic and other persuasions that wish to maintain the perpetual virginity of Mary deny that Jesus had those family members, a nigh impossible tenet to maintain given the clear biblical record without adherence to the tenet of the perpetual virginity of Mary. *See also* Eusebius; genealogy of Jesus; immaculate conception; Infancy Gospels; James; Joseph; Joses; Jude as brother of Jesus; Simon.

Destiny: a pagan god or god ideal which, along with its partner expression "Fortune," is meant to represent good or ill luck. Or, as we might say it, "heads or tails." The prophet Isaiah (Isa. 65:11) represents the god being worshiped with mixed wine at a table setting. The word in Hebrew is a pun on the name of the god Meni *See also* Fortune; Gad as idol; idol(s); Levant pantheon; Meni.

destiny: an expression of one's ultimate life experiences. To where or toward whom are we headed? We cannot go back, so we must be going to some end. And that end is eternity according to Christian doctrine. Other religions, especially most Eastern persuasions, see the future as developed by unbiased fate. For them, the good destiny is absorption into nothingness. Naturally then, the word destiny and others like it have a close association with prophecy. *See also* determinism; fatalism; fate; foreordination; fortune; manifest destiny; predestination.

destroyer: a person or dangerous entity bent on devastation. Jeremiah 12:12, for example, uses the name to identify an enemy ready to wreak havoc on Judah; the aggressor may be locusts but is more likely an invading human army. The term has frequent prophetic application when some sort of disaster is forthcoming. Nevertheless, God remains aware (*e.g.* Job 26:6). *See also* Abaddon; Apollyon.

destroying mountain: a derisive term for Babylon, an empire destined to be eliminated as punishment from God (Jer. 51:25). The name appears to be a bit odd as Babylonia features no mountains. It must be then that the epithet pertaining to the great power of the Babylonians. *See also* Babylon, Babylonians; Babylonia.

Destruction. See Abaddon, Apollyon, destroyer.

destruction of heaven and earth: the final act of God dealing with heaven and earth as we know them today. The particulars are found in Revelation 21:1, but Peter also mentions the earth's demise by fire (2 Pe. 3:7). In the book of Revelation, God declares He will make everything new. Most scholars agree the word "new" (in this context) may be renewal or refurbish—not necessarily destruction and recreation of our planet. Many religions share the idea of end time destructions of one magnitude or another. *See also* creation; eschatology, eschatological; heaven; heaven and earth destroyed by fire; new heaven and earth; world to come, the.

destruction of Jerusalem: the fall of Jerusalem during the Jewish war of A.D. 70. Although there have been, and will be, other invasions of the Holy City, the phrase is usually restricted to that event. The date is of particular importance to those theologians known as "preterists" since much of their evaluation of prophecy centers on this one historical occasion. The episode is a central prophecy of Jesus, especially as he delineated it in his Olivet Discourse. *See also* invasions of Jerusalem; Jerusalem as city; Jerusalem, siege of (literal); Jerusalem, siege of (pantomime); Jewish War; Olivet Discourse, the; preterist(s).

determinism: the theological precept (considered erroneous by orthodox Christianity) that the universe is controlled by natural law alone. Such a concept negates both human free will and God's sovereignty. Prophetic biblical religion insists that God is able and free to produce miracles and to intervene in history any time He deems it desirable and is not bound by deterministic events. If the definition above is reversed, the resulting idea would be that events are fixed by God (*e.g.*, John 6:44), making it resemble predestination to some degree. The quote of part of John 6:64 reads: "For Jesus had known from the beginning which of them did not believe and who would betray him." The implication is that Jesus had determined events before they happened. In philosophy, determinism carries a similar meaning. The core understanding, especially as promoted by J. Stuart Mill, is that we have no free will and our volitions are predetermined. *See also* biblical criticism; Destiny; destiny; fatalism; fate; Fortune; fortune; predestination; reprobation.

Deus otiosus: the Latin phrase announcing that God withdrew into isolation and became inactive following His creative accomplishments.

Deus Volt!: "God wills it!," the battle cry of the Christian Crusaders. *See also Alluha Akbar;* Crusades; Urban II, Pope.

deuterocanonical books: those apocryphal books present in Roman Catholic Bibles, which the church asserts are not exactly inspired but deemed worthy of study. *See also* Apocrypha, the; book(s); Roman Catholic Church; Vulgate.

Deutero-Isaiah: The term asserting that parts of the writings in the book of Isaiah were allegedly composed by a second author. Some scholars see clear seams between chapters 1–39, 40–55, and even 55–66 (Trito-Isaiah). *See also* Isaiah as Old Testament prophecy; Trito-Isaiah.

Deuteronomy as Old Testament book: the fourth book of the Bible and of the Pentateuch. This record is central to Jewish theology as a recapitulation of the law given to Moses. It stresses fidelity of faith, sacrifices, communal living, and obedience to Yahweh. The Mosaic Covenant is outlined and described as a conditional agreement promising blessings to Israel according to their faithfulness. Israel is assured of the land (the Palestinian or Land Covenant), and the Messiah is promised on some future day. Enemies of Israel are to be punished and blessing is accrued to the Jews as the remnant is repentant in latter days. The entry into the Promised Land (Canaan) can be taken as a type for entry into the Millennium. Israel failed, of course, to honor its side of the treaty, necessitating a more permanent non-conditional covenant through Abraham and other assurances of the preservation of the Jews.

deva(s), devi(s): the name for Hindu (primarily) and Buddhist (less often) gods and goddesses. *See also* Buddhism; Hinduism; idol(s).

developmental fulfillment. See progressive fulfillment.

developmentalist theology: an approach to theological understanding which declares that the industrialized nations of the world can lead the way to fiscal and political issues through capitalism in combating poverty in third world countries. The theory is the polar opposite of liberation theology which, in substance, sees the privileged nations as hindrances to their economic development. What is not always acknowledged is that both systems are faulty to some degree. *See also* liberation theology.

devil. See Satan.

devils: usually named as angels (Teraph, Seraph, or Cherub) who were among the fallen in rebellion against heaven somewhere in eternity past. Most class them as "evil spirits" or demons who were cast out of God's presence along with their leader, Satan. Some scholars speculate, however, that demons and devils are not the same entity. *See also* Abaddon; Abezi-Thibod; Adramelech; Anammelech; angel(s); Apollyon; Apophis; Asmodaeus; attending spirits; authorities; Azazel; Azrael; Baal-zebub; Baphomet; Beelzeboul; Beelzebub; Belial; bugbears; clurichauns; Cupay; daemons; deceiving spirits; demon(s), demonic; demonology; Dibbuk; Dubbi'el; evil (unclean) spirit(s); fallen angel(s); familiar spirits; frog(s); Furies; Gadreel;

genie(s); Gregori; devils of Loudon; Dibbuk; disa; Dubbi'el; Eblis; elementals; energumen; exorcism; Furies; Gadreel; Hahgwehdaetgah; Iblis; idol(s); incubus; *Kategor;* Lares; lion; Legion; Lilith; Mastema; Nephilim; Oniropompi; Orisha; Oya; Pandemonium; paredri; Pazuzu; power(s); prefect(s); prince of Greece; prince of Persia; Sammael; Sanat Kumar; Satan; satyr; Seth; Shaytan; sirens; spirits in prison; spiritual warfare; territorial sprits; thrones; tutelary; Typhon; wandering stars; wight(s).

devil's advocate: in general usage, the person who assumes the negative or condemnatory side of an argument or action in order that all angles of the proposal have adequate exposure. In the Roman Church, the devil's advocate is a member or the Sacred Congregation of Rites (established 1587) dealing with the process of beatification and canonization. His job is to point out all deficiencies in the candidate which might bar his or her sainthood. *See also* beatification; postulator; Roman Catholic Church.

Devil's Bible: the *Codex Gigas* meaning "giant book." The production is believed to be the largest extant medieval manuscript surviving today. Originally from what became the Czech Republic, the tome is now in the National Library of Sweden in Stockholm, taken as a prize of war. The catchy name derives from the large and fantastic illustration of the devil placed near the story of the creation.

devil's books: playing cards, since each suit has a king which those opposed to gambling attributed to the evil one.

Devil's Dictionary: a satirical, even witty, lexicon by Ambrose Bierce (1842–1913). Bierce was a renowned journalist and dark critic of contemporary life and literature. His dictionary is considered a spoof and seldom taken seriously.

"Devil's Footprint, The": a natural landmark near Ipswich, Massachusetts. The feature consists of a footprint-shaped form embedded in granite on a neighboring hillside. Local legend says it was made in the autumn of 1740 when the evangelist George Whitefield preached so powerfully that the devil jumped from a nearby church steeple in his hasty exit from town. *See also* Whitefield, George.

devil's mark: a mostly out-of-fashion belief that people who have made a pact with the devil or a demon are often said to bear some kind of mark, scar, or malformation of the body. The superstition implies that those unfortunates said to be dominated by the devil are somehow "marked" to show his ownership. Any spot on the body, be it moles, scars, birthmarks, or whatever could be interpreted as a sign of witchcraft, sorcery, or proof in some way that an individual was in Satan's service. Such marks were a ready tool of the examiners of the bloody Inquisition. The sign was viewed as Satan's way of reminding the afflicted that "You belong to me and don't forget it." Mikhail Gorbachev, president of the Soviet Union in the late 80s and early 90s, was seen by some to bear such a blotch because of a prominent wine-colored birthmark on his upper brow. *See also* Inquisition, the; ordeal(s); Satan; 666.

Devil's Millennium: a period of spiritual adultery highlighted in Revelation's admonition to the church at Thyatira (Rev. 2:18–28). Some say Christ has given Thyatira one thousand years to repent and reject the allure of the Jezebel in her midst. The text does not specifically mention a precise time of grace for that church, but some interpreters have accounted the time as such and call it the "Devil's Millennium."

devil's missionary: a derogatory name applied to many for their anti-religious cast. Foremost among them is perhaps the French author Voltaire (1694 – 1778), a widely read opponent of Christianity. *See also* Voltaire.

devils of Loudon, the: the name attached to the curious incident in the 1600s occurring at Loudon, France, where nuns claimed to be bewitched by the demon Beelzebub. Two notoriously immoral priests were implicated in the possessions and were executed for witchcraft. The story was made into a movie in 1971 called "The Devils." *See also* demonology; demon possession; devils; witchcraft.

devil's tattoo: not a skin design but the beating of drums, as one might drum his fingers in boredom or irritation. The evil perpetrated as worship of Molech in the Valley of Hinnom, among the most sinister in apostate Judah, was accompanied by drumming.

devil's temple: a somewhat dated reference to a movie house or theater. Early Christians held little respect for the theater and the Scots even passed a law (in the 1500s) decreeing that the theater was the actual temple of the devil, where he frequently appeared clothed in a corporeal substance and possessed the spectators. Today's entertainment offerings, of course, are tame compared to those earlier presentations.

Devir: the Jewish designation for the Holy of Holies in the Temple. Solomon's Temple housed the ark of the covenant, but the space was empty in subsequent replacements. God claimed that He would dwell there "in thick darkness" (1 Ki. 8:12). *See also* adytum; ark of the covenant; Hebrew language; Heikhal; Holy of Holies; *Ulam*.

de Vitiguerro, Jean: a religionist who, going by other assumed names (either in the 13th or 16th centuries) is sometimes said to have influenced Nostradamus. He predicted that there would be no Roman pope at the end, and the papacy was to stand leaderless for at least two years. *See also* false prophets; Nostradamus.

devotion, devotional: a state or attitude ranging from simple allegiance to ardent love. One may be devoted to one's pet fish or enraptured by God's glory. Quite often, the word is closely aligned with religious feeling and action that may manifest in prayer, meditation, ecstasy, study (daily devotions), sacred ritual, or the many forms of formal and informal worship. *See also* orarium; worship.

History and Mystery

devout: rendering considerable time to prayer and worship. The general use term throughout most of society is often rendered "religious." *See also* religiosity.

Dewey, John: American intellectual, philosopher, psychologist, and education reformer (1859–1952). Dewey was a strong advocate for democracy, improved methods of teaching and learning, and held many other interests. One of his primary efforts, however, was to campaign for the humanist theory; he was an active member of the Humanist Society. *See also* humanism; Humanist Society.

de Wyon (Wion), Arnold: a Belgian Benedictine (1554–1610) who is also an historian and recorder of the Malachy prophecies. His commentary or transcription is contained in the massive volume entitled *Lignum Vitae,* the "ironwood history" from 1595. He conducted most of his work in the retreat at Monte Cassino. *See also* Benedict, Order of; Malachy; "Prophecy of the Popes"; Roman Catholic Church.

Dharma: "the way of higher truths" in most Eastern religions. The doctrine is particularly significant in Buddhism, Hinduism, Jainism, and Sikhism. Dharma is one of the three jewels of Buddhism. *See also* Sangha; Three Jewels of Buddhism, the.

Dhammapada: an early part of the Pali Canon and companion piece to the Suttanipata. The title can be interpreted as "Way of Truth" and is supposedly the most read anthology of the teachings of Buddha. The text is mostly in verse style and widely quoted. *See also* Buddhism; Gautama Buddha; Pali Canon, the; *Sutta Pitaka*; Suttanipata; Theravada Buddhism.

dhikr: or *zikr,* pronounced "THIK-er," the monotonous repetition of God's name to induce alternate states of consciousness, usually practiced by Sufi Islamists. *See also* Islam; mantra; Sufi.

Diabolical Mimicry, the: the theory that those apparently similar stories of pagan religions and the nativity of Jesus can be explained in a simple formula (*viz.,* that the pagan gods were fantastic and mythological whereas Jesus was an historical figure and his miracles were real). Opponents of the historical Jesus system are the most ready to employ the term. *See also* biblical criticism; bridal chamber ceremony; Christian mythology; criteria of double dissimilarity; Gnosticism, Gnostic(s); *Golden Bough, The;* Harry Potter; historical Jesus, the; Jesus Myth, the; Lewis, Clive Staples; Logos; *preparatio evangelica.*

diachronic: "across time," the study of events as they change over time. Also called the *historic* view, diachronic is not a snapshot in time but a long scrutiny of chronological movement as it changes itself into history. *See also* historicism; synchronic.

Diadochi: the name used to identify the factions of Greek rule through the known world after the death of Alexander the Great. The Jews, Daniel among them, often had to deal with some of them, those of the Ptolemy and Seleucid dynasties especially. Alexander's most able generals eventually partitioned the empire. Cassander took Macedonia and Greece, Lysimachus got Thrace and Asia Minor, Seleucus I ruled Syria and Mesopotamia, and Ptolemy claimed Egypt and Israel, to name the most important. Some of the Diadochi are likely represented in Daniel 11:4. *See also* Alexander the Great; Cassander; Greece; Lysimachus; Ptolemy I Soter; ram and the goat, the; Seleucus I Nicator.

dial-a-prayer: a slang reference from the 50s when one could dial the telephone for a short recorded prayer or inspirational message to uplift the spirit. Or perhaps the call was to satisfy some subtle guilt for one's inattention to spiritual matters. Today the phrase is jargon for any canned religious content outside of live participation in worship and learning, probably implying a sort of artificial religion. Often enough, the term refers to all forms of televangelism as well. *See also* Christianese; pulpit theft; slurs, religious; televangelism, televangelist(s).

dialectic: a method of reasoned argument as old as Socrates and Plato. The dialectic dialogue centers on discussion, debate, and exchange of ideas. The system has loaned its name to any number of philosophies and religious methodologies (*i.e.*, dialectic materialism, nature, behavior therapy, theology, enlightenment, monism, and others). *See also* dialectic monism; dialectic theology.

dialectic imagination: a religious perspective emphasizing the individual and the perceived withdrawal of God away from the sinful world of our habitation. Analogical imagination, on the other hand, stresses the expression of God in all aspects of His sovereignty. Both hypotheses were advanced by Andrew Greely who believed, probably erroneously, that Catholics were more dialectical and Protestants analogical. *See also* analogical imagination.

dialectic materialism: the psychological base of Communism. The forces of material reality are forcing history to its end through the stages of feudalism to capitalism to, ultimately, socialism with no private ownership of goods. Atheism is dialectic materialism's principal conception since it is governed by an impersonal force. *See also* Lenin, Vladimir; Marx, Karl; "opiate of the people"; sociology of religion.

dialectic monism: an ontological religio-psychological thought process that perceives reality as finally a unified whole. It differs from strict monism in that this wholeness is expressed in dualism or extremes of polarity. The idea resembles Taoism and certain Buddhist philosophy. *See also* dialectic; dialectic theology; Taoism.

dialectic theology: more commonly known as "neo-orthodoxy." The movement began as a reaction to the liberalism of the 19th century after World War I. More attention was paid to the principles and tenets of the Protestant Reformation, led by able scholars like Karl Barth, Friedrich Gogarten, Eduaard Thumeysen, F. E. Baur, Friedrich Hegel; Rudolf Bultmann, and Emil Brunner. *See also* Barth, Karl; biblical criticism; Brunner, Emil Heinrich; Bultmann, Rudolf; dialectic; dialectic monism; higher criticism; neo-orthodoxy; theology; Tubingen School.

dialogical critical method: exegesis that examines, not only what a given text says, but also what it omits. *See also* biblical criticism; lower criticism.

dialogical principle of worship: the dynamic of conversation between God speaking (in His own way) and the people responding (as they may) in the act of public worship. *See also* elements of worship; form of worship; liturgy; normative principles of worship; regulative principles of worship; worship.

Diana. See Artemis.

Diaspora: the Jewish name for their scattering, either voluntarily or by forced exile, into the world and away from their homeland in Palestine. Such an episode has transpired a number of times during the history of the nation of Israel. The latest dispersion did not end until 1948, and many Jews still reside outside of the Holy Land. At one point, there were more Jews in New York City than in Israel. By the time of Jesus, there may have been a million Jews in Alexandria, the largest dispersed community outside of Palestine. Today, there are about thirteen million Jews worldwide, of whom eight million are *Diaspora;* five million are in Israel. The two major dispersals occurred at the time of the Babylon Captivity (606–536 B.C.) and the Roman persecutions (A.D 132–1948). According to Amos 9:15, there will not be another. In our age, there are about eight million Jews in *Diaspora* and two million in Israel. Prophecy indicates that someday all Jews will return to the Holy Land. *See also* Babylonian Captivity; Elephantine; exile; *golah;* Jerusalem, siege of (literal); Jerusalem, siege of (pantomime); Judaism; Law of Return; Palestine.

Diatessaron: the formula showing that the Gospels (Matthew, Mark, Luke, and John) are basically in harmony with one another, first systematically explored by Tatian in his book by that name. The term means "the gospel out of four," but the more common theological idea is simply addressed as the "harmony of the Gospels." The idea may hold some understanding that the four Gospels match each other in content, but the true core of diatessaron is that the same subject matter is explored in each. Actually, there are details in the Gospels that are seemingly inconsistent in the several accounts; also, some incidents are mentioned in some Gospels but not the others. The first real attempt to create the diatessaron in written form was by a Syrian writer named Tatian, who produced a study aid that gave similarities and dissimilarities of the Gospels at a glance. Modern harmonies do the same. *See also* harmony of the Gospels; parallelism; Tatian.

diatribe: in ecclesiastical circles (perhaps its mildest form), an imagined dialogue between a student and teacher. The learner asks a question, usually an inane or absurd one. The answer is "by no means" or equivalent language. The term was used by Rudolf Bultmann in 1910, and there are traces of it in some Pauline epistles. More common usage expresses a diatribe as a bitter and contentious debate or argument, which is almost always emotionally charged.

Dibbuk: a demon in Jewish folklore. *See also* Abaddon; Abezi-Thibod; Adramelech; Anammelech; Apollyon; Asmodaeus; Azazel; Azrael; Baal-zebub; Beelzeboul; demon(s), demonic; devils; Dubbi'el; Gadreel; idol(s); Legion; Lilith; Mastema; Pazuzu; Sammael; Sanat Kumar; Sceva; Shaytan; slave girl of Philippi; Syrophoenician woman; woman of Canaan.

dicastry: a Vatican department with a specified jurisdiction such as the Secretary of State, Pontifical Councils, Tribunals, etc. *See also* Pontifical Council; Roman Catholic Church; Tribunal; Vatican, the.

dichotomism. See dualism.

dichotomy: the concept that the human frame possesses body and soul only. Most theologians add a third—that of spirit. *See also* Descartes, Rene; trichotomy.

Didache, the: one of the more reliable noncanonical writings extant in the early church era. The document's full title is *The Teaching of the Lord to the Gentiles through the Twelve Apostles* and was intended to be an instructional handbook for non-Jews covering such subjects as morality, liturgy, and ecclesiology. Its prophetic material is profound and discusses such topics as the Second Coming, immanency, an Antichrist type figure, and resurrection. The treatise was probably written before Revelation and relies on Pauline theology rather than Johannine. Some readers have gleaned a doctrine of "salvation by works" accented from some of the material. If it is expressly there, the tenet is contrary to the standard of salvation by grace alone, which is a theme of the New Testament. There is no mention of the Millennium in the text. *See also* autosoterism; works, salvation by.

didactic method: the examination of ideas via the process of logic, usually by the question and answer process. It was a favored method of Socrates and is still a mainstay of Roman Catholic religious education but—so far as we know—of limited use to the Hebrew and Christian prophets. *See also* catechism; didactic theology; religious education.

didactic theology: a manner of interpreting Bible passages by which the author has supposedly addressed his subject in a forthright and unambiguous fashion. Most Bible learning is not so overt and must be studied systematically instead. Didactic reading, on the other hand, uses temporal, geographical, linguistic, and cultural solutions to present its message from a simple and basic platform of investigation. The system is sometimes called the "Princeton School" of theology (as made famous by Benjamin B. Warfield) as opposed to the more non-specific expression (exemplified by Dewey Beegle). *See also* didactic method; religious education; systematic theology.

Didascalia: "instructions" in doctrine and liturgy for Coptic Christians. The document was supposedly complied of instructions given to the several churches by the apostles immediately after the Jerusalem Council. Content has changed but the work centers on instructions for bishops, deacons, and others concerning church discipline and order. *See also* canon(s) of the church; catechism; Coptic Church; liturgy, Christian; religious education.

didyma. See oracle(s).

Didymus. See Thomas as apostle.

Dies Irae: "day of wrath," a Latin hymn or Medieval poem depicting the last judgment dated no later than the 13th century. The words are calling souls to the throne of God where they are to be judged. In Christian liturgy, it properly fits as a Requiem but the text uncharacteristically mentions an Erythraean Sibyl. *See also* day of the Lamb's wrath, the; eschatology, eschatological; judgment(s); liturgical year; liturgy, Christian; music; Requiem; Sibyl(s).

Diet of Worms: a Roman Catholic convocation led by the young emperor of the Holy Roman Empire and king of Spain, Charles V, and populated by Spanish and German clergy and nobility. The meeting was, in reality, a trial for Martin Luther conducted at the city of Worms in western Germany on April 18, 1521. Luther was asked to recant his anti-papacy rhetoric, but he refused, using the famous words, "Here I stand; I cannot do otherwise, so help me God." The resulting Edict cast Luther as an outlaw, and he was excommunicated him from the Roman Church. *See also* Charles V, Emperor; Holy Roman Empire; Luther, Martin; "Ninety-Five Theses, The"; Protestant Reformation; Roman Catholic Church.

di Gattinara, Cardinal Mercurino: Imperial Counselor to Emperor Charles V (16th century). He was a thoroughgoing apocalypticist and was convinced that his king was to be the last of the world rulers. Di Gattinara was highly influential in his day and helped restore the Roman Catholic Church to some of its former glory by countering some of the effects of the Protestant Reformation. *See also* Charles V, Emperor; Roman Catholic Church.

Dignus es: "A Song of the Lamb" a canticle contrived from Revelation 4:11, 5:9–10, and 13. It is probably more common in Episcopal liturgy. *See also* liturgical year; liturgy, Christian; music.

dimensionality: a concept common to physicists but less so to theologians. The notion is that there are, or almost certainly may be, dimensions of existence outside our familiar four of length, depth, height, and time. The theory can help the understanding intellect of believers who experience God in our observable dimensions only that seem irregular to us humans. He exists as spirit but can manipulate all four dimensions on our plane and even many more (some scientists estimate there may be eleven or more additional dimensions in the universe). He is a unit of being but in a Trinity mode; He speaks from a burning bush that doesn't consume itself; He hears the prayers of billions at once but attends each one singularly; He is far away yet near as a thought; He is love in its purity but capable of unimaginable wrath; He extends salvation to all but not all are saved, and the list goes on and on. In our world of limited knowledge, some elements of our existence make no sense. We confront *contradictions* – direct or irresolvable opposition between two statements, laws, or principles; we meet *paradoxes* – those direct but resolvable opposition problems between true statements, laws, or principles; or we encounter *antinomies* – direct contradictions between two statements, laws, or principles that appear equally true. Some may never find solutions unless we allow for an experience of God's actions that are not limited to our own frames of reference. Empiricism does not help us much in this arena. He is not confined to our four basic physical fundamentals but can roam freely up and down, inside and out, through and beyond our human capacities. As proven by his Creator status, extra-dimensionality can even explain how God has no beginning and no end. We may never know God completely but can, if we invest in the trust and value of dimensionality, know Him better. Dimensionality may also be labeled extra-dimensionalism or super-dimensionalism, and my be identified in some aspects to the space-time continuum. *See also* empiricism; hermeneutic(s); mystery of God.

Dinah: a daughter of Jacob by his wife Leah (Gen. 30:21). She was raped by Shechem, the son of Hamor the Hivite (Gen. 34), a travesty for which her brothers Levi and Simeon wrecked severe vengeance. Those actions had consequences for the prophetic futures of both tribes (*e.g.* Genesis 49). *See also* Levi; Shechem; Simeon.

dingir: the Sumerian word for "god" similar to the Hebrew concept of Elohim. The term is usually transliterated as *digir* and is closely associated with the sky or the heavens. *See also* Sumerian and Babylonian pantheon.

diocese: a Roman Catholic or Anglican collection of parishes overseen by a bishop. In the East, it is the district overseen by a patriarch. *See also* church field; Church of England; cure; Eastern Orthodox Church; eparchy; episcopate; fold; katholikon; ministry; missions, missionaries; parish; patriarchate(s); pentarchy; presbytery; primate; Roman Catholic Church; see.

Diocletian: Roman emperor (A.D. 245–313). Diocletian pursued the most concentrated effort of any Roman ruler to wipe out Christianity completely. His persecutions, with that of Galerius, were essentially the last of the Roman tendencies to destroy the Christians, but they were the most savage. Nearly half of all recorded martyrdoms in the early church period were posted to this era. History records one episode in which he had 17,000 men, women, and children slaughtered in the arena in one month alone. It does seem odd that too many historians allow the Romans to label other cultures as "barbarian" before examining their own subjects. *See also* Christianity in the Roman Empire; king(s); Roman Empire.

Diogenes: Greek Cynic philosopher (ca. 412–ca. 323 B.C.). He despised conventional norms and preferred to live in a barrel (or a large ceramic urn) and exhibit an ideal of unfeeling and unconcern about the regularities of life. Who does not picture him, lamp in hand, wandering the streets of Athens, vainly looking for a single honest man? He walked nude and performed all bodily functions in public to show his contempt for normal living. Diogenes's philosophy did not seem to fuse well with Christianity, but some of the Jewish prophets might have relished his struggle with ethics. *See also* Cynics; philosophy of the Greeks.

Dionysian Artificers: or Sons of Solomon, an early secret society appearing to prominence around 1000 B.C., about the time of the construction of Solomon's Temple. They took their title from the Greek god Dionysus and used private passwords and signs. The members were divided into lodges ruled by a master and dedicated part of their time to helping the indigent. The chief architect of Solomon's Temple, often named as one Hiram Abiff, was supposedly a member. Hiram was killed by three fellow members because he would not reveal the deepest secrets of master masonry, an act which is reputedly reenacted in third degree Masonic ritual today. The Dionysians believed that the temples they built must be constructed on the principles of sacred geometry based on the supreme plan of God. Some unproven sources cite the higher levels of Freemasonry, which equate Hiram with Osiris and perform a ritual depicting him as a sign of death and resurrection of the ancient god and his revivification in the New World Order. The Dionysian influence on Freemasonry is undeniable as their temple in Washington, D.C., depicts. Here they are said to perform the Abiff/Osiris ceremony each time a new United States president is inaugurated. The Dionysian myth spawned splinter groups known as the Ionians and the Cassidens. *See also* Cassidens; "Dionysian Artificers, The"; Dionysus the god; fraternal organization(s); Freemasonry;

hexagram; Hiram Abiff; Ionians; orphic religion; Osiris; religious organizations; secret societies; sect(s).

"Dionysian Artificers, The": an essay by the Portuguese mason Hippolyto Joseph da Costa (1774–1823) published in 1820. In the history, da Costa tried to prove that Freemasonry derived from ancient Greek philosophy and religion and attempted to draw parallels between Masonic initiation and orphic mysteries. The historic claim is that a group of that name surfaced around 3000 B.C. just before the building of Solomon's Temple. They took their name from the Greek god Dionysus (Bacchus), who, with the aid of another group called the Ionians, claimed to be the architects of such marvels as the Temple of Diana at Ephesus. In the Holy Land, they called themselves the sons of Solomon and adopted the king's six-pointed star as their mason's mark. The legendary Hiram of Tyre may have been associated with the group since he, King Solomon, and Hiram Abiff are considered to be the first grand masters of Freemasonry. *See also* Cassidens; Dionysian Artificers; Dionysus the god; Freemasonry; hexagram; Hiram Abiff; Ionians; orphic religion.

Dionysius of Alexandria: influential member of the Alexandrian School (died ca. A.D. 264) who, in accord with the school's basic theology, was an allegorist. To explain his position, he wrote: "I suppose that it is beyond my comprehension... it is too high for me to grasp. So I resorted to allegorism." He did, however, submit that Revelation was canonical but denied its apostolic authorship. He was one of the most ardent anti-millennialists of the church fathers. *See also* Dionysius of Rome.

Dionysius of Greece: one of the few intellectuals of Athens who responded positively to Paul's preaching of Christ. Evidently, he was the Areopagite in charge of morals, manners, and philosophy of the Areopagus in Greece (Acts 17:34).

Dionysius of Rome: a second century bishop of Rome (A.D. 259 – 268) who entered into a controversy with Dionysius of Alexandria concerning the divine nature of Christ. To this pope fell the task of rebuilding the Roman Church following the persecutions of Emperor Valerius but before the toleration of Galerius. Oddly enough, Dionysius is recorded as owning gladiators and enjoying the games of the arena. It was not until the fifth century, when Rome was invaded by the so-called "barbarians," that those same "pagans" put an end to the bloody and violent spectacles. *See also* Dionysius of Alexandria; Edict of Toleration; Roman Catholic Church.

Dionysius the Areopagite: a writer living around 500 A.D. mistakenly named for the Areopagite converted from Paul's preaching at Athens (Acts 17:34). He is known in history, since we don't know his real name, as Pseudo-Dionysius, one who holds few claims to fame except his concoction of angelic ranking produced from his own mind and research. According to his arrangement in *The Celestial Hierarchy*, angels are classed as Seraphim, Cherubim, thrones, dominions (or Denominations), Virtues (or authorities), powers, principalities, archangels, and angels. The terms are not inventions as all classes are mentioned in the Bible but not in one place. The ranking is set out highest to lowest and Dionysius even explains the functions of each division. *See also* angel(s); authorities; Cherub, Cherubim; Eastern Orthodox Church; Seraph, Seraphim.

Dionysus the god: or Bacchus (Roman depiction), or the ancient Greek deity of wine and drama. He was more than simply a drunken parody of excess and revelry but rather the god of polished and festive social intercourse. In fact, he served as the social leveler, patron of creativity, negotiator for nations and classes, slave emancipator, striver to good morality, and the comforting wine-giver to all. He was the son of Zeus and the mortal Semele, but the mother was killed by the jealous Hera, causing Zeus to save the baby and preserve him in his thigh until birth. Thereafter, Dionysus was depicted as much human as divine. In a further version of the birth story, Dionysus was born of Zeus and Persephone, queen of the underworld. The jealous Hera ordered the fierce Titans to kill him by ripping the child to pieces. Dionysus tried to defend himself by changing forms, the last being a bull when he was overcome. After they dismembered him, the Titans ate the limbs, excepting the heart. Killing a bull, drinking its blood, and ingesting its raw meat became a religious practice to devotees. A pomegranate tree sprang from his blood so his worship also came to be associated with trees. Zeus destroyed the Titans with lightning bolts in retaliation. From their ashes, humanity was created as a mixture of divine and holy. The preserved heart was used to impregnate Semele causing Dionysus to be born again. Thus, in either account, he is counted as one of the "resurrection gods." *See also* Dionysian Artificers; idol(s); Olympian pantheon; "resurrection gods"; underworld.

diophysitism. See dyophysitism.

Diotrephes: a proud and domineering man who opposed hospitality to itinerate missionaries and teachers in the early church. He even excommunicated those who desired to host such evangelistic workers. Diotrephes was also spreading malicious gossip about the apostle John, as well as being discourteous to the local churches. Diotrephes was self-centered, a malicious gossiper, and seems to conduct a personal vendetta against the apostle John. John condemned his actions in his third epistle. Another mentioned in the same letter (3 Jn. 7), Demetrius, is of more noble character as is another member named Gaius who was recipient of the letter. *See also* Demetrius the Christian; Gaius; hospitality.

diphysitism: the doctrine that God has two natures, one divine and the other human. These two attributes, however, coexist in a single person. As dogma of the church, it won out over its opposite allegation, that of Monophysitism, as declared by the Council of Chalcedon in A.D. 451.

The key phrase that seemed to push diphysitism over Monophysitism was perhaps the formula: "two natures, without confusion, change, division, or separation." Even though the doctrine was a technical victory for the Western Church, all of Christianity did not recognize the decision of the bishops at Chalcedon. *See also* Council of Chalcedon; Monophysitism.

diptych: an icon consisting of two flat surfaces joined with a hinge. If the object was used as an exercise book notes or lessons could be written since there was wax inside. Such articles were used in the Byzantine churches and some were quite elaborate and expensive. *See also* art, religious; Eastern Orthodox Church; furniture and furnishings of the modern church; icon, iconography.

dirge: a specific liturgical form employed mostly in mourning for the dead. The music or march is characterized by the traditional 3 : 2 metric pattern—a measure of three major beats in the first stanza but only two in the second stanza. The same form is used in the slow-paced, plodding step of the pallbearers walking in a halting march of three steps, then two, as they proceed to the burial site. Some Jewish scholars claim that the 450 false prophets of Baal strutted in a dance before Elijah (1 Ki. 18:26). *See also* burial; chant; death; dance; exequy; funeral; jeremiad; *kinah;* kontakion; lament; liturgy, Christian; liturgy, Jewish; music; obit; obsequy; Requiem; requiescat; threnody; vigil.

Dis: the place of the dead, according to old Roman religion and which served as another name for the god of the underworld. It was a cheerless and unhappy place in shadows similar to the Greek Hades or Hebrew *Sheol.* Many Roman grave markers carried the theme by inscriptions like: "I was not, I was, I am not, I care not." Such hopelessness is one reason Christianity was acceptable to many of the ancient Romans. *See also* Abraham's bosom; afterlife; Annwn; Aralu; Arcadia; Asgard; Avalon; death; Duat; eschatology, eschatological; grave; Elysium; eternal life; future life, doctrine of the; Gehenna; Hades; happy hunting ground; heaven; hell; Hy-Breasail; Hyperborea; intermediate state; Jade Empire, the; Jahannam; Janna; lake of fire; life after death; limbo; *Limbus Puerorum;* Manes; Mictlan; new heaven and new earth; Nirvana; Olympian pantheon; Otherworld; Paradise; paradise of God; Pardes; Perdition; Promised Land, the; Pure Land, the; purgatory; Shambhala legends; *Sheol;* soul sleep; space doctrine; Summerland; Thule, land of; Tir na nOg; underworld; Upper Gehenna; Utopia; Valhalla; world to come, the; Xibala.

disa: *disir* (plural) ghosts or spirits associated with fate, according to Norse legend, which can be benevolent or antagonistic to mortals. *See also* attending spirit(s); banshee; bogle; brownies; bugbears; clurichauns; daemons; deceiving spirits; demons, demonic; devils; dryad(s); elemental(s); fairy, fairies; familiar spirits; Furies; ghost(s); ghoul; gnome(s); Green Man, the; hobgoblins; homunculus; household deities; huldafolk; idol(s); Lares; leprechaun(s); Loa Loas; Manes; mythological beasties, elementals, monsters, and spirit animals; nereid; nisse; Norse and Old Germanic pantheon; nymph(s); nyx; Oniropompi; Orisha; Oya; para; paredri; penates; Robin Goodfellow; satyr; Seelie Court, Unseelie Court; selkie; Sidhe; sirens; spirit warfare; sylph(s); teraphim; territorial spirits; Trickster; Tuatha de Danann; tutelary; undine; Valkyries; wight(s).

discalced: religious orders who go about barefoot or wearing only sandals. *See also* Isaiah stripped and barefoot; sandal(s); shoe(s).

discerning the spirits: the ability to distinguish between the Spirit of God and the spirits of demons. Such a capability is to be desired by every Christian and is considered a gift of the Holy Spirit (1 Cor. 12:8–10; Eph. 4:11). In many instances, if a believer "feels" something is wrong or not squared with goodness, it probably is. *See also* charisms; demonology.

disciple(s): a follower of Christ. The first to be so named were a group of twelve chosen by Jesus to be his primary teaching and missionary band, but all servants of Christ in any age are properly called disciples. The first selected were Andrew, Bartholomew (Nathaniel), James (son of Zebedee or "the greater,") James (son of Alphaeus or "the less,") John, Philip, Judas (son of James), Judas Iscariot, Matthew (Levi), Simon Peter, Simon the Zealot, Thaddeus (Jude or Lebbaeus), and Thomas (Didymus). All except John were martyred according to most legends (which may or may not be reliable). Millions of followers have claimed the title since. *See also* Andrew as apostle; apostle(s); James; John as apostle; Judas; liturgical year; martyr(s); Matthew as apostle; Matthias; Nathaniel; Peter as apostle; Philip; prophets as martyrs; shepherding (discipleship); Simon; Thomas as apostle.

Disciples of Christ: a post-Great Awakening denomination—called Campbellites at that time—formed by the efforts of Alexander Campbell and Barton W. Stone. They are an offshoot of the Christian Church from the same era. The Disciples favor open Communion, non-creedal faith, and religious freedom. In 1906 a branch split from the main denomination to become the Churches of Christ, and in 1969 the Christian Church/Church of Christ separated. *See also* Campbell, Alexander; Campbellites; Christian Church (denomination); church bodies in America (typed); Christian Church (denomination); Churches of Christ; Clarke, James Freeman; denomination(s), denominationalism; Garfield, James Abram; Great Awakenings, the; Restoration Movement in America; Smith, Gerald Lyman Kenneth; Stone, Barton W.; United Churches.

disciplina arcane: supposed secret religious truths that are purposefully withheld from non-believers and immature novices. *See also* deep secrets, so-called; deep things of God; esotericism; Gnosticism, Gnostics; mystery; mystery of God; mystery religion(s); secret wisdom.

Discordianism: a religious-philosophical brand of worship to the goddess of chaos, Discordia (or Eris). The cult is similar to Zen Buddhism and claims that order and disorder are illusions produced by the central nervous system. *See also* cult(s); idol(s); Olympian pantheon; pandemonium; parody religions.

disembodied state. See intermediate state.

disestablishmentarianism: any campaign or effort to abolish an established national church within a nation. The antithesis of that idea is antidisestablishmentarianism. Various laws and regulations have been established in attempts to promote disestablishment in free societies through the years. Included are the Cyrus Cylinder (539 B.C.), the Edict of Toleration (A.D. 311), Edict of Milan (313), Compact of Basel (1436), Edict of St. Germain (1562), Edict of Torda (1568), Warsaw Confederation confession (1573), Union of Utrecht (1579), Edict of Nantes (1598), Letter of Majesty in Bohemia (1609), Massachusetts Body of Liberties (1641), Puritan *Booke of General Lawes and Liberties* (1648), Maryland Edict of Toleration (1649), Edict of Toleration at Brandenburg (1664), Act of Toleration in Parliament of England (1689), Chinese Act of Toleration (1692), Toleration Act of Ernest Casimir in Budingen (1712), Tolerance Edict of Catherine II of Russia (1773), Portent of Toleration (1781) and Edict of Tolerance (for Jews in 1882) by Joseph II in the Holy Roman Empire, Edict of Elector Clemens Wenceslaus of Saxony (1784), Edict of Versailles (1787), Freedom of Religion (First Amendment to the United States Constitution in 1791), Edict of Friedrich Wilhelm III of Prussia (1812), Edict of Toleration in Hawaii (1839), Edict of Toleration for Jews to settle in the Holy Land (1844), Tolerance Edict of Frederich William IV of Prussia (1847), Edict of Toleration by Tsar Nicholas II of Russia (1905), and the Toleration Act of 1689 in England. The Fourteenth Amendment to the United States Constitution (the Equal Rights Amendment) was proposed as far back as 1923 but never ratified by the states. Other antidiscrimination laws other than freedom of religion have been enacted to guarantee human rights ranging in subject to ethnicity, acceptance, gender, disability, family status, education, occupation, housing, salary, age, civil rights, homelessness, bullying, voting rights, pregnancy, rehabilitation, hate crimes, etc. *See also* Abington School District vs. Schempp; Allegheny County vs. ACLU; antidisestablishmentarianism; *Book of the General Lawes and Libertyes;* caesaropapacy; civil religion; collegialism; Cyrus Cylinder; divine right of kings; Edict of Milan; Edict of Nantes; Edict of Toleration; Emerson vs. Board of Education; Establishment Clause and Free Exercise Clause; Geghan Bill; Government Regulation Index (GRI); "hate crimes"; Johnson Amendment; Lemon vs. Kurtzman; Massachusetts Body of Liberties; *Pontifex Maximus; princeps; principis;* public square; regalism; Shubert vs. Verner; social issues; state church; ultramontanism; Toleration Act of 1649; ultramontanism; Virginia's Religious Disestablishment law.

disfellowshiping: an ecclesiastical action (generally Protestant) that denies further participation by one of more of its body. The offenders are officially removed from the membership by vote, ostracism, or some other means if the congregation or religious group is convinced the offending member will defame or hinder its functions. The Roman Catholic synonym would be excommunication. *See also* Christianese; church abuse; church discipline; churching; defrocking; excommunication; in-fighting; shunning.

disobedience: refusal to obey commands, authorities, or laws, including those of God. The prophets and other teachers were commonly engaged in promoting obedience to the Law of God and to the certified civil authorities. The most pronounced prophet to disobey his calling was probably Jonah, who resisted God's direction to preach in Nineveh. His rebellion was to no avail, however, because the Holy Spirit does intercede with a recalcitrant disciple when the Father's call will not be denied. *See also* social issues.

dispensation(s): 1. a system of dispensational theology by which history is arbitrarily divided into segments according the moral and religious characteristics, which are said to be defined by the seven churches of Revelation in chapters 2 and 3. C.I. Scofield named the historical eras representing these seven as: innocence (Garden of Eden and faithful Adam), conscience (fallen Adam to Noah), human government (Noah to Abraham), promise (Abraham to Moses), law (Moses to Christ), grace (the church age from Christ's First Advent to his Second), and the kingdom age (the Millennium). In contemporary understanding (especially accepted among dispensational premillennialists) the seven eras are often approximated by Ephesus representing the Apostolic Age (A.D. 40–100); Smyrna as the Persecuted Era (100–313); Pergamum as the Compromising Age (313–630); Thyatira as the Impious Age (630–1328); Sardis as the Violent Age (1328–1648); Philadelphia as the Reformation Era (1648–1914); and Laodicea as the present age postulated to end at the time of the Second Coming of Christ. Such arbitrary divisions of history are not new. From the time of Daniel onward, visionaries attempted to reinterpret prophecy and to calculate the lengths of several passing eons. The author of *3 Enoch* divided human history into ten weeks. Seven of the dispensations are past. The eighth was to be an era of universal righteousness ruled by the saints. The ninth is to be a period of judgment. The tenth will see the former heaven and earth pass away and new ones appear and resurrection accomplished. Another scheme divided history into seven millennia corresponding to the creation week. 2. in canon law, granting permission to break a law, release one from a vow, or for other reasons in certain cases. The church may grant dispensations to relieve hardship or in peculiar circumstances as charitable and just. Roman Catholicism is the most active user of dispensations. *See also* Blackstone, William Eugene; church age theory, the; Darby, John Nelson; dispensation of the fullness of time(s);

dispensational premillennialism; dispensational theology; economy; *oikonomo;* Roman Catholic Church; Scofield, C.I.; seven churches of Asia Minor, the; "six-day theory, the"; six (or seven) ages of the world.

dispensation of the fullness of time(s): a phrase considered by most theologians to represent a period of time in which heaven and earth are governed by Jesus. The concept appears in Ephesians 1:10 with *times* (plural) and in Galatians 4:4 with *time* (singular). There are both major and minor differences among interpreters from Mormonism, Protestantism, Roman Catholicism, Jehovah's Witnesses, and other sects as to precisely what the expressions mean within the details. *See also* dispensation(s); Millennium, millennial.

dispensational premillennialism: the system of belief that asserts that the Millennium will begin at the return of Christ to earth as the King of kings. The theory is based on Revelation 20:1-6, but unlike the covenant or historical premillennialism, it refers frequently to relevant Old Testament Scripture to support or enhance the doctrine. Dispensational premillennialism differs chiefly from historic premillennialism in that the former ascribes to the pre-Tribulation rapture scenario whereas the latter does not. *See also* covenant (historical) premillennialism; dispensation(s); dispensational theology; *Late Great Planet Earth, The;* rapture.

dispensational theology: a system of segregating periods of history into religious or societal divisions, which are said to characterize the moral and spiritual atmosphere of each age. Typically, the seven churches of Revelation 2 and 3 are said to represent seven definite, if somewhat imprecise, periods of church history. The premise is commonly known as *dispensationalism* or the *church age theory.* The principles of dispensationalism were invented by the British-born John Nelson Darby and popularized in America by C.I. Scofield. The ideas gained popularity with the publication of *The Scofield Reference Bible* in 1909 and its subsequent editions. Scofield named the historical eras representing the seven Revelation churches as: innocence (Garden of Eden), conscience (Adam to Noah), human government (Noah to Abraham), law (Moses to Christ), grace (the church age from Christ's First Advent to his Second), and the kingdom age (the Millennium). In contemporary understanding (especially accepted among dispensational premillennialists) the seven eras are often approximated by Ephesus representing the Apostolic Age (A.D. 40–100); Smyrna as the Persecuted Era (100–313); Pergamum as the Compromising Age (313–630); Thyatira as the Impious Age (630–1328); Sardis as the Violent Age (1328–1648); Philadelphia as the Reformation Era (1648–1914); and Laodicea as the present age postulated to the time of the Second Coming of Christ. In any case, it is probable that any commendations or condemnations presented to one church are likely relevant to all the others. *See also* Apostolic Brethren; Blackstone, William Eugene; Chafer, Lewis Sperry; church age theory, the; church decline; Dallas Theological Seminary; Darby, John Nelson; dispensation(s); dispensational premillennialism; economy; Edwards, Morgan; history of the Church; Irving, Edward; Jurieu, Peter; MacDonald, Margaret; *oikonomo;* philo-Semitism; Scofield, C.I.; *Scofield Reference Bible,* The; seven churches of Asia Minor, the.

disputation: a method of debate common to learning practices of the Middle Ages. A topic for discussion was proposed, then argued or discussed until the idea was satisfactorily covered. When Martin Luther tacked his "Ninety-Five Theses" to the Whittenberg chapel door, he was following a natural custom of the times and calling for a debate with educational purposes. *See also* polemics; religious education.

dissention: disagreement, quarreling—an all too common faction between and within religious congregations and organizations. *See also* social issues.

dissipation: a waste of life in foolish or evil pleasure—a lack of moral restraint. *See also* after one's own lusts; body; carnal;

concupiscence; debauchery; demimondaines; depravity; flesh; hedonism; human condition, the; human nature, the; immorality; moral uncleanliness; orgies; sin(s); sinful nature, the; social issues; unclean; wicked, wickedness, worldly.

ditheism: sometimes dytheism, the belief that Christ had two wills, however one may define the will of the mind. *See also* dualism.

dittography: the unintended repetition of a letter, letters, word, or groups of words when copying a manuscript. *See also* accideme; alliteration; apostrophe; apothegm; assonance; autograph; Bible; Bible manuscripts; Bible translations; biblical criticism; chiasmus; conflict story; *constructio ad sensum;* context; contextualization; double sense fulfillment; doublets; doubling; edification; eisegesis; epanadiplosis; epigrammatic statements; etymology; exegesis; folio; form criticism; gattung; gloss; gnomic sayings; grammatical-historical interpretation; *hapax legomena;* haplography; hermeneutic(s); higher criticism; homographs; homonyms; homophones; *homoteleuton;* hyperbole; idiom; *inclusio;* interpolation; interpretation; inverted nun; irony; isagogics; *itture sopherim;* jot and tittle; kere; *kethib;* "L"; liberalist interpretation; literal interpretation; litotes; loan words; lower criticism; "M"; Masoretic Text; minuscule(s); mystery of God; omission; onomastica; onomatopoeia; palimpsest; papyrus; paradigm; parallelism; parchment; *paroimia; paronomasia;* pericope; personification; Peshita; pointing; point of view; polyglot; principles of interpretation; proof texting; pun(s); "Q"; redaction; revelation, theological; rhetorical criticism; rhetorical devices; riddle; satire; *scripto continua;* scriptorium; *sebirin;* simile; similitude; source criticism; sources, primary and secondary; special points; strophe; superscription; symbol(s); synecdoche; syntax; synthetic parallelism; text; textual criticism; *tiggune sopherim;* Time Texts; Torah; translation; transposition; trope; type(s); typology; uncial(s); vellum; verbicide.

Diurnal: a prayer book for the monastic Daily Office, excepting matins. Some call the guide a Monastic Breviary since it covers material for daytime devotions on a regular schedule. *See also* monasticism; prayer(s).

Divali: 1. an important Hindu holiday (official in some places) called the Festival of Lights. The occasion occurs in the autumn (in the northern hemisphere) and the spring (in the southern hemisphere) celebrating the victory of light over darkness, good over evil, knowledge over ignorance, and hope over despair. Millions of lights dot the cities, homes, and businesses. 2. the Jain religion recognizes a festival of the same name and celebrated in the same time frame. The Jain holiday notes the achievement of Nirvana for the last Mahavira Omniscient teacher). 3. the Hindu philosophy of enlightenment. *See also Dasa Laksana;* Hinduism; Jainism.

Dives: the legendary name of the rich fool in hell vilified in Jesus' parabolic story of the interaction between Father Abraham and the beggar Lazarus (Lk. 16:19–31). Actually, the name Dives is erroneous since the story does not name the rich man. The Latin adjective *dives* ("rich") was improperly translated as a noun in the Vulgate to the effect that the selfish man carried that name afterwards. *See also* Abraham's bosom; hell; Lazarus.

dividing (middle) wall of partition. See middle (dividing) wall of partition.

divination: the pseudoscience of attempted fortune-telling or the prediction of future events by mystical means, of which there are hundreds of methods. Divination practices include necromancy, astrology, haruspex, casting of lots, psychometry, hydromancy, lecanomancy, spiritism, occultism, tarot, palmistry, and innumerable other mantic-religious means. Such techniques were employed in the ancient world to aid in the proper framing of laws, founding of colonies, conduct of wars, futures of dynasties, healing of disease, processing legal affairs, and the like. The practitioners employed a host of shamans, diviners, visionaries, astrologers, tongues-speakers, exorcists, incantation priests, etc., to facilitate their designs. Their methods included the use of ecstatic visions, portents, auguries, auspices, astrology, the movement and sound of leaves in the trees or on the ground, the flow of water, glossolalia, omens, various bird habits (like the flight pattern, the chirping of wrens, the flight of crows, the croaking of ravens), casting lots, "spontaneous prose" (incantation or extemporaneous speaking), omen sticks (like *I Ching*), dreams, auras, fire and soot, appearance of the roots of trees, cloud formations, "palm knowledge" (covering a variety of hand manipulations and magic), aeromancy, food (its formation, consumption, appearance, or excrement), card reading, sounds, sand or dust patterns, belomancy, bibliomancy, wave action, smoke patterns, scrying, demonology, haruspicy, animal behavior or appearance, necromancy, pendulum action, pyramidology, runes and letters, crystallomancy, Ouija, tea leaves, charms and spells, and any number of magical antics as prolific as the human mind can produce them. All such operations are the opposite of the true prophetic purpose and forbidden to God's people. True faith and belief, with reference to biblical prophecy alone, are the acceptable modes for investigating the future plan of God. "The idols speak deceit, diviners see visions that lie; they tell dreams that are false, and they give comfort in vain" (Zech. 10:2). An exception was made in early Hebrew history when the casting of the Urim and Thummin was permitted if performed by the high priest of Israel and crucial to the safety of the nation. Despite its unscientific pedigree, the ancients were quite serious in its use and practicality. Cicero, the Roman historian, is quoted as saying: "I see no race of men, however polished or educated, however brutal and barbarous, which does not believe that warnings of future events are given and may be understood and announced by certain persons." New Agers also trust the practice if done properly. Even so, divination seemed never to have achieved the respect regularly enjoyed by other prophetic practices of the time, especially what was deemed to be the authentic transmission of pronouncements of a divine being. *See also* anthropomancy; anthroposophy; apotropaic magic; aretology; Ariosophy; astral plane; astral projection; astrolabe; astrology, astrologers; athame; audition; augury; automatic writing; bagua; belomancy; *besom;* bibliomancy; black arts; black mirror; blood moon(s); cartomancy; chiromancy; clairaudience; clairsentience; clairvoyance; cleromancy; cone of power; conjure; crop circles; cryptesthesia; crystallomancy; crystal skulls; divine; dream(s); dreams and visions; ecstasy; enchantment; enneagram; esoteric sects; evil eye; extrasensory perception (ESP); foreknowledge; foretelling; geomancy; grimoire; gris-gris; hepatoscopy; Hermetic wisdom; Hermetic writings; hex; hierscopy; horoscope(s); hydromancy; idol(s); idolatry; ifa; incantation; juju; labyrinth walk; lecanomancy; literomancy; locution; magic arts; magic, magick; magic square; magnetism; *mana;* mantic wisdom; mantra; miracles(s); monition; necromancy; New Age religion; numbers, symbology of; occult, occultic; omen; oneiromancy; oracle(s); otherworldly journeys; ouija board; out-of-body experiences (OBEs); pentagram; philosophers' stone; planchette; planets as gods; portent; precognition; prediction; premonition; prodigy; prognostication; prophecy, general; psi; psychic healing; psychic reading; psychometry; psychonautics; prognostication; prophecy; psychomancy; psychometry; pyramidology; remote viewing; retrocognition; revelation; rhabdomancy; scrying; séance; secret wisdom; sorcery, sorceries; spell; spell names; spiritism; superstition; tarot; telegnosis; telepathy; telesthesia; theurgy; third eye, the; thoughtform; totemism; vision quest; visions; visualization; voodoo; voudou; wanga; warlock(s); Web-Bot; witchcraft; wizard(s); *ya sang*; yoga; Zen; zodiac; *zos kia* cultus.

divine: 1. that which is holy and god-like. 2. an occasional name for a clergyperson. 3. to inquire for an answer or understand a mystery solution. *See also* abbot; agapetae; archbishop(s);

archimandrite; bishop(s); camerlengo; canon(s) of the church; cardinal(s); catholicos; chaplain(s); chorepiscope; clergy; curate; divination; ecclesiastic(s); episcopate; friar(s); hegymanos; holiness; holy; man of God; metropolitan; minister(s); monk(s); monsignor; pastor(s); patriarch(s); preacher(s); prefect(s); prelate(s); prior, prioress; prophesy; patriarchs; priest(s); starets.

***Divine Comedy,* the:** the masterpiece work of Alighieri Dante, the most noted Italian poet of the Middle Ages. The epic was originally called simply his *Commedia* (holding a more precise meaning of drama as opposed to absurdity or humor), but the appellation *Devina* was added by his biographer Boccaccio. Dante's classic is an allegory of the afterlife contained in three volumes: *The Inferno, The Purgatorio,* and *The Paradisio.* The work was published to immediate and enduring success, even before the author's death in 1321. Dante's allegorical visit to hell and related regions represent the "Noble Soul" of mankind suited for heaven but describes in gruesome detail the suffering of the damned and some estimate of the glory of the redeemed. Dante was certainly not shy about placing his enemies and friends in one or another of his states of eternal being. The Inferno is home to a number of Roman church leaders, notably popes Nicholas III, Boniface VIII, and Clement V. *See also* Alighieri, Dante; *Apocalypse of Paul;* Virgil.

divine council: a heavenly assembly of gods commonly believed to exist in the ancient East. In the Jewish version, Yahweh presides over such a gathering governing lesser divines as His emissaries (Ps. 82; Job 1–2; Zech. 3). Ancient alien theorists see the council as minor gods who "left their first estate" (Gen. 6) and "...were stripped of their immortality and died like mortal men" (Psalm 82). *See also* angel(s); council of God; council of heaven; council, the heavenly; court of heaven; Elohim; Heavenly Council; heavenly court; Nephilim; Watchers, the.

divine filiation: the Roman Catholic doctrine affirming the divine sonship of Christ. *See also* Roman Catholic Church.

Divine Imperative, the: the theological statement that God seeks worshippers. The will to recruit believers unto Himself is part of His nature and made possible by supplying the Holy Spirit to all who choose to follow Him and by providing the power of the Spirit or making him available to humanity. God's eagerness to save rests totally with divine determination and intent (1 Jn. 4:10). Stephen Vincent Benet called such a God "the Hound of Heaven." *The Divine Imperative* is also a book written by the Swiss theologian Emil Brunner. *See also* Barth, Karl; Bonhoeffer, Dietrich; Brunner, Emil Heinrich; Bultmann, Rudolf; categorical imperative, the; dialectic theology; didactic theology; neo-orthodoxy.

Divine Institutes, The: the most recognized work of the Christian apologist Lactantius, written between the years A.D 303–311. The treatise is anti-pagan in theme and upholds the reasonableness of Christianity. *See also* Lactantius.

Divine Light Mission: American organization of Guru Maharaj Ji (b. 1958). The cult leader was proclaimed a Messiah by his followers and was quite popular in the 1970s. The near-defunct group is now known as *Elan Vital*. *See also* cult(s).

Divine Liturgy: or Holy Liturgy, the formal worship of the Eastern Orthodox Church; similar to Mass in Roman Catholicism. *See also* Eastern Orthodox Church.

Divine Office. See canonical hours.

Divine Proportion, the: sometimes called "God's building block" or "the golden number," or some other similar descriptive phrase. The Greeks called it "the golden mean" as part of their philosophical understanding of the universe. The concept (stated as PHI) says all of creation and the solar system, including plants, animals, art, music, architecture, and even human beings are formed proportionally to which all of nature conforms. Just as pi (π) is the ratio of the circumference of a circle to its diameter, the PHI (ϕ) is the ratio of line sequences when they are divided geometrically into one larger and one smaller length. Always, the proportions of the main line and its segments, when multiplied by the mathematical formula, equal to the number 1.618. The Fibonacci sequences [a series of numbers in which the next number in line always name the sum of the two previous] (011235813, etc.)] also equals PHI because the ratio of each pair of successive numbers is 1.618. The Bible and theology are said to use the PHI as well. The ark of the covenant and Noah's ark, as examples, are proportionately 1.618 in their described dimensions. Even the mysterious number 666 in Revelation 13 is interpreted by some mathematicians as PHI in some esoteric form. For one illustration of the latter, if one calculates the sine of 666 degrees, the result is one-half of the true PHI or, the anti-PHI. *See also* apocalyptic calculation; 888; "fingerprint of God, the"; numbers, symbology of; Pythagorean Theorem; OMO DEI; 616; 666; theomatic number(s); 37.

divine right of kings: an ancient and ingrained belief or construct declaring that a national monarch is answerable to God alone and not to the people whom he governs. Opposition to the autocracy of such kings and emperors have usually resulted in bloody rebellions and convoluted political finesse over the centuries to gather more freedoms for the nation or individuals. *See also* disestablishmentarianism; caesaropapacy; civil religion; collegialism; disestablishmentarianism; Establishment Clause and Free Exercise Clause; "Glorious Revolution, the"; King; king(s); King, a; *lex rex* principle; Queen; queen(s); regalism; state church.

Diviner's Tree: the tenebinth venerated as the tree that spawned the children of the gods. Its shade provided a favored place for idol worship in ancient times. *See also* idol(s); idolatry; Levant pantheon.

Divine Science, Church of: a New Thought offshoot organized in the 1880s by Malinad Cramer and some helpers. *See also* cult(s); idolatry; mind science; New Thought Movement; Religious Science.

divine services: the official name for worship experiences in a military setting. The phrase applies no matter the time, location, or religious practice being observed. Divine services are conducted by trained and designated lay leaders, chaplains, or the cognizant commanding officer. In the Navy, at least, while divine services are in session is the only instance in which the church pennant may be flown above the national ensign. *See also* chaplain(s); liturgical year; liturgy, Christian; liturgy, Jewish; worship.

divinization. See theosis.

division of Israel: a prediction presented in Daniel 11:39, which foresees the betrayal of Israel by the "king who exalts himself." The threat forecasts that unwelcome rulers will be placed over the people and the land will be sold at a price. The implication is that such actions will be duplicated by the Antichrist and False Prophet during the Tribulation. In another sense entirely, the division of Israel can be described the tribal land assignments allotted by Joshua during the conquest of Canaan. At the time, all the allotted land was sporadically or incompletely subdued and the borders were prone to shift for various reasons. Even today, Israel is segregated with the existence of the West Bank and Gaza Strip. Yet another division is programmed for the Millennium as recorded in the book of Ezekiel. *See also* forest of the south; Galilee; Gilead; Idumea, Idumean(s); Israel; Judah; Judea; Kinneret; Palestine; provinces of Palestine; Samaria; Transjordan; tribes of Israel, the; West Bank.

divorce: the legal and personal dissolution of a marriage. In all civil cases, government legalities are involved with the granting and stipulations of divorces but church authority may also be involved when appropriate. In general, most religious traditions look with disfavor on the ending of a marriage but abide it in certain circumstances; some rules are more draconic than others but most permit the practice for abandonment, adultery, or fornication. Remarriage of divorced persons in the religious community is a related but separate problem with its own set of restrictions and allowances. *See also* adultery, adulteries; annulment; fornication; matrimony; social issues.

Dixon, Jeanne: celebrated psychic of the recent past (1904–1997). She announced that the Antichrist was born somewhere in the Middle East on February 5, 1962. If so, he would be almost 50 years of age around the turn of this decade. Dixon had predicted a planetary alignment on February 4 of that year, and the Antichrist would be born the following day. She also announced Armageddon in the year 2020, with the Second Coming between 2020 and 2037 following failed predictions from 1962. *See also* psychic(s).

docetism: a Gnostic-type belief expressed as the concept that Jesus "appeared" to have a body but really did not. The idea was an attempt to deal with the problem of how a righteous God could be so intimately involved with a sinful world and actually physically suffer for it in a fleshy body. The name comes from *dokein*, with a meaning of "to seem"—play-acting, much as a modern-day actor may portray the life of an earlier century as a museum docent or stand-in character.

Doctor Mirabilis: a 1964 publication by James Blish, a novel about the history of science which the author recognizes as the life story of Roger Bacon. It touches on the struggle of science against the established church. *See also* Bacon, Roger; philosophy of religion; Skeptic's Credo.

Doctors of the Church: a title afforded only the greatest church leaders and theologians of the early Roman Catholic and Easter Orthodox churches. There have been eight so named as a base list—five from the Roman Catholic persuasion and three from Greek Orthodoxy. The Latin scholars are counted as Ambrose of Milan, Augustine of Hippo, Jerome of Stridon, and Gregory the Great (Pope Gregory I). Eastern Orthodoxy claims John Chrysostom of Antioch and Constantinople, Basil the Great, and Gregory of Nazianzus. Who composed the list and how its authenticity is established is unknown. Various popes have added names over the years to stretch the list to its highest count. Protestantism recognizes great scholarship, of course, but generally refrains from arbitrary exalted titles except those earned academically or informally bestowed for practicality in the field. *See also* Ambrose; Augustine, Aurelius; Basil; Cappadocian fathers; Chrysostom, John; Eastern Orthodox Church; Gregory of Nazianzus; Gregory I, Pope; Jerome; Roman Catholic Church.

doctrine(s): the tenets of faith that one holds dear to the formulation of the individual's belief system. Or those elements of orthodoxy as may be promulgated by a church or other authoritative religious group. It is possible to hold to false dogma, as well as to espouse sound doctrine. False doctrine is strongly condemned in 1 Timothy 1:3 and elsewhere throughout the Scripture, so careful study and prayer should govern the seeker's road to faith formation. *See also* dogma, dogmatism; tenet.

Doctrine and Covenants: one of the three prominent books of the Church of Jesus Christ of Latter-Day Saints (the Mormons). The work sprang from Joseph Smith while he was still resident in Kirkland, Ohio, in 1835 and addresses key organizational and doctrinal standards for the body. The distinctions of the Melchizadek and Aaronic priesthoods are delineated, and the power structure of the church and its peculiar polity is explained. *See also* Book of Mormon; Church of Jesus Christ of Latter-Day Saints, the; Community of Christ (Mormon); Moroni; *Pearl of Great Price,* the; Smith, Joseph; Young, Brigham.

documentary hypothesis: a system of Pentateuch analysis invented by the German scholar Julius Wellhausen, also called the Graf-Wellhausen theory. "Form criticism" is another description of the formula or processes similar to it. According to the procedure, the first five books of the Bible are composed of "documents," each of which was set out by a separate author or redactor. Those designated J and E (Yahwist and Elohist) stand for divine names encountered before the eighth century B.C. The D (Deuternonomist) were there before 622 B.C. The P (Priestly) appeared after the Babylonian Exile in the sixth century B.C. These designations have been further refined by later theologians. Notwithstanding the debate as to the authenticity of the documentary hypothesis, there is little doubt that there have been additions to some of the Old Testament books, particularly the historical ones, inserted by later copyists or editors. Josephus did not mention these modifications, surely because they were not extant in his earlier copies of the texts, or were not recognized as such. *See also* biblical criticism; form criticism; lower criticism; Wellhausen, Julius.

dobbies: family spirits who, in exchange for milk and oat cakes, will provide protection and good luck to the household. One can, however, turn nasty if provoked or neglected. *See also* bugbears; household deities.

Doeg: an Edomite, Saul's chief shepherd. He was a spy at Nob and responsible for the massacre of the priests in the community there after they had aided the fleeing David and his men (1 Sam. 22:18–19). Allusion is made to Doeg and his ignominious act in Psalm 52. *See also* Abiathar; Ahimelech; Nob.

dog(s): a canine animal long considered a faithful companion and helper to man, but sometimes classed as a despised nuisance. In most instances, when the name is encountered in Scripture, it identifies the latter idea, but it can also pinpoint a man of extraordinary malfeasance—a despicable or evil person (*e.g.*, Ps. 22:16, 20). Sometimes the term describes a male shrine prostitute (Job 36:14). Revelation 22:15 names those among the outsiders from the Holy City as dogs. To be labeled a dog or a pig, or even a fool (Raca) was the gravest of insults. Jesus hinted, at least once (Mk. 7:24-30), that Gentiles like the Syrophoenician woman could be described that way in the common assumptions of the day among the Jews. See also adultery, adulteries; adulteress; animals, birds, and insects, symbology of; fornication; idolatry; prostitute, prostitution; Raca; Religious Babylon; sacred prostitution; Syrophoenician woman.

dogma, dogmatism: doctrine or those codified laws and creeds of belief that are usually presented as unchangeable. Dogmatism is the attitude or stance of an apologetic (defender of the faith) that is unyielding or not subject to change no matter what the facts of the discussion may dictate. Such a state of mind invariably stifles discussion, learning, and appreciation for theology. Even so, dogmatism is often, if inconsistently, considered to be a synonym for doctrine itself. *See also* doctrine(s); tenet.

Dogon Nommos: ancestral spirits or deities, hailing from the star Sirius B and worshiped by the Dogon tribe of Mali in West Africa. The word *nommos* derives from the Dogon word meaning "to make one drink" and the spirits are described as frog-like and said to resemble mermen and mermaids. They also appear in Babylonian, Accadian, and Sumerian myths. The Egyptian goddess Isis is sometimes depicted as a mermaid. *See also* attending spirits; dryad(s); mythological beasties, elementals, monsters, and spirit animals; nereid; reptilian theory; undine.

Dogrib: the Dene Aboriginal Canadian people of the Northwest Territories commonly called the "First Nation." Their tradition says there are three Dogrib prophets who claimed to have brought Christianity to the people via dances and trance-like states. *See also* dance.

Dome of the Rock: (*Qubbat al-Sakara*) the third most holy shrine of Islam said to be the site from which Mohammed ascended on horseback to heaven (a late assertion). The structure was commissioned by Caliph Abdal-Malik in A.D. 691 and is often mistakenly identified as the Mosque of Omar. That misunderstanding is a two-pronged error because the construction was not intended as a mosque and Omar (Umar) had nothing to do with its design. The construction, oddly enough, was mostly done by Christian architects and was erected as a monument to Mohammed's victory over Christianity. It was an intentional design by Abdal-Malik, who desired it to be the unrivaled building of the time, even meant to overshadow the famous *Hagia Sophia* Church in Constantinople. One of its unique features includes all the *Qur'an* sayings about Jesus written in Arabic calligraphy since reproductive art is forbidden by Islam. Central to this motif is Koran 4:171—Islam's warning to Christians: "people of the book: do not transgress the bounds of your religion. Speak nothing but the truth about God. The Messiah, Jesus the son of Mary, was no more than God's apostle and His Word which he cast to Mary as a spirit from Him. So believe in God and His apostles and do not say 'Three.' Forbear, and it shall be better for you. God is but one God. God forbid that He should bear a son! His is all that the heavens and the earth contain. God is the all-sufficient protector." The place was called the *Templum Domini* ("the Temple of the Lord") by the Knights Templar when their order controlled the Temple Mount. They made the Muslim shrine a Christian church. Reports circulate that the assassins of Thomas Becket were taken there to be buried by members of that fraternity. The completed domed structure, renowned for its exterior architecture and interior décor, has eschatological significance because it quite possibly occupies the plat of ground where the Jewish Temple of Jerusalem was built and is possibly to be rebuilt. Disturbance of the structure would surely engulf the Middle East, and probably the world, into dire consternation and warfare. *See also al-Aqsa* Mosque; Becket, Thomas; Dome of the Spirits; *Haram esh-Sheif;* Islam; Jerusalem, landmarks of; Mohammed; mosque; Noble Sanctuary, the.

Dome of the Spirits: also "Dome of the Tablets" or *Qubbat al-Arwah,* a small Arabic cupola set some 150 feet north of the Dome of the Rock. The structure is in direct line from the Eastern Gate toward the Western Wall on a flat foundation stone. Given its situation, it could become an object of great contention should the Jews decide to erect a third Temple in the same area. *See also al-Aqsa* Mosque; Dome of the Rock; Islam; Jerusalem, landmarks of; *Qubbat al Arwah.*

Dome of the Tablets. See Dome of the Spirits.

Dominguez, Francisco Atanasio. See de Escalante, Silvestre Velez and Dominguez and Francisco Atanasio.

Dominic: Roman Catholic churchman (1170–1221) who organized the order of monks called the Dominicans. Before his death, his order numbered sixty houses located almost everywhere in Europe. Dominic bore heavy responsibility for the Albigensian massacres. He is considered the patron saint of astronomers. *See also* astronomy, astronomers; Dominicans; Francis of Assai; friar(s); Roman Catholic Church.

Dominicans: the "Order of Preachers," a Roman Catholic monastic affiliation founded by Dominic of Seville for the purpose of winning back heretics to the church through preaching. Like the later Franciscans, the members were mendicants. Because of their emphasis on education and preaching, the Dominicans produced some of the greatest theologians and scholars of the Roman Church. A few of the most recognized include Albertus Magnus, Catherine of Siena, Girolamo Savonarola, and Thomas Aquinas. They also produced four popes. *See also* Albertus Magnus; Assumptionist Orders; Aquinas, Thomas; Augustinian Order; Barnabites; Benedict, Order of; Black Canons; canon(s) of the church; canons regular; Capuchin Order; Carmelites; Carthusians; Celestines; Cistercians; clergy; Dominic; Franciscans; friar(s); liturgical year; Minim; monasticism;

monk(s); orders; Paulist Fathers; Premonstratensian Order; priest(s); religious organizations; Roman Catholic Church; Savonarola, Girolamo; Servite Order; Spirituals of the Franciscan Order; Tetzel, Johann; Trappist Order.

dominions: those angelic beings described as situated in the so-called "middle" selections (dominions, Virtues, and powers) with a higher sect above and one below. They may be the same as authorities since there is no fully accepted standard formula for classifying angels. *See also* angel(s); archangel(s); authorities; Bene Elohim; Chashmallim; Chayoth; Cherub, Cherubim; *elohim;* Erelim; Galgallim; Hashmallim; Hayyot; Husk(s); Ishim; *mal'ak;* Ophanim; powers; principalities; Seraph, Seraphim; thrones; Virtues.

dominion theology: or New Apostolic Reformation, the belief that someday the world will be under the authority of Jesus Christ. He will have *dominion,* and Christianity will be the dominant religious expression. The idea is a form of postmillennialism but is more radical in that it makes the Church responsible for both private and public activism. To dominionists, obedience to God's law must be enforced within society now, often construed in some circles as strict adherence to the ancient Law of Moses. *See also* demotic millennialism; eschatology, eschatological; idealist eschatology; Manifest Sons of God; postmillennial, postmillennialism; Reconstructionism; Reformed Reformation Movement; replacement theology; seven mountains dogma; theology; theonomy; Whitby, Daniel.

domino effect: the principle that explains how one catastrophic event can cause another as episodes cascade one after the other. In prophecy, some view the domino effect as the method by which the world will end—in a series of calamitous occurrences, each catastrophe playing off the others.

Domitian: Roman emperor from A.D. 81–96, a severe persecutor of the Christians. Most conservative scholars agree that the book of Revelation was written during his reign. *See also* Christianity in the Roman Empire; king(s); Roman Empire.

domocide: literally, "death by government." Despotic rulers or regimes are commonplace in human history everywhere on the globe. Atrocities upon the innocent by those who rule them are among the most dreadful of all human actions as exemplified in modern history by Hitler, Saddam Hussein, Soviet Russia, and many others. Lenin and Stalin alone accounted for some six million deaths. Herod the Great should be numbered among those who practiced domocide when he attempted the slaughter of the innocents in an attempt to murder the Christ child, along with vast numbers of his own citizens and family. His actions to murder children were anticipated with prophetic prelude (Jer. 31:15; Mt. 2:18).

don: from "dominus," a Spanish title for a nobleman. Today the term has rested on the leader of an English university or college. It is also the unofficial name for the head of a crime syndicate or a verb for dressing with a hat or clothing. *See also* canon(s) of the church; ecclesiastic(s); dean; Mafia; provost.

Donation of Constantine: a document supposedly from the emperor Constantine in which he named the Roman papacy as the true descendant of Peter who was to act as "first pope," or at least, the "first among equals." The letter was put forward as having originated when Constantine moved the Roman capital to Constantinople in A.D. 330. The treatise helped the bishops of the West, starting with Pope Sylvester I, in their struggle for papal supremacy over the East and the other Sees. The article was an egregious forgery, but by the time the deception was proven, the effect was irreversible. Much later, Pope Julius II even commissioned the Vatican workshop of the painter Raphael to portray the donation on the Basilica of Old Saint Peter's to help him try to counter some of the effects of the Reformation. It was a futile effort because, by then, every competent scholar in Europe knew that the *Donation* was spurious. *See also* apostolic succession; Donation of Pippin; "Pseudo-Isidorian Decretals"; Roman Catholic Church.

"Donation of Pippin": a gift to the Roman Church from Pippin, king of the Franks and grandfather of Charlemagne, which aided Pope Stephen to wrest control of the papal states from the Lombards (A.D. 756). Pippin's armed and financial assistance secured the return of the Vatican unmolested, which was heavily inspired by the pope's assertion that the *Donation of Constantine* was legitimate. *See also Donation of Constantine;* Pippin III; "Pseudo-Isidorian Decretals"; Roman Catholic Church.

Donatism: the teaching of Donatus, bishop of Casae Nigrae and named a saint, which states that the sacraments of the Roman Catholic Church, particularly the mass and baptism, are not effectual to the recipient unless the minister or priest conducting them is truly worthy. As a group, the Donatists (fourth through fifth centuries) refused the legitimacy of church leaders who turned over copies of Christian Scriptures to be burned under the persecution of Diocletian. Anyone who did such a despicable act was labeled *traditor*—carrying the Latin meaning of "one who hands over" but from which we get our word "traitor." The Donatists supported baptismal regeneration and held some idea of the separation of church and state. The most dynamic Donatist leader was Tyconius (A.D. 370–390) who looked for the end of the world in 380. The sect was declared heretical by the pope in 1184, after which many fled to Holland, Germany, Bohemia, Spain, and Italy. *See also* Adoptionism; appropriation; Anomoeans; appropriation; Arianism; Arius; complementarian view of the Trinity; dualism; Dynamic Monarchianism; dynamism; eternal subordination of the Son; "four fences of Chalcedon"; *homoiousios; homoousios;* hypostatic union; incarnation; *kenosis;* kenotic view of Christ; modalism; Monarchianism; monophysitism; Nestorianism; *ousia;* patripassianism; Pelagianism; Pelagius; *perichoresis;* psilanthropism; Roman Catholic Church; sacerdotalism; Socianism, Socinians;

subordinationism; theanthroposophy; *Theophorus*; Trinity; two natures, doctrine of the; Tyconius; unipersonality.

"dones": modern slang for those members who have left the established church, sometimes in substantial numbers. While the reasons for their exodus may be personal and varied, polls indicate that the chief motivator may not have been burn out, doctrinal differences, personality clashes, or some other disenchantment, but disfavor with the "politics" of the fellowship. Politicizing the church polity and its function rather than administration via biblical principles usually leads to bitterness or disloyalty among the constituents. *See also* Christianese; "nones"; "no-shows"; NOTA; slurs, religious; "spiritual but not religious."

Doniphan, Alexander William: a Missouri lawyer and soldier (1808–1887). As a brigadier general in the Missouri militia, Doniphan was ordered to execute Joseph Smith during that state's objective to drive out the Mormons. He refused to comply with the directive and was vindicated when the warrant was withdrawn by cooler heads. Doniphan also led Missouri volunteers in the Mexican War, claiming victories in New Mexico and Mexico. He is credited with the longest march in army history—3600 miles in seven months.

donkey: a small but sturdy beast of burden when domesticated. In the wild, an ass is a prophetic example of strength, rebellion, lack of discipline, or feral behavior (as in Hosea 8:9). By contrast, a tame donkey could be a sign of humility, as exemplified by Jesus when he rode one of the species into Jerusalem at his Triumphal Entry (Zech. 9:9; Lk. 19:28–44). The animal owned by the warlock Balaam actually spoke the Word of God to him (Num. 22:21–33). Such livestock of commerce were valuable as a means of transport and labor. *See also* animals, birds, and insects, symbology of; ass; donkey walk; flocks and herds; horse; mule.

donkey walk: the Russian Orthodox ceremony practiced at Epiphany when the patriarch of the church rides a donkey in procession led by the tsar; or when the tsar rides and the prelate leads. The ritual is one of the two main observances of the faith each year. *See also* donkey; liturgical year; Russian Orthodoxy.

Donnelly, Ignatius: author, land speculator, and political reformer (1831–1901). Donnelly was first a Republican in the House of Representatives (1862), then Greenback candidate for vice president, then organizer and vice presidential candidate of the Populist party (1892). He may be classed as a sort of "secular prophet" in that his books (*Atlantis: the Antediluvian World*—(1882), *The Great Cryptogram*—(1888), and *Caesar's Column*—(1891)) were seminal in their content. The first claimed civilization grew from the mythical Atlantis, the second tried to prove that the plays of William Shakespeare were actually written by Francis Bacon, and the third predicted such marvels and the dirigible and television. *See also* Atlantis; Bacon, Sir Francis.

doom: 1. to make certain some action planned or experienced will fail. 2. fate, condemnation, ruin. *See also* destiny; fatalism; fate.

doomsday: the anticipated calamitous end to the universe caused by some cataclysmic event uncontrolled by human intelligence or technology. In the minds of many, doomsday is the same as Armageddon, but they are distinct events. Context determines doomsday as to whether it is devastation with human involvement or God's destruction of the old order to make possible the new. *See also* apocalyptic, apocalypticism; Doomsday Clock, the; doomsday cult(s); eschatology, eschatological.

Doomsday Book: despite its rather formidable title, the document was an ambitious accounting of all property, produce, and land seizures in England and parts of Wales in the year 1086 A.D. The record was ordered by William the Conqueror as an aid to distributing the wealth of the defeated Anglo-Saxons to his own nobility. The evidence was known then as "the Great Survey." Some 13,000 towns and villages were assessed in meticulous detail. Perhaps the apocalyptic title derived from the idea that, like the eschatological judgment of the ages, the contents of the bookkeeping could not be altered.

Doomsday Clock, the: a timepiece model instituted and maintained by the board of directors of the *Bulletin of the Atomic Scientists* at the University of Chicago. The clock has been in existence since 1947 when the world was made aware of its great risk for nuclear disaster. It is intended to show (according to the judgments of the scientists) how close the world is to annihilation, midnight being zero hour. Settings have varied over the years,—some closer and others more optimistic. On January 17, 2007, it showed two minutes till midnight. The Cuban missile crisis of 1962 was perhaps the closest the world has ever come to nuclear disaster, but that crisis was resolved before the clock could be officially changed. Today, the worldwide dangers cover environmental and other threats besides nuclear weapons. When the clock strikes twelve, life on earth will be over, virtually speaking; World War III. *See also* apocalyptic, apocalypticism; apocalyptic calculation; apocalyptic fervor; doomsday; Google Translate message.

doomsday cult(s): any fringe religious group that stresses end-of-the-world doctrines, often with a minimum display of hope but plenty of gloom, despair, and faulty theology. Such associations are obsessed with apocalyptic and millennialist theory that is unsustainable from the biblical record. Inevitably, their beliefs lead to catastrophe and terror as they try to precipitate Armageddon, or preach it to a fever pitch of fear-mongering. *See also* apocalyptic, apocalypticism; cult(s); doomsday; doomsday fervor; sect(s).

door(s) of Revelation: mention of a number of doorways, each with its own eschatological purpose, in the book of Revelation. The church at Philadelphia is promised an open door that none can shut as an assurance that the perseverance and opportunities open to that congregation would continue (Rev. 3:8). The church at Laodicea is told that Christ is knocking on the door to their church, yearning to enter for fellowship (Rev. 3:19). A door to heaven is seen standing open from which a voice invites the writer John to enter "in the Spirit" to view the throne room of God and to learn of future events (Rev. 4:1). Another open door is implied when the heavenly voice invites the two faithful witnesses to "Come up here" (Rev. 11:12). Matthew 24:33 warns that the time of Christ's appearing is near, even at the doors. *See also* "Come up here"; eschatology, eschatological.

doors of evangelism: a rather diverse and intriguing metaphor for three types of Christian discipleship as they relate to church participation and dedication. The references turn on the analogy of the front door, the side door, and the back door of a church. Front door Christians are steady and regular in both attendance at worship and conscientious in their devotion and works—they enter gladly through the front door. Side door Christians prefer more "outside" activities away from the sanctuary such as home Bible studies, alternate mission activities, parties, fellowship get-togethers, and the like—they are more contented entering the side door. Back door Christians are those trending to slowly or quickly lapse in their dedication, fading into inactivity, or slipping away from the mainstream purpose of the Christian life—they are headed out the back door. *See also* backsliding; Christianese; evangelist(s), evangelism; lapsed; slurs, religious.

Dorcas. See Tabitha.

Dormition of the Theotokos: the Eastern Orthodox recognition of the death, burial, resurrection, and ascension of Mary, the mother of Jesus. The worship center of the celebration may be the Greek island of Tenos which holds the shrine of Mary to which miraculous cures of attributed. *See also* Assumption of Mary; Church of the Holy Sepulcher; Eastern Orthodox Church; feasts and special days of high liturgical faiths; liturgical year; liturgy, Christian; Marianist; Mariolatry; *Theotokos*.

Dositheos the Samaritan: (Dositheus), a first-century Samaritan impostor claiming to be the lawgiver promised by Moses. He was named as a co-founder of the religion known as Mandaeanism because he knew John the Baptist (who was revered by the Mandaeans) and was said to be a teacher of Simon Magus. He was said to have also had association with the Essenes and contributed to the doctrines of the Gnostics. *See also* Gnosticism, Gnostic(s); Mandaeanism; Samaritan(s); Simon Magus.

dot within a circle: an occultic ideogram, closely associated with Rosicrucianism and Freemasonry that can represent the all-seeing eye or the light of knowledge. It was supposedly the seal of the Egyptian city of Heliopolis and the alchemist symbol for gold. It can also represent the scientific rendition of the solar system. *See also* alchemy; Freemasonry; idolatry; occult, occultism; Order of the Rosy Cross.

Douay-Rheims Bible: the foundational translation of the Bible specifically for the Roman Catholic Church (started in 1582). The rendition rendered the Bible from Latin to English with the Vulgate as almost its only source. The intent was to refute the doctrines of the Reformation Protestants and was intended to be a defense of Catholic theology. The "Douay" name promotes the Old Testament; "Rheims" is primarily the New Testament translation in those French cities. *See also* Bible translations; Roman Catholic Church.

double bind: a mental or psychological dilemma upon hearing two "truths" from a single teacher for which no appropriate answer can be formed. In modern terms, a double bind can be expressed as a "heads I win; tails you lose" situation. There is no logical escape from one. The expression can also be expressed as a cognitive dissonance that fits many practices of dangerous cults for it is impossible to reconcile two totally incompatible beliefs or attitudes at the same time.

double-edged sword: Revelation's description of Christ both at the beginning of the book (Rev. 1:16) and at the end (Rev. 19:15) as having such a weapon protruding from his mouth. The sword brings to mind Christ's truthfulness when speaking, and more vividly, his ability to punish evildoers via his sharp and pointed language delivered in absolute veracity. Since the design is two-edged, it is an offensive weapon capable of slashing on the forward motion and gashing on the return swing. Psalm 149:6–7 is a succinct expression of the sword symbolism: "May the praise of God be in their mouths and a double-edged sword in their hands, to inflict vengeance on the nations and punishment on the peoples..." *See also* sword.

double-minded: the mental process of some who are changeable, uncertain, unstable, or insincere of belief. Such thinking was condemned by Christian apologists (Jas. 1:8).

double portion: a multiplying of anything by two. In prophecy, the phrase is almost always associated with Elisha, who desired a "double portion" of the spirit of Elijah, his mentor. Some have noted there were eight miracles performed by Elijah before his rapture, but only fifteen for Elisha before his death—one short of the double. The final manifestation then occurred when the dead man was revived after touching the bones of Elisha (2 Ki. 13:20–21). To covet a "double portion" of the Spirit is considered to be a grave and heavily responsible obligation. *See also* Elisha; Elisha's miracles.

double predestination: a specific understanding of a single doctrine of Calvinism stating that God has deliberately chosen some to be saved but others to condemnation. The effect is the same in the end for both instances but the doctrine as stated leaves no choice in the matter of salvation for the individual. *See also* BACON; Calvinism; conditional election; election; eternal security; fall from grace; Five-Point Calvinism; free will; grace; "once saved, always saved"; perseverance of the saints; predestination; total depravity; TULIP; Westminster Confession.

double reference, prophecy of. See double sense fulfillment.

double sense fulfillment: a prophecy which may have more than one fulfillment. One stage of completion may be present in one era only to be repeated or supplemented in another. An example of this phenomenon can be seen in Daniel's prophecy concerning the one who would defile the Temple of God (the abomination of desolation event). The first fulfillment was satisfied with the actions of Antiochus Epiphanes, but the desecrating act also carried a more remote eventuality in the actions of the Antichrist. To cite a second illustration, the prophecy of Hosea 11:1 is a clear reference to the Israelite Exodus from Egypt: "When Israel was a child, I loved him, and out of Egypt I called my son." Matthew (Mt. 2:15), however, uses the same prophecy (or part of it) to reference Jesus as the personal Messiah by comparing the holy family's return from Egypt to escape the evil intentions of Herod the Great. Most Jews, and others, claim that the verse is taken out of context and expanded to a place it should not be. To the Gospel writers and most evangelists, however, it makes perfect sense to use the theme as New Testament prophecy fulfilled, for God is not constrained in His projection of the prophetic values. In yet another context, the calling could even refer to the appeal to a sinner to repentance. The literary device is also known as double fulfillment, multiple sense prophecy, repeated fulfillment, or progressive fulfillment. *See also* antitype; lower criticism; multiple sense prophecy; prophecy types; repeated fulfillment; single sense fulfillment.

double sense interpretation. See allegorism.

doublets: sayings having the same meaning but expressed in different ways. Many of the Psalms are so constructed. *See also* doubling.

doubling: the practice of repeating verses or exposition in the Scriptural structure either for clarity or emphasis (*i.e.*,

Exodus 16:8 and 16:12). The practice can be shadowed in the poetic structure of some of the Psalms. *See also* accideme; acrostic poem; alliteration; antithetic parallelism; apostrophe; apothegm; assonance; autograph; Bible; Bible manuscripts; Bible translations; biblical criticism; chiasmus; climatic parallelism; colon; conflict story; *constructio ad sensum;* context; contextualization; dittography; double sense fulfillment; doublets; edification; eisegesis; epanadiplosis; epigrammatic statements; etymology; exegesis; folio; form criticism; gattung; gloss; gnomic sayings; grammatical-historical interpretation; *hapax legomena;* haplography; hermeneutic(s); higher criticism; homographs; homonyms; homophones; *homoteleuton;* hyperbole; idiom; *inclusio;* interpolation; interpretation; inverted nun; irony; isagogics; *itture sopherim;* jot and tittle; kere; *kethib;* "L"; liberalist interpretation; literal interpretation; litotes; lower criticism; "M"; Masoretic Text; minuscule(s); mystery of God; omission; onomastica; onomatopoeia; palimpsest; papyrus; paradigm; parallelism; parchment; *paroimia; paronomasia;* pericope; personification; Peshita; poetry (biblical); pointing; point of view; polyglot; principles of interpretation; proof texting; pun(s); "Q"; redaction; revelation, theological; rhetorical criticism; rhetorical devices; riddle; satire; *scripto continua;* scriptorium; *sebirin;* simile; similitude; source criticism; sources, primary and secondary; special points; strophe; superscription; symbol(s); synecdoche; syntax; synthetic parallelism; text; textual criticism; *tiggune sopherim;* Time Texts; Torah; translation; transposition; trope; type(s); typology; uncial(s); vellum; verbicide.

doubting Thomas: religious slang for one, including those who are believers, who is continuously skeptical about his or her spiritual condition or the reliability of faith matters. The phrase springs from the experience of the apostle Thomas (Jn. 20: 24–29) who openly expressed his disbelief in the resurrection of Jesus for a time. In fact, many who heard or saw the story of the resurrection were doubtful or uncertain of its authenticity until it was demonstrated to them. Jesus blessed those who saw and believed but expressed even greater grace on those who did not see and yet believe. *See also* Christianese; slurs, religious; Thomas as apostle.

dove: a bird of the Columbidae family prominate in biblical reference. For most practical purposes, a dove and a pigeon are the same though the former is usually considered to be somewhat smaller. The dove has long been a prophetic symbol of innocence, naiveté, or someone who is senseless or silly. It has held a place in symbol for gentleness, love, purity, peace, and religious expression in both ancient and modern poetry and legend for ages. Mated doves are known to coo lovingly at each other for hours. The bleeding-heart dove, for example, has a greenish-blue back but a breast of bright red. It is said that when Christ hung on the cross, this dove flew from the heavens and gently brushed against the spear wound in his side. Christ's blood stained its body, and from then, every dove of the species carries a few blood-red feathers. The dove is also a recognized symbol of the Holy Spirit (*e.g.*, John 1:32) and a modern-day widespread sign for peace, often depicted with a sprig of olive in its beak. Less frequently, the dove is a symbol for Israel where some translations call it a turtle (Ps. 74:19; S of S). Doves were the often recognized as the familiars of the Sibyl priestesses and known to impart prophetic utterances with their persistent cooing. Both dove and pigeon were considered acceptable sacrifices for the poor, including the family of Jesus. The context and intent of the writer largely determine the meaning of the word. Dove's dung (called "seed pods" in some translations) was sold at inflated prices during the siege of Samaria and necessarily eaten to stave off starvation (2 Ki. 6:25); the same was true during the capture of Jerusalem in A.D. 70. The name for Jonah the prophet means "dove." *See also* angel(s); animals, birds, and insects, symbology of; bird; columbine; mythical beasties, elementals, monsters, and spirit animals; names (titles) for the Holy Spirit; Sibyl(s); symbology of; pigeon.

Dowie, John Alexander: founder of a theocratic commune at Zion City, near Chicago, in the late 19th century called the Christian Catholic Apostolic Church, or "Zionites." Dowie was a Congregationalist preacher from Australia (though born in Scotland) and called himself "Elijah the Restorer." Later, he was the "First Apostle," evidently an increase in status within the community membership. The group practiced immersion baptism, abstinence from pork, and obligatory tithing. They were millennial in outlook and continually set dates for the return of Christ. The experiment began its collapse with a scandal involving moral and financial irregularities. Dowie claimed to be the forerunner to Christ's Second Coming and practiced faith healing. He was an eloquent and persuasive leader prone to wear full Hebrew-priest-type regalia but his financial scams kept him in and out of legal troubles. At one point, the false *Mahdi* Mirza Ghulam Ahmad challenged Dowie to a prayer war to prove who was truly the chosen of God. The loser was to be proven his false claims by dying first. Dowie died in 1907 and Ahmad in 1908. Dowie was succeeded by his son-in-law William Glenn Voliva (who predicted the end of the age for September of 1935) but the community never prospered thereafter. *See also* Ahmad, Mirza Ghulam; Christian Catholic Apostolic Church; communal communities; Congregationalists; cult(s).

Dow, Lorenzo: itinerate preacher (1777–1834) who journeyed as far as the Gulf Coast from New England and to Ireland overseas on his mission to promote his brand of Protestantism. Dow was generally described as ill-tempered, eccentric, and quarrelsome and was even sued for libel by the Methodists at one point. He traveled from Connecticut to Alabama and Mississippi, then to the Emerald Isle in a desperate attempt to convert that staunchly Roman Catholic island to Protestantism. Dow ended his days out of favor and selling a "snake oil" product he had invented. *See also* missions, missionaries; Presbyterians; revivalism; "souper."

Downgraders: certain theologians and clergy who wavered in their theology of Jesus during the 1880s concerning the miracles of Jesus. They instead began to concentrate on the Lord's teaching and morality so as not having to deal, seemingly, with a more difficult theological issue of the supernatural.

Dowry of the Dead. See *Book of the Dead*.

Doxology, doxology: a short praise hymn, a number of which are found in Revelation. Perhaps the most familiar doxology is a popular one attributed to Bishop Thomas Ken from *Morning and Evening Prayers*, Stanza ten: "Praise God from whom all blessings flow! Praise Him, all creatures here below! Praise Him above, ye heavenly hosts! Praise Father, Son, and Holy Ghost!" The composition is actually the final stanza of Ken's hymn entitled "Awake, My Soul, and with the Sun." Romans 11:33–36 is another New Testament example of a doxology, one that was perhaps a worship article of the early church. Revelation is replete with doxology type praises. *See also Gloria Patri*; Ken, Thomas; liturgical year; liturgy, Christian; music; Greater Doxology; *Old 100*; praise.

Doyle, Arthur Conan: renowned Scottish physician and author (1859–1920) who produced the Sherlock Holmes stories while living in London. Doyle held a long-standing interest in mystical matters and was a member of the Society for Psychical Research, a Freemason, and a dedicated spiritualist. What is not so well recognized is that he predicted earth catastrophes of all sorts. His most astonishing prognostication is that a land mass (Atlantis?) would arise from the sea causing a devastating tsunami. The destruction of earth, however, will not be total according to his interpretation. *See also* spiritualism.

Draco: the Dragon, or great serpent constellation of the sky. In Egyptian religion, the giant serpent Apepi pursued the sun-god Re in his regular crossing in the sky. Thuban, at that time the northern-most star in the snake's tail, prompted the Egyptian builders to position the Great Pyramid in the north side of so it could be seen. Precession has since caused it to change location. In Orphic tradition, the world emerged from a snake-entwined egg when the creator god Phanes appeared. One ancient belief saw Draco spinning around the celestial North Pole with the head locked in place and the body and tail flailing about in centrifugal force, spreading his evil or creative matter onto the world. So, the snake is quite frequently a creation entity. In other cultures, Draco is the Laden that guarded the golden apples of the Hesperides and killed by Hercules as one of his labors; Hercules's constellation lies nearby. The Greco-Roman people said that the Dragon was slain by Minerva and tossed into the sky in its convoluted and twisted form. He had been one of the Titans who battled the Olympians for ten years. Other tales have him as the demon son of Gaia, Typhon. Almost all cultures of the world hold some variation of the man/woman/snake/tree image similar to the Genesis account of creation and other ancient beliefs. The snake may be good, evil, or neutral, depending on the variety of doctrine. Christianity shows the snake (dragon) as decidedly evil and representing the devil. Jesus warned us to be wise as serpents and innocent of doves (Mt. 10:16). *See also* dragon; Egyptian pantheon; Gaia (Gaea); idol(s); Minerva; mythological beasties, elementals, monsters, and spirit animals; Olympian pantheon; Orphic religion; ouroboros; Re (Ra); reptilian theory; serpent; Titans; Tryphon.

dragon: a mythical creature often used to portray evil, violence, or sometimes, cleverness. Revelation 12 is the best example wherein Satan is pictured as a fierce and destructive red dragon or overgrown serpent on steroids. Some other passages may also denote the enraged dragon in the person of Antichrist when he has assumed much of Satan's power and authority. Ezekiel's prophecy against Egypt mentions a "great monster" (Ezk. 29:3) or "great dragon" (King James Version) that is destined to be stilled by Yahweh. *See also* accuser of our brothers; angel of light; animals, birds, and insects, symbology of; anointed cherub; Apophis; Baalzebub; Baphomet; Beelzeboul; *Bel and the Dragon;* Belial; Behemoth; Cupay; Day Star, Draco; Evil One, the; father of lies; Ghede; goat; god of this age, the; guardian Cherub; Hahgwehdaetgah; Hydra; Iblis; idol(s); *Kategor;* kingdom of the air; kingdom of this world; king of Babylon, king of Tyre; Leviathan; Light-Bringer; lion; Lucifer; Mastema; Morning Star, the; mythological beasties, elementals, monsters, and spirit animals; ouroboros; prince and power of the air; prince of demons; prince of this world; Python, python; Rahab; red dragon; reptilian theory; ruler of the kingdom of the air; Sanat Kumar; Satan; seed of the serpent; serpent; Shaytan; son of the morning, son of the dawn; tail of the dragon; woman clothed in (with) the sun, the.

Dragonnades: a major factor in the persecution of the Huguenots of France. Roman Catholic authorities billeted the rowdy army called Dragonnades in private homes much to the consternation of the owners. The soldiers were an aid to harassment and were used to hasten the emigration of the dissenters. *See also* Huguenots; Inquisition, the; religious organizations; Roman Catholic Church.

drama. See music.

dramatic atonement. See victor motif.

Draper, John Williams: world-renowned physician, scientist, historian, philosopher, chemist, and educator (1811–1882). Draper was a multifaceted genius in all areas of his expertise and internationally reputed in each of them, the subject of religion being no exception. He wrote *History of the Conflict between Religion and Science* in 1874. The book is a strong attack on mysticism and revelation as sources of knowledge. *See also* clergy scientists; mysticism, mystics; revelation, theological; Wesleyan Church.

"drawing down the moon": the Wiccan process of occult action within the witches' magic circle. The spells produced there by the participants are believed to tap into the energy of the gods and goddesses much like some sort of cosmic battery. Many covens use the basic text of Wicca, the *Book of Shadows,* for ritual guidance in order to manipulate the elements. *See also Book of Shadows;* coven(s); elemental(s); esbat; idolatry; Sabbat; thoughtform; Walpurgis Night; Wicca; witch(es); witchcraft.

dream(s): the occasional drama of the mind in repose. In the realm of prophecy, the dream is a mental action in which the seer is instructed or motivated by God through nocturnal revelations. The experience is differentiated from a vision in that the dreamer is sleeping whereas a vision is available to the seer in a more or less conscious state. The most expansive exposition of dreams and visions in an eschatological sense is undoubtedly Joel 2:28. Even Peter used part of this prophecy in his Pentecost sermon (Acts 1:17–21). The ancients believed that the dream of the incumbent closest to dawn was more likely to be prophetic but dreams of any sort were usually taken quite seriously. In ancient Babylon, for example, dreams (like omens) were actively solicited by the religious and political leaders. They could be induced, it was believed, either spontaneously or by ritual. There was even a manual of instruction, dating from about 450 B.C., to explain how this was to be accomplished. Messages would arrive from the underworld via a Wind Messenger, perhaps with help from a Dream Ladder, to the client who was waiting, stupefied with incense, on a rooftop. The message would then have to be interpreted which required a whole new class of specialists. Their conviction was phrased in Latin as *in somnis veritas* – "in dreams there is truth." *See also* audition; beatific vision; crushing rock that became a mountain; Daniel's dream of the kingdom beasts; Daniel's interpretation of Nebuchadnezzar's tree dream; dreams and visions; ecstasy; flight into Egypt; foretelling; Gabriel; generational prophecy; Jacob's ladder; locution; mantic wisdom; Morpheus; omen; oneiromancy; Oniropompi; oracle(s); portent; prophecy; revealer of mysteries; revelation, theological; sleep; stratified man, dream of the; succubus; vision(s).

"Dream of the Rood, The": one of earliest extant Christian poems in English literature. The verses describe the pending crucifixion of Christ from the perspective of the tree that is to supply the material for the deed. The wood is horrified that it will be used for such an ignoble death of the innocent, leaving to Christ the necessity of explaining that such a sacrifice will lead to redemption, and therefore is honorable. *See also* cross; crucifix; crucifixion; Holy Rood; rood.

dreams and visions: two miraculous methods (that some call oneiromancy) by which God sometimes imparts His message to the prophets or other servants. When discussed, the pair of words is usually addressed together even though there are technical differences between the two functions. The prophet Joel promises that such activity will characterize the day of the Lord: "And afterward, I will pour out my Spirit on all people. Your sons and daughters will prophesy, and your old men will dream dreams, your young men will see visions" (Joel 2:28). Biblical characters who experienced dream revelations in some context include Jacob, Solomon, Joseph (both Joseph the son of Jacob in Egypt and the husband of Mary), and the Magi. Those experiencing visions include Jacob, David, Isaiah, Daniel, Ezekiel, Ananias, Cornelius, Peter, Paul, and John. Some dreams and visions can, of course, be classed as false and even satanic. Scripture warns the faithful to test those spirits and scrutinize the deceptive prophet: "I have heard what the prophets say who prophesy lies in my name. They say, 'I had a dream! I had a dream!'

How long will this continue in the hearts of these lying prophets, who prophesy the delusions of their own minds? They think the dreams they tell one another will make my people forget my name, just as their fathers forgot my name through Baal worship" (Jer. 23:25–27). Any dream or vision that promotes false teachings, evil premonitions, or night terrors and nightmares is condemned and subject to the restrictions of Deuteronomy 18:10: "Let there not be found among you him who observes dreams [omens]." Discernment and wisdom are necessary to distinguish between true prophecy and that which is false. *See also* audition; beatific vision; discerning the spirits; dream(s); ecstasy; foretelling; generational prophecy; locution; mantic wisdom; multivalent language; omen; oneiromancy; oracle(s); portent; prophecy; vision(s).

Dresden Codex: the *Codex Dresdensis*, perhaps the most intriguing document known to have survived from the ancient Mayan culture. The original text is located today in Dresden, Germany. Two more records are to be found in museums in Madrid and Paris. The *Codex* mainly recounts natural phenomenon that were critical to Mesoamerican agricultural pursuits. The last chapter, however, seems to reveal the famous Mayan doomsday predictions for the year 2012. Most experts agree that our present age will disappear according to the very last prophecy of the last page due to dramatic and rather sudden weather change. *See also* Aztecs; Chilam-Balam; eagle and the condor, the; Inca; Itza-Maya; Katun Prophecies; Maya; Mesoamerica; *Popul Unh;* 2012 prophecy, advocates of; 2012, prophecy of; Toltecs.

drive-by evangelism: a type or style of persuasive evangelism on the personal level in an attempt to quickly and dramatically solicit persuasion to an acceptance of faith in Christ. The idea is to "save" or "convert" or "witness to" the listener with a "hard-sell" message that is often intimidating and awkward. More often than not, the presentation produces resentment or shallow commitment rather than a true and loving influence to the faith. *See also* Christianese; evangelist(s), evangelism; slurs, religious.

dross: the useless char or stubborn deposit (slag) after some metal has been smelted or persistent scraps left in the pot after cooking. Ezekiel 22:17–22 and 24:6 describe the house of Israel and Jerusalem as dross that cannot be removed after melting silver, lead, copper, or tin, thus leaving a residue that is useful for nothing and coincidentally ruining the container. *See also* offscourings.

drought: the prolonged lack of sufficient rainfall and dew causing agricultural hardship and famine. The prophet Elijah was adept at withholding rain as are the two super witnesses in Revelation 11. Drought was a frequent chastisement from God, and perhaps still is, on certain occasions.

Druid's egg. See serpent's egg.

Druidism: an ancient priestly paganism associated with Celtic culture in Gaul, Great Britain, and Ireland prominent during the second century and beyond. Druid practices are eerily similar to those of ancient Egypt; some even say identical. Druid beliefs centered in nature with elements of animism. The groups were accused of practicing human sacrifice, but the sources for that idea may be unproven. Legend says they burned their victims in a large "wicker man" edifice, "the burning man." The Druid priesthood was more than a religion as they were the supreme judges, administrators, and community authority among the people who were knowledgeable in nature study, philosophy, and jurisprudence and were highly respected everywhere. Henry Rowlands even claimed they were descended from Noah! Prominence was certainly not limited to men as women were also numerous and powerful; it is said Saint Patrick prayed that God would protect him from the Druidesses. The name for Ireland, Eire, is chosen from the triune goddesses Eire, Banba, and Fotla, the latter pair frequently mentioned in poetry and saga. The societal position of the Druids has been compared to the Brahmins of India and the Pythagoreans of Greece. Druid influence was powerful because they were educated, disciplined, and powerful, firmly fixed in the social caste as intellectuals (the middle class consisting of Bards, Vates, and Druids). The Druid chieftain was an ollamh. Members were exempt from military service and never paid taxes. Unfortunately, they were forbidden from recording their vast learning, probably because of religious taboo and for fear their philosophy would be weakened by records instead of reliance on the severe discipline required for necessary memorization by their aspirants to the sect. They reputedly revered various aspects of the outdoors, particularly the mystic elements of the oak and probably the mistletoe that grew on them. A drink made from the mistletoe was believed to promote fecundity to any barren animal and could overcome all poisons. Climbing the oaks to retrieve mistletoe was a religious ritual, followed by sacrificing a pair of white bulls. Most were skilled in hypnotism and could concoct a "drink of oblivion" to induce forgetfulness. Physician types were adept in the use of "healing stones,", surgery (including the brain), therapeutic baths, and medicinal herbs. Firewalking was also practiced as well as elaborate baptismal demonstrations. Shape-changing was not uncommon. They were specialists in haruspicy and many other forms of augury and incantation. The hazel, yew, and rowan trees were also important, all of which can be considered phallic symbols. The birch and aspen were suitable for making sacred objects like wands and grave paraphernalia. High Druids were considered "the wise ones of the oaks" and filled with "oak knowledge." They carried bardic wands or small tree branches with little silver bells as tokens of their office. Rare was the Druid who could not perform amazing feats of natural transformation or diplomatic skills. Even walking between two opposing armies could halt a battle. For the Druids, the power of life and the afterlife involved the magical or philosophical notion of Truth. To them, it was synonymous with the godhead and they viewed the concept as divine reason much as the Hindus acknowledged *satyakriya,* the Christians understood the *logos,* or the Greeks cherished their philosophy of the *sophia.* Druidism was severely repressed by the Romans who have left us virtually the only information we have of the sect (much of it probably prejudiced) and the Christians virtually finished them off. Remarkably, the victories of Christian missionaries over the Druids are represented in native literature as basically a magical one because many Druids converted to Christianity. There are present-day imitations of their religion, however. Druidism holds a number of sacred days, but the principal ones are Beltane on May 1 to celebrate the arrival of summer and Samhain on November 1 to acknowledge winter. The persecutions of Romans and Christianity have given way to a revived romanticism concerning Druidism in our time. In 1781 English Druidist enthusiasts established an Ancient Order of Druids, organized along the lines of Freemasonry. Even none other than Winston Churchill was initiated into the Albion Lodge of the Ancient Order of Druids in 1908. The accepted sacred writings of the sect include the *Mabinogion* and *Lebor Gabala Erenn* (the "Book of Invasions"). By 1819 an "Eisteddfod" had been founded as a major institution with an annual convention held every August in Wales. Vincenzo Bellini (1801 – 1835) wrote his opera *Norma* on a Celtic theme followed by Angelo Catelani in 1841 with another opera, *Carattaco.* A dedicated Druid magazine launched in 1830 and Stonehenge still draws an annual assembly of white-robed participants. New Age religion was quick to ride the coattails of modern Druidism with an array of colorful ideas and credos. One of the most notable witches of all time, Sybyl Leek, capitalized on the subject matter for many of her books. Even "New Age Christianity," promoted by the Toronto-based astrologer Alexander Blain-Ewart, has seized on the theme. To some degree, the Druids have become the unofficial poster child for the environmental movement preaching harmony with nature, fighting to protect endangered species of animal and plant life, and promoting the environment. *See also* Beltane; bogle; Burning Man Festival; Celtic folklore and religion; Christmas tree; Cicero, Marcus Tullius; cosmic tree; crane bag; Easter; filidh; Hallowmas; Halloween; idolatry; Imbolc; Lammas; Leek, Sybil; Ludhnasadh; memeton; Merlin; oak; Ogham; phallic worship; Presbyterians; Samhain; sect(s); serpent's egg; Sidhe; stone circles; Stonehenge; tonsure; Yule.

Drusilla: the Jewess wife of the Roman governor Felix. She abandoned her first marriage to take Felix, a Gentile idolater, so she and her husband must have suffered some anguish under the prophetic preaching of Paul (Acts 24:24–25). Drusilla was the youngest daughter of Herod Agrippa I. She and Felix had a son named Agrippa who was killed in the eruption of Mount Vesuvius. *See also* Felix of Rome; Herod Agrippa I.

Druze: a monotheistic religion and society located mostly in Syria, Israel, Lebanon, and Jordan. They call themselves *ahi al-Tawhid*, a name that actually means "people of monotheism" or "people of unity." The practice itself includes elements of Judaism, Gnosticism, Neoplatonism, Pythagoreanism, and other philosophies, but the central thrust stresses the role of the mind and truthfulness. The religion began with a Persian named Muhammad bin Ismail Nashtahin ad-Darzi whom followers believed to be God incarnate. The accepted sacred text is the *Epistles of Wisdom*. *See also* Alawis; Islam; Ismailis; Quarmatians; sect(s); Syria.

dryad(s): or hamadryad—a nymph similar to the water sprites but which live in trees, mostly oaks. *See also* attending spirit(s); banshee; bogle; brownies; bugbears; clurichauns; daemons; deceiving spirits; demons, demonic; devils; disa; Dogon Nommos; dryad(s); elemental(s); fairy, fairies; Furies; ghost(s); ghoul; gnome(s); Green Man, the; Gregori; hobgoblins; homunculus; household deities; huldafolk; idol(s); Lares; leprechaun(s); Loa Loas; Menes; mythological beasties, elementals, monsters, and spirit animals; nereid; nisse; nymph(s); nyx; oak; Oniropompi; Orisha; Oya; Olympian pantheon; para; paredri; penates; Robin Goodfellow; satyr; Seelie Court, Unseelie Court; selkie; Sidhe; sirens; spiritual warfare; sprite(s); sylph(s); teraphim; territorial spirits; Trickster; Tuatha de Danann; tutelary; undine; wight(s).

dry bones, valley of. See Ezekiel's vision of the valley of dry bones.

dry ground, the: a common name for the earth in pseudepigraphal writing.

dual covenant theology: 1. the idea that Jews do not need to accept Jesus Christ as Messiah in order to be justified. The nature of New Testament salvation and their own Torah customs will suffice for justification. 2. both the Old and New Testaments are valid for the Christian church today; the Old has not been abrogated or superseded by the New. *See also* covenant theology.

dual hermeneutics: a system of interpretation by which nonprophetic Scripture is understood literally but prophetic Scripture is interpreted nonliterally. It was a frequent device of Augustine but is not recognized by most conservative scholars as a legitimate expository technique. *See also* biblical criticism.

dualism: or ditheism and dichotomism, the theological concept where there are two independent divine beings or eternal principles, one of which is evil and the other good. Mankind can exhibit both of these contingencies, which inevitably cause internal struggle and social stress of the faith process. Dualism is a main feature of Zoroastrianism, from which some of Jewish and Christian doctrine has been developed. It is not, however, a cardinal belief of either of those faith expressions. *See also* Adoptionism; appropriation;

Anomoeans; appropriation; Arianism; Arius; Cerdo; complementarian view of the Trinity; Donatism; Dynamic Monarchianism; dynamism; eternal subordination of the Son; "four fences of Chalcedon"; *homoiousios; homoousios;* hypostatic union; incarnation; *kenosis;* kenotic view of Christ; modalism; Monarchianism; monophysitism; Mandaeanism; Manicheanism; Mithraism; Nestorianism; *ousia;* patripassianism; Pelagianism; Pelagius; *perichoresis;* psilanthropism; sacerdotalism; Socianism, Socinians; subordinationism; theanthroposophy; *Theophorus*; Trinity; two natures, doctrine of the; unipersonality; Zoroaster, Zoroastrianism.

Duat: according to ancient Egyptian lore, the seven mansions or palace which served as the dwelling-place of the gods. Or, the place could denote the underworld for that early culture. The locale was guarded by the *arrit*, the seven massive doors that allowed access. *See also* Abraham's bosom; afterlife; Amente; Annwn; Aralu; Arcadia; Asgard; Avalon; Dis; Egyptian pantheon; Elysium; eschatology, eschatological; eternal life; future life, doctrine of the; Gehenna; Hades; happy hunting ground; heaven; hell; Hy-Breasail; Hyperborea; intermediate state; Jade Empire, the; Jahannam; Janna; lake of fire; life after death; limbo; *Limbus Puerorum;* Mictlan; new heaven and new earth; Nirvana; Otherworld; Paradise; paradise of God; Pardes; Perdition; Promised Land, the; Pure Land, the; purgatory; Shambhala legends; *Sheol;* soul sleep; space doctrine; Summerland; Thule, land of; Tir na nOg; underworld; Upper Gehenna; Utopia; Valhalla; world to come, the; Xibala.

Dubbi'el: a demon. Legend names him as the prince of Persia (Dan. 10:13). *See also* Abaddon; Abezi-Thibod; Adramelech; Anammelech; Apollyon; Apophis; Asmodaeus; Azazel; Azrael; Baal-zebub; Beelzeboul; Beelzebub; demon(s), demonic; devils; Dibbuk; Gadreel; idol(s); Legion; Lilith;

Mastema; Pazuzu; prince of Persia; Sammael; Sceva; slave girl of Philippi; Sumerian and Babylonian pantheon; Syrophoenician woman; woman of Canaan.

due time, in: a hint from Peter that God will intervene to judge and reward the populations of the earth. The time will be of God's choosing when it is time to do so (1 Pe. 5:6) and will be at no other time. *See also* apocalyptic, apocalypticism; apocalyptic calculation; apocalyptic time; appointed time, the; end time; *en takhei;* eschatology, eschatological; "forcing the time"; *kairos*; TEOTWAWKI; time; time is near, the; time of fulfillment; times and the seasons, the.

Dukhobors: an agrarian commune for Russian pacifists. They were called the "spirit fighters" and existed primarily as a resistance to state interference with religious practice. Worship was simple, consisting of an altar with symbolic bread, salt, and a water jar. *See also* communal communities; sect(s).

Dumah: or Duma, a symbolic name for Edom. The term means "silence" or "stillness" and is likely a play on words for the Edomites which suggesting a coming calamity upon that nation that will subject her to desolation (Isa. 21:11–12). Even in English, the term sounds like a pun for "dumb." *See also* Edom.

dumb. See mute.

Dungeons and Dragons: a once-popular fantasy role-playing competition in which users assume an imaginary but realistic role character to enact realistic mystical adventures. The game reputedly calls for the assumption of demonic names, spells, and the like which can deeply affect the mind. Some parents have reported suicide and suicidal tendency by their children when heavily involved in the play. Popularity for the game seems to be lowering with the latest generation who prefer dabbling in such cults as Hare Krishna, Scientology, "the Moonies," and others of the stripe. *See also* cult(s); fantasy role-playing games.

Dunkards: officially, the Church of the Brethren (of which they are an offshoot), commonly called "Dunkers." The name evolved from their unique method of baptism in which the administrator immerses the candidate three times face-first (once for each name in the Trinity). The Dunkards are of German background but settled in Germantown, Pennsylvania, on land donated by William Penn. Germantown is now incorporated into Philadelphia. The Dunkards strive to live peacefully and simply, bolstered by their rejection of military service, oaths, legal contracts, alcohol and tobacco, frivolous amusements, and the like. They also religiously practice foot-washing and Communion. *See also* church bodies in America (typed); Church of the Brethren; denomination(s), denominationalism; Inner Light Churches; Pennsylvania Dutch; sect(s).

dulia: and *hyperdulia,* a Latin term used sometimes by Catholic theologians when discussing the worship or adoration of saints and angels (*doulia* in Greek). The practice is considered an inferior veneration of saints and angels as compared with the worship of God *(latria)*. For Protestants, the word simply applies in its true meaning as a reference to slavery. *See also* angelotry; hyten; *latria;* Mariolatry; Roman Catholic Church; slave, slavery; veneration of the saints.

Dunster, Henry: English Cambridge-educated scholar (1609–ca. 1659) who was immediately installed as the first president of Harvard, which was not then a recognized academic college, when he arrived in America. The institution excelled under his leadership for which he received no stipend, except small taxes he was obligated to collect himself. Dunster was forced to resign in 1654 when he began to show signs of Baptist principles in his beliefs; he then moved from Cambridge to Scituate, Massachusetts where he pastored until his death. *See also* Baptists; Bray, Thomas; Glover, Jose; Mather, Increase.

duotheist. See bitheist.

du Puy, Raymond: (Raimond Dupuy) second and most active grand master of the warrior knights known as the Knights of Saint John (the Hospitallers). *See also* knighted orders; Roman Catholic Church.

Dura: the Babylonian plain on which Nebuchadnezzar erected his giant statue and demanded its worship. Daniel's three friends, Shadrach, Meshach, and Abednego, defied the order and were cast into the fiery furnace, only to be miraculously rescued.

Durer, Albrecht: an accomplished artist (A.D. 1471–1528) particularly noted for his apocalyptic images. Perhaps his most celebrated works are a series of fifteen eschatological wood engravings, which include the remarkable yet disturbing *Four Horsemen of the Apocalypse* and *Saint Michael and the Dragon*. The former is contained in the British Museum and the latter in the *Bibliotheque Nationale* in Paris. This pair of engravings is approximately 15×11 inches, and both are frequently used to illustrate prophecy books and articles even today. He was most likely the illustrator for Sebastian Brant's popular satirical poem at the time entitled *The Ship of Fools*. Durer was a devout Roman Catholic but a great admirer of Martin Luther. *See also* art, religious; Roman Catholic Church.

Dussehera: the Hindu annual celebration of the victory of Lord Rama (representing good) over the demons (representing evil). *See also* Hinduism.

dust: the fine grains of dirt composing the land's surface or a name for the soil itself. Figuratively, dust can symbolize: 1. despair or anguish (Ps. 119:25). The ancients were prone to throw dust into the air or on their heads as an act of frustration or mourning, often accompanied by tearing of their clothing. The same action could also indicate a gesture of abandonment, contempt, or hatred (Acts 22:23). Jesus instructed his disciples to "shake the dust off of your feet" (Mt. 10:14) when departing from a city that refused their message; 2. a metaphor sometimes paired with ashes (*i.e.*, "dust and ashes"), which can represent humility (as in Genesis 18:27) or sorrow and repentance (as in Joshua 7:6); 3. a large number of people or things (Ps. 78:27); 4. something very small and unimportant (Ps. 18:42); 5. the product from which man was created (Gen. 2:7) and the material to which we will return (Gen. 3:19; Eccl. 12:7); 6. a circumstance denoting a humble position to which one is brought down (Ps. 44:25) or a degrading position from which one is brought up (1 Ki. 15:2); 7. the grave (Job 20:11) or *Sheol*; 8. anything worthless (Zeph. 1:17); 9. a situation seen as hopeless or something completely destroyed (2 Ki. 13:7), expressed as "brought to dust;" 10. humiliation (Isa. 49:23); 11. defeat (Job 10:9). *See also* "ashes to ashes"; sand; stars; sackcloth and ashes.

duty faith: the teaching or doctrine, somewhat universal in its bearing, that everyone everywhere has an obligation (duty) to believe the gospel. *See also* warrant of faith.

"dwelling of God is among men, the." See "tabernacle (dwelling) of God is among men, the."

dweomer: or dwimmer, a type of ancient magic including sorcery, spell-casting, trickery, and the like. The term is particularly relevant to the Norse primitives and Celtic practices. *See also* Celtic folklore and religion; enchantment; ensorcell; magic, magick; magnetism; New Age religion; sorcery, sorceries; spell; spell names; thoughtform.

Dwight, Timothy: erudite American theologian (1752–1817) with a distinguished career in writing and education. Dwight was ready for college at age eight but entered Yale at thirteen. As an adult, he pastored at the Congregationalist church at Greenfield Hill in Connecticut and was finally named president of Yale University. His grandfather was none other than Jonathan Edwards. Dwight's famous epic poem (authored 1785) is some 10,000 lines long, entitled *Conquest of Canaan*. The work compares America's Revolutionary

War to the Israelite conquest of Canaan. Unfortunately, he succumbed to date-setting by predicting the end of the age in the year 1999 but remained an active revivalist supporter. *See also* clergy patriots; Congregationalists; Great Awakenings, the; revivalism.

dyarchy: those representatives of the priestly office and that of royalty, who are considered to be of equal rank. Something like a dyarchy is outlined for Israel in the revelations to Joshua and Zerubbabel in Zechariah 4–7.

Dyer, Mary: a Quaker martyr in early colonial America (?–1660). Dyer felt compelled to proclaim acceptance for the Quakers in the American colonies. She concentrated her efforts in the Puritan stronghold of Massachusetts. After being expelled twice with a warning, she was hanged by the theocratic authorities. Dyer was a friend, supporter, and fellow fugitive with Anne Hutchinson. See also Hutchinson, Anne; martyr(s); Society of Friends.

dynamic equivalence: a theory of Bible translation proposed by the linguist Eugene Nida (1914 – 2011) that emphasizes the emotional reaction of the reader more than the literal language being studied. If a word or phrase in the observer's native language appears strange or imprecise to the interpreter, it is best to find an equivalent dynamic idea to explain it. Much as the word "heart," for example, is commonly used to describe a person's full range of life, emotions, ideas, and essence, the new Bible word can likewise take on meaning for the reader in a more personal sense. Dynamic equivalence is a way of turning ambiguities into subjective reality and is entirely foreign to proven biblical interpretative methods. The sensibilities of culture and internal "feeling" of the reader are more important than the true meaning of the passage. *See also* allegorical interpretation; analogical interpretation; Bible translations; eisegesis; exegesis; biblical criticism; form criticism; grammatical-historical interpretation; hermeneutic(s); interpolation; interpretation; liberalist interpretation; literal interpretation; lower criticism; principles of interpretation; textual criticism; translation.

Dynamic Monarchianism: a doctrine that purports to preserve the unity of God by putting Christ outside the Godhead no matter what attributes are ascribed or removed from the Son. Christ was "clothed" with power (*dynamis*) at his baptism event and became the Messiah. The Monarchianism view later became more commonly known as Adoptionism. *See also* Adoptionism; appropriation; Anomoeans; Arianism; Arius; complementarian view of the Trinity; Donatism; dualism; dynamism; eternal subordination of the Son; "four fences of Chalcedon"; *homoiousios; homoousios;* hypostatic union; incarnation; *kenosis;* kenotic view of Christ; modalism; Monarchianism; monophysitism; Nestorianism; *ousia;* patripassianism; Pelagianism; Pelagius; *perichoresis;* psilanthropism; Sabellianism; Socianism, Socinians; subordinationism; theanthroposophy; *Theophorus*; Trinity; two natures, doctrine of the; unipersonality.

dynamism: the term used to identify Jesus' effectiveness in his earthly ministry. By God's power he was endowed with the spirit and energy to heal, teach, debate, and raise the dead. The beginning of his dynamism is usually considered to be his baptism and its physical end at the crucifixion. *See also* Adoptionism; appropriation; Anomoeans; Arianism; Arius; complementarian view of the Trinity; Donatism; dualism; Dynamic Monarchianism; dyophysitism; eternal subordination of the Son; "four fences of Chalcedon"; *homoiousios; homoousios;* hypostatic union; incarnation; *kenosis;* kenotic view of Christ; modalism; Monarchianism; monophysitism; Nestorianism; *ousia;* patripassianism; Pelagianism; Pelagius; *perichoresis;* psilanthropism; Sabellianism; Socianism, Socinians; subordinationism; theanthroposophy; *Theophorus*; Trinity; two natures, doctrine of the; unipersonality.

dyophysitism: a theological word used to name the doctrine that Christ had a dual nature within his being. The word arose from the Greek meaning "two natures." Sometimes the term is used to name the Nestorians. *Dyoenergism,* a related term, refers to "two energies," the doctrine that teaches the existence of dual dynamics in the person of Jesus—one human and the other divine. *See also* Adoptionism; appropriation; Anomoeans; Arianism; Arius; complementarian view of the Trinity; Donatism; dualism; Dynamic Monarchianism; eternal subordination of the Son; "four fences of Chalcedon"; *homoiousios; homoousios;* hypostatic union; incarnation; *kenosis;* kenotic view of Christ; miaphysitism; modalism; Monarchianism; monophysitism; Nestorianism; *ousia;* patripassianism; Pelagianism; Pelagius; *perichoresis;* psilanthropism; Sabellianism; Socianism, Socinians; subordinationism; theanthroposophy; *Theophorus;* Trinity; two natures, doctrine of the; unipersonality.

dystheism: the belief that God exists but that He is not wholly good and possibly evil (misotheism). *See also* eutheism; misotheism, misotheist.

dystelelogical theory: an argument for the non-existence, or at least, an uncaring or no-good God because there is evil and cruelty in the world. If God is all-powerful and loving, why does He allow such a state of affairs? The position is opposite the teleological presupposition which presents positive thinking for God's governance. *See also* teleology.

Dystopia: an imaginary community or condition where everything is as bad as it can get—a condition brought on by anarchy, human misery, squalor, oppression, disease, and overcrowding. Some have phrased the situation as "hell on earth" and the polar opposite of *Utopia*. A modern fascination with the dystopian theme is surely present in our society, extant in art, literature, film, and the fixation of many of the younger generation on such themes as zombie apocalypse, alien invasion, and vampire and werewolf fears, all of which has been absorbed into the modern psyche. *See also* apocalyptic themed books and movies; hell; Utopia.

BIBLIOGRAPHY

Abanes, Richard. *End-Time Visions: The Doomsday Obsession.* Nashville, TN: Broadman & Holman Publishers, 1998.

Ackroyd, P.R., A.R.C. Leaney, A.R.C., and J. W. Packer, eds. Cambridge, UK: The University Press, 1972–1974. *The Cambridge Bible Commentary on the New English Bible: The Book of Daniel*; Author: Raymond Hammer; Date: 1976; *The Cambridge Bible Commentary on the New English Bible: Ecclesiasticus*; Author: John G. Snaith Date: 1974; *The Cambridge Bible Commentary on the New English Bible: The First and Second Books of Esdras*; Author: Richard J. Coggins and M. A. Knibb Date: 1979; *The Cambridge Bible Commentary on the New English Bible: The Shorter Books of the Apocrypha;* Editor: J.C. Dancy Date: 1972; *The Cambridge Bible Commentary on the New English Bible: The Wisdom of Solomon*; Author: Ernest G. Clarke Date: 1974; *The Cambridge Bible Commentary on the New English Bible: The Book of the Prophet Ezekiel;* Author: Keith Carley Date: 1974.

Alcorn, Randy. *Heaven.* Wheaton, IL: Tyndale House Publishers, 2004.

Ali, A. Yusuf, ed. *The Holy Qur'an.* Brentwood, MD: Amana Corp., 1983.

Alighieri, Dante. *The Divine Comedy.* New York, NY: Modern Library, 1950.

Anderson, Robert A. *Signs and Wonders: A Commentary on the Book of Daniel.* Grand Rapids, MI: William B. Eerdmans Publishing Co., 1984.

_____. *The Coming Prince.* 10th ed. Grand Rapids, MI: Kregel Publications, 1977.

Ankerberg, John and Jimmy DeYoung. *Israel Under Fire: The Prophetic Chain of Events that Threatens the Middle East.* Eugene, OR: Harvest House Publishers, 2009.

Apel, Willi. *Harvard Dictionary of Music*. 14th printing. Cambridge, MA: Harvard University Press, 1962.

Archer, Gleason L., Paul D. Feinberg, Douglas J. Moo, and Richard R. Reiter. *The Rapture: Pre-, Mid-, or Post-Tribulational?* Grand Rapids, MI: Zondervan Corporation, 1984.

Armstrong, Hart. *Christ's Twofold Prophecy—The Olivet Discourse: A Topical Study of Our Lord's Great Prophetic Utterance on the Mount of Olives*. Wichita, KS: Christian Communications, Inc., 1993.

Armstrong, Karen. *A History of God: The 4,000 Year Quest of Judaism, Christianity, and Islam*. 12th printing. New York, NY: Alfred A. Knopf, Inc., 1993.

Ashley, Leonard R. N. *The Complete Book of Devils and Demons*. New York, NY: Skyhorse Publishing, 2011.

Ausubel, Nathan, ed. *A Treasury of Jewish Folklore*. New York, NY: Bantam Books, Inc., 1980.

Baker, Robert A. *A Summary of Christian History*. Nashville, TN: Broadman Press, 1959.

Ballard, H. Wayne and B. Donald Keyser. *From Jerusalem to Gaza: An Old Testament Theology*. Macon, GA: Smyth & Helwys Publishing, Inc., 2002.

Bamberger, Bernaul J. *Fallen Angels: Soldiers of Satan's Realm*. The Jewish Publication Society, Philadelphia, PA: 1952.

Barret, David V. *A Brief History of Secret Societies*. Philadelphia, PA: Running Press, 2007.

Blackstone, William E. *Jesus is Coming: God's Hope for a Restless World*. Grand Rapids, MI: Kregel Classics, 1989.

Blenkinsopp, Joseph. *A History of Prophecy in Israel*. Philadelphia, PA: The Westminster Press, 1983.

Benware, Paul N. *The Believer's Payday*. Chattanooga, TN: AMG Publishers, 2002.

_____. *Understanding End time Prophecy: A Comprehensive Approach*. Chicago, IL: Moody Publishers, 1995.

Beasley-Murray, George R. *Jesus and the Last Days: The Interpretation of the Olivet Discourse.* Vancouver, BC: Regent College Publishing, 1993.

Biltz, Mark. *Blood Moons: Decoding the Imminent Heavenly Signs.* Washington, D.C.: WND Books, 2014.

Blau, Joseph L. *Men and Movements in American Philosophy.* Englewood, NJ: Printice-Hall, Inc., 1966.

Braden, Charles Samuel. *These Also Believe.* New York, NY: The Macmillan Company, 1963.

Braswell, George W. Jr. *Islam: Its Prophet, Peoples, Politics, and Power.* Nashville, TN: Broadman and Holman Publishers, 1996.

Bright, Bill and John N. Damoose. *Red Sky in the Morning: How You Can Help Prevent America's Gathering Storms.* Orlando, FL: NewLife Publications, 1998.

Brown, William. *The Tabernacle: Its Priests and Its Services.* Peabody, MA: Hendrickson Publishers, Inc., 1996.

Bruce, F. F. *The Books and the Parchments: How We Got Our English Bible.* Westwood, NJ: Fleming H. Revell Company, 1963.

_____. Revised by David R. Payne. *Israel and the Nations: The History of Israel from the Exodus to the Fall of the Second Temple.* Downers Grove, IL: InterVarsity Press, 1997.

Bullinger, E. W. *The Witness of the Stars.* Grand Rapids, MI: Kregel Publications, 2003. Reprint of the 1894 edition.

Bush, George. *The Valley of Vision; or The Dry Bones of Israel Revived: An Attempted Proof (From Ezekiel, Chapter 37:1-14) of the Restoration and Conversion of the Jews.* New York, NY: Saxton and Miles, 1844.

Byfield, Ted, ed. *The Veil is Torn A.D. 30 to 79, Pentecost to the Destruction of Jerusalem.* Canada: National Library of Canada Cataloguing in Publication Data, 2003.

Cahn, Jonathan. *The Harbinger: The Ancient Mystery That Holds the Secret of America's Future.* Lake Mary, FL: Frontline, 2011.

———. *The Harbinger Companion with Study Guide.* Lake Mary, FL: Frontline, 2013.

Calaway, Bernie L. *Discernment from Daniel.* Baltimore, MD: PublishAmerica, Inc., 2002.

———. *Oracles from Olivet: The Eschatological Jesus.* Baltimore, MD: PublishAmerica, Inc., 2008.

———. *Revealing the Revelation: A Guide to the Literature of the Apocalypse.* Bethesda, MD: International Scholars Publication (Rowman & Littlefield Publishing Group), 1998.

———. *Revelation for Regular Readers.* Baltimore, MD: PublishAmerica, Inc., 2004.

Calaway, Bernie L. and Jan Ledford. *Operation Revelation: A Teen's Script to Earth's Final Curtain.* Baltimore, MD: PublishAmerica, Inc., 2006.

Capps, Benjamin. *Time-Life Books: The Old West—The Indians.* New York, NY: Time-Life Books, 1973.

Carson, D. A. *The God Who is There: Finding Your Place in God's Story.* Grand Rapids, MI: Baker Books, 2010.

Carter, Stephen L. *The Culture of Disbelief: How American Law and Politics Trivialize Religious Devotion.* New York, NY: Basic Books, 1993.

Charles, R. H., ed. *The Apocrypha and Pseudepigrapha of the Old Testament.* 2 vols. Oxford: Clarendon Press, 1979.

Charlesworth, James H., ed. *The Old Testament Pseudepigrapha.* 2 vols. Garden City, NY: Doubleday & Company, Inc., 1985.

Chitwood, Arlen L. *Mysteries of the Kingdom.* Norman, OK: The Lamp Broadcast, Inc., 2011.

Chouinard, Patrick. *Forgotten Worlds: From Atlantis to the X-Woman of Siberia and the Hobbits of Flores.* Rochester, VT: Bear & Company, 2012.

_____. *Lost Race of the Giants: the Mystery of their Culture, Influences, and Decline throughout the World.* Rochester, VT: Bear and Company, 2013.

Clouse, Robert G., Robert N. Hosack, and Richard V. Pierard. *The New Millennium Manual: A Once and Future Guide.* Grand Rapids, MI: Baker Books, 1999.

_____, ed. *The Meaning of the Millennium: Four Views.* Downers Grove, IL: InterVarsity Press, 1977.

Coleman, Robert. *Songs of Heaven.* Old Tappan, NJ: Fleming H. Revell Co., 1980.

Connelly, Douglas. *The Book of Revelation Made Clear: A User-Friendly Look at the Bible's Most Complicated Book* (formerly *The Book of Revelation for Blockheads).* Grand Rapids, MI: Zondervan, 2007.

Cornfield, Gaalyah and Daniel Noel Freedman. *Archeology of the Bible: The First Thousand Years.* New York, NY: Harper and Row Publishers, Inc., 1976.

Cook, Edward M. *Solving the Mysteries of the Dead Sea Scrolls: New Light on the Bible.* Grand Rapids, MI: Zondervan Publishing House, 1994.

Couch, Mel, ed. *Dictionary of Premillennial Theology.* Grand Rapids, MI: Kregel Publications, 1996.

Couch, Paul. *The Shadow of the Apocalypse: When All Hell Breaks Loose.* Berkley Books: New York, NY, 2004.

Crim, Keith, ed. *Abingdon Dictionary of Living Religions.* Nashville, TN: Abingdon Press, 1981.

Crocket, William, ed. *Four Views of Hell.* Grand Rapids, MI: Zondervan Publishing House, 1992.

Cruden, Alexander. *Cruden's Complete Concordance.* Chicago, IL: The John C. Winston Company, 1930.

Davidson, Mark. *Daniel Revisited: Discovering the Four Mideast Signs Leading to the Antichrist.* Nashville, TN: Thomas Nelson Publishing, 2015.

Davies, J. G., ed. *The New Westminster Dictionary of Liturgy and Worship.* Philadelphia, PA: Westminster Press, 1986.

Davis, John J. *Biblical Numerology: A Basic Study of the Use of Numbers in the Bible.* Grand Rapids, MI: Baker Book House, 1968.

Dearman, J. Andrew. *Religion and Culture in Ancient Israel.* Peabody, MA: Hendrickson Publishers, 1992.

De Haan, M. R. *Daniel the Prophet: Thirty-Five Simple Studies in the Book of Daniel.* Grand Rapids, MI: Zondervan Publishing House, 1947.

de Lange, Nicholas. *Judaism.* Oxford, England: Oxford University Press, 1986.

Dixon, Jim. *Last Things Revealed: Hope for Life and the Everafter.* Colorado Springs, CO: Biblica Publishing, 2011.

Dostoyevsky, Fyodor. *The Brothers Karamazov.* New York, NY: Sinet, 1980.

Duck, Daymond R. *Revelation: God's Word for the Biblically Inept.* Lancaster, PA: Starburst Publishers, 1998.

Efird, James M. *Left Behind? What the Bible Really Says about the End time.* Macon, GA: Smyth & Helwys Publishing, Inc., 2005.

Ellis, Peter Berresford. *A Brief History of the Celts.* London, UK: Robinson, 2003.

_____. A *Brief History of the Druids.* Philadelphia, PA: Running Press Book Publishers, 2002.Evans, Mike. *The Final Generation.* Phoenix, AZ: Time Worthy Books, 2012.

_____. *The Temple: The Center of Gravity.* Phoenix, AZ: Time Worthy Books, 2015.

Faid, Robert W. *A Scientific Approach to Biblical Mysteries plus A Scientific Approach to More Biblical Mysteries.* Carmel, NY: Guideposts via special arrangement with New Leaf Press, 1993.

Farrar, Steve. *Get in the Ark: Finding Safety in the Coming Judgment.* Nashville, TN: Thomas Nelson Publishers, 2000.

Finegan, Jack. *Myth and Mystery: An Introduction to the Pagan Religions of the Biblical World.* Grand Rapids, MI: Baker Book House, 1989.

Finkel, Irving. *The Ark Before Noah: Decoding the Story of the Ark.* New York, NY: Doubleday, 2014.

Finley, Robert. *The Time Was at Hand.* Xulon Press, 2011.

Finto, Don. *Your People Shall Be My People: How Israel, the Jews and the Christian Church Will Come Together in the Last Days.* Bloomington, MN: Chosen Books, 2014.

Fortson, Dante. *As the Days of Noah Were: The Sons of God and the Coming Apocalypse.* USA: Impact Agenda Media, 2010.

Friedman, Stanton T. *Flying Saucers and Science: A Scientist Investigates the Mysteries of UFOs.* Pompton Plains, NJ: New Page Books, 2008.

Gardner, Laurence. *The Shadow of Solomon: The Lost Secret of The Freemasons Revealed.* San Francisco, CA: Weiser Books, 2005.

Garlow, James L. *The Covenant: A Bible Study.* Kansas City, MO: Beacon Hill Press of Kansas City, 1999.

Gehman, Henry Snyder, ed. *The New Westminster Dictionary of the Bible.* Wheaton, IL: Tyndale House Publishers, 1970.

Gibbon, Edward. *The Decline and Fall of the Roman Empire.* vol. 1. New York, NY: Modern Library, undated.

Glasser, William. *Reality Therapy: A New Approach to Psychiatry.* New York, NY: Harper & Row, Publishers, 1965.

Goll, Jim W. *The Seer: The Prophetic Power of Visions, Dreams, and Open Heavens.* Shippensburg, PA: Destiny Image Publishers, Inc., 2004.

Goodrich, Norma Lorre. *Ancient Myths.* New York, NY: New American Library, 1960.

Grun, Bernard. *The Timetables of History.* 3rd rev. ed. New York, NY: Simon & Schuster, 1991.

Guillermo, Jorge. *Sibyls: Prophecy and Power in the Ancient World.* New York, NY: Peter Mayer Publishers, Inc., 2013.

Haag, Michael. *The Templars: The History and the Myth.* London: Harper Collins, 2009. e-books.

Hamon, Bill. *Prophetic Scriptures Yet to Be Fulfilled.* Shippensburg, PA: Destiny Image Publishers, Inc., 2010.

Hamp, Douglas. *Corrupting the Image: Angels, Aliens, and the Antichrist Revealed.* Defender Publishing, LLC, 2011.

Hanegraaf, Hank. *The Apocalypse Code: Find Out What the Bible Really Says about the End Times and Why It Matters Today.* Nashville, TN: Thomas Nelson Publishers, 2007.

Hancock, Graham. *The Sign and the Seal.* New York, NY: Simon & Shuster, Inc., 1992.

Heinlein, Robert A. *Job: A Comedy of Justice.* New York, NY: Ballantine Books, 1984.

_____. *The Number of the Beast.* New York, NY: Ballantine Books, 1980.

Heiser, Michael S. *Angels: What the Bible Really Says about God's Heavenly Host.* Bellingham, WA: Lexham Press, 2018.

Hester, H. I. *The Heart of the New Testament.* 10th printing. Liberty, MO: The William Jewell Press, 1950.

Hildebrand, Lloyd B. *2012: Is This the End?* Alachua, FL: Bridge Logos Foundation, 2009.

Hitchcock, Mark. *2012, the Bible, and the End of the Word.* Eugene, OR: Harvest House Publishers, 2009.

_____. *The End: A Complete Overview of Bible Prophecy and the End of Days.* Cold Stream, IL: Tyndale House Publishers, 2012.

Horn, Thomas, ed. *Pandemonium's Engine: How the End of the Church Age, the Rise of Transhumanism, and the Coming of the Ubermensch (Overman) Herald Satan's Imminent and Final Assault on the Creation of God.* Crane, Mo: Defender Press, 2011.

Horn, Thomas and Thomas Putnam. *Petrus Romanus: The Final Pope is Here.* Crane, MO: Defender Press, 2012.

Howard, Kevin and Marvin Rosenthal. *The Feasts of the Lord: God's Prophetic Calendar from Calvary to the Kingdom.* Orlando, FL: Zion's Hope, Inc., 1997.

Howard, Michael. *Secret Societies: Their Influence and Power from Antiquity to the Present Day.* Rochester, VT: Destiny Books, 2008.

Howard, W.F. *Christianity According to Saint John.* London, UK: Duckworth Printing, 1958.

Howells, Robert. *The Last Pope: Francis and the Fall of the Vatican... St. Malachy's Prophecies.* London, UK: Watkins Publishing, 2013.

Humphreys, Fisher and Philip Wise. *Fundamentalism.* Macon, GA: Smyth & Helwys Publishing, Inc., 2004.

James, E. O. *The Ancient Gods.* Edison, NJ: Castle Books, 2004.

Jeffrey, Grant R. *The New Temple and the Second Coming: The Prophecy That Points to Christ's Return in Your Generation.* Colorado Springs, CO: Waterbrook Press, 2007.

Jeremiah, David. *Is This the End? Signs of God's Providence in a Disturbing New World.* Nashville, TN: W Publishing Group, 2016.

Jerome. *Jerome's Commentary on Daniel.* Grand Rapids, MI: Baker Book House, 1958.

Johnson, Ken. *Ancient Book of Jasher: Referenced in Joshua 10:13; 2 Samuel 1:18; and 2 Timothy 3:8.* Biblefacts Ministries, 2008.

———. *Ancient Paganism: The Sorcery of the Fallen Angels.* 2009.

———. *Ancient Prophecies Revealed: 500 Prophecies Listed in Order of When They Were Fulfilled.* 2010.

Kaufmann, Walter. *Religions in Four Dimensions: Existential, Aesthetic, Historical, Comparative.* New York, NY: Reader's Digest Press, 1976.

Kinley, Jeff. *The End of America?: Bible Prophecy and a Country in Crisis.* Eugene, OR: Harvest House Publishers, 2017.

Kirsch, Jonathan. *A History of the End of the World: How the Most Controversial Book in the Bible Changed the Course of Western Civilization.* San Francisco, CA: HarperSanFrancisco, 2006.

Klein, John and Adam Spears. *Devils and Demons and the Return of the Nephilim.* Bend, OR: Covenant Research Institute, 2005.

Knight, Christopher and Robert Lomas. *The Second Messiah: Templars, the Turin Shroud, and the Great Secret of Freemasonry.* Gloucester, MA: Fair Winds Press, 1997.

LaHaye, Tim and Jerry B. Jenkins. *Left Behind.* 12 vols. Tyndale House Publishers, Inc., 1995.

Landay, Jerry M. *The House of David.* New York, NY: E. P. Dutton & Co., Inc., 1973.

Lang, J. Stephen. *1,001 Things You Always Wanted to Know about Angels, Demons, and the Afterlife.* Nashville, TN: Thomas Nelson, 2000.

Larson, Bob. *Larson's Book of Cults.* Wheaton, IL: Tyndale House Publishers, Inc., 1982.

Latourette, Kenneth Scott. *A History of Christianity A.D. 1500—A.D. 1975*. vol. 2 rev. ed. San Frincisco, CA: Harper and Row, 1975.

Law, Terry. *The Truth About Angels*. Lake Mary, FL: Creation House, 1994.

Lehmann, Arthur C. and James E. Myers. *Magic, Witchcraft, and Religion: An Anthropological Study of the Supernatural*. Palo Alto, CA: Mayfield Publishing Company, 1985.

L'Engle, Madeleine. *A Wrinkle in Time*. Ariel Books: Farrar, Straus and Giroux, 1963.

Leon-Dufour, Xavier. *Dictionary of Biblical Theology*. 2nd rev. ed. New York, NY: Seabury Press, 1967.

Lindsey, Hal. *The Late Great Planet Earth*. Grand Rapids, MI: Zondervan Publishing House, 1970.

The Living Bible Encyclopedia in Story and Pictures. 16 vols. New York, NY: H. S. Struttman Co. Inc., 1968.

Lockyer, Herbert. *All the Parables of the Bible: A Study and Analysis of the More than 250 Parables in Scripture*. Grand Rapids, MI: Zondervan Publishing House, 1963.

Ludwigson, R. *A Survey of Bible Prophecy*. Grand Rapids, MI: Zondervan Publishing House, 1977.

Lumpkin, Joseph P. *The Books of Enoch: The Angels, the Watchers, and the Nephilim: (With Extensive Commentary on the Three Books of Enoch, the Fallen Angels, the Calendar of Enoch, and Daniel's Prophecy)*. Blountsville, AL: Fifth Estate Publishers, 2011.

_____. *The Prophecy of Saint Malachy: The Soon Coming End of Days*. Blountsville, AL: Fifth Estate Publishers, 2012.

MacBain, Alexander. *Celtic Mythology and Religion*. Glastonbury, UK: The Lost Library, 1917.

MacCulloch, Diarmaid. *Christianity: The First Three Thousand Years*. New York, NY: Penguin Books, 2009.

Martin, Walter. *The Kingdom of the Cults.* Minneapolis, MN: Bethany House Publishers, 1997.

Matthews, Victor H. *Manners and Customs in the Bible.* rev. ed. Peabody, MA: Hendrickson Publishers, Inc., 1996.

Maus, Cynthia Pearl. *Christ and the Fine Arts: An Anthology of Pictures, Poetry, Music, and Stories Centering in the Life of Christ.* rev. ed. New York, NY: Harper & Brothers Publishers, 1959.

Mayer, F. E. *The Religious Bodies of America.* 4th ed. Saint Louis, MO: Concordia Publishing House, 1961.

McCullar, Michael. *A Christian's Guide to Islam.* Macon, GA: Smyth & Helwys Publishing, Inc., 2008.

McDowell, Josh. *The New Evidence That Demands a Verdict.* Nashville, TN: Thomas Nelson Publishers, 1999.

McGuire, Paul and Troy Anderson. *The Babylon Code: Solving the Bible's Greatest End-Times Mystery.* New York, NY: FaithWords (a division of Hachette Book Group), 2015.

McKay, David O., (trustee-in-trust). *The Book of Mormon.* Salt Lake City, UT: The Church of Jesus Christ of Latter-Day Saints, 1961.

McNeill, John T. *The History and Character of Calvinism.* New York, NY: Oxford University Press, 1962.

Mead, Frank S. *Handbook of Denominations in the United States.* 9th ed. Revised by Samuel S. Hill. Nashville, TN: Abingdon Press, 1990.

Merrill, Eugene H. *Kingdom of Priests: A History of Old Testament Israel.* Grand Rapids, MI: Baker Book House, 1987.

Miller, Aaron David. *The Much Too Promised Land: America's Elusive Search for Arab-Israeli Peace.* New York, NY: Bantam Books, 2008.

Miller, Stephen M. *The Complete Guide to Bible Prophecy.* Uhrichsville, OH: Barbour Publishing, Inc., 2010.

Mills, Watson E., ed. *Mercer Dictionary of the Bible.* Macon, GA: Mercer University Press, 1997.

Missler, Chuck. *Prophecy 20/20: Profiling the Future through the Lens of Scripture.* Nashville, TN: Thomas Nelson Publishers, 2006.

Mistele, Bryan P. *The Truth about Prophecy in the Bible.* Redmond, WA: Beyond Today Publishing, 2005.

Moody, Raymond A. Jr. *Life After Life* and *Reflections on Life After Life.* Carmel, NY: Guideposts, 1975.

Moore, Maree. *The Dove, the Rose, and the Sceptre: In Search of the Ark of the Covenant.* Queensland, Australia: Joshua Books, 2004.

Morgan, Giles. *Freemasonry: Its History and Mysteries Revealed.* New York, NY: Shelter Harbor Press, 2015.

Munro-Hay, Stuart. *The Quest for the Ark of the Covenant.* London, New York: I. B. Tauris, 2005.

Murphy, Derek. *Jesus Harry Potter Christ.* Portland, OR: Holy Blasphemy Press, 2011.

Needham, Matthew. *The End of the World: What You Should Know about the Last Days, the Antichrist, the Judgments of God, and the Glorious Return of Jesus Christ.* Citta Sant'Angelo, Italy: Evenagelista Media, 2012.

Nixon, Thomas C. *The Olivet Discourse: The Mystery Revealed.* Bloomington, IN: 1st Book Library, 2003.

Noel, Ruth S. *The Mythology of Middle-Earth.* Boston, MA: Houghton Mifflin Company, 1978.

Oates, Wayne. *The Psychology of Religion.* Waco, TX: Word Books, 1973.

Odell, Margaret S., ed. *Smyth & Helwys Bible Commentary: Ezekiel.* Macon, GA: Smyth & Helwys Publishing, Inc., 2005.

Pace, Sharon. *Judaism: A Brief Guide to Faith and Practice.* Macon, GA: Smyth & Helwys Publishing, Inc., 2012.

Pack, David C. *The Bible's Greatest Prophecies Unlocked: A Voice Cries Out*. Park One Publishing, 2010.

Pagels, Elaine. *Revelations: Visions, Prophecy, and Politics in the Book of Revelation*. New York, NY: Penguin Books, 2012.

Patterson, Bob. *Discovering Revelation*. Carmel, NY: Guideposts Associates, Inc., 1987.

Payne, J. Barton. *Encyclopedia of Biblical Prophecy: The Complete Guide to Scriptural Predictions and Their Fulfillment*. 2 vols. Grand Rapids, MI: Baker Book House, 1973.

Pearson, Patricia. *Opening Heaven's Door: What the Dying May Be Trying to Tell Us About Where They're Going*. Toronto, Canada: Vintage Canada, 2015.

Pentecost, J. Dwight. *Things to Come: A Study in Biblical Eschatology*. Grand Rapids, MI: Zondervan Publishing, 1976.

Perry, Richard H. *The Complete Idiot's Guide to the Last Days: An Apocalyptic Look at the Future*. Indianapolis, IN: Alpha Books, 2006.

Petrement, Simone. *A Separate God: The Christian Origins of Gnosticism*. San Francisco, CA: Harper San Francisco, 1984.

Pfeiffer, Charles F., Howard F. Vos, and John Rea, eds. *Wycliffe Bible Encyclopedia*. vols. 1 and 2. Chicago, IL: Moody Press, 1975.

Pfeiffer, Robert H. *The Books of the Old Testament*. New York, NY: Harper & Row, Publishers, 1957.

Phillips, Graham. *The Templars and the Ark of the Covenant: The Discovery of the Treasure of Solomon*. Rochester, VT: Bear & Company, 2004.

Philpott, Kent. *A Manual of Demonology and the Occult*. Grand Rapids, MI: Zondervan Publishing House, 1976.

Piper, Don and Cecil Murphy. *90 Minutes In Heaven: A True Story of Death and Life*. Grand Rapids, MI: Revell, 2004.

Price, Isabella. *Visions of the End: The Christian Book of Revelation and Other Apocalyptic Prophecies*. Smashwords, 2014.

Price, Paula A. *The Prophet's Dictionary: The Ultimate Guide to Supernatural Wisdom*. Tulsa, OK: Whitaker House, 2006.

Price, Randall. *The Coming Last Days Temple*. Eugene, OR: Harvest House Publishers, 1999.

_____. *The Temple and Bible Prophecy: A Definitive Look at Its Past, Present, and Future...*Eugene, OR: Harvest House Publishers, 2005.

Read, Piers Paul. *The Templars: The Dramatic History of the Knights Templar, the Most Powerful Military Order of the Crusades*. Cambridge, MA: De Capo Press, 1999.

Reddish, Mitchell G., ed. *Apocalyptic Literature: A Reader*. Peabody, MA: Hendrickson Publishers, 1995.

_____. *Smyth & Helwys Bible Commentary: Revelation*. Macon, GA: Smyth & Helwys Publishing, Inc., 2001.

Rhodes, Ron. *The End Times in Chronological Order: A Complete Overview to Understanding Bible Prophecy*. Eugene, OR: Harvest House Publishers, 2012.

_____. *Unmasking the Antichrist: Dispelling the Myths, Discovering the Truth*. Eugene, OR: Harvest House Publishers, 2012.

Roberts, Scott Alan. *The Rise and Fall of the Nephilim: The Untold Story of Fallen Angels, Giants on the Earth, and Their Extraterrestrial Origins*. Pompton Plains, IL: New Page Books, 2012.

Rogerson, John. *Chronicle of the Old Testament Kings: The Reign-by-Reign Record of the Rulers of Ancient Israel*. London: Thames and Hudson, Ltd., 1999.

Rose Book of Bible Charts, Maps, and Time Lines (10th anniversary edition). Peabody, MA: Rose Publishing LLC, 2005.

Rosenthal, Marvin. *The Prewrath Rapture of the Church*. Nashville, TN: Thomas Nelson Publishers, 1990.

Ross, Hugh. *Beyond the Cosmos: What Recent Discoveries in Astronomy and Physics Reveal about the Nature of God.* Colorado Springs, CO: NavPress, 1996.

Rossing, Barbara R. *The Rapture Exposed: The Message of Hope in the Book of Revelation.* New York, NY: Basic Books, 2004.

Rowling, J. K. *Harry Potter.* 7 vols. New York, NY: Scholastic Press, 1997.

Rutledge, Fleming. *The Battle for Middle Earth: Tolkien's Divine Design in The Lord of the Rings.* Grand Rapids, MI: William B. Eerdmans Publishing Co., 2004.

Ryle, James. *A Dream Come True.* Lake Mary, FL: Creation House, 1995.

Sapp, David. *Sessions with Revelation: The Last Days of Evil.* Macon, GA: Smyth & Helwys Publishing Inc., 2014.

Sims, Albert E. and Charles Dent. *Who's Who in the Bible.* New York, NY: Philosophical Society Library, Inc., 1960.

Sitchin, Zecharia. *There Were Giants on the Earth: God, Demi-gods, and Human Ancestry: The Evidence of Alien DNA.* Rochester, VT: Bear & Company, 2010.

Smith, Lee and Wes Bodin. *Religion in Human Culture: The Jewish Tradition.* Allen, TX: Argus Communications, 1978.

Smith, T.C. *Reading the Signs: A Sensible Approach to Revelation and Other Apocalyptic Writings.* Macon, GA: Smyth & Helwys Publishing, Inc., 1997.

Sora, Steven. *The Lost Treasure of the Knights Templar: Solving the Oak Island Mystery.* Rochester, VT: Destiny Books, 1999.

Sproul, R.C. *The Last Days According to Jesus.* Grand Rapids, MI: Baker Books, 1998.

Stewart, Randall. *American Literature and Christian Doctrine.* Baton Rouge, LA: Louisiana State University Press, 1958.

Stone, Perry. *Deciphering End-Time Prophecy Codes.* Lake Mary, FL: Chrisma House, 2015.

Strong, James. *The New Strong's Concordance of the Bible.* pop. ed. Nashville, TN: Thomas Nelson Publishers, 1985.

Surburg, Raymond F. *Introduction to the Intertestamental Period.* Saint Louis, MO: Concordia Publishing House, 1975.

Sweeney, Marvin A. *Reading Ezekiel: A Literary and Theological Commentary.* Macon, GA: Smyth & Helwys Publishing, Inc., 2013.

Tan, Paul Lee. *The Interpretation of Prophecy.* Rockville, MD: Assurance Publishers, 1974.

Tatford, Frederick A. *Daniel and His Prophecy: Studies in the Prophecy of Daniel.* reprint. Klock & Klock in the U. S. A., 1980.

Tenney, Merrill C., ed. *The Living Bible Encyclopedia in Story and Pictures.* New York, NY: H. S. Stuttmann Co., Inc., 1968.

Terry, Milton S. *Biblical Apocalyptics: A Study of the Most Notable Revelations of God and of Christ.* Grand Rapids, MI: Baker Book House, 1898.

Thorsen, Don. *An Exploration of Christian Theology.* Peabody, MA: Hendrickson Publishers, Inc., 2008.

Trafton, Joseph L. *Reading Revelation: A Literary and Theological Commentary.* vol. 12. Macon, GA: Smyth & Helwys, 2005.

Unger, Merrill F. *Archaeology and the Old Testament.* Grand Rapids, MI: Zondervan Publishing House, 1954.

von Daniken, Erich. *Chariots of the Gods?* New York, NY: Bantam Books, 1968.

Walter, Philippe. *Christian Mythology: Revelations of Pagan Origins.* Rochester, VT: Inner Traditions, 2003.

Walvoord, John F. *Major Bible Prophecies.* Grand Rapids, MI: Zondervan Publishers, 1991.

_____. *The Revelation of Jesus Christ.* Chicago, IL: Moody Press, 1966.

Ward, Kaari, ed. *Jesus and His Times.* Pleasantville, NY: Reader's Digest Association, 1987.

Weisburger, Bernard A., chief consultant. *Reader's Digest Family Encyclopedia of American History.* Pleasantville, NY: Reader's Digest Association, Inc., 1975.

Westminster Standards, The. Suwanee, GA: Great Commission Publications, 1978.

Whale, J.S. *Christian Doctrine.* Cambridge, UK: Cambridge University Press, 1966.

Whitson, William, trans. *The Life and Works of Flavius Josephus.* New York, NY: Holt, Rinehart, and Winston, (undated).

Willmington, H. L. *Willmington's Book of Bible Lists.* Philadelphia, PA: The Westminster Press, 1987.

Winward, Stephen. *A Guide to the Prophets.* Atlanta, GA: John Knox Press, 1976.

Wohlberg, Steve. *End Time Delusions: The Rapture, the Antichrist, Israel, and the End of the World.* Shippensburg, PA: Destiny Image Publishers, Inc., 2004.

Wood, Leon J. *A Survey of Israel's History.* Grand Rapids, MI: Academie Books, 1986.

Wright, G. Ernest, principal advisor. *Great People of the Bible and How They Lived.* Pleasantville, NY: Reader's Digest Association, 1974.

Zagami, Leo Lyon. *Confessions of an Illuminati: The Time of Revelations and Tribulation Leading Up to 2020* (Vol 2). San Francisco, CA: CCC Publications, 2016.

Other Works By The Author

Revealing the Revelation: A Guide to the Literature of the Apocalypse

Discernment from Daniel

101 Fun Fables (color illustrations by author)

Prophecy *A—Z: The Complete Eschatological Dictionary*

Operation Revelation: A Teen's Script to Earth's Final Curtain (with Jan Ledford)

Revelation for Regular Readers

Oracles from Olivet: The Eschatological Jesus